Nathaniel Hawthorne
in His Times

For all our happiness
in Salem
from the Non Quiet Non silent
and indecent of Salem)
with all my Love

Charles

7/14/98

JAMES R. MELLOW

Nathaniel Hawthorne
in His Times

THE JOHNS HOPKINS UNIVERSITY PRESS
BALTIMORE AND LONDON

Originally published in 1980 by Houghton Mifflin Company
Johns Hopkins Paperbacks edition, 1998
9 8 7 6 5 4 3 2 1

The Johns Hopkins University Press
2715 North Charles Street
Baltimore, Maryland 21218-4363
The Johns Hopkins Press Ltd., London
www.press.jhu.edu

Passages from The English Notebooks by Nathaniel Hawthorne, edited by
Randall Stewart, are reprinted by permission of The Modern Language Association.
Copyright 1941 by The Modern Language Association of America; copyright ©
renewed 1969 by Cleone Odell Stewart.

Library of Congress Cataloging-in-Publication Data

Mellow, James R.
  Nathaniel Hawthorne in his times / James R. Mellow.
     p.   cm.
  Originally published : Boston : Houghton Mifflin, 1980.
  Includes bibliographical references (p.   ) and index.
  ISBN 0-8018-5900-X (pbk. : alk. paper)
   1. Hawthorne, Nathaniel, 1804–1864—Biography.   2. Novelists, American—
19th century—Biography.   I. Title.
PS1881.M4   1998
813'.3—dc21
  [B]   98-2623
                                                                    CIP

A catalog record for this book is available from the British Library.

Every dream has at least one point at which it is unfathomable; a central point, as it were, connecting it with the unknown.

— Sigmund Freud, *The Interpretation of Dreams*

Contents

Illustrations

Part One

Mr. Hawthorne Calls Again

"AND IN THE EVENING. . . . a great ring came at the front door. I opened it," Elizabeth Palmer Peabody remembered, "and there stood your father in all the splendor of his young beauty, and a hooded figure hanging on each arm . . ." She was recalling for her nephew Julian, in 1882, her first meeting with his father, fixing on a moment out of the flux of time — a Saturday night, early in November 1837 — when Nathaniel Hawthorne and his sisters, Elizabeth and Louisa, nervous and smiling, stood at the door of the Peabody home on Salem's Charter Street.

The Hawthornes had been summoned by Miss Peabody — writer, teacher, intellectual busybody — who felt it was time she met the reticent Salem author whose anonymous stories she had read in the *New-England Magazine*. The stories had recently been republished — and the author identified — in a volume titled *Twice-told Tales*, brought out by a Boston firm, the American Stationers' Company. The book had received several favorable reviews — Professor Longfellow of Harvard, writing in the *North American Review*, had hailed the author as a "new star" rising in the literary heavens. Hawthorne, thirty-three, just emerging from a lengthy period of seclusion, seemed on the verge of a promising career.

It was Lizzie Peabody's contention that the Hawthorne women — the Widow Hawthorne and her two daughters — had been remiss in not introducing the eligible young man into society. She regarded it as one of the principal functions of the women of a household to provide a man with those social occasions which might further his career or introduce him to suitable women and, perhaps, a future wife. But the entire Hawthorne family was strangely reclusive. The Widow Hawthorne, whose husband, Nathaniel, a sea captain, had died in far-off Surinam in 1808, had immured herself in her Herbert Street house with an "all but Hindoo self-devotion to the manes of her husband" — or so, at least, Lizzie felt. "Madame" Hawthorne was never to be seen on the streets of Salem; on rare occasions, one might catch a glimpse of her taking the cool evening air in her garden, dressed in uncompromising widow's black and in the fashion of another era. She seldom received guests, saw only her children and immediate family. Season after season, she kept to her chamber. Her meals were taken in her room, alone.

Even Lizzie Peabody, a determined hostess, found it difficult to establish relations with so eccentric a household. The entire family, it seemed, had adopted the widow's unsociable behavior. Elizabeth, the elder daughter, also stayed in her room, reading all day, eating her meals by herself, emerging only to take long solitary walks. It was rumored in Salem that a "love-disappointment" had caused the older Hawthorne daughter to live in such a peculiar manner; a young man she had met in Newburyport had failed to call at Salem, as he had promised. But Lizzie Peabody, having had such disappointments in her own life, took a practical view of affairs of the heart. She well remembered Elizabeth Hawthorne from childhood days; the two girls had done their lessons together in Mrs. Peabody's dame school. Lizzie had thought then that Elizabeth Hawthorne was a "brilliant little girl" and "a great genius." It was unlikely that she would be overwhelmed by some minor flirtation.

Lizzie Peabody's recollections of Nathaniel Hawthorne were much less vivid. From that earlier time, years before, when the Peabody and Hawthorne families had been backyard neighbors on Herbert and Union streets, she remembered only a little boy with "clustering locks" and broad shoulders, dancing about the yard. Now, young Hawthorne was living as a virtual hermit in a household of conventual women. Lizzie Peabody felt it was a waste of talent and opportunity. Only Louisa Hawthorne seemed to have acquired a taste for sociability — at least to the extent of dealing with local tradesmen, for the management of the household had largely fallen to the younger of the Hawthorne daughters. But even that measure of sociability, Lizzie Peabody discovered, had its limits.

When she first read such stories as "The Gray Champion" and "The Devil in Manuscript," in the pages of the *New-England Magazine*, Lizzie Peabody decided that the author was probably "some old 'New-Light' Quaker who had outgrown his sectarianism." She had written a letter to this supposedly old man (though she did not send it), asking him how he knew that "sensitive natures are especially apt to be malicious." Then she had read a laudatory review that revealed the identity of the mysterious author as one "Nathaniel Hawthorne." Lizzie was next convinced that the real author was the brilliant Elizabeth Hawthorne, who, she supposed, had adopted a masculine identity for purposes of authorship. With her usual peremptoriness, Lizzie paid a call at Herbert Street. There, she was promptly informed by Louisa that the author was, indeed, her brother, Nathaniel. Lizzie, whose impregnable frankness could be abrasive, remarked, "But if your brother can write like that, he has no right to be idle." Louisa merely laughed. "He never is idle," she said. Louisa went upstairs to report on their guest, and in a few moments returned with a message from her sister: if Miss Peabody would call some evening, Elizabeth Hawthorne would be happy to see her. "But," Lizzie remembered, "she did not appoint any particular evening, and a year passed."

Elizabeth Palmer Peabody was an author of some note. Her *Record of a School: Exemplifying the General Principles of Spiritual Culture*, published a year before, had attracted much attention in educational circles. Among her friends were the literati of Salem, Concord, and Boston — including the eccentric poet Jones Very, the Concord sage Ralph Waldo Emerson, and the peppery young Boston historian George Bancroft. Nathaniel Hawthorne made no attempt to pursue an acquaintance with the influential caller. But when *Twice-told Tales* was published, he sent an inscribed copy to "Miss Elizabeth Peabody, with the respects of the Author." This tentative gesture had prompted the request that Hawthorne and his sisters call at the Peabody home.

On that first visit, Lizzie, the eldest of three Peabody sisters, had greeted the guests alone; her younger sister Mary was to join them later. The youngest of the Peabody daughters, the invalid Sophia, had already gone to bed. Lizzie, welcoming Elizabeth Hawthorne, had been immediately struck by the attractiveness of her former schoolmate. Recalling the meeting for her nephew, she remembered Elizabeth Hawthorne's "black hair in beautiful natural curls, her bright rather shy eyes, and a rather excited, frequent, low laugh." Elizabeth Hawthorne looked "full of wit and keenness, as if she were experienced in the world; not the least sentimental in air, but strongly intellectual." Louisa Hawthorne, on the other hand, had nothing vivid or noteworthy in her character; Lizzie passed her over with the noncommittal observation that "Louisa was quite like other people."

It was Nathaniel Hawthorne who made the most forceful impression on his hostess: handsome, sensitive, with a fierce shyness, as if he were determined neither to relax his guard nor to reveal a weakness. "But as soon as he forgot himself in conversation," Lizzie remembered, "all this passed away, and the beauty of the outline of all his features, the pure complexion, the wonderful eyes, like mountain lakes seeming to reflect the heavens, made a wonderful impression." As soon as she could decently excuse herself, Lizzie Peabody had rushed upstairs. "Oh Sophia," she told her youngest sister, "Mr. Hawthorne and his sisters have come, and you never saw anything so splendid — he is handsomer than Lord Byron! You must get up and dress and come down."

Sophia had laughed and refused: "I think it would be rather ridiculous to get up. If he has come once he will come again."

Nathaniel Hawthorne did call again. On his second visit — an afternoon call a short while later — he sat chatting with Lizzie Peabody in the crowded drawing room that overlooked the ancient Salem burying ground. On this occasion, Sophia Peabody deigned to come downstairs. "My sister Sophia . . ." Lizzie announced, as Sophia, pale, hesitant, clad in a white wrapper, stood in the doorway. Lizzie Peabody remembered that first meeting of Hawthorne and Sophia with a vividness scarcely touched by time. Hawthorne rose and looked at the young woman intently. "He did not realize how intently, and afterwards, as we went on talking, she would interpose frequently a remark, in her low sweet voice. Every time she did so, he looked at her with the same intentness of interest. I was struck with it, and painfully. I thought, what if he should fall in love with her; and I had heard her so often say, nothing would ever tempt her to marry, and inflict upon a husband the care of such a sufferer." Lizzie Peabody's romantic recollection of the incident was generous; early in her acquaintance with Hawthorne, Peabody relatives suspected that Hawthorne regarded Lizzie herself as a marital prospect.

Sophia Peabody was not, by the standards of the time, a beautiful woman. "In person she was small, graceful, active, and beautifully formed," her son Julian was to write of her. "Her face was so alive and translucent with lovely expressions that it was hard to determine whether or not it were physically lovely; but I incline to think that a mathematical survey would have pronounced her features plain; only no mathematical survey could have taken cognizance of her smile."

When she first met Hawthorne, Sophia was twenty-eight. From the time she had reached the age of puberty, she had been subject to attacks of migraine that, at their onset, heightened her sensitivity to such a degree that even the clatter of knives and forks at the dinner table produced pain so unbearable she was forced to take her meals in her room. Suffering from undetermined ailments, she became another of those unfortunate nineteenth-century females who were treated by their families as both hostages and pets. An active life was proscribed; marriage, certainly, was regarded as an improbability. But she had a lengthy career as a medical patient, suffering through one experimental cure after another. Lizzie Peabody recalled her sister's heroic submission to the medical profession: "The endurance of her physical constitution defied all the poisons of the *materia medica* — mercury, arsenic, opium, hyoscyamus, etc. etc." Sophia survived the doctoring; her prolonged illness seems never to have weakened her religious faith or her indomitable optimism. The "silent ministry of pain," as she referred to it, gave her an ethereal and not unattractive quality; it added grace to her somewhat plain features.

On the afternoon of that first encounter, sitting on the sofa, contemplating with her soft, gray eyes the superb figure of Mr. Hawthorne — so attentive and deferential toward her — Sophia felt a momentary recoil. Hawthorne's presence, so Julian years later reported his mother had told him, "exercised so strong a magnetic attraction upon her, that instinctively, and in self-defense as it were, she drew back and repelled him. The power which she felt in him alarmed her; she did not understand what it meant, and was only able to feel that she must resist."

In Lizzie Peabody's account, Sophia had had an immediate opportunity to demonstrate her self-possession. It was decided that Hawthorne would call that evening to escort Lizzie to a visit at the Hawthorne home.

Hawthorne turned to the small, frail figure on the couch and asked, "And Miss Sophia, will not you come too?"

Sophia smiled and shook her head. "I never go out in the evening, Mr. Hawthorne."

"I wish you would," Hawthorne responded, with more than a touch of urgency in his voice.

———

Versions of the truth, private records, personal fragments — bits of wreckage borne on the surface of the broad, indifferent stream of time. Lizzie Peabody's perfect vignette has the classic elements of a romance: the chance meeting, the instant recognition — love at first sight. Her story carried along with it the inaccuracies, the tricks of memory and personal prejudice, that would never be corrected during the long passage of the years. Yet her story had its basis in fact.

In Julian Hawthorne's narrative, Sophia eventually recognized the certainties of a moment long past. "In the end," Julian maintained, "she realized that they had loved each other at first sight." But Julian's version had been colored by his status as the dutiful son of a famous father and his adoring wife.

There is the ample testimony of Nathaniel Hawthorne's love letters to Sophia — ardent, imploring, rapt — the letters of a man who came late to the great love of his life. In time, Hawthorne began to view his love for Sophia as his salvation. "Now, dearest, dost thou comprehend what thou hast done for me?" he asks in an early letter. "And is it not a somewhat fearful thought, that a few slight circumstances might have prevented us from meeting . . . ?"

What are stories but attempts to fix the permanence of the moment, to salvage it from the rushing impermanence of time? When Hawthorne first met Sophia, the circumstances of his life were of a quite different nature from those that could be accommodated by Lizzie Peabody's brightly painted tale — more complex and more ordinary, in fact, than she seemed able to grasp. It was a story out of life, and not unromantic in its way: one of those narratives, drawn from the welter of everyday experience, that seldom appealed to Nathaniel Hawthorne, the writer of fiction. With his instinct for the unspoken motives of the heart and mind, with his brooding imagination, he looked for something more than the circumspect life of Salem's streets and parlors as his literary domain. He had staked out for himself a realm of dreams and fantasies — a territory apart from ordinary life, though it, too, might have its special truths.

A Remarkably Hard-Headed Race

THE SALEM into which Nathaniel Hawthorne was born on July 4, 1804, was still in its prosperous days. Its great families — the Crowninshields, Storeys, and Pingrees — still remained. Their houses, many of them designed by Samuel McIntire in the chaste and elegant Federal style of the 1790s, stood like emblems of virtuous wealth on Essex and Chestnut streets. Since the Revolution and the first years of the Republic, the Salem trade had shifted to the Orient and the Indies, and the mansions of the wealthy merchant families stationed along the quiet elm-shaded streets were the repositories of the arts of the East — Chinese vases on the mantlepieces, delicately painted Chinese fire screens, blue-and-white export ware from Canton gracing the tables. There was still a market for the luxuries that the port of Salem offered: Ceylon tea, Chinese silks and porcelains, Dutch gin, Jamaican rum. The growing commerce of a new country was in the process — a process to be hastened by the War of 1812 — of moving to the larger ports of Boston and New York. But the forests of masts and rigging along the Derby and Crowninshield wharves gave evidence that Salem was a busy seaport. Throngs of rough sailors, small tradesmen, and petty clerks crowded the streets. Heavy drays overloaded with cargo, their drivers cursing at straining horses, rumbled along the piers. Everywhere hung the sharp odor of pitch, mingled with salt sea air. Not far from the scene of this feverish commercial activity, Nathaniel Hawthorne was born in the second-story bedroom, above the parlor, of a small, gambrel-roofed house on Union Street.

The coincidence of his birthday with the nation's was to have its effect on Hawthorne's life. The house on not-so-illustrious Union Street was within sound of Salem Common, and throughout his childhood and well into later life, Hawthorne took special pleasure in the great national birthday celebrated on the green, poplar-lined triangle of the common. The blustering oratory with its air of self-congratulation, the parades and military bands, the punctual artillery salutes, had their appeal and fascination for him. A solitary young man of reticent habits, he nonetheless became a connoisseur of popular events — Fourth of July celebrations, military musters, country fairs, and traveling raree shows. He developed a taste for the casual gossip of local taverns, preferring it to polite parlor discourse. He had a marked preference for democratic, rather than aristocratic, occasions.

The Hathorne family — it was Nathaniel Hawthorne who added the *w* to the ancient spelling some time after he left college — provided the future writer with an ambiguous heritage, stretching back to the days of colonial settlement. For Hawthorne, the history and fortunes of his family became a kind of literary property, all the more dramatic since the family, in its brush with Salem history, had suffered a decline.

William Hathorne, the first of the American settlers in the family, had been a member of John Winthrop's historic Massachusetts Bay Colony, arriving between 1630 and 1633 and settling in Dorchester. By 1636, he had moved to Salem, where he distinguished himself as a major in the Salem militia. Eventually, he became speaker and, subsequently, deputy of the House of Delegates. In religion, William was a man of pious but uncompromising principles, remembered by his descendant for having ordered, in orthodox Puritan fashion, that a heretic Quaker woman, Anne Coleman, be whipped out of town. Hawthorne admired a family tradition that held that the stalwart William had once defied an order from King Charles II to return to London with the aged Governor Bellingham to explain the unruly conduct of His Majesty's fractious colony. Hawthorne treasured the transcript of a letter, purportedly written by his ancestor two centuries before, the copy of which he had obtained himself, in 1856, from the State Paper Office in London. The letter, written in 1666, signed Samuel Nadhorth — a possible pseudonym — is addressed to Sir William Morice, one of the king's secretaries of state. With an unusual combination of political tact and abrasive integrity, the writer exonerates himself and his fellow colonists by citing the hardships of life in a "waste and howling wilderness," the continuing loyalty of the colonists to the crown, and, more pointedly, their undeniable services to His Majesty's treasury. He goes on to condemn the abuses of the royal commissioners who are attempting to deprive the colonists of their liberties — "sacred and civil" liberties, that had been granted them by a royal charter. To offset the colonists' refusal to comply with the king's wishes, the writer notes that a present of two great masts and a shipload of twenty-eight large masts is being sent to the king. The colonists had been "forced to take up money at interest" in order to make this "small present"; nonetheless, they are "not without hope of a favorable acceptance, which will be to their souls as a cloud of latter rain." Hawthorne could scarcely have overlooked — or failed to admire — that the exquisite courtesy of the letter-writer's style concealed a number of sharp barbs.

William Hathorne's son John reached an even greater eminence — and notoriety — as one of the judges in the Salem witchcraft trials, that outbreak of hysteria and harsh justice in which the testimony of eight "afflicted girls" brought about the hanging of nineteen unoffending victims and the death by torture of another. It was a family legend that one of the victims, before her execution on Gallow's Hill, had placed a curse on Judge Hathorne and his descendants.

Hawthorne was to remain fascinated by those darker regions of the human mind that had been exposed in the courtroom presided over by his seventeenth-century ancestor. Witches and witches' Sabbaths, diabolical persuasions, the guilt of unmentioned crimes, whether real or circumstantial, were to become the themes of many of Hawthorne's stories and romances. Long after Judge Hathorne, in 1717, in his seventy-sixth year, was laid to rest in Salem burying ground, Nathaniel Hawthorne, in the preface to *The Scarlet Letter*, offered to take on himself the family curse that "the dreary and unprosperous condition of the race, for many a long year back, would argue to exist."

The Hathorne family had, indeed, fallen on poorer days. In his will, John Hathorne had requested the repayment of certain sums he had borrowed from his surviving sons, Ebenezer and Joseph — an indication, perhaps, of financial embarrassment in his old age. Joseph inherited the family farm in Salem township, Ebenezer having died, probably of smallpox, in 1717, before his father's will was probated. Joseph remained a simple farmer. His son Daniel, born in 1731, achieved fame as a privateer during the Revolutionary War. But "Bold Daniel," as he was known both in a popular ballad and in the family annals, did little to increase the Hathorne wealth. In 1772, after selling the family homestead, he bought a small house and property on Union Street from the Pickmans, relatives of his wife, Rachel. It was there that Nathaniel Hawthorne's father — named Nathaniel before him — was born, on May 19, 1775.

The witch curse, evidently, did not apply to the female descendants of the Hathorne line, for at least two of Daniel's daughters married well. Rachel, his first child, married Simon Forrester, a protégé of the captain's and an intemperate and moody man, who was to become one of the richest merchants in Salem. Another daughter, Sarah, married John Crowninshield, a member of an equally illustrious mercantile family. Nathaniel and his older brother Daniel both took to the sea, but neither achieved much financial distinction. The younger Daniel Hathorne was lost at sea in 1804. Throughout his brief maritime career, Nathaniel Hathorne captained other men's ships, usually those of his brothers-in-law, never his own.

On August 2, 1801, Nathaniel Hathorne married Elizabeth Clarke Manning, the daughter of a neighbor, Richard Manning, who lived on nearby Herbert Street. The Mannings were a prospering family of four sons and four daughters that could trace its lineage back to the colonial period, having arrived in America in 1679. Through industry and acumen, Richard Manning, a blacksmith by trade, had established himself as the proprietor and manager of the Boston and Salem Stage Company. He had also invested considerable sums in land grants in Maine, then a territory of Massachusetts. His daughter Betsey, an attractive but shy young woman with "remarkable eyes, full of sensibility and expression," was five years her husband's junior. Nathaniel Hathorne was remembered as "a warm-hearted and kindly man, very fond of children," but "somewhat inclined to melancholy, and of a reticent disposition." It was said that he was "a great reader, employing all his leisure time at sea over books." The couple's first child, a daughter whom they named Elizabeth, was born on March 2, 1802, seven months after their marriage, a circumstance that may have accounted, in part, for Elizabeth Hawthorne's later reclusive tendencies. In family circles Elizabeth was known as Ebe or Abby, names acquired from her brother, Nathaniel, who found it impossible to pronounce Elizabeth. A second daughter, Maria Louisa, was born on January 9, 1808.

Elizabeth Hawthorne's recollections of her father must have been sparse; she was only six when he died. But her family sentiments were fierce, a good deal more intense than her brother's. She seemed particularly intent on discrediting any suggestion of a taint of melancholy or morbidity in her father or her famous brother or in the family in general. When, later in life, Elizabeth Palmer Peabody suggested to her niece Una Hawthorne that there might have been a trace of insanity in the Hawthorne lineage, Ebe reacted huffily. Her annoyance was plainly visible in a letter to Una: "You may tell E.P.P., or anyone else, that I never heard of insanity in the Hawthorne family; we are a remarkably 'hard-headed' race, not easily excited, not apt to be carried away by any impulse; in short, we are just what E.P.P. is not, and what she cannot comprehend that any one else can be." It was another example of Lizzie Peabody's famous and forthright insensitivity — for Una, who had had a nervous breakdown, was not likely to be consoled by her Aunt Lizzie's pointing out that her troubles were hereditary and, therefore, probably incurable.

Hawthorne had only the barest acquaintance with his father, who was usually at sea. On the day of his son's birth, Nathaniel Hathorne was in midocean, aboard the *Mary and Eliza*, returning from a voyage to the East Indies. It was, as he recorded in his logbook, a day of fresh breezes that turned to "fresh gales" by evening; he had been nearly seven months at sea. A Salem colleague remembered Nathaniel Hathorne as "the sternest man that ever walked a deck!" Yet, far from home, he seems to have encouraged a friendship or two. An inscription in the logbook relating his voyage from Bengal to Salem aboard the Crowninshield ship the *America* carries the inscription, "Nathaniel Hathorne's Book, Presented by his Esteemed Friend, Mr. Robert Robbinet, Oct. 25, 1795, Calcutta." Hawthorne particularly treasured the 1795–1796 logbook; it described a historic voyage of sorts, for as part of its cargo the *America* was transporting the first elephant brought to the United States. Hawthorne deliberately asserted his ownership of the precious book, printing out his name, the date, and place — *1820, Salem* — and enclosing it in a bold black-and-white decorative border, set in the middle of his father's carefully inscribed title page.

Nathaniel Hathorne's handwriting was crisp and sharp, though tending toward the usual flourishes of eighteenth-century calligraphy, and his descriptive style was terse. Amidst the regular reports of smooth seas and "small" rains, among the notations of ships sighted — the *Resolution* of seventy-six guns, the brig *Bermuda* of sixteen guns — an imaginative son might catch a glimpse of his father's life and the scenes he had witnessed. There was, for example, his father's brief account, entered on February 24, 1796, of Ascension Island, high, barren, and volcanic: "Coming from eastward, you may come within a cable's length of the shore without danger." Useful information, as was the brisk inventory of a not-very-attractive port: no wood and very little water, "some goats on the island and a great many Rats." The rocks appeared to be "burnt and are so rotten that they may be broken to pieces by the hand of any Person." Hawthorne also learned that his father was given to composing poetry during his long sea voyages: "In the Midst of all these dire allarms / I'll think dear Betsey on thy Charms . . ." The son recopied the father's sentimental verses in his own, tighter hand, correcting the spelling.

Late in 1807, Nathaniel Hathorne sailed for Surinam (then Dutch Guiana), on the brig *Nabby*. Somewhere, perhaps at Cayenne, in French Guiana, he came down with yellow fever. By the time he reached port at Paramaribo, he was fatally ill, and he died there, in a boardinghouse. He died intestate, with little to leave his family — that little reduced by the medical and burial expenses. The report of his death did not reach Salem until April 1808. Ebe Hawthorne recalled the April day: "I remember very well that one morning, my mother called my brother into her room, next to the one where we slept, and told him that his father was dead. He left very little property and my Grandfather Manning took us home." Ebe made no mention of her four-year-old brother's response.

Although Hawthorne frequently remarked on his paternal ancestors and their lives, he exhibited a marked reticence — or, perhaps, reverence — concerning his father. Nathaniel Hathorne is virtually never mentioned in Hawthorne's letters or journals, although once, in studying an engraving made from a portrait of himself, Hawthorne was pleased to notice a striking resemblance to a miniature of his father. He seems to have regarded it as some species of magic, as if the engraver had managed to expose the hidden resemblance, although the original artist had not caught it.

One does, however, encounter that mysterious father — or his surrogate — in Hawthorne's fiction. There is something tentative and often ominous about the figures who stand in paternal relationships to Hawthorne's sensitive young protagonists. An air of unresolved paternity seems to cling to Hawthorne's heroes; distinctions between true fathers (many of whom are dead) and substitute fathers are often blurred. Young Goodman Brown's real father is dead, but he has a meeting with a shadowy and diabolical father figure on the road to the witches' Sabbath. The two "might have been taken for father and son," Hawthorne asserts. The wounded Roger Malvin, of "Roger Malvin's Burial," has acted as a father to the fatherless Reuben Bourne and exercises "a father's authority" when he sends the boy away rather than risk his life in the forest, where he is waiting to die. Ilbrahim, "The Gentle Boy" of Hawthorne's early story by that name, is adopted by the settler Tobias Pearson, who finds him weeping at the grave of his father, a Quaker who has been executed by the Puritans. David Swan's paternity is "respectable," though its status is vague; he is "on the high road from his native place to the city of Boston, where his uncle, a small dealer in the grocery line, was to take him behind the counter." On the way, he is nearly adopted by a wealthy and elderly couple who have lost a son.

Grandfather Manning, fifty-four at the time of his son-in-law's death, was still the active, industrious head of the large and sociable Manning clan. Hawthorne remembered him vaguely but appreciatively as a "kindly figure," whom he associated with the practical, plain-spoken Samuel Johnson. But Richard Manning's reign lasted only five years after Nathaniel Hathorne's death. He died of a stroke at an inn in Newbury on April 19, 1813. According to the obituary in the *Salem Gazette*, which commented on the suddenness of the event, "He left his family in perfect health, on Saturday, on a journey eastward, had proceeded as far as Newbury, and on the following morning was arrested by the hand of death, being found in his bed in a fit of apoplexy."

The management of the Manning stagecoach lines and stables and the considerable properties in Raymond, Maine, fell to his four sons, Richard, William, Robert, and Samuel. Young Nathaniel, a handsome and lively child, and the only nephew of the late-marrying Manning males, was "particularly petted." For her niece Una, Elizabeth Hawthorne recalled that period with affection and perhaps a tinge of envy: "We were indulged in all convenient ways, and under very little control, except that of circumstances. There were aunts and uncles, and they were all as fond, especially of your father, and as careful of his welfare, as if he had been their own child."

It was Hawthorne's uncle Robert Manning, however, who became the paternal figure for Hawthorne and his sisters. The third of the Manning brothers and a twenty-four-year-old bachelor (he did not marry until he was forty), Robert traveled constantly between Salem and Raymond, managing, with his brothers, the buying and selling of Maine properties. A dedicated horticulturalist, Robert Manning became increasingly interested in the cultivation of fruit trees, and developed extensive orchards in North Salem and in Maine. In 1823, in Salem, he opened his Dearborn Street Pomological Garden for the sale of his choice varieties. His *Book of Fruits*, first published in 1838, was for years the standard text on the tested varieties of pears, peaches, apples and cherries suitable for cultivation in New England. At his death, in 1842, Robert Manning was regarded as America's leading pomologist.

Uncle Robert took on his role as self-appointed guardian with enthusiasm. An 1813 letter to his nephew, written from Maine, clearly expresses his pleasure and affection. "Nathaniel — O how I am bedear'd and beuncle'd by great Boys and girls. Why, when I read your letters, I went to the glass to see my white hairs, I felt as if I was 40 or 50 years old, but no matter for that, be good children and the older 'Dear Uncle' grows, the more he will love you. Nat, you want to learn to swim, and so you shall when Uncle comes home, but you must study the hard lessons, learn all you can at school, mind your mother, dont look cross, hold up your head like a man, keep your cloth[e]s clean, and when Uncle comes home we shall enjoy ourselves as we did in good old times." The Widow Hawthorne, unlike the rest of the Manning clan, was retiring in disposition; she was evidently inadequate to the task of bringing up her children, and usually deferred to the advice of her brothers. Robert Manning took upon himself the direction of his nephew's education, much to Hawthorne's regret, for although he was an avid reader, he was never a ready scholar. Throughout his childhood and youth, Hawthorne's letters to Robert Manning were polite and deferential, responsive to his uncle's commands, but he seems to have chafed under Uncle Robert's benevolent tyranny. At the age of sixteen, he could boldly write his mother, "In five years, I shall belong to myself."

The eldest of the Manning brothers, Richard, moved to Maine after his father's death. Despite the fact that he suffered from a crippling ailment (possibly tuberculosis of the bone) and was forced to use crutches most of his adult life, Richard managed the family real estate in Maine, operated a store in Raymond, and traded in horses and lumber. Richard, too, married late — at the age of thirty-three. A man of energetic disposition, he sometimes gave way to bitterness over his physical condition. In 1815, several months before his marriage, he complained to Hawthorne's mother, "As to my lameness, I have given over all thoughts of ever getting better of that, but I do not forget to complain of my hard fortune, and very often, curse the day in which I was born." If his afflictions were to continue another five years as they had for the five years passed, he claimed, "I should wish that a veil of Oblivion might be drawn over me, and my name blotted out from among the Sons of Men." The rhetoric has a flourish appropriate to an inveterate reader, as Richard Manning was, but it does not conceal a pessimism that was distinctly real. (Hawthorne, too, was to find the veil — though not the "veil of Oblivion" — a useful symbol for those obscure, private emotions that separate one man from another.) In his last years, Richard Manning was confined to a wheelchair. He died in 1830, too soon to see his nephew become a famous author.

Hawthorne's remaining Manning uncles had less direct influence on his life. In 1820, William, who operated the stage lines in Salem, hired his nephew as a secretary-clerk. The salary of a dollar a week, so Hawthorne wrote his mother, was "quite convenient for many purposes." Samuel was a horse-trader, working in the family stables; his quiet, avuncular generosity was a source of spending money. In his later years, he frequently took trips for his health as well as for business; his nephew sometimes went along as a traveling companion.

Hawthorne spent much of his childhood in a household of active women. He lived with his grandmother, Miriam Manning, two aunts, his mother and sisters, and Hannah Lord, a Manning niece who worked as a servant. Among the Herbert Street women, he sometimes felt isolated — particularly when his mother and sisters were away in Maine. On one such occasion, writing to his Uncle Robert, who was visiting in Raymond, he expressed his hope that his sister Ebe would return to Salem, since he had "nobody to talk to but Grandmother, Aunt Mary and Hannah and it seems very lonesome here." He was critical, too, of his grandmother's stingy household management, mentioning that they had "a pot of excellent guaver jelly" and another of preserved limes, which would surely go to mold because his grandmother was "keeping them against somebody is sick and I suppose she would be very disappointed if everybody was to continue well and they were to spoil." There was also a question about the oranges, "which are rotting as fast as possible and we stand a very fair chance of not having any good of them because we have to eat the bad ones first as the good are to be kept till they are spoilt also."

Toward his Aunt Mary, who remained a spinster throughout her life, Hawthorne displayed a sometimes teasing affection, conjuring up unlikely suitors. It was Mary who encouraged her nephew and her older niece in their reading habits, by sharing with them her library card for the Salem Athenaeum. Another of Betsey Hawthorne's sisters, Priscilla, was also living in the Herbert Street house when the Hawthornes moved there. But in 1817, Priscilla Manning, at the age of twenty-seven — in one of those mergers of commerce and romance typical of the nineteenth century — married John Dike, a thirty-four-year-old widower and a coal and wood merchant who regularly bought his lumber from the Mannings' Maine properties.

Hawthorne, then, spent his early years in a bustling household, with the daily activities of the stagecoach business close at hand. Family anecdotes of his childhood are few. One story credits him with a rather severe case of fastidiousness at an early age: a neighboring lady fussed over him too much, and the child shouted, "Take her away! She is ugly and fat, and has a loud voice!" Apparently he had a dramatic instinct for the lugubrious; on unexpected occasions he would declaim a line from *Richard III*: "Stand back, my Lord, and let the coffin pass!" Ebe Hawthorne remembered a series of days when her brother returned from school with new accounts of his scraps with a boy named John Knights. When asked why he fought so much, he answered forthrightly, "I can't help it. John Knights is a boy of very quarrelsome disposition." As a youngster, he had a pet monkey; when it died it was solemnly buried in the backyard. (Louisa, too young to understand such sorrows, thought the creature had been "planted.") He had a lifetime affection for cats, though in his childhood he seems to have given them rough use. Having tossed a kitten over a fence once, he was admonished and told the kitten would never trust him again. "Oh, she'll think it was William," he answered, without a blush of shame. (William was a playmate.) One of Hawthorne's favorite cats, when he was older, was perversely named Beelzebub.

Hawthorne seems to have developed a streak of pragmatism at a young age — and a distaste for family handouts. Ebe Hawthorne remembered, "He never wanted money, except to spend; and once, in the country, where there were no shops, he refused to take some that was offered to him, because he could not spend it immediately. Another time, old Mr. Forrester offered him a five-dollar bill, which he also refused; which was uncivil, for Mr. Forrester always noticed him very kindly when he met him."

II

When he was nine, Hawthorne was invalided for more than a year. Ebe Hawthorne recalled that her brother had injured his foot when playing bat and ball. (She also remembered a recurrence, but "strangely" could not recall the date.) The initial period of lameness had his family considerably worried; they feared that he might be permanently disabled. They called in the local physicians — Dr. Gideon Barstow, Dr. Oliver Kittredge, even Dr. Nathaniel Peabody — but the doctors had no success. Hawthorne had been enrolled in a private school run by Joseph Worcester (later to become the noted lexicographer), but his education was, for the moment, suspended. On December 9, 1813, in the run-on fashion of childhood and with the misspelling and lack of punctuation that indicated some needed training in grammar, he wrote his Uncle Robert, then in Maine, with an air of satisfaction, "It is know 4 weeks yesterday since I have been to school and I dont know but it will be 4 weeks longer before I go again." He described his condition: "I have been out in the office two or three times and have set down on the step of the door and once I hopped out into the street. Yesterday I went out into the office and had 4 cakes Hanna carried me out once but not then . . ." As the weeks passed and his condition did not improve, Mr. Worcester was asked to come to the Manning house and hear his pupil's lessons in the evening.

His family was plainly concerned about his slow recovery. Ebe Hawthorne wrote plaintively to her Uncle Robert, "I don't know as Nathaniel's foot will ever get well if you don't come home, he won't walk on it, and the doctor says he must; so do come home soon." On his tenth birthday, Hawthorne evidently sensed the full frustration of his disability. His Aunt Priscilla, writing to her brothers in Maine, reported, "Nathaniel is no better, he realized the severity of his confinement more on *Independent Day* than he ever had done before. William was engaged, I was at Andover and he could not even ride out, to witness the *celebration of that event,* in which he has taken *such delight.*" His Uncle Richard, who felt a special sympathy, was plainly disappointed when his nephew was still too lame to make a trip to Maine. As an inducement, perhaps, he wrote Robert Manning, "Tell Nathaniel I am much pleased with his present, and when he comes down here, I shall give him a nice Fowling Piece that once belonged to his Father."

Hawthorne spent his invalid year hobbling about on crutches or lying on the floor, reading. It was during his two long confinements, Ebe recalled, that her brother acquired his habit of constant reading. She seems to have thoroughly approved of their rather desultory form of education. "He was both beautiful and bright, and perhaps his training was as good as any other could have been," she later claimed. "We were the victims of no educational pedantry. We always had plenty of books, and our minds and sensibilities were not unduly stimulated. If he had been educated for a genius, it would have injured him excessively. He developed himself. I think mental superiority in parents is seldom beneficial to children. Shrewdness and good-nature are all that is requisite."

Hawthorne's Aunt Priscilla, however, was not of the same opinion. She pleaded with her brother Robert to encourage the boy to study — using an appropriate horticultural metaphor: "Be so good Robert as to favour him with your advice (which I think will not fail to be influential) with regard to attending to writing, and some of his lessons, regularly . . . However rich the soil, we do not expect fruit, unless good seed is sown, and the plants carefully cultivated." Hawthorne, in an autobiographical fragment written for a friend, suggested that his protracted invalidism had involved some malingering on his part. He had a "natural repugnance" for schooling, he said, and Providence had favored him in that respect: "I never did go half as much as other boys, partly owing to delicate health (which I made the most of for the purpose) and partly because, much of the time, there were no schools within reach." But there were other, more somber, moments when he did not expect "to live to be twenty-five."

In mid 1814, a new doctor, a Dr. Smith of Hanover, prescribed a form of hydrotherapy that consisted of dousing the injured foot with cold water every morning. By late August, there was some improvement, though Hawthorne was still on crutches. Priscilla Manning wrote her brother that Nathaniel appeared to be in "good health and spirits, and we even flatter ourselves that there is some alteration in the appearance of his foot . . . He amuses himself with playing about the yard, and in Herbert Street nearly all day." It was not until the following January, however, that his mother was able to write Richard Manning, "Nathaniel has entirely recovered the use of his foot, and walks as well as he did before he was lame. His joy was great when he found he could walk without his crutches. It is indeed a subject of thankfulness to us all, he was lame fourteen months."

For several years, various members of the Manning family had planned to move to Maine, leaving William in charge of the Salem operations. In 1814, Betsey Hawthorne and her sister Mary considered buying a farm at Bridgton, near Raymond, but after many postponements, the plan was given up. During the summer of 1816, she and her family lived as boarders with one of the tenant farmers on Manning property in Maine. That October, much to his regret, Hawthorne returned to Salem to continue his schooling, leaving his mother and sisters behind. A year later, Robert Manning began plans to build, near Lake Sebago outside Raymond, a home large enough to accommodate himself and his spinster sister Mary, while his mother and sisters remained behind for an extended stay. The house, though, was not completed until 1818 and was thereafter known in the family as "Manning's Folly," not because of its costly or extravagant construction, but because it was so seldom lived in. In late October 1818, however, Betsey Hawthorne and the children moved to Maine, presumably to take up permanent residence in Uncle Robert's folly.

Hawthorne considered his childhood years in Maine one of the happiest periods of his life, though he had few companions his age except for his sisters. In the summers, he was free to roam the woods at his own will, hunting for partridges and hen hawks with his father's ancient fowling gun. The brooks were full of trout. In the winter, he skated, often in complete solitude, on the frozen lake, the dark pines looming on the horizon as the sun set. When he was cold, he installed himself in one of the many vacant cabins along the lake and settled on the broad hearth in front of a crackling log fire. The slow progress of the days and the seasons, the sense of isolation, seemed to agree with him.

There were few dramatic events. Once, during a blizzard in the spring of 1819, there was a local tragedy involving a neighboring couple, Mr. and Mrs. Tarbox. The husband had started out to get provisions in nearby Raymond. When he did not return, his wife went in search of him. They were found the following morning, frozen to death, a few feet from each other. Richard Manning adopted one of the five orphans. Hawthorne, who had already made some tentative attempts at writing poetry, reportedly wrote a ballad on the subject, though it has not survived. Far less dramatic was the trouble with the Merino ram later that spring. Hawthorne wrote his uncle in May that the ram had "threatened to kill Louisa without any provocation and has behaved so bad that Mother did not think it safe to keep him and Mr. Ham has got him." Rounding out his news from Maine, he added, "I have shot a partridge and a henhawk and caught 18 large trout out of our brooke."

For the most part, Hawthorne's life in Maine was undisturbed by the irksome question of education. During the winter of 1818–1819, however, he was forced to go to school at nearby Stroudwater, under the direction of the Reverend Caleb Bradley, a Harvard graduate. Restless and unhappy, he waited until Uncle Robert had returned to Salem, then threatened to leave the school on his own. His mother and his more amenable Uncle Richard allowed the boy to come home.

Hawthorne nonetheless read a good deal during this period and was to form some opinions about his own education. He could recall reading, on rainy days in Maine, "in Shakespeare and 'The Pilgrim's Progress,' and any poetry or light books within my reach." Interestingly, in view of his later development as a writer of allegories, his two favorite books of these earlier years were Spenser's *Faerie Queene* and Bunyan's *Pilgrim's Progress,* which he read and reread (and frequently alluded to) throughout his life. He could recall his pleasure as a small boy, standing on tiptoe to pull down books from his Grandfather Manning's shelf, shutting himself off in the pages of some barely comprehensible work, but understanding it more through sensibility than intellect. Only a solitary child, "left much to such wild modes of culture as he chooses for himself while yet ignorant what culture means," Hawthorne maintained, could develop the special intimacy with an author that he thought was worth having.

In later life, Hawthorne idealized his Maine childhood, stressing the natural setting: "Those were delightful days, for that part of the country was wild then, with only scattered clearings, and nine tenths of it primeval woods." He once told a friend, "I lived in Maine like a bird of the air, so perfect was the freedom I enjoyed." But he had, by then, acquired that doubleness of mind that marked him as a writer: the ability to recognize the rare, glowing occasions that life offered — and the price that it exacted. For he added, "It was there I first got my cursed habits of solitude."

The Maine idyll was over in his fifteenth year. In the summer of 1819 he was back in Salem, separated from his mother and sisters, and enrolled in Mr. Archer's school on Marlborough Street. He was plainly unhappy. Aunt Mary reported to her sister on July 6, "Nathaniel [had] a solitary Independence and birthday this year, he requested that he might not begin going to school until after the 5th of July . . . He sighs for the woods of Raymond, and yet he seems to be convinced of the necessity of preparing to do something." Three weeks later, Hawthorne wrote his mother, "I have begun to go to school and can find no fault with it except it's not being dear enough, only 5 dollars a quarter, and not near enough for it is up by the Baptist Meeting House. I am as well contented here as I expected to be, but sometimes I do have very bad fits of homesickness." In September, he wrote Louisa with similar complaints: "I shall never be contented here, I am sure. I now go to a 5 dollar school, I have been to a 10 dollar one. 'O, Lucifer, son of morning, how art thou fallen!'" He was reading a good deal, so he informed Louisa: *Waverley, The Mysteries of Udolpho, The Adventures of Ferdinand Count Fathom, Roderick Random,* and the first volume of *The Arabian Nights.* He sent his sisters some recent samples of his poetry:

> *Oh, earthly pomp is but a dream,*
> *And like a meteor's short-lived gleam;*
> *And all the sons of glory soon*
> *Will rest beneath the mould'ring stone.*
> *And genius is a star whose light*
> *Is soon to sink in endless night,*
> *And heavenly beauty's angel form*
> *Will bend like flowers in winter's storm.*

He was visited, it seems, by thoughts out of season — as unusual as flowers in a winter storm — on the vanity of human wishes and the sad fate of genius. "Though those are my rhymes, yet they are not exactly my thoughts," he explained to Louisa. "I am full of scraps of poetry; can't keep it out of my brain." Another stanza read:

> *I saw where in the lowly grave*
> *Departed Genius lay;*
> *And mournful yew-trees o'er it wave*
> *To hide it from the day.*

"I could vomit up a dozen pages more if I was a mind to," he added, with the same depreciation and irony that were to characterize his attitude toward his work when he became a mature writer — even a famous one.

Separated from his family, failing to recognize that his Uncle Robert, however fussing and meddling, was concerned for his future, Hawthorne appears to have developed a certain truculence toward the Mannings. He was coming of age. In March 1820, he wrote his mother confidentially that things were not going well in the Herbert Street household. "I am extremely homesick. Aunt Mary is continually scolding at me. Grandma'am hardly ever speaks a pleasant word to me. If I ever attempt to speak a word in my defense, they cry out against my impudence. However, I guess I can live through a year and a half more, and then I shall leave them. One good effect results from their eternal finding-fault. It gives me some employment in retaliating, and that keeps up my spirits."

He was anticipating the arrival of Louisa, who was being sent to school in Salem. In writing her, he could gracefully concede, "Though you and I could never keep the peace when we were together, yet I believe it [was?] almost always my fault." Still, he was experiencing some ambivalence in the matter; he clearly hoped that his mother would "upon no account think of returning to Salem," and he told Louisa bluntly, "I don't much want you to come either." In his letter to his mother, he cautioned that it might be better if Louisa boarded with his Aunt Priscilla in the Dike household: "Then Aunt Mary can't have her to domineer over."

He may have been experiencing some difficulty in asserting his masculine independence under the domestic regime of his aunt and his grandmother. That he would have preferred the relaxed supervision of his mother is clear from his letter. "Oh, how I wish I was again with you, with nothing to do but go a-gunning. But the happiest days of my life are gone," he claimed, adding, "Why was I not a girl that I might have been pinned all my life to my Mother's apron?"

In his March letter, Hawthorne also informed his mother that he had "begun to fit for college under Benjamin L. Oliver, Lawyer. So you are in danger of having one learned man in your family. Mr. Oliver thought I could enter college next commencement, but Uncle Robert is afraid I should have to study too hard. I get my lessons at home, and recite them to him at 7 o'clock in the morning."

With Louisa's return to Salem, his loneliness was somewhat abated. Both of them were enrolled in Mr. Turner's dancing school. In the fall, Hawthorne gallantly escorted his sister to a ball at which the young women were required to wear white dresses with short sleeves, and long white kid gloves. Louisa's gown of India muslin had been bought for her by her aunt Rachel Forrester.

In the afternoons, Hawthorne worked as secretary and bookkeeper for his Uncle William in the stagecoach office, but he ventured into the literary life as well. He became publisher, editor, and author of a newspaper, *The Spectator*, patterned after the famous journal of Addison and Steele. The issues, which were written out by hand in painstakingly careful penmanship, included essays on high-minded subjects — "On Wealth," "On Benevolence," and "On Industry" — in which the writer confessed, "An Author does not write the worse for knowing little or nothing of his subject." *The Spectator* was a short-lived project: the first issue was dated August 21, 1820, and the last, September 25. It contained a family gossip column, samples of poetry, and comic notices, one of which advertised for a husband for Aunt Mary.

Hawthorne's studies with Mr. Oliver left him little time for editorship and poetry. In October, he wrote Ebe that he had "almost given up writing Poetry. No man can be a Poet and a Book Keeper at the same time. I do find this place most horribly dismal and have taken to chewing tobacco with all my might, which I think raises my spirits. Say nothing of it in your letters . . ." He was of two minds about college, apparently, and weary of his uncle's authority. "I do not think I shall ever go to college," he told Ebe, "I can scarcely bear the thought of living upon Uncle Robert for 4 years longer. How happy I shall feel to be able to say, 'I am Lord of myself!' You may cut off this part of my letter and show the other to Uncle Richard."

It was a restless period in his life, the time when a young man experiences the full brunt of rising sexual impulses and feels the need of privacy. Yet at the age of seventeen, in the crowded Manning household, Hawthorne was obliged to share his bed. In a letter to his mother, written in March 1821, Hawthorne mentioned, "I dreamed the other night that I was walking by the Sebago; and when I awoke was so angry at finding it all a delusion, that I gave Uncle Robert (who sleeps with me) a most horrible kick."

That he was given a certain latitude by his Uncle Robert is suggested by the fact that when the celebrated actor Edmund Kean was appearing in Boston, Hawthorne was allowed to go to a performance of *King Lear*, staying overnight and returning the following day. He wrote his mother about the performance, "It was enough to have drawn tears from millstones. I could have cried myself if I had been in a convenient place for such an exploit." He added, "It is now going on two years since I saw you. Do not you regret the time when

I was a little boy? I do almost." He boasted that he was now "as tall as Uncle Robert."

That summer, Salem was much exercised about the trial of Stephen Clark, a young man who had been convicted of arson and sentenced to die under an old law that made barn-burning a capital offense. Although the clergy preached clemency, Clark was hanged. This instance of hard Salem justice evidently gave rise to thoughts about the dangers of misspent youth. Aunt Mary, writing to her sister, was disposed to draw a conventional moral: if poor Stephen Clark had attended a Sabbath school, "he might have escaped the dreadful End to which he has come." Whether there was a connection or not, Hawthorne wrote his mother at the time that he was going to meeting so constantly that he found it difficult to stay awake during the sermons. His response to Clark's fate was curious. "I did not go to see Stephen Clark executed," he wrote his mother. "It is said that he could have been restored to life some time after his execution. I do not know why it was not done."

The theme of the man who attempts to escape the immutable laws of nature and cheat death — either by some magic art or medical wizardry — persists throughout Hawthorne's writings from the early "Dr. Heidegger's Experiment" to the unfinished *Dolliver Romance.*

It had been decided that Hawthorne would enroll in the fairly new college of Bowdoin, in New Brunswick, Maine, not too far distant from Raymond. "I am quite reconciled to going to college," Hawthorne informed his mother, "since I am to spend the vacations with you. Yet four years of the best part of my Life is a great deal to throw away." He also touched lightly on the possibilities of a future profession:

> The being a minister is of course out of the Question. I should not think that even you could desire me to choose so dull a way of life. Oh, no, mother, I was not born to vegetate forever in one place, and to live and die as calm and tranquil as — a puddle of water. As to lawyers, there are so many of them already that one half of them (upon a moderate calculation) are in a state of actual starvation. A physician, then, seems to be "Hobson's choice"; but yet I should not like to live by the diseases and infirmities of my fellow Creatures. And it would weigh very heavily on my conscience if, in the course of my practice, I should chance to send any unlucky patient "ad inferum," which being interpreted is "to the realms below." Oh that I was rich enough to live without a profession! What do you

> think of my becoming an author, and relying for support upon my
> pen? Indeed, I think the illegibility of my handwriting is very
> author-like. How proud you would feel to see my works praised by
> the reviewers, as equal to [the] proudest productions of the scrib-
> bling sons of John Bull. But authors are always poor devils, and
> therefore Satan may take them . . .

The tone is jocular; the letter, no doubt, was intended to test his
mother's sentiments. He seems also to have been concerned about
keeping his tentative ambitions secret from his practical-minded
Manning relatives, for in a cautionary postscript he added, "Do not
show this letter."

In the merest, offhand manner, the letter also contains the suggestion of another idea that becomes a persistent theme in Hawthorne's
work: the hint that writing involved an almost diabolical form of
knowledge, an acquaintance with the darker passions, the hidden
sins and guilts of others — that an author was, in a sense, in league
with the devil.

⌐ III ⌐

Despite Hawthorne's premature worries that he would be wasting
four precious years at college, he may well have been looking forward to his escape from Salem and the rule of women. At Bowdoin,
he would be thrown into the company of young men his own age.
Late in 1821, he made the long, tedious stage journey to Brunswick,
accompanied by his Uncle Robert, who wanted to be sure his
nephew passed the entrance examinations and that he would be
suitably housed. Hawthorne passed the entrance requirements satis-
factorily, though without any great distinction; he also found suitable quarters in Maine Hall, one of the few dormitory facilities on
the still-raw country campus. He elected to take his meals in the
nearby home of Samuel Newman, the young and capable professor
of Greek and Latin at Bowdoin, a man who encouraged in his students a taste for literary values as well as a thorough grounding in
the classical languages.

On the journey to Bowdoin, Hawthorne had become acquainted
with three student passengers — Alfred Mason and Jonathan Cilley,
both from Maine and entering their freshman year, and Franklin
Pierce, of New Hampshire, a returning sophomore. Mason became
Hawthorne's roommate for the first two years — an economy, since
the two students could share the expense of firewood, $1.00 a cord,
throughout the frigid Maine winters. Mason was preparing for a career in medicine, a career cut short when, at the young age of

twenty-four, Mason contracted a disease at Bellevue Hospital, in New York, where he had begun his internship. Cilley, a high-spirited young man, planned to become a lawyer and would eventually embark on a promising political career, serving as the congressman for his district in Maine.

With Pierce, Hawthorne formed a lifelong friendship. Younger than Hawthorne by some four months, slender, affable, with a congenial disposition that seemed to draw out the more circumspect Hawthorne, Pierce was the son of a Revolutionary hero, General Benjamin Pierce, who instilled in his son his own zeal for the Republic. Young Pierce exhibited an aptitude for the military — at least to the extent of becoming an officer in the Bowdoin Cadets, a short-lived military corps numbering about forty students who regularly practiced drill and paraded on the campus. (Hawthorne enlisted in the unit as a mere private; it was the only military service he ever knew.) But Pierce, too, was studying for the law and later moved into politics, his way smoothed by his father's powerful political connections in New Hampshire. From the beginning, Hawthorne was impressed with what he discerned as Pierce's leadership qualities. He also admired — and perhaps envied — his friend's warm relationship with his father.

Through Alfred Mason, Hawthorne was introduced to another law student, Horatio Bridge, with whom he established an unequivocal friendship. Bridge's father was a Maine politician and lawyer, a former probate judge who had retired early for reasons of health. Boisterous and easygoing in his youth, but prudent in his later life, Bridge was to have a distinguished governmental career, first in the navy and then as a paymaster general in the Navy Department in Washington. He seems to have been immediately taken with Hawthorne's affable manner and by his Byronic good looks. He described the young Hawthorne as "a slender lad, having a massive head, with dark, brilliant and most expressive eyes." Others, too, were struck by Hawthorne's piercing light gray eyes, which, in certain moods and in certain lights, deepened into purplish-blue. They were like "blue-gray sapphires," according to one acquaintance; another, the English novelist Charles Reade, claimed they were the most magnificent eyes he had ever seen in a human head. At his mature height, Hawthorne was five feet, ten and a half inches tall, broad-shouldered, but with a light, athletic build. He had a noticeable habit, according to Bridge, "of carrying his head a little to one side; but his walk was square and firm." A family story had it that when Hawthorne was at Bowdoin, an astonished Gypsy woman, meeting him on a woodland path, had stopped and asked, "Are you a man or an angel?"

There was also something indefinably feminine in Hawthorne's nature, suggested by his full, sensuous lips, perhaps, or by his characteristic passivity and reserve with others. Oliver Wendell Holmes complained that trying to talk with Hawthorne was like "love-making." Hawthorne's "shy, beautiful soul had to be wooed from its bashful pudency like an unschooled maiden." Horatio Bridge, far less assertive than Holmes, never seemed troubled by Hawthorne's sometimes unsettling silences. In his *Personal Recollections of Nathaniel Hawthorne*, written many years later, Bridge made an effort to counteract the image of the morbidly shy author that had crystallized about Hawthorne's name. "He was neither morose nor sentimental," Bridge claimed, "and, though taciturn, was invariably cheerful with his chosen friends; and there was much more of fun and frolic in his disposition than his published writings indicate." But, then, Hawthorne could relax with companions like Bridge; with literary celebrities and rival authors he seldom opened up. Bridge was also struck by Hawthorne's "great pluck and determination." He vividly recalled an incident in which the usually aloof Hawthorne was being kidded by his classmates. The occasion was so rare in itself that the bantering went too far. Hawthorne put up with it for a while, then resolutely planted himself in front of the most combative of his classmates and said quietly that the kidding would have to stop. There was such "danger in his eye," Bridge recalled, that no one questioned his seriousness.

It was Bridge who first recognized Hawthorne's literary talent, predicting a great future for his friend. He could have come to that conclusion only from intuition — and from the regularity with which Professor Newman praised and read aloud Hawthorne's classroom compositions. Hawthorne wrote little and, with one possible exception, published nothing during his college years. (The exception, reportedly, was an anonymous article about a spurious insect attacking New England fruit trees; it was sent to a horticultural magazine, where it would perplex his Uncle Robert.)

Throughout the early, discouraging years of his professional life, Hawthorne was to rely on Bridge's encouraging letters — for Bridge was convinced of Hawthorne's inevitable fame. With Hawthorne, loyalties once formed were never abandoned; he always remembered Bridge's encouragement. Years later, dedicating his collection of stories *The Snow-Image* to his friend, Hawthorne affectionately recalled their college days. "If anybody is responsible for my being at this day an author, it is yourself," he wrote, addressing Bridge. "I know not whence your faith came; but, while we were lads together at a country college — gathering blue-berries, in study-hours, under those tall academic pines; or watching the great logs, as they tumbled along the current of the Androscoggin; or shooting pigeons and gray squirrels in the woods; or bat-fowling in the summer twilight . . . two idle lads, in short (as we need not fear to acknowledge now), doing a hundred things that the Faculty never heard of, or else it had been the worse for us — still it was your prognostic of your friend's destiny, that he was to be a writer of fiction."

Bowdoin, chartered in 1794, was a small remote college modeled on the plan of Harvard, though hardly so distinguished — or so expensive. When Hawthorne registered in 1821, it had a faculty of 8 professors, several of them Harvard graduates, and a student body of about 120, nearly all of whom came from Maine or nearby New Hampshire, Vermont, and Massachusetts. The curriculum of prescribed courses included a heavy concentration in Greek and Latin, with required weekly translations, and studies in the various branches of mathematics and philosophy. The scientific curriculum included natural history and geology. Professor Parker Cleaveland, who, with the necessary economy of a small school, taught mathematics, philosophy, chemistry, and mineralogy, was a recognized authority in the field of geology. Bowdoin paid little attention to modern literature or the modern languages. Hawthorne, in his senior year, resorted to an outside tutor for his study of French.

The president of the college was the Reverend William Allen, a stern disciplinarian, a Congregationalist, still holding to the strict Calvinist doctrines of his generation. Equally unpopular with the students was the newly ordained preacher, the Reverend Asa Mead, who, not without cause, harangued his students at chapel services about the evils of drinking. The bane of Hawthorne's college years — aside from the compulsory religious services — were the weekly declamations required of the students throughout the year. More often than not, Hawthorne avoided these and incurred the resulting fines. According to Bridge, Hawthorne's aversion to public speaking could be traced back to a schoolboy experience in Salem, when he had got up on a platform to recite and had been laughed at by the other boys.

Still, Hawthorne's reluctance in regard to public speaking did not keep him from joining the informal Pot-8-O Club, which met weekly at Ward's Tavern, conveniently located at the edge of the campus, and at which recitations of poems or dissertations on chosen topics were required. Jonathan Cilley and Alfred Mason were among his fellow members. The refreshments at these gatherings consisted of "Roasted potatoes, butter, salt and cider or some other mild drink." The club's constitution, with something less than the truth, announced, "Ardent spirits shall never be introduced." In his first published novel, *Fanshawe,* the setting of which was undoubtedly Bowdoin, Hawthorne makes it clear that he was thoroughly acquainted with the student's clandestine drinking sessions in the local taverns. Bridge, too, in his memoirs, notes that it was the common practice on campus for students to keep a clean container — meant for carrying kerosene for their lamps — for the purpose of carrying wine and beer to the dormitories.

Despite its provincial situation, Bowdoin could boast of rather distinguished alumni from Hawthorne's college years. In Hawthorne, it had educated one of the country's most renowned authors; in Pierce, a President. Cilley, in his brief career, served with distinction in the Maine legislature and in Washington; and Bridge, who was to hold appointed offices in Washington during Pierce's administration and later, listed in his memoir a dozen or more of his college contemporaries who went on to achieve transient fame in politics. Calvin Stowe, the undisputed scholar of Franklin Pierce's class, became a noted preacher and reformer, though he achieved more lasting recognition as the husband of Harriet Beecher Stowe. Henry Wadsworth Longfellow, who did not enroll until the sophomore year of the class of 1825, became the most popular poet of his day. Despite their literary inclinations, he and Hawthorne were barely acquainted during their Bowdoin years. Their friendship, lengthy and untroubled, dated from a later period in their lives. At least once, however, the two appeared on the same program of compulsory "Exhibitions." On the evening of October 29, 1824, Longfellow delivered the opening Latin discourse, "Angli Poetae" (The English Poets). Hawthorne, eighth on the program, gave an address, "De Patribus Conscriptis Romanorum" (Of Roman Senators).

Longfellow, only fifteen when he entered Bowdoin, was a precocious and exemplary student, something of a grind. He never incurred fines, as did his older brother, Stephen, who already exhibited the lack of purpose and the tendency to drink that later ruined his life. Longfellow briefly joined the Bowdoin Cadets, but soon grew tired of the parading and resigned when the cadets degenerated into a social club. He was readily invited to join the Peucinian Society, the most respected and conservative literary club on the campus. The Peucinians favored John Quincy Adams. Hawthorne, Cilley, Pierce, Bridge, and the more convivial Stephen Longfellow were Atheneans, advocates of the Democratic Party and supporters of General Jackson in the 1824 elections. It was some indication of Longfellow's diligence that on graduating, at the age of eighteen, he was offered a position as the first professor of a newly established chair of modern languages, a post voted on by the trustees of Bowdoin — one of whom was Longfellow's father, a well-to-do Portland lawyer and politician. Even before his graduation, Longfellow had acquired a reputation as a poet and essayist, his contributions sought after by the editors of the *American Monthly Magazine* and the *United States Literary Gazette*.

By contrast, Hawthorne's college career was undistinguished. "I was an idle student," he later recalled, "negligent of college rules and the Procrustean details of academic life, rather choosing to nurse my own fancies than to dig into Greek roots and be numbered among the learned Thebans." His Bowdoin years gave him what he appeared to need most — a time to think and be, freedom from the rule of women and the authority of his Uncle Robert. Still, he could admire the will power and determination of his friend Pierce, who had to come to grips with a youthful tendency to dissipation and drink. In his junior year, told that he had the lowest standing in his class and would undoubtedly fail, Pierce applied himself, surviving on four hours' sleep a night, until he had pulled up his rank to third in his class.

Hawthorne's surviving letters to his sisters and family during these years are chatty; they seldom mention his academic studies. "My occupations this term have been much the same as they were last," he wrote Louisa in April 1822, "except that I have, in a great measure, discontinued the practice of playing cards. One of the students has been suspended lately for this offence, and two of our class have been fined. I narrowly escaped detection myself and mean for the future to be more careful." He was not careful enough, however. On May 30, he wrote his mother frankly, "All the card players in College have been found out, and my unfortunate self among the number. One has been dismissed from College, two suspended, and the rest, with myself, have been fined 50 cts. each . . . When the President asked what we played for, I thought proper to inform him it was 50 cts., although it happened to be a Quart of Wine, but if I had told him of that he would probably have fined me for having a blow." Somewhat solipsistically, he added, "There was no untruth in the case, as the wine cost 50 cts. I have not played at all this term. I have not drank any kind of spirits or wine this term, and shall not until the last week."

President Allen wrote Mrs. Hawthorne about her son's misdemeanor, though taking a lenient view. "Perhaps he might not have gamed," he wrote, "were it not for the influence of a Student, whom we have dismissed from college." Hawthorne was indignant: "I was full as willing to play as the person he suspects of having enticed me, and would have been influenced by no one. I have a great mind to commence playing again, merely to show him that I scorn to be seduced by another into anything wrong." Whether he was involved or not, Hawthorne regularly informed his family about the nonacademic activities at Bowdoin. "If I had time," he wrote Louisa, "I would tell you a mighty story, how some of the students hung Parson Mead in effigy, and how one of them was suspended. Mother need not be frightened, as I was not engaged in it."

Like most students, Hawthorne was often short of money, and his letters home are punctuated with requests. Unfortunately, his mother had moved back to Salem in 1822, and Hawthorne could seldom afford the time or the expense to make the journey to Salem. He was popular with his college friends and was often asked to their homes, particularly by Bridge, whose family lived in Augusta. "I am invited by several of the students to pass the vacation with them," he wrote in the spring of 1823. "I believe I shall go to Augusta, if Mother and Uncle R. have no objections. The stage fare will be about five dollars and I should like about ten dollars as spending money, as I am going to the house of an Honorable." But he fretted about not seeing his family. At the end of his junior year, he wrote Louisa, demanding that she manufacture some excuse — to be written to President Allen — requesting that he be sent home before the term was over. "I am almost dead of homesickness," he claimed, "and am apprehensive of serious injury to my health if I am not soon removed from this place." He offered several ingenious rationalizations: "The latter part of the term preceding Commencement is invariably spent in dissipation, and I am afraid that my stay here will have an ill effect upon my moral character, which would be a cause of grief to mother and you." Louisa, he suggested, should claim that his mother was "out of health" or that his Uncle Robert was taking a journey for his health and wanted his nephew to accompany him. "Write immediately, write immediately, write immediately . . ." he demanded. "If you can think of a true excuse, send it; if not, any other will answer the same purpose." His mother, he was sure, would have no objections; if she did, Louisa's eloquence would bring her around. "If I do not get a letter by Monday, or Tuesday at the farthest," he threatened, "I will leave Brunswick without liberty."

Few of Hawthorne's letters to his family during these college years, however, reflect such a pitch of restlessness. For the most part, they are the letters of a young man not overly concerned about the future; their tone is frequently bantering. He complains about his "want of decent clothes" or his lack of money; he boasts of the rare occasion when he complied with the college rules and declaimed in chapel. "I made a very splendid appearance in the chapel last Friday evening, before a crowded audience," he writes his sister after his appearance on the platform with Longfellow. "I would send you a printed list of the performances if it were not for the postage." He wants more news from his sisters: "You ought to give me a more particular account of yourselves and all that concerns you, as, though it might appear trifling to others, it would be interesting to me. I suppose Louisa has by this time returned from Newburyport, and gives herself the airs of a traveling lady."

In December 1824, his Uncle Robert married Rebecca Dodge Burnham. Hawthorne was not able to attend the ceremonies. Perhaps his reasons were genuine; perhaps he merely used his studies as an excuse. (He was to have a number of excuses for not attending Robert Manning's funeral, many years later, and sent his apologies by way of his sister, rather than writing directly to the widow.) He wrote his Aunt Mary, on this occasion, in a joking vein, "I sincerely sympathize with Uncle Robert and the family in the pleasure they must feel at the approaching event. I wish that it were possible for me to be present, in order that I might learn how to conduct myself when marriage shall be my fate. Then he twitted his maiden aunt: "I console myself with the hope that you, at least, will not neglect to give me an invitation to your wedding, which I should not be surprised to hear announced. Elizabeth says that you are very deeply in love with Mr. Upham. Is the passion reciprocal?"

It was, apparently, late in his college career that he informed his sister Elizabeth he had "made progress in my novel," an indication to her, at least, that Hawthorne had begun to think seriously of becoming a writer. He may also have begun work on a series of short stories and sketches, *Seven Tales of My Native Land*, which he later hoped to publish as a book. Elizabeth recalled that it was during the summer vacation of 1825 — just before his September graduation — that he had first showed her the stories. There are few indications that he had decisively settled upon any particular profession.

Chiefly, his final letters from Bowdoin express a sense of boredom and dissatisfaction, an eagerness to be finished with college. Hawthorne's uncle John Dike, on a business trip to Maine, visited him at the college, and the pair had made a trip to Raymond. Hawthorne found his reception at Richard Manning's home unaccountably cold and complained of it in a letter to his younger sister: "Uncle Richard seemed to care nothing about us, and Mrs. Manning was as cold and freezing as a December morning." On his return, President Allen had called him to his office to inform him that, although he had passed his grades, his failure to meet the college requirements in declamations meant that he was not eligible to make one of the many commencement addresses that were a feature of the gradua-

tion ceremonies. Hawthorne was not displeased. "I am perfectly satisfied with this arrangement," he wrote home, "as it is a sufficient
testimony of my scholarship, while it saves me the mortification of
making my appearance in public at commencement." Still, he was
not so belligerent on the subject that he was unconcerned about the
opinion of the Mannings. "Perhaps the family may not be so well
pleased with it. Tell me," he asked, "what are their sentiments on
the subject?"

He was much more unhappy about the good accounts his Uncle
John had been spreading in Salem.

> I am not very well pleased with Mr. Dike's report of me [he wrote].
> The family had before conceived much too high an opinion of my
> talents, and had probably formed expectations which I shall never
> realize. I have thought much upon the subject and have finally
> come to the conclusion that I shall never make a distinguished fig-
> ure in the world and all I hope or wish is to plod along with the
> multitude. I do not say this for the purpose of drawing any flattery
> from you, but merely to set Mother and the rest of you right, upon a
> point where your partiality has led you astray. I did hope that
> Uncle Robert's opinion of me was nearer to the truth, as his deport-
> ment towards me never expressed a very high estimation of my
> abilities.

Hawthorne was always to be cautious of praise, diffident about success, inordinately careful in his self-evaluations; and he was often
closer to the truth than his adulators.

He did, in fact, graduate with the multitude — eighteenth in a
class of thirty-nine. No member of his family seems to have been
present at the ceremonies on September 7. His name, along with
thirteen others, including his friend Bridge's, did not appear on the
"Order of Commencement."

Among the speakers on that day was the exemplary student Henry
Wadsworth Longfellow, graduating fourth in his class. In that atmosphere of routine aspirations and anticlimax, amidst the drone
of conventional sentiments, young Longfellow's speech, "Our Native
Writers," struck a decisive note. "Yes! — and palms are to be won
by our native writers!" the young poet declared, " — by those, that
have been nursed and brought up with us in the civil and religious
freedom of our country. Already has a voice been lifted up in this
land . . ." On that bright summer day, standing on the platform
against a backdrop of green native pines, Longfellow, no doubt addressing his cautious father as well as the world, asserted that the
lack of a "polite literature" in America could be traced to "the want
of that exclusive attention, which eminence in any profession so im-

periously demands." He went on, "We are a plain people, that have had nothing to do with the mere pleasures and luxuries of life: and hence there has sprung up within us a quick-sightedness to the failings of literary men, and an aversion to everything that is not practical, operative and thorough-going." It was clear that Longfellow had ambitions for remedying that state of affairs.

These were ambitions that Hawthorne must have shared, though with more diffidence and uncertainty.

The Long Seclusion

I T WAS my fortune or misfortune . . ." Hawthorne later wrote, "to have some slender means of supporting myself; and so, on leaving college, in 1825, instead of immediately studying a profession, I sat myself down to consider what pursuit in life I was best fit for. My mother had now returned, and taken up her abode in her deceased father's house . . . in which I had a room. And year after year I kept on considering what I was fit for, and time and my destiny decided that I was to be the writer that I am."

Behind that laconic statement lies one of the more curious chapters in the career of a great American writer. On leaving Bowdoin, Hawthorne entered upon what he termed his "long seclusion," a decade in which he served his apprenticeship as a writer immured behind the family walls. Much of his boyhood and youth had been spent away from his native Salem; as a consequence, he had few acquaintances and friends there. "I doubt whether so much as twenty people in the town were aware of my existence," he remembered.

In later years, he was to be of two minds about his Salem life, uncertain whether it should be construed as "fortune or misfortune." At times, he viewed it simply as a very tolerable period, one in which he "seemed cheerful and enjoyed the very best bodily health." His lengthy seclusion had neither made him "melancholy or misanthrophic," nor had it unfitted him for "the bustle of life." At such moments, he was inclined to trust the instinct that had taught him the disciplines of solitude.

On other occasions, however, he viewed those Salem years as a form of limbo, a long and weary imprisonment. In his youth, Hawthorne displayed none of the irascible temperament of the genius and little of that pose of the artist-as-romantic-hero. He remained remarkably level-headed about his profession. Still, there were to be moments in his career — solemn moments — when the matter-of-fact surfaces of life seemed to open up, revealing chasms below. Revisiting his upstairs room in the Herbert Street house as a mature writer, he was to have some gloomy reflections. "If ever I should have a biographer," he mused, "he ought to make great mention of this chamber in my memoirs, because so much of my lonely youth was wasted here, and here my mind and character were formed." In his small chamber under the eaves, he had "sat a long, long time, waiting patiently for the world to know me, and sometimes wondering why it did not know me sooner, or whether it would ever know me at all — at least, till I were in my grave. And sometimes . . . it seemed as if I were already in my grave . . ." Ebe Hawthorne, recalling those years, maintained, "It was only after his return to Salem and when he felt as if he could not get away from there and was conscious of being utterly unlike every one else in the place that he began to withdraw into himself."

She also recalled that her brother's habits "were as regular as possible." In the mornings, and occasionally in the afternoons, Hawthorne wrote. If the weather was fair, he took solitary walks, usually to the shore at Juniper Point, by the "old ten-gun battery," which stood in ruins. He became a connoisseur of flotsam, examining the bits of driftage, the tangles of kelp and eel grass along the shore. Sometimes he walked to the shaded hills of North Salem, crossing the North Bridge — for Salem proper, in Hawthorne's time, was still an extended peninsula, separated on the north by the North River and on the south by the Mill Pond and the South River. There, in the summertime, he might take a brisk dip in a secluded cove, screened by maples and walnut trees. Returning homeward, past Cold Spring, he took note of the pretty picture of three little girls, none of them older than nine, paddling in the fountain, giggling as he passed. The scene, he maintained, "would have been prettier, if they had shown bare legs, instead of pantelettes." In the evenings — usually at twilight and whatever the weather — he took an hour-long walk. Occasionally he went to Gallow's Hill, where the witches had been hanged and their bodies flung into an ignominious grave. In the fading light of a summer evening, the hill seemed burnished with the golden flowers of the woodwax, growing there in abundance. On stormy nights, he ventured out into the rain-blackened streets of Salem, pleased by the gleaming reflections of shop windows. On winter evenings, Elizabeth recalled, Hawthorne ate "a pint bowl of thick chocolate (not cocoa, but the old-fashioned chocolate) crumbed full of bread; eating never hurt him then, and he liked good things. In summer, he ate something equivalent, finishing with fruit in the season of it." For most of his life, Hawthorne tended to be abstemious in the matter of food, as with all of his own physical wants and comforts. A friend, who once offered to brush off his greatcoat, never forgot Hawthorne's almost comic rejoinder: "No, no," he insisted, "I never brush my coat, it wears it out!"

In the evenings, Elizabeth Hawthorne recalled, they sometimes discussed political affairs, "upon which we differed in opinion; he being a Democrat and I of the opposite party. In reality, his interest in such things was so slight that I think nothing would have kept it alive but my contentious spirit." She also remembered that her brother might find a book so absorbing that he did not talk at all. But Hawthorne's silences on those occasions may well have been the result of his unwillingness of argue with his sister. He once remarked, not altogether facetiously, "The only thing I fear is the ridicule of Elizabeth." Elizabeth Hawthorne, writing about her brother for her niece Una, pointedly remembered, "Your Papa used to call me the severest critic he knew, and sometimes he told me I was not amiable in my tastes; but I believe that was because I excessively admired Milton's Satan, and had other predilections of a similar kind, as I have still."

However reclusive she was by nature, Ebe Hawthorne had an avid interest in the affairs of Salem and the world. She read the newspapers faithfully, kept abreast of American politics, and had her ideas on most topics of the day. Her opinions seemed to ripen with age and solitude. Having been forced to read nothing but religious books on Sundays — one of the "restraints imposed upon my childhood" — she had little interest in theological writing. "The only argument for the inspiration of the Bible that has any weight with me," she maintained, "is that it is readable, which other religious books are not." She distrusted the eastward bent of the transcendentalists — their "orientation," so to speak. "All that Emerson, Thoreau and others say about the Vedas, Confucius, etc. is evidently mere humbug," she claimed. "I have a better opinion of their taste than to suppose that they really do think as they profess to." She considered philosophy a waste of time; thought it far more advisable to read newspapers and glean one's philosophy from works of poetry and fiction. She worshiped Shakespeare and thought Samuel Johnson was the most useful of lifetime literary companions. She was surprised to learn that the history texts she had read in her youth were now dismissed as faulty. She thought about it, then came to some conclusions on the subject: "It is remarkable, but I think it generally proves true, that useful knowledge, unless for immediate practical application, is the most useless of all. After a little while you will find out that there was some element of falsehood in it, and that what reality it possessed was only temporary."

Hawthorne respected his sister's wit and originality of mind. He was willing to concede — though perhaps with a man's slight edge of disdain — that Ebe "knows the world marvelously, considering it is only through books." There were periods, he claimed — sometimes for three months at a time — when he scarcely saw his sister. "We do not live at our house," he maintained; "we only vegetate. Elizabeth never leaves her den; I have mine in the upper story." Daytime interviews with his sister were so rare that he could "never imagine her in sunshine." She seemed almost a creature of the night. "I really doubt whether her faculties of life and intellect begin to be exercised till dusk — unless on extraordinary occasions. Their noon is at midnight," he said.

The Widow Hawthorne and his sister Louisa, a bit more conventional, sometimes sat in the parlor with him after tea. Hawthorne's relationship with his mother was ambivalent. In later life, he suggested that their temperaments clashed and that his dealings with her were uneasy. But his letters to her throughout childhood and his college years are always trusting and open, confident of her sympathy, and frank about his minor vices, his drinking and card-playing. The truth, perhaps, is that Hawthorne's feelings about his mother, like those toward his father, were subjects too sacred to be openly examined or discussed.

With Louisa, aside from their childhood squabbles, Hawthorne's relationship was altogether easier — more sociable and normal than that with the opinionated Elizabeth. Nor was the Herbert Street household so completely isolated as Hawthorne sometimes painted it. On certain evenings, he and Louisa invited friends, including David Roberts, a young Salem lawyer, to play whist. Hawthorne, who had a fondness for private or comic names, dubbed him the Chancellor. The other was Horace Conolly, a recent graduate of Yale, the adopted son of a Hawthorne relation, old Suzy Ingersoll. Hawthorne called him the Cardinal, presumably because of his unctuous manner — or merely because he had studied for the ministry. In this whist-playing circle, Hawthorne and Louisa were the Emperor and the Empress.

During his Salem years, Hawthorne "read endlessly all sorts of good and good-for-nothing books." Although he had the use of Aunt Mary's library card, Elizabeth remembered that it was one of her brother's "peculiarities" that he would never visit the Salem Athenaeum himself, "nor look over the catalogue to select a book, nor indeed do anything but find fault with it; so that it was left entirely to me to provide him with reading." If he claimed to have little interest in contemporary history, Hawthorne nonetheless read histories of New England; the annals of Boston, Scituate, and Plymouth, and Felt's *Annals of Salem*, are among the books withdrawn for him from the Athenaeum during these years. He read the papers of Thomas Hutchinson, the unfortunate governor of the Massachusetts Bay Colony who had fled to England on the eve of the Revolution. He read tracts of such religious sects as the Shakers. He had an especial interest in Howell's *State Trials*, with its ancient accounts of criminal justice in England. He pored over the heavy folios for hours and later claimed he got "more delectation out of them than tongue could tell." He boasted once that if he had five lives, he could spend all of them devising tales from the odd personal histories, the bizarre narratives that were woven into the dry annals of English justice.

He asked Elizabeth to get out such French books as the Athenaeum contained: the writings of Montaigne, Corneille, Racine, Voltaire, and Rousseau. Cervantes' *Don Quixote* was a perennial favorite and often alluded to in his own writings. Among American authors, he read the writings of Hamilton, Jefferson, and Franklin. He developed an admiration for Cotton Mather's *Magnalia Christi Americana*, that "strange, pedantic history, in which true events and real personages move before the reader with the dreamy aspect which they wore in Cotton Mather's singular mind."

He read Samuel Johnson; but the "stalwart Doctor's grandiloquent productions," except for those "two stern and masculine poems," *London* and *The Vanity of Human Wishes*, were not much to his taste. In later life, Hawthorne wrote that Johnson "meddled only with the surface of life, and never cared to penetrate farther than to plough-share depth; his very sense and sagacity were but a one-eyed clearness." Yet Hawthorne felt that Johnson, the practical man, the talker, the humorist, had been a very valuable companion in his youth, a counterweight to his own "native propensities" toward dreaminess and fantasy. He was particularly moved by a penitential episode in the life of the great doctor. Johnson, a grown man, had stood bareheaded in the market square at Uttoxeter, doing public penance for a tormenting sin he had committed against his father in his youth.

He read Wordsworth and the younger, tragic poets of the Romantic movement — Keats, Shelley, and Byron — all of whom had died during his college years. Although he was, in his youth at least, a diffident poet, Hawthorne developed no great admiration for poetry as a genre, only for certain poets — most often those, like Longfellow or Coventry Patmore, who were of a conservative and sentimental cast of mind. "I am not a man of metre," he once claimed with a spark of pride. On idle occasions, he read through the past volumes of *The Gentleman's Magazine* and other periodicals and felt "the peculiar weariness and depression of spirits which is felt after a day wasted."

"He read a great many novels," Elizabeth Hawthorne remembered; "he made an artistic study of them." In his youth, he read Scott's romantic novels and once expressed a wish that he hadn't so that he "might have the pleasure of reading them again." For light reading and Gothic romances, he turned to the works of Mrs. Radcliffe and Horace Walpole and the novels of the American writers Charles Brockden Brown and John Neal, borrowed from a local circulating library. In his later life, almost as an antithesis to his own literary talents, he expressed a preference for authors like Dickens and Trollope, whose genius for picturesque and realistic detail, for the throb of contemporary life, seemed far different from his own kind of imaginative genius.

Hawthorne was always fond of the lure of the exotic. He read Hakluyt's *Voyages*, Pinckard's *Notes on the West Indies*, Temple's *Travels in Various Parts of Peru*, and Heber's *Travels in India*, as well as the travel writings of the American botanist John Bartram. He had an avid interest in biographies, autobiographies, memoirs. "Of all things, I delight in autobiographies," he once told his publisher, James T. Fields, who had sent him a copy of the memoirs of Anna Mowatt, the actress. Taciturn and reserved about his own life, he had the true author's interest in gossip and the private affairs of others.

It is not altogether clear whether *Fanshawe*, Hawthorne's first published novel, was, in fact, his first novel, the novel on which he reported making progress while in college. Elizabeth's account of her brother's early writings is ambiguous. She speaks of the several stories Hawthorne had showed her in the summer of 1825 — among them a tale of witchcraft titled "Alice Doane," and another called "Susan Grey." They were part of the collection he intended to call *Seven Tales of My Native Land*. Most of the stories Hawthorne subsequently burned in a fit of dissatisfaction with his early efforts and with his lack of success. But Ebe also spoke of *Fanshawe* as the "smaller book" he wrote after his return to Salem. The first novel, begun at Bowdoin, may have been burned with the earliest stories. Ebe had read the stories and thought them much better than the novel. "There was much more of his peculiar genius in them than in *Fanshawe*," she remarked. According to her account, Hawthorne had had the novel published at his own expense — $100. It was issued simply as *Fanshawe: A Tale*, without benefit of the author's name, in October 1828, by the Boston publisher Marsh and Capen.

There is a good deal of Sir Walter Scott in *Fanshawe*. It has a beautiful and beleaguered heroine in Ellen Langton; a thorough-going villain in Butler, a pirate who has strayed inland for criminal purposes; an abduction; a wild chase through dark woods; and two heroes: Edward Walcott, a handsome young extrovert, and Fanshawe, the retiring, mysteriously ailing student who seems "unconnected with the world, unconcerned in its feelings, and uninfluenced by it in any of his pursuits." The setting of this improbable story is Harley College, Hawthorne's fictional counterpart of Bowdoin, a "seminary of learning" set in a remote corner of an unnamed New England state. The president of this institution is the amiable Dr. Melmoth, whose only escape from a shrewish wife is his quiet study. Childless Dr. Melmoth is an ideal surrogate father to his students; his rule is "mild and gentle."

The heroes, Walcott and Fanshawe, represent the dual aspirations of a young man, both the active and the contemplative sides of Hawthorne's nature. Walcott, a stock romantic figure, has the manners of "polished society" and a "considerable command of money." He is also a respectable scholar and an erstwhile poet. His youthful follies, "sometimes perhaps approaching near to vices," may be related to Hawthorne's own bouts of wine-drinking and card-playing at Bowdoin. But he is impulsive and something of a hothead, given to action first and then reflection — traits Hawthorne may have borrowed from his college friends Cilley and Bridge.

With a touch of self-serving irony, perhaps, Hawthorne arranges his story so that the unassuming Fanshawe faces down the villain, rescues Ellen, and wins her love. There are elements of Hawthorne in Fanshawe, the "solitary being" who confines himself to his chamber and his studies except for one hour, "the sunset hour," when he walks along the river bank where he hopes to meet Ellen. Fanshawe, weary of his studies, asks himself, "Where was the happiness of superior knowledge?" It is a question that probably mirrored Hawthorne's own sentiments. Yet in Fanshawe's "inmost heart," Hawthorne assures the reader, "there would have been discovered that dream of undying fame, which, dream as it is, is more powerful than a thousand realities."

Although Fanshawe is fully conscious of his growing love for Ellen, a passion that might draw him out of his solitude and into the world, he resolves not to seek Ellen's love, "the result of which, for a thousand reasons, could not be happiness." The "thousand reasons," in fact, turn out to be a single implausible one: Fanshawe's conviction that he will die young, and of the most improbable of causes — a passion for study so intense that it does, in due course, bring him to an early grave. Fanshawe's fate is one of the earliest instances in Hawthorne's fiction of the unwritten prohibition against love and marriage that thwarts many of Hawthorne's heroes. The epitaph inscribed on Fanshawe's tombstone, *"The ashes of a hard student and a good scholar,"* has significance. It is the paraphrase of an epitaph for another Nathaniel — Nathanael Mather — written by his brother Cotton Mather in the pages of his *Magnalia Christi.*

Ellen Langton and Edward Walcott marry four years after Fanshawe's untimely death; they live a life of "calm and quiet bliss." Walcott is cured of those "passions and pursuits that would have interfered with domestic felicity." He never regrets "the worldly distinction" that might have been his if he had not married.

Fanshawe was an uneven and derivative performance, but as a first published effort by a young writer, it had distinctiveness of style and sometimes displayed a happy facility for description. The brief vignettes of minor characters, such as Hugh Crombie, reformed-pirate-turned-tavernkeeper, and of Dr. Melmoth and his termagant wife, are done with a surer hand than are the portrayals of the principals of the story. The reviews were generally kind. An unsigned review in the *Yankee and Boston Literary Gazette* declared, "Many parts of it are powerful and pathetic, and there are not a few specimens scattered about the work of excellent descriptive pencilling." Sarah Josepha Hale, in the *Ladies' Magazine*, admonished the public, "Purchase it, reader. There is but one volume, and trust me that it is worth placing in your library." William Leggett, writing in the *Critic*, announced, "The mind that produced this little, interesting volume, is capable of making great and rich additions to our native literature." A markedly unfavorable review appeared in the *New England Galaxy*: "Fanshawe . . . A love story with this title has just been published by Marsh and Capen. It has, like ten thousand others, a mystery, an elopement; a villain, a father, a tavern, almost a duel, a horrible death, and — heaven save the mark! . . . an end."

The *Galaxy*'s review came closest to the author's own opinion, for Hawthorne became the book's severest critic. Some years after publication, Hawthorne reclaimed the copy he had given his sister and, so Elizabeth maintained, "no doubt burned it." He insisted that his family keep his authorship a secret. Elizabeth disapproved, but yielded to his wishes. "We were in those days . . ." she remembered, "absurdly obedient to him. I do not quite approve of either obedience or concealment." Hawthorne also wrote his friend Bridge, asking him to destroy the copy he had been given.

For the remainder of his life, Hawthorne concealed his authorship of the novel. Years later, when James T. Fields inquired about his earliest novel, Hawthorne refused to supply any information. "I cannot be sworn to make correct answers as to all the literary or other follies of my nonage," he told Fields, "and I earnestly recommend you not brush away the dust that may have gathered over them. Whatever might do me credit, you may be pretty sure that I should be ready enough to bring forward. Anything else, it is our mutual interest to conceal." He seemed as intent on covering his tracks as if he had committed a crime.

———

"What is more potent than fire!" exclaims Oberon, the fictional author of one of Hawthorne's early stories, "The Devil in Manuscript." To the amazement of his stunned friend, the unnamed narrator of the story, Oberon has thrown a pile of his manuscripts into a blazing fire. His desperate act is a measure of his frustration. He has just recited for his friend a litany of his woes in his attempts to find an American publisher for his work. "One man publishes nothing but school-books," he complains, "another has five novels already under examination . . . another gentleman is just giving up business, on purpose, I verily believe, to escape publishing my book. Several, however, would not absolutely decline the agency, on my advancing half the cost of an edition, and giving bonds for the remainder." Oberon has found only one "honest" man among the seventeen to whom he has shown his book, "and he tells me fairly, that no American publisher will meddle with an American work, seldom if by a known writer, and never if by a new one, unless at the writer's risk." Hawthorne's tale, in fact, spoke for an entire generation of authors faced with the burgeoning and uncertain American publishing industry, which faltered with every financial crisis and which, in every season, found it more profitable to reprint, without paying authors' fees, the works of popular English writers. Because there were no copyright laws, piracy was rampant on both sides of the Atlantic.

"I have become ambitious of a bubble, and careless of solid reputation," Oberon tells his friend in his discouragement. At this stage of his career, the very thought of his tales causes a revulsion that verges on the physical. "I tell you there is a demon in them!" Oberon exclaims. Staring at the burning manuscripts, he imagines that he sees the leering face of the devil in the midst of the bright flames.

Hawthorne's frustrated author, however, has his final, ironic success: the bonfire of his manuscripts sets the roof afire. He knows the exhilaration of defeat. Amidst the uproar and confusion, the sound of alarms, the shouting of the crowds in the street below, the showers of sparks in the sky, he exults: "My tales! . . . the chimney! The roof! The Fiend has gone forth by night, and startled thousands in fear and wonder from their beds! Here I stand — a triumphant author! Huzza! Huzza! My brain has set the town on fire!"

"The Devil in Manuscript" is one of Hawthorne's autobiographical tales. He based the story on an incident in his own early career, when he had burned his manuscripts in a fit of discouragement. That had been the fate of his first projected story sequence, *Seven Tales of My Native Land* — with the exception of two stories, one of them, "Alice Doane," a tale of wizardry and murder, which had been in the "kinder custody" of a publisher "and thus by no conspicuous merits of their own, escaped destruction." Oberon, as Bridge recalled, was the name Hawthorne had adopted for himself in college; and it was to Bridge — as Oberon does to the narrator of the tale — that Hawthorne confided his sense of failure as an author. Hawthorne had destroyed his manuscripts, so he wrote Bridge, "in a mood half savage, half despairing." In later years, however, he could speak of the condemned manuscripts as "very dull stuff," which he had burned "without mercy or remorse," marveling only that they "should yet have possessed inflammability enough to set the chimney on fire!"

Still, there is more to "The Devil in Manuscript" than the ingenuity of an author shaping art from the experience of painful failure. First published in 1835, it stands roughly at the turning point of Hawthorne's career, after a decade of obscurity. It has the flaws of a young writer — the courtliness and implausibility of the dialogue; the failure to grasp or delineate character in brief strokes. Yet it puts forward one of those elemental metaphors that persist throughout Hawthorne's work: the symbolic nature of fire in both its domestic and diabolical aspects — the comforting warmth of the hearth, the purifying rites of the flame, the damnation of hellfire. Hawthorne frequently referred to the benign aspects of fire; his low-key essay "Fire-Worship," for example, is an ambling, topical commentary on the replacement of the fireplace by the new "air-tight" stove of nineteenth-century households. But he was far more drawn to the dramatic possibilities of the symbol. Fire is the central metaphor of a late story, "Earth's Holocaust," in which an uncontrollable mob of reformers, in a rage for destruction, proceed to burn what they consider the vanities of the world, one by one. Fire is also the symbolic inferno — in the rustic but awesome image of the limekiln — in which Ethan Brand is purified of his "unpardonable sin." Given this literary obsession, there is a certain appropriate symbolism in the circumstance that at the outset of his career Hawthorne consigned his unwanted manuscripts to the flames. There may also have been an element of poetic inevitability in the fact that, some three years after publication, the remainder of the first — and only — edition of his unwanted novel, *Fanshawe*, was destroyed in a fire in the Marsh and Capen store.

Elizabeth Hawthorne, discussing her brother's years of solitude in Salem, tried to counter the image of her brother as a morbid recluse. In the process, she cast an interesting light on the personal sources of Hawthorne's imagination. Whenever there was a public gathering, Elizabeth remembered, Hawthorne always went out. "He liked a crowd," she claimed. Political meetings, military drills, firemen's musters, were an irresistible attraction. "When General Jackson, of whom he professed himself a partisan, visited Salem in 1833," Elizabeth recalled, "he walked out to the boundary of the town to meet him, not to speak to him — but only to look at him, and found only a few men and boys collected, not enough, without the assistance that he rendered, to welcome the General with a good cheer." Conscious of her brother's essential reticence, she added, "It is hard to fancy him doing such a thing as shouting."

There were other occasions in the routine life of Salem that inevitably drew Hawthorne out of his solitary room. "A great conflagration," Elizabeth recalled, "attracted him in a peculiar manner." Whenever the alarms sounded, she said, Hawthorne was sure to be found at the scene, "looking on, from some dark corner, while the fire was raging." The final episode of "The Devil in Manuscript" — the gaping crowds, the alarms, the tolling of steeple bells, the bursts of flame and smoke, the showers of sparks against a black and wintry sky — were not simply the dark imaginings of the author; they had the force of experience.

In spite of Hawthorne's dissatisfaction with his first published effort, *Fanshawe* was to have an effect on his career. In 1829, a year after its publication, Hawthorne was in correspondence with Samuel G. Goodrich, Boston publisher and editor of the respectable gift-annual *The Token*. Goodrich had read the romance and felt that it indicated "extraordinary powers." Having learned the name of the author, he wrote Hawthorne, asking for contributions to his annual. A canny businessman, usually delinquent in his payments to authors, Goodrich was the first noteworthy publisher to take an interest in Hawthorne's career. He offered to help the budding author find a publisher for another projected sequence of stories that Hawthorne intended to call *Provincial Tales*. In a letter to Goodrich, written in December 1829, Hawthorne remarked that one of his stories was based on local superstitions. He went on to explain: "I do not know that such an attempt has hitherto been made; but, as I have thrown away much time in listening to such traditions, I could not help trying to put them into some shape." Early in his career, there was an innovative streak in Hawthorne's literary ambitions, an urge to provide a structure or a framework for his tales, one that would allow him to publish his stories as something more than a mere collection. *Provincial Tales* was his second attempt to shape a story sequence out of the thin and rocky soil of New England legend, and it was no more successful than his first. "I am obliged to you for your willingness to aid me in my affairs," Hawthorne wrote Goodrich in his December letter, "though I perceive that you do not anticipate much success. Very probably you may be in the right."

Nonetheless, Goodrich promised to use his influence with some Boston publisher who might "take hold of the work" and publish it with "a fair chance of success." But he was clearly more interested in securing contributions to his forthcoming edition of *The Token*, published each fall to take advantage of the Christmas sales, though always postdated for the following year. He was impressed with the stories Hawthorne had sent him. "As a practical evidence of my opinion of the uncommon merit of these tales," he wrote, "I offer you $35 for the privilege of inserting 'The Gentle Boy' in the 'Token'; and you shall be at liberty to publish it with your collection, provided it does not appear before the publication of the 'Token.' "

Hawthorne, who was reluctant to break up his story sequence, sent the publisher two alternative pieces, one of which at least — a sketch, "Sights from a Steeple" — appeared in *The Token* in the fall of 1830. Hawthorne suggested that his contributions be identified as "By the author of Provincial Tales," even though he had no publisher and suspected that his book might "never see the light at all." He rationalized, "An unpublished book is not more obscure than many that creep into the world." *Provincial Tales*, in fact, was never published, and Goodrich printed "Sights from a Steeple" anonymously.

The following spring, when Goodrich was once more seeking contributions for his gift annual, Hawthorne allowed him to use several of the stories he had previously withheld. On May 31, the editor responded enthusiastically, saying that he had made "very liberal use of the privilege" Hawthorne had given him. "I have already inserted four of them," he wrote, "namely 'The Wives of the Dead,' 'Roger Malvin's Burial,' 'Major Molineaux,' and 'The Gentle Boy.' As they are anonymous, no objection arises from having so many pages by one author, particularly as they are as good, if not better, than anything else I get."

Considering the meager financial rewards — for Goodrich paid Hawthorne less than $1.00 a page, when he paid at all, for stories that he admitted were of "uncommon merit" — this was probably cold comfort for the author.

༂ II ༃

"Once a year, or thereabouts," Hawthorne boasted to a friend, with uncharacteristic immodesty, "I used to make an excursion of a few weeks, in which I enjoyed as much of life as other people do in the whole year's round." Early in his career, Hawthorne had discovered that the summer was an unfavorable time for writing. He found it difficult to concentrate. His creative instincts, it seemed, needed a touch of frost before they revived. He once confessed that it was only when the autumn leaves began to color that he could bear to settle down to his desk. In the summers, he traveled.

At first, these summer excursions were family affairs. Most often he accompanied his Uncle Samuel on trips that seemed part business and partly a matter of health. Like his brothers, Samuel Manning suffered from an advancing tubercular condition for which travel was considered a restorative. Samuel Manning was quite evidently a convivial man. In August 1829, Hawthorne wrote to his uncle, already in New Haven, to say that he would be pleased to join him. He had, he conceded, seen very little of his Aunt Mary: "She drinks nothing but sweetened water, and never offers me any porter; so that there is not so much inducement to visit the house as when you were here."

In his family letters and later, in a series of notebooks, Hawthorne recorded the experiences of his summer travels. In time, the detailed observations of his notebooks were to be used as source material for incidents and characters in his stories. It was clear that his summer excursions were intended to furnish him with materials for his writing. Even his family letters adopted the detailed and droll manner of the literary observer. "We did not leave New Haven till last Saturday . . ." he wrote Louisa on the return trip to Salem with his Uncle Samuel, "and we were forced to halt for the night at Cheshire, a village about fifteen miles from New Haven. The next day being Sunday we made a Sabbath day's journey of seventeen miles and put up at Farmington. As we were wearied with rapid travelling, we found it impossible to attend divine service, which was (of course) very grievous to us both." He added slyly, "In the evening, however, I went to a Bible class with a very polite and agreeable gentleman, whom I afterward discovered to be a strolling tailor of very questionable habits."

Much of Hawthorne's pleasure during these summer jaunts came from his observations of odd village types, of gentlemen of "questionable habits," most of whom were to be encountered at the local taverns. It was obvious that Uncle Samuel enjoyed the congeniality of a saloon — and Hawthorne was seldom loath to join him. He would not "marvel much," Hawthorne informed his sister, "if your Uncle Sam pushes on to Canada, unless we should meet with two or three bad taverns in succession."

But it was also the freedom of the road, the release from familial constraints, that Hawthorne enjoyed. Strangers in small towns, during this period, were certain to attract attention, and Hawthorne, with his handsome looks, his air of amusement and amiability, appears to have attracted more than the usual curiosity.

A young man in new circumstances, it seemed, acquired all sorts of strange identities:

> I meet with many marvelous adventures [he wrote Louisa]. At New Haven, I observed a gentleman staring at me with great earnestness, after which he went into the bar-room, I suppose to inquire who I might be. Finally, he came up to me and said that as I bore a striking resemblance to a family of Stanburys, he was induced to inquire if I was connected with them. I was sorry to be obliged to answer in the negative. At another place they took me for a lawyer in search of a place to settle, and strongly recommended their own village. Moreover, I heard some of the students at Yale College conjecturing that I was an Englishman, and to-day, as I was standing without my coat at the door of a tavern, a man came up to me, and asked me for some oats for his horse.

Not all of his summer excursions can be determined from surviving letters. A few, like a month's sojourn at Martha's Vineyard, possibly in the summer of 1830, or a brief stay in Swampscott in 1833, can be inferred from later sketches and stories, such as "Chippings with a Chisel" and "The Village Uncle," and from the recollections of his sister Elizabeth. A journey through New Hampshire with his Uncle Samuel in August 1831 is confirmed by a letter. Occasionally, it appears, Hawthorne found it difficult to pry his uncle loose from the hospitality of the road. "One of your Uncle Sam's old acquaintances keeps the tavern at Concord," Hawthorne wrote Louisa, "so that it was like the separation of soul and body to get him away."

At Canterbury, New Hampshire, where there was a prosperous settlement of Shakers, Hawthorne developed a distinct interest in the Shaker way of life and its literary possibilities. This visit was to result in two notable early stories, "The Shaker Bridal" and "The Canterbury Pilgrims." Observing some of the Shaker rites, he formed a favorable opinion of the thirty or forty Shaker women, some of whom he pronounced "quite pretty." The Shaker costume, however — light dresses, with muslin kerchiefs crossed over the women's breasts, stiff muslin caps — made them look "pretty much as if they had just stept out of their coffins." His view of the Shaker men was caustic; there was nothing remarkable about them "except their stupidity, and it did look queer to see these great boobies cutting all sorts of ridiculous capers with the gravest countenances imaginable." Still, he conceded, the Shakers had "a good and comfortable life, and if it were not for their ridiculous ceremonies, a man might not do a wiser thing than join them." Perhaps it was the influence of a tumblerful of superb cider — "as much as a common head could cleverly carry" — that encouraged such thoughts. "I spoke to them about becoming a member of the Society," Hawthorne advised Louisa, "but have come to no decision on that point." For some months afterward, he was apt to tease his sisters with his intention of adopting the celibate life of the Shaker community.

In the summer of 1832, Hawthorne planned an extensive trip to northern New York and on into Canada. An outbreak of cholera in Canada, though, made him defer his plans. In June, he wrote to his friend Franklin Pierce, in New Hampshire, expressing his disappointment. "I was making preparations for a northern tour," he wrote, "when this accursed Cholera broke out in Canada. It was my intention to go by way of New York and Albany to Niagara, from thence to Montreal and Quebec . . ." With a touch of irony, he added, "I am very desirous of making this journey, on account of a book by which I intend to acquire an (undoubtedly) immense literary reputation."

The chief purpose of his letter, however, was to congratulate his friend Pierce on his recent election as speaker in the New Hampshire legislature. Far from being uninterested in politics, Hawthorne went on to sketch — prophetically — a complete career for his college friend. "I sincerely congratulate you on all your public honors, in possession or in prospect," he wrote. "If they continue to accumulate so rapidly, you will be at the summit of political eminence, by that time of life when men are usually just beginning to make a figure . . . If I were in your place, I should like to proceed by the following steps; after a few years in Congress, to be chosen Governor, say, at thirty years old — next a Senator in Congress — then minister to England — then to be put at the head of one of the Departments (that of War would suit you, I should think) — and lastly — but it will be time enough to think of the next step, some years hence." It says something about Hawthorne's grasp of American politics that he should have sketched out so accurately Pierce's route to political success. Pierce served in the House and Senate for nine years; he was offered the cabinet post of attorney general by the Polk administration (but declined it); he was a brigadier general in the Mexican War; and, finally, in 1852, he was elected President — that last step Hawthorne had stopped short of predicting.

Somehow, the consideration Hawthorne gave to his friend's bright prospects served only to reflect on his own obscure future. "You cannot imagine how proud I feel," Hawthorne wrote Pierce, "when I recollect that I myself was once in office with you on the standing committee of the Athenaean Society. That," he concluded somewhat regretfully, "was my first and last appearance in public life."

In September, Hawthorne began his journey, probably the most extensive he made during this period of his life. His travels can be reconstructed on only scanty documentary evidence: a letter written to his mother from Burlington, Vermont, in mid September; a printed certification that Nathaniel Hawthorne had "passed behind the Great Falling Sheet of Water to Termination Rock" at Niagara Falls, on September 28, 1832. Circumstantial details of at least one lengthy northern excursion are related in a series of fragmentary travel pieces, "Sketches from Memory, By a Pedestrian," published three years later in the November and December 1835 issues of the *New-England Magazine*. The sketches were obviously intended to provide a narrative framework for at least two stories based on local legends — "The Ambitious Guest" and "The Great Carbuncle." Their separate publication represents another of those editorial defeats which Hawthorne suffered early in his career. The persistence with which he attempted to set his allegorical tales within some realistic narrative setting indicates the urgency of his effort to merge his talent for imaginative fiction with his very real gifts as an observer of the social scene.

Hawthorne's travels had taken him from Bartlett, New Hampshire, through the valley of the Saco River, in the heart of the White Mountains. The wild scenery, the "old crystal hills" hung with clouds, impressed him; on the slopes he noticed "the red path-ways of the Slides, those avalanches of earth, stones and trees, which descend into the hollows, leaving vestiges of their track, hardly to be effaced by the vegetation of ages." In his Burlington letter to his mother, he complains of his ride, at four o'clock on a showery morning, to Mount Washington, over "the very worst road that ever was seen, mud and mire, and several rivers to be forded." For two nights and three days, he stayed with a party of travelers at the inn and postal station of Ethan Crawford near Crawford's Notch. It was perhaps while traveling through the White Mountains — if he had not heard it before — that Hawthorne learned the old Indian legend of a great carbuncle, a stone of immense size, whose dazzling light, seen from the distance, had lured generations of adventurers into vain searches. It was there, too, that he probably was told the story of the doomed Willey family that, some years before, had been buried in an avalanche.

"The Ambitious Guest," the story based on that New Hampshire legend, is not one of Hawthorne's memorable tales; the ominous note of impending tragedy is too insistently sounded from the beginning. The final catastrophe, when the isolated mountain family and the stranger who has taken lodgings with them flee for shelter and are buried in the landslide, though the house remains standing and unscathed, is distinctly anticlimactic. Fate hangs too heavily over the tale; but it offers, in the character of the youthful stranger, a glimpse of Hawthorne's feelings about his own unsatisfied ambitions, his obscure destiny. Hawthorne's young man is driven by "a high and abstracted ambition," the precise nature of which is never stated. "He could have borne to live an undistinguished life," Hawthorne notes, "but not to be forgotten in the grave." Like Hawthorne, he has led a solitary existence, is modest and somewhat shy. He feels a kinship with the isolated mountain family. In the evening by the fireside, with the dreary wind moaning outside, the young man reveals his vague ambitions. "As yet, I have done nothing," he acknowledges with a touch of self pity. "Were I to vanish from the earth to-morrow, none would know so much of me as you." Yet he boasts, "But I cannot die till I have achieved my destiny. Then let Death come! I shall have built my monument!"

With heavy-handed irony, Hawthorne buries the family and the "high-souled youth" under a landslide that becomes their monument. The bodies are never recovered, and the very existence of the stranger is a mere conjecture — "His name and person utterly unknown; his history, his way of life, his plans, a mystery never to be solved; his death and his existence, equally a doubt!" The tone is melodramatic, but the implications are clear: Hawthorne, with a perverse severity, had savaged his own bright dreams in those of his ambitious young man.

At Burlington, the "Inland Port" of his later sketch, Hawthorne was unimpressed by the silvery unruffled surface of Lake Champlain. The lake, steaming in the bright sunlight, gave off a faint, sickly smell. "One breeze from the Atlantic, with its briny fragrance," Hawthorne suggested, with his coastal prejudice, "would be worth more to these inland people than all the perfumes of Arabia." The ships along the wharves looked flimsy and unseaworthy; the sailors — if one might call them that — were dressed in pantaloons and long-tailed coats, more like gentlemen than the self-respecting "old salts" he knew in Salem.

Burlington was a port of entry for the Canadian trade, and Canadian banknotes circulated as freely as the American dollar. "British and American coin are jumbled in to the same pocket," Hawthorne quipped, "the effigies of the king of England being made to kiss those of the goddess of liberty." The busy public square, with its white houses and brick-front shops, some of them tin-roofed and glistening in the sunlight, had a cosmopolitan air. There were merchants from Montreal, clusters of British officers, French-Canadians from the provinces, Green Mountain boys from Vermont. And everywhere, Hawthorne noted, there were hordes of emigrant Irish — "infinite tribes, overflowing by every outlet into the States."

Traveling south, below Utica he embarked on a dirty canal barge that would take him westward along the Erie Canal, the great manmade waterway that had been promoted by De Witt Clinton and officially opened only seven years before. Hawthorne touted Clinton as an "enchanter" who had "waved his magic wand from the Hudson to Lake Erie, and united them by a watery highway." Towns had sprung up, cities of brick and stone with churches and theaters, luxuries and refinements, where there had been nothing before. There were "gay dames and polished citizens" where once there had been only remote cabins and backwoodsmen. In his travels, Hawthorne was sensitive to the incursions of the future; he imagined a time when "the wondrous stream may flow between two continuous lines of buildings, through one thronged street, from Buffalo to Albany."

Still, there were, along the route, remote stretches of dense forests with here and there a rude cabin beside fields of blackened tree stumps. From one of these, a woman, sallow-faced, stared wearily out of her window, looking "like Poverty personified, half clothed, half fed, and dwelling in a desert, while a tide of wealth was sweeping by her door." As the three dray horses plodded along the towpath, Hawthorne, seated on deck, enjoyed the varied traffic along the waterway: double-ended barges carrying salt and flour eastward to Albany; three glum Indians, in a poorly constructed boat, staring fixedly and silently at the passing canal boat. "Perhaps," Hawthorne mused, "these three alone, among the ancient possessors of the land, had attempted to derive benefit from the white man's mighty projects, and float along the current of his enterprise." Once, they overtook a boatful of Swiss immigrants traveling toward Michigan, singing and laughing in their brightly colored costumes of scarlet, yellow, and blue. Hawthorne spied a pretty young woman "with a beautiful pair of naked white arms," who turned and shouted a teasing remark to him. "She spoke in her native tongue," he remembered, "and I retorted in good English, both of us laughing heartily at each other's unintelligible wit. I cannot describe how pleasantly this incident affected me."

But life aboard the canal boat, traveling westward at a snail's pace, was more often monotonous and confining. Meals were taken on board in the main cabin; the same room served as the sleeping quarters for the twenty or more passengers — both the men and the women — with a crimson curtain, "the sexual division of the boat," being let down at night. The sleeping berths were mere shelves, "hardly so wide as a coffin," Hawthorne pointedly observed. There was barely room to turn over in one's sleep.

In his description of his fellow passengers Hawthorne took special note of a traveling Englishman with a scribbling bent, taking notes in a memorandum book, which Hawthorne was sure would result in a future travel book. But did the Englishman, in fact, exist, or was he merely invented by Hawthorne for the purpose of setting down his own malign sketches of his countrymen? In his sketch "The Canal-Boat," Hawthorne imagined the Englishman's account of his fellow passengers: the Virginia schoolmaster, Yankee by birth, whose erudition was no better than a schoolboy's Latin theme, "made up of scraps, ill-selected and worse put together"; the Massachusetts farmer, whose religion was "gloom on the Sabbath, long prayers every morning and eventide, and illiberality at all times." The most acid sketch was reserved for a sharp-eyed Detroit merchant, a mixture of "daring enterprise and close-fisted avarice," who had been three times bankrupt and "richer after every ruin." "Here . . ." Hawthorne observed under his borrowed persona, "Here, in one word (Oh wicked Englishman to say it!), here is the American!" Hawthorne's scribbling Englishman, whether real or imaginary, represented a clear gain in literary technique; he brought an insidious humor, a talent for social analysis, a point of view to the usual banalities of travel-writing.

An equally devastating sketch was that of the American Woman, in the person of an attractive Western belle, who, having noticed that she was being observed, blushed deeply and retired to the sanctuary of the female quarters: "Here was the pure, modest, sensitive, and shrinking woman of America; shrinking when no evil is intended; and sensitive like diseased flesh, that thrills if you but point at it; and strangely modest, without confidence in the modesty of other people; and admirably pure, with such a quick apprehension of all impurity." It is a sketch by a man with healthy instincts who feels some cause for complaint with strait-laced American mores in his encounters with the opposite sex — and perhaps with the prudish and feminine editorial standards of American magazines.

The sketch is all the more ironic, considering that the Western belle, who blushes where no impurity was intended, figures quite prominently in one of the frankest sexual episodes that Hawthorne was ever to write and one that evidently escaped the notice of readers when it was published anonymously in the *New-England Magazine* in December 1835, and again when it escaped censorship in the 1854 edition of *Mosses from an Old Manse*. In the person of the narrator, and not the visiting Englishman, Hawthorne, with the sensitivity to auditory stimuli that marks him as a writer, describes the bedtime preparations after the curtain has been drawn in the long cabin. He presents the scene with that mounting attention to incidental detail that figures in the most ardent sexual fantasies:

> My head was close to the crimson curtain . . . behind which I continually heard whispers and stealthy footsteps; the noise of a comb laid on the table, or a slipper dropt on the floor; the twang, like a broken harp-string, caused by loosening a tight belt; the rustling of a gown in its descent; and the unlacing of a pair of stays. My ear seemed to have the properties of an eye: a visible image pestered my fancy in the darkness; the curtain was withdrawn between me and the western lady, who yet disrobed herself without a blush.
>
> Finally, all was hushed in that quarter. Still, I was more broad awake than through the whole preceding day, and felt a feverish impulse to toss my limbs miles apart, and appease the unquietness of mind by that of matter . . .

One night — traveling the "long level," the seventy miles between Utica and Syracuse — Hawthorne witnessed an eerie scene. They were passing through what had been an immense swamp, now drained into the canal. What remained were pools of stagnant water and the bleached, ashen trunks of dead and decaying trees. "In spots where destruction had been riotous," Hawthorne noted, "the lanterns showed perhaps a hundred trunks, erect, half overthrown, extended along the ground, resting on their shattered limbs or tossing them desperately into darkness." The scene was "ghostlike — the very land of unsubstantial things, whither dreams might betake themselves, when they quit the slumberer's brain." It was an image of future ruin. The wild nature of America, Hawthorne claimed, "had been driven to this desert place by the encroachments of civilized man." In the older societies of Europe, he suggested, "decay sits among fallen palaces; but here, her home is in the forests."

By contrast, the city of Rochester was all bustle and energy, a mushrooming town crowded with "pedestrians, horsemen, stage-coaches, gigs, light wagons, and heavy ox-teams, all hurrying, trot-ting, rattling and rumbling, in a throng that passed continually, but never passed away." He was surprised at the number of public houses: "some were farmers' taverns — cheap, homely and comfort-able; others were magnificent hotels, with negro waiters, gentle-manly landlords in black broadcloth, and foppish bar-keepers in Broadway coats . . ." There were lottery offices everywhere, plas-tered with red-and-yellow handbills, offering "splendid fortunes to the world at large"; it seemed a town built on transience and prom-issory dreams.

By the time Hawthorne's unidentified traveler — half Hawthorne and half invention — reaches Niagara, late in September, it is some-thing of an anticlimax. He has been anticipating the great American scenic event, yet is unaccountably hesitant. "Never did a pilgrim approach Niagara with a deeper enthusiasm than mine . . ." he confesses, yet he delays the moment of seeing it, "because my treas-ury of anticipated enjoyments, comprising all the wonders of the world, had nothing else so magnificent, and I was loth to exchange the pleasures of hope for those of memory so soon." When, finally, he reaches the village of Manchester by the Falls, he does not rush — "like a madman" — to the scene. "On the contrary," he recalls, "I alighted with perfect decency and composure, gave my cloak to the black waiter, pointed out my baggage, and inquired, not the nearest way to the cataract, but about the dinner-hour. The interval was spent in arranging my dress." Lingering over his dinner with an "unwonted and perverse epicurism," he steps out on the broad pi-azza, pacing back and forth, puffing on a cigar, and studying the "very ordinary village." Finally, he makes his way toward Goat Island. At the toll house, he delays further, signing his name in the large tourist's ledger, studying an odd collection of curiosities — the skin of a huge sturgeon, samples of minerals, Indian moccasins, and other handicrafts made from deerskin and embroidered with beads. He selects a gnarled walking stick, made by a Tuscarora Indian, carved with images of a snake and a fish. Then, on an afternoon of glorious sunshine, he makes his visit.

With the roar of the cataract resounding in his ears, he ventures across the bridge to the pine-shrouded island. There, turning back and standing on the verge, he views the American Falls, a dazzling rainbow rising from the perpetual mists. Then he proceeds around the island to view the Horseshoe Falls, edging his way out, cau-tiously, along the narrow bridge, only two or three feet wide, at the edge of the descending sheet of water. Standing there on the flimsy bridge, a small figure in a flapping cloak, he takes in the vast sweep of the whitening water.

But he cannot conceal from himself that this first glimpse is a disappointment. He envies the old-time explorers who came upon the scene unprepared, drawn only by the distant roar. He had come, unfortunately, with his mind filled with imagined pictures, "haunted with a vision of foam and fury, and dizzy cliffs, and an ocean tumbling out of the sky — a scene, in short, which Nature had too much good taste and calm simplicity to realize." A "wretched sense of disappointment" weighs upon him after this first encounter with the American Sublime. It is only after several nights of sleeping with the "dull, muffled thunder" of the falls as a background music to his dreams that he feels his old enthusiasm revive.

In his sketches, it is the pedestrian Hawthorne who appears — the sometime traveler, the occasional man of the world, the observer of the American scene. This Hawthorne affects an air of diffidence and casual interest, is somewhat debonair. At times, he poses as the dandy, fussy about his appearance, a bit disdainful of his compatriots. Yet Hawthorne is never the outsider, the stranger. He is another character in the scene, the amused and amusing commentator on what he once described as "a text of deep and varied meaning" — the circumstance of being American.

〜 III 〜

But there is another Hawthorne: the solitary writer and journalizer, spending the long hours in the upstairs bedroom in the Herbert Street house; the student of his own vague dreams and emotions; the man of a sometimes morbid turn of mind. He is the captive of time, the sensitive man who, in a moment of weariness, scribbles in an undated entry in his journal: "A recluse, like myself, or a prisoner, to measure time by the progress of sunshine through his chamber." In such moments, the record of his solitary life seemed reduced to the barest essentials, the slow passage of the sunlight across the bedroom carpet, along the furniture of his mind.

The darker side of Hawthorne's mind seemed reserved for his early tales. The presiding themes there — the secret springs of shame, the hidden nature of guilt, the communion of sinners — speak of the tormented mind. But the style is always fastidious and elegant; it scarcely ever verges on prurience or despair. His researches into the interior self bring him to a shadowy world of "shapeless half-ideas which throng the dim region beyond the daylight of our perfect consciousness." Morality — the codes of a particular society at a particular time — does not become his real province as a writer, as it did for Dickens or Trollope, whose grasp of society and the real world he so much admired. Hawthorne was seldom to be a judgmental writer. Often enough, with Hawthorne's sinners, the deed is only hinted at. The crime may occur in some penumbral past, but the conscience will be explored with the skill of a surgeon probing diseased flesh. The mystery of sin is what absorbs him.

The author and his tales are much like the narrator — and dreamer — of an early sketch, "The Haunted Mind," which stands, almost, as the prelude to his early fiction. Hawthorne's dreamer has started up from his midnight sleep, is held fast in that moment between dreaming and waking, that "intermediate space, where the business of life does not intrude, where the passing moment lingers, and becomes truly the present." A clock strikes in the frosty air; then another, nearer by. Through the window, in the cold moonlight, he sees a vista of snow-covered roofs and the frozen street. The dreamer thinks, comically, "on the luxury of wearing out a whole existence in bed, like an oyster in its shell, content with the sluggish ecstasy of inaction." Hawthorne is a master of the whims, evasions, subterfuges of the mind. He is also aware of its sudden plunges into darkness. His dreamer thinks "how the dead are lying in their cold shrouds and narrow coffins, through the drear winter of the grave." That gloomy thought invites "a gloomy multitude."

"In the depths of every heart," the troubled sleeper declares, "there is a tomb and a dungeon, though the lights, the music, and revelry above may cause us to forget their existence, and the buried ones, or prisoners, whom they hide. But sometimes, and oftenest at midnight, those dark receptacles are flung wide open." In Hawthorne's fictional world, the phantom images that arise at that zero hour, "the devils of a guilty heart," are often presented in an abstracted or allegorical form: "What if Remorse should assume the features of an injured friend? What if the fiend should come in woman's garments, with a pale beauty amid sin and desolation, and lie down by your side? What if he should stand at your bed's foot, in the likeness of a corpse, with a bloody stain upon the shroud?" But they are all — the injured friend, the exotic woman, the murdered man — recurrent images in the tales. For Hawthorne, as a youthful writer, there were, perhaps, the two avenues to experience: to be much in the world, to be busy with the world's business, to be observant of the social scene, "the lights, the music, and the revelry above"; or to retire into solitude, to explore the secrets of the self, to analyze the private promptings of one's own mind and the world of fantasy and daydreams that one found there. Few things are more poignant in Hawthorne's early career than his attempt to bring those tendencies into a balance and equilibrium.

In "The Haunted Mind," his disturbed dreamer casts his eye about for some commonplace and reassuring sign of the living world — "the table near the fire-place, the book with an ivory knife between its leaves, the unfolded letter, the hat and the fallen glove." He conjures up, in a merger of wish and dream, a different companion — not the lustful woman of the nightmare, but a purer vision: "As your head falls back upon the pillow you think — in a whisper be it spoken — how pleasant in these night solitudes, would be the rise and fall of a softer breathing than your own, the slight pressure of a tenderer bosom, the quiet throb of a purer heart, imparting its peacefulness to your troubled one, as if the fond sleeper were involving you in her dream." The quest for that "fond sleeper" was to be more a necessity of life than of his fiction.

In "Young Goodman Brown," Hawthorne relates the story of a young newlywed, who, bidding good-bye to his beautiful young wife, Faith, sets off for a secret appointment in the woods. Faith, her lace cap fluttering with pink ribbons, pokes her head out the door to give her husband a parting kiss. She pleads with him to remain at home that night. "A lone woman," she says, "is troubled with such dreams and such thoughts that she's afeard of herself, sometimes." Hawthorne makes the most of this ambiguous confession; Goodman Brown, mistaking as jealousy his wife's fears about her own vulnerability, chides her for doubting him already, when they have been only "three months married."

Goodman Brown's secret mission is to attend a midnight convocation of witches in the forest. His sponsor, whom he meets along a darkening and gloomy pathway, is an older man who carries a walking stick carved in the shape of a writhing black serpent and who may well be the devil himself. Yet he bears a strange resemblance to Goodman Brown's father. In a moment of misgiving, Goodman Brown remonstrates with his diabolical sponsor. "My father never went into the woods on such an errand, nor his father before him," the young man says. "We have been a race of honest men and good Christians, since the days of the martyrs." The devil contradicts him with an air of sweet reasonableness: "I helped your grandfather, the constable, when he lashed the Quaker woman so smartly through the streets of Salem. And it was I that brought your father a pitch-pine knot, kindled at my own hearth, to set fire to an Indian village, in King Philip's war." Moreover, he claims, he is on the best of terms with those people whom Goodman Brown has been taught to revere — the deacons of the church, the town selectmen. Even the governor, the devil intimates — then breaks off. "But these are state secrets," he says. Hawthorne may be indulging in a bit of wry humor at this point, merging history and fiction. In borrowing from his own family background and introducing (as he shortly does) the historical figures of Goody Cloyse and Martha Carrier, two of the accused women of the witchcraft trials, he slyly vindicates old John Hathorne. The fictional premise is that there were, indeed, witches abroad in the land at the time of his stern Hathorne ancestors.

At the witches' Sabbath, Goodman Brown learns that his wife is to be the other initiate at the infernal ceremonies. The two converts stand before the burning altar; Faith is veiled. The devil exhorts them in a black sermon: "Depending upon one another's hearts, ye had still hoped, that virtue were not all a dream. Now are ye undeceived! Evil is the nature of mankind. Evil must be your only happiness. Welcome, again, my children, to the communion of your race!" But just at the moment of initiation, when Goodman Brown pleads with his wife to resist the devil, the entire scene dissolves. The reader is left to wonder whether it has been a dream or a reality. The ambiguity is central to the story; in Hawthorne, the actual deed or the mere imagination of it each has an effect. In the morning, Goodman Brown returns to Salem village a different person — "a stern, a sad, a darkly meditative, a distrustful, if not a desperate man."

Hawthorne is fascinated by the perverse normality of the world after some great crisis of the heart or mind. The bland sunshine of an ordinary day greets Goodman Brown. The minister whom he had witnessed at the witches' revels is calmly taking a walk before breakfast; Goody Cloyse is catechizing a little girl who has brought her a pint of morning's milk; Faith comes skipping to greet her husband, her pink ribbons fluttering. He gives her a stern look and passes on without a greeting. In this Yankee fable of the end of innocence, the young American Adam, having tasted the fruit of the tree of knowledge of good and evil, becomes a ruined man. He has been initiated into "the deep mystery of sin"; he can sense the "secret deeds" of others. Goodman Brown shrinks from society, becomes silent and morose until the end of his days. When he dies, no comforting verse is carved on his tombstone — "for his dying hour was gloom."

In another story, "The Minister's Black Veil," Hawthorne explores again the secrets of the heart that set a man apart from his neighbors. The Reverend Mr. Hooper, one Sunday, appears before his congregation wearing a black veil over his head. Never an energetic preacher, his discourse on this particular day is on "secret sin, and those sad mysteries which we hide from our nearest and dearest, and would fain conceal from our own consciousness." His delivery on this occasion acquires a dreadful force in the minds of his startled parishioners. The veil, which he has vowed to wear for the remainder of his life, estranges him from the villagers, his congregation, even his intended bride, Elizabeth. He lives "shrouded in dismal suspicions; kind and loving, though unloved, and dimly feared; a man apart from men, shunned in their health and joy." The veil, however, has one salutary effect: it enables the minister to sympathize with every dark affection. "Dying sinners cried aloud for Mr. Hooper, and would not yield their breath till he appeared." On his own deathbed, the minister refuses the efforts of his mourners to remove the veil. "I look around me," he says in his final breath, "and lo! on every visage, a Black Veil!"

It is not without interest that in publishing his odd little tale Hawthorne appended a note saying that the idea for the story had been taken from life. A Reverend Mr. Moody, of York, Maine, had "made himself remarkable by the same eccentricity," Hawthorne claimed. As a young man, the minister had accidentally killed a friend, and "from that day till the hour of his own death, he hid his face from men." The man who is guilty of the death of another — or believes himself to be — is a frequent character in Hawthorne's fiction.

Of equal psychological relevance is the distinction Hawthorne made, in an early notebook entry, between the mask and the veil. Commenting on Emperor Augustus' dying exclamation, "Has it not been well acted?" Hawthorne made a mental note for himself: "An essay on the misery of being always under a masque. A veil may sometimes be needful, but never a masque." He was to speak of his own guarded reserve in similar terms in the preface to *Mosses from an Old Manse*. "So far as I am a man of really individual attributes, I veil my face," he wrote. He was not, he maintained, one of those authors "who serve up their own hearts delicately fried, with brain-sauce, as a tidbit for their beloved public." Yet he was willing to deliver — in the form of his cautious fables, parables, allegories — some of the less palatable truths of the human condition. Like the Reverend Mr. Hooper, Hawthorne had his sympathies with "all dark affections."

Astonishingly, Hawthorne seems to have achieved a mastery of that elusive theme of the dark affections quite early in his career. "My Kinsman, Major Molineux" is practically seamless in its perfection. (That it was a quite early story is determined from the fact that Samuel Goodrich specifically referred to "My Uncle Molineaux" as among the first manuscripts Hawthorne had sent him.) Hawthorne's country-bred hero, Robin, barely eighteen, is another of his youths in search of a father figure; though in this case Robin has left his family, including his father, a country preacher and farmer, for an unnamed city where his relative the major resides. The elderly major, wealthy and childless, had shown a great interest in Robin and his elder brother during a visit to their father's farm and hinted that he would be willing to help establish one of the boys in life. Robin has been elected to take advantage of the major's charity.

At the outset of the story, Robin's physical attractiveness is pointedly mentioned; he is one of those handsome, well-set-up youths who can expect to be treated favorably even by total strangers. He is on good terms with the world. But he soon learns that the moment he makes enquiries about his well-to-do kinsman, the responses turn decidedly hostile. Hawthorne is particularly good at suggesting emotions that are barely held in check — the surliness, among the patrons of a tavern, that could easily edge over into violence, the loutish laughter of men in a barbershop.

Few things are more subtle than the ease with which Hawthorne uses a conventional fictional situation to exploit the tentative sexual adventurousness that accompanies his young hero's coming of age. While searching for his kinsman's mansion, on a back street, Robin encounters an attractive young prostitute in a scarlet petticoat, who, claiming to be the major's housekeeper, attempts to seduce him. The economy with which Hawthorne indicates the boy's gullibility, the woman's attractiveness, her obliging manner, and the steeliness of her grip, is remarkable. "The fair and hospitable dame took our hero by the hand; and though the touch was light, and the force was gentleness, and though Robin read in her eyes what he did not hear in her words, yet the slender waisted woman, in the scarlet petticoat, proved stronger than the athletic country youth. She had drawn his half-willing footsteps nearly to the threshold . . ." Equally notable are the brief auditory and visual effects by which Hawthorne establishes the whole ambience of the tale with a kind of clean economy: the repeated image of the elderly man with the sepulchral cough, his cane tapping out his passage down the nightmare streets; the grim-featured man, painted up as if for a carnival, one side of his face black, the other red — a surreal image — who tells him to wait, that his famous kinsman will pass by within an hour. "Strange things we travelers see!" Robin exclaims, a remark no doubt drawn from Hawthorne's own encounters with "questionable" types on the road.

In a slightly different way, the dénouement of "My Kinsman, Major Molineux," like that of "Young Goodman Brown," is one of Hawthorne's infernal midnight scenes in which figures of authority, once honored and respected, are exposed in their disgrace before a young initiate. In a bizarre torchlight parade, led by the two-faced man, Major Molineux does indeed pass — but drawn in a cart, tarred and feathered, a political scapegoat, a man forced into public penance for unspecified crimes. In the midst of the tumult and uproar, caught up in the shouting merriment, Robin finds himself laughing at his kinsman — the loudest reveler of them all.

Throughout Hawthorne's work, from his earliest tales to his last completed novel, there is a recurring theme of the end of innocence, an awareness of a kind of midnight knowledge after which nothing remains the same. It is a knowledge of one's self and others, a knowledge of the world and human nature that changes life irremediably. In *The Marble Faun*, summing up the theme of a lifetime, Hawthorne refers to that shock of recognition when the young and inexperienced, who may have heard about evil but know it only as an "impalpable theory," have their "first actual discovery that sin is in the world." In Hawthorne, it is always a shared experience. "In due time," he writes, "some mortal, whom they reverence too highly, is commissioned by Providence to teach them this direful lesson; he perpetrates a sin; and Adam falls anew."

In "My Kinsman, Major Molineux" there is an awful moment of recognition between the major and young Robin. As the motley procession passes, Robin, fascinated, studies the figure of his sponsor, "an elderly man, of large and majestic person, and strong, square features, betokening a steady soul; but steady as it was, his enemies had found the means to shake it. His face was pale as death, and far more ghastly, the broad forehead was contracted in his agony, so that his eyebrows formed one grizzled line; his eyes were red and wild . . ." When their eyes meet, Robin, witnessing the "foul disgrace of a head that had grown gray in honor," feels "a mixture of pity and terror." He, too, has been irrevocably judged in that moment of humiliation. He suddenly feels a distaste for "town life." Turning to the obliging stranger — presumably an older, more experienced man — who has waited with him for the parade, he asks the way to the ferry. The stranger insists that Robin put off his return home for a few more days. "Or," he suggests, "if you prefer to remain with us, perhaps, as you are a shrewd youth, you may rise in the world, without the help of your kinsman, Major Molineux."

Hawthorne's tale is a conventional story of initiation, of the rites of passage and the toppling of a familial authority. But in its eerie economy, it has a force that seems uneasily personal; it has both the uncomfortable laughter of relief and the sense of tragedy at witnessing the fall from grace of a once-honorable figure. The concluding remark of the story echoes Hawthorne's own complaint, years before, about the burden of living on his Uncle Robert's charity for another four years — his Uncle Robert being that parental authority whose assessment of his character, Hawthorne was sure, was far more accurate than that of his more indulgent family members. In his letter, Hawthorne had exclaimed, with the exasperation of youth, "How happy I shall feel to be able to say, 'I am Lord of myself!' " In his fictional treatment, that impatient urge acquired the force of necessity, and brought with it a kind of sorry, even shameful, wisdom.

Monsieur Du Miroir

IN COLLEGE, Hawthorne had made a secret bet with his classmate Jonathan Cilley. The details of the wager, dated November 14, 1824, had been placed in a sealed envelope and given to their mutual friend, Horatio Bridge, who was to serve as arbiter. Across the envelope, Hawthorne had written, "Mr. Horatio Bridge is requested to take charge of this paper, and not to open it until the fifteenth day of November, 1836, unless by the joint request of Cilley and Hawthorne."

On the specified day, Bridge opened the envelope and found two written pledges. Cilley's read: "If Nathaniel Hathorne is neither a married man nor a widower on the fourteenth day of November, One Thousand Eight Hundred and Thirty-six, I bind myself upon my honor to pay the said Hathorne a barrel of the best old Madeira wine. Witness my hand and seal. Jonathan Cilley."

Hawthorne's pledge was equally succinct: "If I am a married man or a widower on the fourteenth day of November, One Thousand Eight Hundred and Thirty-six, I bind myself, upon my honor, to pay Jonathan Cilley a barrel of the best old Madeira wine."

Bridge wrote to both parties. In his letter to Hawthorne, he particularly stressed that Hawthorne should lay claim to his barrel of Madeira; in his letter to Cilley, Bridge mentioned that their friend was about to publish a book.

Cilley, who was deeply involved in a bitterly contested campaign for a congressional seat from his district in Maine, wrote Hawthorne in a style of brusque camaraderie. "Now you are indeed a writer of great repute," he wrote from Thomaston, "and soon to be the author of a book. I did not mistake your vein in that particular, if I did in the like matrimonial. Damn that barrel of old Madeira; who cares if I have lost it! If only you and Frank Pierce and Joe Drummer and Sam Boyd and Bridge and Bill Hale were together with me, we would have a regular drunk, as my chum in college used to call it, on that same barrel of wine."

Significantly, the wager had not depended on which of the two young men would marry first, but whether Hawthorne, alone, would be married by the agreed-upon date. That Hawthorne made the bet at just the time when his Uncle Robert, at the late age of forty, was preparing to marry would seem to be significant, as well. What prompted Hawthorne to make so unusual a wager is not known. Evidently, some awareness of himself, of his disinclination toward marriage, or distrust of it, must have figured in his determination to respond to Cilley's challenge by predicting that he would not marry until late in his life. By 1836, his friend Cilley had been seven years married and was a father. Hawthorne, at thirty-two, had steadfastly remained a bachelor.

Hawthorne was clearly ambivalent about marriage during his years of seclusion. His sister Elizabeth contended that he would never marry. She was well aware of minor flirtations that occurred when her brother was away on trips. She recalled that in 1833, after a sojourn of two or three weeks in Swampscott, her brother had come home "captivated in his fanciful way, with a 'Mermaid,' as he called her. He would not tell us her name, but said she was of the aristocracy of the village, the keeper of a little shop. She gave him a sugar heart, a pink one, which he kept a great while, and then (how boyish, but how like him!) he ate it." The Swampscott girl, renamed Susan, figures in a story Hawthorne wrote at the time, "The Village Uncle." The candy heart appears in a rather rhapsodic passage: "Oh Susan," the narrator expostulates, "the sugar heart you gave me, and the old rhyme — 'When this you see, remember me' — scratched on it with the point of your scissors! Inscriptions on marble have been sooner forgotten, than those words shall be on that frail heart." The story was published anonymously in *The Token* of 1835. Hawthorne evidently thought better about his romantic outburst; when the story was reprinted in *Twice-told Tales*, he carefully removed the mention of the supposedly indelible inscription. Susan, so Hawthorne told Ebe, "had a very great deal of what the French called *espièglerie*," a roguishness that he found charming. Elizabeth, quite accurately, saw no reason to worry about the affair. Hawthorne always had such "fancies" whenever he went away from home; if he had talked less about his "mermaid," she might have taken him more seriously.

Susan is one of Hawthorne's early, sunny heroines. The aged narrator's recollection of his first glimpse of her is vivid. It is twilight on the shore, the waves roll in, the wind sweeps by, a silver moon brightens the sky. She is standing on a bridge, "fluttering in the breeze like a sea bird that might skim away." He imagines her, fancifully, as a daughter of the wind, or a mermaid. "And yet it gladdened me, after all this nonsense," he says, "to find you nothing but a pretty young girl, sadly perplexed with the rude behaviour of the wind about your petticoats."

Hawthorne's account of the married life of Susan and the narrator is highly romanticized, a fantasy of domestic bliss in a cottage by the sea that would appeal to the largely feminine readership of gift-annuals. But the relationship he describes has something personal about it, the dream of a solitary bachelor: "She kindled a domestic fire within my heart, and took up her dwelling there, even in that chill and lonesome cavern, hung round with glittering icicles of fancy. She gave me warmth of feeling, while the influence of my mind made her contemplative. I taught her to love the moonlight hour, when the expanse of the encircled bay was smooth as a great mirror . . ." Susan was Hawthorne's image of the redemptory woman, a chaste and idealized love.

There are other instructive marriages in his early tales. In "The Canterbury Pilgrims," Hawthorne deals with a fictional pair of lovers, Josiah and Miriam, and a real setting, the Shaker community of Canterbury, New Hampshire, which he had visited in 1831. His young couple are fleeing the community and its harsh rule of celibacy. On their way, they meet a company of pilgrims — a failed poet, a ruined businessman, a disgruntled farmer accompanied by his wife and two small children — who are on their way to join the Shakers. In an effort to persuade the young lovers to return to the community, each of the pilgrims tells the story of his life and disappointments in the world. The poet and the businessman are easy caricatures; the tales of their disaffection are predictable. But the farmer and his unhappy wife are more realistic; their pathetic story has the hard currency of truth. The farmer married young — "just such a neat and pretty young woman as Miriam," he tells the Shaker youth. He had expected little more out of life than his own hard work could earn for him and his family. "I thought it a matter of course that the Lord would help me, because I was willing to help myself," he says. But even these small hopes have been disappointed: "My means have been growing narrower, and my living poorer, and my heart colder and heavier, all the time; till at last I could bear it no longer."

The farmer's wife tells Miriam a sorry tale of gradual estrangement. "By-and-by," she warns the young girl about Josiah, "he'll grow gloomy, rough, hard to please, and you'll be peevish, and full of little angry fits, and apt to be complaining by the fireside so your love will wear away, by little and little, and leave you miserable at last. It has been so with us; and yet my husband and I were true lovers once, if ever two young folks were."

The young couple nonetheless decide to take their chances among the world's people — although with "chastened hopes." The moral of Hawthorne's tale — or "parable," as he refers to it — is that ideal associations such as the Shaker community offer only a "cold and passionless security" which is little better than the grave, that such refuges are likely to become the havens of the queer and the dissatisfied. But Hawthorne is not sanguine, either, about the course of true love, however ardent; the unhappy fate of the farmer and his wife will be re-enacted.

Still, Josiah and Miriam are among the more fortunate lovers in Hawthorne's early tales. Love and marriage are more apt to be followed by death, madness, blighted hopes, dismal failures; a theme of dark nuptials runs steadily through the early stories. In "The Shaker Bridal," Martha Pierson, out of love for her childhood sweetheart, Adam Colburn, has followed him to the Shaker settlement at Goshen. She endures the celibacy required by the community, living as a sister to the man she desperately loves. Now the time has come when the aged elder of the settlement, Father Ephraim, proposes to hand over the rule of the community to the pair of former lovers, who are still in the "summer of their years." At the ceremony — a sublimation of the real ceremony Martha yearns for, as Hawthorne clearly suggests in his title — Martha suddenly dies, her heart unable to endure "the weight of its desolate agony."

A farcical variation of the theme occurs in "The Wedding-Knell." Mrs. Dabney, a worldly twice-widowed woman, returns to New York to marry an elderly bachelor, Mr. Ellenwood, whom she had long ago loved but turned down for a wealthier and older suitor. At the church, she is stunned by the tolling of the funeral bells and the appearance of a funeral procession coming down the aisle. Her bridegroom, dressed in his shroud, has arranged a mock funeral in order to symbolize the waste of his life and the inappropriateness of his marriage at a time when he should more aptly be preparing for death.

The chill, funereal note intrudes at moments of bliss in several of Hawthorne's early stories. In "The Minister's Black Veil," the Reverend Mr. Hooper, wearing his veil, casts a pall over the wedding ceremony of the "handsomest couple in Milford Village." In "The May-Pole of Merry Mount," another beautiful young couple, members of a hedonist sect, are captured by the Puritans just at the moment when their wedding is about to take place. They barely escape death. Even the happy marriage of "The Village Uncle" is framed as a recollection at the point of death; among the local stories the aged narrator recalls is "the sad, true tale of a young man on the eve of marriage, who had been nine days missing, when his drowned body floated into the very pathway, on Marblehead neck, that had often led him to the dwelling of his bride." In "The White Old Maid," the mysterious spinster who for years has followed every coffin to its grave suddenly appears at a wedding ceremony, "just as the priest was uniting a false maid to a wealthy man, before her lover had been dead a year." The tentative romance of the young stranger and the sweet daughter of the mountain family in "The Ambitious Guest" is buried in the avalanche. In "The Prophetic Pictures," a couple about to be married have their wedding portraits painted. The artist — like many of the artists in Hawthorne's stories — has the gift of seeing into the "inmost soul" of his subjects. He captures the look of madness in the bridegroom and the expression of grief and sorrow in the bride that prefigure the fate of the bridal couple. For a young writer, the theme of dark nuptials may have been an easy device. But it occurs with such persistence in Hawthorne's early stories that it also suggests a more deep-seated psychological prohibition against marriage and happiness.

In his personal life, if not in his work during these years, he was apt to take a more casual attitude on the subject. In a letter to his cousin John Dike, Jr., who had moved to Ohio and there become engaged, Hawthorne could write with all the aplomb of a man of the world on the subject of marriage and short engagements. "Courtship is said to be a very pleasant business," he told Dike, "but actual happiness is certainly far preferable to anxiety and expectation." He went on, "If I were in your situation, I should bring matters to a conclusion as speedily as I could, for fear of some undesirable accident. Besides, it is a good thing to be married young, before you and your bride have contracted any stubborn habits. I have heard it remarked that the marriages which take place before twenty-five years of age generally turn out the best . . . So I advise you to get married before cold weather comes on." The letter may have been Hawthorne's little joke; it was written in 1830, when he was a seasoned man of twenty-six — past the age of taking his own advice.

Hawthorne's friend Horatio Bridge, during these years, was also the recipient of his advice on morals and marriage. Bridge might complain, "But, after all, the worst accusation I can make against myself is that I have no settled plan of existence, even now, at the age of thirty," but he did not strenuously object. "I sometimes think seriously of matrimony for ten minutes together, and should perhaps perpetrate it if I did not like myself too well." He added, "My morals have improved exceedingly in the past year; your advice in a former letter was very efficient in this improvement."

With friends, Hawthorne's advice was reluctantly given. "I take advice from you kindly," Bridge remarked in his letter. "I am a vain man, and a proud one; and I would spurn with scorn the interference of any one whom I suspected of giving me advice with any other than the most friendly feelings." But he was not inclined to be morbid about his transgressions. "A little wickedness will not hurt one," he claimed, "especially if the sinner be of a retiring disposition. It stirs one up, and makes him like the rest of the world." Bridge was perhaps offering Hawthorne some gentle advice in return.

ᴄ᷍ᴐ II ᴄ᷍ᴗ

Far more often, however, Hawthorne wrote Bridge about his professional disappointments. Since 1830, his stories and sketches had been appearing anonymously in gift-annuals, newspapers, magazines — *The Token*, the *Salem Gazette*, the *New-England Magazine*, the *American Monthly Magazine*, *Youth's Keepsake*. He had begun to acquire a sub rosa reputation with publishers, reviewers, and discriminating readers. Throughout this period his stories had always appeared anonymously or had been identified only as by the author of "The Gentle Boy" or "The Gray Champion." Occasionally, as he did with "The Devil in Manuscript," he employed a fanciful pseudonym, like Ashley A. Royce. Publishers were only too happy to accommodate Hawthorne in this respect; it allowed them to publish several stories by the same author in a single issue. Yet on Hawthorne's part it was more than deference to an established editorial custom; he positively insisted on anonymity. In January 1832, writing to the Philadelphia publishers of *The Atlantic Souvenir*, to which he hoped to contribute, Hawthorne identified himself as the author of "My Kinsman, Major Molineux," "Roger Malvin's Burial," and "The Gentle Boy," all in the current issue of *The Token*, but said, "I should not wish to be mentioned as the author of those tales."

Horatio Bridge cautioned him about the practice. "I've been thinking how singularly you stand among the writers of the day," he wrote Hawthorne, "known by name to very few, and yet your writings admired more than any others with which they are ushered forth. One reason for this is that you scatter your strength by fighting under various banners. In the same book you appear as the author of 'The Gentle Boy,' the author of 'The Wedding-Knell,' 'Sights from a Steeple,' and besides throw out two or three articles with no allusion to the author . . . Your articles in the last 'Token' alone are enough to give you a respectable name, if you were known as their author."

Nor was Hawthorne well paid for his contributions. Goodrich paid less than $1.00 a page. For the twenty-seven stories and sketches that Hawthorne contributed to *The Token* between 1831 and 1837, he probably received no more than $380.00. With Park Benjamin, the editor of the *New-England Magazine*, Hawthorne fared no better and maybe a good deal worse. In 1834, unable to find a publisher for his two-volume collection of stories and interconnecting narrative, *The Story Teller*, he turned it over to Benjamin for serial publication. Only two of the episodes, however, appeared as Hawthorne had intended them, in the November and December issues of the magazine. After that, a number of them were published independently, for when Benjamin moved to New York, to co-edit the *American Monthly Magazine*, he took the remaining unpublished manuscript with him. Benjamin had paid no more than a dollar a page at the *New-England Magazine*; it is doubtful that Hawthorne received anything for his contributions to the *American Monthly*. Writing to Bridge about the affair, he complained bitterly, "Thus has this man, who would be considered a Maecenas, taken from a penniless writer material incomparably better than any his own brain can supply." Paid little — and sometimes not at all — Hawthorne was understandably soured on American publishers.

Still, early in 1836, when Goodrich recommended him for the editorship of the *American Magazine of Useful and Entertaining Knowledge*, a Boston-based publication owned by the Bewick Company, Hawthorne reluctantly accepted the post. He was promised a salary of $500 a year. The position required that he write and edit virtually the entire contents of the magazine, often tailoring his pieces to the wood engravings that the Bewick Company supplied. He accepted the offer, which meant moving to Boston, on the strength of the promise that he would begin receiving his salary promptly, and on Goodrich's assurance that the publishers of *The Token* — which Goodrich had recently sold (though he remained as an editorial adviser) — would send him money that was still due for contributions to the previous edition.

In January 1836, Hawthorne moved to Boston, boarding with the family of Thomas Green Fessenden, at 53 Hancock Street. Fessenden was an amiable, somewhat abstracted, sixty-five-year-old literary character, the author of a sporadically published satirical poem, *Terrible Tractoration*, which Hawthorne had first read in college. He was also the indefatigable editor of *The New England Farmer* (which had featured an article on Robert Manning's orchards), a former member of the Massachusetts state legislature, and an inventor of sorts, whose Patent Steam and Hot-Water Stove bubbled and hissed noisily in his apartment. Childless, he lived with his considerably younger but devoted wife, Lydia, and an equally devoted niece, Catherine Ainsworth.

Hawthorne came to feel a certain affection for the old man. In the evenings, the pair would discuss poetry in the disorder of Fessenden's study, with books and manuscripts and agricultural pamphlets and newspapers strewn about the tables and floors. Fessenden consulted his boarder about his latest stanzas for a new edition of *Terrible Tractoration*. In his youth, he had been a well-known poet, highly praised in London; but more recently he had fallen into what Hawthorne considered a benevolent neglect. Fessenden, he observed, "was peculiarly sensitive and nervous in regard to the trials of authorship: a little censure did him more harm than much praise could do him good." Occasionally, the old poet would take up a bass viol that stood in the corner, consoling himself with music, playing some "old-fashioned tune of soothing potency." He seems to have developed a fondness for Hawthorne. Praising the virtues of his youthful and efficient wife — without whom, he confessed, he would have long since been in his grave — he heartily advised Hawthorne to acquire a "similar treasure" for himself.

Hawthorne's burdensome duties as editor of the *American Magazine* left him little time — and no money — for other entertainments during his winter evenings in Boston. He was obliged to fill up entire issues with brief biographies, articles, and essays on such subjects as the Revolutionary hero, General Benjamin Lincoln, the city of Jerusalem, explorations in Canada, French soldiering, piracy, and longevity. Out of kindness, he also devoted an article to Fessenden's poetry. Sometimes he resorted to reprinting passages from the books of Mrs. Trollope or Charles Lamb or the poems of Wordsworth. "I am so busy with agents, clerks, engravers, stereotype printers, devils — and the devil knows what all — that I have not much time to write," he complained in a letter to Louisa soon after his arrival. He did mention that he had been invited to a literary party, but had declined. "It is holden weekly by two blue-stockings. I shall go by and by."

He also picked up some political gossip about a prominent Whig politician that he passed on to the Whig-sympathizing Elizabeth in a letter written a few days later: "Daniel Webster drinks and is notoriously immoral; he is enormously in debt (one man having indorsed $100,000 for him) and altogether a disreputable character — so say the Whigs." All of which, perhaps, only increased Hawthorne's own admiration for the orator and politician.

Since the Bewick Company was so niggardly that it did not have a membership for him with the Boston Athenaeum, he could read books only there and not take them out. He turned to his sister Elizabeth for assistance in filling up the monthly quota of articles and essays. "Concoct, concoct, concoct," he wrote her. "I make nothing of writing a history or biography before dinner. Do you the same." She drew out books from the Salem Athenaeum, sent him lengthy quotations, which he printed intact, and undertook a needed biography of Alexander Hamilton. Even so, Hawthorne had to work at a strenuous pace to fill the pages of the voracious publication. "I have written all but a half page with my own pen," he complained to Louisa, "except what Ebe sent. Let her send more; for I have worked my brain hard enough this month." His letters to Elizabeth were usually frantic requests for more material — a biography of Jefferson, a subject he did not find congenial, and abstracts or extracts of anything serviceable she might come across in her reading — "provided always," he added, "that it be not too good; and even if it should be, perhaps it will not quite ruin the Magazine; my own selections being bad enough to satisfy anybody. I can't help it."

He was annoyed with Goodrich, who had promised to pay him the $45 owing to him from *The Token* but had given him only further promises. "My mind is pretty much made up about this Goodrich," he wrote Louisa bitterly. "He is a good-natured sort of man enough, but rather an unscrupulous one in money matters, and not particularly trustworthy in anything." He did not feel obliged to Goodrich for the editorship of the *American Magazine,* for Goodrich was a director and stockholder in the Bewick Company. "Of course it was his interest to get the best man he could; and I defy them to get another to do for a thousand dollars what I do for 500; and furthermore, I have no doubt that Goodrich was authorized to give me 600. He made the best bargain he could, and a hard bargain, too." Hawthorne added, "This world is as full of rogues as Beelzebub is of fleas."

Nor was he being paid by the publishers of the *American Magazine.* "For the Devil's sake," he told Louisa, "if you have any money send me a little. It is now a month since I left Salem and not a damned cent have I had, except five dollars that I borrowed of Uncle Robert — and out of that I paid my stage fare and other expenses . . . It is well that I have enough to do; or I should have had the blues most damnably here; for of course, I have no amusement." His present stock, he said, was "precisely 34 cents," and he noted, "All that I have spent in Boston, except for absolute necessaries has been 9 cents on the first day I came — 6 for a glass of wine and three for a cigar." Since then, he had been forced into the most stringent economies.

By May, when he received a mere $20, he was threatening, "Unless they pay me the whole amount shortly, I shall return to Salem, and stay till they do." Nonetheless, he remained on long enough to complete the August issue. And despite his having threatened to break off his relationship with Goodrich, he did undertake a further commission from the publisher. Goodrich had embarked on a series of juvenile books under the rubric of Peter Parley — books that were immensely profitable for the publisher but seldom so for the writer. In May, Goodrich proposed that Hawthorne write one of the series, *Peter Parley's Universal History*, and Hawthorne, after asking Elizabeth to collaborate with him, agreed. "Our pay, as Historians of the Universe," he informed Elizabeth, "will be 100 dollars, the whole of which you may have. It is a poor compensation. Yet better than the *Token*; because the kind of writing is so much less difficult." It was a meager reward for the effort, and when, after the manuscript was completed in September, Goodrich suggested another volume in the series — this one on the "manner, customs and civilities of all countries" — offering $300, Hawthorne turned him down. By then, after months of frustration and overwork, he had resigned as editor of the *American Magazine* and was back in Salem. It is not certain whether Hawthorne received even the half-year's salary that would have been due him. The Bewick Company went into receivership — "compelled to this course by the tightness of the money market, and losses which they had sustained," so Hawthorne was informed by letter. He was assured that he would be paid promptly by the assignee, Samuel Blake, Esquire.

―――――

Horatio Bridge had thought Hawthorne's move to Boston a wise one. Not that he regarded the editorship of the *American Magazine* as so advantageous; but it might lead to something better. "Besides," he wrote Hawthorne at the time, "it is no small point gained to get you out of Salem . . . There is a peculiar dullness about Salem — a heavy atmosphere which no literary man can breath. You are now fairly embarked with the other literary men, and if you can't sail with any other, I'll be d——d."

Now that Hawthorne was back in Salem, Bridge became increasingly worried about the tone of his friend's letters. "You have the blues again," Bridge wrote Hawthorne that fall. "Don't give up to them, for God's sake and your own and mine and everybody's. Brighter days will come, and that within six months." Nearly a week later, responding to another of Hawthorne's letters, Bridge complained of its "desperate coolness." He wrote, "I fear that you are too good a subject for suicide, and that some day you will end your mortal woes on your own responsibility . . . I wish you to refrain till next Thursday, when I shall be in Boston, *Deo volente*. I am not in a very good mood myself just now, and am certainly unfit to write or think. Be sure and come to meet me in Boston."

Bridge's optimism about Hawthorne's prospects was more than easy encouragement; he had, in fact, taken steps to assure "brighter days" for his friend. Earlier that fall, Hawthorne had decided once again to publish a volume of stories. It is perhaps an indication of his uncertainty about the publishing business that, despite his displeasure with Goodrich, he once more applied to the publisher for help. What Hawthorne had in mind this time was a collection of his previously published stories — without the narrative framework that had proved such a stumbling block in the past.

From the beginning, Bridge expressed a great interest in the project and its progress. "I hope to God," he advised, "that you will put your name upon the title page, and come before the world at once and on your own responsibility. You could not fail to make a noise and an honorable name, and something besides." He added, "Should there be any trouble in a pecuniary way with the publishers, let me know, and I can and will raise the needful with great pleasure."

Bridge was better than his word; he wrote directly to Goodrich, asking about the terms of publication, but stipulated that Hawthorne should not be told about his intervention. On October 20, Goodrich replied, "I received your letter in regard to our friend Hawthorne. It will cost about $450 to print 1000 volumes in good style. I have seen a publisher, and he agrees to publish it if he can be guaranteed $250 as an ultimate resort against loss. If you will find that guaranty, the thing shall be put immediately in hand." Goodrich doubted that Bridge would be "called upon for a farthing"; he wished to know only if he would take the risk. "The generous spirit of your letter is a reference," he assured Bridge. Hawthorne would receive the usual terms — royalties of 10 percent on the retail price.

Bridge immediately offered the guaranty, but even so Goodrich had difficulty in placing the book. Eventually, he turned to his parent organization, the American Stationers' Company, which published *The Token* and the Peter Parley books. Although he was, in fact, a director of the firm, he had to make one concession in order to get Hawthorne's book published, relinquishing his copyright on the stories that had previously appeared in *The Token*. On December 12, J. B. Russell, agent for the American Stationers' Company, wrote Hawthorne to assure him that his book was not being "unreasonably delayed or neglected." They had been searching for a "good printer."

In gratitude, Hawthorne considered dedicating the volume to Goodrich. But when he wrote Bridge about this plan, Bridge managed to forestall him. "I fear you will hurt yourself by puffing Goodrich *undeservedly*," he wrote, "— for there is no doubt in my mind of his selfishness in regard to your work and yourself. I am perfectly aware that he has taken a good deal of interest in you, but when did he ever do anything for you without a *quid pro quo*? The magazine was given to you for $100 less than it should have been. The 'Token' was saved by your writing." He urged Hawthorne not to "mar the prospects" of his first book "by hoisting Goodrich into favor." Hawthorne took his advice.

Throughout the ensuing winter, Bridge gave a good deal of thought to Hawthorne and his prospects. On Christmas Day, he wrote his friend a long and reflective letter:

> The bane of your life has been self-distrust. This has kept you back for many years . . . I have been trying to think what you are so miserable for. Although you have not much property, you have good health and powers of writing, which have made and can still make you independent. Suppose you get but $300 per annum for your writings. You can, with economy, live upon that, though it would be a d——d tight squeeze. You have no family dependent upon you, and why should you "borrow trouble?" This is taking the worst view of your case that it can possibly bear. It seems to me that you never look at the bright side with any hope or confidence. It is not the philosophy to make one happy.

Bridge, it seems, considered his friend's bachelorhood a temporary blessing in disguise. Marriage would be a case of borrowing trouble. The subject of marriage, inevitably, was in the air, since, only the month before, Bridge had opened the letter containing Cilley and Hawthorne's marital wager. "I doubt whether you ever get your wine from Cilley," Bridge cautioned. "His inquiring of you whether he had really lost the bet is suspicious; and he has written me in a manner inconsistent with an intention of paying promptly; and if a bet grows old, it grows cold.

"And so Frank Pierce is elected Senator," Bridge went on, by way of offering a hopeful example. "There is an instance of what a man can do for himself by trying. With no very remarkable talents, he, at the age of thirty-four, fills one of the highest stations in the nation. He is a good fellow, and I rejoice at his success. He can do something for you perhaps. The inclination he certainly has." It was understandable that Bridge felt a certain ebullience; it must have seemed that he and his classmates were part of a generation about to move into public life. Frank Pierce was a senator; Cilley was engaged in a run-off campaign for a congressional seat; Hawthorne was about to publish a book.

Bridge, too, was engaged in a risky business enterprise that would either make him or break him — the building of a dam across the Kennebec River at Augusta. He estimated that the venture would cost him $20,000; in fact it involved a good deal more — the risking of the family capital. The times were not exactly propitious; the financial panic of 1836–1837, which had caused many business failures, made the raising of additional capital for the dam project extremely difficult. Moreover, there had been minor mishaps at the construction site. With the winter weather, ice was gathering in the river, and it was uncertain whether portions of the dam would hold. Still, Bridge was optimistic — and generous. "I expect next summer to be full of money," he told Hawthorne, "a part of which shall be heartily at your service if it comes."

ᔐ III ᔐ

Twice-told Tales, by Nathaniel Hawthorne, was published on March 6, 1837. In his selection of the eighteen reprinted stories that made up the volume, Hawthorne clearly tried to anticipate the tastes of the reading public. He included a good number of the pleasant and sometimes innocuous descriptive sketches that were favored in gift-annuals like *The Token* — "Sights from a Steeple," "A Rill from the Town-Pump," "The Vision of the Fountain," "Little Annie's Ramble," "Sunday at Home." Stories that probed some deeper problem of character — "The Wedding-Knell," "Wakefield," "Mr. Higginbotham's Catastrophe" — were generally farcical or comical and resolved with happy endings. Both "The Gentle Boy" and "The May-Pole of Merry Mount," although they dealt with harsh Puritan justice — or injustice — were sentimental in tone. Only "The Minister's Black Veil," "The Prophetic Pictures," and, possibly, "The Hollow of the Three Hills" hinted at the darker side of his imagination.

Hawthorne's more profound and troubling stories — "My Kinsman, Major Molineux," "Young Goodman Brown," "The Wives of the Dead," "Roger Malvin's Burial," stories that later critics would regard as among his early masterpieces — were excluded. So, too, were relatively innocent sketches that hinted at the personal experiences of the author — "The Devil in Manuscript," "Monsieur du Miroir." In the transition from anonymity to public acknowledgement of his authorship, Hawthorne carefully edited out of his stories any passages that might offend. He deleted a remark in "The Gentle Boy" which indicated that the Quaker boy, Ilbrahim, had been struck "in a tender part" when he was assaulted by the neigh-

borhood children. In reprinting "Mr. Higginbotham's Catastrophe,"
Hawthorne dropped altogether the introductory framework that described, among other things, the Story Teller's encounter with a
troupe of traveling actors — "the fantastic and effeminate men, the
painted women, the giddy girl in boy's clothes, merrier than modest." (The narrator has been completely bewildered by "a young
person of doubtful sex," and muses, "If a gentleman, how could he
have performed the singing-girl, the night before . . . Or if a lady,
why did she enact Young Norval, and now wear a green coat and
white pantaloons in the character of Little Pickle?" In broad-
minded fashion, he decides the dress is pretty and "the wearer be-
witching.") *Twice-told Tales* was clearly a guarded performance, intended to put its author before the public in the most acceptable
light.

Horatio Bridge's early response was predictably optimistic. He
thought the appearance of the book decidedly good and the title "excellent." "I have never read 'The Gentle Boy' till today," he wrote
Hawthorne, "when it had the credit of making me blubber a dozen
times at least during the two readings which I have given it." In
the course of his congratulations, he included a brief personal announcement: "As for me, I shall probably go to New York for several
weeks, if my 'Mill Dam' continues to look as well as it does now.
Though I have forty or fifty thousand at stake, I do not sleep the
worse for it. If I lose, I shall try for the appointment of Purser in the
Navy, and with a good chance of success." As a rousing conclusion,
he predicted, "Good times for both of us are coming. You have broken the ice; the ice can't break me." He tactfully refrained from any
mention of his part in the publication of *Twice-told Tales*; it was not
until the sales of the book had earned back his guaranty that he informed Hawthorne.

Obviously hoping for favorable comment, Hawthorne sent a first
copy of the book to another former classmate, Henry Wadsworth
Longfellow. Longfellow had only just recently taken up his position
as Smith Professor of Modern Languages at Harvard, following a
period of study abroad — an unhappy sojourn in which his young
wife, Mary, had died in Rotterdam of complications following a miscarriage. He had not yet acquired his immense fame as America's
most popular poet, but he had already established a reputation as a
writer and linguist. Hawthorne had admired his *Outre-Mer: A Pilgrimage Beyond the Sea*, a volume of travel sketches published two
years before. The two men had not seen each other since their final
days at Bowdoin, twelve years before. But Longfellow, at thirty, was
another of those college associates, facing toward success, against
whom Hawthorne measured his own lack of direction. His letter

was characteristically deferential. "We were not, it is true, so well acquainted at college that I can plead an absolute right to inflict my 'twice-told' tediousness upon you," Hawthorne wrote on March 7, the day following publication, "but I have often regretted that we were not better known to each other, and have been glad of your success in literature, and in more important matters. I know not whether you are aware that I have made a good many idle attempts in the way of Magazine and Annual scribbling. The present volume contains such articles as seemed best worth offering to the public a second time; and I should flatter myself that they would repay you some part of the pleasure which I have derived from your own Outre-Mer."

It was a conventional literary letter, meant to elicit a conventional literary favor — though without asking for it outright — and it had the desired effect. Longfellow wrote a lengthy review of *Twice-told Tales*, full of generous praise, that was published in the *North American Review*. But before the review appeared, Hawthorne's gesture had established communication with an influential colleague. Although he was never a prolific correspondent, Hawthorne on this occasion pursued his advantage. On June 4, writing again to Longfellow, he noted, "When I last heard from the publishers — which was not very recently — the book was doing pretty well. Six or seven hundred copies had been sold." Referring to the depressed state of the economy, he added, "I suppose, however, these awful times have now stopped the sale."

He also provided Longfellow with a dramatic glimpse of his life since Bowdoin: "I seldom venture abroad till after dark. By some witch-craft or other — for I really cannot assign any reasonable why and wherefore — I have been carried apart from the main current of life, and find it impossible to get back again." He and Longfellow had touched lives at an unhappy moment in each of their careers. Longfellow, still mourning the death of his wife, was burdened with regret and guilt for having taken her abroad against the advice of friends and family; Hawthorne was beginning to sense the full weight of his isolation. Longfellow, in a letter, vaguely referred to his misfortunes; Hawthorne responded, from his own self-concern: "You tell me you have met with troubles and changes. I know not what they may have been, but I can assure you that trouble is the next best thing to enjoyment, and that there is no fate in this world so horrible as to have no share in either its joys or sorrows. For the last ten years, I have not lived, but only dreamed of living." Whatever his reserve, Hawthorne was not unwilling, it appears, to speak openly about his personal life when it might serve a useful purpose by piquing his fellow writer's interest.

On June 19, having received an advanced copy of Longfellow's review, he wrote gratefully, "I frankly own that I was not without hopes that you would do this kind office for the book; though I could not have anticipated how very kindly it would be done. Whether or no the public will agree to the praise which you bestow on me, there are at least five persons who think you the most sagacious critic on earth — viz., my mother and two sisters, my old maiden aunt, and finally, the sturdiest believer of the whole five, my own self."

Longfellow's review, published in the July 1837 issue of the *North American Review*, began on a note of exuberance: "When a new star rises in the heavens, people gaze after it for a season with the naked eye, and with such telescopes as they may find." Longfellow predicted that critics would soon be deciding upon the "magnitude" of Hawthorne's star and "its place in the heaven of poetry." His own assessment followed: "To this little work we would say, 'Live ever, sweet, sweet book.' It comes from the hand of a man of genius."

Longfellow stressed the agreeable blend of poetry and romance he found in Hawthorne's tales and sketches. He then launched into a lengthy disquisition on poetics, which, though it had some tangential references to Hawthorne's prose, was actually more appropriate to his own evolving poetic style. As a proponent of a native American literature, he praised Hawthorne for having chosen his themes from New England legends. "There is no tradition of the Rhine nor of the Black Forest," Longfellow stated, a bit chauvinistically, "which can compare in beauty with that of the Phantom Ship." (The latter legend, drawn from Mather's *Magnalia Christi*, was to be the source of one of his own later poems.) In extolling Hawthorne's virtues, he was, in fact, outlining his own poetic program.

Somewhat perversely, Longfellow chose to emphasize the personality of the author. The *Twice-told Tales*, he stated, was one of those volumes which "excite in you a feeling of personal interest for the author." The picture of the author that he drew from Hawthorne's stories — helped, probably, by Hawthorne's revealing letters — was rather more congenial than factual: "A calm, thoughtful face seems to be looking at you from every page; with now a pleasant smile, and now a shade of sadness stealing over its features. Sometimes, though not often, it glares wildly at you, with a strange and painful expression." It was clear that Longfellow preferred the gentle and civilized Hawthorne — and not the brooding recluse. The excerpts that Longfellow offered the reader — passages from "The Vision of the Fountain," "Sunday at Home," and the entire sketch, "A Rill from the Town-Pump" — were meant to illustrate the book's "vein of pleasant philosophy" and its "quiet humor."

Through his years of anonymous publication, Hawthorne had received little attention — and that, fairly recently. The most gratifying praise, undoubtedly, had been a notice of his stories in the 1836 *Token* that had appeared in the London *Athenaeum*. The review, by Henry F. Chorley, whom Hawthorne was to meet years later, had spoken favorably of his "two stories of darker colour," "The Wedding-Knell" and "The Minister's Black Veil." Even that mild approval struck a responsive chord in the writer, whose ambition it had been to see his works "praised by the reviewers, as equal to the proudest productions of the scribbling sons of John Bull." Hawthorne, bragging, had written home to Ebe at the time, "My worshipful self is a very famous man in London — the Athenaeum having noticed all my articles in the last Token, with long extracts."

The earliest reviews of *Twice-told Tales* were brief but cordial. The *Salem Gazette* declared that "the beautiful simplicity and elegance" of Hawthorne's style placed him "among the very first of American writers." The unsigned review in the *Knickerbocker* magazine, which included lengthy excerpts from the tales, echoed the same idea. Hawthorne, it claimed, had "few equals, and with perhaps one or two eminent exceptions, no superior in our country." Encouraging as these notices would have seemed to an author, Hawthorne must have felt that Longfellow's considered and lengthy article was the reward for his long years of anonymity.

Unaccountably, the review in the *American Monthly* did not appear until a year after publication. Since fragments of Hawthorne's abortive *Story Teller* continued to surface in the magazine from time to time, the *American Monthly* might have been considered friendly to the author. The anonymous reviewer — perhaps Park Benjamin himself, or his co-editor, Charles Fenno Hoffman — began by imitating Longfellow's critique: "A rose bathed and baptized in dew — a star in its first gentle emergence above the horizon — are types of the soul of Nathaniel Hawthorne." Like Longfellow, the reviewer also discerned the character of the author in his tales, though he came up with a more remarkable image — that of "a stricken deer in the forest of life."

Perhaps reacting to Longfellow's claim that Hawthorne's tales were "national in their character," the critic took a different tack. Hawthorne was too much the essayist, his interests too limited in their range to speak "for many kinds and classes of men." American literature, in general, the reviewer claimed, seemed to attract writers of "the gentler order." There were many Apollos in American writing, but, as yet, no Jove and no Jovian thunder. Intellects "of a hardier and more robust kind" seemed inevitably drawn to politics and commerce.

What had begun as praise turned into an arraignment; Hawthorne was consigned to the functional role of a "minor" writer, softening up the public for greater things. "Never can a nation be impregnated with the literary spirit by minor authors alone," the reviewer pontificated. "They may ripple and play round the heart, and ensnare the affections, in their placid flow; but the national mind and imagination are to be borne along only on the ocean-stream of a great genius." Ironically, Hawthorne's tale "The Threefold Destiny," quite probably one of the fragments of *The Story Teller*, appeared in the March 1838 issue, along with the review of *Twice-told Tales*. Not unpredictably, it was the last of Hawthorne's contributions to the magazine.

If Hawthorne had hoped to ensure the financial success of his book by the cautious selection he made of its contents, he was unsuccessful. Although Goodrich reported on April 8 that the book was selling well "and making its way to the hearts of many," within two months the sales had reached only 600 or 700 copies out of the first edition of 1000 volumes. Hawthorne's 10 percent of the $1.00-a-volume price was meager. Early in 1838, the American Stationers' Company went under, another of the casualties of the panic of 1837, and the balance of the edition, some 100 volumes, was remaindered. Horatio Bridge had tried to be realistic about prospective sales for a first book. Hawthorne had evidently complained that the response was unsatisfactory. Bridge answered, "Your book will do good, if the papers *are* cold about it. Most of the coldness is due to the fact that the stories are 'Twice-Told'; and this I know from remarks of some of my friends, who declined buying because the book was not original!" Bridge had a point: at least five of the tales and sketches Hawthorne had selected had appeared in the still-current edition of *The Token*. Another, "Dr. Heidegger's Experiment," had been published as recently as the January 1837 issue of the *Knickerbocker*. To an extent, Hawthorne had undercut the sales of his book by relying on too-recently published work.

More important, in long-range terms, was the critical response to the book. It created the public image of a dreamy and imaginative author, a stylist above all — and a fragile, somewhat feminine talent that needed proper wooing. Longfellow had suggested that readers had to understand Hawthorne's character in order fully to appreciate his tales. The reviewer in the *American Monthly* went even further: "To be read fitly, he should be read in the right mood and at the proper hour. To be taken up in haste and opened at random, would do him great wrong."

Had Hawthorne made his first appearance before the public in the manner he had originally intended — framing his imaginative stories within a totally conceived narrative structure — he would have created something quite different and innovative within the tame, borrowed forms of American fiction. Moreover, the moodier aspects of his imagination would have been balanced by his talent for hard, detailed, and often comic observation. Hawthorne had attempted to achieve something like that balance in *Twice-told Tales* by interspersing his stories with pleasant sketches. But in his effort to ingratiate himself with the reading public, he had succeeded too well.

For years, the image of the retiring author was to plague him. In the preface to the third edition of *Twice-told Tales*, written fourteen years later, Hawthorne was to speak, drily, of the "mild, shy, gentle, melancholic, exceedingly sensitive, and not very forcible man" that his reading public and his critics held up to him as a kind of mirror image. He wondered out loud whether he might not have tried unconsciously to fill out the "amiable" outline of the character assigned to him; he even wondered whether he could discard that image without shedding "a few tears of tender sensibility."

But at the time *Twice-told Tales* was first published, Hawthorne was his own most concerned and valuable critic. In his June 4 letter to Longfellow, he gave a carefully reasoned evaluation of his literary efforts:

> They would have been better, I trust, if written under more favorable circumstances. I have had no external excitement — no consciousness that the public would like what I wrote, nor much hope nor a very passionate desire that they should do so. Nevertheless, having nothing else to be ambitious of, I have felt considerably interested in literature; and if my writings had made any decided impression, I should probably have been stimulated to greater exertions . . . I have another great difficulty, in the lack of materials; for I have seen so little of the world, that I have nothing but thin air to concoct my stories of, and it is not easy to give a lifelike semblance to such shadowy stuff.

That summer — and for many years ahead — Hawthorne was to make a conscientious attempt to remedy that lack.

⎇ IV ⎇

In Washington, the installation of the new Democratic administration of Martin Van Buren, the chosen candidate of old General Jackson, opened up some opportunities for Hawthorne's future. Both Franklin Pierce, as a newly elected senator, and Jonathan Cilley, now a congressman, began a search for some suitable administrative post for their friend. At first, an editorial position with one of the administration newspapers seemed a possibility; but then, when his friends learned that a large naval and scientific expedition was being considered for funding, they turned their efforts to securing for him the position of official historian of the cruise. The purpose of the proposed expedition was a lengthy exploration of the South Seas and the coastal regions of Antarctica. Franklin Pierce, acting promptly, wrote to Jeremiah N. Reynolds, the promoter of the expedition, asking for his support and influence on Hawthorne's behalf. Pierce frankly hoped Reynolds would discuss the matter with Churchill Cambreleng, the Tammany politician and a close friend and adviser of Van Buren's, and perhaps with the President himself. He noted the publication of *Twice-told Tales* and the favorable reviews, but felt it necessary to indicate that Hawthorne was in no way temperamental or undependable. "He is a man of decided genius," Pierce explained, "without any whims or caprices calculated to impair his efficiency or usefulness in any department of literature."

Bridge, aware of Hawthorne's unsettled mood, was both encouraging and cautious. "I think I can do something with men of influence in this State, and perhaps in yours also," he wrote Hawthorne. "For instance I am well acquainted with George Bancroft." He could answer for "the whole Maine delegation," he told his friend.

Still, Bridge, who had more active connections with politics and politicians than his friend, felt it necessary to warn Hawthorne, "But, after all, it will still be very doubtful if you succeed. Therefore do not set your heart too thoroughly upon it." Throughout the spring and early summer, he alternately buoyed up Hawthorne's hope and advised caution in his expectations. Early in April, he informed Hawthorne that he had written to Bancroft, who was pursuing a double career as a historian and as a spokesman for the Democratic Party, requesting that Bancroft put in a good word for Hawthorne with the secretary of the navy. "I don't know whether he will comply, but I think I tickled him in the right place. He can't well help doing the handsome thing by you." But then again he advised, "It is absolute folly to think of despairing, should you fail in this. There is many a good day in store for you yet, if you never go to the South Seas, of which, however, I have little doubt."

Jonathan Cilley was active on another front. In Washington, he had made the acquaintance of a debonair young editor of a new magazine, John O'Sullivan, to whom he promptly recommended the author of *Twice-told Tales*. O'Sullivan was an engaging Irishman from a family with a somewhat shadowy political past; his father had served as a diplomat under several previous administrations and not without blotches on his integrity, since he was charged with bribery and extortion on several occasions. Young O'Sullivan, who had graduated from Columbia, grew up in an atmosphere of national politics and with a taste for literature that was unerring in many respects.

In the spring of 1837, with a brother-in-law, O'Sullivan found the financial backing for a new political and literary magazine, *The United States Magazine and Democratic Review*, which, under O'Sullivan's able editorship, was to become the most prestigious journal of its kind in America. With a combination of shrewdness and unembarrassed flattery, O'Sullivan managed to secure contributions from the most important authors of the period — Lowell, Whittier, Bryant, Poe, Longfellow, Thoreau, Bancroft, and Orestes Brownson. The magazine was intended to counteract the influence of such established Whig journals as the *North American Review*; former President Jackson was its first subscriber. Another crotchety former President, John Quincy Adams, when asked to write for the journal, refused, claiming it was a contradiction in terms; literature was, by nature, aristocratic and hardly democratic. Longfellow, a later contributor, thought the young editor, with his "weak eyes and green spectacles," an outright "Humbug," part of the "new politico-literary system" that was intent upon puffing every Locofoco author, and abusing all others.

O'Sullivan, writing to Hawthorne early in April 1837, airily sketched out the program of his new publication. The magazine, he boasted, would be "of the highest rank of magazine literature, taking *ton* of the first class in England for model. The compensation to good writers will be on so liberal a scale as to command the best and most polished exertions of their minds." Hawthorne was promised from $3.00 to $5.00 per page for his contributions — a good deal more than he had ever been offered. But he was to find that, like a good many of O'Sullivan's schemes, it was one more castle in the air. Throughout the near-decade that Hawthorne contributed to the *Democratic Review*, as it was eventually called, the generous payments were usually in arrears. Largely out of charity, Hawthorne remained a frequent contributor, sending O'Sullivan some of his most notable stories — "The Celestial Rail-road" and "Rappaccini's Daughter," for example. His regular appearances in the review gave his literary reputation a political complexion that was to prove unfortunate on at least one occasion. Hawthorne's first impression of the twenty-four-year-old editor, when he met him, was not promising; he thought O'Sullivan charming but superficial. Yet he took to him as only a cautious and reticent man can take to someone with a blithe sociability and a gift for prodigality that was all too likely to prove costly to his very best friends. Throughout his life, O'Sullivan borrowed generously and invested heavily in get-rich-quick schemes. O'Sullivan and his gaudy career might well have been some fantastical creation of Hawthorne's own mind — one to which he remained steadfastly loyal.

By mid April Horatio Bridge's optimism about the Reynolds expedition had begun to wane. Reynolds, who fully expected to be appointed head of the scientific corps, had grown impatient with the delays and entered into a bitter public controversy with Mahlon Dickerson, the secretary of the navy, charging the navy with incompetence and mismanagement. Bridge rightly concluded that Reynolds' airing of the dispute would prove a "stumbling block" to Hawthorne's appointment, and though he and Hawthorne's friends continued to work for the appointment throughout the spring and summer, Hawthorne never received the commission. The expedition was put under the command of Charles Wilkes, formerly head of the Navy Department's Depot of Charts and Instruments. The four-year cruise, which circumnavigated the globe between 1838 to 1842, explored the northwest coast of America, charted some 300 islands in the South Pacific and the coastal regions of Antarctica bordering the Indian Ocean. Wilkes himself was to write the official five-volume *Narrative* of the expedition. (Reynolds, who volunteered to go at his own expense, was pointedly excluded.) Hawthorne's friends had worked strenuously on his behalf, but in the shifting ground of American politics, they had applied to the wrong sponsor. Still, the attempt had provided Hawthorne with his first glimpse of the machinery of political power.

By late April, Bridge was suggesting that Hawthorne pay him a visit in Maine. "I want you to spend two or three months this summer with me in my bachelor lodgings at Augusta," he wrote Hawthorne on the 28th, "We can be all to ourselves, and I am a famous cooker of breakfast and tea. And then we will make an excursion or two. Think of this seriously." In May, after a visit to Washington that made it clear that Hawthorne's appointment was most unlikely, he began to encourage his friend about his writing. "Are you writing another book?" he asked on May 17. "You ought to follow up so good a beginning, if beginning this may be called. I wish you would come to Augusta and write all summer in my poor domicile . . . God knows whether there will be another opportunity, after this summer, for you and me to be together again."

There was, however, another cause for Bridge's ambivalence about the naval expedition. Hawthorne, during these months, seems to have been contemplating marriage — something of a deterrent to his taking a sea voyage lasting four years. Who the young woman was is not clear; it may well have been the haughty young Salem heiress who was to figure dramatically in his life several months later. (Family accounts obscure the date at which he met her.) Or it may have been another of those passing infatuations that Ebe Hawthorne claimed her brother was prone to. Bridge's constant inquiries throughout the spring suggest that it was an affair of some importance. "Are you seriously thinking of getting married?" he asked on April 14. "If you are, nothing that I could say would avail to deter you." Bridge was, plainly, not optimistic about the circumstances. "I am in doubt whether you would be more happy in this new mode of life than you are now," he added, conscious of Hawthorne's depressed frame of mind. "This I am sure of, that unless you are fortunate in your choice, you will be wretched in a tenfold degree. I confess that personally, I have a strong desire to see you attain a high rank in literature. Hence my preference would be that you should take the voyage *if you can*. And after taking a turn round the world, and establishing a name that will be worth working for, if you choose to marry you can do it with more advantage than now." Two weeks later, he queried Hawthorne again: "What has become of your matrimonial ideas? Are you in a good way to bring this about?" In May, commenting on the likely failure of the Reynolds expedition, he remarked, "If so, we had better keep out of it, especially if you can marry a fortune, and I finish my Mill Dam" — an intimation, perhaps, that Hawthorne's intended came from a wealthy family. "I wish you would tell me if you were in earnest about marrying," Bridge pleaded.

A week later, on May 24, in response to a letter from Hawthorne indicating that he would make the trip to Maine, Bridge replied with pleasure. "When you come," he answered, "make your arrangements so that you can stay two or three months here. I have a great house to myself, and you shall have the run of it. As for old acquaintances, rely upon it they will not trouble you." Hawthorne, quite evidently, was in a despondent mood — whether from his lack of success or from the failure of his love affair is uncertain. "It is no use for you to feel blue," Bridge recommended. "I tell you that you will be in a good situation next winter, instead of 'under a sod.' Pierce is interested in you, and can make some arrangement, I know . . . So courage and *au diable* with your sods!" He concluded, "I have something to say to you upon marriage, and about Goodrich, and a thousand other things. I shall be inclined to quarrel with you if you do not come, and that would be a serious business for you, for my wrath is dreadful."

Hawthorne arrived in Augusta on the night of July 3, the eve of his thirty-third birthday. Bridge's house, the paternal mansion of some twenty rooms, stood on high ground some distance from the Kennebec River and the site of his dam. An older couple, Captain Harrison and his wife, their infant daughter, and a servant-girl named Nancy lived in one wing of the house, separated from Bridge's bachelor quarters. The only other occupant was Bridge's French tutor, Monsieur Schaeffer — a blond, bantam-sized Alsatian, twenty-one years old and slightly cross-eyed — who taught French in a school at Augusta.

Throughout his six- or seven-week stay, Hawthorne made detailed and lengthy entries in his notebook. His conversations with Bridge, his own nightly French lessons or talks with Monsieur Schaeffer, reports on fishing trips and evenings spent in the local tavern, descriptions of scenery and the odd characters who came into his purview — are all set down in programmatic fashion, as if Hawthorne was determined to come to grips with the outside world.

Monsieur Schaeffer was a subject of particular attention. Ungainly, poorly dressed, diminutive in his coarse blue coat and thin cotton pantaloons, he cut a poor figure and was not taken seriously by his students at school. Bridge claimed he was "an infidel" and a philosopher; Hawthorne found him well informed and intelligent. Monsieur Schaeffer was pitiably unhappy with his situation, however. "So lonely as he is here," Hawthorne noted on July 5, "struggling against the world, with bitter feelings in his breast, and yet talking with the vivacity and gaiety of his nation . . ." After a day of teaching French "to blockheads who sneer at him," he would return late, in a fit of exasperation. If Bridge was still awake, he would storm into his bedroom, standing by the bedside, exclaiming, *"Je hais — Je hais les Yankees!"* and giving vent to the "stifled bitterness of the whole day." Yet in the mornings, before sunrise, Hawthorne could hear him humming and shuffling about in the next room. After an early morning walk, he would return for breakfast, "cheerful and vivacious enough," eat a hearty meal, and set out for school, singing a happy song as he started down the gravel path.

Hawthorne studied his friend Bridge with equal care. Bridge, he noted, had more gentlemanly qualities than any of his other acquaintances: "polished, yet natural, frank, open and straightforward," and with a highly developed awareness of the sensitivities of others. Bridge was "well-acquainted with the world" and had many opportunities for being so; yet he never seemed ill-tempered or cold in his feelings. Hawthorne surmised that he would settle down into some "singular course of life." "He seems almost to have made up his mind never to be married — which I wonder at," Hawthorne observed, "for he has strong affections, and is fond both of women and children."

They were three characters, Hawthorne wrote, "each with something out of the common way, living together somewhat like monks." Yet he felt he could become attached to their odd way of life — "so independent, and untroubled by the forms and restrictions of society." Hawthorne willingly acknowledged that he, too, was "a queer character." He sensed that this visit to his friend might be "the longest space, probably, that we are ever destined to spend together; for fate seems to be preparing changes for both of us. My circumstances, at least, cannot long continue as they are and have been; and Bridge, too, stands betwixt high prosperity and utter ruin."

Bridge's prosperity — or possible ruin — stood not far distant from the house; the half-finished dam forded out from both sides of the river toward an incompleted center. Hawthorne was not optimistic about its prospects; it looked "as much like the ruins of a Dam destroyed by the spring freshets, as like the foundation of a Dam yet to be." It had, in fact, survived the spring torrents but had encountered another problem. The corporation had been reorganized by the Maine legislature and was authorized to increase its capital stock, but with the economic slump, sales were not promising. Nonetheless, the work was proceeding, and Bridge hoped that the dam and subsidiary locks would be completed by the fall. In the mornings, through the window, Hawthorne could hear the voices of the Irish and Canadian workers, the ring of the hammers, floating up from the river. Then, strangely, in the bright green summer landscape, there would be a roar of thunder — the sound of blasting in a nearby quarry.

Like most deep-grained Yankees, Hawthorne was a bit disdainful of the hordes of easygoing, vocal Irish who had crowded into the area, living in squatters' colonies of sod huts and shacks; the men spending their money on drink and brawling in the streets; the women tending to their squawling but healthy offspring. Bridge told him that sometimes as many as twenty adults and children would be crowded into one small square hut. Hawthorne was more admiring of the Canadians, mostly French, who were "frugal and thrifty," and who had come to earn their money and would return across the border. Since Bridge could speak French, he was frequently sought out as an arbiter in the inevitable disputes between the workingmen. Hawthorne, who had known Bridge only as "a free and wild young man," was impressed by his friend's maturity.

Hawthorne was also admiring of the obstinacy of the Irish and of their clannishness. He went with Bridge one day to a village of ramshackle huts. Bridge was determined to find out who had stolen the fence rails from one of his fences, but had little luck; no one would admit to any knowledge of the theft. Bridge, he realized, had the right to evict the squatters and tear down their crude shelters. "It is not a little striking to see how quietly these people contemplate the probability of his exercising it — resolving, indeed, to burrow in their holes as long as may be, yet caring about as little for an ejectment, as those who could find a tenement anywhere." He was particularly observant of the women, many of them pretty and modest-looking, but overburdened with children and wearing drab clothes that made them look "aged before their time." The married women, he noticed, would have nothing to do with the "knot of whores" who had drifted to the campsite and spent their evenings hanging around the local taverns.

Augusta had been named the state capital only a decade before, and there was a good deal that was raw about the city and its manners. At Barker's Tavern in the Mansion House, politics and cigar smoke hovered in the air. Governor Robert Dunlap, an accessible celebrity, was mildly stared after when he crossed through the bar; his counselors lounged on benches or sat on the front porch. A rough and easy democracy pervaded the place; stage drivers were asked to drink with the up-and-coming politicos. Bridge had learned to move in such a society; he had been obliged to pull strings, apply pressure, in order to get his dam capitalized. Hawthorne gave a terse description of the lively scene — but from a peculiar angle: "The decanters and wine-bottles on the move; and the beer and soda-founts pouring out continual streams, with a whiz . . . Rubicund faces; breaths smelling of brandy water. Occasionally, perhaps, the pop of a champagne cork."

One day, while standing on the tavern stoop with Bridge and several others, he noticed a laborer with a "depressed, neglected air," asking after a woman named Mary Ann Russell. His question aroused a good deal of mirth among the bystanders, since Mary Ann

Russell had been one of the several whores ousted from the tavern several nights before. The local pimp, a sly-looking Negro referred to as the "Doctor," asked him pointedly, "Do you want to use her?" Others asked if Mary Ann Russell was his daughter. Finally, he admitted that she was his wife and had run away after being thrown in jail for striking a child. "A man generally places some little dependence on his wife," he explained, "whether she's good or bad." After standing the Doctor to a drink, the husband and the pimp had gone off in search of the woman. "I would have given considerable to witness his meeting with his wife," Hawthorne noted in his journal. "On the whole, there was a moral picturesqueness in the contrasts of this scene — a man moved as deeply as his nature would admit, in the midst of hardened, gibing spectators, heartless towards him. It is worth thinking over and studying out." He was also, perhaps, turning over in his mind the hazards of marriage. "Query — in relation to the man's prostitute wife," he jotted down at the end of his journal entry: "How much desire and resolution of doing her duty by her husband can a wife retain, while injuring him in what is deemed the most essential point."

In the evenings, Hawthorne took his French lessons from Monsieur Schaeffer or sat up late talking expansively with him "of Christianity and Deism, of ways of life, of marriage, of benevolence — in short all deep matters of this world and the next." There was a large element of the theatrical in Monsieur Schaeffer; he might break out into an English ditty, act out scraps of French tragedies, or imitate a Catholic priest intoning the liturgy. He had "frenchified" all their names: Bridge was Monsieur du Pont; Hawthorne, Monsieur de l'Aubépine — a name that Hawthorne liked well enough to borrow for publication with his story "Rappaccini's Daughter" when it appeared in the *Democratic Review*. Monsieur Schaeffer, however, had his more serious moments. One evening, he confessed to Hawthorne that, although he had traveled widely, he had never yet "sinned" with a woman. On another occasion, having mentioned that one of his students had translated Hawthorne's "The Minister's Black Veil" into French as an exercise, he revealed that, unlike the Reverend Mr. Hooper, he would have no objection to exposing "his whole heart — his whole inner man — to the view of the world." Hawthorne, nonplussed that a reader had taken the moral of his story so literally, did not encourage Monsieur Schaeffer to do so; nor was it likely that he would discard the veil from his own well-guarded personality.

A strange bachelor existence, Hawthorne conceded in his notebook, yet it seemed agreeable to the three of them. "We appear mutually to be very well pleased with each other," he commented.

"Of female society," he added, "I see nothing. The only petticoat that comes within our premises appertains to Nancy." He seems to have studied the pretty, dark-eyed servant girl rather carefully. She had a pleasant good morning and a shy smile for him when she came in to make the beds; he noticed her thoughtful glances as she stood, bare-armed at the washtub, gazing out the window at Bridge or someone else crossing through the dooryard. In the afternoons, dressed in silks, she strolled in the yard, "not unconscious," so Hawthorne noted slyly, "that some gentleman may be staring at her from behind our green blinds." In the evenings, Nancy walked in the village. "Thus passes her life," Hawthorne observed, "cheerfully, usefully, virtuously, with hopes, doubtless, of a husband and children."

His life, at the moment, was in a kind of summer stasis: the mornings succeeded one another, green and cool and misty; the muffled shouts of the workmen, the sounds of construction, hovered in the air. He and Bridge made fishing excursions along the Kennebec and the small brooks in the vicinity, Bridge patiently casting for trout and catching chub, Hawthorne lounging on the river bank or swimming in icy, secluded pools. He noted down in his journal the odd types he encountered — "remarkables," he called them — the belligerent Irishwoman standing at the door of her hovel, alternately threatening and buttering up Bridge, declaring that no one would throw her out of her home until her potatoes were dug; the crusty pilot of a small boat, taking heavy tugs at a bottle of whiskey — as did Bridge and himself — while discussing politics and the banking crisis. On a trip to nearby Gardiner, he studied the unfinished mansion of Robert Hallowell Gardiner — a granite castle on the hillside, with circular towers and a lofty entrance. All work on it had come to an end because of ruinous business failures; the owner was living in a little cottage near his unfinished palace. Hawthorne wondered what sort of house excited the greater contempt — Gardiner's granite folly or "the board-built and turf-buttressed hovels" of the "wild Irish," which had sprung up like mushrooms along the river.

In late July, Jonathan Cilley paid a visit to Augusta. In college, Cilley, two years older than Hawthorne, had seemed almost an older brother. An odd bond between them, perhaps, was the fact that Cilley's birthday was July 2 — two days before Hawthorne's — and that Cilley's father had died in 1808, the same year as Nathaniel Hathorne. After a twelve-year interval, Hawthorne studied the young hothead who had now become thin, sharp-featured, and sallow-faced at thirty-five. "He is a singular man," Hawthorne recorded; "shrewd, crafty, insinuating, with wonderful tact, seizing on each man by his manageable point, and using him for his own purposes, often without the man's suspecting that he is made a fool of." Fiercely ambitious and a renegade Democrat who had battled the state's Democratic machine, Cilley had created many political enemies — especially Judge John Ruggles, the local power-broker under whom he had studied law after graduating from Bowdoin. Cilley spoke openly of his political goals, of the disreputable things charged against him as a politician, and the manner in which he had cleared himself of the charges. Hawthorne judged that his friend could be "bold and fierce as a tiger" when the occasion demanded; Cilley would conceal "like a murder-secret, anything that it is not good for him to have known."

Even so, Hawthorne had yielded to warm, if wary, feelings about his old classmate, particularly when Cilley, with tears in this eyes, had spoken of the death of a much-loved daughter, "and how it had affected him, and how impossible it had been for him to believe that she was really to die." After their meeting, Hawthorne reported, "I believe him to be about as honest, now, as the great run of the world — with something even approaching high-mindedness . . . Upon the whole, I have quite a good liking for him."

It may have been Cilley who sponsored Hawthorne's visit to the Charlestown Naval Yard a month later, following his return from Maine. Hawthorne's notebook dates the visit as taking place on Friday, August 26, 1837, but gives no indication of its purpose. Quite probably it was another, belated, attempt to muster support for Hawthorne's appointment to the naval expedition. Hawthorne and Cilley dined aboard the revenue cutter *Hamilton*, in company with Colonel Isaac Barnes, the naval officer for the Boston Custom House. Hawthorne admired the well-appointed cabin, with its maple furnishings, and the substantial meal — chowder, fried fish, corned beef — and the champagne afterward. He was introduced to John "Roaring Jack" Percival, a hero of the War of 1812, white-haired and weather-worn. Hawthorne savored the crusty opinions of the old veteran, "full of antique prejudices against the modern fashions of the younger officers; their moustaches, and such fripperies." Percival also engaged in a spirited political debate, arguing against Cilley's point of view "with much pertinacity." Hawthorne seems to have enjoyed the gruff talk and the sometimes grisly accounts of old naval battles a good deal more than the thorough inspection of the naval yard he and Cilley were given after dinner. They were accompanied by Commandant John Downes, a veteran officer "with rather more of the ocean than the drawing room about him." Downes had been commodore of the frigate *Potomac* during its 1831 round-the-world cruise — a cruise for which Jeremiah Reynolds had served as historian.

On the following day, Hawthorne paid a visit to his relative Ebenezer Hathorne, a forty-eight-year-old bachelor who was working at the Boston Custom House. Eben's grandfather and "Bold Daniel" had been brothers. The "pride of ancestry" was Eben's avocation; he knew a good deal of family lore. He was a quick-tempered and nervous man; his hands shook as he shuffled through the old papers and family records on his desk. Hawthorne particularly recalled his account of Philip English, one of the victims of the witchcraft hysteria who managed to take his accused wife to New York. According to Eben, one of English's daughters later married a son of his enemy, Judge Hathorne — an item of ancestral gossip that was to prove useful years later when Hawthorne came to write *The House of the Seven Gables.* Hawthorne was astonished, however, when his elderly cousin passed from family legend to the subject of politics, giving vent to "the most arrant democracy and locofocoism, that I have happened to hear; saying that nobody ought to possess wealth longer than his own life, and that then it should return to the people &c. It was queer." Hawthorne's amazement is slightly suspect; he was to express a similar view in the preface to *The House of the Seven Gables,* where he claimed that one of the morals of the story was "the folly of tumbling down an avalanche of ill-gotten gold, or real estate, on the heads of an unfortunate posterity." And in the novel itself, Clifford Pyncheon asserts, "What we call real estate — the solid ground to build a house on — is the broad foundation on which nearly all the guilt of this world rests." Ebe Hawthorne recalled that her brother had had some "queer" economic views himself: "One odd, but characteristic notion of his was that he should like a competent income that would neither increase nor diminish. I said that it might be well to have it increase, but he replied, 'No, because then it would engross too much of his attention.' " She added, perhaps with a touch of asperity: "Afterwards, when he lived more in the world, he must have felt that an increasing income could in no circumstances be objectionable."

ᜒ V ᜒ

"Four precepts," Hawthorne wrote in an undated entry in his notebook toward the end of his long seclusion in Salem: "To break off custom; to shake off spirits ill-disposed; to meditate on youth; to do nothing against a man's genius." His earliest journal, begun in 1835, is made up of such brisk admonitions, with random notes and ideas for stories, descriptions of walks to Salem Neck and through Dark Lane. There are accounts of his readings, snippets of information culled from periodicals, bits of local gossip and legend.

The early entries have their personal interest: "Follow out the fantasy of a man taking his life by installments, instead of at one payment — say ten years of life alternately with ten years of suspended animation," he writes at the end of his own decade of solitude. "To picture the predicament of worldly people, if admitted to Paradise," he writes elsewhere.

Other entries strike a distinctly private note: "In this dismal and squalid chamber FAME was won," he writes in a famous entry in the fall of 1836. The occasion, probably, was Park Benjamin's highly favorable review of his *Token* stories, in the October issue of the *American Monthly Magazine*, a review that had revealed Hawthorne's name to the public for the first time. Hawthorne's entry was slightly premature; his real fame came later in life and only after many disappointments. In a more considered moment, he writes, "Fame — some very humble persons in a town may be said to possess it — as the penny-post, the town-crier, the constable etc.; and they are known to every body; while many richer, more intellectual, worthier persons are unknown to the majority of their fellow citizens. Something analogous in the world at large." There is a tone of weariness and dissatisfaction in some of the entries. "A lament for Life's wasted sunshine," he scribbles. "To think, as the sun goes down," he writes again, "what events have happened in the course of the day — events of ordinary occurrence. As the clocks have struck, the dead have been buried etc." The days seemed to slip by, chronicled only by such terminal events.

In his lonelier moments, in his solitary walks, in the quiet of his dim bedroom, he was a man communing with himself, attempting to catch a glimpse of his own identity. "To make one's own reflection in a mirror the subject of a story," he writes. It was the germ of one of his more revealing sketches.

"Monsieur du Miroir" is one of the exceptional inventions among Hawthorne's early tales and sketches. At first glance, it is merely a clever idea, one that a practiced or sensible writer might leave as a random notebook jotting. But Hawthorne, having decided to flesh out the notion in a full-fledged sketch, created a minor — if somewhat overlong — tour de force. The basic conceit of the story is a man's recognition of his mirror image as that of another, a mysterious and dumb personage, to whom he is fatefully bound through life. That Hawthorne was a handsome man and possessed of a nor-

mal vanity is clear from his letters and from the accounts of his
contemporaries; yet he was, perhaps, more self-conscious than vain.
Most of his references to his own physical appearance are modest
and jocular. The narcissistic situation of "Monsieur du Miroir" went
further than personal vanity. The experience of seeing himself in the
mirror, on which the story was based, was a means of catching some
glimpse of his own identity, of distancing himself from his personal
ruminations, of attempting to stand outside himself as a concerned,
somewhat amused observer. For Hawthorne, character was fate,
and throughout his writings, the mirror image is used repeatedly as
a passing metaphor for insight into one's own character or one's
fate. (Hawthorne was to make similar use of the midcentury invention, the camera, although he invariably made slighting remarks
about photographs of himself. In at least one of his novels, *The
House of the Seven Gables*, the camera is a perverse instrument of
recognition that never lies about the secret personality of its subject.)

The tone of "Monsieur du Miroir" is mildly ironic; the narrator,
approaching his middle years, is curious about this "other," who
turns up, uninvited, at glittering theatrical performances and in
crowded ballrooms. "He has been imprudent enough," the narrator
complains, "to show himself within the dusty panes of the lowest
pot-houses, or even more disreputable haunts. In such cases, meeting each other's eyes, we both looked down, abashed."

The narrator and his reflected image seem doomed to live, enjoy,
suffer, and die in unison. "Here, in my chamber, for instance, as the
evening deepens into night," the narrator reports, "I sit alone —
the key turned and withdrawn from the lock — the key-hole stuffed
with paper, to keep out a peevish little blast of wind. Yet, lonely as I
seem, were I to lift one of the lamps and step five paces eastward, M.
du Miroir would be sure to meet me, with a lamp also in his hand."
The narrator indulges in an idle fantasy, never to be gratified: "If I
must needs have so intrusive an intimate, who stares me in the face
in my closest privacy, and follows me even to my bed-chamber, I
should prefer — scandal apart — the laughing bloom of a young
girl, to the dark and bearded gravity of my present companion." The
sexual implication is amusing and slightly daring — considering the
staid literary conventions of the period. But does it conceal an unconscious echo of the wish Hawthorne had made years before, that
he might have been a girl, "pinned all my life to my Mother's
apron?"

Despite its surface amiabilities, "Monsieur du Miroir" has its bitter philosophical moments. "And when the coffin lid shall have
closed over me," the narrator speculates, "and that face and form,

which, more truly than the lover swears it to his beloved, are the sole light of his existence, when they shall be laid in that dark chamber, whither his swift and secret footsteps cannot bring him — then what is to become of poor M. du Miroir! . . . Will he linger where I have lived, to remind the neglectful world of one who staked much to win a name, but will not then care whether he lost or won?"

It is a plain admission of his own disappointed hopes, his sense of failure, neatly woven into the fabric of his allegory on the fateful marriage between the private mind and the public image.

On November 13, 1837, Hawthorne received a letter inviting him to the funeral of Thomas Green Fessenden, who had died on the previous Saturday. Hawthorne had admired the aged poet, whose youth had been wasted on impractical schemes and inventions, and the remainder of whose life had been given over to literary drudgery, editing one magazine or newspaper after another. Fessenden's true bent, Hawthorne felt, had been indicated early in his career with his poem "Jonathan's Courtship," a genial satire on country manners. But a small measure of success with political satire, *Democracy Unveiled*, a Federalist tract repeating old newspaper slanders against Thomas Jefferson and others, had encouraged Fessenden to waste his time on the transient and ephemeral topics of the day. Hawthorne clearly felt that Fessenden was unequipped to be a satirist; he had none of that "ferocity of the true blood-hound of literature — such as Swift, or Churchill, or Cobbett — which fastens upon the throat of its victim." Now, Fessenden was dead, at sixty-six, little remembered after a brief burst of fame, his true talents largely wasted.

One thing Hawthorne particularly regretted when he came to write the biographical essay on Fessenden, which he sent as one of his last contributions to the *American Monthly*. He had been unable to get Fessenden to talk about his past life and his associations with the notable writers and politicians of his time. "Indeed," Hawthorne noted in his essay, "lacking a turn for observation of character, his former companions had passed before him like images in a mirror, giving him little knowledge of their inner nature." Fessenden seemed to lack entirely the tendency of the aged to reminisce about the past; his eyes were fixed on the future. On one of Hawthorne's last visits to the poet in Boston, the old man, lying flushed and dizzy in his bed, was full of glowing schemes for moving to Illinois, insisting that Hawthorne join him.

On the 14th, Hawthorne journeyed to Boston to attend the funeral, following the coffin to Mount Auburn Cemetery. It was a gloomy day; snow — the first of the season — had been falling since early in the morning. In the dull light, the gray stones and the drifting snow made the cemetery seem like "the dreariest spot on earth." Only a few friends were there to help carry the coffin to the sepulcher; on its passage from the hearse, it was covered with snow. The mourners descended the steps and were given a last look at the body. "Dark would have been the hour," Hawthorne wrote, "if, when we closed the door of the tomb upon his perishing mortality, we had believed that our friend was there."

Fessenden, Hawthorne claimed in his essay, had been "a man of genius," worthy of being well remembered in the "literary and political annals of our country." But it was all too likely that on that bleak Tuesday, with the drifting snow blurring the scene, blotting out the weathered stones, he had seen the cold extinction of a literary career.

Part Two

Miss. Sophia A. Peabody,

with the affectionate
regards of her friend,
Nath. Hawthorne.

1838

The Sophistry of Passion

FATE SEEMS TO BE preparing changes for both of us," Hawthorne had written in his notebook in the summer of 1837, at the beginning of his visit with Horatio Bridge. His judgment was prophetic, for within the year his life was radically altered. He was to gain that experience of the real world which he felt he lacked as a writer through a series of events that might have daunted the worldliest of men.

On November 11, the evening that Thomas Green Fessenden lay dying in Boston, Hawthorne and his sisters paid their first call on the Peabody family in Charter Street. Lizzie Peabody had issued her invitation on the pretext of wanting to discuss the *Democratic Review*, to which she hoped to become a contributor. Sensing that her guests were nervous, she had ushered them into the parlor and lit the astral lamp. When she turned, she found the Hawthornes sitting stiffly, all in a row. To break the ice, she encouraged them to study the new edition of Homer's *Iliad*, with designs by John Flaxman, that Professor Cornelius Felton of Harvard had just sent her. The Hawthornes had drawn up their chairs and Lizzie had proceeded upstairs, hoping to tempt Sophia to come down — but without success. Otherwise, the evening had gone extremely well; the talk had been animated and congenial. Mary Peabody, arriving at nine — so Lizzie remembered — had immediately grasped the situation and made a considerable effort to charm the reclusive Hawthornes. Hawthorne, hesitant and reserved, had felt the pleasure of being mildly lionized. It was clear that the Peabody sisters regarded the author as a social catch.

A few days later, Mary Peabody, writing to her brother George in New Orleans, described their visitor: "He has lived the life of a perfect recluse till very lately — so diffident that he suffers inexpressibly in the presence of his fellow-mortals — but he has a temple of a head (not a tower) and an eye full of sparkle, glisten and intelligence." She and Elizabeth were planning to send *Twice-told Tales* to their brother if Mr. Bancroft, who was traveling to New Orleans, would carry the book with him. Mary thought George would find the stories diverting. The author, she informed her brother, "has promised to come again and if we can get fairly acquainted I think we shall find much pleasure in him."

It may well have been true, as Lizzie Peabody remembered it, that on his second visit Hawthorne had stared fixedly at the frail figure of Sophia Peabody, sitting demurely in the parlor. Clasping his hands together and with a "look of entreaty," he may have pointedly asked Sophia to acompany Elizabeth to Herbert Street that evening. But only in the most subliminal way could Hawthorne have sensed the seriousness of the occasion; for he had already met, and considered himself in love with, another young woman — a Salem heiress of undisputed attractiveness, whose worldliness and perversity were to involve him in a near-duel with a friend.

Mary Crowninshield Silsbee was the daughter of Nathaniel Silsbee, a retired United States senator and one of the wealthier merchants of Salem. As a child, Mary had been oversensitive, pretty, vain, and spoiled; as a young woman, she had pretensions to culture and aspired to be mistress of a glittering salon. Her father's wealth and social position afforded her the necessary opportunities. As a girl of eighteen, she had begun traveling to Washington with her father and mother when Congress was in session. At other times of the year, she was in residence in Salem and Boston; she had early acquired an imperious social manner.

Lizzie Peabody, in particular, disliked the young woman and considered her "a great coquette, a mischief-maker, a fearful liar." Mary Silsbee, she claimed, was possessed by a "sort of moral insanity . . . She was a coarse-minded woman. She liked to create difficulties and intrigues." Another feminine contemporary, Lydia Haven, a friend of the Peabody sisters, described the heiress's manners as "a torrent of affectation," and her style of dress as showy and irregular. Mary Silsbee seemed to be in a state of perpetual dishabille, "her head caught in a snarl of laces," her figure "rigged out in a gown that had the appearance of just kindling into a blaze."

It was part of Lizzie Peabody's indictment against Mary Silsbee that she had interfered in the love affair of Elizabeth Crowninshield, a cousin of Mary's and five years her senior. In Washington, Elizabeth Crowninshield had fallen in love with a visiting English nobleman, to whom she became engaged. Whether out of jealousy or a perverse spirit of intrigue, Mary Silsbee wrote a number of anonymous letters that effectively ended the affair. The Englishman returned to England and never married; Elizabeth Crowninshield remained a spinster until the age of forty-nine, when she made a marriage of friendship with the elderly, unromantic Reverend William Mountford.

At about the age of eighteen or nineteen, Mary Silsbee had had a romantic involvement with a much older man, Jared Sparks, a former minister, the publisher of the *North American Review*, and a celebrated and opinionated teacher and scholar who had rescued and was editing the papers of George Washington. Lizzie Peabody considered him exceedingly brilliant and handsome; he was another of those intellectual men she hoped to serve. When she learned that Sparks intended to edit a series of American biographies, she immediately flooded him with suggestions for authors and insisted that he should call the series *Sparks' Library of American Biographies*, "because your name is so up in the world as having inexhaustible historical resources & being honest & indefatigable as to facts . . ." Sparks's prominence — and his looks — are verified by the portraits of him painted by Rembrandt Peale, Gilbert Stuart, and Thomas Sully. He was to achieve later renown first as a professor at Harvard University and then as its president.

His relationship with Mary Silsbee, the "Star of Salem," was a subject of some concern among his friends. An older, bluestocking friend, Ann Gillam Storrow, was pointedly critical of his becoming a "worshipper" at the shrine of "a woman to whom common report gives so little that is intrinsically interesting and valuable though so much that is glaring and attractive. I hate to think that you are assailable through your vanity . . . I cannot bear to have you let a reigning Belle lead you captive." Two years of study and research in Europe (Sparks was the editor of a pioneering study, *The Diplomatic Correspondence of the American Revolution*) cooled his passion. Sparks, it appears, broke off the affair with Mary Silsbee; in 1832, at the age of forty-three, he married Frances Allen, a wealthy young woman from Hyde Park.

At the time Hawthorne met her, probably early in 1837, Mary Silsbee was twenty-eight. According to Lizzie Peabody, Mary Silsbee had learned of the young Salem author through John L. O'Sullivan, the gadabout editor of the *Democratic Review*. Eager to add another trophy to her guest collection, she had induced O'Sullivan to arrange a meeting. But a hostess as ambitious as Mary Silsbee could certainly have found the means to invite a promising author to her Salem home without the agency of O'Sullivan, who presumably did not become acquainted with Hawthorne until after April 1837. As early as October 1836, Park Benjamin, writing in the *American Monthly*, had identified Hawthorne as the author of several tales in the current *Token*, and by March 1837, with the publication of *Twice-told Tales*, Hawthorne had achieved enough local celebrity to have come to Mary Silsbee's attention.

Hawthorne's lack of social experience, evidently, had not prepared him for the young woman; he was quite plainly dazzled by her interest and flattery. It is quite possible that she was the cause of Horatio Bridge's repeated inquiries about Hawthorne's marital intentions throughout the spring of 1837. In that case, Mary Silsbee would have been the young woman Hawthorne had in mind when he wrote Longfellow, in June, exhibiting some urgency about the choice of a profession, claiming that he saw "little prospect but that I must scribble for a living." He told the poet, "I have now, or soon shall have, one sharp spur to exertion, which I lacked at an earlier period."

Whether Hawthorne knew the wayward history of the Salem heiress is uncertain, but he was both charmed and perplexed by her. He was to write her a number of letters, which she later burned at his request. In headstrong fashion, Mary Silsbee proceeded to acquaint Hawthorne with a few of the more intimate events of her private life, some details of which were apparently fabricated. She assured him "that he was the only human being to whom she could reveal the secrets of her inmost soul." An accomplished coquette, attempting to play the role of a fascinator, she was alternately confidential and coolly mysterious, suggesting that there was some "secret spring" to their relationship that Hawthorne would either discover "soon" — or "never." Hawthorne — so Lizzie Peabody recalled — was plainly fascinated and flattered by the confidences of the woman. Yet when she, in turn, tried to draw him out, expecting him to respond with a similar intimacy, Hawthorne's reticence became an obstacle. He let her down lightly, telling her "in the gentlest and most considerate manner, that it was impossible for him to regard himself as an object of so much interest as to warrant his dissecting himself for her benefit." Mary Silsbee, faced with Hawthorne's rebuff, tactfully withdrew. But she appears to have resented it.

There may also have been another dimension to his relationship with the attractive Miss Silsbee. Her father had been an important figure in the United States Senate, only slightly overshadowed by his colleague, Daniel Webster. Nathaniel Silsbee still had powerful connections in Washington. A self-made man, having risen in the world from a lowly seaman to a prosperous merchant, Silsbee had been chairman of the Commerce Committee in the Senate and an influential voice regarding naval affairs. He had also taken a decisive role in the development of the United States Customs Service. At a time when Hawthorne was still hoping to secure an appointment to the Reynolds expedition, Silsbee might be a powerful ally — or a dangerous enemy.

The details — and the dénouement — of Hawthorne's affair with Mary Silsbee were known to the Hawthorne family. Elizabeth Peabody, in her burgeoning friendship with Hawthorne and his sisters, learned them in some detail. Late in life — in 1882 — she related them to her nephew. Julian Hawthorne drew on his diary notes of his aunt's recollections for his biography of his parents, *Nathaniel Hawthorne and His Wife*, but in recounting the affair, he discreetly referred to Mary Silsbee and John Louis O'Sullivan, who was also involved, as simply "Mary" and "Louis." Critics, then and later, disregarded his account as an undocumented and romanticized fiction. It was not until 1958, when Norman Holmes Pearson, who was editing the Hawthorne letters, published "Hawthorne's Duel," an article in the *Essex Institute Historical Collections*, that the authenticity of Julian's account, in its essential details, was established.

In Julian's undeniably romantic version, Mary Silsbee summoned Hawthorne one evening to a "private and mysterious interview."

> After much artful preface and well-contrived hesitation and agitated reluctance, she at length presented him with the startling information that his friend Louis [John Louis O'Sullivan], presuming upon her innocence and guilelessness, had been guilty of an attempt to practice the basest treachery upon her; and she passionately adjured Hawthorne, as her only confidential and trusted friend and protector, to champion her cause. This story, which was devoid of a vestige of truth, but which was nevertheless so cunningly interwoven with certain circumstances known to her auditor as to appear like truth itself, so kindled Hawthorne's indignation and resentment, that, without pausing to make proper investigations, he forthwith sent Louis a challenge.

Hawthorne had only recently become acquainted with O'Sullivan and could hardly have formed a careful evaluation of the man. In later years, after a long friendship, he would speak of something feminine in O'Sullivan's character, referring to his "vivid affections" and his "quick womanly sensibility." O'Sullivan was "too much like a woman, without being a woman." Hawthorne thought of him as a soiled angel, led astray by temporary ambitions and political affiliations. Quite possibly, Hawthorne was aware of O'Sullivan's unreliability from the beginning. Yet, however extravagant and unthinking O'Sullivan might prove, Hawthorne discerned in him a basic honesty. The devil, Hawthorne claimed, had "a smaller share in O'Sullivan than in other bipeds who wear breeches."

At the time that he issued his challenge, Hawthorne had reason to feel indebted to O'Sullivan, who had begun to publish him in the *Democratic Review*. And, by reason of his influential political connections in Washington and New York, O'Sullivan could also be a very useful friend. Mary Silsbee's ploy had placed Hawthorne in the worst of situations. For reasons of natural human vanity, he would not want to believe that the woman he was in love with was a gratuitous liar. Nor could he ignore her request to "champion her cause," as Julian quaintly described it, without a personal sense of cowardice. There was also the question of what Mary's father might think of his failure to act.

Despite the superficialities of his character, O'Sullivan was a knowledgeable man. Rather than accepting the challenge outright, he investigated the situation, and then, in Julian's account, wrote Hawthorne "a frank and generous letter, in which, after fully and punctually explaining to him the ins and outs of the deception that had been practiced upon him," O'Sullivan refused to accept the challenge. Instead, he "claimed the renewal of Hawthorne's friendship."

Hawthorne's decision to go to Washington, early in 1838, was probably connected with the unhappy affair. Perhaps he wanted to discuss the matter face to face with O'Sullivan. On February 5, in a gloomy mood, he wrote to Horatio Bridge:

> It is my purpose to set out for Washington in the course of a fortnight or thereabouts but only to make a short visit. Would it be utterly impossible, or extremely unadvisable, for you to come to Boston or this place, within that interval? Not that you can do me the least good; but it would be a satisfaction to me to hold a talk with the best friend I ever had or shall have (of the male sex) — and there may be cause for regret on your part, should we fail of a meeting. But I repeat that you cannot exercise the slightest favorable influence on my affairs — they being beyond your control, and hardly within my own.

At the end of his letter, he added, "Be mum!"

It is uncertain whether Hawthorne, in fact, made the journey to Washington. But Julian Hawthorne reported, somewhat dramatically, that his father had had an interview with O'Sullivan, in which the editor left Hawthorne's vanity "not a leg to stand upon." Horatio Bridge, who was well aware of Hawthorne's resoluteness, recalled that O'Sullivan had had to give "ample explanations" before Hawthorne was persuaded by Pierce and Cilley, who were serv-

ing as his advisers, to give up his challenge. Finally convinced that
he had been manipulated, Hawthorne had confronted the Salem
heiress and, in Lizzie Peabody's colorful words, "crushed her."

⌁ II ⌁

In Washington, Jonathan Cilley's abrasive temperament had
brought him a reputation as a Yankee firebrand. Hawthorne, in his
brief meetings with Cilley after his election to Congress, observed
that Cilley's political career had made changes in his character that
had not been so noticeable in their college years. Cilley's "harsher
traits" — his iron resolution, his terrible energy — "had grown
apace with his milder ones." But Hawthorne felt instinctively that
these were the traits of leadership, qualities that encouraged political supporters. Cilley was a radical Democrat.

A burning political issue of the period was the banking controversy. Until the election of Andrew Jackson, government funds
had been deposited in the Bank of the United States, which was
under the direction of the autocratic and high-handed Nicholas
Biddle. That system gave the bank — and Biddle — a virtual iron
hand over the fiscal policies of the country and over rates of credit.
Moreover, it had given rise to a great deal of corruption; it was a
common practice for bank officials to bribe legislators, by way of
private loans, to vote for legislation favorable to the institution. It
was also common practice for them to use the same form of persuasion with the publishers and editors of influential newspapers.
One of the notable scandals during the Jackson administration had
been the case of Colonel James Watson Webb, publisher of the
Morning Courier and New York Enquirer, a Whig paper that had nevertheless supported Jackson in his battle against the unpopular
Bank of the United States. When, later, Webb suddenly reversed his
stand and became one of the bank's supporters, it was discovered — as the result of a congressional inquiry — that Webb and his
paper had been the recipients of three loans from the bank, amounting to $52,975. The transactions were a matter of public record, pub-
lished in the report of the House committee.

Jackson's policy, successful only after a bitter struggle, was to deposit government monies in various state banks. He had achieved
this success only through his broad popularity and with the support
of the nation's rival private banks. The net result, however, was a
ruinous inflation, a flood of paper money and easy credit, that resulted in the panic of 1837. The newly elected Martin Van Buren,
faced with this dilemma, pushed for the establishment of an independent federal treasury that would, in effect, bring about a di-

vorce between the government and the banking industry. It was an unpopular move among conservative Whigs and conservative Democrats, both of whom had profitable ties with the business community. Van Buren was immediately branded as a captive of the Locofocos.

Conservatives of both parties warned that Van Buren's assault on the state banking system was an attack on both states' rights and the prerogatives of capital. On the floor of the House, the Whig congressman from Massachusetts, Caleb Cushing, argued that the destruction of the present banking system would revolutionize society and the property rights of the country. "Will not the same desperado spirit, which strikes at one form of property, strike at another?" he asked. "If it ravages the North, will it spare the South?" he added, clearly enlisting the support of Southern slave-holders. The banking issue was being grafted onto the growing crisis of the slavery question.

It was against this backdrop of heated political controversy and the entrenched Southern custom of dueling that Jonathan Cilley played out the last act of his political career. The Senate and the House, during these years, had each become a hotbed of challenges and duels. Cilley's colleague Congressman John Fairfield of Maine, writing home to his wife, reported regularly on the duels and near-duels that occurred during his brief tenure of two years. One of these, a duel between Jesse Bynum of North Carolina and Daniel Jenifer of Maryland — an affair that had required six shots, though so poorly aimed that not even an injury had resulted — had been fought over nothing more than the question of whether an attempt to interrupt a long-winded speech should have been called "ungentlemanly."

A seedy and disreputable Washington correspondent, Matthew Davis, writing under the byline "The Spy in Washington," charged in the pages of the *Courier and Enquirer* that he had indisputable proof that a member of Congress had offered to sell his influence with a government committee in relation to an upcoming contract. On February 12, 1838, Henry A. Wise, congressman from Virginia and a master of political invective, moved that a committee be established to investigate the charges. In the course of the debate, Cilley opposed Wise's motion, claiming that if Davis had charges to make, he should make them under oath, and make them distinctly, not "vaguely." In an aside, he added that he did not know the editor of the *Courier and Enquirer*, but that if this was the same man who had changed the policies of his paper after receiving "facilities to the amount of some $52,000," then he did not think such charges were "entitled to much credit in an American Congress." His remarks were reported in the *Washington Globe*. Ironically, as it developed, the charges involved a senator; ironically, too, the implicated senator was John Ruggles, Cilley's old political enemy. Under the circumstances, the inquiry belonged in the Senate, not the House.

On February 21, in the hall of the House of Representatives, Cilley was handed a note from Colonel Webb. It was delivered by William Graves, representative from Kentucky. In the note, Webb demanded to know if the report in the *Washington Globe* was true, and if the "editor" to whom Cilley had referred was himself. Cilley refused the note, claiming the traditional congressional privilege that remarks made on the floor of the House in debate were not subject to legal charges or challenges. In refusing, he made it clear he had intended no disrespect to his fellow congressman, the bearer of the note.

Whether as a matter of real principle or the result of a plot among Southern Whigs to embarrass a troublesome administration Democrat, Graves chose to see Cilley's refusal as a slur upon his own honor and that of his friend, Colonel Webb. He wrote Cilley demanding clarification. Cilley responded that he chose not to be drawn into controversy on the subject of Colonel Webb. "I neither affirmed nor denied anything in regard to his character," he asserted. Graves, playing the opportunities, replied that Cilley's response was "inexplicit, unsatisfactory, and insufficient." He demanded that Cilley disclaim any slur upon the honor of Colonel Webb, and stated that he expected a "categorical answer."

Although Cilley had tried to stave off a duel on such unwarranted charges, his answer was emphatic. "Your note of this date has just been placed in my hands," he wrote Graves. "I regret that mine of yesterday was unsatisfactory to you; but I cannot admit the right on your part to propound the question to which you ask a categorical answer, and therefore decline any further response to it." On the following day, February 23, Graves sent a formal challenge to Cilley at his boardinghouse on Third Street. It was delivered by Henry Wise, serving as Graves's second. Cilley had no recourse but to accept. In his reply he named as his second George W. Jones, the delegate from the Wisconsin territory.

At thirty-five, and at the peak of his career, Cilley was an isolated figure, having come to power without the support of his own state party. He could hardly expect assistance from the Southern factionalists. Julian Hawthorne, in his account of Cilley's duel and its effect on his father, claimed that Hawthorne's challenge to O'Sullivan, supposedly still moot at the time, had had an influence on Cilley's decision to meet Graves's challenge. Cilley, Julian claimed, had responded to a taunt that if his friend Hawthorne had not hesitated to enter into a duel, Cilley should be equally bold. The more likely truth is that Cilley in his isolated position had been maneuvered into the confrontation by political forces. But it is also plausible that Hawthorne, for whom the theme of circumstantial guilt in the death of a comrade or friend had already become an abiding literary theme, may have felt himself in some way implicated.

Between two and three o'clock in the afternoon of February 24, the contending parties gathered on the outskirts of Washington City, on the road to Marlboro in Maryland. The meeting place had been kept secret, much to the chagrin of the bloodthirsty Colonel Webb, who had gone, fully armed, to Cilley's boardinghouse, prepared to antagonize Cilley and fight him on the spot.

In a field along the Maryland road, close to the state border, the two principals and their seconds met. Each man was allowed two friends and an attending surgeon. The only others present were the carriage drivers and a few spectators. Among Cilley's chosen friends was the hotheaded North Carolinian, Jesse Bynum, an old hand at such occasions. It was a bright, sunny day, with the chill of winter still in the air. There was a blustering wind, which proved not to be to Cilley's favor when the two men drew lots for position. Cilley, allowed the choice of weapons, had selected rifles.

The seconds, Jones and Wise, paced off the distance in the field. Cilley and Graves took up their positions, rifles cocked and with the triggers set. At the given signal, both men fired. Both were wide of the mark. Cilley, perhaps intentionally or through nervousness, had fired before his rifle was fully raised.

The seconds consulted in midfield. Since the contestants had satisfied a point of honor, Wise claimed it was necessary only that Cilley assign some acceptable reason for his refusal to accept Webb's note. Both men might then honorably withdraw. Cilley responded with the answer he had given earlier: he was not bound to receive Webb's note, but no disrespect had been intended toward Graves, for whom he held "the highest respect and most kind feelings." Graves's answer was that this left him in exactly the same position as when he had made his challenge.

Another round was exchanged — without harm. Once more, the seconds met in the middle of the field but arrived at no point of reconciliation. Jesse Bynum grimly remarked that "if either of those gentlemen fall by continuing the contest, the community will put their blood on our hands." Dr. Jonathan Foltz, Graves's attending physician, insisted that the contest should be ended. Wise suggested that if the next shot did not settle the matter, the distance should be shortened.

On the third try, Cilley was struck. Clutching his hip with his left hand, he fell to the ground. He was unconscious when his friends reached him. According to Foltz, the rifle ball had passed clean through the body, midway between the lower ribs and the spine. In five minutes, Cilley was dead.

His death was the occasion for innumerable Sunday sermons and editorials on the evils of dueling. In the House, a Committee of Inquiry was established to investigate the "late duel." Its report, rendered some months later, confirmed that the ritual had been conducted with all the punctilious attention to form expected of gentlemen on the field of honor. But its conclusion was that the entire challenge had been out of order. Graves was expelled for "a breach of the highest constitutional privileges of the House"; Wise and Jones were censured.

On February 27, the day of Cilley's funeral, Bridge's friend Senator Reuel Williams, writing from Washington, hinted at dark matters not made public: "He died like a hero, in defense of his honor and his principles . . . Cilley was too promising and too independent to be allowed to remain in the way of the Whigs and his death is the result of more deep and general policy than has been and perhaps may ever be made public."

Hawthorne was stunned by the news. He had remembered, from a visit with Cilley in Thomaston, a gentler, more private figure, not the unbending and somewhat ruthless public man. They had talked, then, about Cilley's family life. In Thomaston, Hawthorne had smiled at the image of the ambitious politician, now a rude farmer, driving his cow home in the evening along a muddy road. Cilley had kept bees and told Hawthorne how "he loved to sit for whole hours by the hives, watching the labors of the insects, and soothed by the hum with which they filled the air." Hawthorne, remembering Cilley's bitterly fought congressional election, considered it, now, a "fatal triumph."

He was despondent; the strain of his love affair and the death of his friend had their effect. In her meddling way, Elizabeth Peabody sensed Hawthorne's mood and tried to apply comfort and irritating constructive advice in equal measure. Her suggestion was that Hawthorne take up German as a diversion from his troubles. After one of her visits to the Hawthorne household, she wrote a long, chatty letter to Ebe: "I saw how much your brother was suffering on Thursday evening, and am glad you think it was not a trial, but rather the contrary to hear my loquaciousness. I talked because I thought it was better than to seem to claim entertainment from him, whose thoughts must be wandering to the so frightfully bereaved. There seems so little for hope and memory to dwell on in such a case (though I hope everything always from the Revelation of Death) that I thought perhaps it would be better if he could divert himself with the German."

Elizabeth Peabody had her views about men and careers. "I see that you both think me rather *enthusiastic*," she went on, "but I believe I say the truth when I say that I do not often *overrate*, and I feel sure that this brother of yours has been gifted and kept so choice in her secret places by Nature thus far, that he may do a great thing for his country." She plainly did not approve of Hawthorne's hoping for some political appointment that would be beneath him; but understanding that he had been "so long uneasy" and that man "needs labor to tame his passions and train his mind to order and method," she was willing to concede that his seeking such an appointment might be advisable. Then she went on to state: "The perilous time for the *most highly gifted* is not *youth* . . . the perilous season is *middle age*, when a false wisdom tempts them to doubt the divine origins of the dreams of their youth." It was then that men of genius listened to the counsels of the worldly and fell *"to the level"* of their associates. She was all the more melancholy at the thought of Hawthorne's "owing anything to the patronage of men of such thoughtless character as has lately been made notorious. And it seems to me they live in too gross a region of selfishness to appreciate the ambrosial moral *aura* which floats around our ARIEL." Despite her embarrassing enthusiasm, Lizzie Peabody, in her meandering, well-meaning, contradictory fashion, had grasped a truth: Hawthorne had passed — or was passing through — his "perilous season."

At the request of John O'Sullivan, Hawthorne wrote a memorial essay on Jonathan Cilley for the *Democratic Review*. Although he could refer to his own notes and impressions of the man and friend, Hawthorne was uncertain about many of the factual details of Cilley's life. Tactfully, he wrote to the postmaster at Thomaston, requesting information about the date of Cilley's marriage, his wife's name and parentage; he did not want to trouble the bereaved family. On March 21, he also wrote to Longfellow in Cambridge, asking for his classmate's recollections. "It has fallen to my lot," he said, "to write a biographical sketch of him; and I fear it will be a thorny affair to handle."

That weekend Longfellow paid Hawthorne a visit in Salem. The poet called on Sunday morning and found Hawthorne "still a-bed in his Herbert Street house in the outskirts of dull Sunday-looking Salem." After dinner, they met again in a nearby coffee house. "Passed the afternoon with him," Longfellow wrote in his journal, "discussing literary matters. He is much of a lion here; sought-after, fed, and expected to roar. A man of genius and fine imagination. He is destined to soar high." They had undoubtedly discussed the tragic death of Cilley, but the talk may have drifted to other matters as well. Earlier, Longfellow had suggested that they collaborate on a book of fairy tales and legends for children. Although the subject was to recur in their letters for approximately a year, the collaboration never took place. On Monday, before Longfellow returned to Cambridge, they had drunk a bottle of champagne together.

It was not until mid April that Hawthorne finished his essay on Cilley, sending it with apologies for lateness. He had been delayed, he said, "by various causes — partly because I could not get all the information I wanted — partly because the task was so painful that I put it off as long as I could. I fear you will find it very coldly written; and you will perceive that some tact has been necessary from the peculiar nature of Cilley's early political struggles. I should like to have seen the report of the Committee of Investigation; but if there be anything to subjoin, you can put it in a note."

In his essay, Hawthorne tempered his account of Cilley's hard-fisted political rise — his disputes with the local party and his former mentor, Judge Ruggles — with the private views he had garnered in Maine of the quiet farmer, husband, and father. He touched only briefly on the circumstances of the fatal duel, referring to the unnamed cause, Colonel Webb, as "a person of disputed respectability." His final judgment on the events was given in the most forthright — even, perhaps, dangerous — terms: "A challenge was never given on a more shadowy pretext; a duel was never pressed to a fatal close in the face of such open kindness as was expressed by Mr. Cilley; and the conclusion is inevitable, that Mr. Graves and his principal second, Mr. Wise, have gone further than their own dreadful code will warrant them, and overstepped the imaginary distinction, which, on their own principles, separates manslaughter from murder."

Publicly, Hawthorne depicted his friend as the civic hero and martyr — albeit a man with human faults and frailties. His private opinions, rendered in his own journals, were a good deal more ambivalent; for along with Cilley's warm affections and frankness, Hawthorne had also underscored his craftiness, his insinuating manner, and wonderful tact. In reviewing his notes, Hawthorne must have felt the grim irony of his private assessment of Cilley: "Hardly anybody, probably, thinks him better than he is, and many think him worse. Nevertheless, unless he should fall into some great and overwhelming discovery of rascality, he will always possess influence; though I should hardly think that he could take any prominent part in Congress." A terrible and brief fame, nonetheless, had overtaken Jonathan Cilley.

ᨡ III ᨢ

In his letter to O'Sullivan, Hawthorne requested a favor for Elizabeth Peabody. He asked if O'Sullivan would consider publishing an article she had recently written, titled "On the Claims of the Beautiful Arts." He had read the first part of the essay and felt it had merit. "She is something too much of a theorist," he added, "but really possesses knowledge, feeling, eloquence and imagination." He felt that Elizabeth's review of her friend Emerson's book, *Nature*, which had appeared in the February issue of the *Democratic Review*, was particularly poor; he wished she had done herself better justice. Hawthorne made it clear that O'Sullivan was not obliged to publish Lizzie's new article, but he would appreciate it if the editor would at least look it over.

He had been seeing much of the Peabody sisters. With Elizabeth, particularly, he developed a wary intimacy, despite her enthusiasm and her presumptuous habit of offering unasked-for advice. Hawthorne would describe her, in a later letter to O'Sullivan, as "a good old soul" who would "give away her only petticoat, I do believe, to anybody that she thought needed it more than herself."

From the beginning, Lizzie Peabody had attempted to draw him out. Hawthorne responded cautiously, talking of the seclusion of his former life and of his strange household. His sisters, he told Lizzie, "are out of the world so completely that they do not know its customs." Lizzie tried to remedy the situation by assiduously cultivating Hawthorne's intellectual sister, Ebe. The two women began exchanging visits, books, and bouquets of flowers — for which Elizabeth Hawthorne had a particular fondness. Under the glow of this attention, Ebe managed to shed her solitary habits to the point of sharing walks with Lizzie — and, on occasion, with Mary.

In her talks with Hawthorne, Lizzie sometimes discussed Sophia. ("What a peculiar person your sister is," Hawthorne had once remarked.) Lizzie had frankly talked about Sophia's invalid condition, her chronic headaches, her surprising stamina. Unknown to Sophia, Lizzie had also shown Hawthorne her sister's Cuba Journal, a series of letters Sophia had written home while on a trip for her health, years before. Hawthorne seemed in awe of the mysteriously elusive and tranquil invalid. "She is a flower to be worn in no man's bosom," he told Elizabeth.

Hawthorne, she conceded, was never a ready talker: "But every word was loaded with significance though there was nothing oracular in his manner." She remarked, "I never saw anybody who listened so devouringly." It was a quality Hawthorne would have needed, since Lizzie was herself a torrential talker. She was convinced that Hawthorne was "profoundly social," but that the strange circumstances of his family life kept him from taking a proper role in society.

Lizzie Peabody touched on Hawthorne's reputation as a recluse in an unsigned review of *Twice-told Tales* that she wrote for the March 24, 1838, issue of *The New Yorker*, a weekly edited by Park Benjamin. In a glowing tribute to Hawthorne's "genius," she admitted that the author's "knowledge of the world is evidently not the superficial one acquired by that perpetual presence in good society — so called — which is absence from all that is profound in human feeling and thought." She went on, somewhat disingenuously, "We will venture our reputation for sagacity on the assertion that he is frank and communicative in his character, winning thereby the experience of whatsoever hearts come in his path." She praised "Sunday at Home," "Sights from a Steeple," and "Little Annie's Ramble," from which she quoted a paragraph. But she was critical of stories like "The Prophetic Pictures," which she felt were too obviously written with the popular audience in mind: "We cannot avoid saying that these subjects are dangerous for his genius. There is a meretricious glare in them, which is but too apt to lead astray. And for him to indulge himself in them, will be likely to lower the sphere of his power. First-rate genius should leave the odd and peculiar, and especially the fantastic and horrible, to the inferior talent . . . Doubtless, we are requiring of genius some self-denial."

In later life, when Lizzie Peabody finally considered writing her reminiscences, she was convinced that she would be able to give "the most true psychological biography" of Hawthorne. She would explain "all the apparent inconsistencies that may have arisen from unscrupulous biographers." Her interpretation would be based on the early period of her acquaintance with the writer, in 1838 and 1839. It was then, she felt, that Hawthorne had given her a kind of intellectual autobiography, an account of the "growth of his mind." But she had waited too long; her definitive portrait was never written.

She had never doubted Hawthorne's genius, though she was never to have a high opinion of his grasp of politics or society. But she sensed in the imaginative writer something awe-inspiring — that "double action" of Hawthorne's mind which had the capacity to balance "the appearance of the moment in the light of the *great whole.*" In her transcendental eagerness, Lizzie gave it a German coloring: "The thinking in eternity and in time, *at once*, as Leibnitz says everyone does, more or less," she explained. In her generous fashion, she had sensed the writer's animating principle: a need to fix the moment permanently in all its hard factuality — and the inevitable defeat as the moment slipped into time.

Convinced that Hawthorne lacked social experience, Lizzie introduced him to such opportunities as Salem offered. She encouraged the author to attend the Saturday "evenings" held by the elderly spinster Miss Susan Burley at her home on Chestnut Street. Miss Burley, a friend of the Peabody sisters since their childhood, was a local patroness of the arts and had an extensive library that she made available to her friends. Though Hawthorne accompanied the Peabody sisters to Miss Burley's, he referred to her social evenings good-naturedly as the "Hurley-Burley."

In her efforts to promote the Salem author, Lizzie gave Emerson a copy of Hawthorne's "Foot-prints on the Sea-shore," which had appeared in the January 1838 issue of the *Democratic Review*. Emerson was not impressed; he was never to have a high opinion of fiction — or of fiction-writers. "I complained that there was no inside to it," he commented in his journal. "Alcott and he together would make a man." Emerson was much more interested in Lizzie's other Salem protégé, the eccentric, twenty-five-year-old poet Jones Very, who wrote mystical sonnets and had "ideas" about Shakespeare. Thin and sharp as a blade, with pursed lips, and eyes that, incorrigibly, seemed focused elsewhere, Very was a religious fanatic, an exalted boor, and a man at the edge of insanity. He was a favorite in the Peabody household; Sophia, who adored him, regularly referred to him as the "angelic Very." She fumed when he was not appreciated at Miss Burley's salon. "They do not understand Very there," she complained to Lizzie. She could be thrilled by the "level rays of celestial light" that beamed from Very's face when the poet was doing nothing more than conversing of an afternoon in the Peabody parlor. Still, she could disagree with Very's diagnosis that her "resignation and acceptance of pain" was prolonging her illness, and with his prescription that if she would only give up her "wilfulness" she could be free of her ailments.

Hawthorne often encountered Very at Miss Burley's and at the home of Caleb Foote, the editor of the *Salem Gazette*. When he first met him, through Lizzie Peabody, Hawthorne was stunned; Very seemed the absolute personification of his own fictional Eliakim Abbott, the itinerant preacher of his *Story Teller* sequence, a man totally inward, burning with self-involvement in the name of a higher cause. Hawthorne confessed to admiring Very's sonnets, but later characterized the poet as a man standing "alone, within a circle which no other of mortal race could enter, nor himself escape from." Hawthorne had, in fact, met the poet when he was on the verge of a mental breakdown that would result in his literal confinement. Within the year, Very decided that he was the "Second Coming," and began showing up in Salem parlors ready to baptize friends "with the Holy Ghost and with fire." When the zealous caller arrived at the Charter Street house, one Sunday morning, Lizzie Peabody, alone on the first floor, meekly submitted to Very's benediction. When the poet asked, "with a slightly uneasy missionary air," how she felt, Lizzie confessed that she had experienced no change. "But you will," Very asserted. Lizzie recalled, "I was silent but respectful, even tenderly so."

If Very had confined his mission to his friends, he might have escaped notoriety in Salem. But when he decided to baptize the local clergy, he was trundled off to the newly opened Charlestown Asylum, where he remained for a month. Ministers like Charles Wentworth Upham were convinced that Very had been infected by Emerson's transcendental heresies. Emerson, who had just received Very's dissertation on Shakespeare, was distressed to learn that the poet might be insane, but declared that his writings certainly were not. "Such a mind cannot be lost," he said.

Hawthorne, in a comic scene witnessed by Sophia and Lizzie, submitted to Very's missionary benediction in the Peabody parlor. "It was very curious," Lizzie reported to Emerson. "Hawthorne received it in the loveliest manner — with the same abandonment with which it was given — for he has that confidence in truth — which delivers him from all mean fears."

Meanwhile, the friendship between the Peabody and Hawthorne families continued to grow. During the spring and summer of 1838, Lizzie was teaching in West Newton, but Sophia kept her informed about her encounters with Hawthorne and his sisters. She reported in detail on one of her visits to Herbert Street: "Louisa came to the door and took me upstairs. As Elizabeth did not know I was coming, I thought I should not perhaps see her . . . I asked for her immediately, and Louisa went to inquire and came back with astonishing intelligence that she would be there in a few minutes. There, now,

am I not a privileged mortal?" Sophia had stayed an hour discussing Wordsworth and Coleridge — and Alexander Pope, whom,
she was surprised to learn, Ebe greatly admired. "Now, what think
you of my triumph?" she asked. "I think I should love her very
much. I believe it is extreme sensibility which makes her a hermit-
ess. It was difficult to meet her eyes; and I wanted to because they
are uncommonly beautiful, I think."

For Lizzie's benefit, Sophia also reported on a call she and Mary
had paid on Mary Crowninshield Silsbee, for the purpose of seeing a
much-talked-about painting Miss Silsbee had commissioned. From
Sophia's description, the painting was that of a woman, clearly intended to be a portrait of Mary Silsbee, and the figure of a mysterious bandit or huntsman. "We were put into the drawing-room by
the woman before Miss Mary appeared," Sophia related in her letter
of May 1. "She received us very simply and pleasantly, and I was
very agreeably impressed with her. But the picture. I should call it a
huntsman, and not a bandit. It was some time before I saw it — except the resemblance to Miss Silsbee which is at first very striking."
Sophia had wanted to be alone with the painting to study it, and
confessed that she would gladly have "put Miss Mary out of the window" in order to do so. She was even more annoyed when they were
interrupted by a Salem dandy, Forrester Barstow, who, with his "intolerably pretty face and little, comfortable, plump figure and indifferent chitchat," had sat directly in her line of vision.

What particularly struck Sophia about the painting, presumably
by the Boston artist Catherine Scollay, was the figure of the
huntsman, whose physical characteristics, as she described them,
bore a resemblance to Hawthorne — especially to his characteristic
manner of cocking his head to one side when he was attentive. "I
hardly know how to communicate my thoughts about it," Sophia
told Lizzie, "yet I seemed to have a volume to say to you. What very
much impressed me was the motion in his hushed attitude — the
head almost imperceptibly bent on one side to listen. So full of life
and grace and energy . . . I like to see the head and features as
small as is quite consistent with *nobleness*. How delicate is his
contour — yet manly."

Sophia had had occasion to study Hawthorne with some care, for
he was regularly visiting the Peabody parlor. Yet there were aspects
of his character that puzzled her. She related to Lizzie a conversation they had had about Helen Barstow, one of the more intellectual
young women of Salem and one of the regulars at Miss Burley's evenings. Hawthorne had said that he thought Helen "was not natural," Sophia wrote. "But he expressed a sense of her brilliant powers, her wit and acuteness, and then he said he thought 'women

were always jealous of such a kind of remarkability' (that was his word) 'in their own sex' and endeavored to deprecate it." She asked, "I wonder what has given him such a horrid opinion of us women — But enough of Mr. Hawthorne."

౿ IV ౿

"In love-quarrels," Hawthorne wrote in his notebook, "a man goes off on stilts, and comes back on his knees."

The charged interview at which he supposedly "crushed" Mary Silsbee was not the last that Hawthorne saw of that young woman. But for several months during the summer of 1838 they were separated by circumstances. He was to take an extended trip — a mysterious journey through western Massachusetts, during which he chose to suspend all contact with his family and friends. At around the same time, Mary Silsbee was making a prolonged summer tour with her father and sister. Nathaniel Silsbee was a widower. His wife had died three years earlier; her failing health, in fact, had been the principal reason Silsbee had resigned his Senate seat. On May 31, Silsbee took his two daughters "on a tour of diversion" through the Midwest. It began with two weeks in Washington, where Silsbee renewed acquaintance with his former colleagues. From there, the family traveled leisurely westward, visiting Cincinnati and Louisville. They were graciously received at Ashland, Henry Clay's country house near Lexington, then proceeded northward as far as Detroit. After a stay at Saratoga Springs, the Silsbees returned to Salem on August 21. Whether Silsbee intended the journey as a cooling-off period in his daughter's relationship with the Salem author, or for purposes of escaping Salem rumors, is not clear. (Longfellow, on a visit to the city, had observed, "Salem is a hornet's nest of gossips. How they buzz and sting.") Perhaps the trip was meant to ease his daughter's strained nerves, for not long after her return to Salem, Mary Silsbee fell ill, her condition serious enough that a physician had "forbidden her the slightest use of her eyes to read or her mind to understand." Even a kind note from her former suitor, Jared Sparks, had been too much of an exertion for her to open. It had been answered by a relative.

Hawthorne, who was not back in Salem until late September, learned the news of the heiress's recovery from Lizzie Peabody. Dr. Peabody had been the physician in attendance at the Silsbee household. On October 19, Lizzie wrote Ebe Hawthorne, "In my hurry last evening, I forgot to say that M. Silsbee is downstairs — I asked the Dr. if she was ready to see company — and the Dr. said 'She hardly feels like it, I guess.' " Heedless of her father's announcement, Lizzie continued, "But nevertheless, I guess your brother would not be refused if he were to send in his name — and very likely it would be a pleasure that would help on her recovery — especially if he contradicts her all the time in the *piquante* manner of an *accomplished coquette.*"

That Lizzie had thrust herself into the affair at some point seems evident from a fragment of a letter she wrote Ebe Hawthorne, possibly in the late fall of 1838 or early in 1839. Whether she had been privy to some of Mary Silsbee's letters or was simply referring to Hawthorne's letters to herself is uncertain, but Lizzie had obviously come to some conclusions about Hawthorne's state of mind, and Hawthorne had taken offense. It is clear that Hawthorne's sisters were concerned and had discussed the matter with Lizzie.

". . . to say that they were evidences of his 'unequal spirits' last spring," the tantalizing fragment begins, "— and that when I came to suspect that M.C.S. was coquetting — I interpreted [their hieroglyphics?] — by means of that — in some measure. If you supposed that I meant to say these letters were an outpouring of distressed feelings in a confidential way — all I can say is — that your supposition was false — They were not confidential at all — not so much so as I thought would be *natural* considering the very character of our acquaintance . . ."

She continued, "You cannot think how ridiculous it makes me appear in his eyes, to represent to him that I think him sentimental *from his letters* — Yet I could not tell him *the truth* — which is that I never did cite his letters as proof of the same — without seeming to contradict his sisters point blank — a thing which he would not bear. So you see, it must remain with you to undo this mischief." The loss of Hawthorne's "confidence and correspondence," Lizzie wrote Ebe, "would be to me more painful than is wise or reasonable perhaps — and certainly entirely unnecessary — Yet his sensitiveness to ridicule being perhaps the most active principle that regulates his conduct — I do not feel sure — that it would not be enough to make him give up even a much dearer friend than I am to him." Lizzie plainly was trying to avoid a serious breach in their relationship.

Despite the news of Mary Silsbee's recovery, Hawthorne was not eager to see her. It was only weeks later, at the insistence of O'Sullivan and in response to an invitation from Mary herself, that he paid her a visit. On November 5, he wrote O'Sullivan:

> In accordance with your exhortations, I have seen our fair friend. Her manner of receiving me incomparably good — perfectly adapted to the circumstances — altogether beyond criticism. It

might seem that I should have the vantage ground in such an interview — having been virtually invited to it by herself, after expressing a desire and determination to break off all intercourse — and having expressly stated, moreover, that any future intercourse should not be on the ground of friendship. But it was no such thing. All the glory was on her side; and no small glory it is, to have made a wronged man feel like an offender — and that, too, without permitting any direct allusion to the matter in dispute — and to have put on just so much dignity as to keep me precisely at the distance she chose, tempered with just so much kindness that I could not possibly quarrel with her.

He had, it seems, gained some insight into the strategies of recrimination.

She was dressed in better taste and looked more beautiful than ever I saw her before [he reported], and she, and her deportment and conversation were all of a piece, and altogether constituted a perfect work of art — meaning the phrase in no bad sense.

He was sure that the interview had not produced the effect Mary Silsbee had hoped for; it had brought him no satisfaction, either. "I came away with, I think, the most dismal and doleful feeling that I ever experienced — a sense that all had been a mistake — that I never really loved — that there was no real sympathy between us — and that a union could only insure the misery of both." He recognized that he had reached the end of the affair. "Surely," he added, "having this feeling, it is my duty to stop here, and to make her aware that I have no further aims."

Yet, he could not bring himself, quite, to fix all the blame on Mary.

It is fit that I do her all manner of justice as respects her treatment of me. Looking back at her conduct, with the light that her last letter has given me, I am convinced that she has meant honorably and kindly by me — that I have nothing to complain of in her motives, though her actions have not been altogether so well judged.

I now put a different interpretation on the "secret spring" which I was to discover "soon" or "never." It cannot be her father's disapprobation; for I had reason to suppose that he knew something of the affair and sanctioned it. That "spring" was within her own heart and I was to discover it by reflecting on something that she had formerly revealed to me. I have reflected, and think that I have penetrated the mystery.

He had at least discovered that he had been more dazzled than in love, perhaps. In his letter to O'Sullivan, he had been more gentlemanly than the experience warranted. It was Lizzie Peabody's recollection that in that awkward interview, without Hawthorne's encouragement, Mary Silsbee had told him that she would marry him when he had an income of $3000. Hawthorne had answered that he never expected to have so much.

Echoes of the affair with Mary Silsbee cropped up in subsequent letters to O'Sullivan. In the following May, Hawthorne reported to O'Sullivan on an odd commission and an interesting piece of news:

> . . . A week or two since, the enclosed letter was sent me, to be transmitted to you, and as it may gratify you to know Miss Silsbee's very words, I here copy them — "In examining many packages of letters I was about to burn, the enclosed is the only one I found left in Mr. O'Sullivan's handwriting. Judging that your kindness will do me the favor to direct and forward it to him — as I do not know where he may be found — I take the liberty of enclosing it to your care, the rest of my task being accomplished. Respectfully, M. C. Silsbee." By "the rest of her task," I suppose she means the destruction of my own letters, which I had requested her to burn. I hardly expected to be the medium of another communication between our fair friend and yourself, but now certainly the last knot of our entanglement is loosed.

So the affair ended in the ashes of his own letters. "What a trustful guardian of secret matters fire is!" he was to write on another occasion. "What should we do without Fire and Death?"

The interesting item of news that he had to communicate to O'Sullivan was that Mary Silsbee was to be married within the week — "an event which I am almost sorry to think, will cause a throb in neither of our bosoms." Jared Sparks, who had been widowed in 1835, was once more in Boston, having been recently appointed McLean Professor of Ancient and Modern History at Harvard, a distinguished post — and one, presumably, more in keeping, financially and socially, with Mary Silsbee's ambitions. Sparks was fifty when he resumed his courtship; the couple were married on May 21, 1839.

"Our fair friend" was to make another fleeting appearance in one of Hawthorne's letters to O'Sullivan. A year later, on April 20, 1840, Hawthorne wrote, "Did I tell you in my last that our friend, Mrs. S., has had a miscarriage? Such seems to be her fate, in her life as a whole, and in all details."

At a later time, and in happier circumstances, Hawthorne was to write a story of a "poisonous" young woman, the daughter of an eminent man, and her love affair with an intense young student. "Rappaccini's Daughter," which clearly draws on his affair with Mary Silsbee, appeared in the December 1844 issue of O'Sullivan's *Democratic Review*. There, Hawthorne outfitted it with a spurious editorial preface, depicting the story as the work of M. de l'Aubépine, a French author with "an inveterate love of allegory." The preface asserts that Monsieur de l'Aubépine "contents himself with a very slight embroidery of outward manners — the faintest possible counterfeit of real life." It goes on to explain that the tale had originally appeared in *La Revue Anti-Aristocratique*. The spoof on the title of the *Democratic Review* allows Hawthorne to bestow some pseudonymous praise on the editor of the journal, the "Comte de Bearhaven," who "for some years past, led the defence of liberal principles and popular rights, with a faithfulness and ability worthy of all praise." Thus, in a jocular manner, the preface and the tale bring together all three of the participants in the Silsbee affair.

"Rappaccini's Daughter" takes place in Italy, at some indefinite point in time. The hero, Giovanni Guasconti, another of Hawthorne's fatherless and beautiful young men, has come to the University of Padua, leaving behind his mother and sisters. He has a letter of introduction to Pietro Baglioni, a professor of medicine at the university and an "ancient comrade" of his father's. Baglioni, like all Hawthorne's surrogate fathers, develops a crucial interest in the young hero.

The poor young Giovanni takes a room in an ancient mansion. His bedroom overlooks the lush but sinister garden of a neighbor — an Eden of malignant-looking flowers and herbs. The owner is Dr. Giacomo Rappaccini, a doctor and scientist of undisputed fame in Padua. A widower, he lives with his only daughter, Beatrice. The garden is locked to the outside world; only Rappaccini and Beatrice tend it. From the beginning, Giovanni is aware of the poisonous nature of this Eden. He sees that Rappaccini wears thick gloves while cultivating the plants, and that when he ventures near a particularly luxuriant specimen growing near the central fountain, he wears a protective mask. Beatrice, however, seems to have a strange immunity to her noxious environment; she is the only one who can walk about the garden without concern — and she is the only one who tends the deadly specimen plant with the profusion of purple blossoms.

Hawthorne's description of the young woman is striking. Giovanni hears her voice first — "a voice as rich as a tropical sunset" that makes him think of "deep hues of purple or crimson and of perfumes heavily delectable." When she steps out into the garden in response to her father's call, he sees that she is as exotic as the flowers she tends, "with a bloom so deep and vivid that one shade the more would have been too much." Hawthorne stresses the bond between the young woman and the poisonous shrub at the center of the garden. Giovanni, rubbing his eyes, doubts "whether it were a girl tending her favorite flower, or one sister performing the duties of affection to another."

Giovanni becomes enamored of the seemingly unobtainable Beatrice and, from the beginning, takes a highly idealized view of her. Through old Lisabetta, the servant-woman in his house — and possibly through the collusion of Rappaccini — Giovanni is shown a secret entrance to the garden. Hawthorne, well aware of the vagaries of desire, describes the coolness with which Giovanni invades the garden for the first time: "How often is it the case, that, when impossibilities have come to pass . . . we find ourselves calm, and even coldly self-possessed, amid circumstances which it would have been a delirium of joy or agony to anticipate. Fate delights to thwart us thus. Passion will choose his own time to rush upon the scene." In his meetings with Beatrice — for the two begin to see each other secretly and regularly — Giovanni is disconcerted by the young woman's lack of sophistication. She has a virginal reserve: "By all appreciable signs, they loved; they had looked love, with eyes that conveyed the holy secret from the depths of one soul into the depths of the other . . . yet there had been no seal of lips, no clasp of hands, nor any slightest caress." There are moments when Giovanni is forced to put down "horrible suspicions that rose, monster-like, out of the caverns of his heart." He has seen evidence of some fatal quality in Beatrice; a bouquet of flowers he has given her seems to wilt in her hand.

Giovanni's mentor, Professor Baglioni, warns him about Rappaccini, describing his colleague as a man who "cares infinitely more for science than for mankind. His patients are interesting to him only as subjects for some new experiment." Rappaccini would "sacrifice human life, his own among the rest, or whatever else was dear to him" in the interest of science. The doctor, in other words, is one of the recurrent villains in Hawthorne's fiction — the sinister gardener, the alchemist, or scientist bent upon experiments that are a perversion of nature, the man who has lost touch with the common values of humankind. Baglioni, convinced that Rappaccini is poisoning the young man through the influence of his daughter, gives Giovanni a powerful antidote in a silver vial.

One day, Giovanni discovers incontrovertible proof that he has, himself, become infected by his association with Beatrice and the poisonous atmosphere of Rappaccini's garden. He breathes on a spider that has been building a web in the corner of his room, and the insect falls dead. (Unfortunately, Hawthorne was apt to push his allegorical method into episodes that come perilously close to comedy for later generations of readers; only the authority and seductiveness of his style allow him to avoid this danger at many points.)

In his rage, Giovanni confronts Beatrice. In a melodramatic scene, he berates the girl, who professes her innocence, blaming her father's "fatal science." "No, no, Giovanni," she declares, "it was not I. I dreamed only to love thee, and be with thee a little time, and so let thee pass away, leaving but thy image in mine heart." When Giovanni, softening, suggests they drink the antidote, Beatrice seizes the vial and drinks first. Just at this operatic moment, Rappaccini arrives on the scene, acknowledging that he has been aware of their meetings. Here, Hawthorne equates the emblematic figure of the malevolent scientist with that of an artist (who also "improves" on nature). "As he drew near, the pale man of science seemed to gaze with a triumphant expression at the beautiful youth and maiden, as might an artist who should spend his life in achieving a picture or a group of statuary, and finally be satisfied with his success." Rappaccini has provided his daughter with the perfect bridegroom.

The antidote, of course, proves fatal, and Beatrice dies. Her final words to Giovanni are, in fact, an accusation: "Oh, was there not, from the first, more poison in thy nature than in mine?"

Despite the Gothic trappings — the perverted scientist, the poisonous effusions, the antidotes in silver vials — despite the near-comic improbabilities and the moments of unabashed melodrama, Hawthorne informed his plot with the psychological awareness he had garnered from his unhappy affair with Mary Silsbee. He was fascinated by the ambiguity and deceptiveness of evil. Sometimes, he suggests, one's nighttime fears and apprehensions are closer to the truth than the hard facts seen in mundane light. Giovanni, after a nocturnal vision of Rappaccini's evil garden, looks out on it in the different light of day and is "surprised, and a little ashamed, to find how real and matter-of-fact an affair it proved to be." But, as the allegory intends, his first vision proves the correct one. Hawthorne also deftly exposes those psychological maneuvers by which the mind contrives to overlook blatant evidence. Giovanni readily dismisses his fears about Beatrice. Her peculiarities are forgotten; "by the subtle sophistry of passion," they have been transmuted into a "golden crown of enchantment." They make her "unique" and all the more attractive.

The affair with Mary Silsbee had brought Hawthorne an acute awareness of the "sophistry of passion." As Beatrice's final accusation suggests, Hawthorne had also come to accept his own complicity in the affair. He and Mary Silsbee had deserved each other. The real world was a realm of such complicity; distinctions of good and evil tended to blur. In fiction — particularly in his early allegorical stories — the lessons could be more sharply drawn. Hawthorne tended to approach allegory as the perfect method for drawing off some universal truth from the transient events of real life. The price he paid, however, was a certain woodenness in his characterizations; they are personifications of good or of evil. "Rappaccini's Daughter" is distinctive among his tales — as opposed to his novels or romances — in its complexity.

Hawthorne did not write the story until some years later, when he was in love and recently married. It is part of the peculiar economy of Hawthorne's imagination that the image of Beatrice — furnished on the one hand by the perverse character of Mary Silsbee — should have been transformed by the more agreeable qualities of the woman he married. Sophia Peabody — frail, secluded in life, an invalid — was not the exotic bloom that Mary Silsbee was. But she, too, merged with the character of Beatrice as both woman and flower. Sophia, however, was the purer bloom — a "flower to be worn in no man's bosom."

Is it more than coincidence that Hawthorne had come to know her through a "Lisabetta" — Elizabeth Peabody, her sister? By an equally odd coincidence, Sophia's father was a doctor of some repute in Salem. And like Senator Silsbee — in this odd circle of repetitive identities — he was also named Nathaniel.

The Quiet, Silent, Dull Decency of Salem

IN THE MIDST of the difficulties of writing his memorial essay on Jonathan Cilley, Hawthorne penned a complaining note to Catherine Ainsworth, the devoted niece of Thomas Green Fessenden, who was still living with the poet's widow in Boston. Hawthorne owed her a letter. "I am tired to death of pen, ink and paper," he wrote on April 12, 1838, excusing his tardiness, "and would never touch either of the three again, if I were not a scribbler by profession." It was a hasty note, and there was a suggestion of coyness in Hawthorne's next remarks: "I have heard recently the interesting intelligence that I am engaged to two ladies in this city. It was my first knowledge of the fact. I do trust that I shall not get married without my own privity and consent." He concluded, "Excuse this nonsense, and answer it with some of your wisdom."

Since he had not yet broken off all relationship with Mary Silsbee, she may well have been one of the two women whose names were linked with his in Salem gossip. His regular appearances at the Peabody home, and his developing friendship, first, with Elizabeth and then with her sister Sophia, had also created some speculation in the minds of the Peabody family and its numerous relatives and friends. Aunt Sophia Pickman, in fact, suggested to her niece Mary that an engagement must be in the offing; she was convinced that Elizabeth Peabody was the object of Mr. Hawthorne's attentions.

When Nathaniel Hawthorne first met the Three Graces of Charter Street — Elizabeth, Mary, and Sophia Peabody — each of the sisters was past the conventional marital age. Each was serious, intelligent, and interesting; none was beautiful. They had been raised in an atmosphere of intellectual curiosity, cultural enthusiasms, and the genteel poverty that went with the profession of schoolteaching. It was as a schoolteacher in a North Adams academy for girls that their mother, Elizabeth Palmer, had met her future husband, Nathaniel Peabody, then a gentle, mild-mannered teacher of Latin at Phillips Academy in Andover, whom she married in 1802. The birthplaces of the Peabody daughters indicated the vagrant, impecunious nature of the family fortunes. Elizabeth Palmer Peabody, the eldest, was born on May 16, 1804, in Billerica, where her mother and father had opened a boarding school for girls. Mrs. Peabody, however, had high expectations for her husband's future. With the ambition and perseverance that were to characterize her daughters as well, she pushed her husband into taking up the medical profession. Mary Peabody, the second daughter, was born on November 16, 1806, in Cambridgeport, where the family had moved while Mr. Peabody pursued his medical studies at Harvard. Much to Mrs. Peabody's chagrin, her husband developed an interest in dentistry — a less prestigious profession than medicine. It was as a dentist — although he also served as a general practitioner — that Nathaniel Peabody hung out his shingle in Salem, while his wife, once again, ran a dame school. In Salem, on September 21, 1809, their third daughter, Sophia Amelia, was born.

The Peabody girls inherited the perennial optimism, the boundless faith in the Almighty, and the persistence of their mother. The Peabody boys, all born in Salem, took on the easy, fumbling nature, the general ineffectualness of their father. Nathaniel Cranch Peabody was born in 1811, George Francis in 1813, and Wellington in 1815. The latter was named after the hero of the recent Battle of Waterloo; the Peabodys, it seems, harbored no ill will against the English for the intervening War of 1812.

Like her mother, Elizabeth Palmer Peabody began her career as a schoolmistress, at the age of sixteen. In the pejorative sense, she remained one all her life: authoritative, fussing and fussy, pedantic, eager to instruct the world. In her lengthy career, she was to be the champion of every liberal effort, a worker for every moral reform. At the age of ninety, she had become the survivor of all the lost causes of a generation.

Men of intellect were Lizzie Peabody's passion. In 1820, while teaching at a school run by Mrs. Richard Cleveland in Lancaster, she struck up a friendship with the handsome Jared Sparks, then the thirty-one-year-old headmaster. It was a purely intellectual relationship; Sparks willingly supplied her with books from his extensive library. Later, for nine years, she served as the secretary — mostly unpaid — for the eminent Unitarian preacher, Dr. William Ellery Channing, whose liberal interpretations of the Bible created a stir among hard-bitten orthodox Calvinists. Barely peeping over his Federal Street pulpit, the diminutive Channing preached the God of love and understanding and, in a resounding voice, argued the perfectibility of man — doctrines that confirmed Lizzie Peabody's seamlessly optimistic view of this world and the hereafter.

In the meantime, Lizzie also took on the custody of another brilliant but fallible man. In 1833, at Mrs. Rebecca Clarke's boardinghouse at Somerset Court, near the Massachusetts State House, Lizzie and Mary were conducting a private school for girls. There, Lizzie became acquainted with Horace Mann, who had recently become a widower. Mann, prematurely white-haired at the age of thirty-six, was going through a mental and spiritual crisis following the death of his wife, Charlotte. His friends feared that the man who had begun a brilliant career as a lawyer and reformer would end in the grip of personal despair. The hours and the days that followed his wife's death, five months before, were "a history of suffering such as no mortal can ever record," Mann recorded in his journal. The deeper his despondency, the more angelic the memory of his wife became — as if the purified image served as a brake on the impossible-to-acknowledge hostility the mourner felt welling up within himself. The anniversaries of Charlotte's death became periods of isolation and withdrawal, recurrent bouts of self-pity, illnesses both mental and physical. Mann began to doubt the existence of God and the afterlife. His punitive doubts about the immortality of his departed wife became intolerable to him. He was a man almost paralyzed by grief.

At Mrs. Clarke's dinner table — the other guests were Jared Sparks (whose first wife, mysteriously, took her meals in her room), a young lawyer, George Hillard, and the landlady's daughter, Sarah Ann — Mary Peabody found Horace Mann "intolerably witty," with an anecdote for every occasion. That verdict may reflect Mary Peabody's low standards of wit; she was, like all the Peabody women, implacably high-minded, and Mann was relatively humorless. Mary was plainly dazzled by the gaunt widower with his shock of white hair, his lean emaciated features, his deep-set, troubled eyes beneath a broad, projecting brow. At first, Mary Peabody was unaware that Mann's attempts at levity were paid for by periods of bleak depression.

Elizabeth Peabody was also dazzled by Mann. She was convinced that she might succeed where even his closest male friends had failed. She took up the bereaved Mann with the dedication she gave to every worthy cause. She brought him to her friend Dr. Channing for counsel and consolation; she prodded him into resuming his legislative career. In 1834, Massachusetts Whigs were fearful of the coalition of "Jackson men, Anti-Masons, workeys, Fanny Wright men and infidels of all descriptions" looming on the political horizon. Mann, suffering through another of his tormenting anniversaries, allowed his name to be placed in nomination for the state Senate, at the urging of Lizzie Peabody and his concerned friends. He had not yet become an abstinence man, but his stand on temperance made him unpopular with many interests in the state. Nonetheless, in a sweep of the Whig forces during an off-year election, he won his seat. Elizabeth, with justifiable pride, could write to her sisters, early in January 1835, "The Senate sat today and our friend Mr. M—— is an *honourable.*" It was from this base of power that Mann began the reform of the state's educational system that later made him famous.

There was a strain of priggishness in Mann's character that became evident with the years. In time, any man who smoked or who drank "ardent spirits" was irrevocably lowered in his estimation. He regarded the theater, which he had once enjoyed, as a "rallying point of dissipation." Elizabeth herself was to come up against this obdurate strain in his nature; Mann criticized her sharply for including, in a commentary she had written on the *Iliad*, a "disrobing scene . . . such as usually have curtains drawn between them and the public eye."

Elizabeth's attentions to the lonely widower had not gone unnoticed by their mutual friends. When he withdrew into his periods of mourning and illness, she sent gifts of flowers and fruits. Avoiding the impropriety of visiting in his sickchamber, she sent him encouraging letters. When Mann, who was the soul of rectitude, became aware that there was talk, he felt it necessary to explain to Lizzie that his affection for her was strictly that of a brother toward a sister. Elizabeth clearly understood the message. Mann's manner had been "unembarrassing." Still, she could not help, in her disappointed way, from turning it around in her mind when she confided in her sister Mary. "Not that it would not be possible for Mr. M—— to make me love him exclusively," she wrote in a flurry of negatives, "but I could not do it unless he had or did try for it. And his situation — his greying hairs and his sorrowfulness ever precluded from my imagination that possibility. I know what the feeling of *love* is — for I have been sought and all but won . . . strong as my friendship is — deep as my interest in Mr. M—— is, it is a totally different thing."

In most of Elizabeth's relationships with intelligent and, presumably, eligible men, there was always something oblique about her understanding of both their intentions and her own.

Where Elizabeth was forward and meddling, Mary Peabody had the virtue of patience. Where Elizabeth offered advice, Mary provided comfort and support. Small and slender, Mary was considered the most attractive of the Peabody sisters, but she was, in fact, somewhat plain. Her dark brown hair was parted severely in the middle; her eyes were a sober gray-green, compared with Elizabeth's vivacious blue. Mary had the habit of quietness, which contrasted with Elizabeth's steady stream of talk. Whatever attractions she possessed would not have been useful in beguiling Horace Mann; he considered it a poor thing in a man to be concerned about physical beauty in a woman. Mann found the role of champion more congenial and once came to Mary's defense by criticizing Elizabeth for her tyrannical attitude toward her younger sister.

Mary's forbearance was put to the test not long after she met Mann. In December 1833, she and Sophia sailed for Cuba. The trip had been arranged by Elizabeth, largely for the benefit of Sophia, whose health, it was felt, would be improved by a tropical climate. The original plan had been that either Elizabeth or Mary would serve as governess and teacher for the children of a wealthy Cuban planter, Dr. Morrell, on his plantation at San Marcos, a day's journey from Havana. In return, Sophia would accompany her sister as guest of the Morrells. Mary, with that sense of familial obligation and Christian duty which characterized her life, made the sacrifice of a lengthy absence from Mr. Mann.

The Peabody sisters and Mother Peabody were incorrigible letter-writers. During the year and a half that the two sisters were in Cuba, a voluminous correspondence was established with Salem. In her letters to her mother and sister, Sophia, with additions by Mary, wrote about their life at La Recompensa, the Morrell plantation. The letters, full of detailed accounts of social life and pleasant pastimes and vivid descriptions of the flora and the fauna of the region, were read aloud to admiring friends and relatives. Later, Lizzie had them reassembled (and sometimes recopied) and bound into three volumes as a Cuba Journal, a family keepsake. Lizzie, too, kept her own Cuba Journal, a continual series of letters that she periodically dispatched to her absent sisters.

There was a steady stream of guests and visitors at La Recompensa; the Morrells were lavish in their hospitality. The two young Salem women sat with the family and the guests on the spacious verandah, looking out over the green lawns and the lush countryside. In the soft nights, there was music in the parlor. Mary, however, often felt "languid" and apathetic. Her duties as teacher for the two rambunctious Morrell boys, Edward and Carlito, were tiring; and in the evenings when there were no guests, she read aloud to Dr. Morrell and his wife. "I am going to write a book — the name of it is Homesickness," she wrote Lizzie. Sophia, on the other hand, seemed to flourish; Dr. Morrell had taken an interest in her health and had given her his "gentlest and safest horse" to ride. Mary informed her mother, "Sophia continues to take a great deal of exercise and grows fat all the time. I would give the world if you could take a peep at her plump cheek."

Occasionally, she wrote Lizzie about the near-feudal conditions of the country and the luxurious style of life that the Morrells took for granted. She wrote, too, of the degrading poverty of the poor in Havana and the bleak lives of the slaves. At La Recompensa, the slaves were seldom mistreated, but she had seen a large group of them, newly arrived from Africa, being driven along the road in chains. She found it difficult to forget such sights. She had talked about slavery with Mrs. Morrell, who was sympathetic to her views but claimed that it was necessary to maintain a strict system of rules and punishments among the blacks in order to avoid riot and murder. Mary readily sensed the fear and hostility that talk of abolition aroused in the Cuban planters. Writing to Lizzie, she expressed her hope that Mr. Mann was not one of the extreme abolitionists who advocated intermarriage; that would only alienate even the most moderate slave-holders from the cause.

When it came to her own, more intimate feelings, Mary was more guarded. But quite probably she had Horace Mann in mind when she wrote Lizzie, "I used to think that never to any human being would I show the inward workings of my soul, and to wish that I had the power of disguising every emotion — it was that which gave me the habit of preserving a calm exterior. Since that time, I have often wished that I had the power to manifest my feelings." Now, she confessed, she had "an ideal image of one to whom I should open every avenue of my heart for the asking — and with that image have been connected all my visions of happiness in this world." She wrote, "Time must prove whether that ideal ever takes a human form."

In all likelihood, she was disturbed when Lizzie confessed to an episode with Mr. Mann, early in their acquaintance, when she and Mary were living at Mrs. Clarke's boardinghouse. Lizzie and Mann had been alone in the parlor, when the widower broke down in grief and laid his head upon her breast, begging pardon for taking such a liberty. "Again — again — and again," Lizzie wrote, "he pressed me to his heart — and with floods of tears — *thanked me* — and when I came upstairs, I should have told you the whole, but you were sure that *his was just the character that soon got over grief* — and I was just the character to be led too far by my feelings . . ." Lizzie explained, "I have got *torrent feelings*, I allow — but they are *feminine* and they are *sentiments*, not *passions* and they should be treated therefore with delicacy. They do not come *from the blood* — but from the intellectual soul and they are pure." It may have been only small consolation that Lizzie also wrote, "It is the supreme delight of my heart when one of us has a friend that the other may have the same — and I do not wish to be preferred — but I am rather better pleased that you should be preferred."

⁓ II ⁓

Since childhood, Sophia Peabody had been the overprotected darling of the family. Julian Hawthorne, in his biography of his parents, maintained that, as an infant, Sophia had had a particularly bad time in teething and was "incontinently dosed with drugs, from the harmful effects of which she never recovered." Since Dr. Nathaniel Peabody was both dentist and physician, the unstated implication is that it was Sophia's father who had contributed heavily to her later invalidism. That circumstance may have been in the back of Hawthorne's mind when he invented the poisonous Dr. Rappaccini.

It was not until her thirteenth or fourteenth year, however, that Sophia began to suffer from the migraine headaches which made her abnormally sensitive to the slightest noises. During the attacks, she was shielded from the rowdiness of her younger brothers; was sealed off in the curtained and cushioned sanctuary of her bedroom. As a child, she had been somewhat impish, forward, and quick-witted. Her repeated bouts with illness seem to have tempered but not erased these qualities. Nor did she develop the morbid, complaining temperament of many invalids. She had a disposition toward optimism and was inclined to view her illness as a test of faith. There was a strain of innocence and naïveté in her that remained through life. "She was enthusiastic, prone to extremes, and to making sweeping judgments of people and things, founded upon intuitive impressions" — so her son remembered. Hawthorne, early in their relationship, tried to curb her extravagant use of adjectives, but without much success. ("I have been trying to clip off my superlatives ever since I knew him," Sophia confessed later in life.) She was pliable, yet surprisingly independent-minded in her judgments of others, and was not inclined to take a reputation at face value. She had resilience; she never gave way to self-pity.

Born into a family of teachers, Sophia was better educated than many women of her time, first by her mother, then by her sister Elizabeth. As a child, she was somewhat precocious. At the age of twelve, writing to her sister Elizabeth from Lancaster, where she was enrolled in Mrs. Cleveland's school, Sophia announced, "I myself am going to study Gibbon as well as Mary." She was studying chemistry, which she found "exceedingly interesting," and was equally enthusiastic about astronomy. She also exhibited an early tendency to bump up against social conventions. "Elizabeth Stillwell told Mrs. Cleveland that I went alone in the woods with Frank Dana," she wrote Lizzie, somewhat defiantly. "Mrs. Cleveland said she did not think it any harm but still she should not like it because other folks would talk about it."

Sophia became proficient in Greek, Latin, and Hebrew. In Salem, she was taught French by Monsieur Louvrier; she studied Italian as well. Early in her life, she indicated an aptitude for drawing and painting that was encouraged by the family. She pursued the study seriously. In periods of health, she even gave drawing lessons to Elizabeth's and Mary's students. She also taught Italian and French to her brothers Nathaniel and George.

Despite her family's worries about her health, Sophia traveled. At the age of eighteen, she visited her aunt Mary Tyler, a teacher in Brattleboro, Vermont. On such occasions, Mother Peabody's letters were apt to be fussing and concerned. "We think that your stay must not exceed six weeks from the time you left," she wrote Sophia. "Aunt T. is kind, hospitable and likes to see you enjoy yourself; but . . . you have not health enough to make yourself useful in the family or the school." She warned her daughter, "The high state of excitement you are in is not exactly the thing for your head. I am delighted to see you alive to the simple pleasures of nature. That heart must be the least corrupt which can enjoy them most; but you enjoy too fervently for your health. Come home now and live awhile upon the past."

Given Sophia's sheltered upbringing and her too-trusting nature, her mother was afraid that her daughter would meet with some inevitable disappointment in the outside world. "Well, darling of my heart, how are you?" she wrote Sophia on another occasion. "Well enough to enjoy the delightful friends who have called you to their fireside? I want you to be happy, but I want you to find happiness a *sober certainty;* that is, I want you to remember that the millennium is not yet — and that the very best among us are fallible, very fallible beings."

In a gentle way, Mother Peabody attempted to remind her daughter of the rewards of family life — to which, it was assumed, Sophia must resign herself. "The love which settles down on the household circle . . ." Mother Peabody advised with New Testament echoes, "is deeper, steadier, more efficient than any other love. Sickness never wearies it; it forgives waywardness, it hopes all things." She had not intended to "preach a sermon," she informed her daughter, but "when I think of your sensitive nature, your shattered nerves, your precarious health — can I do less than long, by precept upon precept, by caution upon caution, to try to induce you to arm yourself at all points against disappointment?"

In 1828, the peripatetic Peabody family moved to Colonnade Row in Boston, where Elizabeth and Mary had opened a school for girls, taking in, as a partner, William Russell, a highly touted educator and teacher of elocution. In Boston, Sophia was placed under the care of another doctor — Dr. Walter Channing, the brother of Elizabeth's friend William Ellery Channing. He put her on a regimen that was intended to relieve her pain without achieving any radical cure, prescribing "regular bodily and intellectual exercise daily," as well as occasional visits to the seashore. She had been tried on a number of drugs — mercury, arsenic, and opium among them — and Channing suggested hyoscine, which acted as a depressant. According to Elizabeth, this did her less harm than any of the other drugs, and Sophia was able to come downstairs and listen to the lectures of Francis Graeter, the drawing teacher in her school. Lizzie also arranged for her to take a brief course of lessons from the successful landscape painter Thomas Doughty, who had moved to Boston from Philadelphia. In Boston, she was introduced to the portrait painter Chester Harding, who gave her lessons and, surprisingly, asked the young invalid to pose for him. Elizabeth managed to borrow one of Washington Allston's paintings, which Sophia faithfully copied. Elizabeth was proud to report that when the two paintings were displayed side by side, even the experts could not tell which was the original. Allston, a brother-in-law of the Channings and one of the most admired painters of his time, made a visit expressly to see the much-talked-about copy. He complimented Sophia, saying it was "far superior" to anything he had expected. For a time, Sophia had even felt well enough to share a separate studio with a friend, Mary Newhall. She had by then become an accomplished copyist, and Elizabeth, always eager to promote her family, helped to sell her sister's paintings.

Whatever Sophia's physical frailties, there was a vein of iron in her character. The Peabody family had hoped that the trip to Cuba, advised by Dr. Channing, would bring an improvement in her health. Away from her overprotective family, under the milder rule of her sister Mary and Dr. Morrell, Sophia seemed to thrive in her new freedom. In January 1834, shortly after arriving at the Morrells' coffee plantation in San Marcos, she wrote her mother, "I ride on horseback before breakfast, nay before sunrise, and then lie down two hours, and as soon as the shadows grow long, ride again till dusk." She outlined the cosmopolitan regimen at the Morrell plantation: breakfast at half-past nine (when the family spoke French); dinner at half-past three (in Spanish), and tea at eight. "Every morning there is a golden sunrise," she added, with her usual effusiveness, "every evening a golden sunset. The stars are of every color of the rainbow and the January moon is the brightest of the year." She exulted in the tropical climate and the scenery — the long avenues of palms, the lime hedgerows bordering the estates. In her rides at dusk, she discovered a species of night-blooming cereus that filled the air with a heady fragrance. She drew a detailed sketch of it in one of her long journal-letters to her family and wrote, "Nothing more could be asked for in a flower — I wished for no more excepting that it were *immortal — deathless* . . ."

She drew and painted. The Morrells were charmed by the facility of her portrait sketches. Their daughter, Louisa, a dark-haired girl of sixteen, was fascinated by the pale young woman from New England. Sophia enjoyed the lively social life at La Recompensa; she looked forward to the visits of dark-eyed young brothers, Fernando and Manuel de Layas, from the neighboring plantation. In the evenings, she sat out on the cool verandah, listening to the family chatter. Sometimes she encouraged Manuel de Layas to sing for her.

Mother Peabody became alarmed at Sophia's exuberance. Sophia cautiously responded, "I will observe your advice — but there is no danger of losing health or hand among such a proud, lazy, ignorant race as the young Spanish Dons, who, generally speaking, ride when it is fair & go to bed when it rains." The only exceptions they had met were the de Layas boys, who had "cultivated their minds." Mary added her reassurances: "I assure you I am very cold and calculating in my intercourse with the world, and my prudence shall be a shield to Sophia's inexperience. She shall not marry any of these 'Spanish flies' as Mr. Grund would call them."

"What think you dearest mother, I did in the evening?" Sophia wrote later. "You will never imagine in the world. I *waltzed*!! and though I was very dizzy the first time, I whirled round without discomfort before I gave up!" Mother Peabody wrote back in worried terms, "My dear one, do not let that Don tempt you to waltz. It may destroy all that has been done. I trembled to read of its effects, for though they did pass off, repeated shocks might do you serious injury. Tell the young man your mother fears to let you, and that ought to silence him." Mary came to the rescue, explaining that Sophia "sleeps well, and can take a great deal of exercise, and is in excellent spirits, but still there is the headache — It often *yields* after violent exercise (not of the waltzing kind) of walking or horseback-ing — but it is by no means removed." Mother Peabody was ap-parently soothed. "And if you are made well — tolerably well," she wrote Sophia, "how richly shall we all be repaid for anxieties and separations."

At twenty-four, Sophia had even been guilty of a certain indiscre-tion. On the voyage to Cuba, she had struck up an acquaintance with James Burroughs, a forty-year-old agent for the sugar-planters, and the brother-in-law of Elizabeth's Boston landlord, Mr. Rice. Sophia, who felt no reason to be guilty, reported on Burroughs' at-tentions, and described him as a great "convenience" and "the very spirit of kindness and gentleness." Elizabeth had heard poor reports of the man; when she learned that Sophia had gone so far as to write letters to Burroughs and accept gifts from him, she was sharply critical of Mary's supervision. Burroughs, it appears, had proposed marriage during the voyage. Sophia refused him, but was nonetheless flattered. Without telling Mary, she agreed to maintain a "sisterly" relationship, and wrote him innocent letters. Burroughs had indiscreetly discussed the relationship and had even read aloud a passage from one of Sophia's letters in a Havana boardinghouse. From Boston, Lizzie fulminated, "He knew better than to expose S. to be talked about for he knows the country and I do not believe he is a person who ought to talk sentiment to any lady." She turned on Mary: "But you ought to have insisted on seeing and knowing the whole. I should have done so — or quarreled outright — and even at the expense of being called a highhanded tyrant." From there, Lizzie went on to old wounds; Mary had never understood her. "You think I have no guide but passion . . ." Lizzie complained. "However I live in hope that this separation may produce *an acquaintance* which our intimate association has prevented."

Mrs. Richard Cleveland, wife of the American vice-consul in Ha-vana, family friend, and mistress of the school in Lancaster, openly discussed the "affair" when she returned to Boston and Salem on a trip. Throughout the late summer and fall, the "rascal" Burroughs was the source of minor eruptions in Lizzie's letters. She had heard that he was going to New Orleans. "I hope you will make out to exchange all the goods and chattels and get back every scrap, espe-cially of Sophia's letters," she wrote Mary. Several weeks later she reverted to the subject: "I am thankful James returned Sophia's let-ters — did he return every one and are they all burnt?"

Sophia's brief assertion of independence and the agitated family squabble were thoroughly over and settled, however, by late April 1835, when she and Mary returned to America aboard the *William*

Henry. The voyage was a cold and stormy one. According to Lizzie, it undid all the good Sophia had obtained from her trip. Whether because of the upsetting journey or the return to her circumscribed Salem life, Sophia's headaches had returned with their old ferocity.

All during her sisters' absence in Cuba, Elizabeth's long, chatty letters from Boston had described her activities. She was readying her *Key to History, Part III: The Greeks* for publication. She had started a series of evening readings for women; they were discussing the writings of Harriet Martineau. Lizzie had been deeply disappointed when her school for girls had failed in 1830; Russell, who had a taste for regal living, had mismanaged the finances and then left for a new teaching position in Germantown, a rich suburb of Philadelphia. (No books had been kept, however, and Lizzie had no legal recourse.) Now she was full of enthusiasm and new plans for opening a school for boys in which she hoped to enroll the children of Mr. Rice, and "the little Blisses," the sons of the Widow Bliss, who was one of the regulars of her reading group. But in the fall of 1834, Amos Bronson Alcott, the pedlar-turned-educator, began his radical experiment, the Temple School, with classes held in two spacious rooms on the top floor of the Masonic Temple on Tremont Street. Lizzie gave up her own risky venture and took a seemingly more secure position as Alcott's assistant, teaching half a day for whatever Mr. Alcott could afford to pay. With her usual selflessness and good will, she encouraged the parents of her own prospective students to send their children to Alcott's new school.

It was Alcott's ambition not merely to nurture the minds of his students, who were drawn from the most influential families of Boston, but to develop their fledgling souls as well. The imagination, Alcott claimed, was not a faculty that was cultivated enough in American education: "And yet if there is any fact settled by the history of our race, it is, that imagination has been the guiding energy of light and life to humanity." His remedy was to center his educational method on discussions, moral instructions, and a course of readings in selected texts: the Bible, above all, supplemented by *Pilgrim's Progress, The Faerie Queene, Paradise Lost,* and the poems of Wordsworth and Coleridge.

In her spare time, Lizzie transcribed Alcott's conversations with the children. It was in order to promote Alcott's educational methods that, in 1835, Lizzie published her *Record of a School: Exemplifying the General Principles of Spiritual Culture.* With her usual luck, a large part of the first edition was burned in a fire; it was hardly the financial success she had hoped for. Nor did Alcott manage to pay her her salary. Under the circumstances, it was advisable for her to move in with the Alcotts in exchange for bed and board. She straightaway acquired another duty — minding Alcott's daughters, Anna and Louisa. A third daughter, born in June 1835, was named Elizabeth Peabody Alcott in gratitude. (It was a short-lived honor; within a year, the Peabody-Alcott friendship soured and the child was subsequently renamed Elizabeth Sewall Alcott.)

Lizzie soon found that living with Alcott and his wife, Abigail, was not the congenial experience she had expected. The philosopher-educator turned out to be narrow and intolerant in his views and rigorously critical of anyone who held opinions different from his own; his tirades against other educators and writers made Lizzie "think less well of many persons, himself included and myself also." Nor would he allow her to discuss controversial subjects with his boarding students; he did not want them subjected to views other than his own. But Lizzie had also begun to feel some alarm about recording Alcott's conversations with the children about the Gospels. These talks were being prepared for publication. Alcott had chosen to discuss the mysteries of birth with his young charges. Although she had taken part in the rather mild investigations, Lizzie, as a maiden lady, advised against reporting such conversations on a subject that, she maintained, even the prophets had spoken of in veiled terms in order to avoid "physiological inquiries." She refused to go on transcribing the talks. Much to her chagrin, Sophia, who had come to Boston on a visit and was staying with the Alcotts, had become absolutely dedicated to the pair and offered to serve as the recording secretary in Lizzie's place. Lizzie, who was regularly detailing her complaints about life at Front Street in her letters to Mary, also seems to have complained that Alcott did not pay her; Mary, evidently, responded with some remark about the high-minded reformer never managing to pay "poor men's bills."

The break came when Lizzie discovered that Mrs. Alcott had entered her room, read her private correspondence with Mary, and taken it to show her husband. In a long, aggrieved letter to Mary, Lizzie poured out her woes: Alcott, without having admitted to reading her letters, had come to her room and bitterly attacked her and Mary, pointedly referring to Mary's remark about poor men's bills. When questioned about the phrase, Alcott insisted that Mary had made it in a conversation with his wife the winter before and that she must have repeated it in her recent letter. Mrs. Alcott, more forthright in a separate wrangle, had predicted "eternal damnation" for Lizzie for what she regarded as "the greatest crime she ever knew of — that is, the existence of a correspondence of this sort." Lizzie wrote to Mary, "They take it for granted that all you think — I think, and moreover that I have made you think what you do." Both Alcotts, she reported, were convinced she had discussed their private affairs with her acquaintances. When Lizzie complained of their "breach of honor," the Alcotts retorted that she should scarcely "speak *the word honor*," having done "things so much worse." Under the circumstances, Lizzie wrote Alcott from her room, saying their relations were at an end.

To make matters worse, Sophia had rebelliously taken the side of the Alcotts, claiming, in Lizzie's presence and in front of their friend Sarah Ann Clarke, that Lizzie had been guilty of similar "deviations from principle," having read the letters of one of her own friends. Moreover, she was convinced that the Alcotts had never done such a thing before and never would again, "not on account of the bad consequences to themselves, but because they are *so good*." Lizzie was hurt, but charitable. She assured Mary that she would take the "tenderest care" of Sophia, who was expected to return to Salem within a few days. "I would not have her know — especially now — how much she has contributed to bring about the present crisis." She herself intended to leave as soon as possible. Since Sophia would be able to "keep up her adoration of Mr. Alcott," and maintain her friendship with both Alcott and his wife, the world need never know the real cause of the break. She planned to tell no one.

In a calmer frame of mind, in August, Lizzie wrote Alcott a long letter about her objections to the forthcoming *Conversations with Children on the Gospels*. "I feel more and more," she warned Alcott, "that these questionable parts ought not to go into the printed book, at least that they must be entirely disconnected with *me*." She told him, "I should like, too, to have the remarks I made on the Circumcision omitted. I do not wish to appear as an interlocutor in that conversation either." She also asked that Alcott explain, in a preface, that the subject had been raised on his responsibility and that the recorder "did not entirely sympathize or agree . . ." Lizzie went on, "You as a man can say anything; but I am a woman, and have feelings that I dare not distrust however little I can *understand them* or give any account of them."

Her caution was perfectly appropriate. When *Conversations* was published in two volumes in 1836 and 1837, the staid *Courier* of Boston labeled it an "indecent and obscene book." Alcott opened the spring term of his school with a mere ten students — "all I fancy that this good and wise city intend to lend me during this quarter," he complained to Emerson. When he admitted a black girl to his decimated classes, he added insult to injury, as far as Boston was concerned. Alcott, who in philosophical matters invariably practiced what he preached, refused to dismiss the child. Heavily in debt, he struggled on, eking out a living with a few straggling students and by giving parlor lectures. Writing to his mother after the inevitable demise of the school Alcott noted, "You may ask what I am about now. I reply, still at my old trade, *hoping* . . ."

Lizzie stalwartly came to his defense when the press and the public were against him. Her support could sometimes be a liability, however. Writing in the *Register and Observer*, she frankly admitted that Alcott's methods lacked logic: "He not only cannot lead his companions on the narrow line of reasoning as Socrates did; but he cannot go upon it himself." But, she claimed, this was "no defect" in teaching children. "Their young brains ought not to be exercised in chopping logic. Their pure imaginations should wander free into the eternal reason." In Lizzie Peabody's rationale, any cause worth supporting could always be lofted, straightaway, into the upper reaches of the Eternal.

Throughout the spring and summer of 1838, while she was teaching in West Newton, Lizzie could hardly have missed the glowing appreciations of "Mr. Hawthorne" that cropped up in Sophia's letters from Salem. Not that Sophia lacked for enthusiasms; her "adoration" of Bronson Alcott had given way to an even greater devotion to Emerson. "I think Mr. Emerson is the greatest man — the most complete man — that ever lived," she wrote her sister. "*As a whole* he is satisfactory. Everything has its due with him. In all relations he is noble." Her letters were also full of exultant praises of George Washington, whose biography she was reading. There may have been a touch of weariness in Lizzie's response: "I agree with you about Washington entirely." Attempting to forestall further discussion, perhaps, she advised, "Talk to Hawthorne about it."

Sophia's accounts of Hawthorne were sober, but warmly appreciative. The author was calling regularly at Charter Street, and Sophia's letters went into detail on every visit. On April 20, not long after Lizzie's departure, Sophia, who was suffering with another bout of headaches, reported that she had lain down one afternoon, her head aching from a variety of "corkscrews, borers, pincers, daggers, squibs and bombs," when the bell rang. "I was just as sure it was Mr. Hawthorne as if I had seen him . . . I descended, armed with a blue, odorous violet. Mr. Hawthorne would not take off his coat or stay, because he had the headache and an engagement . . . He said he had written to you, and that it was a great thing for him to write a letter. He looked very brilliant notwithstanding his headache." Sophia had showed him a little temple mosaic she had made, and Hawthorne had pronounced it "very pretty." He also announced that he planned to go to Boston in a short time and would have a little forget-me-not that Sophia had painted set as a brooch. Sophia continued, "Mary invited him to come with his sister on Saturday evening and read German, but it seems to me he does not want to go on with the German."

A few days later, when the author called again, Sophia was too ill to see him. But Mary entertained him in the parlor. Sophia had kept her door open, trying, at least, to overhear the conversation. "But was it not a pity I should lose such a long visit?" she complained to Lizzie. "No amount of *pain* would have prevented me from going out, but such exhaustion entirely mastered me. Mary said he looked very brilliant." Strangely, she reported, she had dreamed about Hawthorne all night and in her dream Hawthorne had kept changing into Charles Emerson, Waldo's younger brother who had died two years earlier. In another journal-letter she reported on a conversation in which Hawthorne said "he wished he could have intercourse with some beautiful children — beautiful little girls; he did not care for boys." Two days later, Sophia ruminated, "What a beautiful smile he has. You know, in 'Annie's Rambles,' he says that if there is anything he prides himself upon it is in having a smile that children love. I should think they would, indeed."

For several days Hawthorne did not appear. The *"furor scribendi,"* Sophia reported, was upon him; she was eagerly looking forward to the results of his efforts, since one of the stories related to her. In her Cuba Journal she had described a visit to a wealthy Spanish family who had a Murillo painting of the Magdalen, so grimy with age that she had offered to clean it. The result was a revelation: glowing colors that had been obscured for generations. Hawthorne told her that he had "imagined a story" for which the cleaning episode had provided the inspiration. "To be the means, in any way, of calling forth one of his divine creations is no small happiness is it?" Sophia wrote Lizzie. "How I do long to read it."

Occasionally, that spring, there were moments when Sophia experienced a kind of curious exaltation, moments when she had out-of-the-ordinary insights. Whether they were drug-induced, the result of her medication, is not certain, but she described one of them in an April letter to Lizzie. "Last night, after I was left in darkness — soft, grateful darkness," she wrote, "my meditations turned upon my habit of viewing things through the 'couleur de rose' medium, and I was questioning what the idea of it was . . . when suddenly, like a night-blooming cereus, my mind opened, and I read in letters of paly golden-green, words to this effect: The beautiful and good and true are the only real and abiding things — the only proper *use* of the soul and nature. Evil and ugliness and falsehood are *abuses*, and in their nature monstrous and transient." Sophia, like her sister, was prone to such transcendental experiences, when the mind bloomed like an exotic flower.

There were moments, too, when she verged on coyness. "I have been reading of the ruins of Persepolis this morning," she wrote Lizzie. "The wonders of the East surpass belief. Shall I ever stand upon the Imperial Palace of Persepolis? Who knows but when I am dried into an atomy like Mrs. Kirkland, I may go to the East too. And when I go, perhaps my husband will not be paralytic. Oh I forget. I never intend to have a husband. Rather, I should say, I never intend any one shall have me for a wife."

In May, when Hawthorne returned from the brief trip to Boston, Sophia related another of his visits. "I was lost in a siesta, when Mr. Hawthorne came," she informed Lizzie in a journal-letter dated May 8 to 13. "I was provoked that I should have to smooth my hair and dress while he was being wasted downstairs. He looked extremely handsome with sufficient sweetness in his face to supply the rest of the world with." Hawthorne took from his pocket the little forget-me-not, "set in elegant style in purest gold beneath block crystal." Sophia was delighted with it. "It is beautiful isn't it?" Hawthorne had remarked. "He thought it too fine for himself to wear," Sophia informed Lizzie, "but I am sure it is modest as a brooch could be."

Lizzie may have expressed some hint of jealousy, for in the same letter Sophia expressed surprise "at the idea of our cutting *you* out of all things. Mr. H's coming here is one sure way of keeping you in mind, and it must be excessively tame after the experience of your society and conversation, so that I think you will shine more by contrast." Lizzie, however, was not altogether placated. She remained unhappy about Hawthorne's tardiness as a correspondent. "I was quite disappointed not to find any letter from Hawthorne," she complained to Sophia early in June. "I hope you sent mine in time enough. When you see him, tell him I was *very much disappointed* — knowing that he had one at hand. I can only be consoled by having one *very soon*. His last letter was queer and written in some sort of excitement when he was fighting with some unhappiness, I know. He said in it he had written me a different sort of letter which he had concluded not to send — and I wrote him to send it by all means."

Under the circumstances, it was understandable that Sophia's references to Hawthorne and his visits became more circumspect. In July, she was explaining her feelings in the same sisterly terms that

Lizzie had used in describing her relationship with Mr. Mann. "I feel as if he were a born brother," she wrote Lizzie on July 23. "I never, hardly, knew a person for whom I had such a full and at the same time perfectly quiet admiration. I do not care about seeing him often; but I delight to remember that *he is* . . . I feel the most entire ease with him, as if I had always known him. He converses a great deal with me when you are not present — just as he talks more to you when we are not present."

But the principal news of her July letter was that Hawthorne was about to embark on a mysterious journey. "He said he was not going to tell anyone where he was to be the next three months — that he thought he should change his name so that if he died no one would be able to find his grave stone. He should not tell even his mother where he could be found — that he neither intended to write to anyone *nor be written to.*

"Perhaps," Sophia added meaningfully, "he desired us to tell you this last resolve. He said he hardly thought he should go to Newton. He seems determined to be let alone."

Yet Hawthorne had attended Miss Burley's Saturday tea — probably for a leave-taking call. There, he had spoken of her — Sophia — to Mary Pickman, "a splendid compliment he paid which Miss Rawlins told me with actual tears of delight in her eyes. She said she knew she was cross and a cheat to tell me when Mary was so anxious to tell me herself, but she could not help it." It was clear that among Peabody relatives like Aunt Rawlins, every attention paid to the Peabody sisters was carefully observed.

Hawthorne had been no less flattering to Sophia when he had visited her on the same Saturday morning. He had intended to return her Cuban Journal, he told her, but her works were "so voluminous" that he decided to send them later. "He told me . . ." Sophia wrote Lizzie, "that I was the Queen of Journalizers. This matter of my Journal seems like a baseless vision. It is all moonshine to me for I cannot realize that it is anything so *mirabile.* But I shall ever thank my stars that I have given him so much pleasure. He looked like the sun shining through a silver mist when he turned to me and said that. It is a most wonderful face."

Pieces of a puzzle: when Hawthorne was in Boston, early in May, he had stayed at the Tremont House. That he and Lizzie Peabody had had a meeting then — probably innocent, but perhaps meaningful — is clear from Sophia's May 8 letter to Lizzie: "He said he had seen you and told me of your sending to the Tremont House for him and his happening to be there. He thought it 'providential' that he should meet you as he did. I told him that you were a most fortunate person — always accomplishing what you wished somehow or other. The weather he said was altogether too bad to go out to Newton." Not a confidential matter, probably, since Hawthorne would not have mentioned it to Sophia, but a meeting that Lizzie had pursued, since Hawthorne was not concerned enough to go to Newton. In her next letter, Sophia reported on Hawthorne's disappointment — slightly overstated — when Lizzie failed to make an expected visit to Salem. Sophia had greeted him in the parlor: "His first question was 'Where is Elizabeth?' He was not at all inclined to bear the disappointment of your not being here, after all. He thought it 'too bad,' 'insufferable,' 'not fair,' and wondered what could be the reason. I told him your excuse, and that there was a letter for him, which Mary soon brought. He put it into his pocket without breaking the seal. He looked very handsome, and was full of smiles."

There are mysterious commissions involving letters from Elizabeth Peabody to Elizabeth Hawthorne. Sophia, in an undated letter written during the summer (probably before Hawthorne left on his journey), speaks of a visit she and Mary had made to Herbert Street, expressly for the purpose of smuggling a letter to Ebe Hawthorne in a volume of Walter Scott. "Mary put E's letter into Scott and directed it to her," Sophia reported, "so I hope she received it without any one knowing it according to your desire." Something evidently went wrong in this confidential correspondence, and Ebe and Lizzie appear to have been at odds. In a letter dated July 31, Lizzie directed Sophia, "Tell E. Hawthorne that if she will write to me I will at least burn up the letter that she first wrote and we will make a bargain about the last of the correspondence."

In Hawthorne's earliest journal, there is an intriguing entry that can safely be dated as some time after an entry of December 6, 1837, and before a description of the supper table at the Tremont House that probably relates to Hawthorne's Boston trip. The notation is terse and forceful: "A story to show how we are all wronged and wrongers, and avenge one another; as a man is jilted by a rich girl, and jilts a poor one." When Sophia began publishing *Passages from the American Note-Books*, two years after Hawthorne's death, she rigorously deleted anything that might reflect adversely upon her husband's character (for example, his references to drinking). She also omitted anything that might seem demeaning to members of the family. When she came to this passage, she pointedly deleted the graphic example of the jilted man and published only the much-weakened suggestion for a story about wrongdoing — a clear indication that the missing fragment had some damaging personal significance.

Lizzie's pursuit of the reluctant Hawthorne at the Tremont House, her secret correspondence with Ebe Hawthorne, her mounting disappointment at not hearing from Hawthorne, and her moments of apparent jealousy in her letters during the summer of 1838, suggest a complicated involvement between herself and Hawthorne. It is not always possible to determine the specific causes of the outbursts of injured innocence and self-pity that erupt in Elizabeth Peabody's letters. Sometimes the occasion is nothing more than a disagreement over a philosophical issue. But there was in her July 31 letter to Sophia a notable complaint on the subject of "veracity," which, in part, related to a discussion about a recent visit to Washington Allston. However, in Lizzie's letters, there is always the impression that emotions are apt to spill out more forcefully than the subject at hand requires. "I do not tell lies — *but the truth*," she scolded Sophia, "— and few people are so transparent. I always speak the truth as it appears to me — and with no regard to consistency . . . Something must be allowed to one's self for the infirmities of nature and it is better to be called selfish and old-maidish than to lose one's soul."

Circumstantial evidence seems to support the case that there was a quite personal involvement between Lizzie Peabody and Hawthorne during that uneasy spring of 1838 when Hawthorne wrote Catherine Ainsworth the rumor that he was engaged to two Salem ladies. A particularly virulent later version of the rumor occurs in a gossipy letter written by Mrs. Caroline Dall, a minor Boston author and a friend of Lizzie's. Mrs. Dall claimed that Hawthorne was, in fact, engaged to Lizzie. "Sophia never knew of her sister's engagement to N.H.," she wrote Thomas Niles, a Boston publisher, in 1894, "but Hawthorne lived in terror lest E.P.P. should tell her. Many an hour of bitter weeping has she passed in my house because of his insulting letters about it — after he was married."

It is difficult to know how much credence to place in Mrs. Dall's charges, for she went on to claim: "It was a very unhappy thing that he married Sophia. It would have been worse had he married Elizabeth; she was old enough to have been his mother." Lizzie, of course, was Hawthorne's age.

It is at least plausible that Hawthorne, on the rebound in his affair with Mary Silsbee, may have found comfort and understanding in Lizzie's company and that Lizzie, awkwardly, had thought it meant more than Hawthorne had intended. But it is also possible that, in a rash moment, Hawthorne proposed to Lizzie Peabody — and then recanted.

༄ III ༄

Shortly after his thirty-fourth birthday and before his mysterious journey, Hawthorne made an entry in his notebook concerning Ladurlad, the hero of Robert Southey's poem "The Curse of Kehama." Ladurlad had visited "a certain celestial region" where, in Hawthorne's words, "the fire in his heart and brain died away for a season, but was rekindled again on returning to earth." Hawthorne wrote, "So may it be with me in my projected three months' seclusion from old associations."

His trip was intended as something more than an escape from the complacencies of Salem; quite probably it was a flight from his recent personal crises — a period of solitude when he would be "let alone." Undoubtedly, Cilley's death and its aftermath had contributed to his decision. His unhappy affair with Mary Silsbee was quite probably another precipitating factor. His decision to remain incommunicado may have been a means of extricating himself from an awkward involvement with Lizzie Peabody.

There would have been, too, a sense of other conclusions in his life. In mid June, Hawthorne had said good-bye to his friend Bridge, recently commissioned as a purser on the cruiser *Cyane*, anchored in Boston Harbor and making ready for an extended cruise. On the 16th, a day of steamy heat, Hawthorne was rowed out to the *Cyane*. Bridge, standing proudly on deck in his new uniform — a braided blue coat, white pantaloons, cloth cap — greeted him heartily. Hawthorne was introduced to the ship's officers, and there were drinks in the mahogany-paneled stateroom. Later, he and Bridge went into Boston for a quiet farewell dinner, accompanied by iced champagne and claret, at the Tremont House.

The two friends had strolled through the Boston streets, Hawthorne noting the many naval officers in town. They passed a darkened theater, the walls plastered with notices of past performances — a circumstance Hawthorne thought significant enough to record in his journal. If he had sensed anything melodramatic in the occasion — his parting dinner with Bridge — his laconic entry gave no evidence of it. He and his friend were not to see each other for several years; Bridge's tour of duty on the *Cyane* would last until 1841.

On July 23, Hawthorne set out on his trip to western Massachusetts. He journeyed from Salem to Boston by coach, and there took the afternoon train for Worcester, where he stayed overnight at the Temperance Hotel. His detailed journal entries during the trip do not suggest unhappiness or gloom; they are the record of an observer keenly intent on capturing the human types he met. On the coach ride to Northampton, for example, he encountered an itinerant essence-pedlar, new to his trade, a cautious man who "spoke of the trials of temper to which pedlars are subjected, but said that it was necessary to be forbearing, because the same road must be travelled again and again." Hawthorne set down the remark as if it were a prescription for life.

On the morning of the 26th, continuing his stage journey from Pittsfield to Bennington, Hawthorne noticed a pair of newlyweds among the passengers. His own marital hopes seemingly in limbo, he studied them with particular care. Hawthorne was riding up front with the driver, but he caught a glimpse of the couple during one of the stops. They were leaning against the back of the coach, oblivious of everything but themselves, "perusing their mutual comeliness." The man had a black beard and thick black brows that formed a straight line across his forehead; Hawthorne took him to be a shopkeeper, probably from New York. The woman was evidently the more infatuated of the two, "referring her whole being to him." She had a pensive look and was slender, with a "genteel figure." En route, the driver, peering into the cab, reported that the bridegroom had his arm around his bride. Hawthorne assumed that he was taking little liberties. Throughout the journey, the blissful couple dined on love and gingerbread, Hawthorne noted — "and dined heartily, notwithstanding." But with an innate suspicion of their happiness, he wished he might see them a year later and note the change in their behavior.

True to the ostensibly inevitable chain of associations that pursued his everyday thoughts as well as his fictions, the notice of the wedded couple was followed by a mention of death. As an afterthought to his account of his first few days of travel, Hawthorne mentioned a tame crow that had flown down from the peak of a barn and followed after the coach. With a raucous cawing and a great flapping of its black wings, the bird pursued them, hopping from fence post to fence post, flying from tree to tree. The driver said the crow had scented a basket of fish, hidden under the seat. Hawthorne's darker imagination conjured up a different situation. "This would be a terrific incident," he noted in his journal, "if it were a dead body that the crow scented, instead of a basket of salmon. Suppose, for instance, a coach travelling along — that one of the passengers suddenly died — and that one of the indications of his death was the deportment of the crow." In his fantasy, the character cast for death was a man.

When the coach reached North Adams, in the bright forenoon,

Hawthorne decided that he liked the aspect of the town "indifferently well" and planned to make it his headquarters. Something about the landscape, as they approached the town, had struck him: the near-mountain scenery, with the long ridge of Mount Greylock in the distance, the thickly wooded areas cut by rushing streams. Here and there, they had passed factory buildings — lumber and textile mills — with the girls peering out the windows as the stage passed. At each of the factory sites, there were clusters of two or three meanly constructed boardinghouses, "supremely artificial establishments," set down in the wilderness.

On his first afternoon in North Adams, he registered at the local inn, then walked out along a narrow road into the woods. There, in a secluded spot, he stripped and bathed, stretching out full length in the "brawling waters." But even the bath in a chilling stream was unable to wash away the premonition of disaster that clung to him. The narrow road wound perilously close to the edge of a steep precipice. Hawthorne noticed a segment of the road sunk deep by continuous traffic. "Soon, probably," he confided to his notebook, "there will be an avalanche, perhaps carrying a stage-coach or a heavy wagon down into the bed of the stream."

On his first evening in North Adams, Hawthorne broke his resolution about not writing to anyone. In a letter to David Roberts, his old card-playing associate of Herbert Street days and still a practicing lawyer in Salem, Hawthorne explained that he had not intended to write, "but as it is possible that there may be some very important intelligence awaiting me, I am induced to break my resolution." He told Roberts, "If any letters have arrived for me, or if any should come to hand within ten days or a fortnight, I will thank you to direct them to this place . . . Please also to write yourself, and tell me any news that may have transpired since my departure." There is no indication of what the "very important intelligence" was. Perhaps he was expecting some word from the absent Mary Silsbee.

"Do not tell anybody that you have heard from me," he advised, "or that you know anything of my whereabouts. You will see me again (God willing) in the course of six months."

———

At the North Adams House, Hawthorne settled into the sleepy life of the small town. With an amused eye, he noted the grizzled and creaky veterans of the Revolutionary War, sunning themselves prominently, demonstrating that they were "still above ground." He even took notice of a meeting of the county commissioners, held in the barroom, for the purpose of deciding on the building of a new road. He took long walks in the surrounding countryside, bathing regularly in the cold streams.

He visited Williamstown, five miles distant, and attended the commencement exercises of the college. The town had a carnival atmosphere, the streets crowded with townspeople and visiting farmers. He watched an impromptu wrestling match between a drunk and a local farmer. Near the meeting house, he stood in the jostling crowd, where a caravan of hucksters had drawn up their carts and were putting up stands, selling watermelons, cider, and beer. Hawthorne particularly observed a middle-aged New York pedlar, who, in the midst of a continuous, cajoling, wheedling speech, kept an eye on the small boys climbing up on his cart, and interjected in his loud voice — "Fall down, roll down, tumble down — only get down" — with barely a pause in his banter.

He noticed, too, a crowd of Negroes, most of whom had emigrated across the New York border. The blacks formed a small society of their own amidst the larger crowd. Hawthorne noted the look of scorn on one of the young Negro women as she watched a drunk black man staggering up the meeting-house steps. "On the whole," he wrote, "I find myself rather more of an abolitionist in feeling than in principle."

Life in North Adams seemed open, boisterous, and unself-conscious. "The people here," he recorded, "show out their character much more strongly than they do with us — there was not the quiet, silent, dull decency as in our public assemblages — but mirth, anger, eccentricity, all showing themselves freely."

He had settled into the comfortable, undemanding society of men. There was something about the life of rural taverns and barrooms that appealed to him: the dim light, the yeasty smells of beer and cider that clung to the walls, the blazing fires on the hearths. There were the scattered conversations and bursts of low-down laughter, the sudden arousals of interest with the arrival of new patrons, the little knots of conversation — about crops, local politics, the weather — that finally unraveled into silence. The tavern was a place for studying mankind, a place where human nature seemed fixed in a kind of amber light. Inevitably, local rumors and local scandals came to rest there — usually in their most down-to-earth form, and Hawthorne was a practiced listener.

"Remarkable characters," he set down at the head of his notebook jottings. There was an ex-lawyer named Haynes, a victim of many misfortunes, who had lost his practice from too much drink, and an arm and part of his foot through accidents. Haynes was dirty and unkempt and had a black iron hook. "My study is man," Haynes told Hawthorne, sizing him up. "I do not know your name," he said, "but there is something of the hawk-eye about you too." Hawthorne sensed, under the barroom bonhomie, the core of strength in the man. Haynes was a student of phrenology and, for the price of a drink, would give a reading. Hawthorne submitted his own head for examination under the ex-lawyer's grimy hand. "This man was created to shine as a bank-president," he announced to the tavern crowd. But he then took the tavernkeeper aside and warned him, "Make that chap pay in advance for his board." There was Otis Hodge, a strapping blacksmith who loved his glass "and comes to the tavern for it, whenever it seems good to him, not calling for it slily and shyly, but marching sturdily to the bar."

Hawthorne took up with a traveling surgeon-dentist who was also a licensed Baptist preacher. Tall, slender, in his midtwenties, he had a self-satisfied air. "We talk together very freely," Hawthorne noted in his journal, "and he has given me an account, among other matters, of all his love-affairs which are rather curious, as illustrative of the life of a smart young country-fellow as relates to the gentle sex. Nothing can exceed the exquisite self-conceit which characterizes these confidences . . . and he seems strangely to find as much food for his passion in having been jilted once or twice, as in his conquests. It is curious to notice his revengeful feeling against the false ones."

He ventured into the life — and death — of the small towns in the region, even attending one or two funerals. One evening toward sunset, he took his place, with a barroom crony, Orrin Smith, a widower, at the head of a funeral procession for a ten-year-old boy. The coffin had been laid on a bed of straw in a horse-drawn wagon, and the procession wound slowly up the cypress-crowned hill to the cemetery. Hawthorne noted the stifled sobs of the mother, as the coffin, lowered into the grave, had to be raised again because of some obstacle. Smith — "a dissolute and mirth-making middle-aged man, who would not seem to have much domestic feeling" — had tactfully strewn the coffin lid with straw to deaden the ugly, final sound of the first clods of earth.

Late in August, he and a Mr. Leach, a patron at the North Adams House, had made a trip to Shelburne Falls, some twenty-two miles distant. Midway on their journey, they stopped at a tavern on the summit of Green Mountain, where they encountered an old gray-bearded man, with a "strange outlandish accent," giving a demonstration of his diorama. The "Old Dutchman," as the patrons referred to him (though he was actually German), was returning from a visit to Saratoga Springs. Hawthorne carefully recorded the "Dutchman's" performance, as if he had some intuition of its later usefulness: "We looked through the glass orifices of his machine, while he exhibited a succession of the very worst scratchings and daubings that can be imagined — worn out, too, and full of cracks and wrinkles, besmeared with tobacco smoke . . . There were views of cities and edifices in Europe, and ruins — and of Napoleon's battles and Nelson's sea fights; in the midst of which would be seen a gigantic brown, hairy hand — the Hand of Destiny — pointing at the principal points of the conflict, while the old Dutchman explained."

He was equally deliberate in describing another episode, a jaunt he took with Mr. Leach one moonlit night in North Adams. They had walked along a mountain road to the site of a burning limekiln, a stone tower some eighteen or twenty feet tall, with a hillock mounded up beside it for carts to draw the loads of marble to the top. The watcher, a dark-bearded figure in shirtsleeves, had been stretched out on the ground, but started up abruptly as they approached. He turned out to be sociable and eager to have their company during his lonely vigil. When he opened the iron door at the base of the tower, the glow of the flames lit up the area with an infernal light. Hawthorne and Leach climbed to the top of the kiln, peering down at the red-hot slabs of marble, burning with a bluish flame that flared up, sometimes, a yard high.

There was something about Hawthorne's nature — some air of compassion or understanding — that brought out the confidences of his acquaintances. Leach told him a personal story, about a young girl whom he had considered marrying, but who confessed that she had already had relations with another man. When Leach "began to talk with her on this subject, intending gently to reprehend her," the girl had become greatly agitated and wept bitterly — "her thoughts flying immediately to her guilt . . . She told so much, or betrayed so much, that he besought her to say no more. 'That was the only time, Mr. Leach,' she sobbed, 'that I ever strayed from the path of virtue.'

"Much might be made of such a scene," Hawthorne confided to his notes, "— the lover's astoundment, at discovering so much more than he expected." Twelve years later, Hawthorne recalled these moments of his North Adams sojourn — the burning limekiln, Leach's account of the wayward girl, the earlier encounter with the old Dutchman and his diorama — and used them in one of his more problematic tales, "Ethan Brand," the grim story of a man who sets out to discover the unpardonable sin.

In his notebook that evening Hawthorne made a further notation. "Mr. Leach spoke to me as if one deviation from chastity might not be an altogether insuperable objection to making a girl his wife."

Was it Hawthorne's astonishment that was reflected in the two exclamation marks he set down at the end of Leach's confession?

Hawthorne did not extend his journey to the six months he had
mentioned in his letter to David Roberts. When he left North
Adams, the second week in September, he made a brief tour through
Connecticut, stopping at Canaan and at Litchfield. In Litchfield, he
remarked on the neatness of the frame houses and the churches, the
ample streets and the village green, and the odd habit of situating a
city on the most elevated ground without the least shelter from the
winds. A last entry in the record of his travels was the recollection of
a Negro man he had seen at the Temperance Hotel in Hartford: "respectably dressed, and well-mounted on horseback, travelling on his
own hook, calling for oats and drinking a glass of brandy and water
at the bar — like any Christian." Another traveler, standing at the
bar, had remarked that he wished he had "a thousand such fellows
in Alabama." "It made a queer impression on me," Hawthorne
noted, "— the negro was really so human — and to talk of owning a
thousand like him."

Finally, he recorded the simple facts: "Left North Adams, Sept.
11th; Reached Home, Sept. 24th, 1838."

ᒧ IV ᒤ

Hawthorne had not been long back in Salem when he found himself
involved in projects that Mary and Elizabeth Peabody had initiated
for his benefit. Horace Mann, after two years in the Massachusetts
Senate, and much to the disappointment of his supporters, gave up
his political ambitions to accept a salaried post as secretary of the
newly formed Board of Education of the Commonwealth of Massachusetts. Mary Peabody was thoroughly pleased by the change.
"How could there be a more beautiful transition of office than
yours?" she wrote him. "After being the breaking-up plough of temperance, you are now to tell the people what to do with their sober-
ness." When she learned that Mann intended to publish a series of
standard texts for school libraries throughout the district, she immediately recommended Hawthorne, referring to him as "a young
man in this town . . . a man of first rate genius" who had it in mind
"to make an attempt at creating a new literature for the young."

Throughout the spring of 1838, Hawthorne had kept in mind the
possibility of collaborating with Longfellow on a book of fairy tales.
"Seriously," he had written Longfellow in March, "I think that a

very pleasant and peculiar kind of reputation may be acquired in this way . . . and what is of more importance to me, though none to a Cambridge Professor, we may perchance put money in our purses." The proposed book had even progressed to the point of acquiring a tentative title, *Boy's Wonder-Horn*. Shortly after his return from North Adams, Hawthorne broached the subject once more. He wrote the poet in October, using a low pun: "Have you blown your blast? — or will it turn out a broken-winded concern? I have not any breath to spare, just at present." Despite the fact that Longfellow had originally suggested the idea, the poet seems to have backed down or lost interest — and the collaboration never took place. Hawthorne may have oversold himself; Longfellow, furthermore, seems to have regarded him as a bit of an odd character. Writing to his friend George Washington Greene, soon after receiving Hawthorne's letter, Longfellow described the Salem author as "a strange owl; a very peculiar individual, with a dash of originality about him, very pleasant to behold."

Undaunted, Hawthorne decided to proceed on his own. Writing Longfellow later — and continuing his musical motif — he complained: "Assuredly, you have a right to make all the music on your own instrument; but I should serve you right were I to set up an opposition — for instance, with a corn-stalk fiddle . . . Really, I do mean to turn my attention to writing for children, either on my own hook, or for a series of works projected by the Board of Education — to which I have been requested to contribute." But the collaboration with Mann's Board of Education did not materialize, either. From the beginning, Horace Mann was cool to the proposals of the Peabody sisters. He had read Hawthorne's *Twice-told Tales*; Lizzie, actively promoting the author, had pressed a copy on him. In a letter to her, Mann agreed that the book was "beautifully" written, but contended that for schoolchildren what was needed was "something nearer home to duty and business." For Mann, popular literature was suspect unless heavily dosed with moral and didactic intentions. Mann was to take a similar tack with Richard Henry Dana, whose *Two Years Before the Mast* he claimed would be suitable for schoolchildren if the author would rewrite it extensively to include more "exact information" regarding the geography and customs of the countries covered, as well as to add "moral sentiments suited to the class of readers for which it is intended." After a visit from Mann, in which the educator — with an air of sweet reasonableness — suggested all sorts of improvements, Dana, astonished and insulted, was moved to write: "In short, there is no end to the stupid, gauche, narrow things this man contrived to say. If some enemy had employed him to come & try my patience to the utmost, he could not have executed his task better." He concluded that Mann was "a schoolmaster gone crazy."

Lizzie Peabody, in the meantime, had begun to explore other avenues. Her friend the historian George Bancroft, a successful and influential politician, had been appointed collector of the Port of Boston by President Van Buren. Elizabeth could lay claim to friendship with both Bancroft and his new wife; the lean and politic historian, a widower, had only recently married Elizabeth Bliss, the widow who had been one of the regulars at Lizzie's reading parties. If Lizzie was reluctant to see Hawthorne enter the political arena, she nonetheless felt that some office in the Custom House might be available. With her usual determination, she set about securing it for him. However, she seems to have bungled in her approach. Her initial interviews with Bancroft, at his home on Winthrop Place in Boston, did not prove satisfactory. A thoroughly committed and opportunistic politician, Bancroft had doubts concerning Hawthorne's party loyalties and effectiveness. Taking a different tack, Lizzie, on November 6, wrote directly to Mrs. Bancroft:

> After I was left alone with Mr. Bancroft — the day I called to see you — we had some conversation about my friend Hawthorne so desultory that I have felt somewhat troubled about it since — I find that he is by no means indifferent to the possibility of getting an office in the Custom house — I told him Mr. Bancroft mentioned the Inspector of Customs as if that was yet to be disposed of — and that he spoke of writing to him. This evening I saw him & he remarked Mr. Bancroft had not written yet. He also said he did not doubt he should write more — After he had an office that would narrow his leisure — and spoke with much earnestness of the necessity of action among men . . . I was myself so sorry to have him leave the quiet of nature which has done so much for his genius to go into the coarse arena of public life . . . that I did not say as clearly perhaps as I ought to have done — that there is nothing about him in any way to unfit him for acting an ordinary part in life. He is upright, faithful and intelligent . . .
>
> Mr. Bancroft asked if he was "interested in politics" and I thought looked disappointed when I said I thought not — and you know I talked to you about his ignorance of such subjects. Nevertheless, as a matter of *Sentiment* as well as *habit* — he is certainly on the administration side of the question. All I have a right to say is — that the cast of his mind determining him to imaginative literature and thinking — he has little interest and takes no personal part in electioneering and local subjects of party division . . . Yet were it a matter of duty — he would doubtless make these investigations and do his part.

The problem with Lizzie Peabody's advocacy was that in her outright honesty, trusting in the good faith of friends, she explained too much and raised uncomfortable issues. Whether as a result of Lizzie's bumbling, in this instance, or because of his own later career, Hawthorne adopted a policy of never volunteering information in pursuit of political office. His system was to answer honestly only those questions which were directly asked.

Lizzie's letter has the air of a woman who, stumbling in her efforts to help a friend, feels obliged to set things right — without, it seems, much assistance from Hawthorne, who was being decidedly stiff. Whatever her methods, she was successful: Bancroft offered Hawthorne a choice of positions. In a reserved letter, written on January 11, 1839, Hawthorne accepted the post of measurer, at a salary of $1500 a year. "After due reflection," Hawthorne wrote Bancroft, "I have determined to accept the office which you had the goodness to offer me, in the Inspector's department of the Custom House. On enquiry of Gen. McNeil and Mr. Jameson, I find that the post vacated by Mr. Harris is considered more laborious and responsible than an ordinary Inspectorship, and they were both of the opinion that I should prefer the duties of the latter." He added, "I hope to be able to remove to Boston within a fortnight, and it would then be agreeable to me to enter upon office."

Hawthorne's eulogy of his dead friend Jonathan Cilley had been of service. Bancroft duly noted the fact in his letter to the secretary of the treasury, Levi Woodbury, announcing his decision: "I have appointed Nathaniel Hawthorne Esquire of Salem (Biographer of Cilley) a Measurer in place of Paul R. George, dismissed, and request your approval of his appointment." Bancroft's succinct note offers an interesting consideration: that Hawthorne had received his appointment at the expense of the prior political appointee. He was later to become a victim himself of the time-honored American system of political patronage.

If he had seemed aloof from the fray when Lizzie Peabody was doing her best to secure him an appointment, he was not loath to present himself as a man of affairs once he had accepted the position. "I have no reason to doubt my capacity to fulfill the duties," he wrote Longfellow, "for I don't know what they are; but as nearly as I can understand, I shall be a sort of Port-Admiral, and take command of vessels after they enter the harbor, and have control of their cargoes . . . They tell me that a considerable portion of my time will be unoccupied; the which I mean to employ in sketches of my new experience, under some such titles as follows . . . 'Voyages at Anchor' — 'Nibblings of a Wharf-Rat' — 'Trials of a Tide Waiter' . . .''

In December of that year, Hawthorne was awaiting the publication of a quite different book, a special edition of one of his earliest and most popular tales, "The Gentle Boy." The edition had been sponsored by Miss Burley, the Salem hostess. It was to carry, as a frontispiece illustration, an engraving taken from a drawing by Sophia Peabody. Not long after she and Hawthorne had met, Sophia had shyly presented her sketch and asked, "I want to know if this looks like your Ilbrahim?" Hawthorne had studied the drawing calmly and carefully. "He will never look otherwise to me," he answered.

When *The Gentle Boy: A Thrice Told Tale* appeared, a slight volume bound in gray paper wrappers, it carried Hawthorne's glowing tribute to the artist. "No testimonial in regard to the effect of this story," he wrote in his preface, "has afforded the Author so much pleasure as that which brings out the present edition. However feeble the creative power which produced the character of Ilbrahim, it has wrought an influence upon another mind, and has thus given to imaginative life a creation of deep and pure beauty." After noting that Sophia's sketch had been praised by "the first painter in America" — meaning Washington Allston — Hawthorne went on, "If, after so high a meed, the Author might add his own humble praise, he would say, that whatever of beauty and of pathos he had conceived, but could not shadow forth in language, has been caught and embodied in the few and simple lines of the sketch." Unhappily, Sophia was distressed with the quality of the engraving, which was heavy-handed, changing the expression of the boy's eyes and mouth. At her insistence, after the first few copies had been printed, the edition was held up while the plate was retouched.

Their relationship was deepening. Hawthorne, early in December, agreed to sit for a portrait sketch by Sophia. In a letter, she referred to it: "When I was drawing you last evening, I was obliged first to observe your actual countenance and then see it in my mind before I could make it visible again." There was a "certain still stream" in the mind, she claimed, in which every real form was reflected "in ideal perfection." This was a truer reflection "than what passes before our careless glance when we think we see all." She explained, "This is why I said I had never beheld your face before I tried to reproduce it. Now I shall recognize it, I am certain, through all Eternity."

Among the random, undated notes of Hawthorne's earliest journal, there is one that appears to refer to the same occasion: "S.A.P. — taking my likeness, I said that such changes would come over my face, that she would not know me when we met again in Heaven. 'See if I dont!' said she, smiling. There was the most peculiar and beautiful humor in the point itself, and in her manner, that can be imagined."

Elizabeth Hawthorne had once warned about her brother that he "would never marry at all, and that he would never *do* anything: that he was an ideal person." It was an odd statement; perhaps it reflected only Ebe Hawthorne's possessive attitude. At the age of thirty-four, the "ideal person" had begun to display the symptoms of a man in love.

In the Wide Desert of the World

MY DEAREST SOPHIE, I had a parting glimpse of you, Monday forenoon, at your window — and that image abides by me, looking pale and not so quiet as is your wont. I have reproached myself many times since, because I did not show my face, and then we should both have smiled . . . I fear that you were not quite well that morning. Do grow better and better — physically, I mean, for I protest against any spiritual improvement, until I am better able to keep pace with you . . . And sleep soundly the whole night long, and get up every morning with a feeling as if you were newly created . . . so that we may walk miles and miles, without your once needing to lean upon my arm."

So Hawthorne wrote Sophia Peabody on March 6, 1839. It was the first of the nearly 100 letters he wrote her during their lengthy courtship — the first, that is, that survives. But Hawthorne's letters to Sophia represent only half the correspondence; Sophia's responses — her "maiden letters," as Hawthorne called them — were burned, years later, on the eve of their departure for Europe.

The little gallantries of a lover, and an enduring concern: these were the principal features of his early letters. The worrisome image of the sheltered invalid, of Sophia Peabody, pale and troubled, glimpsed through the high window of the Charter Street house, remained with Hawthorne throughout their courtship. Up to their wedding day — and after — Sophia's health was always a cause of anxiety. According to family accounts, Sophia had made up her mind not to marry unless she was well. Lizzie Peabody recalled, "She said if it was the will of God that they should marry, He would make her well. He said, Far be it from me to snatch before Providence wills it." Hawthorne had reasons for deferring any announcement. There was, first of all, the chagrin of his all-too-recent affair with Mary Silsbee and the embarrassment it must have caused to his family. And Sophia's invalid condition, more than likely, would only have underscored any opposition his sisters might feel toward the marriage. According to Julian, Ebe Hawthorne had more than intimated that any move toward marriage might have disastrous consequences for the precarious health of their mother.

There was, furthermore, the question of Hawthorne's vocation: as a professional writer — poorly paid when he was paid — he could hardly hope to support a wife, much less an invalid. For the time being, he and Sophia decided to keep their engagement a secret; there were too many contingencies. In writing to Sophia, Hawthorne's habit of adding lengthy postscripts for succeeding days may have been a way of cutting down on the frequency of his correspondence. A too-regular delivery of letters to the Peabody household would arouse gossip in Salem.

By March 1839, Hawthorne was settled into the routine of his new job as measurer of coal and salt for the Boston Custom House. He had taken a room in a boardinghouse on Somerset Place, walking to work in the mornings, returning in the evenings to sit by the fireside and write his letters to Sophia. At first, he found bracing the long hours in the open air on the wharves of Boston Harbor and East Cambridge, taking the inventory of incoming cargoes. It was a scene of activity and noise: the squawling of the gulls, the screech and whine of the pulleys as the heavily laden tubs of coal and salt were hoisted, the regular shouts of the work crews calling, "Tally, Sir." He enjoyed the physical labor, the tonic effect of the salt air, when, in the heat of summer, the sun beat down on the glinting water.

He looked forward to her letters, usually delivered to the Custom House. "My blessed Dove," he wrote, "Your letter was brought to me at East Cambridge, this afternoon — otherwise I know not when I should have received it . . . I put it in my pocket . . . for I always feel as if your letters were too sacred to be read in the midst of people — and (you will smile) I never read them without first washing my hands."

He had begun to acquire a reputation as a sober worker. George Bancroft had spoken highly of Hawthorne to Ralph Waldo Emerson — so Lizzie Peabody eagerly reported to Sophia when she visited Emerson in Concord, "The Mount of Transfiguration," as Lizzie designated it. "I was hardly seated here . . ." Lizzie wrote, "before Mr. Emerson asked me what I had to say of Hawthorne, and told me that Mr. Bancroft said that Hawthorne was the most efficient and best of the Custom House officers. Pray tell that down in Herbert Street." Lizzie had brought along a copy of *Twice-told Tales* and had pressed it on the Concord philosopher. Mr. Emerson seemed "all congenial" about Hawthorne, though he had not read him sufficiently. "He is in a good mood to do so, however," Lizzie claimed, "and I intend to bring him to his knees in a day or two, so that he will read the book, and all that Hawthorne has written." Her good intentions did not bear any magnificent fruit. Emerson was still not inclined to take Hawthorne's fictions seriously. A few months later, reading Dickens' *Oliver Twist*, he conceded that Dickens had *"flash,"* but "like Cooper & Hawthorne, he has no dramatic talent. The moment he attempts dialogue the improbability of life hardens to wood and stone." Emerson, with some accuracy, lodged the same complaint against Hawthorne's dialogue.

For Hawthorne, in his new employment, there were times that seemed less than agreeable. On cold winter days, with a wind whipping along the open wharves, during the long hours of tallying, he had to pace the deck to keep warm or seek shelter in a cabin. On occasion, too, he was required to settle disputes between the captains and the work gangs. "I would you could have beheld the awful sternness of my visage and demeanor," he wrote Sophia, "in the execution of this momentous duty." The worst days were those of enforced inactivity, when the weather was bad or when there were no new ships in port. Then he sat out the long hours in the Custom House, reading newspapers, listening to the drone of talk among the other officers and the political cronies and hangers-on who cluttered up the day. He broke up the time as best he could, with a walk to the picture galleries at the Boston Athenaeum, or a few hours spent in its reading room. (The helpful Miss Burley had arranged membership privileges for him.) Then it was back to the Custom House, to sit idly by the stove. "I do think that it is the doom laid upon me, of murdering so many of the brightest hours of the day at that unblest Custom House, that makes such havoc with my wits . . ." he wrote. "A salt, or even a coal ship is ten million times preferable; for there the sky is above me."

Occasionally, it seemed he had two lives, one stuck fast in solid reality, the other lived more enjoyably elsewhere. "I have a mind, some day, to send my dearest a journal of all my doings and sufferings," he wrote Sophia; "my whole external life, from the time I awake at dawn, till I close my eyes at night. What a dry, dull history would it be! But then, apart from this, I would write another journal of my inward life throughout the self-same day — my fits of pleasant thought, and those likewise which are shadowed by passing clouds — the yearnings of my heart towards my Dove — my pictures of what we are to enjoy together. Nobody would think that the same man could live two such different lives simultaneously."

Hawthorne was keeping a random journal of his Custom House days, but his literary efforts had come to a standstill. "My thoughts sometimes wander back to literature," he told Sophia, "and I have momentary impulses to write stories. But this will not be, at present. The utmost that I can hope to do will be to portray some of the characteristics of the life which I am now living, and of the people with whom I am brought into contact, for future use."

In his journal, Hawthorne described the pitiable life of an old man, poor and seedy, in patched clothes, who fished for flounder at the end of the dock, letting his catch get sun-dried and useless. "He has no business, no amusement, but just to crawl to the end of Long Wharf, and throw his line over." He also set down the odd ghost stories told to him by a co-worker and fellow Salemite, William Pike. Pike, who was to become a lifelong friend, intrigued Hawthorne with his stubborn affability. In his late twenties, short, stout, bull-necked, Pike occasionally preached and sometimes gave religious instructions to the inmates in the state prison. He suffered badly from asthma and from strange, perhaps psychological, seizures, which left him paralyzed and unable to call for help whenever he lay down flat in his bed. In his Boston boardinghouse, fearful that he would suffocate, he was forced to sleep sitting upright. Hawthorne, impressed with Pike's somewhat plodding intelligence, had expected great things from his friend, but later in life confessed his disappointment. "You will never, I fear . . . make the impression on the world that, in years gone by, I used to hope you would," he frankly told Pike. "It will not be your fault, however, but the fault of circumstances. Your flower was not destined to bloom in this world."

Sometimes, in his journalizing, Hawthorne merely recorded the desultory view: "Objects on a wharf — a huge pile of cotton bales, from a New Orleans ship, twenty or thirty feet high, as high as a house. Barrels of molasses, in regular ranges; casks of linseed oil. Iron in bars landing from a vessel . . . Long Wharf is devoted to ponderous, evil-smelling, inelegant necessaries of life . . ." It was a photograph out of time, salvaged for unspecified later use.

Writing to Longfellow in May 1839, Hawthorne complained that his friend neither came to see him nor made any inquiries about him. He conceded that he had done nothing further toward publishing a new volume of tales and said that he wanted to discuss the matter with the poet. "If I write a preface," he said, "it will be to bid farewell to literature; for as a literary man, my new occupations entirely break me up."

Three days later, on May 19, he wrote O'Sullivan to the same effect. O'Sullivan was having financial troubles with the *Democratic Review* and assumed that Hawthorne's failure to contribute was due to delinquent payments for his previous articles. Hawthorne reassured him, "That I have not recently contributed, is owing to no disinclination thereto; but the fact is, I am quite done for and broken up as a literary man, so long as I retain this office." And it was clear that he would be thoroughly occupied for the remainder of the summer and autumn. "The more business the better," he wrote, "for, by the omission of Congress to pass a certain regulation, I shall be entitled to the whole fees of my office, amounting to $3000, instead of the paltry $1500. If ever I come to be worth $5000, I will kick all business to the devil — at least till that be spent." It was "the absolute decree of fate," Hawthorne claimed, that had made him give up writing for the *Democratic Review*. "I have no refuge, save to declare myself no longer a literary man."

It was in the same May 19 letter that Hawthorne reported the impending marriage of Mary Silsbee and Professor Sparks. "My visits to Salem," he told O'Sullivan, "have been so short and hurried, that I have found no time to call on her these three months." He understood, nonetheless, that he was "still in good odor" with the Salem heiress. "As for me," he wrote, "I have neither resentments nor regrets, liking nor dislike — having fallen in love with somebody else."

⌒ II ⌒

The first year of courtship marked the progressive deepening of his feelings toward Sophia. His letters, chatty and ardent by turns, replaced the journal he had intended to keep. He recorded the events of his days as a form of communication between them. She was constantly in his thoughts. "Mine own Dove," he wrote her on April 2, "I have been sitting by my fireside ever since tea-time, till now it is past eight o'clock; and have been musing and dreaming about a thousand things, with every one of which, I do believe, some nearer or remoter thought of you was intermingled." At first, he stressed the spiritual aspects of their relationship. "When we shall be endowed with our spiritual bodies," he wrote her, "I think they will be so constituted, that we may send thoughts and feelings any distance, in no time at all, and transfuse them warm and fresh into the consciousness of those whom we love." It was an unusual acknowledgement for Hawthorne, a man who had, until recently, been inclined to think more upon guilt than on spiritual glory.

He was also continuously concerned about Sophia's health, warning her not to go out in the east wind or overtax herself or attempt to take walks with his sister Ebe, who was indefatigable and wanted "to walk half round the world" whenever she went out of doors. "How I wish I could give you a portion of my insensibility!" he wrote her. "And yet I should be almost afraid of some radical transformation, were I to produce a change in that respect. God made you so delicately, that it is especially unsafe to interfere with His workmanship." It was unusual for Hawthorne to talk about God, with or without a capitalized pronoun.

By May, he was writing to her in a comic tangle of words: "Oh my dearest, I yearn for you, and my heart heaves when I think of you — (and that is always, but sometimes a thought makes me know and feel you more vividly than at others, and *that* I call 'thinking of you') — heaves and swells (my heart does) as sometimes you have felt it beneath you, when your head, or your bosom, is resting on it. At such moments, it is stirred up from its depths. Then our two ocean-hearts mingle their floods . . ." Passion, it seems, had mangled his usually fastidious syntax.

Writing on July 24, at 8:00 P.M. — for often, in his letters to Sophia, Hawthorne carefully noted both the date and hour — he found a far more suitable soubriquet than "My Dove." "I am tired this evening, as usual, with my long day's toil," he wrote, "and my head wants its pillow — and my soul yearns for the friend whom God has given it! — whose soul He has married to my soul. Oh, my dearest, how that thought thrills me! We *are* married! I felt it long ago; and sometimes, when I was seeking for some fondest word, it has been on my lips to call you — 'Wife'! . . . Are we not married? God knows we are." In that melting of his innate reserve which became a fact of his love letters, he added, "I have really thought sometimes, that God gave you to me to be the salvation of my soul."

That idea, in fact, became an absolute conviction: Sophia had saved him from a lonely fate. "I used to think," he wrote her gratefully, "that I could imagine all passions, all feelings, all states of the heart and mind; but how little did I know what it is to be mingled with another's being! Thou only hast taught me that I have a heart — thou only hast thrown a light deep downward, and upward, into my soul. Thou only hast revealed me to myself; for without thy aid, my best knowledge of myself would have been merely to know my own shadow . . . Indeed, we are but shadows . . . till the heart is touched. That touch creates us — then we begin to be."

It was as if their love had been the perfect matching of two solitudes. It seemed to Hawthorne that in the reflection of Sophia's love he found a different, better, view of himself; in her dauntless optimism he discovered a counterweight to his own gloomy suppositions. In her lifelong devotion to his genius, he was to find the antidote for his own diffidence. It was little wonder that he should think of their love as something unassailably permanent, an island rising out of the stream of time. "You will always be the same to me," he wrote her, "because we have met in Eternity, and there our intimacy was formed." There was, perhaps, a note of desperation in his claim.

In his growing dependence on their relationship, Hawthorne was not always able to brush away thoughts of impending disaster. "If it were possible that you should vanish from me," he wrote Sophia, "I feel and know that my soul would be solitary forever and ever. I almost think that there would be no 'forever' for me . . . You are my first hope and my last."

Sometimes he countered such moods with vivid pictures of their future life: "If we had but a cottage, somewhere beyond the sway of the East Wind, yet within the limits of New England, where we could be always together, and have a place to *be* in — what could we desire more?" He added, verging into suggestive terrain, "Then how happy I would be — and how good! I could not be other than good and happy, when your kiss would sanctify me at all my outgoings and incomings (and when I should rest nightly in your arms.)" His vision of their life was tethered to the exercise of their talents: "And you should draw, and paint, and sculpture, and make music, and poetry too, and your husband would admire and criticise; and I, being pervaded with your spirit, would write beautifully, and make myself famous for your sake, because perhaps you would like to have the world acknowledge me . . . I shall always read my manuscripts to you, in the summer afternoons or winter evenings; and if they please you I shall expect a smile and a kiss as my reward — and if they do not please, I must have a smile and kiss to comfort me."

But Hawthorne plainly wanted a wife of flesh and blood, capable of physical passion. In the gentlest, most seductive way possible, his claims for the spiritual nature of their affections gave way to the mildest references to the nuptial bed. In August, he wrote Sophia about reading Harriet Martineau's *Deerbrook*, a romance in which he found "some truth" but too much idealized fantasy for his taste. "Your husband is presently going to bed . . ." he teased. "Will not his wife come and rest in his bosom . . . What a happy and holy fashion it is that those who love one another should rest on the same pillow. I smile at this sentence, but I wrote it innocently, nonetheless. Good night, my wife. Receive your husband's kiss upon your eyelids." In a later letter, the suggestion was more pointed: "Dove, come to my bosom — it yearns for you as it never did before. I shall fold my arms together, after I am in bed, and try to imagine that you are close to my heart. Naughty wife, what right have you to be anywhere else? How many sweet words I should breathe into your ear in the quiet night — how many holy kisses would I press upon your lips."

Considering his hasty visits to Salem and their brief meetings, it was a relief when Sophia, early in October, came to Boston to stay with her sister Mary, who was boarding with the family of Francis Dana Channing. Prose — even the ardent prose of his letters — was merely a weak conveyor of his feelings. Now, they could meet with a sense of comfort and perhaps of intimacy, even in a roomful of friends. "Ownest Dove," Hawthorne wrote her after one such evening, "did you get home safe and sound, and with a quiet and happy heart? How could you go without another press of lips? Yet Providence acted lovingly towards us on Tuesday evening, allowing us to meet in the wide desert of this world and mingle our spirits in a conjugal embrace . . . I want you very much in my arms tonight. I mean to dream of you with might and main. How sweet those kisses were on Tuesday evening!"

Yet with sensitive, shy people, there were bound to be misunderstandings. Hawthorne had playfully mentioned Sophia's "indifference" to his letters, and she had been hurt. "Dearest, I beseech you," he pleaded, "grant me freedom to be careless and wayward — for I have had such freedom all my life. Oh, let me feel that I may even do you a little wrong without your avenging it (oh how cruelly) by being wounded." Early in the spring, Sophia had written him about a disturbing dream. In it, she had received a letter from him, addressed to her as "My dear Sister," in which there had been a question raised about the "continuance" of their friendship. Hawthorne, overreacting, but knowing the value of dreams, immediately sensed some reluctance on Sophia's part, some holding back — as if she preferred to keep the relationship from becoming sexual. "I wish you had read that dream-letter through," he wrote her, "and could remember its contents. I am very sure that it could not have been written by me, however, because I should not think of addressing you as 'My dear Sister' — nor should I like to have you call me brother — nor even should have liked it from the very first of our acquaint. We are, I trust, kindred spirits, but not brother and sister." His disappointment showed plainly in the sharpness of his tone: "Mine own Dove, you are to blame for dreaming such letters, or parts of letters, as coming from me. It was you that wrote it — not I." And he added, "Pray, for my sake, that no shadows of earth may ever come between us, because . . . my only hope of being a happy man depends upon the permanence of our union."

Hawthorne, too, had a troublesome dream. It was on an evening when he had returned to Salem. He had felt a "vague weight" upon his spirit, "a sense that something was wanting to me here." He was prone to such feelings now, whenever he returned to his Herbert Street bedroom. Taking up a letter he had begun earlier in the evening, he added:

I have been asleep; and I dreamed that I had been sleeping a whole year in the open air; and that while I slept, the grass grew around me. It seemed, in my dream, that the very bed-clothes which actually covered me were spread beneath me, and when I awoke (in my dream), I snatched them up, and the earth under them looked black, as if it had been burnt — one square place, exactly the size of the bedclothes. Yet there was grass and herbage scattered over this burnt space, looking as fresh, and bright, and dewy, as if the summer rain and the summer sun had been cherishing them all the time. Interpret this for me, my Dove — but do not draw any somber omens from it. What is signified by my nap of a whole year? (It made me grieve to think that I had lost so much of eternity) — and what was the fire that blasted the spot of earth which I occupied, while the grass flourished all around?

Bare earth in a grassy plot might easily be interpreted as a new grave. But the dream is also one of renewal: fresh growth sprouting up from the scorched earth. For Hawthorne, fire was the terrible element that both consumed and refined. He could use it, too, as a more temperate metaphor, describing the girls of Salem on a summer afternoon as looking "warm and voluptuous — not languidly voluptuous, but with a mild fire." (Sophia, speaking of Hawthorne's 1838 journey, echoed his phrase about the fire in the mind that "died away." "I trust it did not 'rekindle' on his return," she added, then spoke deprecatingly about the beginning of their romance: "At all events a fire did kindle then, of a certain kind, in his and in my heart and brain.")

Hawthorne's letter was written on May 26. It had been a year since his unhappy affair with Mary Silsbee — less than a week after she had married a man named Sparks.

Sophia Peabody did, in fact, have a brother who could claim a large measure of her affection during the period when she became acquainted with Hawthorne. And in November 1839, Sophia was summoned home to Salem; George Peabody, invalided for two years, was close to death. It was the second fatal illness in the family. In 1837, Wellington, the youngest Peabody son, had died of yellow fever contracted while working in a New Orleans hospital. George Peabody had been with his brother at the time of his death and had returned to Salem disheartened and ill himself. The Peabody family thought George was suffering from yellow fever, but later discovered that his slow and painful death had resulted from "consumption of the spinal marrow."

At first, Sophia had been kept ignorant of George's true condition;

but her bedroom was next to her brother's, and she could hardly ignore his groans of pain at night or the relief that came only with
morphine. She had written Elizabeth about her feelings: "I never
have thought, you know, that it was any trial to bear my own
pain — I could always manage it and arrange it in the grand economy of events; but I must yet learn to be patient and serene at the
sight and consciousness of his . . . The slow and ever increasing suffering is the most appalling prospect that can be."

Taking up the family vigil by the bedside, she was all the more
conscious of the drastic change in her brother. George was twenty-
five; in his youth he had been a proud athlete. Now the young phy-
sique and the fine profile were wasted by disease; his features were
taut with pain. Hawthorne, well aware of Sophia's love for her
brother, worried about the effect of the emotional strain on her precarious health. He warned her to be prepared for the worst — "if
this may be called worst which is in truth best for all — and more
than all for George." On November 14, he wrote her: "May God
sustain you under this affliction. I have long dreaded it for your
sake. Oh, let your heart be full of love for me now, and realize how
entirely my happiness depends on your well-being. You are not your
own dearest — you must not give way to grief." He was distinctly
conscious of some failure on his part. "My dearest," he added, "this
note seems cold and lifeless to me, as if there were no tenderness nor
comfort in it. Think for yourself all that I cannot speak."

As the agonizing wait continued, he wrote her comfortingly, yet
he could not avoid interjecting his own claims. It was as if, under
the cover of a very real concern for Sophia, some element of jealousy
managed to stir toward consciousness. "Oh be strong for the sake of
your husband," he wrote her on the 17th. "Let all your love for me
be so much added to the strength of your heart. Remember that
your anguish must likewise be mine." Then, on the 20th, he wrote,
"Dearest, there is nothing in me worthy of you. My heart is weak in
comparison with yours." Still, he found it necessary to tug at her affections: "Mine own wife, what a cold night this is going to be! How
am I to keep warm, unless you nestle close to my bosom."

Five days later, after a hurried weekend visit to Salem, Hawthorne wrote from Boston, "I came off in the two o'clock cars,
through such a pouring rain, that doubtless Sophie Hawthorne set it
down for certain that I should pass the day and night in Salem . . .
I feel that I ought to be with you now; for it grieves me to imagine
you all alone in that chamber, where you 'sit and wait' — as you
said to me this morning. This, I trust, is the last of your sorrow,
mine own wife, in which you will not have all the aid that your husband's bosom, and the profoundest sympathy that exists within it,

can impart." If there was some reason for Sophia to think that he might have remained in Salem overnight, then there was, quite probably, the possibility that he could have. Yet, despite his worries over Sophia's grief, he had returned to Boston in a drenching rain. It was on the evening of November 25 — possibly while Hawthorne was writing his letter — that George Peabody died.

Hawthorne was concerned and sympathetic; yet beneath his calm advice, and probably for the most judicious reasons, he tried to erase from Sophia's mind the memory of a beloved brother. The tone of a letter written after the funeral, is clinical. "Dearest," he wrote Sophia on November 29, "for some little time to come, I pray you not to muse too much upon your brother, even though such musings should be untinged with gloom and should appear to make you happier. In the eternity where he now dwells, it has doubtless become of no importance to himself whether he died yesterday, or a thousand years ago; he is already at home in the celestial city — more at home than ever he was in his mother's house. Then, my beloved, let us leave him there for the present."

⌒ III ⌒

Late in October, before George Peabody's final illness, Hawthorne was invited by George Hillard and his wife to move to new quarters. Hillard, a Boston lawyer four years Hawthorne's junior, was a friend of the Peabody sisters. Before his marriage to Susan Howe, in 1835, he had been one of the regulars at Mrs. Clarke's boarding-house. Hillard had a congenial and undemanding personality and a ready, somewhat sly wit. He recently had formed a partnership with Charles Sumner, a Harvard graduate and, like himself, another of the favored students of Mr. Justice Story. Tall, strapping, and a bit vain, Sumner had just returned from a highly successful European tour, dressed in fashion by the best English tailors. He had settled into his law practice with a humorless determination. "Sumner," Hillard reported, "is behaving like a very good boy, nailed to his desk like a bad cent to a grocer's counter." Hawthorne appreciated Hillard's easy, accommodating manner; the two were to become good friends.

In the fall, when Hillard decided to take a house at 54 Pinckney Street, on Beacon Hill, he asked Hawthorne whether he would consider lodging there. Hawthorne was enthusiastic. "What thinks my Dove of this?" he wrote Sophia immediately. "Your husband is quite delighted, because he thinks matters may be managed so that once in a while he may meet his own wife within his own premises. Might it not be so? Or would his wife — most preposterous idea!! —

deem it a sin against decorum to pay a visit to her husband?" It was Hawthorne's little joke — since, obviously, Susan Hillard would serve as a necessary, but perhaps lenient, chaperone. His arrangement with Hillard would give him a private parlor and an adjoining bedroom, with breakfasts taken with the Hillards. Before his move, Sophia and Mary had helped select a Brussels carpet and furnishings for his new quarters. By mid November, he was installed and reporting that Susan Hillard was taking excellent care of him, feeding him eggs and baked apples and other delicacies: "Altogether I am as happily situated as a man can be, whose heart is wedded, while externally he is still a bachelor."

If Hawthorne assumed that his new lodgings would afford him privacy, he was soon disillusioned. The Hillards were a sociable couple and there were frequent visitors. Moreover, his position at the Custom House left him open to invitations from his superiors, particularly Bancroft and General John McNeil, the surveyor of the port, who was married to Franklin Pierce's half sister. Sophia, too, added to his burden by offering him a ticket to Emerson's lecture series "The Present Age," given at the Masonic Temple in Boston. Hawthorne declined. "My evenings are very precious to me," he explained, on December 2, "and some of them are unavoidably thrown away in paying or receiving visits, or in writing letters of business; and therefore I prize the rest as if the sands of the hourglass were gold or diamond dust." He confessed, "I have never had the good luck to profit much, or indeed any, by attending lectures, so that I think the ticket had better be bestowed on somebody who can listen to Mr. Emerson more worthily."

With the approaching holidays, he was all the more besieged. "I was invited to dine at Mr. Bancroft's yesterday with Miss Margaret Fuller," he wrote three days later, "but Providence had given me some business to do; for which I was very thankful. When my Dove and Sophie Hawthorne can go with me, I shall not be afraid to accept invitations to meet literary lions and lionesses." In midmonth, there was another claim on his time. "Your husband has received an invitation, through Mr. Collector Bancroft, to go to Dr. Channing's tonight. What is to be done? Anything, rather than to go." He did, however, manage a call on Sophia's sister, then in Boston. "Mary and your husband talked with the utmost hopefulness and faith of my Dove's future health and well-being . . ." he wrote Sophia. "I love Mary because she loves you so much — our affections meet in you, and so we become kindred."

On New Year's Eve, Sophia wrote him from Salem. She had injured her hand slightly, and her penmanship was awkward. "I cannot tell you how much I love you in this backhanded style," she wrote him. "My love is not in this attitude — it rather bends forward to meet you." She continued, "What a year has this been to us! My definition of Beauty is that it is love, and therefore includes both truth and good. But those only who love as we do can feel the significance and force of this." She was, she said, "full of the glory of the day. God bless you this night of the old year. It has proved the year of our nativity. Has not the old earth passed away from us — are not all things new?"

Hawthorne, writing from Boston on New Year's Day, echoed the thought: "What a year the last has been! Dearest, you make the same exclamation; but my heart originates it too. It has been the year of years. Do you not feel, dearest, that we live above time and apart from time, even while we seem to be in the midst of time?" Two days later, he wrote again. There had been a series of freezing days. "Did we walk together in any such cold weather last winter?" he asked. "I believe we did. How strange that such a flower as our affection should have blossomed amid snow and wintry winds — accompaniments which no poet or novelist, that I know of, has even introduced into a love-tale." With the pardonable excess of a lover, he wrote, "Nothing like our story was ever written — or ever will be — for we shall not feel inclined to make the public our confidant."

In his New Year's Day letter, Hawthorne had asked Sophia to make out a list of books she would like to have in their library. He intended, when opportunity and cash allowed, to fill up their new bookcase. "I want to feel that I am buying them for the both of us," he told her. Sophia, in turn, informed him that she was painting two pictures for the new apartment. Hawthorne responded jubilantly on January 3, "You cannot think how much delight those pictures are going to give me . . . I never owned a picture in my life; yet pictures have always been among the earthly possessions (and they are spiritual possessions too) which I most coveted." There was an element of gallantry in his letter, for Hawthorne had seldom expressed, either in his letters or journals, an overwhelming interest in painting. It was after he met Sophia, who had a knowledgeable taste in such matters, that he slowly developed a real interest in the visual arts. Even then, he was more intrigued by the palpable, three-dimensional character of sculpture than by painting. "Moonlight is Sculpture — Sunset, and sunlight generally, Painting," he wrote in his notebook. It was one of the early, cryptic references to the subject that followed on his meeting with Sophia.

When Sophia's landscapes arrived, they were suitably hung — one above the mantelpiece in the parlor, the other on the opposite wall. "I gaze at them by all sorts of light," he wrote appreciatively; "day-light, twilight and candle-light; and when the lamps are extin-guished, and before getting into bed, I sit looking at these pictures by the flickering fire-light." He was convinced that the two figures in the copy of a landscape by Menaggio — a lady and a cavalier stand-ing on a bridge — represented Sophia and himself.

Throughout the spring and summer, Hawthorne's letters to So-phia included a litany of complaints about unwanted invitations and unexpected visitors. "I have met with an immense misfortune . . ." he wrote her. "I have received an invitation to a party at Gen-eral McNeil's . . . Why will not people let your poor persecuted hus-band alone? . . . I cannot go. I will not go." On another occasion, he wrote her, "My days have been so busy, and my evenings so invaded with visitants, that I have not had a moment's time to talk with thee . . . Night before last, came Mr. Jones Very; and thou knowest that he is somewhat unconscionable as to the length of his calls." (The visit from Very would have been particularly awkward, for Haw-thorne had already complained to Mary Peabody that Very "wants a brother." The poet was pestering him in an attempt to convert him. "What shall I do?" he had asked Mary.) There was, as well, a visit from George Hillard's brother, fresh from London, who "wasted my precious hours with a dull talk of nothing." And Horace Conolly, the whist-playing Cardinal of his Herbert Street years, had showed up with a young Cambridge law student who "came to do homage to thy husband's literary renown." Hawthorne protested, "I do wish the blockheads, and all other blockheads in this world, could com-prehend how inestimable are the quiet hours of a busy man."

Sophia, with the best of intentions, added to his burdens. She urged him to attend the services of Father Edward Taylor, the famous and fiery preacher who was the minister of the Seamen's Bethel in Boston, and the original of Herman Melville's Father Map-ple. Although God loomed large in Hawthorne's letters to Sophia, He did not figure prominently in Hawthorne's Sunday mornings. In answering Sophia, Hawthorne blatantly stalled. "Most absolute lit-tle wife," he asked, "didst thou expressly command me to go to Fa-ther Taylor's church this very Sabbath? . . . Now belovedest, it would not be an auspicious day for me to hear the aforesaid Son of Thunder." Two weeks later, he confessed that he had reneged again. He promised to hear Father Taylor at another time, but extracted a promise from Sophia in return, that she would not be disappointed if he failed to appreciate her man of God. "Promise me this," he wrote, "and at some auspicious hour . . . Father Taylor shall have an opportunity to make music with my soul. But I forewarn thee, sweetest Dove, that thy husband is a most unmalleable man — thou art not to suppose, because his spirit answers to every touch of thine, that therefore every breeze, or even every whirlwind, can up-turn him from his depths. Well, dearest, I have said my say, on this matter."

In June, Sophia was planning a visit to the Emersons in Concord. The invitation had come as a result of her recent efforts in sculpture. In Boston, Sophia had studied briefly under the intense young sculptor Shobal Vail Clevenger. While her brother George lay ill, she had made a portrait bas-relief of the invalid to serve as a remembrance. The medallion proved so successful, at least in the minds of family and friends, that she was encouraged to attempt another. This time, the relief portrait was of Charles Emerson, the adored brother of Waldo, who had died in 1836 on the eve of his marriage to a young Concord woman, Elizabeth Hoar. The portrait suffered, undoubtedly, from the fact that Sophia worked from miniatures and recollections of those who had known the younger Emerson. Yet when the final cast was taken, Emerson wrote her a warm letter of appreciation. "Elizabeth [Hoar] is very well content with the cast," he affirmed, "though she thinks it has lost some of its precision, as well as the agreeable tint of the clay. All our friends find the likeness — some of them slowly — but all at last. We all count it a beautiful possession . . . You must now gratify us all by fixing a time when you will come to Concord and hear what we have to say of it."

In Sophia, Emerson evidently recognized that he was dealing with one of the worshipers at his shrine. Writing her about her impending visit, he felt it necessary to disabuse her of her notions: "In regard to certain expressions in your letter, I ought to say, you will presently be undeceived. Though I am fond of writing, and of public speaking, I am a very poor talker and for the most part very much prefer silence. Of Charles's beautiful talent in that art I have had no share; but our common friend, Mr. Alcott, the prince of conversers, lives little more than a mile from our house, and we will call in his aid, as we often do."

In mid June, installed in the Emersons' spacious and four-square house on the Lexington Road, Sophia, warmed by the sympathetic appreciation of Emerson and his wife, Lidian, wrote Hawthorne in glowing terms about the country town. Hawthorne replied on the 22nd, "Would that we could build our cottage this very now amid the scenes which thou describest. My heart thirsts and languishes to be there, away from the hot sun, and the coal-dust and the steaming docks, and the thick-pated, stubborn, contentious men, with whom I brawl from morning till night." Sophia had evidently told the Emersons of her engagement, for Hawthorne responded, "It gladdens me . . . that thou meetest with sympathy there and that thy friends have faith that thy husband is worthy of thee." Since Sophia was enjoying herself, Hawthorne encouraged her to prolong the visit, adding, "I do not press thee to stay, but leave it all to thy wisdom." He was, himself, not eager to pursue any deeper acquaintance with the resident philosopher of the little New England town. "I must not forget to thank Mr. Emerson for his invitation to Concord," he concluded, a bit evasively, "but really it will not be in my power to accept it."

In July 1840, Elizabeth Peabody realized one of her more feasible ambitions: she rented a house at 13 West Street in Boston and there opened a bookstore. Her shop, during the next few years, became a center for much of the intellectual and cultural life of the city. The front room, lined with shelves, served as the book room, reverting to the family parlor after shop hours, and Elizabeth stocked it with English and foreign-language books and periodicals. There, one could find the latest issues of *Blackwood's* and *La Revue des Deux Mondes*. At the suggestion of her friend Washington Allston, she also carried art supplies. On Wednesday evenings, Lizzie held a weekly reception to which everyone of any intellectual disposition in Boston was invited.

It was in the parlor on West Street, also, that Margaret Fuller held her regular series of "conversations," an early feminist gesture meant to counteract the poor contemporary standards of female education. The weekly meetings, as Margaret Fuller announced, would provide "a point of union to well-educated and thinking women, in a city, which, with great pretensions to mental refinement, boasts, at present, nothing of the kind." Her first series on Greek mythology, begun in November 1839, before Lizzie had opened her shop, had gone remarkably well. Conducting her discourses along Socratic lines, Margaret Fuller, a Minerva of "exceeding plainness," in Emerson's private view, had discussed Prometheus as the symbol of pure reason, Venus as the paradigm of instinctive womanhood, and Bacchus — "the answer of the earth to the sun" — as the principal exemplar of the life of triumph and divine frenzy. Emerson, who attended one of the early meetings, found her delivery distinctly nasal, but noted that Margaret's circle of illuminati "comprised some of the most agreeable and intelligent women to be found in Boston and its neighborhood." For her second course of conversations, to be held in the West Street bookstore during the winter of 1840,

Margaret had proposed the topic "The Fine Arts." Under Lizzie's auspices, as well, she instituted another series of conversations to which gentlemen would be admitted.

The house on West Street made it possible for the entire Peabody family to be together once again. Mother Peabody, the doctor, and Sophia were planning to move to Boston. Hawthorne, delighted by the prospect, was nevertheless concerned about Sophia's health. He wrote her on July 10, "Do not thou make thyself sick in the bustle of removing; for I think there is nothing more trying, even to a robust frame and rugged spirit." He signed himself "De l'Aubépine."

The West Street house became a hive of family activity. Sophia was given her own upstairs studio room. Her copies of old master paintings were displayed for sale in the parlor. Dr. Peabody used the residence as a drugstore for dispensing his homeopathic remedies. For a time, Mary conducted a morning school for children. In the afternoons, she gave French lessons to Boston matrons. She was also conducting regular classes in drawing, based on a new method employing cubes and cones. At West Street, there was even room enough for the Peabody family to take in boarders.

Among her other occupations, Lizzie Peabody decided to become a publisher, issuing tracts and pamphlets for various morally minded Boston organizations, including the Anti-Slavery Society. One of her earliest projects, however, was the publication of a volume of children's stories on historical subjects, *Grandfather's Chair*, written by Hawthorne. The idea for the book had come from Hawthorne's spinster second cousin, Suzy Ingersoll. During one of his visits to Salem, he had been given a tour of inspection of the old, many-gabled Ingersoll house on Turner Street. When the "Duchess," as Hawthorne called her, peremptorily asked why he was not writing, Hawthorne complained of a lack of subjects. "Oh there are subjects enough," Suzy Ingersoll maintained. "Write about that old chair," she said, pointing to a Pilgrim relic standing next to the fireplace. "You can make a biographical sketch of each old Puritan who became in succession the owner of the chair." The idea struck Hawthorne as a good one. Writing Horace Conolly about the visit, Hawthorne had already decided on the title. His long-postponed plans for writing a children's book had received the necessary impetus.

In June, Conolly visited Hawthorne in his rooms in Boston and claimed to have seen the completed manuscript. The book was a slight volume, relating in five brief episodes the history of the chair from its arrival aboard the ship *Arbella* through the governments of Winthrop, Bellingham, Dudley, and Endicott. It allowed Hawthorne, for once, an opportunity to use his previously aborted plans for a sequence of tales within the framework of a continuing narrative. In this case, the narrative thread was provided by the old grandfather, who related the stories to his grandchildren. With a rare burst of energy, Hawthorne continued the exercise, writing two more sequels, *Famous Old People* and *Liberty Tree*, which carried the history forward to the heroes of the Revolutionary War. In November, he wrote jokingly to Longfellow: "By occupying Grandfather's chair, for a month past, I really believe I have grown an old man prematurely."

Lizzie Peabody published the first volume in December, by arrangement with Wiley and Putnam, and the succeeding volumes followed in January and March of 1841. In his preface to *Grandfather's Chair*, Hawthorne spoke coolly of the book as a "ponderous tome" and expressed his doubts about the success of his venture. To make an entertaining narrative out of the "unmalleable material" of early American history, he claimed, was as unlikely as manufacturing "delicate playthings out of the granite rocks on which New England is founded."

ᘓ IV ᘔ

Boston in the 1840s was a city in intellectual ferment. Emerson, as responsible as any man for the demand for change, was to give one of the most colorful, if sardonic, accounts of the strange assortment of social and religious reformers who seemed to gravitate toward the Hub. In a famous bit of reportage, he described the convention of the Friends of Universal Reform, sponsored by the zealous abolitionist William Lloyd Garrison and held in the Chardon Street Chapel beginning in November 1840:

> If the assembly was disorderly, it was picturesque. Madmen, madwomen, men with beards, Dunkers, Muggletonians, Come-outers, Groaners, Agrarians, Seventh-day-Baptists, Quakers, Abolitionists, Calvinists, Unitarians and Philosophers — all came successively to the top, and seized their moment, if not their hour, wherein to chide, or pray, or preach, or protest. The faces were a study. The most daring innovators and the champions-until-death of the old causes sat side by side.

Emerson's account had all the detachment of a man who was never a joiner. Yet Emerson had yielded to a gregarious impulse on one occasion, becoming a founding member of Hedge's Club, a loosely knit cabal of intellectuals that, beginning in the fall of 1836, held irregular meetings in Boston and Concord. The club had taken its name from Frederick Henry Hedge, a liberal Unitarian minister

"Bold Daniel" Hathorne, Nathaniel Hawthorne's grandfather. Engraving by Schoff.

Nathaniel Hathorne, Hawthorne's father. Engraving by Schoff.

Robert Manning, Hawthorne's maternal uncle, from a miniature in the collection of the Essex Institute, Salem, Massachusetts.

The campus at Bowdoin College, ca. 1820. Lithograph by an unknown artist from a painting by J. G. Brown.

Hawthorne's silhouette, one of a series made of the Bowdoin graduating class of 1825.

Jonathan Cilley. Unidentified nineteenth-century lithograph.

The Manning House *(center)*, Herbert Street, Salem. "In this dismal and squalid chamber, FAME was won," Hawthorne confided in his notebook in 1836.

Sophia Peabody. Engraving by Schoff from a portrait presumably painted by Chester Harding.

Mary Crowninshield Silsbee (Mrs. Jared Sparks).
Portrait by Francis Alexander, 1830.

Hawthorne at thirty-six. Portrait by Charles Osgood, 1840.

Undated sketch of "Mamma" Peabody, by
Sophia Peabody Hawthorne.

Mary Peabody Mann. Daguerreotype
taken soon after her marriage to Horace
Mann in 1843.

Elizabeth Palmer Peabody in old age.

Henry Wadsworth Longfellow. Daguerreotype by Southworth
and Hawes, ca. 1848.

Fanny Appleton Longfellow.

The Night-blooming Cereus. Sketch from Sophia
Peabody's Cuban Journal, May 1834.

The Old Manse, Concord.

The breakfast room at the Old Manse.

of Bangor, Maine, whose visits to Massachusetts prompted the irregular meetings of the society.

At its very first meeting, the topic of discussion had been the failure and timidity of the Unitarian faith. Considering the fact that the original membership consisted largely of dissatisfied Unitarian ministers, the subject was not an unusual one. Although Emerson still paid his pew fees and occasionally preached in the Concord church where his step-grandfather, Ezra Ripley, was pastor, he had all but given up his own ministry. In two years' time, Emerson would be considered a renegade and a heretic. His Divinity School Address, delivered at the Harvard Divinity School in July 1838, rocked the clerical community of New England. In the very sanctuary of the Unitarian faith, Emerson had boldly called for the restoration of God to His heaven and the dismissal of the cult of Jesus as the intermediary between the individual soul and its creator. Orthodox ministers considered the address blasphemous and the speaker an infidel and a heretic.

Among the other dissatisfied clergymen of Hedge's Club were George Ripley, another Harvard graduate, who was edging toward resignation from his Purchase Street Church; Theodore Parker, a liberal preacher from West Roxbury; and the young James Freeman Clarke, the clergyman-son of Mrs. Rebecca Clarke, who ran the Boston boardinghouse. Although the members had cordially invited the "Bishop" of the Unitarian Faith, William Ellery Channing, to join, the cautious Dr. Channing had not been receptive. His more radical clergyman-nephew, William Henry Channing, however, regularly attended the meetings — though not, it seemed, with any benefit to his polemical abilities. Theodore Parker, in an uncharitable moment, claimed that the younger Channing pounded an argument exceedingly hard, but since the head of the nail was always downward, Channing never drove a point home.

In time, the character of the club discussions altered considerably; the yeasty philosophical notions of Kant, Fichte, Schelling, and Hegel were regularly debated at its meetings. Blended with these was a good deal of French social philosophy — the writings of the utopian and communitarian philosophers Saint-Simon, Victor Cousin, Charles Fourier. By the 1840s, the association had received a new title, the Transcendental Club. Members were surprised, so Emerson commented, "at this rumor of school or sect, and certainly at the name of Transcendentalism, given nobody knows by whom, or when it was first applied." The name, however, stuck.

The Transcendental Club was not so unremittingly intellectual as it might have seemed; its meetings were frequently the occasions for oyster suppers in Boston and picnics in Concord. Nor was it exclusively clerical. Among its other members were Jones Very, John Sullivan Dwight, a minister-turned-musicologist, and the indefatigable Bronson Alcott, never a man to miss a discussion. With novel liberality for its time, it also welcomed women to its ranks; Ripley's wife, Sophia, and his sister Marianne frequently attended its meetings, as did Margaret Fuller and Elizabeth Peabody. The only major exception to this openness was the fulminating orator and editor Orestes Brownson, who so harangued the membership on every point that after one or two sessions he was no longer informed of forthcoming meetings.

In 1840, the members of the club decided to sponsor a publication, intended to promulgate its views and opinions. The first issue of *The Dial* appeared in July. For the first two years of its four-year existence, Margaret Fuller served as the hard-working, unpaid editor; after that, Emerson reluctantly took on the job. When its commercial publisher, Weeks Jordan and Company, went into bankruptcy, the burden was taken on by Lizzie Peabody. Lizzie made one necessary economy; she kept the print-run close to the number of subscribers. Emerson had been profligate with complimentary copies.

Later that same year, the club experienced another ferment when George Ripley, having resigned his ministry, promoted a scheme for an ideal community of laborers and intellectuals. Ripley had found the seemingly perfect site for his utopia — a dairy farm of some 170 acres, a setting of lush green pastures and pine woods located in West Roxbury on the banks of the Charles River.

It was Ripley's opinion that at Brook Farm he would effect the social reforms that the church was too timid to accomplish. In a formal invitation to Emerson to join the community, he carefully inventoried his aims: ". . . to insure a more natural union between intellectual and manual labor than now exists; to combine the thinker and the worker, as far as possible, in the same individual . . . to do away with the necessity of menial services by opening the benefits of education and the profits of labor to all." It was a large order, and he intended to do no less than "prepare a society of liberal, intelligent and cultivated persons, whose relations with each other would permit a more wholesome and simple life than can be led amidst the pressures of our competitive institutions." It was to be one of the great, unsung failures of nineteenth-century American reform.

The Association, as Ripley called it, would be organized as a joint stock company, each share to be $500. Ripley envisoned a community of about ten families, expecting that the capital needed would be $30,000 for the land, buildings, and equipment. A year's labor of 300 days would guarantee each member his bed and board. Associates who did no work would be charged $4.00 a week for board, fuel, light, and laundry. Each share would entitle the member to the tuition of one pupil at the Association school. Shareholders would be entitled to vote on all matters relating to the funding of the project. It was an ideally organized scheme.

Emerson, however, held back. When George Ripley and his wife, accompanied by Margaret Fuller and Alcott, visited him on October 16 to discuss the plan, Emerson was unusually aloof and hesitant in his responses. In his journal, he was a good deal more forthright: "I wished to be convinced, to be thawed, to be made nobly mad." Instead, he found Ripley's scheme merely "arithmetic and comfort." He described Brook Farm as "only a room in the Astor House hired for the Transcendentalists." In carefully reasoned terms, he set down his objections: "I do not wish to remove from my present prison to a prison a little larger. I wish to break all prisons." He did not wish to hide his "impotency," he claimed, in the thick of a crowd. "Moreover," he added, "to join this body would be to traverse all my long trumpeted theory, and the instinct which spoke from it, that one man is a counterpoise to a city." His journal entry on that cool October evening was the war cry of the individualist against the encroaching age of conformity.

Oddly enough, it was the rehabilitated solitary, Nathaniel Hawthorne — wary of reformers and do-good schemes — who gave Ripley's project his earnest consideration. In Boston, he and Sophia had attended meetings of the Transcendental Club. In Brook Farm, Hawthorne thought he saw his escape from his burdensome Custom House job. The farm might be the ideal place to begin his honeymoon with Sophia. He would labor and write; he would no longer be dependent on the whims of publishers and the public. With considerably more optimism than the chary Emerson, Hawthorne invested $1000 of his Custom House savings; it was the price of two shares, one for himself, the other for Sophia.

In November, when it seemed clear there would be a change of administration and a victory for the Whigs, Hawthorne wrote David Roberts with the condescending air of a man who has escaped political disaster: "The Custom House officers begin to suspect that Harrison will be the next President. Poor devils, they are in a miserable condition. I have sent in my resignation, and adhere to it, though Bancroft requested me to take it back." On the 20th, he wrote Longfellow that he was still detained at his post: "Bancroft represented to me that by resigning before the close of the year, I should make him a great deal of trouble; and so my good nature was wrought upon to hold the office a while longer."

By the end of the month, he had clearly determined to commit

himself to the Brook Farm experiment, but with his usual cir-
cumspection he intended to try it out before subjecting Sophia to
the vagaries of communal living. Writing to her from Salem on
November 27, he mentioned that he had planned to visit Miss Burley's that evening, but that he heard the elderly hostess was in Boston. "Perhaps thou wilt see her there. I wonder if she will not come
and settle with us in Mr. Ripley's Utopia. And this reminds me to
ask whether thou hast drawn those caricatures — especially the one
of thy husband, staggering, and puffing, and toiling onward to the
gate of the farm, burthened with the unsaleable remnant of Grandfather's Chair. Dear me, what a ponderous leaden load it will be."

His escape from the Custom House, from politics and politicians — whose consciences, he once told Sophia, could stretch like
India rubber — was not without its embarrassments. A somewhat
belligerent letter to George Bancroft, in which he once more insisted
on his resignation, indicates that he had had a disagreement over
his salary. Although, in his letter to Longfellow, Hawthorne suggested that his duties were "nominal" and his salary as well, he
evidently claimed — and received — his whole year's salary. Both
Bancroft and the Custom House paymaster, a Mr. Frothingham,
were evidently annoyed. Writing to Bancroft on January 8, Hawthorne regretted that his actions should have caused the collector
"any disturbance or displeasure." He explained, "As I had received
no more than the amount legally due me, and as it came to me
through the regular channel, and was obtained by no deception on
my part — and, moreover, as I was willing that the correctness of
my position should be tested by law — it struck me as a very singular proposition that I was bound in honor to pay back any part of
the money, or to serve a longer term for what was already my own."
His next sentence coolly suggested that he had the collector over a
barrel and knew it, for Bancroft clearly did not want a public airing
of the case. Hawthorne, in fact, was astonishingly cheeky: "Still, I
felt myself under a moral obligation, arising from your past kindness, not to do what you seemed to suppose might compromise you
with the Secretary or the public."

Hawthorne was not disposed to let the matter go at that. "I understand that Mr. Frothingham considers himself much aggrieved by
my conduct — but surely without reason," he added, "for it never
occurred to me that he would take the responsibility of paying large
sums of money without your knowledge, or against your positive orders. Nor, in making up my mind on the course to be pursued, did I
once think of Mr. Frothingham, any more than of the desk on which
he counted out the money. I trust, therefore, that he will revise his

opinion (not expressed to myself, but whispered to others) as to the dishonorableness of my proceedings."

On his periodic visits to Salem, now, Hawthorne felt the full weight of his dissatisfaction with his earlier, solitary life. In mid March, writing to Sophia from his native town, he spoke of it as a place of banishment. "Methinks all enormous sinners should be sent on pilgrimage to Salem," he told her, "and compelled to spend a length of time there, proportioned to the enormity of their offenses. Such a punishment would be suited to sinners that do not quite deserve hanging, yet are too aggravated for the States-Prison."

Unlike Emerson, who saw Brook Farm as the exchange of one prison for another, Hawthorne, with less insight perhaps, thought of it as an escape.

ᴄ⁊ V ᴄ⁊

"Here is thy poor husband in a polar Paradise!" Hawthorne wrote Sophia on April 13, the day after his arrival at Brook Farm. He had had a cold journey, traveling by stage from Boston. It had been a day of lead-gray skies; snow had begun to fall in the morning. By the time he reached West Roxbury, the drifts were piled high. He trudged up the slope of the hill to the isolated farmhouse on the Dedham-Watertown Road. There was, fortunately, a hearty blaze in the kitchen fireplace. "I know not how to interpret this aspect of nature," he told Sophia; "whether it be of good or evil omen . . . Through faith, I persist in believing that spring and summer will come in their due season; but the unregenerated man shivers within me."

However polar in appearance, the precincts of Brook Farm were a good deal more ordinary. The farmhouse, promptly christened the Hive, and its outbuildings provided the only accommodations when Hawthorne first arrived. In time, other buildings were erected to house the growing community, which, during Hawthorne's brief stay, expanded to include some fifty members, including boarders and children. The Association, which had not been legally formed when the core of original members gathered at the farm in April, had also leased a house on the opposite side of the road to serve as a school; this proved to be the most economically successful venture of the enterprise.

A small group was on hand when Hawthorne arrived: Ripley, his wife and sister, Mrs. Minot Pratt and her three children (her husband, a printer, joined them later), and the gentle, fussing George P. Bradford, a classmate of Emerson's at Harvard, with whom Hawthorne struck up an easy and immediate friendship. Most of the early family, which numbered some twenty members, had settled in two weeks before, and living accommodations were already cramped. The farmhouse parlor served as the communal dining room and sitting room, with the kitchen behind it. On the opposite side of the downstairs hall was the apartment of Almira Barlow, a vivacious young matron recently separated from her husband. She and her three sons were boarders. The upper rooms were set aside as sleeping quarters.

Within a very short time, it was necessary to add two wings to the structure to accommodate such necessities as a laundry and a separate parlor and sitting room. George Ripley's extensive library, which was intended to serve partially in lieu of his investment in shares, was arranged on shelves in the wide hallway. In the new construction, a large upstairs room was outfitted as a men's dormitory and promptly dubbed Attica. A day nursery was initiated; there, mothers could leave their children while tending to their chores. During the first months of Hawthorne's residence, the men worked in the fields, the women took charge of the household duties. Later, there was to be a more complex division of labor.

In an early burst of enthusiasm, Hawthorne, writing to his sisters, signed himself "Nathaniel Hawthorne, Ploughman." He found the daily regimen highly satisfactory. "The whole fraternity eat together," he told his family, "and such a delectable way of life has never been seen on earth, since the days of the early Christians. We get up at half-past four, breakfast at half-past six, dine at half-past twelve, and go to bed at nine." To Sophia, he wrote roguishly of his initiation into farming. "Belovedest, I have not yet taken my first lesson in agriculture, as thou mayest well suppose — except that I went to see our cows foddered, yesterday afternoon. We have eight of our own; and the number is now increased by a transcendental heifer belonging to Miss Margaret Fuller. She is very fractious, and apt to kick over the milk pail. Thou knowest best, whether in these traits of character she resembles her mistress." He felt some amusement in twitting Sophia about her enthusiasm for the bluestocking writer and reformer, who had, like Emerson, decided against joining the venture. Hawthorne referred to West Street and Margaret's conversations, which Sophia was attending, as the "Babel of talkers." He even went so far as to wish that "Miss Margaret Fuller might lose her tongue! — or my Dove her ears, and so be left wholly to her husband's golden silence."

In his first letter, he noted for Sophia's amusement, "Thy husband intends to convert himself into a milk-maid, this evening; but I pray heaven that Mr. Ripley may be moved to assign him the kindliest cow in the herd — otherwise he will perform his duty with fear and trembling." On the following day, April 14, he conceded that he had not, after all, milked any cows, because "Mr. Ripley was afraid to trust them to my hands, or me to their horns, — I know not which." And he added, "But this morning, I have done wonders. Before breakfast, I went out to the barn, and began to chop hay for the cattle; and with such 'righteous vengeance' (as Mr. Ripley says) did I labor, that in the space of ten minutes, I broke the machine. Then I brought wood and replenished the fires; and finally sat down to breakfast and ate up a huge mound of buckwheat cakes."

Mr. Ripley, he went on, then "put a four-pronged instrument into my hands, which he gave me to understand was called a pitch-fork; and he and Mr. Farley being armed with similar weapons, we all commenced a gallant attack upon a heap of manure." The manure pile, which Hawthorne ever after referred to as the "gold mine," became a constant refrain in his letters. Among the several failings of the community was the choice of the site itself; for though the verdant green pastures of Brook Farm had evoked the admiration of Ripley and his wife, they were suitable chiefly for pasturage and dairy farming. The rich topsoil was only a few inches deep; below that was gravel, unsuited for the subsistence farming the community was planned for. Tons of costly fertilizer had to be bought and supplemented with muck, laboriously dug from the marshy river in dry seasons. After a morning's encounter with the manure pile, Hawthorne confessed he would not let Sophia come "within a half mile" of him. Still, he boasted, "I shall make an excellent husbandman. I feel the original Adam reviving in me."

Four days later, he wrote, "Thy husband has milked a cow!!!" He went on to add further details about Margaret Fuller's heifer, which, having been ostracized by the herd, clung to him for protection. In order to get rid of her, he had to give her two or three gentle pats with a shovel. "She is not an amiable cow; but she has a very intelligent face, and seems to be of a reflective cast of character. I doubt not that she will soon perceive the expediency of being on good terms with the rest of the sisterhood."

The daily work was strenuous and unremitting, and he had to admit that since his arrival, he had been no farther than twenty yards from the house and barn. "But I begin to perceive that this is a beautiful place. The scenery is of a mild and placid character . . . There is a brook so near the house, that we shall be able to hear its ripple in the summer evenings; and whenever we lie awake in the summer nights."

At first, he enjoyed the physical exertion; he preferred working out of doors and complained when his chores kept him close to the house. But the weather at the end of April turned dreary, and he came down with a cold serious enough to keep him bedridden for several days. His brain, he said, was "in a thick fog" and his head seemed "stuffed with coarse wool." The family, he reported, "has been dismal and dolorous throughout the storm." A colony of wasps had wintered over in his room and were beginning to stir, "doubtless with the intention of stinging me from head to foot." He had a sense of being a thousand miles distant from the world. "I read no newspapers," he wrote her, "and hardly remember who is President; and feel as if I had no more concern with what other people trouble themselves about, than if I dwelt in another planet."

By May 4, he had recuperated: "All this morning I have been at work under the clear blue sky, on a hillside. Sometimes it almost seemed as if I were at work in the sky itself; though the material in which I wrought was the ore from our gold mine." The farm was growing more and more beautiful, he wrote, and the hills were turning green. The parlor was "dressed in evergreen, as at Christmas." At night there was sometimes music in the parlor, and, inevitably, discussion. "We had some tableaux last evening," he wrote, "the principal characters being sustained by Mr. Farley and Miss Ellen Slade. They went off very well."

Sophia, who paid a brief visit to Brook Farm in late May, was incorrigibly enthusiastic, though she cautioned her "husband" not to work too hard. "My life," she wrote him in one of her rare surviving love letters, "— how beautiful is Brook Farm! I was enchanted with it and it far surpassed my expectations. Most joyfully could I dwell there for its own beauty's sake." In a postscript, written on the following day, May 31, she burst out in a full declaration of love: "Every thought I seize seems of no value if I cannot share it with thee. Every deed is indifferent which cannot meet thy sympathy. Thou art literally my All-the-World . . . It is astonishing how much more I love thee every day."

In June, with work on the manure pile still continuing, Hawthorne's letters registered some complaints: "I think this present life of mine gives me an antipathy to pen and ink, even more than my Custom-House experience did . . . After a hard day's work in the gold mine, my soul obstinately refuses to be poured out on paper. That abominable gold-mine! Thank God, we anticipate getting rid of its treasures in the course of two or three days! . . . It is my opinion . . . that a man's soul may be buried and perish under a dung-heap, or in a furrow of the field, just as well as under a pile of money."

In Salem, Hawthorne's sisters waited impatiently for a visit from their brother. When he failed to come in May, Louisa scolded, "If you only knew how we anticipated your coming home, and how impatient we are when you do not come at the usual time, you would not think you could be spared."

During the previous winter, Hawthorne had had his portrait painted by the Salem artist Charles Osgood; it was a highly flattering picture — a handsome young man in his prime, wearing a wing collar and black cravat, posed against a rich brown backdrop. The hair dark and tousled, the forehead broad, the eyes vivid with expression; yet somehow Osgood, either through a trick of the light or for effect, had painted the eyes brown instead of Hawthorne's striking gray-blue. The lips had just a trace of a smile, but were perhaps too full, too feminine, too rosy. Hawthorne had the portrait sent to his family; he told them that since they had the likeness, they might "very well dispense with the original."

His mother thought the portrait "perfect"; Ebe found it "excellent." Louisa suggested that the color was "too high . . . But perhaps it is a modest blush at the compliments which are paid you to your face." She made it plain, however, that it was not a satisfactory substitution for a visit. "It is a comfort to look at the picture, to be sure; but I am tempted to speak to it sometimes, and it answers never a word; and when mother looks at it, she takes up a lamentation because you stay away so long and work so hard."

In June, when Hawthorne failed to make another promised visit, Louisa became testy: "I had not written before, because we had been looking for you every day, and we do most seriously object to your staying away from home so long. Do you know that it was nine weeks last Tuesday since you left home? — a great deal too long." It was clear that his family thought the Brook Farm adventure unnecessary. "I am sure it cannot be [good] for your health to work from half-past four till seven," Louisa wrote, "and I cannot bear to think that this hot sun is beating upon your head . . . What is the use of burning your brains out in the sun, when you can do anything better with them? Ebe says she thought you were only to work three hours a day for your board, and she cannot understand your keeping at it all day." In a softened mood, Louisa threatened to pay a visit to Brook Farm; she wanted to get out into the country and ramble in the woods, and she expected Hawthorne might accompany her. "I am bent upon coming up to see you this summer," she informed him. "Do not you remember how you and I used to go a-fishing together in Raymond? Your mention of wild-flowers and pickerel has given me a longing for the woods and waters again." Louisa fretted, too, about the state of his clothing. His mother was sewing buttons on his thin pantaloons; he had not mentioned whether he needed more working shirts. "Mother apostrophizes your picture," she said, "because you do not come home." Late in June — perhaps to forestall a visit from Louisa, as well as to soothe family feelings — Hawthorne made a hurried visit to Salem.

By August, however, he was once again negligent. Louisa wrote him in an adamant tone. "I have waited for a letter from you till I am tired and cannot wait any longer," she complained on August 3. "I have been to the post-office and received the same answer so often that I am ashamed to go any more. What do you mean by such conduct, neither coming or writing to us. It is six weeks today since you left us, and in all that time we have heard nothing from you except when Uncle Robert saw you in Boston . . . We do not like it at all . . . Mother is very vehement about it." Hawthorne was finding it difficult to escape from the posessiveness of his sisters. It was one more reason that he delayed informing his family about his engagement.

Hawthorne was feeling guilty about his neglect of his family and confessed as much in a letter to Sophia written on August 22. He noted that he had received Louisa's letter "scolding me most pathetically for my long absence. Indeed, I have been rather naughty in this respect; but I knew that it would be unsatisfactory to them and myself, if I came only for a single day." He was planning to spend the next weekend in Boston with Sophia, and then the week after in Salem — "longer or shorter according to the intensity of the occasion for my presence." Perhaps he was feeling all the more guilty, since, in late July, he may have spent a week or two at the seashore with his fellow Brook Farmer Frank Farley, who was suffering from a severe mental depression. Both George Ripley and Farley had requested that Hawthorne accompany him. The trip was evidently unsuccessful; in his August 22 letter, Hawthorne reported that Farley had left the community. "He was quite out of his wits, the night before," Hawthorne told Sophia, "and thy husband sat up with him till long past midnight. The farm is pleasanter now that he is gone; for his unappeasable wretchedness threw a gloom over everything."

In the same letter, Hawthorne expressed his growing doubts about Brook Farm as the hoped-for setting of their honeymoon. Although the farmers had been in residence since spring, the deeding of the property was still hanging fire, and it appeared doubtful that Ripley would come to a settlement with the owner. Nor did he think that Ripley and the Association would muster enough capital to make the operation functional. "Thou and I must form other plans for ourselves," he told Sophia, "for I can see few or no signs that Providence purposes to give us a home here. I am weary, weary, thrice weary of waiting so many ages." He doubted that he would remain through the winter "unless with an absolute certainty that there will be a home ready for us in the spring. Otherwise, I shall return to Boston — still, however, considering myself an associate of the community; so that we may take advantage of any more favorable aspect of affairs."

More than a week later, writing from Salem, Hawthorne mentioned that his life in West Roxbury now seemed eerily distant: "I should judge it to be twenty years since I left Brook Farm; and I take this to be one proof that my life there was an unnatural and unsuitable, and therefore an unreal one. It already looks like a dream behind me." But he felt equally displaced in Salem. "I have been out only once, in the daytime, since my arrival," he wrote. "How immediately and irrecoverably (if thou didst not keep me out of the abyss) should I relapse into the way of life in which I spent my youth! . . . The sunshine would never fall on me, no more than on a ghost."

Hawthorne was never a man to underestimate the burdens of the personal past; he understood the insidious tenacity of old habits, old moods. In the cloistered atmosphere of the family household, he acknowledged his wholehearted dependence on Sophia. It was more than gallantry that caused him to write: "If, in the interval since I quitted this lonely old chamber, I had found no woman (and thou was the only possible one) to impart reality and significance to life, I should have come back hither ere now, with the feeling that all was a dream and a mockery. Dost thou rejoice that thou has saved me from such a fate?"

He was trying to resume his literary career. With the exception of his children's stories, he had published little since 1839. Only a single tale, "John Inglefield's Thanksgiving," had appeared in the *Democratic Review*; as he confessed to O'Sullivan, he no longer considered himself a literary man. He was forced to make the same admission to George Hillard, who had asked for a contribution to *The Token*, which he was then editing. Hawthorne wrote the Boston lawyer from Brook Farm on July 16, "I have not written that infernal story. The thought of it has tormented me ever since I came here." He regretted the failure, but asked, "What could be done? An engagement to write a story must in its nature be conditional; because stories grow like vegetables, and are not manufactured like a pine table. My former stories sprung up of their own accord, out of a quiet life. Now, I have no quiet at all."

He had other projects in mind, however. Throughout the summer of 1841, he was negotiating with James Munroe, a Boston publisher, about editing a series of volumes, a library of foreign and American authors, that the firm planned to issue. Hawthorne, at the time, thought it a plausible opportunity. Then, too, he was pushing for a new edition of his children's stories, the *Grandfather's Chair* sequence, with, perhaps, an additional volume of biographical sketches. The plan was to have the new edition illustrated with Sophia's drawings. Since the future of Brook Farm did not appear promising, he was counting on his publishing ventures. "I confess that I have strong hopes of good from this arrangement with Munroe," he wrote Sophia from the farm, "but when I look at the scanty avails of my past literary efforts, I do not feel authorized to expect much from the future. Well; we shall see. Other persons have bought large estates and built mansions with such little books as I mean to write; so perhaps, it is not unreasonable to hope that mine may enable me to build a little cottage — or, at least, to buy or hire one . . . Dearest, how much depends on these little books!"

Sophia, however, had heard poor reports about Munroe and wrote him with some concern. Hawthorne, in Salem, responded on September 10, trying to calm her fears. He could not believe the stories about Munroe, he told her, "because such an abominable rascal never would be sustained and countenanced by respectable men. I take him to be neither better nor worse than the average of his tribe. However, I intend to have all my copyrights taken out in my own name."

Sophia and her judgments had begun to assume a particular importance to his work and his professional plans. From Salem, he wrote her with detailed suggestions for the illustrations: Governor Shirley, seated in the "great chair," receiving the Acadian exiles; Cotton Mather, "venerable in a three-cornered hat and other antique attire, walking the streets of Boston, and lifting up his hands to bless the people, while they all revile him." It is not clear whether Hawthorne had then decided to bring out an expanded edition of his *Twice-told Tales*, one that would include the stories and sketches he had written since the 1837 volume. But he had already begun to send copies of the later stories to Sophia for consideration. Moreover, he had written her earlier, "I doubt whether I shall write any more for the public, till I can have a daily or nightly opportunity of submitting my productions to the criticism of Sophie Hawthorne. I have a high opinion of that young lady's critical acumen, but a great dread of her severity." When Sophia expressed some doubts about three of his tales, Hawthorne responded in an amiable manner. "Sweetest," he wrote her from Salem on September 10, "thou dost please me much by criticizing thy husband's stories, and finding fault with them. I do not very well recollect Monsieur du Miroir, but as to Mrs. Bullfrog, I give her up to the severest reprehension. The story was written as a mere experiment in that style . . . I recollect that the Man of Adamant seemed a fine idea to me . . . but I failed in giving shape and substance to the vision which I saw. I don't think it can be very good." It is some indication of Hawthorne's growing deference to Sophia's judgment that he did not include any of the stories in the new edition of *Twice-told Tales*. Since Sophia's letter has not survived, it is difficult to determine the basis of her criticism of "Monsieur du Miroir." She may have objected to the autobiographical elements woven into the story; perhaps she felt the reference to the narrator's appearance in a "pot-house" was not genteel. "Mrs. Bullfrog" is a cleverly written but stale joke about marriage, involving a "very lady-like sort of gentleman" who is overly fussy and fastidious. On his wedding trip, the coach overturns and he discovers that his bride's glossy ringlets are a wig and her flashing teeth are false. "The Man of Adamant" is a dour, somewhat banal allegory about a man who quits society and lives in a cave. His hardness of heart is improbably symbolized when he becomes a petrified monument that survives the ages and is discovered by a group of children. Sophia's objections to both stories may well have been on grounds of quality.

Back at Brook Farm by September 22, Hawthorne was dissatisfied; even the weather, he wrote Sophia, had conspired against him — "cold, chill, sullen, so that it is impossible to be on friendly terms with Mother Nature." He was adapting himself to the "queer community," but no longer as a laborer, merely as a boarder. Even so, with time on his hands, he did not find the atmosphere congenial for work. "I doubt whether I shall succeed in writing another volume of Grandfather's Library while I remain at the farm," he wrote. "I have not the sense of perfect seclusion, which has always been essential to my power of producing anything." He was philosophic: "Perhaps it will be quite as well that I find myself unable to set about literary occupation for the present . . . Meantime, I shall see these people and their enterprise under a new point of view, and perhaps be able to determine whether thou and I have any call to cast in our lot among them."

Sophia was still distrustful of Munroe; Hawthorne, in a lengthy letter written on September 27, countered with his own feelings of confidence: "I am not, nor shall be, in the least degree in his power . . . He might announce his projected library, with me for the editor, in all the newspapers in the universe; but still I could not be bound to become the editor, unless by my own act . . . My dearest, instead of getting me within his power by this delay, he has trusted to my ignorance and simplicity, and has put *himself* in *my* power. Show the contrary, if thou canst."

When the weather brightened he took long walks, enjoyed the countryside, found harvests of wild grapes. He was still of two minds about living in the community. "Didst thou know what treasures of wild grapes there are in this land?" he wrote Sophia. "If we dwell here, we will make our own wine." His ambivalence made his position even more awkward, when, a short time later, he was made a trustee of the Association. "From the nature of my office," he wrote Sophia, "I shall have the chief direction of all the money affairs of the community, the making of bargains, the supervision of receipts and expenditures etc. etc. etc." Given the tentative nature of his own plans, it was an important office. As if to emphasize his decisiveness, he told Sophia firmly, "My accession to these august offices does not at all decide the question of my remaining here permanently. I told Mr. Ripley that I could not spend the winter at the farm, and that it was quite uncertain whether I returned in the spring."

Meanwhile, he was disturbed by Sophia's having expressed an interest in the new vogue of mesmerism, or "animal magnetism," as it was called. Lizzie Peabody was convinced that if Sophia submitted to being hypnotized, she might be cured of her headaches. Hawthorne's response was unusually sharp and, at the same time, pleading. He begged her to take no part in such experiments. "I am unwilling that a power should be exercised on thee, of which we know neither the origin nor the consequence . . ." He asked, "Supposing that the power arises from the transfusion of one spirit into another, it seems to me that the sacredness of an individual is violated by it; there would be an intrusion into the holy of holies — and the intruder would not be thy husband!" He seemed to see such practices as almost a kind of sexual violation. It was not that he was a skeptical scientist who disbelieved in mesmerism or the more common fad for séances and spirit-rappings. "The view which I take of this matter," he told Sophia, "is caused by no want of faith in mysteries; but from a deep reverence of the soul, and of the mysteries which it knows within itself." His letter was apparently effective; Sophia did not worry him with reports of miraculous cures through mesmerism.

As a mere observer of the community, now, Hawthorne recorded his daily activities. He lent a hand with harvesting the potatoes and gathering in the apples. He noted a new arrival, a young seamstress from Boston, half-girl and half-woman, who obviously intrigued him: "If she were larger than she is, and of less pleasing aspect, I think she might be intolerable; but being so small, and with a white skin, healthy as a wild flower, she is really very agreeable . . . On continued observation and acquaintance, you discover that she is not a little girl, but really a little woman, with all the prerogatives and liabilities of a woman."

The little seamstress was to serve him later; she was the original of Priscilla in *The Blithedale Romance*. His journal account of her is not entirely laudatory; he appreciated the sunniness of her disposition; but, somewhat disappointedly, he realized "her intellect is very ordinary, and she never says anything worth hearing."

On a bright day late in September the entire community suspended work for a picnic and costume party, held in honor of six-year-old Frank Dana's birthday. In a clearing in the woods, Hawthorne and George Bradford came upon a wild dance of a Swiss girl, an Indian squaw, a Jim Crow Negro, and one or two foresters. Then, like sobering presences, Emerson and Margaret Fuller wandered into the glade. The four adults sat down for a lengthy discussion in the midst of the wild revels and childish antics. Emerson may have been referring to the episode in an undated entry in his journal: "Margaret Fuller talked of ballads, and our love for them; strange that we should so value the wild man, the Ishmaelite . . . and yet every step we take, everything we do, is to tame him . . . Margaret does not think, she says, in the woods, only 'finds herself expressed.' " A mild enough record of a pleasant afternoon.

But the scene had struck Hawthorne forcefully: "It has left a fantastic impression on my memory, this intermingling of wild and fabulous characters with real and homely ones, in the secluded nook of the woods. I remember them with the sunlight breaking through the overshadowing branches, and they appearing and disappearing confusedly — perhaps starting out of the earth, as if the every day laws of Nature were suspended."

During his last month at Brook Farm — for he planned to leave by November — Hawthorne recorded in precise detail his country walks along thoroughfares and untraveled roads. Autumn lay over the countryside — a yellow blaze of maples and the dark brown of oaks. China asters were in bloom along the roadsides; the sweet fern was turning russet. "The cawing of the crow resounds among the woods, at this season," he noted. "A sentinel is aware of your approach a great way off, and gives the alarm . . ." He stood in an upland pasture, staring off toward Cow Island; light glanced off the meandering Charles River. Flocks of birds descended upon the meadows in sudden flurries of excitement; in brooks and pools, shoals of small fish darted about restlessly. The mood of autumn clung to him, a sense of fruitfulness and of finalities. "Passing an orchard," he noted, "you hear an uneasy rustling in the trees, not as if they were struggling with the wind. Scattered about, are barrels to contain the apples, and perhaps a great heap of golden or scarlet apples is collected in one place."

On October 27, he set down a final entry: "Fringed gentians — found the last, probably, that will be seen this year, growing on the margin of the brook."

꒰ VI ꒱

Throughout the fall and winter of 1841–1842, Hawthorne continued to be busy with publishing projects, shuttling back and forth between Boston and Salem. Munroe did not, after all, reissue his children's stories. But on October 11, Hawthorne signed a contract with the firm for a two-volume edition of *Twice-told Tales*, which included twenty-one more sketches than had appeared in the 1837 edition. The terms of the agreement allowed for an edition of 1500 copies (though only 1000 copies were published in December), with royalties of 10 percent on the $2.25 price of the set. Hawthorne decided against editing Munroe's proposed library of foreign and American authors.

The three volumes of his children's stories, plus a fourth, *Biographical Stories for Children*, which he evidently wrote after his departure from Brook Farm, were published by Tappan & Dennet, with Sophia's illustrations, early in the new year. The negotiations resulted in what Lizzie Peabody later described as "a very temporary quarrel" between herself and her future brother-in-law, brought on by the fact that she "did not want to take any percentage on Grandfather's Chair." But the quarrel quite obviously had lasted longer than Lizzie remembered. In June 1841, Hawthorne was communicating with her in formal, third-person terms: "Mr. Hawthorne particularly desires that the bargain with Mr. Munroe, in respect to the remaining copies of Grandfather's Chair etc. may be concluded on such terms as Miss Peabody thinks best, without further reference to himself." As late as February 1842, he was still writing her in the same manner regarding transactions with Tappan & Dennet. On February 19, he wrote Lizzie, "If Mr. Hawthorne had felt himself solely, or chiefly, interested, he would have advised the sale of the first edition of those books, long since, at any price that could have been obtained for them. But, as he hoped that Miss Peabody would see the justice to both parties, of taking to herself the publisher's share of the profits, he did not feel himself authorized to speak so strongly as he otherwise might. He *now* recommends that they should be got rid of on *any* terms."

The unusual spate of publication succeeded in bringing Hawthorne's name before the public after a lapse of three years. The *Grandfather's Chair* series received appreciative notices in *Godey's Lady's Book and Magazine*, and the London *Athenaeum*. The reviews of *Twice-told Tales*, published in December, were distinctly favorable, though many of them harked back to the image of the reticent author of the earlier collection. Nathan Hale, Jr., in the *Boston Miscellany*, stressed the quiet, meditative temperament of the writer and called the stories "unique in their form and language." Longfellow, in the April issue of the *North American Review*, echoed his earlier praise. But once again he emphasized the sensibility of the author and the delicacy of his touch. Hawthorne's genius, Longfellow stated, "is characterized by a large proportion of feminine elements, depth and tenderness of feeling, exceeding purity of mind." Orestes Brownson in his own periodical, the *Boston Quarterly Review*, discovered in Hawthorne's writings "a pure and living stream of manly thought and feeling, which characterizes always the true man, the Christian, the republican and the patriot" — all of which were ideals Brownson heartily espoused. But Hawthorne, he contended, owed his country something more; he ought to "attempt a higher and bolder strain than he has thus far done."

Only Edgar Allan Poe, discussing the tales in a lengthy, two-part critique in the April and May issues of *Graham's Magazine*, saw Hawthorne from a different angle, praising his innovative qualities rather than his sensibility. "His *originality*," Poe remarked, "both of incident and of reflection is very remarkable; and this trait alone would ensure him at least *our* warmest regard and commendation." He said further, "Mr. Hawthorne's distinctive trait is invention, creation, imagination, originality — a trait which, in the literature of fiction, is positively worth all the rest . . . Mr. Hawthorne is original at *all* points." Part of Poe's generosity may have been prompted by his having discovered that Hawthorne's reputation was not being touted by "one of the impudent *cliques* which beset our literature." As a critic of American culture — and one with increasingly paranoid obsessions — he was preparing to expose such cliques "at the earliest opportunity."

The stories that Poe singled out for praise — "The Hollow of the Three Hills," "The Minister's Black Veil," "Fancy's Show Box," "The Wedding-Knell" — interestingly enough, were stories of darker intention than the more popular sketches; all of them were complementary with Poe's own tastes as a tale-writer. It is quite probable that Poe's generosity, at the moment, was determined by the fact that he did not consider Hawthorne an immediate threat as a rival.

Unfortunately for Hawthorne, the sales of the new edition were dismally disappointing. A year later, when he asked George Hillard to inquire about the status of the book from Munroe, he complained, "Surely the book was puffed enough to meet with a sale. What the devil is the matter?" Much to his chagrin, he learned that Munroe still had 600 copies on hand. The book had not even sold well enough to cover the costs of publication. Two years later, considering a proposition for buying up the edition, he was even more abrupt. "I wish the devil had the books," he said, "— for I suppose he is a member of the 'Trade.'"

With a woman's instinct, quite early in their engagement Sophia had raised the issue of informing Hawthorne's mother and sisters. Hawthorne then had begged the question; he was reluctant to tell his family. He preferred to leave the matter to Sophia's "exquisite sense of what is right and delicate." In June 1840, he promised, "We will talk it over at an early opportunity. I think I can partly understand why they appear cool towards thee; but it is for nothing in thy self personally, nor from any unkindness towards my Dove . . . But there are some untoward circumstances. Nevertheless, I have faith that all will be well, and that they will receive Sophie Hawthorne into their heart of hearts; so let us wait patiently on Providence."

But as late as February 1842, he was still stalling. He explained that there was a kind of "strange reserve" among the various members of the family with regard to emotional matters. "We are conscious of one another's feelings, always; but there seems to be a tacit law, that our deepest heart-concernments are not to be spoken of. I cannot gush out in their presence — I cannot take my heart in my hand, and show it to them."

Now that their plans had been formed — they had set a date for the end of June and had found a house — the issue of telling Hawthorne's family became imperative. It was not until May, on a visit to Salem, that he informed his sisters. Even then, he deferred breaking the news to his mother. Ebe's letter of congratulations to Sophia, written on May 23, read more like an indictment. The "approaching union" Ebe wrote, made it "incumbent upon me to offer you the assurances of my sincere desire for your mutual happiness. With regard to my sister and myself, I hope nothing will ever occur to render your future intercourse with us other than agreeable, particularly as it need not be so frequent or so close as to require more than reciprocal good will, if we do not happen to suit each other in our new relationship." With blunt candor, Ebe added:

I write thus plainly, because my brother has desired me to say only what was true; though I do not recognize his right to speak of truth, after keeping us so long in ignorance of this affair. But I believe him when he says that this was not in accordance with your wishes, for such a concealment must naturally be unpleasant, and besides, what I know of your amiable disposition convinces me that you would not give us unnecessary pain. It was especially due to my mother that she should long ago have been made acquainted with the engagement of her only son; it is much more difficult to inform her of it at this late period.

Hawthorne's announcement to his sisters had been followed by a gracious letter from Sophia. Hawthorne wrote her about it: "Dearest Heart, Thy letter to my sisters was most beautiful — sweet, gentle and magnanimous . . . If they do not love thee, it will be because they have no hearts to love with." He added, "Three evenings without a glimpse of thee! And I know not whether I am to come at six or seven o'clock tomorrow evening — or scarcely, indeed, whether I am to come at all . . . I met Mr. Emerson at the Athenaeum yesterday. He tells me our garden etc., makes fine progress. Would that we were there."

The house that they would be moving to, an old parsonage in Concord that stood near the North Bridge over the Concord River, had been suggested by Emerson and Elizabeth Hoar. Emerson was thoroughly acquainted with the place; it had been built for his grandfather, the Reverend William Emerson, and later occupied by his step-grandfather, the Reverend Ezra Ripley. Emerson had played there as a child; much later, in the upstairs study, he had written his book *Nature*. In September 1841, Ezra Ripley had died at the age of ninety — an old and doomed oak whose fall made "some sensation in the forest," Emerson recorded in his journal. The house had become vacant. As a gesture of friendship, Emerson had his young protégé and boarder, Henry David Thoreau, plant a vegetable garden for the expected newlyweds.

In the meantime, Sophia informed her friends, among them Margaret Fuller, about the forthcoming marriage. "We shall be married in June, the month of roses and of perfect bloom," Sophia wrote Margaret on May 11. She also informed her of their decision to live in Concord, adding, "Mr. Hawthorne, last evening, in the midst of his emotions so deep and absorbing, after deciding, said that Margaret can now, when she visits Mr. Emerson, spend part of the time with us." Margaret's response was full of generous praise. "If ever I saw a man," she answered on June 4, "who combined delicate tenderness to understand the heart of a woman, with quiet depth and manliness enough to satisfy her, it is Mr. Hawthorne." She was visiting in Concord and wished that the wedding couple could have enjoyed the glorious early June days there. "The whole earth is decked for a bridal," she said.

It was not until early June that Hawthorne finally informed his mother. His delay, it seemed, had been unnecessary. He wrote Sophia on June 9:

> Scarcely had I arrived here, when our mother came out of her chamber, looking better and more cheerful than I have seen her this some time, and enquired about the health and well being of my Dove . . . Foolish me, to doubt that my mother's love would be wise, like all other genuine love. And foolish again, to have doubted my Dove's instinct . . . It seems that our mother had seen how things were, a long time ago. At first her heart was troubled, because she knew that much of outward as well as inward fitness was requisite to secure thy foolish husband's peace . . . My sisters, too, begin to sympathize as they ought; and all is well.

For some time now, his letters to Sophia registered his growing impatience and his growing ardor. He could no longer be satisfied with "holy kisses." His letters hinted — tactfully, but with a definite sexual undercurrent — at other demands. "We have left expression — at least such expression as can be achieved with pen and ink — far behind us," he told her. "Even the spoken word has long been inadequate. Looks — pressures of the lips and hands — the touch of bosom to bosom — these are a better language; but bye-and-bye, our spirits will demand some more adequate expression even than these."

Yet, as the day of their marriage drew near, Hawthorne felt — or suspected — some final reluctance in Sophia.

> Thou hast not been out of my mind a moment since I saw thee last [he wrote her on June 20] — and never wilt thou be, so long as we exist. Canst thou say as much? Dearest, dost thou know that there are but ten days more in this blessed month of June? And dost thou remember what is to happen within those ten days? Poor little Dove. Now dost thou tremble and shrink back, and beginnest to fear that thou hast acted too rashly in this matter . . . Ah, foolish virgin. It is too late; nothing can part us now . . . Year by year thou must come closer and closer to me; and a thousand ages hence, we shall be only in the honeymoon of our marriage . . . Sweetest wife, I cannot write to thee. The time for that species of communication is past.

Hawthorne's suspicions were correct. Sophia suffered a mild relapse and a return of her headaches. Mary Peabody informed him that their wedding would have to be postponed for a week. Hawthorne wrote Sophia, his disappointment clear, but he tried to be reassuring:

> I had hoped, as thou knowest, for an earlier day; but I cannot help feeling that Mary is on the safe and reasonable side. Shouldst thou feel that this postponement is advisable, thou wilt find me patient beyond what thou thinkest me capable of. I will even be happy if thou wilt only keep thy mind and heart at peace . . . My ownest, if it will at all reconcile thee to the postponement of the ceremony, I will go to Concord tomorrow or next day, and see about our affairs there . . .
>
> P.S. I enclose an order for a case of wine, which is to be given to the baggage-wagoner, when he comes for the furniture. He can present it and receive the case.
>
> P.S. 2nd. I love thee! I love thee! I love thee!
>
> P.S. 3rd. Dost thou love me at all?

On July 8, Hawthorne sent a brief note to the Reverend James Freeman Clarke: "My Dear Sir: Though personally a stranger to you, I am about to request of you the greatest favor which I can receive of any man. I am to be married to Miss Sophia Peabody tomorrow; and it is our mutual desire that you should perform the ceremony. Unless it should be a decidedly rainy day, a carriage will call for you at half past eleven o'clock in the forenoon. Very respectfully yours, Nathaniel Hawthorne."

July 9, after several days of clouds and rain, was promising. At the appointed time, the sun was shining into the Peabody parlor on West Street. The ceremony was a simple one, with only the family and a few friends in attendance, among them Sarah Clarke, Sophia's artist-friend, and the sister of the minister. Hawthorne's sisters did not attend. Directly after the ceremony, the bride and groom left for Concord in a carriage.

From Concord, Sophia wrote her mother reassuringly: "Dear, dear Mother, Every step the horses took, I felt better and not in the least tired. I was not tired at the tavern and not tired when I arrived. My husband looked upon me as upon a mirage which would suddenly disappear. It seemed miraculous that I was so well."

Hawthorne sent a brief message to his family. Even on this occasion, he could not quite dismiss the association of death and marriage that seemed a part of his imaginative inheritance. "The execution took place yesterday," he wrote Louisa. "We made a Christian end, and came straight to Paradise, where we abide at this present writing. We are as happy as people can be, without making themselves ridiculous, and might be even happier; but, as a matter of taste, we choose to stop at this point."

Part Three

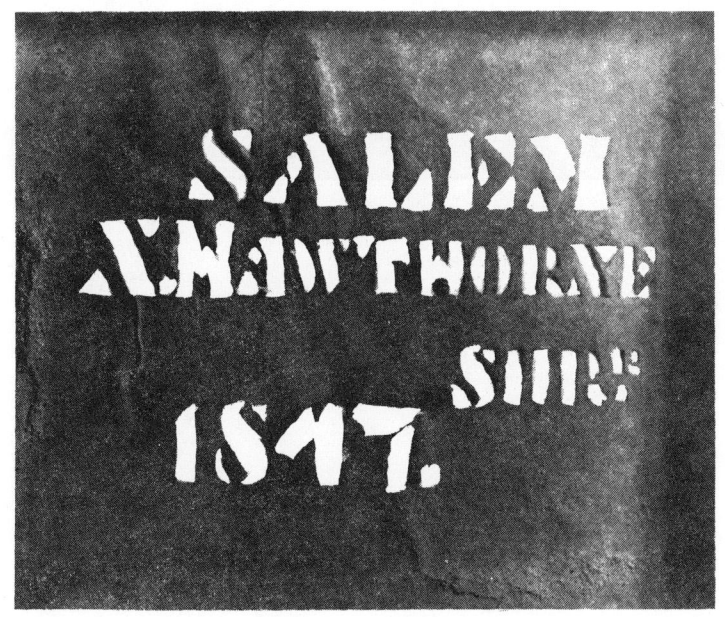

A New Adam and Eve

THE WEATHERED gray parsonage that the newlyweds had rented
was set back from the public road, at the end of a long avenue of
Balm of Gilead trees. Hawthorne readily appreciated the retired situation of the house, which did not stand "so imminent upon the
road that every passer-by can thrust his head, as it were, into the
domestic circle." At the end of the avenue, passing figures looked
"too remote and dim to disturb the sense of privacy." Built in 1770
for the Reverend William Emerson, it was situated near the sluggish
Concord River, which curved around the back, or westward-facing
side, of the house. In the setting sun, the glint of the river's placid
waters could be glimpsed through the orchard.

It was from the small upstairs study — through the wavering
glass panes of the study windows, in fact — that the Reverend
Emerson had looked out on the North Bridge and had watched the
retreat of the British regulars on that historic day in April 1775.
When Hawthorne took the house, the new monument, a granite
obelisk commemorating the battle, was visible from his study window. The parsonage had other associations with that Revolutionary
day; two nameless British soldiers lay buried near the old stone wall
that separated the parsonage's north field from the route of the
battle. Hawthorne was especially interested in the legend that one
of the unfortunate soldiers, lying wounded after the skirmish, had
been bludgeoned to death by the parson's young assistant, who was
carrying an ax. As a secret sharer of other men's guilt, Hawthorne
wondered whether the young man who had committed the terrible
deed — probably from a "nervous impulse, without purpose, without thought" — had been tortured forever by that bloodstain, contracted "before the long custom of war had robbed human life of its
sanctity."

In 1776, the Reverend Emerson, who had patriotically enlisted as chaplain for the rebel forces, died of "camp-fever" in Rutland, Vermont. The parsonage next became the residence of the long-lived Reverend Ezra Ripley. With an economy that could be practiced only by the pure of heart, the Reverend Ripley married the Widow Emerson, thus acquiring, with his new parish, a convenient home and a wife well practiced in clerical life. Three young Ripleys were added to the five children fathered by the Reverend Emerson.

It was Ezra Ripley, who, at an advanced age, had laid out the apple orchard behind the parsonage — much to the amusement of his neighbors, who suspected that he would never survive to enjoy its fruit. However, the clergyman had lived on, and the orchard had flourished and even turned a profit. Hawthorne inherited its bounty, though the trees were now ancient and mossy and long past their prime. But in season, in the still afternoons when scarcely a breath of wind stirred, he could hear the thump of the apples falling — "from the mere necessity of perfect ripeness." He inherited, too, rows of currant bushes, summer-bearing cherries, and pear trees that "flung down bushels upon bushels of heavy pears." The vegetable garden Thoreau had planted — rows of beans and Indian corn, hills of summer squash — was coming into harvest. Through no effort of his own, Hawthorne had fallen heir to the abundance of nature. Having been a Brook Farmer, he did not subscribe to the Puritan dictum that "toil sweetens the bread it earns." In Concord, he relished the "free gifts of Providence."

The house and its clerical history intrigued him, and he promptly adopted the local habit of referring to it as the Old Manse. It was, he said, "the very spot for the residence of a clergyman; a man not estranged from human life, yet enveloped, in the midst of it, with a veil woven of intermingled gloom and brightness." The description was just as applicable to the once-solitary writer, who, on a "memorable summer afternoon," rode with his bride past the stone gateposts and up the rutted avenue, overgrown with weeds, to the front door of their new home. They had repossessed an abandoned Eden — one blessed by nature's bounties, but with a reminder of an ancient fratricide buried just beyond its boundaries.

They had taken their Eden furnished — at $100 a year. The furniture consisted of old-fashioned bedsteads, ancient mirrors in black frames, large and roomy chests of drawers, small, well-worn tables, and a collection of "high-backed, short-legged rheumatic chairs." The only disagreeable feature was the gallery of prints of grim New England divines, looking like "bad angels," that hung in the upstairs study. The pictures were promptly banished to the roomy attic.

Hawthorne's scanty bachelor furnishings, his bookcases and books from Pinckney Street, had been sent ahead for the upstairs study. From her meager earnings as a painter, Sophia had bought their bedroom furniture secondhand. She had repainted the bedstead herself; on the headboard, in the manner of Flaxman, a copy of Guido Reni's *Aurora*; on the footboard, an allegorical figure of Night. Elizabeth Hoar had made the house ready for their wedding day. When they arrived, there were flowers everywhere — a vase of white lilies in the bedroom, a bouquet of "fairy flowers" in Hawthorne's study. The Peabody family, fearful of any strain on Sophia's health, had arranged for a young Irish cook, Sarah, to work for the newlyweds. She had been waiting down by the river for their arrival, and had come running back through the orchard, flustered and flushed, breathing heavily, effusively wishing her new mistress joy on her wedding day. It was not until after six that Hawthorne and Sophia had their supper. Then Elizabeth Hoar had come, shyly, bringing a gift of four pounds of newly made butter.

"Everything is as fresh as in first June," Sophia informed her mother on the following day. "We are Adam and Eve and see no persons round." She added, "Dearest Mother, I have a letter to write to you about you and me — but not yet, I am going to keep quiet and find whether this wonderful revival be sound and real . . . I am the happiest person on earth."

"Dear Sophie," Mother Peabody answered Sophia's outpouring, "I could fill sheets with what my heart is full of, on several subjects; but I am more and more convinced that this world is not the place to pour out the soul without reserve." She went on in her mixture of homely affection and encouragement, "I never doubted that you would be most happy in the connection you have formed; you are kindred spirits, and it must be so." Then came the message: "Yet, however happy you may be in each other, you will feel a void, if the enlarged circle of love is not occupied with objects worthy to be there. True love increases our capability of loving our fellow-beings."

For the first several months of the honeymoon — and a good while after — Sophia's letters were rhapsodic. "Say what you will," she wrote her mother, "there never was such a husband to enrich the world since it sprang out of chaos. I feel precisely like an Eve in Paradise. We have not done much but enjoy each other yet."

Mrs. Peabody replied, "My dearest — I have a thousand things to say, which are silly perhaps, but mothers cannot always be wise.

When I gave you up, my sweetest confidante, my ever lovely and cheering companion, I set myself aside and thought only of the repose, the fulness of bliss, that awaited you under the protection and in the possession of the confiding love of so rare a being as Nathaniel Hawthorne. Still, my heart was rebellious, and sunk full low when I entered the rooms so long consecrated to you; and I had to reason with myself and say, 'I have not lost her, but gained a noble son.' "

Sophia answered with confidences of her own: "I wish I could be a wife and daughter at the same time so that your dear heart might not feel desolated of me. While I was at home, I never dared once to refer to our separation, for I knew that it was too tender and overcoming a subject for both you and me to talk about." Her happiness was clearly evident in her letter: "It is four weeks tomorrow since we came and it seems at the same time one moment and a thousand years."

Mrs. Peabody was resigned. "I housekeep, paint, sew, study German, read, and give no room for useless regrets and still more useless anxieties," she assured her daughter. "We are all religiously doing all we can, for ourselves and others." But although she did not intend to give way to useless anxieties, she nevertheless fussed about Sophia's health. Sophia replied, "My peerless Mother, it sounds strangely to have you speak of being summoned to 'my sick bed' . . . I seem to be translated out of the former Sophia Peabody's body-corporate entirely . . . Nothing can be farther from my purposes than to be upon a sick bed." When Mother Peabody hinted that her daughter might be too submissive as a wife, Sophia answered confidently, "Do not fear that I shall be too subject to my Adam, my crown of Perfection. He loves power as little as any mortal I ever knew; and it is never a question of private will between us, but of absolute right . . . We do not forget God, my mother. We constantly together thank Him."

Mother Peabody, who admired her son-in-law's writings, had suggestions for his career: "Mr. Hawthorne, who is writing to make the world better, ought to see all that is doing in the world. He ought to mingle as much as possible with the human beings he is doing so much to cultivate and refine." Sophia took a different tack; her husband's "abomination of visiting" still held strong, "be it to see no matter what angel." Yet with company, she maintained, "he is very hospitable and receives strangers with great loveliness and graciousness." But she asked, "Of what moment will it be, a thousand years hence, whether he saw this or that person?" They had, indeed, been seeing a good deal of Emerson and Elizabeth Hoar, Sophia reported. Mr. Emerson claimed that her husband's manner was "regal, like a prince or general," even when he was handing round the bread at table. Elizabeth Hoar had noticed that, despite Hawthorne's shyness, "he always faced the occasion like a man." Mr. Hawthorne, Sophia wrote, "seems to fascinate Mr. Emerson. Whenever he comes to see him, he always takes him away so that no one may interrupt him in his close and dead-set attack upon his ear, and when Mrs. Emerson and I were walking with our respective husbands, the other day, Mr. Emerson soon looked back and said, 'You two ladies must find each other agreeable for I must have Mr. Hawthorne. E[lizabeth] Hoar says that persons about Mr. E. so generally echo him, that it is refreshing to him to find this perfect individual all himself and nobody else." Yet the walks and talks together did not improve Emerson's harsh opinion of Hawthorne as a fiction-monger. "N. Hawthorne's reputation as a writer," Emerson noted in his journal, "is a very pleasing fact, because his writing is not good for anything, and this is a tribute to the man."

During the early years of their marriage, Hawthorne and Sophia kept a journal, alternating their entries, commenting on each other's commentaries, writing for each other's benefit, sometimes in a teasing vein. Sophia's entries tended to be effusive, lyrical; Hawthorne's were hearty, often ironic. Her first, fragmentary entry records a minor quarrel that took place a month after their marriage. In the course of one of their walks together, she had decided to cut through a field of unmown grass, and Hawthorne had asked her not to. Sophia, in a short-lived show of independence, had proceeded to walk through the field; it was the inevitable testing-time of two sensitive but strong-willed people. "I was very naughty and would not obey," Sophia confessed in the journal, "and therefore he punished me by staying behind. This I did not like very well." The reconciliation was swift; they met in the woods at the other side of the field. Sophia recorded the scene: "We penetrated the pleasant gloom and sat down upon the carpet of dried pine leaves. Then I clasped him in my arms in the lovely shade, and we laid down a few moments on the bosom of dear Mother Earth. Oh, how sweet it was! And I told him I would not be so naughty again, and there was a very slight diamond shower without any thunder or lightning and we were happiest."

In his new-found contentment, Hawthorne felt no inclination to write at all — even in the journal. It was not until August 5 — and then only at Sophia's insistence — that he made a first, laconic entry. "A rainy day — a rainy day," he reported, "and I do verily believe there is no sunshine in this world, except what beams from my wife's eyes. At present, she has laid her strict command on me to take pen in hand; and to ensure my obedience has banished me to the little ten-foot-square apartment, misnamed my study; but she must not be surprised, if the dismalness of the day, and the dulness of my solitude, should be the prominent characteristics of what I write." He asked, "And what is there to write about at all? Happiness has no succession of events."

He nevertheless proceeded to record the mundane routine of their lives: the principal visitors — George Prescott, from a neighboring farm, who supplied them with milk from "some ambrosial cow" and regularly brought bouquets for the new bride; Elizabeth Hoar, who seemed "more at home among spirits than among fleshly bodies." Hawthorne noted, "Mr. Emerson comes sometimes and has been so far favored as to be feasted (with a gnome, yclept Ellery Channing) on our nectar and ambrosia." Even "Mr. Thorow" — Hawthorne had difficulties with the spelling of the name — had visited the Old Manse and "listened twice to the music of the spheres, which, for our private convenience, we have packed into a musical box." (Hawthorne did not mention that one evening when they were alone, Sophia had danced a passionate "Chachacha Cracovienne" to the strains of the music box. Hawthorne told her that she deserved the head of John the Baptist.) Their other regular visitor was the butcher, who furnished them with cuts of "delicate calf or lamb, whose unspotted innocence entitles them to the happiness of becoming our sustenance." In his initial journal entry, Hawthorne teased his wife about the first day of their honeymoon: "Would that my wife would permit me to record the ethereal dainties that kind Heaven provided for us, on the first day of our arrival! Never, surely, was such food heard of on earth — at least, not by me."

He noted the changes made in their living quarters: fresh paint and wallpaper in rooms that seemed never to have been redecorated since the house was built. They had had to buy a new cookstove for the antiquated kitchen. The small room opposite the kitchen, with its north window facing the bridge, Sophia converted into a breakfast room that also served as her studio. Directly above was Hawthorne's study. The modest front room, once old Dr. Ripley's sleeping apartment, had been transformed into a cheerful parlor with new wallpaper and the Brussels carpet Sophia had picked for Hawthorne's bachelor quarters. A plaster bust of Apollo, a wedding gift from Sophia's friend Caroline Sturgis, presided over one corner. The opposite parlor, with its old French wallpaper and a stuffed owl ensconced on the mantelpiece (to which Hawthorne had taken an immediate fancy), was first used as a storeroom and then as a second sitting room. Notwithstanding their efforts to redecorate, the house had kept its antique character. Even the introduction of "such modernisms as astral-lamps, card-vases, gilded Cologne bottles, silver taper-stands, and bronze and alabaster card-vases, do not seem at all impertinent," Hawthorne noted.

Hawthorne reflected on his idyllic circumstances. "My life, at this time," he jotted down on August 13, "is more like that of a boy, externally, than it has been since I was really a boy. It is usually supposed that the cares of life come with matrimony; but I seem to have cast off all care."

The routine days drifted into a late-summer abundance. Hawthorne rose early ("I left my Sophie's arms at five o'clock this morning") and fished for bream and perch in the river. His catch was always large enough for breakfast or dinner. He was noticeably uncharitable about the muddy Concord, with its hardly perceptible current, the water too tepid for a refreshing swim. "One dip into the salt-sea would be worth more than a whole week's soaking in such a lifeless tide," he complained. He bathed in it, nevertheless, once or twice a day. Tall blue spires of pickerel weed grew along its sedgy shores, and the scarlet blossoms of the cardinal flower were in full bloom. He made bouquets of them for Sophia.

After breakfast, he tended his garden. The beans were in flower; miraculously — in that miraculous summer — they formed pods overnight. The bees were in a constant hum among the yellow squash blossoms. Cucumbers had begun to yield, and the tomatoes would soon be ripening. The Indian corn was in tassle. Thoreau had overplanted; there was a superabundance of cabbages. Neither he nor Sophia liked the vegetable. It was unreasonable to expect Sarah, the only other member of their household, to eat fifty heads. The peach tree outside the kitchen window was so heavily laden with fruit that Hawthorne had to prop up its branches. "I feel somewhat overwhelmed with the impending bounties of Providence," he wrote in his journal.

After the gardening chores, he went to his study to idle away the time — reading, mostly, and occasionally scribbling in his journal. Sometimes, he merely slept till the dinner hour. Rainy days were a trial. He stared out the windows at the dripping landscape. A willow that brushed against the western windows had already begun to color. With each gust of wind, the leaves fell like a yellow rain. After an intolerable succession of rainy days, he noted the murmurous, monotonous sound effects: "All day long, we hear the water drip-drip-dripping and splash-splash-splashing from the eaves, and bubbling and foaming into the tubs which we have set out to receive it." The clapboards on the Old Manse and the trunks of trees were blackened with rain. The gray surface of the river was shimmering and blurred. On such days, he confessed, he was little better than a gray cloud himself; but Sophia always managed to cheer him up. Once, she read aloud the Sermon on the Mount — so beautifully that "even the Author of it might be satisfied."

On pleasant days, "the chief event of the afternoon and the happiest one of the day" was a walk with his wife. In the calm evenings, he looked back on days "spent in what the world would call idleness and for which I can myself suggest no more appropriate epithet." They were living in a world displaced from time. Distant figures and tradesmen in plodding carriages, passing along the main road, reminded them of a world outside. Sometimes, a black dog would stand at the end of the avenue, looking wistfully toward the house; but when Hawthorne called to it, the dog hurried off with his tail between his legs. Time seemed to drift by on a current as barely perceptible as that of the sleepy river.

By mid August, the newlyweds were receiving. Toward evening on the 13th, George and Susan Hillard arrived for a visit. It gave Hawthorne a new sensation when he heard the coach rumble up the avenue and turn around at the door of the manse. "I felt that I was regarded as a man with a wife and a household — a man having a tangible existence and locality in the world," he noted in his journal. The next morning — a mild but gray Sunday — they had a breakfast of flapjacks and freshly caught bream. At nine, Hawthorne and Hillard set out for a walk to Walden Pond, stopping at Emerson's house. Hawthorne slyly noted that Emerson, "from a scruple of his external conscience," had detained them inside until all his neighbors had gone to church, and then accompanied them on their walk. On their way, they met Edmund Hosmer, the philosophical farmer Emerson admired and about whom he had recently written. Hawthorne felt the publicity had been a mistake; Hosmer, now self-conscious, saw himself as something of a character and a wit. "It would be amusing to draw a parallel between him [Emerson] and his admirer," Hawthorne confided to his notebook. "Mr. Emerson — the mystic, stretching his hand out of cloud-land, in vain search for something real; and the man of sturdy sense, all whose ideas seem to be dug out of his mind, hard and substantial, as he digs potatoes." Emerson was a "great searcher for facts; but they seem to melt away and become unsubstantial in his grasp."

At Walden Pond, Hawthorne was much impressed with the narrow, pebbled beach, the sparkling blue water that seemed so different from the weedy banks of the sluggish river. When Emerson left them, he and Hillard took a refreshing swim. "It does really seem as if not only my corporeal person, but my moral self, had received a cleansing from that bath," Hawthorne wrote. "A good deal of mud and river-slime had accumulated on my soul; but those bright waters washed it all away."

Not long after the Hillards' visit — and only after much fussing and repeated instructions — Louisa Hawthorne arrived for an extended stay. She was still as timorous as ever about travel; but once in Concord, she thoroughly enjoyed herself, making excursions with her brother, picking whortleberries and huge bouquets of cardinal flowers. (In her impetuosity, it seemed to Sophia, Louisa was pulling up sheaves of flowers by the roots.) Louisa was introduced to the occasional visitors at the manse. One of these was George Bradford, the former Brook Farmer who was now living as a simple farmer in Plymouth. Hawthorne found him as comfortable as ever, but still a man "without any one salient point." Bradford, he felt, had the combination of strength and "utmost gentleness," the "uncommon regularity of nature" that he remembered from Brook Farm days. On an unexplainable impulse, he invited Bradford to become a boarder at the Old Manse — an invitation he immediately regretted. "Perhaps," Hawthorne temporized in his journal, "with all his rare and delicate properties, which make him, in some respects more like a shadow than a substance, it is best for us both that he should decline."

"Mr. Thorow" came to dinner on a Wednesday evening during Louisa's visit. They had celebrated the event by cutting open the first watermelons from the garden. Hawthorne studied Emerson's friend carefully; he found the young man "ugly as sin, long-nosed, queer-mouthed." But Thoreau's ugliness seemed perfectly "honest" and more suitable to his nature than beauty. Thoreau was nature's "especial child," full of strange stories and of the secret lore of animals and plants. He led "a sort of Indian life among civilized men" and was unconcerned about earning a regular livelihood. When he walked across a ploughed field, he instinctively picked up arrowheads and spear points — as if the spirits of the red men "willed him to be the inheritor of their simple wealth."

Hawthorne felt Thoreau had more than a "tincture of literature" and a true taste for poetry, particularly for the work of the older poets. But his tastes, Hawthorne decided, were "more exclusive than is desirable, like all other Transcendentalists." He appreciated Thoreau's nature-writing for its careful observation. Thoreau very capably suggested the "wild beauty" of a scene, but he sometimes slipped into passages of "cloudy and dreamy metaphysics."

After the midday dinner, the two men walked along the banks of the Concord. Upriver on the opposite shore a friend was waiting with Thoreau's rowboat. At a signal from Thoreau, the young man "forthwith" paddled across. If Hawthorne noticed the odd circumstance that while Thoreau dined and visited, he had left a friend, out of sight, attending his boat, like a lackey caring for a gentleman's horse, he did not remark on it in his journal. His mention of the circumstance, however, may have been a subliminal confirmation of the "uncouth and somewhat rustic" though courteous manners he had detected in the naturalist. There was something disturbing about Thoreau — the great, staring intensity of his wild blue eyes, the unbending rigor of his character, a certain furtiveness in his behavior — that made him an uncomfortable person to be with, on occasion. Sophia, at first, was put off by his awkwardness; Thoreau was all sharp elbows and ungainly opinions. But she warmed to him in time. (Elizabeth Hoar, the gentlest of women, once remarked, "I love Henry, but I cannot like him; and as for taking his arm, I should as soon think of taking the arm of an elm-tree.")

That afternoon, Hawthorne and Thoreau took a leisurely voyage upstream in the small rowboat. The river was swollen from the recent rains. As they glided noiselessly along, Hawthorne could see banks of flowers submerged beneath the waters. He marveled at the ease with which Thoreau manipulated the craft, and discovered that Thoreau had learned the knack from watching Indians paddling their canoes. The boat had been christened the *Musketaquid*, after the Indian name for the river; Thoreau and his brother John had built it themselves and, three years before, had made a voyage northward up the Merrimack River to Hooksett, New Hampshire. If Thoreau had any sentimental attachment for the craft — his adored brother John having died that January of a tetanus infection — he gave no evidence of it. Hawthorne recorded in his journal that Thoreau, "being in want of money," planned to sell the *Musketaquid* for only $7.00 and that he had agreed to buy it. He doubted, however, that he could as easily acquire Thoreau's skill in rowing it.

On the following day, Thoreau arrived to complete the transaction, and to give Hawthorne a lesson in paddling while Sophia and Louisa looked on. "My little wife . . ." Hawthorne noted in his journal, "cannot feel very proud of her husband's proficiency. I managed, indeed, to propel the boat by rowing with two oars; but the use of the single paddle is quite beyond my present skill." With Thoreau, the boat was "as docile as a trained steed." Hawthorne noted his determination to rechristen the *Musketaquid* the *Pond Lily*, since he intended to use it to bring home cargoes of water lilies for his wife. In his journal, he made a summary judgment of Thoreau: "On the whole, I find him a healthy and wholesome man to know."

He had less agreeable feelings about Emerson's other protégé,

William Ellery Channing II, who paid a call on the evening Hawthorne acquired the *Musketaquid*. His earlier reference to Channing as a "gnome" had probably been a teasing one for Sophia's benefit, since she had known Channing as an unruly boy, the son of her Boston doctor, Walter Channing. Ellery Channing, named after his famous uncle, was now twenty-five, small in stature, moody and unpredictable in disposition. He had recently married Ellen Fuller, Margaret's attractive younger sister. Emerson, who considered Channing a promising, if undisciplined, poet, had been encouraging him to set up housekeeping in Concord. Hawthorne found him only tolerable, concluding that Channing was another of those "queer and clever young men" Emerson was forever picking up "by way of a genius."

Channing's evening call had had a professional purpose. He was eager to become a regular contributor to the *Boston Miscellany*, which had published Hawthorne's "A Virtuoso's Collection" in its May issue and his own essay, "Sundays in the City and Country," in July; he had heard a rumor that Hawthorne might become an editor of the publication. Hawthorne was dismayed to find that "the lad himself seems to feel as if he were a genius; and, ridiculously enough, looks upon his own verses as too sacred to be sold for money. Prose he will sell to the highest bidder." Out of deference to Sophia, probably, he conceded that he liked Channing well enough: "But after all, these originals in a small way, after one has seen a few of them, become more dull and commonplace than even those who keep the ordinary pathway of life." He suspected that once Channing's "mystery" had been fathomed, he would become a very wearisome person indeed. In a later assessment, he decided Channing was "but a poor substitute for Mr. Thoreau." The remark called forth a mild rejoinder from Sophia. "I think perhaps he will prove more worthy & interesting a companion than thou supposest, dearest husband," she added in the journal. "He has to me a pleasanter way of saying things than Mr. Thoreau, because so wholly without the air of saying anything of consequence." It was one of Sophia's stranger recommendations.

One afternoon in mid August, Margaret Fuller paid a surprise visit. Sophia and Hawthorne had been engaged in an intimate tête-à-tête in the parlor, when they heard footsteps in the hallway. "I sprang from my husband's embrace, and found Queen Margaret," Sophia wrote her mother. "We were delighted. 'She came in so beautifully,' as Mr. Hawthorne truly said, and he looked full of gleaming welcome." Margaret had been immediately invited to take off her shawl and bonnet and stay for tea. "She was like the moon, radiant and gentle," Sophia commented.

In her journal, Margaret Fuller remarked on the pleasant situation of the house, the whispering of the trees along the avenue, the peaceful view. "The house within I like," she noted; "all their things are so expressive of themselves and mix in so gracefully with the old furniture." Hawthorne walked her home that evening; she was staying with the Emersons. They stopped to look at the moon, "struggling with clouds." In his happiness, Hawthorne was confidential. Margaret reported: "H said he should be much more willing to die than two months ago, for he had had some real possession in life, but still he never wished to leave this earth: it was beautiful enough. He expressed, as he always does, many fine perceptions. I like to hear the lightest thing he says."

Margaret's arrival in Concord had, it seems, aroused a kind of moonstruck mood among its most responsive citizens. Emerson, too, reported on a nighttime walk with Margaret, down by the river, and seeing "the moon broken in the water interrogating, interrogating." With Emerson, such a lyric moment was apt to proceed to more intellectual topics. "Thence followed the history of the surrounding minds," Emerson continued. "M. said she felt herself amidst Tendencies: did not regret life, nor accuse the imperfections of her own . . . I told her that I could not discern the least difference between the first experience and the latest in my own case. I had never been otherwise than indolent, never strained a muscle, and only saw a difference in the Circumstance, not in the man."

Margaret's version of their moonlight conversation proceeded along other lines. She felt Emerson's distrust of mere, mindless nature. Yet the rhythm of Emerson's thoughts seems to have carried over into her own report: "Looking at the moon in the river he said the same thing as in his letter, how each twinkling light breaking there summons to demand the whole secret, and how 'promising, promising nature never fulfills what she thus gives us a right to expect.' I said I never could meet him here, the beauty does not stimulate me to ask *why?* and press to the centre, I was satisfied for the moment — . . . Then we had an excellent talk: We agreed that my god was love, his truth . . ."

On the 21st, a Sunday, Hawthorne encountered Margaret again. On her evening visit, she had left a book behind, and Hawthorne had returned it to Emerson's house. Cutting back through the woods of Sleepy Hollow, he found Margaret lying beside the wooded pathway. She had been reading and enjoying the peaceful solitude. There was a mood of autumn in the woods, a sense of coolness at the heart of summer's heat, and the distant cawing of crows enhanced the prophetic sense of the "year's decay." An old man passed by them "and smiled to see Margaret lying on the ground and me sitting by her side," Hawthorne reported. "He made some remark about the beauty of the afternoon, and withdrew himself into the shadow of the wood." Hawthorne and Margaret had a lengthy and rambling talk "about Autumn — and about the pleasures of getting lost in the woods — and about the crows, whose voices Margaret had heard — and about the experiences of early childhood, whose influence remains upon the character after the collection of them has passed away — and about the sight of mountains from a distance, and the view from their summits — and about other matters of high and low philosophy."

In the midst of their conversation, they heard an intruder in the woods, a voice calling out for Margaret. Emerson stepped out of the green shade. Hawthorne, in a wry journal entry, remarked on the fact that Emerson, "in spite of his clerical consecration, had found no better way of spending the Sabbath than to ramble among the woods." He gave a brief, possibly facetious, report of Emerson's conversation: "He said there were Muses in the woods to-day, and whispers to be heard in the breezes." At nearly six o'clock, the trio had broken up; Hawthorne made his way back to the Old Manse, where Sophia was waiting tea.

Emerson seems to have left no account of the meeting, but Margaret Fuller, in a journal entry dated Sunday, August 2I, suggests a glow of satisfaction: "What a happy, happy day, all clear light. I cannot write about it . . ." At the conclusion of his journal entry, Hawthorne gave further testimony of the insidiousness of the August moon: "Last evening there was the most beautiful moonlight that ever hallowed this earthly world; and when I went to bathe in the river, which was as calm as death, it seemed like plunging down into the sky. But I had rather be on earth than even in the seventh Heaven, just now."

The cordiality of his meetings with Margaret Fuller was put to the test in very short order. At the "earnest request" of Ellery Channing, Margaret had approached Sophia to see if the Hawthornes would consider taking Channing and his wife as boarders at the Old Manse. Sophia, amenable on the surface, had left the decision to her husband. Hawthorne wrote Margaret a lengthy letter on August 25 — the length, no doubt, intended to cushion his firm refusal. "Dear Margaret," he said, "Sophia has told me of her conversation with you, about our receiving Mr. Ellery Channing and your sister as inmates of our household. I found that my wife's ideas were not altogether unfavorable to the plan — which, together with your own implied opinion in its favor, has led me to consider it with a good deal of attention." His conclusion, however, was "that the comfort of both parties would be put in great jeopardy," and cautioned, "In saying this, I would not be understood to mean anything against the social qualities of Mr. and Mrs. Channing — my objection being wholly independent of such considerations." After the chilly formalities, Hawthorne came up with one of his prettiest excuses. "Had it been proposed to Adam and Eve to receive two angels in their Paradise, as *boarders*," he continued, underlining the crass consideration, "I doubt whether they would have been altogether pleased to consent." He pleaded the added weight of "domestic care" that would be placed on Sophia.

Hawthorne felt it necessary to explain — or explain away — the fact that he had already invited his bachelor friend George Bradford to share his marital paradise. "But in doing so," he added lamely, "I was influenced far less by what Mr. Bradford is, than by what he is not; or rather, his negative qualities seem to take away his personality, and leave his excellent characteristics to be fully and fearlessly enjoyed. I doubt whether he be not precisely the rarest man in the world." Even with such a paragon, Hawthorne tried to explain, he had "some misgivings as to the wisdom of my proposal to him."

Recovering his suavity, Hawthorne acknowledged that his lengthy letter was a "very imperfect expression" of his ideas. In a final bit of cordiality, he maintained, "There is nobody to whom I would more willingly speak my mind, because I can be certain of being thoroughly understood." It was with the grateful air of a man who sees an avenue of escape that he concluded, "I would say more, but here is the bottom of the page."

Margaret understood the situation perfectly well; she viewed Hawthorne's letter as a noteworthy specimen and enclosed it in her journal, along with a letter from Sophia, which has since been lost. "It is a striking contrast of tone," she noted, "between the man and woman so sincerely bound together by one sentiment."

Late in September, on the 27th and 28th, Hawthorne made an excursion with Emerson. Emerson apparently had suggested the trip. "I shall never see you in this hazardous way," he reputedly informed Hawthorne. "We must take a long walk together. Will you go to Harvard and visit the Shakers?" After a killing frost, the weather had turned suddenly mild; it was ideal Indian summer. They set out early on the morning of the 27th, with the village of Harvard, twenty miles distant, as their destination. They planned to visit the Shaker settlement three miles beyond the town on the following morning. It was the longest period the two men had spent together, and for once Hawthorne was not in a taciturn mood. Emerson, alert to the rivalries of the occasion, noted in his journal that their walk had been without incident: "It needed none, for we were in excellent spirits, had much conversation, for we were both old collectors who had never had the opportunity before to show each other our cabinets, so that we could have filled with matter much longer days." Largely, they kept to themselves; Emerson boasted they had not so much as asked for a cup of milk at a farmhouse. They did, however, test a tavern along the way. Emerson complained that such establishments had fallen victim to a new morality. "The Temperance Society," he wrote, "has well nigh emptied the bar-room; it is but a cold place. H. tried to smoke a cigar, but I observed he was soon out on the piazza."

It was probably during their walk that the discussion turned to poetry, with Emerson observing that Landor, "though like other poets he has not been happy in love, has written admirable sentences on the passion." Hawthorne, from his own store of bitter wisdom, answered that disappointment was an effective teacher.

He was not, it would seem, so congenial on the second morning, when they traveled to the Shaker settlement for breakfast. Emerson became involved in a spirited discussion with two of the brethren and clearly felt that with a little more time he might have won out in his argument. But his "powers of persuasion were crippled by a disgraceful barking cold," and Hawthorne seemed inclined "to play Jove more than Mercurius." The two travelers were given a tour of the farm — the orchards and vineyards, the barn and herb room. Emerson was impressed with the industry and ingenuity of the settlers and thought the community a model one. "They are in many ways a very interesting Society," he commented, "but at present have an additional importance as an experiment of Socialism which so falls in with the temper of the times."

Hawthorne did not set down his brief observations until a week after his return and was not so enthusiastic. "Mr. Emerson held a theological discussion with two of the Shaker brethren," he wrote, "but the particulars of it have faded from my memory; and all the other adventures of the tour have now so lost their freshness that I cannot adequately recall them. Wherefore let them rest untold." What he remembered was the sight of some fringed gentians blooming by the roadside and the pleasure of returning to his wife — "the first time that I ever came home in my life; for I never had a home before."

ᑲ II ᑭ

Older Concord residents could not remember a longer winter in twenty years. Hawthorne claimed that it had begun on Thanksgiving Day — a chill gray day that began with rain that soon turned to sleet and snow. The river was sullen and lead-colored. Already, a pond in a neighboring meadow had frozen over and boys had begun to skate. Hawthorne and Sophia celebrated the day by themselves. "A good old festival" Hawthorne noted, "and my wife and I have kept it with our hearts, and besides have made good cheer upon our turkey and pudding and pies and custards . . . There was a new and livelier sense, I think, that we have at last found a home, and that a new family has been gathered since the last Thanksgiving Day." Writing to Louisa, he boasted of his wife's culinary abilities: "She made a plum pudding and some pumpkin pies by the mere force of instinct — having never been taught; and they would have done credit to an old pastry-cook." Their five-pound turkey had been cooked, "sentence by sentence," from the recipe in Miss Leslie's *Directions for Cookery*. He had carved it "in first rate style."

By the year's end, the snow lay deep in the woods; the river was frozen from bank to bank. Sophia reported to her Salem friend Mary Foote that her husband was skating regularly — "a rare sight, gliding over the icy stream." Occasionally, Emerson and Thoreau joined him. Sophia's descriptions were graphic reports on the personal styles of the men: Thoreau, "figuring dithyrambic dances and Bacchic leaps on the ice — very remarkable, but very ugly, methought. Next him followed Mr. Hawthorne, who, wrapped in his cloak, moved like a self-impelled Greek statue, stately and grave. Mr. Emerson closed the line, evidently too weary to hold himself erect, pitching headforemost, half lying on the air." Writing to her sister-in-law Louisa, she noted that "deep snow and steady freezing prevail here." She was happy to say that her husband was in "the glory of health" and often went skating before the sun was up. "Is not that heroic?" she asked. "I went with him once upon the river . . . and slid while he curvilineated about." By way of allaying any anxieties Louisa might have had, she commented, "I think he will be very careful, because he has a wife now and knows she could not well support any accident to befall him." It may also have been her first guarded hint to her in-laws that she was pregnant.

For Louisa's benefit, Sophia outlined their winter regimen. She particularly wanted Hawthorne's sisters to know that she was encouraging her husband to work. "Every morning now he writes till two o'clock alone in his study," she said. "He has written as usual as no one else can write." The results of her husband's latest efforts, she told Louisa, would shortly be appearing in a new magazine, *The Pioneer*, edited by the young poet James Russell Lowell and his friend Robert Carter. (In the premier, January 1843, issue, Lowell had reviewed the Tappen & Dennet combined edition of Hawthorne's children's stories, *Historical Tales for Youth*, and had praised Hawthorne for condescending to write — and so well — for the children's market. "Mr. Hawthorne," he claimed, "is making our New England history as delightful to the children as he has already to the parents.")

At two every afternoon they had their dinner; next, Hawthorne went to the village, stopping at the post office, then spending the afternoon reading in the Concord Athenaeum. It was usually sunset when he returned. They had a new maid, an Irish girl named Molly Bryan, who was the "pink of good nature" and an admirable cook. They took tea early in order to have the long evenings together. Hawthorne generally read aloud while they sat in the study, catching the last of the evening light upon the river. They were reading Milton and Bacon and "other less portentous and world-renowned books."

Hawthorne was amazed at the solitude of their lives; for weeks, it seemed the only footprints in the snow that lay deep along the avenue were his own. Even his daily jaunts to the post office and the village reading room seemed to pass without a word spoken to another soul. "My wife is, in the strictest sense, my sole companion," he wrote in their double-entry journal, "and I need no other — there is no vacancy in my mind, any more than in my heart. In truth, I have spent so many years in total seclusion from all human society, that it is no wonder if I now feel all my desires satisfied by this sole intercourse." But Sophia, he said, had come "from the midst of many friends and a large circle of acquaintance"; and he marveled that she should be content. "Thank God that I suffice for her boundless heart," he wrote; it was another of the pretty compliments they traded back and forth in their journal. But there were times, Hawthorne admitted, when he "sighed and groaned" for the green woods and warm sunshine.

There were few interruptions of the long winter solitude. John O'Sullivan paid an unexpected visit early in January. He arrived one evening when Hawthorne and Sophia were in the study reading Dante. "We have had a delightful visit from him and he says he thinks this is the Paradise of the earth, the happiest house in the world . . ." Sophia wrote to her mother. "No friend is dearer to Mr. Hawthorne than he, and so I have enjoyed their enjoyment of each other . . . I like him very much." Molly Bryan was particularly taken with their visitor.

Hawthorne, who had been attempting — without too much success — to promote Thoreau among his editorial acquaintances, introduced the Concord naturalist to O'Sullivan when they met in the Concord reading room. Thoreau had returned to the manse to have tea. He wrote Emerson, away on a lecture tour, that he was not overly impressed with the Irish editor: "He is a rather puny-looking man, and did not strike me. We had nothing to say to one another, and therefore said a great deal." Despite his feelings, he sent O'Sullivan a lackluster essay, "The Landlord," which he acknowledged he had written largely to sell, and a more serious review of a communitarian pamphlet by J. A. Etzler. Both were published in later issues of the *Democratic Review*, though Thoreau claimed that he had had difficulties over the Etzler review because the editors "could not subscribe to all the opinions."

The other winter disturbance was a letter from Margaret Fuller, written on January 16, this time asking if the Hawthornes would take in Charles King Newcomb as a boarder. After his firm refusal of the Channings, Hawthorne must have been amazed at Margaret's persistence. Newcomb had been one of the young associates at Brook Farm; he was, as well, a recent contributor to *The Dial* and another of Emerson's budding geniuses. Newcomb, Margaret wrote Hawthorne, was in "delicate health" and much in need of work and of "influences both cheering and tranquilizing." He wanted to settle in Concord for the coming summer (he was then living in Providence) and hoped to work on Hawthorne's "farm" while living in the manse as a boarder.

In her letter, Margaret attempted to be ingratiating and amusing. "You must not think I have any black design against your domestic peace," she began. "— Neither am I the agent of any secret tribunal of the dagger . . . Nor am I commissioned by the malice of some baffled lover to make you wretched."

She conceded, "Yet it may look so, when you find me once again, in defiance of my failure last summer, despite your letter of full exposition, once more attempting to mix a foreign element in your well-compounded cup." Margaret insisted, "If you do not want him, simply say no, and trouble not to state the reasons; we shall divine them." She clearly did not want another lecture.

Hawthorne waited more than two weeks before replying. He pleaded the pressures of work: "I have an immense deal of scribbling to do — being a monthly contributor to three or four periodicals." In refusing, Hawthorne obliquely hinted at Sophia's pregnancy. It would not be possible to take in any boarder, he noted, "for a reason at present undeveloped, but which, I trust, time will bring to light." Blithely, he added, "So here is a second negative.

How strange, when I should be so glad to do everything that you had the slightest wish for me to do, and when you are so incapable of wishing anything that ought not to be!" There were, he said, "many roofs besides mine" in Concord; he hoped that Charles Newcomb would settle under one of them so that they might have "long days" together on the river and in the woods.

In his dealings with Margaret Fuller, Hawthorne was never so congenial and confiding as during the first years of his marriage. In his second letter of refusal, he took some pains to give her a glimpse of his marital life and happiness. "I do suppose that nobody ever lived, in one sense, quite so selfish a life as we do," he confessed; ". . . we let the world alone as much as the world does us." He had been skating all winter, he told her, "like a very schoolboy," and went on, "Indeed, since my marriage, the circle of my life seems to have come round, and brought back many of my school-day enjoyments; and I find a deeper pleasure in them now." He was, he said, "boy and man together."

Yet in his congenial sparring with Margaret, he managed to take a swipe at her brother-in-law, Ellery Channing. He claimed he missed Ellery very much on his skating expeditions and wondered whether the would-be poet had deserted Concord altogether. Having recently returned to literary work himself, his reference to Channing was a bit condescending — and perhaps admiring. "How few people in this world know how to be idle!" he said. "It is a much higher faculty than any sort of usefulness or ability . . . I do not mean to deny Ellery's ability for any sort of vulgar usefulness; but he certainly *can* lie in the sun."

In February, there was a family tragedy. One evening, while walking on the frozen Concord River with Hawthorne, Sophia had a bad fall. She was afraid she had lost the baby. Dr. Josiah Bartlett was called in, and, although he was uncertain at first, he later confirmed his opinion to Hawthorne that his wife had, in fact, miscarried. By then Sophia was convinced that "the precious heart is gone." While Sophia was invalided, Mother Peabody paid a visit to Concord. She may have scolded the pair for taking risks; Sophia's letters to her mother after her recovery and Mother Peabody's return to Boston hint at some prior emotional disturbance. On the morning of her mother's departure, Sophia felt well enough to wash the dishes, and she refused to let Hawthorne go to his study until Molly "put it in the nicest order." Molly, Sophia wrote her mother, "washed over all the paint and it soon looked as though there had been no sad scenes enacted there." She dressed up especially, "in a tight dress instead of flowing robes," to greet Hawthorne when he returned. The sun was shining into the western windows of the study: "It required a great deal of credence to believe that anything at all happened to us, so exactly the time seemed to join upon our last presences in the same place."

Hawthorne, in his distress over Sophia's condition, and probably because of his mother-in-law's presence, was out of sorts. In general, he was deferential to Mrs. Peabody, but in private, and to friends like Bridge, his references to his mother-in-law were less than flattering. Sophia found it necessary to assure her mother that Hawthorne had appreciated her visit: "I wish you could see my husband now that I have quite recovered. He was under such a heavy cloud during your visit that he was like the veiled Prophet. Now there is not the slightest need of any sun in the sky, he shines with such a lustre. He was thankful for your presence every moment, but could not testify [to] it as he now could, so drearily he felt. It was the first time I had been taken from him and the world seemed standing on its head to him bouleversing himself with it." In her letter to her mother, Sophia spoke of their renewed happiness since her recovery: "It seems now as if some invisible James Clarke had married us again."

Although they were disappointed at the loss of a child, they were both confident they would have another soon. Hawthorne, writing in their journal on March 31 (it was his first entry after the long winter), acknowledged, "One grief we have had . . . all else has been happiness. Nor did the grief penetrate to the reality of our life. We do not feel as if our promised child were taken from us forever . . . The longer we live together — the deeper we penetrate into one another, and become mutually interfused — the happier we are. God will surely crown our union with children, because it fulfills the highest conditions of marriage."

In her letter to her mother, Sophia also hinted at their growing financial problems. They had been planning to make a trip to Boston — Sophia to stay with her mother and perhaps consult with her Boston doctor; Hawthorne to go on to Salem to pay a long-overdue visit to his family. They were held back, however, for lack of money. James Lowell, Sophia wrote, owed her husband $20 for his contributions to *The Pioneer*, but they had not yet received a penny. Lowell had offered Hawthorne "any price for his articles." But the twenty-four-year-old editor was suffering with a severe eye disease, and early in January had gone to New York to consult a specialist. The treatment involved a curtailment of his reading and writing activities — though he wrote daily letters of instruction to his co-editor, Robert Carter, in Boston. Sophia, who knew Lowell through his engagement to her childhood friend Maria White, sympathized with Lowell's ailment, but was abrupt about his failure to pay. "I feel sorry for him," she told her mother, "but we want it [the money]."

In agreeing to contribute to *The Pioneer*, Hawthorne had attempted to raise his fees — though with his usual diffidence. Replying to Lowell's initial request, he had mentioned that Epes Sargent, the editor of *Sargent's New Monthly Magazine*, had offered him $5.00 a page for his contributions. "If you consider this a fair price," he told Lowell, "it will satisfy me; if not, you may have the article for whatever your arrangements will allow you to pay." Hawthorne's sketch "The Hall of Fantasy" appeared in the second, the February 1843, issue of the new magazine. He also sent a further contribution, his story "The Birthmark," for the March issue. There had been some misunderstanding about payment. Hawthorne, in writing to Carter in February, felt it necessary to explain: "I beg you to assure Mr. Lowell, that I did not intend to make a demand for immediate payment of my last contribution. I merely mentioned a price per page, because he had spoken to me upon the subject; and we get rid of an embarrassment by having such matters definitely fixed." Lowell, perhaps because he found the fee high, had left the matter hanging; he was paying another contributor, John Sullivan Dwight, the music critic, $2.00 per page and $10 for articles of three pages or more.

It was not until March 9 that Hawthorne and Sophia made their trip — although not because Lowell had paid his debt; the money had evidently come from another source. In Salem, Hawthorne found his family tolerably well, though Elizabeth, he reported to Sophia, was "not quite thawed." He wrote, "They speak of thee and me with an evident sense that we are very happy indeed, and I can see that they are convinced of my having found the very little wife that God meant for me." He was plainly uneasy about their separation and cautioned his wife to sleep well, avoid too much company, and to be especially careful when walking through the "snow and slosh" of the Boston streets. In a sleepless state, he imagined himself back at the Old Manse, wandering through the empty rooms, alone. He seemed to picture every object "in a sort of dim, gray light — our bed-chamber — the study, all in confusion — the parlor, with the fragments of that abortive breakfast on the table, and the precious silver forks, and the old bronze image keeping its solitary stand upon the mantelpiece." A presentiment of misfortune seemed to cling to him. Four days later, he wrote Sophia about having a disturbing dream "that our house was broken open, and all our silver stolen."

Sophia sent him the latest news from Boston: *The Pioneer* was to be discontinued with the March issue. Hawthorne was not surprised: "I expected it to fail in due season but not quite so soon. Not improbably we shall have to wait months for our money, if we ever get it at all." He had applied to O'Sullivan for payment, as well, and was disappointed. "Nobody pays us," he complained. "It was very unkind — at least, inconsiderate — in Mr. O'Sullivan not to send some money, my request being so urgent. Perhaps he has written to Concord."

He was forced to turn down a suggestion of Sophia's for lack of funds. "We cannot very well afford to buy a surplus stock of paper, just now," he answered. "By and by, I should like some, and I suppose there will always be opportunities to get it cheap at auction . . . Our earnings are miserably scanty at best; yet, if we could but get even that pittance, I should continue to be thankful, though certainly for small favors." Referring to the recent prophecies of the Millerite sect that the Apocalypse was at hand, Hawthorne claimed, "The world deserves to come to a speedy end, if it were for nothing else save to break down this abominable system of credit — of keeping possession of other people's property — which renders it impossible for a man to be just and honest, even if so inclined."

But principally, his letters to Sophia from Salem recorded his unhappiness at their separation. "I need thee continually at bed and board and wherever I am," he told her, "and nothing elses makes any approach towards satisfying me . . . Four whole days must still intervene before we meet — it is too long — too long . . ."

It had been some time since Hawthorne had seen Henry Wadsworth Longfellow. The poet had been abroad on a leave of absence and did not return until November 1842. "I have been looking to receive somewhat in the shape of a letter of congratulations from you, on the great event of my marriage," Hawthorne had written shortly after the poet's return, "but it does not seem to be forthcoming. Perhaps it is the etiquette that I should congratulate [you] on your return from Outre Mer." The ostensible purpose of his letter was to invite Longfellow to lecture at the Concord Lyceum, for "the magnificent sum of ten dollars." He had himself been invited to lecture and, though in need of money, had declined. His distaste for the public platform was real and lifelong. In a Christmas Eve letter to the poet, Hawthorne somewhat offhandedly invited Longfellow to pay a visit to Concord. "I have some scruples of conscience about asking you to come in mid-winter," he wrote, "for it would be preposterous, I suppose, to expect anybody to be comfortable or contented here, except ourselves. You will have to warm yourself by the glow of our felicity, aided by as large a wood-fire as we can pile into the chimney." He also expressed mild amazement at Longfellow's recent book, *Poems on Slavery*. Although flattering, the tone of his letter suggests that he had misgivings about Longfellow's talents as a polemicist. "I never was more surprised than at your writing poems about Slavery," he commented. "I have not seen them, but have faith in their excellence, though I cannot conjecture what species of excellence it will be. You have never poetized a practical subject hitherto."

The two men, however, did not meet until March, at the end of Hawthorne's Salem and Boston visits. On March 21, the day before he and Sophia were to return to Concord, Hawthorne crossed over to Cambridge to have dinner with the poet. Longfellow had reminded him of the engagement in a letter on the 19th, although curiously he made no mention of an invitation to Sophia. "I want very much to see you, and to tell you how truly delighted I was with your last story, The Birth Mark. Not the comet himself can unfold a more glorious *tail*," he punned. "But you should have made a Romance of it, and not a short story only. More of that on Tuesday."

ᴄᴖ III ᴄᴗ

Unhappily, his relief at returning to the Old Manse was short-lived; a little more than two weeks later, he was thrust into a bachelor's existence. Sophia had received word of Mary's impending marriage to Horace Mann. The announcement had come as a surprise; Mary had hinted nothing about it, and the circumstances were uncharacteristically hurried for a man as cautious as Mann.

Samuel Gridley Howe, after a tempestuous courtship of Julia Ward, finally won her consent; the bridal couple were to go to Europe on their honeymoon. Howe had asked his best and most adoring bachelor friend, Charles Sumner, to accompany them; Sumner, dejected at the loss of his best friend, had declined. (Within a month, Sumner's depression was to deepen considerably more. His equally good friend, Longfellow, resumed his courtship of the beautiful but reserved Frances Appleton, and shortly after announced his marriage.)

Howe had next asked Horace Mann to join him on the wedding trip. Much to Julia Ward's regret, the honeymoon was also to be an educational tour; Howe intended to study European prisons and hospitals — and Mann, who had agreed to go, planned to make a survey of European schools. Having made that decision, Mann, out of perspicacity as well as passion, asked Mary Peabody to marry him — since, as he confided to his journal, "it would be too painful to go & leave so lovely a being & one in whom I had such an interest, behind me." The wedding and the departure date of the steamboat *Britannia* were scheduled for May Day. Mary had written Sophia the news: "I believe no one is quite astonished but you, lovey, no one that knew Mr. Mann's intimacy with us, I mean. How nicely I dusted thy little eyes, Sophy! I would not have had you know that the large joy of knowing and loving him stood so near the large sorrow of apprehension that I should never dwell wholly by his side."

Sophia had returned to Boston on April 7, leaving Hawthorne at the manse. He had seen her off at eleven that morning, watching the carriage lumbering down the drive; then he had gone to the barn to saw wood with a briskness that was greater than usual. For unknown reasons, he made a vow that he would not speak a word to any other human being during his wife's absence. In a short while, however, Thoreau came by to return a book and announce that he was soon leaving for Staten Island, where he would serve as a tutor in the family of William Emerson, Waldo's brother. In his journal, Hawthorne reported on their desultory conversation about "the spiritual advantages of change of place, and upon the Dial, and upon Mr. Alcott and other kindred or concatenated subjects." He admitted that he would be sorry to see Thoreau leave Concord, "he being one of the few persons, I think, with whom to hold intercourse is like hearing the wind among the boughs of a forest-tree." But he approved of Thoreau's making "one step towards a circumstantial position in the world." Whatever his appreciation of the idle life, Hawthorne had not altogether escaped the Puritan work ethic. Thoreau also announced — and Hawthorne duly reported it in the journal — that he had found a house for Ellery Channing and his wife, who would soon be returning to Concord.

It was a dreary span of days. He spent his mornings writing, the afternoons in chopping wood and in journalizing. He went impatiently to the post office, hoping for letters from his wife. In the evenings, he studied German; painfully, he admitted — "Slow work, and dull work, too!" He was attempting to read a story by Ludwig Tieck. Occasionally, "as a soporific," he read *The Dial*. His nights, he contended — purely for Sophia's benefit — were restless. "What is the use of going to bed at all, in solitude?" he asked, after the third night. On the following evening, he reported, his greatest enjoyment in bed had been "to extend myself cross-wise, diagonally, semicircularly, and in all other postures that would be incompatible with a bed-fellow. I believe, too, that during my sleep, I seek thee throughout the empty vastitude of our couch; for I found myself, when I awoke, in a quite different region than I had occupied in the early part of the night."

He saw very little of the maidservant, Molly. She filled the lamps and rang the dinner bell to announce the meals, he claimed. "Once in a while, I hear a door slam like a thunderclap; but she never shows her face, nor speaks a word, unless to announce a visitor, or deliver a letter." There were few visitors to remark about; on some days he had even been able to keep his vow of silence.

Emerson made a Saturday call: "My little wife, I know, will demand to know every word that was spoken; but she knows me too well to anticipate anything of the kind." He at least set down the gist of their talk: Emerson "seemed fullest of Margaret Fuller, who, he says, has risen perceptibly into a higher state since their last meeting. He apotheosized her as the greatest woman, I believe, of ancient or modern times, and the one figure in the world worth considering." Emerson also reported that Ellery Channing's poems would soon be published, though he did not expect any very wide reception of the book. They discussed the departure of Thoreau, on which they agreed. "Mr. Emerson," Hawthorne reported, "appears to have suffered some inconveniency from his experience of Mr. Thoreau as an inmate. It may well be that such a sturdy and uncompromising person is fitter to meet occasionally in the open air, than to have as a permanent guest at table and fireside." They also discussed Brook Farm and the "singular moral aspects" that it presented; they had agreed on the "great desirability that its progress and developments should be observed, and its history written." There was some brief discussion of Charles Newcomb, who had become silent and morose and on occasion had no other response than a sardonic laugh. Newcomb's friends feared that he was passing into a "permanent eclipse." Then he noted, "Finally, between five and six o'clock, Mr. Emerson took his leave, threatening to come again, unless I call on him very soon."

The only other recorded visitor was Thoreau, once again. He came on the 11th, for a final voyage in the rechristened *Pond Lily*. They had bailed out the leaky rowboat and ventured up the river as far as the North Branch. The Concord was swollen from the recent thaws, and there were a considerable number of ice floes. On their return, Hawthorne and Thoreau had boarded one of these — two sharply defined figures silhouetted on an island of ice, floating downstream in the sluggish river of time, a rowboat trailing behind.

Late that afternoon Emerson made good on his threat, returning with a letter from Ellery Channing, "written in a style of very pleasant humor." Hawthorne was impatient for his guest to leave; he was expecting Sophia's return that evening. As soon as the Concord philosopher left, Hawthorne sat down to his journal to update the chronicle of his loneliness. "And thus," he reported, "the record is brought down to the present moment; ten minutes past six. To-night — tonight — yes, within an hour — this Eden, which is no Eden to a solitary Adam, will regain its Eve."

It is highly probable that the rapturous though high-minded little homily about the physical aspects of marital love that Sophia set down in their journal, in the next entry, related to her return. A large portion of it was cut from the page, but the remaining frag-ment speaks of the "inward thought" that makes the body "either material or angelic." Her entry continues, " 'Are ye not the temple of the living God?' says the apostle. Ah, yes, I suppose some persons are the den of the archfiend and through such has this miraculous form come into disrepute. Before our marriage, I knew nothing of its capacities, and the truly married alone can know what a wondrous instrument it is for the purposes of the heart."

———

Throughout the spring, by letter and through visits, Hawthorne maintained contact with Horatio Bridge, who had been appointed purser on the U.S.S. *Saratoga*, docked in the Portsmouth Naval Yard in New Hampshire. The ship was scheduled to make a cruise of West African waters. Bridge would be at sea for some two years. Hawthorne suggested that Bridge write about his experiences for a series of articles in the *Democratic Review*. He offered to edit the pieces and put them in shape for publication. (Later, he advised Bridge to make a book of his travel letters.) In the meantime, the *Saratoga* was under repair, having been badly damaged during a blizzard at sea. Alert to the literary possibilities, Hawthorne, writ-ing on March 25, congratulated his friend on having experienced the storm: "Perhaps a description of the tempest may form a good in-troduction to your series of articles in the Democratic."

He told Bridge, concerning his own recent trip to Salem, "I did not come to see you, because I was very short of cash — having been disappointed in money that I had expected from three or four sources. My difficulties of this sort sometimes make me sigh for the regular monthly payments at the Custom House." He then launched into an apocalyptic complaint: "The system of slack payments in this country is most abominable, and ought, of itself, to bring upon us the destruction foretold by Father Miller. It is impossible for any individual to be just and honest, and true to his engagements, when it is a settled principle of the community to be always behindhand." He had not, after all, received a payment for his contributions to the *Democratic Review*, and he quite probably had O'Sullivan in mind — though the name was later excised from his letter to Bridge. "I find no difference in anybody, in this respect; all do wrong alike.

[O'Sullivan] is just as certain to disappoint me in money matters as any pitiful little scoundrel among the booksellers. On my part, I am compelled to disappoint those who put faith in my engagements; and so it goes round. The devil take such a system."

When Bridge sent him a description of the storm at sea, Hawthorne, in a letter written on May 3, praised it as "very graphic and effective," and offered some pointers on the art of travel-writing:

> I would advise you not to stick too accurately to the bare fact, either in your descriptions or narrations; else your hand will be cramped, and the result will be a want of freedom, that will deprive you of a higher truth than that which you strive to attain. Allow your fancy pretty free license, and omit no heightening touches merely because they did not chance to happen before your eyes. If they did not happen, they at least ought — which is all that concerns you. This is the secret of all entertaining travellers.

Taken at face value, the advice provides one of the more interesting confessions of the blurred distinction between fact and fiction in Hawthorne's literary theory. After the general matters, Hawthorne got down to particulars: "If you meet with any distinguished characters, give personal sketches of them. Begin to write always before the impression of novelty has worn off your mind; else you will begin to think that the peculiarities which at first attracted you, are not worth recording . . . Think nothing too trifling to write down, so it be in the smallest degree characteristic." Only after giving "due time" to observation, Hawthorne advised, should Bridge turn his attention to broader themes — "grave reflections on national character, customs, morals, religion, the influences of peculiar modes of government, etc." Hawthorne seemed to imply that such considerations were best treated as afterthoughts.

Bridge planned to publish his articles anonymously, but Hawthorne boasted, "I by no means despair of putting you in the way to acquire a very pretty amount of literary reputation, should you ever think it worth while to assume the authorship of these proposed sketches. All the merit will be your own; for I shall merely arrange them, correct the style, and perform other little offices as to which only a practised scribbler is *au fait*."

In his letter to Hawthorne, Bridge had complained that life had "lost its charm," that his enthusiasm was dead, that there was nothing worth living for. Hawthorne relayed Sophia's advice that Bridge fall in love — rather incongruous advice, since Bridge was about to leave on a two-year naval cruise. "You would find all the fresh coloring restored to the faded pictures of life," Hawthorne assured his friend; "it would renew your youth — you would be a boy again, with the deeper feeling and purposes of a man." He recommended, "Try it — try it — first, however, taking care that the object is every way unexceptionable; for this will be your last chance in life."

Hawthorne wrote, "Speaking of love, Longfellow was in love with Miss Appleton when he wrote Hyperion." And he added in a moment of serious reflection, "Except yourself, Longfellow is the only college acquaintance about whom I now really care much. Pierce, somehow or other, has faded out of my affections."

The winter had been tediously long; spring was slow in coming. The two seasons, Hawthorne noted in his journal, "are now struggling for the mastery in my study." His window was open; there was a fire in the stove. One beautiful day Sophia, standing in the burgeoning orchard, called up to her husband — "on the strength of the loveliness, though against the rules." The air was full of birdsong, the trees were misted with green. Hawthorne poked his head out the study window but would not join her. Sophia's explanation was typically euphoric: "The Muse had him entrapped in a golden net," she wrote her mother.

They found a renewed happiness in each other following the miscarriage. Sophia was confident she would have another child. It was from that sense of confidence and happiness that one evening, as she stood in her husband's study looking out the window at the sun setting behind the quiet river, she took out her diamond ring and made an inscription on the glass pane: "Man's accidents are God's purposes. Sophia A. Hawthorne, 1843." Hawthorne took the ring and added: "Nath. Hawthorne. This is his study. 1843. The smallest twig leans clear against the sky. Composed by my wife and written with her diamond." Sophia closed off the brief exchange: "Inscribed by my husband at sunset. April 3rd, 1843. In the gold light. S.A.H."

Throughout the spring and summer, Sophia's entries in the journal and her letters to her mother verged on the ecstatic and lyrical. On the beautiful Sunday when the birds had been singing at full throat and her husband had looked out from his study window, she exulted, "There never was such an air, such a sun, such a day, such a sky, such a God!"

In June, after a surprising late frost, there were days of blazing heat and sunshine. "Yesterday glowed like molten brass," Hawthorne wrote on June 23. His garden was thriving; the peas were "in such forwardness, that I should not wonder if we had some of them on the table within a week." The rows of early corn were well up and waving in the wind; he had just set out tomatoes and capers.

A succession of guests descended on the manse. Sophia's mother paid a visit of a few days; then her friend Anna Shaw, with her sister-in-law, Mrs. Francis G. Shaw, stayed overnight. George Hillard and his wife arrived, Susan Hillard to spend several days. Sophia had been writing insistently to Louisa Hawthorne to encourage a visit. With little chance of success, she had also tried to persuade Hawthorne's mother and "the voluntary nun, the lady Elizabeth," to come as well. "We shall not put off your coming dear Louisa for anybody," Sophia wrote again, on their anniversary, July 9. "I know Nathaniel cares more about it than any other visit . . . I think he feels more affection for you all constantly instead of less as time wears on. His loving me does not cast you out of his heart, but rather makes more room there." Hawthorne added a postscript, marked "Private," revealing that his family was short of funds and he was unable to help. "I have received no money yet," he said, "and the Devil knows when I shall. Come if you can, and I will let you have some as soon as possible." Louisa, for one reason or another, delayed and delayed and did not come until early October.

On the first anniversary of their marriage, Hawthorne summed up his feelings. "We never were so happy as now," he wrote in his journal, "— never such wide capacity for happiness, yet overflowing with all that the day and every moment brings to us. Methinks this birthday of our married life is like a cape, which we have now doubled, and find a more infinite ocean of love stretching out before us. God bless us and keep us; for there is something more awful in happiness than in sorrow."

One reason for his happiness was Sophia's preceding journal entry for the same day. She had been experiencing the symptoms of a new pregnancy. "I have not felt very well for two weeks," she wrote, "but it is the very poetry of discomfort, for I rejoice at every smallest proof that I am as ladies wish to be who love their lords . . . Ah, may our little dovelet look like thee!"

In the Hall of Fantasy

I HAVE WRITTEN with pretty commendable diligence," Hawthorne wrote in his journal on March 31, "averaging from two to four hours a day; and the result is seen in various Magazines." His literary efforts, written during the fall and winter of the honeymoon, had been appearing in the pages of *Sargent's New Monthly Magazine* ("The Old Apple-Dealer" and "The Antique Ring" in January and February 1843); *The Pioneer* ("The Hall of Fantasy" and "The Birthmark" in February and March); and in his old standby, the *Democratic Review* ("The New Adam and Eve" and "Egotism; or, the Bosom-Serpent" in February and March). Except for the children's stories he would write in subsequent years, the twenty tales and sketches published in 1843 and 1844 represent the last burst of his interest in short fiction. Given his reluctance to write during the summer, this represents an average of one or two tales or sketches a month, no strenuous effort on Hawthorne's part, though he was apt to write slowly and carefully.

"I might have written more," Hawthorne conceded in his journal, "if it had seemed worth while; but I was content to earn only so much gold as might suffice for our immediate wants, having prospects of official station." With a wife to support and a child on the way, he was not optimistic about earning a living as a writer; it was, in fact, clear that he could not. He was hoping for some official position with the Tyler administration, even though that would mean moving from Concord. "Meantime," he wrote, "the Magazine people do not pay their debts; so that we taste some of the inconveniences of poverty and the mortification — only temporarily, however — of owing money, with empty pockets."

For the remainder of his stay at the Old Manse, he was plagued with financial problems. Since 1838, Hawthorne had had his eye on the Salem postmastership, a political plum he considered "the next best thing to holding no office at all." At that time, no longer contemplating marriage, he had encouraged O'Sullivan to "move Heaven and Earth" to get him the appointment, since the salary could "purchase other comforts as well as matrimonial ones." With the Tyler administration, Hawthorne's hopes had revived. But Tyler, an ex-Democrat who had succeeded to the presidency when the doddering William Henry Harrison, a Whig, died after a month in office, depended for support on an uneasy coalition of moderate Whigs and Democrats. Hawthorne, writing to Bridge late in March 1843, acknowledged, with a touch of irony, that any reward for his "patriotism and public services" would probably be contingent upon a similar coalition in Salem. He was realistic enough to admit that there was "little prospect" of it.

His friend O'Sullivan even took the unusual step of enlisting the support of the influential Henry Wise. It had been Wise who had served as Graves's second in the fatal Cilley duel; and it had been Wise whom Hawthorne had publicly accused, in the pages of the *Democratic Review*, of overstepping the line between "manslaughter and murder." In a long unctuous letter, O'Sullivan pleaded Hawthorne's poverty, his recent marriage, his literary reputation, and his "simplicity of heart" as reasons that he should be given the postmastership. Only at the end of his letter did he refer to the "painful and delicate" topic of Cilley's death, counting on "a generous magnanimity" from Wise. It had been Cilley, O'Sullivan claimed, who had originally pushed for Hawthorne's appointment to the Salem postmastership; now it seemed almost "a bequeathed duty" to Cilley's memory to follow through on the appointment. O'Sullivan's letter was one of the more dexterous productions in that sometimes fictional enterprise, American politics. He had successfully turned a personal embarrassment into a legitimate claim for support from a former political enemy. But it was not until three years later that Hawthorne was finally to obtain a political post.

Hawthorne's literary activities during this period were no more rewarding. Several of the magazines he contributed to — *Sargent's*, the *Boston Miscellany*, and *The Pioneer* — failed after only a few issues. It is doubtful that Hawthorne was ever paid for most of his contributions. O'Sullivan, as usual, was in financial straits. Considering the laxity with which Hawthorne was paid, it was understandable that he was not eager to write for new and untried publications. When Edgar Allan Poe, through Lowell, asked for a contribution to his projected magazine, *The Stylus*, Hawthorne wrote Lowell that he was "greatly troubled" about the possibilities of any immediate contribution: "If I am to send anything to Mr. Poe, I should wish it to be worth his reception; but I am conscious of no power to produce anything good, at present. When you write to him, do make my apologies, and tell him that I have no more brains than a cabbage — which is absolutely true. He shall hear from me after the first frost — possibly sooner." That Hawthorne was suffering from mental weariness is confirmed by his journal. He complained of a "sense of imbecility — one of the dismallest sensations, methinks, that mortal can experience — the consciousness of a blunted pen, benumbed fingers, and a mind no longer capable of a vigorous grasp." Poe's magazine was never published; it was another of his failures. Hawthorne's delay had simply saved him from one more financial disappointment. But his diffidence may have been a mistake. Poe, who savored every slight, seems to have remembered Hawthorne's aloofness.

"It is rather singular that I should need an office," Hawthorne wrote Bridge in May, "for nobody's scribblings seem to be more acceptable to the public than mine; and yet I shall find it a tough scratch to gain a respectable support by my pen." His efforts to find a more profitable connection than that of a random contributor had come to nothing. He had made it clear to the editors of the *Boston Miscellany* and to Epes Sargent that he was available for some more exclusive arrangement with their publications. When, in July, Rufus W. Griswold, co-editor of *Graham's Magazine,* asked for a contribution, Hawthorne was considerably bolder in his approach. "I am advised that the publishers of Magazines consider it desirable to attach writers exclusively to their own establishments," he wrote Griswold, "and will pay at a higher rate for such a monopoly. If this be the case, I should make no difficulty in forswearing all other periodicals for a specified time — and so much the more readily, on account of the safety of your Magazine in a financial point of view." But Hawthorne's approach was no more successful in those quarters than it had been elsewhere.

Sophia complained about the unfairness of their situation. "Oh, for the $1,300 justly due my husband," she wrote Mother Peabody. "It is rather depressing that people do not pay their debts to him. Mr. Lowell, notwithstanding his voluntary promise a fortnight ago to pay his part — has not yet fulfilled it — and an awful pause seems to have swallowed up Epes Sargent." In a later letter, she noted that the *Democratic Review* was now so poor, "it can only offer twenty dollars for an article of what length soever, so that Mr. Hawthorne cannot well afford to give any but short pieces to it. And it is besides sadly dilatory about payment."

An air of diligence clings to the stories Hawthorne wrote during that happiest period of his life, his honeymoon at the Old Manse. The moralizing, sermonizing, generalizing functions of prose — the functions Hawthorne had advised Bridge to hold in abeyance while keeping a journal — are very much in the foreground of "The Hall of Fantasy," "The Procession of Life," "The Christmas Banquet," "A Select Party." Very few of the stories approach the stature of his earlier parables of the human heart, the explorations of human will and individual character that gave substance to *Twice-told Tales*. The newer stories were heavily burdened with allegorical intentions and an underscored morality.

Ironically, the stories that matched the best of his early fiction — stories like "The Artist of the Beautiful" and "Rappaccini's Daughter" — were published in the *Democratic Review*, so there was no lessening of quality in the work he sent O'Sullivan, whatever its length. Hawthorne also gave the *Democratic Review* what must be considered his most popular and enduring allegorical fable, "The Celestial Rail-road," as well as two of his more successful attempts along those lines, "The New Adam and Eve" and "The Intelligence Office." Elsewhere, Hawthorne was likely to tailor the piece to his audience. For the largely feminine readership of *Godey's Lady's Book*, he offered one of his easy and agreeable fables, "Drowne's Wooden Image," an American version of the Pygmalion myth. It is also one of his more pedestrian parables of the artist, a story of a mysterious and beautiful woman who inspires an otherwise ineffectual artist to create his one masterpiece. Hawthorne evidently felt it was just the thing for a readership courted by such popular feminist writers as Sarah Josepha Hale, Catharine Maria Sedgwick, and Mrs. Lydia Sigourney, the "sweet singer of Hartford." In rather condescending fashion, he informed the editor that his going rate was $25 and that *Godey's* might have the piece "at the same valuation, though I do not care to become a regular contributor at that rate. I should have asked the same had it been shorter." It was the only story of Hawthorne's to be published in the influential woman's magazine.

He was far more at home in *The Pioneer*, whose editors boasted they were offering the intelligent reading public a substitute for "the enormous quantity of thrice-diluted trash, in the shape of namby pamby love tales and sketches" that were ordinarily foisted upon the American public. Hawthorne's story "The Birth-mark," which appeared in the March 1843 issue, an unromantic tale of the scientist-perfectionist gone wrong, a man so lacking in the common understanding of the heart that he destroys his young wife in order to remove a minor blemish, was probably the kind of literary antidote *The Pioneer* editors had in mind. "The Hall of Fantasy," which had appeared the month before, was, however, a thin conceit: the fable of a castle in the air, a house of the imagination, to which poets, writers, dreamers, and inventors had access. Hawthorne was to re-cast the idea several times in the next two years.

"The Christmas Banquet," published in the *Democratic Review* for January 1844, was, in fact, another version of "The Hall of Fantasy." So, too, were "The Intelligence Office" and "A Select Party," which appeared in the same magazine in succeeding months. Essentially, the stories were social critiques, catalogues of human types and vanities. Like the vast folio volume in which the clerk of the Intelligence Office inscribes want ads and sales notices, the stories are a record of the "freaks of idle hearts, and aspirations of deep hearts, and desperate longings of miserable hearts, and evil prayers of perverted hearts." Only occasionally do the fables reach the level of terrible appropriateness of the angry man in "The Intelligence Office," who exclaims, "I want my place! — my own place! — my true place in the world! — my proper sphere! — my thing to do . . ." He is the representative of a type Hawthorne had begun to notice in American society, the more vocal brother, perhaps, of Thoreau's man who leads a life of "quiet desperation."

Yet there is a sense in which Hawthorne's social types border on the stereotypical. The same characters appear and reappear in his allegories: the fanatic and the reformer, the theorist, the disgruntled author, the failed politician, the militant feminist. Hawthorne may well have modeled his version of the female reformer on the examples of Margaret Fuller and his sister-in-law Elizabeth Peabody. In "The Christmas Banquet," there seems to be a kind of personal animus underlying his description of the feminist as "a woman of unemployed energy, who found herself in the world with nothing to achieve, nothing to enjoy and nothing even to suffer. She had, therefore, driven herself to the verge of madness by dark broodings over the wrongs of her sex, and its exclusion from a proper field of actions." He was, apparently, a good deal more sympathetic toward the men who found themselves in that predicament in modern society than toward women who could make the same complaint.

Throughout this creative period, Hawthorne was very much preoccupied with the Millerites, Father William Miller and his Adventist followers, who were predicting the Second Coming of Christ and the end of the world. That awesome event, originally scheduled to occur in the fall of 1843, failed to take place, and the Millerites, after a bit of hedging, rescheduled it for 1844. In his angry letter to Bridge about financial practices in America, Hawthorne had referred to these prophecies of doom and retribution. An apocalyptic mood crept into his fiction as well. Father Miller, in his black frock coat, makes an appearance in "The Hall of Fantasy," earnestly proclaiming, to a deeply attentive crowd, the coming destruction of the world. The narrator of that story takes a grim satisfaction in the fact that one blast of the prophet's "relentless theory" would obliterate all the improbable visions of the other prophets, reformers, and utopians gathered in his hall of dreams. In "The New Adam and Eve," Hawthorne imagines that Father Miller's prophecy has come to pass; the story takes place on the morning after the Apocalypse. The prophet also makes a final appearance in another of Hawthorne's stories, this time after his prophesied doomsday has come and gone without effect. In "The Christmas Banquet," he is among the guests at an annual feast of the miserable and disaffected of the world. The discredited preacher has "given himself up to despair at the tedious delay of the final conflagration" — a bizarre disappointment. In a strange blend of fact and fiction, this disgruntled prophet makes a doomed passage through Hawthorne's fiction, like a meteor that consumes itself in the process. An odd obsession for a writer who was, presumably, enjoying the happiest days of his life.

Two fables of the Apocalypse.

"Earth's Holocaust," which appeared in the May 1844 issue of *Graham's Magazine*, is one of Hawthorne's more controlled sketches of this period, a grim catalogue of the world's vanities, worn-out traditions, useless honors. One by one, they are thrown upon a giant bonfire, situated on a broad Midwestern prairie. (Hawthorne, perceptive of the growing commercialism of American life, indicates that the site has been selected by the insurance companies: even the destruction of American society will be presided over by American business.) With marvelous insouciance, he sets the scene in some indistinct period: "Once upon a time — but whether in time past or time to come, is a matter of little or no moment . . ." The great conflagration begins with a rage for democracy; the emblems of nobility and prestige — coats of arms, ribbons of honor, badges of knighthood — are among the first items cast into the flames. An old man complains that, in getting rid of the elite, the reformers have also gotten rid of the patrons of the arts. The crowd shouts him down. When a reformer cries out, "Let him thank his stars that we have not flung him into the same fire!" Hawthorne raises a first innuendo about the tyranny of reform. Next to go are the symbols of vice and luxury — barrels of wine and hard liquor, sheaves of tobacco. Another old man, complaining that "all the spice of life" is being condemned, wishes that the "nonsensical reformers" would fling themselves in, as well. "Be patient," one of the bystanders responds, "— it will come to that in the end. They will first fling us in, and finally themselves." The weapons and munitions of war and the instruments of capital punishment are thrown into the blazing heap. (An army commander, not unsympathetic to the cause, nevertheless remarks that it only means future work for "armorers and cannon-founderies"; every reform, Hawthorne suggests, will have its commercial opportunities.) Then, as the urge for reforms rises to a frenzied pitch, the banks are gutted and the money burned; the title deeds of property and marriage certificates are cast into the flames. Finally come the books. The hundred volumes of Voltaire — a reformer himself — are among the first to go, giving off "a brilliant shower of sparkles, and little jets of flame." Byron's works burn with fitful gleams and "gushes of black vapor." A man whom Hawthorne describes as "a modern philosopher" cheers on the work. "That's just the thing," he cries. "Now we shall get rid of the weight of dead men's thought." For Hawthorne's fanatics, the past, too, is an insufferable burden.

Hawthorne's narrator is confronted by the bitter knowledge that even the human impulse to perfection and reform is perverted by the worst of human motives — jealousy, vengeance, the urge for personal glory and power. He ponders "the fatal circumstance of an error at the very root of the matter! The Heart — the Heart — there was the little, yet boundless sphere, wherein existed the original wrong." The devil, in the guise of a dark stranger, watching the mindless destruction, seems to have the last, cynical word, pointing out that unless the heart, "that foul cavern," is purified, nothing will have been gained. "Oh, take my word for it, it will be the old world yet!" he claims.

In his story "The New Adam and Eve," Hawthorne conceives of a different — perhaps complementary — Apocalypse. This time, the useless emblems and institutions of civilization remain; the inhabitants of the world have all been exterminated — with the exception of his primordial couple. Hawthorne has set the scene of his fantasy in and around Boston: Mount Auburn Cemetery and the recently completed Bunker Hill Monument in Charlestown figure prominently in the tale. Hawthorne's Adam and Eve are complete innocents, a pair of naked anthropologists trying to solve the riddles of a lost society. In Hawthorne's vision, they inevitably prefer nature to the artifices of civilization. They roam the deserted streets of Boston, inspect its empty shops and institutions "with no knowledge of their predecessors, nor of the diseased cirumstances that had become encrusted around them." They have no taste for the wines and liquors they discover; they prefer pure water. Eve throws away pearls and jewels in favor of a perfect rose. They view the Bunker Hill Monument as a "visible prayer," not as the commemorative monument to a great national battle. The piles of paper money discovered in bank vaults are considered mere rubbish.

Hawthorne plays his sketch for every possible irony. His Eve has no overwhelming curiosity that will lead to banishment; she is an archconservative, a bit of a philistine. When Adam lingers in a public library, poring over old volumes, Eve chides him for wasting his time. The author, in an ironic indictment of civilization and its discontents, agrees with her: "All the perversions and sophistries and false wisdom so aptly mimicking the true; all the narrow truth, so partial that it becomes more deceptive than falsehood; all the wrong principles and worse practice, the pernicious examples and mistaken rules of life; all the specious theories which turn earth into cloud-land and men into shadows; all the sad experience, which it took mankind so many ages to accumulate, and from which they never drew a moral for their future guidance — the whole heap of this disastrous lore would have tumbled at once upon Adam's head." Hawthorne's book-burning episode in "Earth's Holocaust" was an ambivalent act; the author clearly saw the printed word as the guardian of all the accumulated wisdom — and folly — of the ages. Adam, initiated into the mysteries of the library, would only repeat the errors of the past: it is one of the more notable nineteenth-century pronouncements on historic determinism.

"The New Adam and Eve" suffers, as do many of Hawthorne's stories from the Concord period, from an insistent working-out of the terms of his social criticism. Sophia, who did not intrude on her husband's work ("I have made a law to myself never to ask him a word concerning what he is writing"), never doubted her husband's tact. Writing to her mother, she claimed: "He follows the Muse. It is the real inspiration, and few are patient and reverent enough to wait for it as he does. In this way (in part) he comes to be so void of extravagance or exaggeration in his style and material." But it is clear that Hawthorne's Concord stories are exaggeratedly "moral." In his happiness, he seems to have been infected by Sophia's high-minded attitudes toward life — and perhaps by the "cloud-land" morality of Concord.

There is a sense, too, that Hawthorne's carefully guarded reticence and isolation served him poorly during this period. The give-and-take of personal relationships and private discussions stand an author in good stead when it comes to his writing. He senses when he has made a point without unnecessary repetition or emphasis. Hawthorne, in these stories, is never quite certain whether he has established his case; he is forever underlining his moral. When

Adam and Eve visit the Hall of Legislature, and Eve sits down in the speaker's chair, Hawthorne spells out the symbolic nature of the act in heavy-handed fashion: "Man's intellect, moderated by Woman's tenderness and moral sense! Were such the legislation of the world, there would be no need of State Houses, Capitals, Halls of Parliament."

Yet "The New Adam and Eve" was one of the more popular tales of an author who had been out of the public eye for a lengthy period. After its appearance in the *Democratic Review*, it was several times reprinted, though the piracies were of no financial benefit to Hawthorne. The personal cast of the story did not escape Hawthorne's family. Not long after it appeared, Louisa wrote Sophia, wondering whether the "new Adam and Eve" of the Old Manse had not seen enough of nature to be ready to return to the artificialities of society. The story, she said, had been reprinted in the *Salem Gazette* and had "excited the wonderment of the people not a little," for Hawthorne had pictured his hero and heroine in a state of nudity. "What an admirable taste in dress they displayed," Louisa commented.

⌐ II ⌐

The winter of Sophia's pregnancy was a severe one. They spent Christmas week together in happy solitude, their cook, Molly, having gone to Boston for the holidays. In the cold mornings, Hawthorne rose early, kindled the fires in the kitchen and breakfast room, put the teakettle on, and roasted the potatoes or cooked the rice, superintending his work while reading a book. After breakfast, Sophia set his study in order, then did whatever chores she could. Later, she took her sewing basket and sat by her husband while he wrote — "with now and then a little discourse" between them. Around one in the afternoon, they walked to the village; at three, they dined. At dusk, Hawthorne sawed wood — his regular exercise for the day. The evenings were spent beside the "air-tight" stove in the study while Hawthorne read Shakespeare aloud. Although their Christmas dinner might have seemed meager to others, Sophia described it as "Paradisiacal"; they had preserved quince and apple, dates, bread and cheese and milk. Except for a brief call from their neighbor Mrs. Prescott, there were no other holiday visitors.

With the new year, the temperature dropped. "In the papers, it is said that there has not been so cold a January for an hundred years!" Sophia wrote her mother. It was a miracle they had survived two weeks of such weather. "Were we not so well acclimated to it, we should probably have become pillars of ice. Our thoughts began to hang in icicles." Molly Bryan, bending over the wash, found her hair covered with frost; for several days she took to singing out loud to keep her mind off the freezing temperatures. It was so cold that when Horace Mann, who was to give a lecture at the Concord Lyceum, asked to stay at the Old Manse, Sophia decided to put him on a cot in Hawthorne's study. The guest room, with its open fireplace, was too frigid for her brother-in-law's worrisome health. Her sister Mary would not be coming with her husband; she, too, was pregnant. Sophia asked for details about Mann's regular diet: cooked apples and milk, syrup for his hot water, a special "dyspepsia bread." She warned Mary in advance, "We can neither of us hear his lecture; for I never have been out in the evening, and Mr. Hawthorne would not leave me to hear Paul preach at this time." They would not risk the possibility of another miscarriage.

With dutiful precision, Horace and Mary Mann's first child, named Horace Mann, Jr., was born on February 25, 1844 — exactly nine months after their marriage. Perhaps the brandy that Samuel Gridley Howe had supplied on the honeymoon had had a beneficial effect. The usually teetotaling Horace had waited until they were "out of the jurisdiction of the American Temperance Society" before losing his inhibitions to the point of joining the Howes in healthy drinks "all round." (Writing expansively "To all whom it may concern," he refused to explain whether the unsteadiness of his hand was due to the brandy or the pitch and roll of the *Britannia*.) Sophia, having learned of her nephew's birth, wrote Mother Peabody in a playful vein, "I suspect that Mary's baby must have opened its mouth the moment it was born, and pronounced a School Report; for its mother's brain has had no other permanent idea in it for the last year."

Her own baby was born a week later, on March 3, after a difficult delivery. Hawthorne wrote Louisa, with obvious relief — and pride, "You and Elizabeth are aunts and our mother is a grandmother to a little girl ,who came head-first into the world at ½ past 9 o'clock this morning, after being ten awful hours in getting across the threshold." He had not seen the baby yet, but reported that it had red hair. Mrs. Peabody, who was visiting, had assured him that the baby was *"lovely."* "Of my own personal knowledge, I can say nothing, except that it already roars very lustily." Sophia, he said, "has had a terrible time, but is now quite comfortable and perfectly happy." He added a cautionary postscript: "In your reply on no account say a word about the *red hair*. We had a name already — Una! Is not it pretty? Una Hawthorne. Una Hawthorne!! It is very pretty." Two hours after the birth, Sophia was given an opportunity to see the baby, and, as she later reported in their journal, she was glad that it was "not a red baby but quite fair." She wrote, "It was a great happiness to be able to put her to my breast immediately and I thanked Heaven I was able to have the privilege of nursing her."

If the happy parents were pleased with the name Una, taken from Spenser's pure heroine, the Hawthorne family was not so satisfied. Hawthorne intercepted a disapproving letter from Louisa and responded gruffly: "Almost everybody has had something to say about it, but only yourselves have found out that it does not sound prettily." There was no use in further criticism, he maintained half-jokingly, "especially from you, whom Sophia has been anxious to please in the whole concoction of this baby." He asked Louisa to write another letter, carefully avoiding any suggestion that she was not pleased with her niece's name. Somewhat outrageously, he claimed that the baby's hair was "a carroty tinge" and that if she only had "a little brown wig," she would be quite pretty.

In a more serious moment, Hawthorne regretted that he had been unable to send his family any money. As soon as he had enough to meet his needs, he promised, he definitely would send something. "I must within no long time," he said, "make some arrangements to establish a more regular income." If any Democrat was elected in the coming fall presidential elections, he said, "all will go well enough. I shall be certain of the Post Office, or of something as good." If not, he wrote, "I shall connect myself permanently with some paper or magazine, which it will not be difficult to do; and I think, without removing from Concord, as the rail-road will soon be opened."

Writing to George Hillard, he noted that fatherhood had brought "a very sober and serious kind of happiness," but he added, with a tinge of regret, that after such an event "the spirit never can be thoroughly gay and careless again." He had, he admitted, been "a trifler" for a preposterously long period, and now he must quit his "cloud-region . . . I have business on earth now, and must look about me for the means of doing it." The birth of his first child had filled him with a new sense of resolution. "It will never do for me to continue merely a writer of stories for the magazines — the most unprofitable business in the world." If no political appointment was forthcoming, he would have to support himself by some form of literary drudgery — "translation, concocting of school-books, newspaper-scribbling etc." Writing to Bridge, aboard the *Saratoga*, he was ebullient. "If you want a new feeling in this weary life," he said, "get married, and make yourself a father. It renews the world from the surface to the center."

In April, Hawthorne visited Salem, seeing his family and, probably, surveying the political situation among the local Democrats. He was also escaping from his father-in-law; Nathaniel Peabody was at the Old Manse on an extended stay. On his way to Salem, Hawthorne reluctantly called on his mother-in-law in Boston. Writing to Sophia, he plainly stated that he had made his "escape" as soon as possible, but he had halfheartedly promised to return for a dinner at West Street. "I wish thy mother could be so inhospitable as never to ask me," he wrote Sophia frankly, "but at all events, I need never go, except when thou art there." He told Sophia that before his return to Concord he planned to "consult" with Mother Peabody about recalling Father Peabody to Boston early. On the subject of his in-laws, Hawthorne did not hide his feelings.

Sophia appreciated her father's visit, but Nathaniel Peabody, a compulsive fixer, had set the household on end with his repairs. Sophia itemized her father's activities for her mother. Her own mood seemed to hover between pride and exasperation:

> He has fixed my chamber bell, mended the bellows, mended the rocking chair (That unfortunate arm, which was forever coming off when one sat down in it . . . One day Mr. Hawthorne did so, and as the crazy old arm came off in his hand, he threw himself into a despairing attitude and exclaimed, "Oh, I will flee my country!" I cannot describe to you, the *wit* of this. I laughed and laughed with many refrains.) He has split all the wood, taken down the partition in the kitchen, pasted all the torn paper on the walls, picked up the dead branches in the avenue, mended baby's carriage, mended the garden gate . . .

But Father Peabody had clearly overstepped his bounds when he arranged to have the garden ploughed while Hawthorne was away. Beneath Hawthorne's surface amiability, there was a steeliness with which his wife was thoroughly familiar. Sophia was concerned enough to complain to her mother. Her husband, she said, would wonder why she hadn't stopped it — "but I did not know of it till a great piece was ploughed. Papa can be very naughty sometimes, you know, in his passion for doing things. The next time he comes, you must scold at him and tell him he may do anything but interfere with Mr. Hawthorne's plans. He *must not* be meddled with."

A month after her husband's return, Sophia was forced to go to Boston for treatments with Dr. Wesselhoeft. Following the birth of Una, she had had a recurrence of her migraine headaches. Late in May, she and the baby made the trip to Boston. Hawthorne accompanied them to see that they were comfortably settled in at West Street. Sophia remained for three weeks, "desperately homesick," but the treatments proved effective.

Before returning to Concord, Hawthorne had picked up Horace Conolly, who was scheduled to be a guest at the Old Manse during

Sophia's absence. On the 25th, Hawthorne and Conolly had crossed the Charles to Cambridge to dine with Longfellow and his wife. The other guests were George Hillard and Fanny Longfellow's brother, Tom Appleton. Hawthorne, writing to Sophia from Concord on the 27th, remarked that he had greatly liked Fanny Longfellow — "Mrs. Longlady (as thou naughtily nicknamest her)." Young and spirited, dark-haired, with all the usual independence of the well-to-do, Fanny Longfellow was in the final weeks of pregnancy. She had looked forward to meeting the author of "Earth's Holocaust," which she had just read in *Graham's* and considered a "capital story." But she found Hawthorne "the most shy and silent of men." As she noted in her diary, "The freest conversation did not thaw forth more than a monosyllable and we discussed art glibly enough. I really pity a person under this spell of reserve." Her brother was to describe the author as "a boned pirate."

Hawthorne and Conolly had stayed late at Craigie House and did not reach the Old Manse until after nine o'clock. The house was "dark and desolate," Hawthorne wrote Sophia. But he was happy to report that Conolly had proved himself a splendid cook, having made "the best dish of fried fish and potatoes" that he had ever had at the manse. They had already had a visit from Ellery Channing, and the three men had gone fishing. Channing, too, was a recent father. Earlier in the month, Ellen Channing had given birth to a baby girl.

A bare two days later, Hawthorne was unhappy with his house guest. In a letter to George Hillard, he complained that Conolly had bored him "so abominably that at last my hospitality gave way, and I fairly besought him to leave me to myself." Writing to Sophia on the same day, he noted that his guest would soon be quitting the manse — "to my unspeakable relief; for he has had a bad cold, which caused him to be much more troublesome, and less amusing, than might otherwise have been the case." He was planning to invite Frank Farley, his former companion at Brook Farm, to pay a visit, but decided to put off writing him until the end of the week. On June 2, there was another visit from Ellery Channing, who, he learned, was quarreling with his wife's wetnurse. "What a gump!" Hawthorne commented. He had been thinking of asking Channing to share the manse with him; now that idea seemed "too hazardous." If Channing could not remain on good terms with his wife's nurse, "he would surely quarrel with me, alone in an empty house; and perhaps the result might be a permanent breach." Hawthorne had some sharp criticisms to make of the younger man: "On the whole, he is but little better than an idiot. He should have been whipt often and soundly in his boyhood . . . But somebody else may take him in hand; it is none of my business."

In a quandary, Hawthorne cast an eye on George Bradford — but immediately had second thoughts. There was something unattractive about Bradford. He was a man of prissy habits who never drank more than half a glass of wine and whose only indulgence was strong tea. He had a perpetual quaver in his voice and such scruples about eating too much that meals were often a trial. He seemed to take shorter steps than a man should. Hawthorne decided that Bradford would be too fastidious to be comfortable with the bachelor conditions at the manse. "A man of his nice conscience," he wrote Sophia, "would be shocked, I suppose, if the whole house were not swept, every day, from top to bottom, or if the dishes of several meals were suffered to accumulate . . . Now such enormities do not at all disturb my composure."

Frank Farley, who arrived on June 5, turned out to be a more acceptable guest. Hawthorne was happy to report that Farley, who had been institutionalized after his breakdown at Brook Farm, was now "in perfect health and absolutely in the seventh heaven." He was, moreover, an admirable cook and had demonstrated his abilities on the first Sunday by preparing a roast veal and rice pudding that had been delicious. Like all male cooks, so Hawthorne informed Sophia, Farley was "rather expensive, and has a tendency to the consumption of eggs in his various concoctions which thou wouldst be apt to frown upon."

As a house guest, Farley had one serious fault: he was a nonstop talker. "He talks and talks and talks and talks," Hawthorne wrote, "and I listen and listen and listen, with a patience for which (in spite of all my sins) I firmly expect to be admitted to the mansions of the blessed." It was only a halfhearted complaint, however, for Hawthorne conceded that he felt a sense of satisfaction in being able to make "this poor, world-worn, hopeless, half crazy man so entirely comfortable as he seems to be here." It was unlikely, he wrote, that he would be able to ask Farley to leave before Sophia returned — perhaps with Mrs. Peabody — so there would be a few days' overlap. In the meantime, Farley was threatening to fatten him up properly for Sophia's arrival. "I have had my dreams of splendor," Hawthorne told her, "but never expected to arrive at the dignity of keeping a man-cook."

On a summer morning in late July, Hawthorne sat down in Sleepy Hollow for the express purpose of recording the ordinariness of the day in its passage through time; to await, as he noted, "such little events as may happen, or observe such noticeable points as the eyes fall upon." He specified the day — July 27, 1844 — and the time — "about ten o'clock in the forenoon." He described the scene in some detail: a field of Indian corn already tasseled out in the open hollow, the encroaching forest of oaks, chestnuts, and white pines. The only sounds that disturbed the silence were the gentle sigh of the wind through the pines, the tinkling of a distant cowbell, the regular interruptions of the village clock — and, once, "the long, melancholy note of a bird, complaining alone, of some wrong or sorrow." He studied the woodland path with its carpet of dry oak leaves, the sunlight filtering through the rank growth of summer, glancing off the thin pine needles; he commented on the "beautiful diversity of green" in his quiet retreat.

In the midst of his thoughts in the green shade, he heard the shrill whistle of a locomotive — a sharp, piercing note, "harsh, above all other harshness." Even from a mile away, it was disruptive. "It tells a story of busy men," he wrote, "citizens, from the hot street, who have come to spend a day in the country village; men of business; in short of all unquietness; and no wonder that it gives such a startling shriek, since it brings the noisy world into the midst of our slumbrous peace." He had recorded the new age of commercialism pushing into the rural retreats of sleepy villages. For the price of fifty cents and an hour's ride, the Fitchburg Railroad — which had officially opened the month before — was annexing the village of Concord to the city of Boston. Hawthorne might resent the noise and the intrusion, but he could also, as he had written Louisa, see the Fitchburg Railroad as opening new options for his own career, making it possible for him to commute to some editorial job in Boston.

In intellectual Concord, he was not the only intelligence aware of the momentous changes in the American way of life. Emerson, too, had heard the whistle of a locomotive in the woods. "Wherever that music comes," he wrote in his journal, "it has a sequel. It is the voice of the civility of the Nineteenth Century saying, 'Here I am.' " Emerson recorded the locomotive hoot as a restless and querying voice: "Whew! Whew! Whew! How is real estate here in the swamp & wilderness? . . . Whew! Whew! Down with that forest on the side of the hill. I want ten thousand chestnut sleepers. I want cedar posts and hundreds of thousands of feet of boards . . . I will plant a dozen houses on this pasture next moon and a village anon." He readily conceded that the new railroad had made man a "chattel," transporting him "by the box & by the ton." Still, with his inveterate optimism, he was sure that some man of genius would convert the new commercial inventions to a higher purpose. True art, he maintained, "springs up between the feet. Somebody shall be born who shall turn to a divine use the railway or the Insurance Office or our caucus or our commerce, in which we seek now only the economical use."

His neighbor Hawthorne had put the new railroad to use in a story, making it an ironic symbol of progress in the spiritual realm. "The Celestial Rail-road," which appeared in the May 1843 issue of the *Democratic Review,* was an updated version of *Pilgrim's Progress.* In Hawthorne's version, the new Christian pilgrim rides the rails to moral perfection without any of the hardships that beset Christian in Bunyan's classic. "The Celestial Rail-road" is a parable of modern spiritual accommodation. A shaky but useful bridge spans the Slough of Despond; it is no longer necessary for the pilgrim to climb the Hill of Difficulty, since a railway tunnel has been cut through it to the other side. The rubble has been used to fill up the Valley of Humiliation, thus sparing the pilgrim another inconvenience. Where Bunyan's pilgrim must carry his heavy burden on his back throughout a wearisome journey, Hawthorne's pilgrims merely send them to the baggage compartment. Even Vanity Fair, that wanton city, has got "religion"; there are churches on every corner. It is a resort for clerics with such names as the Reverend Mr. Shallow-deep and the Reverend Dr. Wind-of-Doctrine. But it is in Vanity Fair that Hawthorne's traveler receives his warning — from one of the hold-outs against the easy spiritual values of the period — that the Celestial Rail-road will never reach its destination. The Lord of the Celestial City, he is told, refuses to grant an "act of incorporation for this rail-road." Every ticket for the Celestial Rail-road is worthless — as Hawthorne's pilgrim discovers at the end of his dream journey.

Hawthorne's sardonic view of the new religious movements of his day, his distrust of the apostles of reform and the proclaimers of the "newness," is severe. In his satire of the clergymen in Vanity Fair, he clearly had some of his clerical contemporaries in mind, since he was delighted when one of them, the Reverend Robert Waterston, seemed cold and aloof during a chance meeting in Boston. "This is so unlike his deportment in times past," Hawthorne wrote Sophia gleefully, "that I suspect the Celestial Rail-road must have given him a pique; and if so, I shall feel as if Providence had sufficiently rewarded me for that pious labor."

During the long rainy days at the Old Manse, Hawthorne sometimes retired to the attic and pored over Dr. Ripley's library of moldering theological tracts. From his reading, Hawthorne formed a distinct opinion of the decline of religious values from the stern and dour Puritanical faith of his forefathers to the easier tenets of contemporary clerics. In his journal, he commented on the difference "between the cold, lifeless, vaguely liberal clergyman of our own day, and the narrow but earnest cushion thumper of puritanical times." He wrote, "On the whole, I prefer the last-mentioned variety of the black-coated tribe."

↶ III ↷

George William Curtis wrote from Concord to his friend and former music teacher, John Sullivan Dwight, "The people here who are worth knowing, I find, live very quietly and retired. In the country, friendship seems not to be of that consuming, absorbing character that city circumstances give it."

Curtis, who was twenty, and his brother, Burrill, two years older, were the sons of a wealthy Rhode Island banker. They had recently settled in Concord after a highly social winter in New York. Young men of principle, they had been mere schoolboys in Mr. Hartshorn's School in Providence when they were struck with admiration for Ralph Waldo Emerson, who had delivered a lecture entitled "The Over-Soul." They were not much older — George being only eighteen — when they joined the Brook Farm community soon after Hawthorne's departure. Among the promising scholars of the utopian community, both were considered remarkably handsome — "like young Greek gods," according to George Ripley. A visitor to Brook Farm, Thomas Wentworth Higginson, later the mentor of Emily Dickinson, had been positively awed by the appearance of George Curtis, in shirtsleeves and boots, escorting a young girl with an "elegant grace which never left him." Curtis was one of those fortunate young men destined for success. He became one of the most prominent Americans of his generation: a famous spokesman of the abolitionist cause, a noted journalist, political editor of *Harper's Weekly*, author of the long-running column, "The Easy Chair," in *Harper's Magazine*. He also became a popular travel-writer, with a taste for the Mideast and the Orient, which he wrote about using the soubriquet "Howadji," a rough transliteration of the Arabic word for "traveler."

Inseparable in childhood, the Curtis brothers were sociable, ingratiating, and musically inclined. During their residence at Brook Farm and on later visits, their impromptu concerts were a welcome form of community entertainment. Standing at the piano in the crowded dining hall, lean and attractive, their faces beaming, they sang such favorites as "The Erl King," "Kathleen Mavourneen," and "Good Night to Julia." It was at the farm that George struck up a lifelong friendship with Dwight, eleven years his senior, and the later publisher of *Dwight's, Journal of Music*, the most influential magazine of musical studies published in America. In the spring of 1844 the Curtis brothers settled in Concord, close to their childhood hero, Emerson. During the days they worked as laborers on Nathaniel Barrett's farm; their evenings were devoted to serious studies.

"My regret at not seeing you was only lessened by the beautiful day I passed with Mr. Hawthorne," Curtis wrote Dwight in the same August 7 letter in which he commented on the quiet Concord citizenry. Hawthorne's life, he told Dwight, "is so harmonious with the antique repose of his house, and so redeemed into the present by his infant, that it is much better to sit an hour with him than hear the Rev. Barzillai Frost!" The baby, he added, "is the most serenely happy I ever saw. It is beautiful, and lies amid such placid influences that it too may have a milk white lamb as emblem; and Mrs. Hawthorne is so tenderly respectful towards her husband that all the romance we picture in a cottage of lovers dwells subdued and dignified with them." Curtis had a talent for painting sentimental pictures: Una was, in fact, guarded by a large and troublesome St. Bernard dog named Leo (a gift from her godfather, John Louis O'Sullivan), which made a nuisance of itself by chasing the neighbor's chickens. But as Curtis conceded, "I see them very seldom."

During the three years Hawthorne lived at the Old Manse, a little caravan of former Brook Farmers stopped in Concord — camping at Emerson's doorstep, so to speak. Almira Barlow, the vivacious and attractive boarder at Brook Farm, together with her son Francis, had moved to Concord. Isaac Hecker, the farm's nervous, God-driven baker, having quit the Association in favor of Bronson Alcott's short-lived communal experiment, Fruitlands, took up residence in Concord. Under the sponsorship of Orestes Brownson, Hecker had begun a spiritual journey to Rome. (After much agonizing reflection, he joined the Catholic Church and founded the Paulist Society in New York.) In Concord, living in Mrs. Thoreau's boardinghouse, Hecker, with some success, pursued a friendship with the stiffish Henry Thoreau; but later, having failed to convert the woodland philosopher to Catholicism, he would complain that Thoreau was a "consecrated crank." George Bradford, the thin giant, a drifting soul and perennial bachelor, had also returned to Concord to serve as the tutor for Emerson's children. Emerson might rail against the new breed of scholars who read newspapers, smoked, took naps in the afternoon, and were "coated over merely with a thin varnish of latin and reading-room literature," but, like Hawthorne, he appreciated Bradford's conversation and his "beautiful" conscience. Another former Brook Farmer, Minot Pratt, having settled in Concord, became one of those philosophical farmers dear to Emerson's heart, a man who contributed papers on agriculture to the Concord Farmer's Club. For several years, Pratt gave annual picnics under the huge elm in the frontyard of his farmhouse. All the dispossessed Brook Farmers and such interested parties as Thoreau and Emerson were invited.

The fate of Brook Farm, therefore, was a subject of some interest in Concord. The Association, plagued with serious financial difficulties, was in the process of being reorganized along lines far different from its transcendental origins. Under the influence of Albert Brisbane, a controversial journalist and propagandist for the ideas of the French social philosopher, Charles Fourier, the bankrupt Brook Farm community was drafting a new constitution based on Fourier's principles of industrial communitarianism. In his public lectures, several of which were delivered at Ripley's utopia, Brisbane had wisely concentrated on the practical aspects of Fourier's philosophy, stressing his ideas on the division of labor and the sharing of profits. He left to the decent obscurity of the French some of Fourier's wilder notions: that when the world was finally organized into Fourierist Phalanxes, the sea would turn to lemonade and men would grow tails. Even less palatable for nineteenth-century minds were some of his libertarian views on sex. Fourier regarded monogamy and sex-for-procreation-only as symptoms of the contemporary world's hypocrisy and mismanagement. He envisioned a thoroughly structured bureaucracy of sex, a court of love that would administer to every form of sexual gratification — normal, abnormal, the rare manias, and the exotic forms of sexual perversion, including large-scale orgies — all in the interest of a smoothly functioning society.

Emerson, who had heard Brisbane lecture in New York, was doubtful: Fourierism, he felt, was "the sublime of mechanics," the "perfection of Arrangement and Contrivance." Still, in contrast with the "small, sour and fierce" schemes of reform that he was already familiar with, Emerson thought Fourierism had a certain largesse. Hawthorne, who had not yet recouped his investment in Brook Farm, also maintained a keen interest in developments in West Roxbury. During the summer of 1844, he had been reading up on Fourier's philosophy. On that idling July day spent in Sleepy Hollow, he had patiently observed a colony of ants, and it had brought to mind his readings in Fourier. The bustling anthill seemed "the very model of a community which Fourierites and others are stumbling in pursuit of. Possibly, the student of such philosophies should go to the ant, and find that nature has given him his lesson there." It was a mild criticism; he apparently expressed himself more force-fully to his wife, who was also reading the French philosopher. So-phia engaged in a lengthy debate on the subject with her mother, during the course of which she conveyed her husband's feelings. Mother Peabody, ordinarily hospitable to any philosophy for the betterment of man, found it difficult to overlook certain aspects of Fourier's system. "The French," she complained, "have been and are still corrupt, and have lost all true ideas relative to woman. There is a sad tendency to the same evil among us." But she wondered, charitably, if Fourier's ideas had not suffered in translation.

Sophia was anxious about setting the record right: "It was not a translation of Fourier that I read. It was the original text — the fourth volume of his works, and though[t] it was so abominable, so immoral, irreligious and void of all delicate sentiment; yet George Bradford told me it is not so bad as some other volumes!!" Sophia conceded some extenuating circumstances: Fourier was writing after the French Revolution, "and this accounts somewhat for the *monstrous* system he proposes, because then the people worshipped a naked woman as the Goddess of Reason." Even so, she added, "It is very plain, from all that I read (a small part) that he had entirely lost his moral sense. To make as much money and luxury and en-joyment out of man's lowest passions as possible — this is the aim and end of his system! . . . My husband read the whole volume and was thoroughly disgusted."

George William Curtis had been studying Fourier as well; he looked forward to that promised future when bands of the enlightened would roam from Phalanx to Phalanx. He was experiencing some sense of isolation in the Concord of the present. He informed Dwight, "Indeed, I think it likely that every year while my home is in the country I may perform a pilgrimage to the city for two or three months for purposes of art and literature and affection." It may well have been that the affectionate or amorous possibilities of Fourier's utopia appealed to younger men like Curtis. Clearly, even intellectual Concord lacked certain satisfactions. "When the band of Phalanxes proceeding into desert and free air, no more allow art to rendezvous in the cities," he continued, "I can take one of the nearest radiating rail-roads and rush from my solitude into the healthily-peopled and cityish-countrified Phalanx."

Several years later, Curtis was to recall his Concord days in a book, *Homes of American Authors*, published in 1853. His roman-ticized essays on the Hawthorne and Emerson households caused a little stir among Concord residents. Mrs. Alcott, for one, was angry about the satiric portrait of her husband, whom Curtis had called Plato Skimpole, borrowing Margaret Fuller's nickname for Alcott. In the main, Curtis' recollections of his associates were genial enough; by the time he wrote them, he had acquired the skills of a polished journalist. In Emerson's study, he recalled, it seemed "always morning," but in his visits to Hawthorne's front parlor, secluded behind its avenue of poplars, it was forever afternoon. His first meetings with the elusive author, he noted, had taken place in the dead of winter at an "aesthetic tea" in Emerson's parlor. The talk that afternoon had been brilliant, but Hawthorne had taken no part in it whatsoever. In the midst of it, Hawthorne had got up and stared out at the white landscape. "So supreme was his silence," Curtis noted, "that it presently engrossed me to the exclusion of all else." When, shortly afterward, Hawthorne had left, Emerson, with a "slow, wise smile," remarked, "Hawthorne rides well his horse of the night."

Of his other visits with Hawthorne, Curtis recalled "a few hazy days, of a tranquil and half-pensive character." In the company of Hawthorne and George Bradford, he had once made an excursion to the top of Wachusett Mountain. Independently of each other, both men — Hawthorne in his notebook; Curtis in a letter to John Dwight — had remarked on a species of white potentilla that grew high on the mountain in such abundance that the pastures were swarming with bees. The excursion, Curtis told Dwight, had been "a fine episode in the summer." It was out of such experiences that Curtis evoked a highly colored account of Hawthorne's responsiveness to nature and society and of his congenial silences: "His own sympathy was so broad and sure that although nothing had been said for hours, his companion knew that not a thing had escaped his eye, nor had a single pulse of beauty in the day or scene or society failed to thrill his heart." (Ellery Channing, however, remembered a different Hawthorne after taking the author to a secluded spot in Gowing's Swamp in Concord, a beautiful pool where Labrador tea and rhodora grew in profusion. "It was a choice walk, to which Thoreau and I did not invite everybody," Channing complained. "When we reached the place, Hawthorne said nothing, but just glanced about him and remarked, 'Let us get out of this dreadful hole!'")

In his Concord recollections, Curtis also described the somewhat comic meetings of the Monday Night Club, which Emerson misguidedly initiated in 1845 in hopes of starting up a little intellectual society. Hawthorne, Thoreau, Bronson Alcott, George Bradford, the two Curtis brothers, and the philosophical farmer, Edmund Hosmer, were among the members who met in Emerson's parlor. The first meeting was strained. "I vaguely remember," Curtis recalled, "that the Orphic Alcott invaded the Sahara of silence with a solemn 'saying,' to which, after due pause, the honorable member for Blackberry Pastures [Thoreau] responded by some keen and graphic observation, while the Olympian host, anxious that so much material should be spun into something, beamed smiling encouragment upon all parties. But the conversation became more and more staccato. [Hawthorne], a statue of night and silence, sat, a little removed, under a portrait of Dante, gazing imperturbably upon the group."

He wrote, "I recall little else but a grave eating of russet apples by the erect philosophers, and a solemn disappearance into night. The club struggled through three Monday evenings."

In his later estimates of Hawthorne, Curtis was to take a harder and more critical line — particularly with regard to Hawthorne's conservative political views. But during the early summers in Concord, he developed a warm appreciation for the taciturn author. "There is no companion superior to him in genial sympathy with human feeling," Curtis wrote Dwight. "He seems to me no less a successful man than Mr. Emerson, although at the opposite end of the village."

Curtis was a member of the large search party, on a grim night in July — it was Hawthorne's third wedding anniversary — that recovered the body of a twenty-year-old girl, Martha Hunt, a schoolteacher, who drowned herself in the Concord River. Curtis' account, written several years later, was a sentimental "village tragedy," the tale of a local maiden, virtuous but unloved, dissatisfied with her station in life. Curtis imagined that Martha Hunt's education in "a fine academy in a neighboring town" had spoiled her for the meaner advantages of Concord; her raw farming family, her probable lifetime occupation as a local schoolteacher. The girl had made at least one earlier attempt at taking her life by walking out into the river, but she had been called back by the agonized pleading of a sister. On July 9, early in the morning, she had gone to the river, where she had been seen walking back and forth along the shore. When she failed to come home that evening, the search party had been got up. Her bonnet and shoes had been found at the spot where she had last been seen, and, floating at the water's edge, her handkerchief.

Hawthorne's version of that night search, written in all probability a day or two later, is full of the grim particulars. Around nine or ten that evening, Ellery Channing had knocked at the door to ask Hawthorne to join the search, using the *Pond Lily*. The pair had traveled downstream, some distance below the bridge. The scene was eerie: the bright lanterns, reflected in the black water; a crowd of dim figures waiting along the shore. There, they had taken on board General Joshua Buttrick and a young man in a blue smock, carrying long poles to test the sludgy river bottom. Ellery Channing was given a rake. Hawthorne rowed upstream, allowing the boat to drift, broadside, down past the area where the bonnet and shoes had been found. It was a place where the river bottom dropped abruptly, "one of the deepest spots in the whole river," Hawthorne noted, "and, holding a lantern over it, it was black as midnight, smooth, impenetrable, and keeping its secrets from the eye as perfectly as mid-ocean would." Once or twice, they had raked up bunches of waterweeds that floated to the surface. From the shoreline, disembodied voices shouted out advice to try one spot or another. On another pass, downriver, the man in the smock gave a sudden start, crying out, "What's this?"

> I felt in a moment what it was [Hawthorne wrote], and I suppose the same electric shock went through everybody in the boat. "Yes, I've got her!" said he; and heaving up his pole with difficulty, there was an appearance of light garments on the surface of the water; he made a strong effort and brought so much of the body above the surface that there could be no doubt of it . . . The fellow evidently had the same sort of feeling in his success as if he had caught a particularly fine fish; though mingled, no doubt, with horror. For my own part, I felt my voice tremble a little when I spoke, at the first shock of discovery, and at seeing the body come to the surface, dimly in the starlight.

The girl's body had been brought to shore and laid on the bank under an oak tree. Hawthorne observed that it was quite rigid: "Her arms had stiffened in the act of struggling and were bent before her, with the hands clenched. She was the very image of a death-agony; and when the men tried to compose her figure, her arms would still return to the same position." One man tried to force the arms down with his foot, a grisly sight in itself. Blood began to stream from the girl's nose; an eye was badly bruised, possibly from having been struck by one of the poles. An old carpenter said that the body would continue to "purge" until the burial. By morning, he claimed, the body would be so swollen, it would be unrecognizable. The girl was placed on a rough bier of boards laid across two fence rails and carried home — Hawthorne aiding the others in the seemingly endless walk. In the farmhouse, she was laid out on a kitchen table, where Mrs. Pratt and Mrs. Lee, a withered old creature of skin and bones, took on the task of preparing the body for burial.

Martha Hunt, Hawthorne learned, had kept a diary "which is said to exhibit (as her whole life did) many high and remarkable traits."

He also was told that when the "tire-women" had stripped the body, they found a cord drawn tight around the girl's waist — for what purpose he could not imagine. Like Curtis, Hawthorne, too, saw Martha Hunt as a victim of circumstance. "I suppose one friend would have saved her; but she died for want of sympathy, — a severe penalty for having cultivated and refined herself out of the sphere of her natural connections."

Hawthorne evidently sensed that the events of that night, that "spectacle of such perfect horror," would be important to him in the future. He was to make extensive use of its details in describing the death of Zenobia in *The Blithedale Romance*. But there, he deleted all the painstakingly recorded details, passing over the struggle to bend the girl's arms, the unremitting bleeding, the carpenter's prediction of swelling. Out of deference to his reading public, he spared them the gruesome details.

When Sophia came to edit her husband's notebooks, she briefly considered publishing Hawthorne's account of the suicide, referring to it as a "wonderful photograph of the terrible night." Presumably she thought better of it. It was not until Julian Hawthorne wrote his biography of his parents that the episode appeared in print. Even then, Thomas Wentworth Higginson, reviewing the biography, scolded the author for publishing such a scene. The result could hardly have been more horrible, Higginson stated, if Julian Hawthorne had "introduced a series of photographs from the Paris morgue."

⌐ IV ⌐

Throughout the fall and winter of 1844–1845, Hawthorne's financial situation worsened. For economic reasons, as well as family ones, he and Sophia and the baby spent Thanksgiving week with his mother and sisters in Salem. It was a notable occasion on at least one count, so Sophia reported to Mrs. Peabody: "For the first time since my husband can remember, he dined with his mother! This is only one of the miracles which the baby is to perform. Her grandmother held her on her lap till one of us should finish dining, and then ate her own meal. She thinks Una is a beauty."

For the next month, the family shifted about. Sophia and the baby went to Boston; Hawthorne remained in Salem, making occasional visits to Boston, where he sometimes stayed overnight with the Hillards because of the crowded conditions at West Street. He was plainly unhappy. He wrote Sophia on December 2, "Thy letter came this morning — much needed; for I was feeling desolate and fragmentary. Thou shouldst not ask me to come to Boston for the purpose of sleeping a night in thy dearest arms because I can hardly resist setting off this minute — and I have no right to spend money for such luxuries." He told Sophia he would wait in Salem until Horatio Bridge, who had returned from his African cruise, reached Boston, probably in a week's time. Part of his reason was financial embarrassment. "It would save him and us the trouble and perplexity of a visit at Concord," he explained.

He was particularly eager to see his friend because of the current political situation in Salem. In a letter written to Bridge in Washington on November 29, Hawthorne welcomed his friend back to his "native soil," then launched into his political prospects. A veteran Democrat, Benjamin Browne, had recently been appointed to the postmastership. The appointment had not yet been confirmed, and there was some doubt whether Browne would be approved. "Very probably, your influence might cause the rejection of the new incumbent; in which case, I think I might have a good chance for the office from Polk." Browne's last-minute appointment, he explained, did not sit well with local Democrats, since he was a member of the Robert Rantoul clique, which was now out of favor because of Rantoul's "dissipated habits." Hawthorne added, "If I am not misinformed, Tyler had actually appointed me, but was afterwards induced to change it." The great likelihood was that Tyler would not press the Browne appointment, but would leave the decision to the incoming Polk administration. "My wife and daughter and myself are all well," Hawthorne concluded. "I have been greatly bothered with pecuniary difficulties, and am so still, but hope unweariedly for better things."

Although he was unhappy about his separation from his wife, Hawthorne felt some relief from his financial problems in Salem. "The good that I get by remaining here," he wrote Sophia, "is a temporary freedom from that vile burden which had irked and chafed me so long — that consciousness of debt, and pecuniary botheration, and the difficulty of providing even for the day's wants. This trouble does not pursue me here; and even when we go back, I hope not to feel it nearly so much as before. Polk's election has certainly brightened our prospects; and we have a right to expect that our difficulties will vanish, in the course of a few months." A short while later, however, he reported upon another embarrassment. The Reverend Charles Upham, who had recently given up a Concord parish to return to Salem and a political career, had been spreading rumors about the Hawthornes' dire financial straits. "He told the most pitiable stories about our poverty and misery," Hawthorne complained, "so as almost to make it appear that we were suffering for food. Everybody that speaks to me seems tacitly to take it for granted that we are in a very desperate condition, and that a government office is the only alternative of the alms-house. I care not for the reputation of being wealthier than I am; but we never have been quite paupers."

Still, the Reverend Mr. Upham and his rumor-mongering were not Hawthorne's only concern. His letter was also an ardent profession of love. "I shall come back to thee with tenfold as much love as ever I felt before," he wrote. "Nobody but we ever knew what it is to be married."

For months, Hawthorne's friends — and Hawthorne himself — had been making a concerted effort to get him a political appointment. Even before George Bancroft's appointment as secretary of the navy for the Polk administration had become a certainty, the politician and historian was being pressed to find some suitable office for his fellow writer. Lizzie Peabody was one of the first to act in her brother-in-law's behalf. During the Thanksgiving stay in Salem, Sophia wrote to her mother, "Pray tell Lizzie not to suggest to Mr. Bancroft that a *moderate* living will suit *best*, since the more salary there may be, the more can be laid aside for those shadowy days when Polk shall be no more . . . Mrs. Bancroft shall be put with Cassiopeia among the constellations if she be instrumental in relieving my husband of this load of anxiety which the muses do not love." Sophia, perhaps, had been infected by her husband's political opportunism, since she had no great liking for the crafty Bancroft, referring to him on various occasions as a "gnome" and as "the Blatant Beast." "I should never wish to be within three feet of him," she had written with unusual harshness after an early meeting. "I cannot express how disagreeable his effect was & I had no intention of not being pleased with him beforehand. It was my instinct to be repelled." She clearly preferred the good offices of Bancroft's wife. For his part, although he was actively seeking a political plum from the new President, Hawthorne had no great enthusiasm for James Polk. Before the election, he had agreed with his sister Elizabeth that the presidency was going from bad to worse, that it would be "Polk next and Clay afterward." His attitude did not improve when the question of his appointment by the new administration dragged on for another year.

By March, when Bancroft's appointment to the cabinet became official, John O'Sullivan was bringing pressure to bear on the new secretary of the navy. Hawthorne was still hoping for the Salem postmastership, and O'Sullivan discussed the matter with Bancroft but was not optimistic. It did not seem that Browne would be removed. "Bancroft spoke of him as an excellent and unexceptionable man," O'Sullivan wrote Hawthorne on March 21. Bancroft, a practical politician, was clearly testing the political waters; it was unlikely that he would want to dismiss a party regular for a political newcomer. O'Sullivan added, "I did not speak of the other places you named at Salem, because you say the emoluments are small." He had broached the subject of consulships in Marseilles, Genoa, and Gibraltar. He asked Hawthorne whether he would consider a consulship in China. "It seems to me that in your place I should like it; and the trade opening there would give, I should suppose, excellent opportunity for doing a business which would result in a fortune." He assured his friend, "At any rate, something satisfactory *shall* be done for you." In his own way, O'Sullivan was mounting a campaign in Hawthorne's behalf. He had commissioned an article about him from an influential critical admirer, Evert A. Duyckinck, an editor with the publishing firm of Wiley and Putnam. He also suggested that Hawthorne have a daguerreotype taken so that a suitable engraving could be made to accompany the article in the *Democratic Review*. "By manufacturing you thus into a Personage," O'Sullivan wrote, "I want to raise your mark higher in Polk's appreciation."

However desperate he was as an office-seeker, Hawthorne was distinctly choosy about the positions he would accept. Convinced that Bancroft was offering him less than he deserved, he flatly turned down a clerkship at the Charlestown Naval Yard. O'Sullivan pointed out that Bancroft had only suggested it as an interim appointment until something as suitable as a librarianship at the soon-to-be-established Smithsonian Institution became available. "You underrate his disposition in the matter," O'Sullivan claimed, trying to allay his friend's suspicions.

Hawthorne surely believed that Bancroft was dragging his feet. Moreover, he suspected — and said as much in a letter to Bridge — that the historian was involved in political double-dealing. Hawthorne had his own political spy in Salem, in the person of Horace Conolly, chairman of a Democratic congressional district committee. According to Conolly, so Hawthorne wrote Bridge, "the hostile party in Salem had received a letter from Bancroft, which had given them great confidence that Browne would not be removed. This letter must have been written almost immediately after Pierce's two letters were received in Washington; and if so, it indicates that Bancroft does not mean to give up his opposition." In an unusually acid aside, Hawthorne accused Bancroft of bad faith in every direction: "If he has been making pledges and fair professions to the enemy, it may be no bad reason for surmising that he will soon desert them, and come over to our side."

His responses at the time carry a certain ironic weight; four years later, when he was himself the victim of a political ouster, Hawthorne was to deny, not entirely truthfully, that he had actively sought political office or that he had campaigned for the ouster of Benjamin Browne. But by then, Browne, ensconced in the postmastership, had become a political ally, having supported Hawthorne's appointment to another party post. Whether out of personal friendship or as a matter of political duty, Hawthorne had also edited Browne's recollections of his life as a privateer and a prisoner in Dartmoor Prison during the War of 1812. Much of the narrative was originally published in installments in the *Democratic Review*. By then, too, Hawthorne had acquired the talent for rationalization by which political careers were sustained — his own no less than Bancroft's.

Earlier in the year, Hawthorne had begun editing Horatio Bridge's notes on his African cruise. On January 19, 1845, he was able to write his friend that he had made "considerable progress" on the book. He wanted more background material, however, and asked expressly for copies of the newspaper the *Liberia Herald*. He suggested that Bridge write some "statesmanlike speculations on the sort of connection that ought to exist between the colony and the mother-country." It is difficult to know precisely what editorial changes Hawthorne made in Bridge's text, or the extent of his rewriting, since the original manuscript has been lost. But it is clear that he aimed at emphasizing both the adventurous and topical elements of Bridge's narrative. From the point of view of factual reportage, Hawthorne made one curious insertion. When Bridge made a mention of African ants, Hawthorne thought it timely to add his own observations about Fourierist principles and the domestic ant colony he had witnessed in Sleepy Hollow the year before.

In March, Hawthorne was suggesting to Evert Duyckinck that Wiley and Putnam publish Bridge's book. Duyckinck was agreeable, all the more so since the firm was eager to bring out a new collection of Hawthorne's stories in a series they were proposing, called the Library of American Books. They offered eight cents a copy, "fully equal to one half the profits," as well as an advance of $100 immediately, for one or two additional unpublished tales. Hawthorne thought the terms "very liberal" but claimed he would have to wait for the proper mood before he could supply the new stories. In the meantime, he pushed Bridge's book, indicating his faith in it by saying he would prefer a percentage of the sales rather than a flat fee for his editorial services. "I look for a considerable circulation," he told Duyckinck; "more than of my own book proper."

Throughout the spring and summer, Hawthorne was forced to apologize for his inability to pull together another collection of stories or to supply the preface he had intended. "I am fit for nothing, at present, higher or finer than such another piece of book-manufacture as the Journal," he wrote Duyckinck on July 1. "My health is not so good, this summer, as it always has been hitherto. I feel no physical vigor; and my inner man droops in sympathy." He had had it in mind to construct "a sort of framework" for his collection, making it "an idealization of our old parsonage, and of the river close at hand, with the glimmerings of my actual life — yet so transmogrified that the reader should not know what was reality and what fancy."

At Duyckinck's request, Hawthorne had sounded out Emerson about the possibility of publishing a book in the Wiley and Putnam series. Emerson, who had been considering a volume of his poems, was not responsive, however. "He seems to think it preferable to publish on his own account — which has always been his method hitherto," Hawthorne informed Duyckinck. As an author attempting to expand his market, and aware of the parochial nature of the publishing industry and its haphazard distribution methods, Hawthorne thought Emerson was making a mistake. "I wish he might be induced to publish this volume in New York," he commented. "His reputation is still, I think, provincial, and almost local, partly owing to the defects of the New England system of publication."

As for Thoreau, whom Duyckinck had also enquired about, Hawthorne was positively discouraging. He was evidently passing through another of his phases of irritation with his younger Concord neighbor. "There is one chance in a thousand that he might write a most excellent and readable book," Hawthorne told Duyckinck, "but I should be sorry to take the responsibility either towards you or him, of stirring him up to write anything for the series. He is the most unmalleable fellow alive — the most tedious, tiresome and intolerable — the narrowest and most notional — and yet, true as all this is, he has great qualities of intellect and character." It was doubtful, Hawthorne claimed, that Thoreau would ever appeal to the popular mind, unless he stuck to writing "a book of simple observation of nature."

His testiness might indicate some unknown unpleasant encounter with the rigorously moralistic Thoreau. Or it may only have been Hawthorne's response to Thoreau's most recent example of social intransigence. Three days later, Thoreau moved into the rude wooden cabin, bought from an Irish family, that he and friends had been reconstructing on the shore of Walden Pond. Hawthorne seems to have regarded Thoreau, with his priggishness and inexperience, as a standing criticism of his own way of life. Thoreau's attitude may have been all the more affecting at a time when Hawthorne was actively seeking a post in the most venal of activities, politics. Some years later, writing to an English friend, Richard Monckton Milnes, Hawthorne recommended Thoreau's writings but testified to the exasperating character of the author. "He is not an agreeable person," Hawthorne wrote, "and in his presence one feels ashamed of having any money, or a house to live in, or so much as two coats to wear, or of having written a book that the public will read — his own mode of life being so unsparing a criticism on all other modes, such as the world approves." By that time, Hawthorne was a man with a house and an adequate number of coats. He was the author, also, of several popular volumes. In Concord, in 1845, when Hawthorne was struggling to lift himself and his family out of near-poverty, Thoreau's moral example must have been especially insufferable.

⌒ V ⌒

On May 9, 1845, Hawthorne set down in his journal, "Borrowed of Horatio Bridge One Hundred Dollars." It was a further indication of his continuing financial straits.

The circumstances of the loan, however, were pleasant enough. Bridge, accompanied by Franklin Pierce, had paid a visit to Concord. In her best pictorial style, Sophia wrote her mother about the call. She and Una had been standing at the nursery window when they caught sight of the two men coming up the avenue. She immediately recognized the "fine elastic figure" of Bridge, but she had never met Pierce before. Bridge waved his hat in the air, in a triumphant greeting, as she raised the window. She was promptly introduced to Pierce. "I saw by a glance that he was a person of delicacy and refinement," Sophia told her mother. At forty-one, Hawthorne's age, Pierce was tall, angular, with surprisingly fine features and lively, almost feminine, eyes. His mouth was uncompromisingly straight. The only unruly feature in his ordinarily prim and fastidious appearance was a shock of tangled brown hair.

"Mr. Hawthorne was in the shed, hewing wood," Sophia continued. "Mr. B. caught a glimpse of him and began a kind of waltz toward him. Mr. P. followed and when they reappeared, Mr. Pierce's arm was encircling my husband's old blue frock. How his friends do love him! Mr. Bridge was wild with spirits." Her glimpse of Pierce had been brief; Hawthorne and his friends spent the evening at the hotel, discussing "business," so Sophia explained. But she had seen enough to decide that Pierce had "natural refinement" — a quality she thought lacking in Bridge. "My husband says that Mr. Pierce's affection for and reliance upon him are perhaps greater than any other person's," Sophia wrote. She noticed that Pierce called Hawthorne "Nathaniel" and that he often looked at her husband with "peculiar tenderness." She greatly appreciated the change of mood that came over Hawthorne in the presence of his friends: "When Mr. Hawthorne returned that night, there was a radiance and relief in his face which I had not seen for some time."

There is little doubt that one order of business, amid the drinks and cigar-smoking at the hotel, had been Hawthorne's political prospects. Hawthorne quite probably also discussed Bridge's forthcoming — though anonymous — appearance as an author. *Journal of an African Cruiser* was scheduled for publication in June, and, as Hawthorne had mentioned to Bridge a week before, it was already stereotyped and ready to go to press. Duyckinck had insisted that Hawthorne's name should appear on the title page in order to enhance the sale value; Bridge, whether out of modesty or because of political considerations, since he was serving as paymaster at the Portsmouth Naval Yard, did not want to be identified as the author. The book would appear as written "By an Officer of the U.S. Navy. Edited by Nathaniel Hawthorne." A first edition of 2000 copies was planned.

In mid June, when the book had not yet appeared, Hawthorne wrote Bridge in glum humor, "I continue to look for it every day. I truly commiserate your situation, standing on the gallows, with the halter about your neck and wondering why the devil they don't turn you off." He himself was still hoping for word on the Salem post office, certain that Bancroft was hedging in his support. Bridge had been pressing Hawthorne to pay an extended visit to the Portsmouth Naval Yard, accompanied by Sophia and Una, so that he could introduce Hawthorne to politicians who might be useful in getting him an appointment. Hawthorne was reluctant to commit himself, hoping that he would have an appointment beforehand. Nor, it appears, did he tell Sophia the purpose of the invitation, preferring to explain it after the fact. "I have said nothing about your plan to Sophia," he wrote Bridge, "knowing that she would not be aiding and abetting towards it, if previously aware of it." By early July, not having received an office, Hawthorne was ready to accept Bridge's offer. Among the other guests he was scheduled to meet there were Senator Charles Atherton of New Hampshire and his wife and Senator (formerly Congressman) John Fairfield of Maine. Franklin and Jane Pierce were also expected during the Hawthornes' stay. Although Pierce had resigned his Senate seat three years before because of his wife's poor health, he still had influential connections in Washington.

Sophia, worried that Bridge, a bachelor, might not be aware of the problems of bringing an infant, wrote him a warning and enquiring letter on the Fourth of July. She had actually written Bridge a few days before, but Hawthorne had objected to some remark she had made and asked her to rewrite her letter. "It was only a freak of fancy that was condemned, however," she explained to Bridge, "and so I write the same letter over again with that omission, for in all matters of taste and fitness [my lord] is absolutely correct." She told Bridge that it would be necessary to bring their maidservant; otherwise it would be difficult for her to make the visit. "I know that your hospitality is as magnificent as that of the Grecian hero who slew an hundred beeves to entertain his guests, but this is not reason why it should be abused. There would still be an advantage in my taking my woman, because she would take the whole care of us, and we should be no additional trouble to your domestics — but are not four of us too many?" She questioned Bridge about the "military arrangements" of the naval yard. "Is there a great deal of martial music and parade," she asked, "so that Una's sleep would be murthered every noon? Her little life is rounded with a sleep every day, and if these naps are prevented, I will not answer for her serenity and agreeableness of behavior."

Hawthorne's journal entries for the Portsmouth visit indicate that he and Sophia stayed at the naval yard for a two-week period, from July 25, to August 9. There is no mention whatsoever of political discussions or of the influential society he had been invited to meet. Instead, Hawthorne confined his remarks to the manners of the naval officers stationed at Portsmouth and the less gentlemanly army officers at nearby Fort Constitution. He noted a youngish lieutenant of marines, a recent convert to "papistry," who was fond of discussion and had "much more intellect than he finds employment for." Always interested in the influence of a wife on a husband, he commented on the middle-aged Commander George Pearson, who had "such cultivation as a sensible man picks up about the world, and with what little literary tincture he imbibes from a bluish wife." He also paid a congenial visit to the Reverend Charles Burroughs, a scholar and bibliophile with a taste for antiquarian items, such as the medieval illuminated manuscript he proudly showed Hawthorne. The elderly Burroughs, rector of St. John's in Portsmouth, was "a man of cheerful gossip, no enemy to a quiet glass of wine."

His final notation was laconic. On August 9, he weighed himself: "170 pounds — greater than at any former period. Una's 25 pounds."

They had not been back in Concord long when they were faced with a crisis. For some time they had known that Samuel Ripley, the son of the old Reverend Ezra Ripley, wanted to move back into the manse. They understood that they would be able to remain until November. Expecting that Hawthorne would receive a political appointment in Salem, Sophia had conceived the idea of moving to Herbert Street until they found suitable quarters. As she explained to Louisa in a letter of August 24, Nathaniel could return to his "ancient study" upstairs, and she and Una would take an unused downstairs room, below the parlor, for their bedroom. She wondered whether old William Manning, who owned the property, would be agreeable to the proposition. "Nathaniel says that room is nothing but an old kitchen; but I do not care in the least how old and ugly it is, just for a few month's residence." She would, however, need a servant-girl to help — and if there was a third-floor room for the girl, she would provide the bedroom furnishings. Sophia made it plain that she would not need to entertain guests while staying at Herbert Street. She would not disturb the family's closely guarded privacy.

Sophia had hardly written to Louisa when Hawthorne learned that they would have to vacate the manse by the early part of October. She sent Louisa a desperate note, and this time her sister-in-law, who had been delaying, answered promptly. "My dear Sophia," Louisa wrote apologetically on September 3, "Your letter which was received this forenoon is too forcible in its appeal to be deferred any longer. I was going to write to you today, at any rate, and tell you that we agree to your plan, if we can ever bring Mr. Manning to any decision — for if any one wants anything of his, it is sure to acquire a new value in his eyes, and he finds out that he wants it himself — however, I have no doubt you can have the room, but he asks ten dollars a quarter for it, and I am afraid will not let it go any lower." Louisa suggested that Sophia would be more comfortable in the downstairs parlor rather than in the kitchen, which was too small and off a very cold pantry. She attempted to be as cordial as possible. "As to your not having any company, my dear Sophia, I hope you do not think we should feel any objection to your friends coming to see you when you wish to see them, we shall be glad to share our parlor with you, as far as it is agreeable to you." The real problem, Louisa thought, would be finding a suitable servant-girl.

For Hawthorne, the forced move could not have come at a worse time. He was strapped for money and did not have enough to pay even his back rent. In desperation, he took a step he had been holding back from; on September 6 he wrote Hillard, asking that he initiate a suit against George Ripley to recover some of the money invested in Brook Farm. What he wanted to recover apparently was the sum of $524.05, which he had advanced toward the building of the house in which he and Sophia had originally planned to live at the farm. The Association note for the investment, signed by Charles Dana and Ripley, was payable on demand. Hawthorne, so far, had received only one interest payment. Hawthorne told Hillard that since he had already dunned Ripley a number of times without results, he wanted the lawyer to proceed "as promptly and forcibly as possible." Ripley, who acknowledged that the money was due Hawthorne, took the position that the debt was owed by the new Brook Farm Phalanx, and it was on this legality that Hawthorne was caught. Hillard initiated the suit in December, and in the following March, Hawthorne was awarded $585 for damages and costs by the Court of Common Pleas. But even that was small consolation, for Hawthorne was never paid. His bitterness about the incident may well be reflected in an undated fragment of a letter, written to a former colleague, possibly Frank Farley, when it was rumored that Brook Farm would go bankrupt: "Let it sink, say I — it has long since ceased to have any sympathy for me — though individually I wish well to all concerned."

Sophia, writing to her mother about their move, confessed that the joys of Concord had begun to wane: "The three years we have spent here will always be to me a blessed memory, because here all my dreams became realities. I have got gradually weaned from it, however, by the perplexities that have vexed my husband the last year and made the place painful to him." She was particularly irritated with Samuel Ripley, "that most anti-angelic of men," who was driving them "out of Paradise." In her indictment there was even a harsh word for her idol, Emerson. "It was only through too great a trust in the honor and truth of others," Sophia complained, that her husband now found himself in such difficulties. "There is owing to him, twice more than money enough to pay all his debts — and he was confident that when he came to a pinch like this, it would not be withheld from him. It is so wholly new to him to be in debt that he cannot 'whistle for it' as Mr. Emerson advised him to, telling him that everybody was in debt, and they were all worse than he was."

As a last resort, Hawthorne wrote Bridge, asking to borrow another $150. With the inevitable hard luck that afflicts people at critical moments, everything went awry. When he did not hear from his friend, Hawthorne feared his letter had gone astray and wrote again, this time on September 28, with only a few days' grace before he had to move. Hawthorne's second desperate request and Bridge's reply to Hawthorne's first letter crossed in the mails. Bridge had been in Boston, but had not been able to get out to Concord as he had planned; he had only just returned to Portsmouth. He could not send the money immediately; he was writing on Saturday night and the banks would not be open until Monday morning. He assured Hawthorne he would send the needed money as quickly as possible. "I almost fancy myself criminal in having been absent from Portsmouth since Tuesday morning . . ." Bridge wrote. "I regret exceedingly that you should have been kept so long in suspense as to the result of your application. The habitual belief which you have in your own bad luck must have made you doubt of its success." The money did not arrive in time; Bridge's first letter reached Concord on October 2, the day the Hawthornes left. Fortunately, John O'Sullivan stopped in Concord on his way to London and paid Hawthorne $100 that was owed him. But although Hawthorne informed Bridge that he had therefore been able to quit Concord "with flying colors," this was hardly the case. O'Sullivan's payment had barely covered some of his back debts and the moving expenses, and Hawthorne had returned to Salem with only $10 in his pocket. He still owed Samuel Ripley for a portion of his back rent. Bridge's contribution was especially welcome when it arrived in Salem a few days later.

If Hawthorne felt any special bitterness about his flight from Concord, he did not express it in the idyllic preface he wrote, months later, for his collection of stories *Mosses from an Old Manse*. He recalled only the happier moments: the privacy of his life with Sophia, the serene days in the midst of nature, the vegetable garden with its abundance, the misty glimpses of the slow Concord River.

If he felt any resentment about his neighbor Emerson's curt dismissal of his financial problems, Hawthorne did not reveal it. Emerson, of course, could afford to take the lofty view; he had gone to law to get his share of his first wife's contested family inheritance and now had a reasonably comfortable income from annuities and bank and railroad stock — aside from his lecturing fees. In his preface, Hawthorne referred only to the "great original Thinker" of the village, calling him "a poet of deep beauty and austere tenderness." Hawthorne confessed that he had gained nothing from Emerson the philosopher, implying that he was too far past the undergraduate age for that. If he offered any rebuke, it was a mild one for the odd types that Emerson, like a magnet, seemed to attract to Concord. "Never was a poor little country village," Hawthorne claimed, "infested with such a variety of queer, strangely dressed, oddly behaved mortals, most of whom took upon themselves to be important agents of the world's destiny, yet were simply bores of a very intense water."

There was more sorrow than anger in his account of his expulsion from Eden: the noisy carpenters who arrived early to make renovations, strewing the lawn with woodchips, tearing down the ancient woodbine that crawled up the southern façade of the house; the painters who threatened to paint the mossy exterior shingles. ("The hand that renovates is always more sacrilegious than that which destroys," Hawthorne maintained.) Sadly, he recalled the last moments of their final day: "We gathered up our household goods, drank a farewell cup of tea in our pleasant little breakfast-room . . . and passed forth between the tall stone gate-posts, as uncertain as the wandering Arabs where our tent might next be pitched."

A Dark Necessity

FROM SALEM, on October 10, Hawthorne wrote Evert Duyckinck, "Here I am . . . in the old, dingy and dusky chamber, where I wasted many good years of my youth, shaping day-dreams and night-dreams into idle stories." He was responding to the editor's "vociferous cry, Mss! Mss!" for the new collection of tales. Hawthorne acknowledged that he was back to old habits: ". . . already, though not a week established here, I take out my quire of paper and prepare to cover it with the accustomed nonsense." But he had not yet been able to write the promised introductory sketch. In two or three weeks time, when he had cleared his mind of "recent anxieties and disturbances," he hoped to have some result for his effort.

His optimism was ill-founded; by Christmas Eve, he was still acknowledging his failure to produce the sketch. "That wretched tale still refuses to unfold its convolutions," he wrote Duyckinck, "— not from any lack of either gentle or compulsory efforts on my part; but I have not now the quiet which has always been my portion aforetime; and therefore nothing prospers with me." He wondered whether he might not have reached "that point in an author's life, when he ceases to effervesce; and whatever I do hereafter must be done with leaden reluctance, and therefore had better be left undone. Do not think me wilfully idle; for it is not so."

Despite Hawthorne's problems, Duyckinck suggested that the book be expanded to two volumes with the addition of earlier stories that had not been published in *Twice-told Tales*. Hawthorne turned with relief to the task of gathering in his "vagrant progeny"; it offered a temporary escape from producing the troublesome introductory sketch. In his reply, he made an odd announcement: "As I never mean to write any more stories (the one now in embryo excepted) we will offer this collection to the public as the last they shall

ever be troubled with, at my hands." Plainly unhappy with his earlier works, he added, "It seems to me absurd to look upon them as
conveying any claim to a settled literary reputation. I thank God, I
have grace enough to be utterly dissatisfied with them . . . I am
ashamed — and there's an end."

In spite of his dissatisfaction, by February 22 he sent Duyckinck
ten tales and sketches for the second volume. Among these, he had
selected two of his finer early tales, "Roger Malvin's Burial" and
"Young Goodman Brown," the latter, certainly, among his masterpieces. He also included two that he had previously passed over
because of Sophia's disapproval — "Mrs. Bullfrog" and "Monsieur
du Miroir." Perhaps he wanted a compensating humor for the collection, or he may have chosen them merely to fill the quota. He still
had not finished his introduction, but he had been giving some
thought to possible titles for the collection. In a postscript, he announced, with Sophia's approval, "We decided on 'Mosses from an
Old Manse.' "

Part of Hawthorne's difficulty during the winter of 1845–1846 was
that he was in a continual state of uncertainty about his political
prospects; the waiting was a trial. Then, too, his living arrangements were not ideal. Unfortunately, the Herbert Street house was
dismally cold; Sophia worried continually about Una's visits to her
grandmother's icy, uncarpeted bedroom. But a principal reason for
Hawthorne's anxiety was that Sophia was pregnant again. Both he
and Sophia were determined that the baby would not be born in the
Herbert Street house, but there was no clear alternative. Nor was
Hawthorne certain how his family would respond to the news of
another addition to the family. In November, when she and Una
were paying a visit to the Mann family in Boston, Sophia sent a
little note to her mother-in-law, pretending it had been written by
Una and announcing the coming birth. She sent it under cover of a
letter to her husband.

Hawthorne, writing on November 10, assured Sophia that she and
Una were greatly missed at "Castle Dismal." "Louisa complains of
the silence of the house," Hawthorne said, "and not all their innumerable cats avail to comfort them in the least. Thy husband thinks
of thee when he ought to be scribbling nonsense and awakes at
deepest midnight to wish thou wert in his arms." He had read Una's
little note, he said, and threw it downstairs. "Doubtless, they find it
a most interesting communication; and I feel a little shamefaced
about meeting them. They will certainly rejoice at the prospect of
another baby and only temper their joy with the serious consider-

ation of how the newcomer is to be provided for." Three days later, he wrote that the news had probably been assimilated on the second floor, since Louisa had been unusually cheerful when he met her at dinner the following day. Other than that, the subject had not been broached at all. As for himself, Hawthorne claimed, "I already love the future little personage." Still, he confessed he felt "a jealousy of him or her on Una's account," and hoped the new baby would not be "better" than the old one. "So take care what thou dost, Phoebe Hawthorne!" he cautioned. He also warned Sophia to be careful in public places, particularly the crowded ferry docks of East Boston: "Thy poor dear little big body is not to be trusted in such a tumult."

Although he adopted a tender, jocular tone with Sophia, he was more forthright in confessing his anxieties to Horatio Bridge. "What a devil of a pickle I shall be in, if the baby should come and the office should not!" he wrote Bridge in February. The tentative "if" referred to the real possibility of a miscarriage. But did it also reveal a certain misgiving on the part of the prospective father — a wish, perhaps, that the baby might not come at such a difficult time? He hadn't, after all, confidently written to Bridge, "What a devil of a pickle I shall be in, when the baby comes, if the office should not."

Hawthorne waited impatiently for some firm word of a political appointment. O'Sullivan kept him informed of President Polk's disposition in the matter; through his contacts with the Salem Democrats he was told of Bancroft's moves. But a minor political appointment in Salem could hardly have been one of the more pressing problems on the new President's mind. The recent annexation of Texas had moved the United States inevitably closer to war with the belligerent Paredes government, recently installed in Mexico City. Polk had ordered American troops, under the command of Brigadier General Zachary Taylor, to the Rio Grande to protect American interests. Moreover, his very effective campaign slogan, "54° 40' or fight," regarding the still-unsettled Oregon border, was having an adverse effect on his attempts to settle the touchy dispute with Great Britain. An expansionist in principle, having adopted John O'Sullivan's catchy phrase, "Manifest Destiny," as his policy, Polk was also concerned about the political vacuum in California, where the provincial government had claimed independence from Mexico. With his narrowing options, Polk could hardly avert the coming war with Mexico; his severest critics, the New England abolitionists, who saw the annexation of Texas as a proslavery move, were making political capital of their charges. There was, therefore, all the more reason for

Polk and Bancroft to proceed cautiously in tampering with their political support in Massachusetts.

Hawthorne, nevertheless, had formidable political backing that reached well beyond Salem. In Washington, Senators Atherton and Fairfield were pressing the administration in his behalf. O'Sullivan was in constant touch with both Polk and Bancroft. Franklin Pierce, viewed favorably enough by Polk to be offered the post of attorney general (which he declined), was writing letters urging an appointment for his college friend. And Bridge, who Hawthorne later felt had provided the most useful assistance, was actively campaigning in his behalf. Hawthorne also had a powerful ally in the Whig camp: Charles Sumner wrote imploring letters to Mrs. Bancroft, asking that Hawthorne be given "some post-office, some custom house, something, that will yield daily bread — anything in the gift of your husband." He concluded, "I wish I could have some assurance from your husband, that Hawthorne shall be cared for."

Bancroft responded sardonically to the barrage. "As to Hawthorne," he wrote Sumner, "I have been most perseveringly his friend." The idea of a wily Democrat dispensing political favors at the request of a virginal Whig was too rare an opportunity to let pass without a neat twist of the knife: "I am glad you go for the good rule of dismissing wicked Whigs and putting in Democrats. Set me down as without influence, if so soon as the course of business will properly permit, you do not find Hawthorne an office holder."

At stake were two positions in the Salem Custom House: the post of surveyor and that of naval officer. It is an indication of Hawthorne's political leverage that two earlier candidates for those offices withdrew in favor of Hawthorne and another well-backed political protégé, John D. Howard. (Hawthorne was to pay a price for this support later, however; local politicians of both parties resented the big guns brought to bear on them for an interloper.) Hawthorne could foresee two stumbling blocks to his success: Polk, so he had been advised, was reluctant to remove the incumbent surveyor, Nehemiah Brown, a Tyler appointee; and there was a second rival for the position of naval officer, Stephen Hoyt, whom Bancroft appeared to favor. Late in February, though, Bancroft wrote the Salem politicos, announcing his opinion that the President "will send in for confirmation Nathaniel Hawthorne as Surveyor of Salem, he being unanimously recommended for that place." The appointment for naval officer was still open. Finding that Hoyt had only weak backing, he advised, "If Hoyt's friends want him appointed, they must make his case a good one."

Despite Bancroft's letter, Hawthorne was wary. In a lengthy letter to Bridge, written March 1, he outlined the situation as he saw it. In case of a draw between the Howard faction and Bancroft's choice, he would himself be appointed naval officer, a position he did not want. He had a plan for smoothing away the differences between the Howard and Hoyt factions. He wrote Bridge:

> If you could authorize me to communicate to a few persons here the intelligence contained in your penultimate letter, I might use it so as to induce them to signify their assent to Hoyt's appointment, as their second choice, in case Howard could not succeed; and this would probably be sufficient as Bancroft is so evidently anxious in Hoyt's behalf. Otherwise I am convinced that I must go into the Naval Office. If you are at liberty, and think it advisable, to take the above course, write me such a letter as may be shown to the Postmaster and one or two others, giving the intelligence anew, and without reference to your former letter, the reception of which, as it has been concealed so long, cannot now be acknowledged.

He had begun to acquire the political aptitudes — the use of a well-timed word, the tactful withholding of information, the mustering of support. "Nothing need be said as to the authority of which you make your statements," Hawthorne went on. "If you consider yourself not authorized to do what I have here suggested, then I had rather you would not write at all, just at present; for my friends here bother me to death, whenever I am known to have received a letter either from you or O'Sullivan — and it is difficult to conceal it, the Postmaster being one of the junto." He assured his friend, "You may depend upon my discretion. I have grown considerable of a politician by the experience of the last few months."

Late in March, Sophia wrote her mother about their future plans; she wanted to be in Boston, close to Dr. Wesselhoeft, during the final stages of her pregnancy. They had decided to take the Carver Street house, which the Horace Manns would shortly be vacating for a home in West Newton. "There is only one solitary drawback," Sophia wrote her mother, "and this is the occasional absence of my husband, should he enter his official station before we return." But Hawthorne would be able to take the train to Salem after breakfast and be home again for dinner. A former maidservant, Mary Pray, who had been housekeeping for Horatio Bridge, would be returning to work for them, so Sophia would not be alone. She was looking forward to the move to Boston and being once more among friends. "Salem is an horrible vacuum in these regards," she told her mother.

On the very next day, March 23, Sophia was able to report: "This morning we have authentic intelligence that my husband is nominated, by the President himself, for Surveyor of the Custom House." Senator Fairfield had written Hawthorne to tell him the news; the salary would be $1200 a year. As her own first official act, Sophia asked her father to go to Earle's, the Boston tailor, and order a suit for Mr. Hawthorne, "the coat to be of broadcloth, of six or seven dollars a yard, the pantaloons of kerseymere or broadcloth of quality to correspond, and the vest of satin — *all* to be black."

With a renewed sense of confidence — and competence — Hawthorne finished the essay for his collection of stories and sent it to Duyckinck, explaining, "The delay has really not been my fault — only my misfortune. Nothing that I tried to write would flow out of my pen, till a very little while ago — when forth came this sketch, of its own accord; and much unlike what I had proposed. I like it pretty well, at this present writing; and my wife better than I." Shortly after, he arranged for copies to be sent to critics and editors in New York, among them Poe, George Curtis, Henry Tuckerman, and Margaret Fuller, who was now a social reporter and literary critic for Horace Greeley's *Tribune*. He also asked for special editions, bound like Wiley and Putnam's edition of Poe's *Tales*, to be sent to Senators Atherton and Fairfield, and another to go to Mrs. George Bancroft, the *Mrs.* significantly underlined. There were two other special requests: a copy to be sent to "a certain Miss Susan Kearney Rodgers" of New York, the fiancée of John O'Sullivan; and one to be sent, by way of Elizabeth Peabody, to Miss Charlotte Marshall of Boston, who was to be the June bride of his friend Horatio Bridge.

In spite of his brightening prospects, Hawthorne was "dismally in want of money." He asked Wiley and Putnam for a $100 advance against the royalties for his book.

ᒧ II ᒧ

The Salem Custom House, with its brick façade, its columned portico atop a steep flight of granite stairs, stood at the head of Derby Wharf, a few blocks from the Union Street house in which Hawthorne had been born. Each day, for three and a half hours in the forenoon, the flag on the ornate cupola hung vertically, flapping lazily in the harbor breezes, signifying that the civil — not the military — authority of the port was in residence. The new surveyor occupied an office in the southwest corner, off the broad entrance hall, with a view commanding the wharves and harbor. Standing at his tall desk, Hawthorne could cast his glance over the cobblestone street in which the tall grass had begun to sprout because of the lack of traffic. The port of Salem was definitely in decline; the larger vessels were now putting in at the deeper harbors of Boston and New York. From the arched windows of his office, Hawthorne could look out at the old wharf, "now burdened with decayed wooden warehouses," with, "perhaps, a bark or a brig, half-way down its melancholy length, discharging hides, or, nearer at hand, a Novia Scotia schooner, pitching out her cargo of firewood." Through a side window, he surveyed the drab shops of ship chandlers, the knots of old salts and wharf rats that hung about the waterside. Hawthorne's office, too, had an air of neglect and seediness: cobwebs hung in the upper reaches of the high ceiling; the floor was strewn with gray sand but was seldom swept. On the half-empty bookshelves, there were random volumes of the *Acts of Congress* and a thick *Digest* of the revenue laws. A long tin pipe ascended to the ceiling and communicated with other rooms; it was the speaking tube through which Hawthorne summoned members of his staff.

More often than not, however, Hawthorne would find his subordinate officers — mostly white-haired and venerable relics of previous administrations — in the central hallway, sleeping in a row, their chairs tipped back against the wall. He drily wondered if any other public official had "such a patriarchal body of veterans under his orders as myself." The talk among the ancient subofficials tended to run to early voyages and sumptuous meals consumed in times past. Occasionally, there was mention of such sea monsters as a huge turtle encountered on voyages to Batavia. "Old Lee . . ." Hawthorne wrote in his journal, "affirmed that he had often heard other shipmasters speak of this same monster; but he being a notorious liar . . . the evidence is by no means perfect."

Hawthorne doubted that even one of these tale-spinners had ever read any of his own stories. He even took some pleasure in the fact. "It is a good lesson — though it may often be a hard one," he wrote of his Custom House experiences, "for a man who has dreamed of literary fame, and of making for himself a rank among the world's dignitaries by such means, to step aside out of the narrow circle in which his claims are recognized, and to find how utterly devoid of significance . . . is all that he achieves, and all he aims at." Ironically, he noted, his own name — stenciled in black letters on crates and bags and bales of dutiable merchandise — was being disseminated around the wide ports of the world. His official custom house stamp, "N. Hawthorne, Sur'r'" had become a "queer vehicle of fame."

Hawthorne was to form easy friendships with a few of the men under his command. With his newly appointed naval officer, John

Howard, he could discuss literary and historical matters; Shakespeare and Napoleon were among Howard's favorite topics. Hawthorne suspected, too, that one of the minor clerks with whom he sometimes discussed literature was secretly writing poems on the Custom House letter paper. He developed a sincere admiration for his venerable superior, old General James Miller, the veteran collector of the port and a hero of the Battle of Lundy's Lane in the War of 1812. He was friendly with Ephraim Miller, the general's son and deputy collector, who was named to his father's post when the old gentleman retired in 1849.

At a later time, writing about his term of office, Hawthorne carefully created the impression that his was not a strict administration. Although it might have been convenient to take an administrative ax to the deadwood on the staff, he maintained that he had barely disturbed the dust that had settled in the sleepy Salem Custom House. But there is a surviving letter, dated May 21, 1846, in which Hawthorne wrote Robert Walker, secretary of the treasury, explaining his dismissal of two inspectors "whom I have found it my duty to report as incompetent." In their places, he recommended the appointments of Stephen Burchmore and Stephen Haraden. Both men, he assured Walker, were "capable and efficient" and "firm friends of the administration." Captain Stephen Burchmore was the brother of Hawthorne's useful political ally Zachariah Burchmore, chief clerk of the Custom House and the influential secretary of the local Democratic Party committee.

"A small troglodyte made his appearance here at ten minutes to six o'clock this morning, who claimed to be your nephew, and the heir of all our wealth and honors," Hawthorne wrote Louisa from Boston on June 22, 1846. "He has dark hair and is no great beauty at present, but is said to be a particularly fine little urchin by everybody who has seen him." Since Louisa and Hawthorne's mother were "out of health" — as Sophia phrased it — the new parents decided not to bring the infant, whom they named Julian, back to the Herbert Street house. Instead, they remained in Boston while Hawthorne commuted daily to Salem.

Judging from his official correspondence, Hawthorne's activities during that summer and fall involved only mundane matters: a report on a faulty hydrometer used to test the proof of alcoholic beverages; a request for repairs to the Custom House portico, which was "considerably decayed." Freed of financial anxieties, he had hoped to have the leisure and inclination to take up his writing once more. He wrote Duyckinck that he was considering a new children's book — "stories to be taken out of the cold moonshine of classical mythology, and modernized, or perhaps gothicized, so that they may be felt by children of these days." But he made no progress on it. The most he had been able to accomplish were a few book notices, written for the *Salem Advertiser* — among them a review of a pirated edition of Dickens' *Traveling Letters* and one of Herman Melville's *Typee*, which he had liked "uncommonly well." "I do not pique myself at all on these critical attempts," he told Duyckinck, who had sent him the Melville book. "They are the fruit of my official hours; and, naturally, I am no critic."

In the fall, they managed to find a house on Chestnut Street, "the most stately street in Salem," Sophia thought, but the house was far too small for their needs, and they regarded it as only an interim stop. Not long after they moved in, Longfellow and George Hillard paid a visit to Salem. Hawthorne and his two friends dined out that evening at the local hotel. The company was enjoyable, but the meal, abominable. Longfellow, a seasoned traveler, commented in his journal, "What a dinner! No German village with a dozen houses in it could have furnished so mean a one."

At Longfellow's insistence, Hawthorne agreed to sit, that fall, for a portrait sketch in crayon by the enterprising Eastman Johnson, whom Longfellow had persuaded to move from Washington to Boston. Longfellow commissioned the artist to do a series of portraits of himself, his family, and acquaintances — among them Emerson and Charles Sumner. Johnson, in his studio in Armory Hall, made his study in brisk and assured fashion, although the sittings were apparently long. His sketch of Hawthorne, then forty-two, was flattering and youthful; only the thinning hair above the high forehead suggested that the author was advancing into middle age. Sophia, however, had no doubts about her husband's beauty. Another Boston painter, Seth Wells Cheney, was also asking to do a portrait of her husband. Sophia, writing to her mother, suggested that Cheney should come to Salem directly, because "Mr. Hawthorne was never so handsome as now."

Their financial situation, she told her mother in the same letter, was not so sunny as they had expected: "We shall not have a cent over our actual expenses this year, both because we had to spend more in Boston, and because Custom House fees have been unusually small this summer, and government is abominably remiss in paying the 'constructed fees' due the officers." They had had their first evening out together since Una was born; Louisa and their maidservant, Dora, had taken care of the children while she and Hawthorne, on the evening of November 16, had accompanied

Emerson — in town to lecture — to the home of a friend, a Mr. Howes.

They had also had a visit from Jared Sparks and his wife, Mary Silsbee Sparks. The Hawthornes, however, were distinctly reluctant to pursue any acquaintanceship. It was not until six or seven weeks later — and after another visit by Sparks — that Hawthorne and Sophia returned the call. Sophia wrote her mother about it in understandably prejudiced fashion: "Last Friday, we went to see them — my husband, Una and I. Mr. Sparks was not at home at first, but after due time, Mrs. Mary appeared — with her child Florence balanced in one arm in a miraculous manner — I thought — It was truly a theatrical entrée, and she said 'I met me child on me way' — Yet I could not but believe it was all a plan from the style. After she had accomplished that manoeuvre, she was as simple as a flower of the field . . . Mr. Sparks came in after a while." It was with satisfaction that Sophia added, "My husband thought Mrs. Sparks' eyes had become smaller and cat-like. Her complexion is now very coarse but she retains a certain beauty."

Late in December, writing to Horatio Bridge, Sophia reported on the new baby, whose father had taken to calling him the Black Prince, because he was swarthy compared to Una. "He is still decidedly, I think, a *brun.*" Sophia wrote, "but his complexion is brilliant and his eyes dark gray with long black lashes like Mr. Hawthorne's . . . His father declares he does not care anything about him, because he is a boy, and so I am obliged to love him twice as much as I otherwise should."

In her letter, Sophia complained about their cramped living quarters: "My husband has no study, and his life is actually wasted this winter for want of one. He has not touched his desk since we came to Salem." She wondered if Bridge might not find himself a better writer, now that he was a husband. Marriage, she claimed, opened up a new world. "I rejoice that you have ceased to be a stray comet and have come into a regular orbit," she wrote. It was a peculiar assertion, since Bridge, shortly after his marriage, had been assigned to another lengthy cruise and was aboard the *United States*. Odder still — considering Bridge's friendship with her husband and his genuine services for Hawthorne — was Sophia's confession that she had been unable to pay a formal call upon Bridge's new wife. She had seen Mrs. Bridge only once, she confessed, and then on a Boston street. "She was with her mother," Sophia wrote, "and I greeted her and shook hands with her very cordially." Bridge's marriage seems to have done little to bring the two couples closer together.

ᏴᎧ III ᎧᏴ

The two-volume edition of *Mosses from an Old Manse* was published early in June 1846, in paper wrappers, at $1.00 a set. A cloth-bound edition of two-volumes-in-one was priced at $1.25. Although the collection had a respectable critical success, it is doubtful that it was financially rewarding. Records of the first edition have not survived, but Wiley and Putnam kept the book in print until the demise of the firm; it ran through six printings by 1853. Hawthorne's royalties for the last three printings were only $144.09.

His private opinion of the book, communicated to his editor, was that it seemed "rather stale." But his wife, he mentioned, "was pleased to like it." He was even less inclined to spend his time on short fiction; for the moment his talents seem to have been more effectively channeled into the realistic introduction for the book, "The Old Manse," a nostalgic account of his private life in Concord. In his preface, Hawthorne confessed his hopes of writing something more substantial during his years at the Old Manse — maybe a novel "that could stand, unsupported, on its edges." Nor had he produced any of the other works that might have been prompted by the historical and clerical associations of his house — "profound treatises on morality — a layman's unprofessional and therefore unprejudiced view of religion — histories (such as Bancroft might have written, had he taken up his abode here, as he once purposed) bright with picture, gleaming over a depth of philosophic thought . . ." Instead, he had written only a series of "trifles." "Unless I could do better," he announced, "I have done enough in this kind."

His graceful remark about Bancroft, whatever he privately felt about the politician, was one of the few references to contemporary American literary figures he allowed to stand in the book. There were several interesting deletions in the reprinted versions of his sketches and tales. In republishing "Rappaccini's Daughter," he dropped the playful introductory tribute to O'Sullivan; he may have wanted to avoid any taint of Democratic politics, now that he was surveyor at Salem. Perhaps at Sophia's urging, he made some lengthy excisions in the text of "Monsieur du Miroir" — references to the narrator's drinking habits and his lax religious views. More significantly, in reprinting "The Hall of Fantasy," he deleted all the spirited references to such literary figures as Washington Irving, Longfellow, Alcott, Emerson, and Poe, as well as to such editorial acquaintances as Rufus Griswold, Tuckerman, and Epes Sargent. Since he would be sending complimentary copies to many of these men, clearly in hopes of editorial notice, he probably considered it better to avoid any suggestion of buying favorable reviews by flattery.

The reviews were, in fact, favorable enough for Hawthorne to write Bridge that the book had "met with good acceptance." The anonymous reviewer in the August issue of *Graham's Magazine* praised the "felicity and evanescent grace" of Hawthorne's humor, which he compared with that of Addison and Goldsmith. The New York critic and writer Charles Wilkins Webber, in the September issue of the *American Whig Review,* calling for an "honestly American" and even an "Aboriginal" literature, was pleased to announce that "Hawthorne is national — national in subject, in treatment and in manner." Webber cited "The New Adam and Eve" and "Earth's Holocaust," and quoted from both. Samuel Dutton, the earnest reviewer of the *New Englander,* was pleased to say that Hawthorne had none of the "diseased self-consciousness" and "laborious self-display" that were so objectionable in many American writers. Dutton preferred Hawthorne's naturalism to his tendency to metaphysics and allegory. Much of Dutton's review, in fact, was a criticism of what he regarded as dangerous transcendental influences in the nation's literature. A pastor of the North Church in New Haven, Dutton regarded Hawthorne's recent life as a kind of Egyptian bondage. "His residence at Concord," the minister claimed, "was, perhaps, either cause or effect of his sympathy with the amiable and highly cultivated, but misty and groping philanthropists of the 'Concord Sect' and the 'Roxbury Phalanx.'" Nor did he approve of the author's recent political career: "It is a waste of a kind of genius, which we cannot well spare, to shut up Nathaniel Hawthorne in a custom house," he stated.

The most critical review of Hawthorne's book came from Edgar Allan Poe, writing in *Godey's Lady's Book* in November 1847 — more than a year after publication. Poe's criticism represented a complete reversal of his praise five years before, when he claimed that Hawthorne was an author who was "original at *all* points." Now, he was maintaining that if Hawthorne were really original, he would have made a more definite mark on his reading public. "But the fact is," Poe stated, "he is *not* original in any sense. Those who speak of him as original mean nothing more than that he differs in his manner or tone, and in his choice of subjects, from any author of their acquaintance — their acquaintance not extending to the German Tieck." What Poe complained of in *Mosses from an Old Manse* was the monotony and sameness of Hawthorne's style and tone, and the author's penchant for allegory, which "completely overwhelms the greater number of his subjects."

Brilliant and bitter, with an erudition that was half-real, half-fake, Poe was among the keenest and most widely read critics of his time. In his reviews of now-forgotten nineteenth-century writers — a long list of ministers and doctors with a hankering after literature, of housewives who aspired to be "poetesses" — Poe took pride in detailing every appearance of a writer in little-remembered nineteenth-century periodicals. He had an obsession, too, about his own reputation in print and ferreted out every two-line mention of himself. Toward women writers he was generous to a fault. Though Boston-born, Poe was Virginia-bred and held strictly to the Southern code of chivalry toward the opposite sex. In defending Mrs. Felicia Hemans' sentimental poems, he made it clear he was doing battle against sneering critics who were "libeling our mothers and our sisters unopposed."

He was also a self-appointed champion of aesthetic standards, a proponent of art for art's sake who found more favor among French writers like Baudelaire than among his countrymen. He considered himself the scourge of the cultural establishment and of all literary quackery. Many of Poe's charges against the literary establishment were well founded: reviewers were often small-jobbers in praise, writing glowing reviews in return for small fees and free books. Publishers not only could commission favorable notices of their books, but place them with accommodating editors. Publications that were overcritical in their reviews were simply dropped from the complimentary list. Poe was well aware of the literary traffic of his time; he himself was well versed in the tricks of the trade and used them in promoting his own reputation.

Poe's sharpest aesthetic judgments were apt to be honed on personal resentments. He had a special animus toward the Boston literary establishment and its organ, the *North American Review*, which once categorized his stories as being of the "forcible-feeble and the shallow-profound school." His half-drunken, nervous performance at a reading and lecture in Boston in 1845 was one of the literary scandals of the period. One member of the audience, Thomas Wentworth Higginson, particularly recalled the poet's riveting personal appearance on the lecture platform — the slight figure, the broad brow and feverishly brilliant eyes, "the look of oversensitiveness which when uncontrolled may prove more debasing than coarseness." Higginson was struck by the "nauseous flattery" with which Poe courted his Boston audience and voiced the suspicion that it masked a deep hostility. "No one," Higginson remarked, "can ever tell, perhaps, what was the real feeling behind the apparently sycophantic attitude."

The later phases of Poe's career were marked by aggravated malice. He conceived a virulent hatred of Longfellow, the darling of the Boston literary establishment. For the alcoholic Poe, harried in his professional life, cadging money, shunting from the editorship of one short-lived publication to another, the affluent, well-connected, dandified Cambridge poet offered an irresistible target. Referring to a luxurious edition of Longfellow's poems (with engraved portrait of the author), Poe scored the "evident toadyism" that awarded to Longfellow's "social position and influence, to his fine paper and large type, to his morocco binding and gilt edges, to his flattering portrait of himself . . ." the merit that the poems themselves did not deserve.

His usual device for cutting down a literary rival was to bring charges of plagiarism against him — charges that were, oftentimes, far-fetched. In the winter of 1844–1845, despite the fact that he was not above borrowing from obscure sources himself, Poe published a series of malevolent articles accusing Longfellow and other contemporary writers of plagiarism. The articles, which appeared first in the *New-York Mirror* and then the *Broadway Journal*, where Poe had become a co-editor and investor, did nothing to improve his reputation. For the most part, Poe's grounds were flimsy ones — coincidental choices of sentimental themes, similar uses of words and phrases that were clichés. Longfellow would not respond, maintaining life was "too precious to be wasted in street brawls." His friends, however, took up the challenge — much to their regret, for they found themselves entangled in a continuing exchange in which Poe mounted more and more sinuously argued charges and countercharges until the entire discussion became muddy, inconclusive, and thoroughly distasteful. Poe's former allies turned away from him. James Russell Lowell, in the course of a biographical note in *Graham's Magazine*, called Poe the "most discriminating, philosophical and fearless critic" in America, but then qualified his praise, adding that Poe *"might be* rather than that he always *is* for he seems sometimes to mistake his phial of prussic-acid for his inkstand." In return, Lowell found himself accused of plagiarizing from Wordsworth. Writing to Charles F. Briggs, a former co-editor with Poe of the *Broadway Journal*, Lowell lamented, "Poe, I am afraid, is wholly lacking in that element of manhood which, for want of a better name, we call character . . . As I prognosticated, I have made [him] my enemy by doing him a service . . . Poe wishes to kick down the ladder by which he rose. He is welcome." Briggs thoroughly understood; having invited Poe to join the staff of the *Broadway Journal,* he had soon found himself eased out of his own position there.

With a paranoid talent for creating real enemies out of previously imagined ones, Poe next attacked the New York literary establishment. With a good deal of advance fanfare, he began publishing in the May 1846 issue of *Godey's Lady's Book* what he claimed was an exposé of the New York literati, revealing the quackery and hypocrisy of New York editors and writers who puffed one another's reputations in print but felt very differently in private. It was clearly an attempt to create a literary sensation after the failure of the *Broadway Journal.* One of the principal victims of Poe's first article was Briggs, who wrote under the pseudonym Harry Franco. Poe claimed that Briggs was "grossly uneducated" and that he could not write "three consecutive sentences of grammatical English." Poe, in turn, was treated to similar invective by Briggs's defenders; his own literary career was pointedly described as "to-day in the gutter, to-morrow in some milliner's magazine." For a year, the trading of insults mounted in New York's newspapers and magazines, until Poe brought suit against the *Evening Mirror* for publishing libelous remarks by one of his literary victims, Thomas Dunn English. Poe won his case and received damages of $225.06, although he had optimistically sued for $5000. But it was an empty victory. For the remainder of his career he was effectively blackballed from most of the prestigious journals and magazines. He might often publish his poems in out-of-the-way publications, but his critical reviews were seldom accepted. His essay "Tale-Writing — Nathaniel Hawthorne," published in the November 1847 issue of *Godey's,* was one of his last important critical articles.

Hawthorne had figured very briefly in Poe's ill-fated quarrel with the New York literati. In the preface to his first article in the series, Poe referred to Hawthorne as having "extraordinary genius" and being a writer who was scarcely recognized by the press or the public. Hawthorne's lack of success, Poe intimated, could be attributed to his being "a poor man" who could not buy literary favors. Also, he was not a "ubiquitous quack," the type that thrived in American culture.

Returning to the subject of Hawthorne more than a year later in his critical essay "Tale-Writing," Poe cited Hawthorne as *"the* example, *par excellence,* in this country, of the privately-admired and publicly-unappreciated man of genius." The publication of *Mosses from an Old Manse* had resulted in a certain amount of critical attention, and Poe was now inclined to diagnose Hawthorne's public failure as the result of his lack of "novelty" and his fatal penchant for allegory. Hawthorne was clearly tainted with the didactic impulse Poe considered the major failing of New England writers. "Allegory," Poe charged, "is at war with the whole tone of his nature." With the instincitve capacity of a touchy artist to overpraise the mediocre productions of a rival, Poe first criticized the "mysticism" of Hawthorne's "Young Goodman Brown," then recommended "the hearty, genial, and still Indian-summer sunshine of his Wakefields and Little Annie's Rambles." He also expressed his concern that Hawthorne was becoming the captive of a clique. "His books," Poe went on to say, "afford strong internal evidence of having been written to himself and his particular friends alone." In his most autocratic manner, Poe administered some praise, offered some critical advice, and, among the sweeter uses of adverse criticism, settled a few old scores against remembered enemies. Hawthorne, Poe stated, "has the purest style, the finest taste, the most available scholarship, the most delicate humor, the most touching pathos, the most radiant imagination, the most consummate ingenuity; and with these varied qualities he has done *well* as a mystic. But is there any of these qualities which should prevent his doing doubly as well in a career of honest, upright, sensible, prehensible and comprehensible things?" In even-handed fashion, Poe then brought down the sharp edge of his ax: "Let him [Hawthorne] mend his pen, get a bottle of visible ink, come out from the Old Manse, cut Mr. Alcott, hang (if possible) the editor of 'The Dial,' and throw out of the window to the pigs all his odd numbers of 'The North American Review.' "

No doubt, the source of Poe's rancor could be found in his ostracism from the literary community. But there may have been other circumstances that rankled him. Five years before, in praising Hawthorne's *Twice-told Tales*, Poe nevertheless claimed he had found an instance of plagiarism involving Hawthorne's story "Howe's Masquerade" and his own allegorical tale, "William Wilson." He made the charge in his usual, irritating, obsequious fashion. "We observe something which resembles a plagiarism," he insinuated, "— but which *may be* a very flattering coincidence of thought." Poe claimed that both Hawthorne's concept and his own were identical, then reprinted passages from both tales that dealt with the confrontation of a character with a cloaked and muffled image who turns out to be himself. The quoted passages did little to confirm his claim. (Since Poe, admittedly, had got the idea from Washington Irving, who, in turn, had it from a subject considered by both Byron and Shelley, probably based on a play by Calderón de la Barca, the charge was slightly preposterous to begin with.)

Hawthorne's is a relatively thin and weak story in which Sir William Howe sees himself as the last of the historic figures in a phantom procession of the provincial governors of Massachusetts; in Poe's far more masterly psychological tale, the disreputable card-cheat, William Wilson, confronts and kills a mirror image that is his own beleaguered conscience. Poe's claim of plagiarism was completely unfounded: "Howe's Masquerade" had first appeared in the *Democratic Review* of March 1838, but "William Wilson" was not published until 1839, in the Christmas annual *The Gift*. It may have been an extenuating circumstance that Poe had made his accusation in a review of the 1842 edition of *Twice-told Tales*, but since he complained there that the tales were already "thrice-told," he was shrewd enough to realize that Hawthorne's story might well have been published earlier than his own.

Hawthorne did not respond to Poe's charges. But he may possibly have had them in mind when, in his sketch "The Hall of Fantasy," he referred to Poe as "belonging to the obnoxious class of critics." Although Hawthorne deleted the references to his contemporaries when he reprinted the piece in *Mosses from an Old Manse*, it was very likely that Poe had seen the original version published in the February 1843 issue of Lowell's *Pioneer*; Poe, too, was a contributor to the periodical. But more immediately, the combative Poe could hardly have ignored the brusque and forthright letter Hawthorne had recently sent him, after having instructed Wiley and Putnam to send Poe a copy of *Mosses*. "I have read your occasional notices of my productions with great interest," Hawthorne wrote the critic on June 17, "not so much because your judgment was, on the whole, favorable, as because it seemed to be given in earnest. I care for nothing but the truth; and shall always much more readily accept a harsh truth, in regard to my writings, than a sugared falsehood."

He added, "I confess, however, that I admire you rather as a writer of tales than as a critic upon them. I might often — and do often — dissent from your opinions, in the later capacity, but could never fail to recognize your force and originality, in the former."

Under the circumstances, it was unlikely that the irascible Mr. Poe would reward Hawthorne with a "sugared falsehood."

⌇ IV ⌇

Not until early in September 1847 did the Hawthornes find a suitable home in Salem — a large house at 14 Mall Street. Three stories high, the house was only one room deep, "so all the rooms face the sun and we shall bask in the sunshine all winter" — as Sophia informed her mother. In her letter, Sophia noted that they hoped to move by the end of the month. She gave a detailed plan of the rooms and said she would use the parlor as a nursery in order to save on firewood. More important, there was a separate suite of rooms, and Mrs. Hawthorne, Louisa, and Elizabeth would be moving into these. There would be no interference in their domestic arrangements, Sophia assured Mrs. Peabody. Louisa kept to herself, and Elizabeth was "an invisible entity," whom she had seen only once in the past two years. Sophia was actually looking forward to the arrangement, since the children could be left with Louisa when she and her husband wanted to enjoy a walk together. But her great satisfaction was that "Mrs. Hawthorne's remainder of life will be glorified by the presence of these children and of her son. I am so glad to win her out of that Castle Dismal and from the mysterious chamber, into which no mortal ever peeped until Una was born and Julian, for they alone have entered the penetralia. Into that chamber the sun never shines. Into these rooms in Mall St., it blazes without ceremony and stint."

In the new house, Hawthorne would have a third-floor-study, all to himself. Sophia was delighted: "He will be as quiet up there as if among the stars — oh blessed consummation. It will be to me a Paradise of Peace to think of him alone and still, yet within my reach. He has now lived in the nursery a year without a chance for one hour's uninterrupted musing, and without his desk being once opened!"

"I am trying to resume my pen," Hawthorne wrote Longfellow not long after moving into the Mall Street house, "but the influences of my situation and customary associates are so anti-literary, that I know not whether I shall succeed." In the privacy of his study, he found himself "dreaming about stories, as of old; but these forenoons in the Custom House undo all that the afternoons and evenings have done." Still, he spent his afternoons in the barely furnished, uncarpeted third-floor room, staring out at the North River. "I should be happier if I could write," Hawthorne said, "— also, I should like to add something to my income, which, though tolerable, is a tight fit. If you can suggest any work of pure literary drudgery, I am the very man for it."

Hawthorne's literary efforts during his three-year term as surveyor were scant. His published pieces consisted only of his introductory sketch, "The Old Manse"; a short story, "The Unpardonable Sin" (later retitled "Ethan Brand"), which he regarded as a fragment of a longer work; and a lengthy but routine historical sketch, "Main Street." Quite possibly, he may also have begun work on two other stories, "The Great Stone Face" and "The Snow-Image," both of which were published in 1850.

The idea for Hawthorne's character Ethan Brand can be traced back to an 1844 notebook entry, made in Concord: "The search of an investigator for the Unpardonable Sin — he at last finds it in his own heart and practice." In a lengthier afterthought, he added, "The Unpardonable Sin might consist in a want of love and reverence for the Human Soul; in consequence of which, the investigator pried into its dark depths, not with a hope or purpose of making it better, but from a cold philosophical curiosity . . . Would not this, in other words, be the separation of the intellect from the heart?"

Hawthorne's parable of a ruthless intellect, uninstructed by compassion, let loose in the world, drew heavily on his journal notes from his troubled 1838 excursion to North Adams. The old "Dutchman" with his traveling diorama, the maimed and disreputable lawyer, Haynes, and an odd little tavern urchin, Joe, provided him with several of his fictional characters. The country husband in search of his prostitute wife and a vagrant grandfather whose granddaughter was brought up in the circus merge in "The Unpardonable Sin" to become a pathetic old man waiting out his life for word of a daughter who has become a world-famous performer. (Rather too conveniently in the story, the daughter, Esther, has met Brand and been corrupted in the course of one of his unnamed "psychological" experiments.) The principal setting of the story — the limekiln, burning infernally in the dark of night — was supplied from Hawthorne's nighttime excursion with Mr. Leach.

The point of Hawthorne's tale was powerful enough; Hawthorne stresses it during the course of Brand's nocturnal vigil beside the limekiln. Brand's heart had withered and hardened: "It had ceased to partake of the universal throb. He had lost his hold of the magnetic chain of humanity." When he throws himself into the burning limekiln, it is as a neat fulfillment of Hawthorne's allegorical premise. Hawthorne had infallibly sensed that the alienated mood of his 1838 excursion might supply the impetus for his story of the alienated intellect. Yet something went wrong with his intention. Despite the suavity of his prose, the mechanics and the moral of the tale are too bluntly exposed. Brand remains largely an "idea" — the cruel intellect with an infernal laugh. The lesser characters, too, are mere wraiths of his more vital notebook "remarkables." Hawthorne clearly had difficulty in bring his story to life.

The publication of "The Unpardonable Sin" had its frustrations, as well. When Lizzie Peabody asked for a contribution to her new publishing venture, an anthology called *Aesthetic Papers*, Hawthorne sent her "The Unpardonable Sin," indicating that it was a fragment from a work in progress and that he would send it elsewhere if she did not find it satisfactory. Sophia, of course, had no reservations about its quality. Forwarding the manuscript through her mother, she described it as if it were a magnificent sermon: "It is a tremendous truth, written, as he often writes truth, with characters of fire, upon an infinite gloom — softened so as not wholly to terrify, by divine touches of beauty."

But Hawthorne had not softened the story enough — at least, for Lizzie's taste. Through her mother, Lizzie suggested that something else might be preferable. Mother Peabody wrote Sophia, "E. says she thinks the 'Unpardonable Sin' is very interesting and full of genius; but of course, if another story is to be written, *at any rate*, she would like to make a choice, if Mr. H. is willing to give her liberty to do so." Lizzie, however, would not give it up "unless for something as great as well as more cheerful." In place of "The Unpardonable Sin," Hawthorne sent his innocuous sketch "Main Street," which appeared in *Aesthetic Papers* in May 1849, where it accompanied Thoreau's virtually unnoticed essay, "Resistance to Civil Government," later famous as "Civil Disobedience."

It is not clear whether Hawthorne engaged in a bit of minor double-dealing with his sister-in-law — or whether he knew in advance that Lizzie would find "The Unpardonable Sin" unacceptable. Without waiting for Lizzie's answer, he sent another copy of the story to Charles Wilkins Webber, who asked for a contribution to his projected magazine, *The American Review*. Hawthorne responded, "At last, by main strength, I have wrenched and torn an idea out of my miserable brain; or rather, the fragment of an idea, like a tooth ill-drawn, and leaving the roots to torture me." Even considering Hawthorne's usual diffidence, his account is dramatic. In telling Webber to feel free to reject the story, however, he made a feeble joke about the fate of his hero: "I am as tractable an author as you ever knew, so far as putting my articles into the fire goes." The story was duly set up in type and the sheets printed, but *The American Review* failed before it was published. Much to Hawthorne's chagrin, Webber, without consulting him, offered it to another periodical, the *Boston Weekly Museum*, which published it in January 1850.

Hawthorne's only other known writings from the period were his incidental reviews for the *Salem Advertiser*, which was then being edited by his friend Horace Conolly. Aside from the Dickens and Melville reviews and one or two other book notices, Hawthorne also wrote two theatrical criticisms, an account of a ball at Ballard Vale, and a review of Longfellow's popular poem *Evangeline*. Hawthorne had a connection with Longfellow's success, for the theme of the dispossessed Acadians had first been suggested to him by Conolly. After using it as the subject for one of his children's tales in *Famous Old People*, Hawthorne had no more interest in it and handed it over to Longfellow, whose book-length poem, published in November 1847, ran to six editions by January and brought the poet approximately $100 a week in royalties during its boom period. Writing Hawthorne, Longfellow thanked him cordially for his "friendly service" in reviewing the book so favorably. He hoped Conolly did not think he had "spoilt the tale he told, in my way of narrating it." He acknowledged, "Still more do I thank you for resigning to me that 'Legend of Acady'! This success I owe entirely to you, for being willing to forego the pleasure of writing a prose tale, which many people would have taken for poetry, that I might write a poem which many people take for prose."

The most consistent writing efforts that Hawthorne managed during his political tenure were his random journal entries on the sleepy life of the Custom House and his regular reports on his two active children. He had, in a sense, become the historian of the nursery. March 19th, 1848 — a Sunday:

> . . . [Julian] climbs into a chair at my knee, and peeps at himself in the glass — now he looks curiously on the page as I write — now, he nearly tumbles down, and is at first frightened — but, seeing that I was likewise startled, pretends to tumble again, and then laughs in my face. Enter Mamma with the milk. He sits on his mother's knee, gulping the milk with grunts and sighs of satisfaction — nor ceases till the cup is exhausted, once, and again, and again. On being undressed, he is [taking an air bath] — he enjoys the felicity of utter nakedness — running away from Mamma with cries of remonstrance, when she wishes to put on his nightgown. Now ensues a terrible catastrophe — not to be mentioned in our seemly history. Now — at ½ past 11, A.M. — he is gone to take his noon-nap.
>
> At about ½ past 12, enter Una and Dora from their walk. Una insisted on going into Dr. Flint's church, where they sat in the gallery, and heard two or three hymns. Also, they went to Mr. Lee's; where Una seems to have made herself very much at home, looking at Josephine's playthings, going to the stone-pot for biscuits, &c. Finally, on their way home, she insisted on being carried in Dora's arms from the Franklin building. Nevertheless, Dora insists upon it that she has been a "nice little girl."
>
> Now, she has gone with Dora into the kitchen — whence, ever and anon, comes the sound of her voice, airy as the sunshine. Mamma has been some time lain down; so that I am alone.
>
> 10 minutes past 1, Enter Mamma with Julian in her arms, his

face like a great red apple, but as yet hardly awake. He sits on his mother's knee, looking dreamily around — putting his fingers in his mouth, probably conscious of another budding tooth. Dora proposes to take Julian out to walk; and Mamma accoutres him for the expedition — he saying "alk; ok" by way of signifying that he understands the matter. "Oh, you little splendor! — Oh, you little splendor of the world!" cries Mamma, overwhelmed with admiration. She puts on his black beaver-hat, with a sable ostrich-feather and paste-buckle. "Oh, enchanting! — was ever anything so beautiful!" . . . Finally a plaid silk cravat is tied round his neck and he sets forth, holding Dora by the hand . . .

Enter Una — "Where is little Julian?" "He has gone out to walk." "No; but I mean where is the place of little Julian, that you've been writing about him." So I point to the page, at which she looks with all possible satisfaction; and stands watching the pen as it hurries forward. "I'll put the ink nearer to you," says she. "Father, are you going to write all this?" she adds, turning over the book, "Father, why do you write down stairs? — you never wrote down stairs before . . ."

His daughter had noticed a change in his writing habits. There were times when Hawthorne found Una's sudden perceptions eerie and disconcerting.

Sometimes his life seemed becalmed — particularly when Sophia was away. "Sweetest wife," he wrote her on one occasion when she had taken the children for a family visit, "I have nothing to tell thee. My life goes on as regularly as our kitchen clock. It has no events, and therefore can have no history." Now and then, when Sophia was absent, he entertained a visitor. Ellery Channing came to spend a week with Hawthorne in the spring of 1847. In a reversal of his earlier view, Hawthorne, writing to Duyckinck, claimed, "The more I know him [Channing], the more I feel he is a remarkable man." Hawthorne tried to promote a manuscript of Channing's *Conversations in Rome between an Artist, a Catholic and a Critic*, derived from a recent trip that Channing had taken in order to escape the nuisance of his wife's second pregnancy. During that Salem visit, the two men had taken "immense walks" every afternoon and sat up till midnight, talking. "He eats like an anaconda," Hawthorne complained to Sophia. "Thou didst never see such an appetite." At the end of the week, he was happy to see Channing go, although he admitted they had had a good time together. Channing, years later, recalling that visit or one he made several months afterward, remembered visiting Hawthorne at the Custom House. Among the surveyor's duties at the time was the testing of the strength of a consignment of rum being shipped to Africa. "I am determined the niggers shall have as good liquor as anyone gets from New England," Hawthorne had boasted.

In the Mall Street house, to be sure, Hawthorne had his own family within call, but it was cold comfort. When Sophia was away, he wrote her self-pitying letters. "Thou canst have no imagination how lonely our house is," he wrote in June 1848, when Sophia and the children were making a prolonged visit to the Mann family in West Newton. "The rooms seem twice as large as before — and twice as quiet. I wish sometime or other, thou wouldst let me take the two children and go away for a few days, and thou remain behind. Otherwise, thou canst have no idea of what it is. And then our great, lonesome bed at night — the scene of so many blissful intercourses — now so solitary." Sophia, it seems, responded in ardent terms, then asked that he destroy that portion of her letter. He answered, "Thou badest me burn two pages of thy last letter, but I cannot do it, and will not; for never was a wife's deep, warm, chaste love so well expressed." At times he sent comic messages to his daughter. He had painted her doll's cheeks a vivid carmine. "Tell my little daughter Una," he advised Sophia, "that her dolly, since her departure, has been blooming like a rose — such an intense bloom, indeed, that I rather suspect her of making free with my brandy-bottle."

Though he might joke, he nonetheless felt Sophia's absences deeply. He was sometimes troubled with dreams of apprehension. He had one during the tedious summer of 1848 while Sophia was visiting the Manns. (It was a dream that tends to corroborate some guilty feeling on Hawthorne's part that Lizzie Peabody had a claim on him.) In the dream, he was standing in a roomful of people. Sophia announced in front of everyone that she was no longer his wife, that she had taken another husband.

> Thou madest this intelligence known with such perfect composure and *sang froid* — not particularly addressing me, but the company generally, that it benumbed my thoughts and feelings . . . But hereupon, thy sister Elizabeth, who was likewise present, informed the company, that, in this state of affairs, having ceased to be thy husband, I of course became hers; and turning to me, very coolly inquired whether she or I should write to inform my mother of the new arrangement! How the children were to be divided, I know not. I only know that my heart suddenly broke loose and I began to expostulate with thee in an infinite agony, in the midst of which I awoke; but the sense of unspeakable injury and outrage hung about me for a long time . . .

A week later, Hawthorne spent his birthday alone. He went to Boston to see the fireworks in the evening, then returned to Salem, close to midnight. Much to his surprise, his sister Elizabeth came to pay him a visit. "I did not wish to risk frightening her away by anything like an exhibition of wonder," he wrote Sophia, "and so we greeted one another kindly and cordially, but with no more *empressement* than if we were constantly in the habit of meeting. It being so late, and I so tired, we did not talk much then . . . Perhaps she will now make it her habit to come down and see us occasionally in the evening." In his letters to Sophia during these absences, there is sometimes a slight undercurrent of recrimination; perhaps his account of Elizabeth's visit was a gentle rebuke, a reminder that his sister had broken a long-standing habit to be with him on his birthday while his wife was still away.

It was understandable, then, that on the eve of Sophia's return, Hawthorne would write her in a mood of exultation. "Soon — soon — thou wilt be at home," he wrote on July 18. "What joy! . . . Kiss our beloved children for me."

———

As a manager and the corresponding secretary of the Salem Lyceum, Hawthorne engaged the lecturers for the organization's regular programs. Often enough, he seems to have sponsored his former Concord associates, who were now becoming celebrities. Twice, during the winter of 1848–1849, he arranged for Thoreau to lecture, offering to put the young man up at his Mall Street house. On November 22, Thoreau gave a talk entitled "Student Life in New England, Its Economy"; the lecture later formed part of *Walden*. Though willing to further Thoreau's career, Hawthorne still had reservations about the Concord naturalist. Longfellow asked Hawthorne to dine at Craigie House on November 23, when Ellery Channing would be his guest. Hawthorne accepted but asked if he might bring along his own house guest, Thoreau. "You would find him well worth knowing," Hawthorne commented; "he is a man of thought and originality, with a certain iron-poker-ishness, an uncompromising stiffness in his mental character, which is interesting, though it grows rather wearisome on close and frequent acquaintance."

The four men dined together in Cambridge on that Thursday afternoon. They were joined by Samuel Longfellow, the poet's younger brother and sometime secretary. As an ever more prolific writer, with a steady stream of correspondence, Longfellow frequently suffered from writer's cramp and needed assistance.

Early in January, Hawthorne engaged Charles Sumner, who had bolted the Whig Party and was becoming an increasingly controversial figure in the antislavery movement. In a recent speech, Sumner had bravely criticized the symbiotic relationship between the slave-holding plantation owners and Northern manufacturers — "the lords of the lash and the lords of the loom," as he called them. (Among the many enemies he had created was Nathan Appleton, the millionaire textile manufacturer and Longfellow's father-in-law. Visits to Craigie House had become impossible when Appleton was there.) Hawthorne also made a reluctant guest of Emerson, whose new lecture series, "England" and "The English," had resulted from his summer tour of England and the Continent. On the road, Emerson preferred living in hotels to visiting friends, but he agreed to stay at Mall Street. "I am a bad guest," he wrote Hawthorne on January 12, "but if you will let me run away suddenly next morning, I will come."

The peregrinating Bronson Alcott had moved back to Boston with his family and had reconvened his public "conversations" in both Boston and Salem. He was also promoting a Town and Country Club, the membership to include all the notable intellectuals of the area. Alcott proposed to serve as both the manager and custodian of the club premises, but the plan never materialized and he had to find other means of providing for his family. To judge from one of Sophia's letters to her mother, Alcott's "conversations" in Salem did not do well, either. On one Monday evening, she reported, there were only six gentlemen and six ladies present. Alcott had paid a visit to Mall Street, and Sophia thoroughly enjoyed it, drawing the philosopher out (no difficult task) to talk about his early experiences as a pedlar. It was from Alcott that Hawthorne learned Thoreau had recently signed a contract for a book. Writing to Thoreau on February 19 to propose a date for a second lecture, Hawthorne offered warm congratulations. Thoreau, evidently pleased, responded, "I am glad to know of your interest in my book, for I have thought of you as a reader while writing it." Unfortunately, the contract, with Hawthorne's former, unsatisfactory publisher, James Munroe and Sons, was to result in a dismal failure for Thoreau, who was left with several hundred copies of *A Week on the Concord and Merrimack Rivers*. In his journal, Thoreau sardonically remarked that he had "a library of nearly 900 volumes, over 700 of which I wrote myself."

In his February letter, Hawthorne suggested that something from the forthcoming book might make an appropriate lecture — "or perhaps that Indian lecture, which you mentioned to me, is in a state of forwardness. Either that, or a continuation of the Walden experiment (or indeed, anything else) will be acceptable." Thoreau's lecture, delivered on February 28, was another segment from the Walden theme. Sophia wrote her mother that she looked forward to it. She had found Thoreau's first lecture "such a revelation of nature in all its exquisite details of wood-thrushes, squirrels, sunshine, mists and shadows . . ." More important, she was warming to the young man, though her husband was still cautious. "Mr. Thoreau has risen above all his arrogance of manner," she informed her mother, "and is as gentle, simple, ruddy, and meek as all geniuses should be; and now his great blue eyes fairly outshine and put into shade a nose which I once thought must make him uncomely forever."

Undoubtedly the greatest thrill for Sophia, during that winter of lectures by celebrities, was the appearance of the powerful orator Daniel Webster, then at the height of his fame, if not of his political power. (In his perennial bid for the presidency, Webster had lost the nomination to Zachary Taylor, who had just been elected.) On the evening of November 16, 1848, the senator from Massachusetts held his Lyceum audience spellbound with a lecture on the Constitution of the United States — "a noble subject," Sophia proclaimed. In her enthusiasm, she mangled her metaphors a bit, referring to the politician as, first, an "old Lion," pacing back and forth across the speaker's platform in a kind of "repressed rage." In a voice ranging from thunderous denunciation to a malicious whisper, Webster attacked the enemies of the Constitution as "Madmen! — and most wicked if not mad!" From a raging lion, he was metamorphosed, in Sophia's account, into something architectural: "He stood like an Egyptian column, solid and without any Corinthian grace, but with dignity and majesty." Webster's every mention of the American flag was answered with "tremendous rolls of applause."

Hawthorne, who had witnessed Webster's performances as a trial lawyer — in Concord on one occasion and, probably, much earlier in Salem, at the trial of the murderers of old Captain Joseph White — had been impressed with Webster's "brute" force. The aging statesman, with his broad brow and deep, cavernous, fiery eyes, had the appearance of a powerful ox. But although Hawthorne willingly acknowledged Webster's charisma, he was wary of his character. In his story "The Great Stone Face," Hawthorne offers a brief vignette of the politician — the only vivid appearance in this maudlin democratic fable — when the "Old Stony Phiz," as he is called, returns to his small home town, a famous native son. Though Webster is actually unnamed in the story, Hawthorne clearly had him and his recent bid for the presidency in mind when he was writing the story. His account of the politician's return is full of the color and vivacity he could bring to a rural scene. There is a cavalcade of eager politicians and farmers on horseback, banners fluttering in the wind, the lively strains of an energetic band, and the candidate, riding in an open barouche, bowing and smiling at his constituents. But amid the local color and the careful observation, Hawthorne also registers his dark suspicions of a flaw in the great man's character. "So wonderfully eloquent was he," Hawthorne writes, "that whatever he might choose to say, his auditors had no choice but to believe him; wrong looked right, and right like wrong." The hero lacks some essential quality: "Something had been originally left out, or had departed. And therefore the marvellously gifted statesman had always a weary gloom in the deep caverns of his eyes, as of a child that has outgrown its playthings, or a man of mighty faculties and little aims, whose life, with all its high performances, was vague and empty."

There was, in fact, something prophetic about Hawthorne's tale, first published in the January 24, 1850, issue of the *National Era*. Barely six weeks later, on March 7, before a packed house in the United States Senate, Webster was to make one of the most controversial and despised speeches of his illustrious career. Endorsing Henry Clay's Compromise Measures of 1850, which included the proposal for an effective Fugitive Slave Law, Webster attacked the fanaticism of the abolitionists, who he felt were fatally dividing the country. Charles Sumner referred to him as a "traitor to a holy cause," another Judas Iscariot or a Benedict Arnold. Even the mild-mannered Emerson, a former admirer, could write, "The word *liberty* in the mouth of Mr. Webster sounds like the word *love* in the mouth of a courtezan." Overnight in American politics, a famous man became infamous: the lesson was not lost on Hawthorne.

ᕲ V ᕬ

Hawthorne's own political dénouement had begun a year earlier. With the election of Zachary Taylor, the old "Rough and Ready" of the 1848 campaign, the Whigs, including Hawthorne's brother-in-law, had been swept into office. Hawthorne, cautiously trusting in the new administration's promise that qualified men would not be removed from office for purely partisan reasons, found himself at the center of a fierce party struggle in which he was finally ousted. The official notice of his removal came by way of the new telegraphic system on June 8, 1849, with the appointment of Captain Allen Putnam as the new surveyor of the Salem Custom House.

Throughout the pitched battle that centered on his dismissal, Hawthorne maintained an attitude of aggrieved innocence, the bewilderment of a man who has been thoroughly wronged. As a shrewd politician, however, he had been anticipating his probable removal for several months. As early as March 5, he wrote his friend and lawyer, George Hillard, a prominent Whig, asking Hillard to use his influence to forestall a move by the Salem Whigs to oust him. Hawthorne argued that he had not been appointed to the surveyorship "as a reward for political services," nor could it be said that he had "acted as a politician" since his appointment. He assured Hillard that local Democrats "look coldly on me for not having used the influence of my position to obtain the removal of Whigs — which I might have done, but which I in no case did." Clearly aware of the precise charges to be brought against him, Hawthorne proceeded to explain that he had not benefited from the ouster of a Whig, since Nehemiah Brown, his predecessor, had been a Tyler Democrat. "Nor," he added, "can any charge of inattention to duty, or other official misconduct, be brought against me; or, if so, I could easily refute it."

Although his tone was sometimes jocular, Hawthorne was obviously concerned. He was only "an inoffensive man of letters," he maintained, who had obtained "a pitiful little office on no other plea than his pitiful little literature," and he ought not to be "left to the mercy of these thick-skulled and no-hearted ruffians." In passing, he referred to his political enemies as "slang-whangers and vote-distributors." He asked Hillard to use his influence among the Boston Whigs to obtain "a few such testimonials as would take my name out of the list of ordinary office-holders; and at least prevent any hasty action." He specifically asked that the letters contain no allusion to the "proposed attack" on him, since the whole thing might fall through of its own accord. "Certainly the general feeling here in Salem would be in my favor," he claimed, "but I have seen too much of the modes of political action to lay any great stress on that."

Writing to Longfellow a few days before his official ouster, Hawthorne complained that he was unable to review Longfellow's recently published *Kavanagh, a Tale*: his previous reviews in the *Salem Advertiser* had brought charges that he had written political articles for that Democratic paper and that he was one of its editors. To his chagrin, he also learned that Horace Conolly, having an eye for political opportunities, had gone over to the enemy side and was attending Whig political caucuses. "I must confess," Hawthorne boasted, "it stirs up a little of the devil within me to find myself hunted by these political bloodhounds. If they succeed in getting me out of office, I will surely immolate one or two of them. Not that poor monster of a Conolly, whom I desire only to bury in oblivion . . . But, if there be among them (as there must be, if they succeed) some men who claim a higher position and ought to know better, I may perhaps select a victim, and let fall one little drop of venom on his heart, that shall make him writhe before the grin of the multitude for a considerable time to come." He was almost looking forward to being turned out of office, he claimed, so that he could indulge in the pleasures of such personal satire. But he was more concerned, he told Longfellow, about his two children, both of whom had scarlet fever. Julian had been seriously ill. "But God spared me that trial . . ." he wrote. "Other troubles may irritate me superficially; nothing else can go near the heart."

On the morning that he received official word of his removal, Hawthorne immediately wrote Hillard from the Custom House, "I am turned out of office! There is no use in lamentation. It now remains to consider what I shall do next." His salary, with "emoluments," he claimed, had allowed him only to support his family and pay off a few of his debts. He asked Hillard if he knew of any editorial positions or if there were possibly some "subordinate office" with the Boston Athenaeum. "Do not think anything too humble to be mentioned to me," he told Hillard, clutching at straws. "The intelligence has just reached me," he said, "and Sophia has not yet heard it. She will bear it like a woman — that is to say, better than a man."

He had accurately predicted his wife's response. Late that night, writing a lengthy letter to her mother, Sophia was coolly assured. "Do not be troubled," she said, "for *we* are not." She saw the crisis as an opportunity for her husband to return to his writing. "He has felt in chains for a long time," Sophia told her mother, "and being a MAN he is not alarmed at being set upon his own feet again — or on his *head* I might say — for that contains the available gold of a mine scarcely worked at all. As Margaret [Fuller] truly once said, 'We have had but a drop or so from that ocean.' "

Later, however, when she learned the details of the behind-the-scenes maneuvering to oust her husband, Sophia's response was one of outright indignation. "The whole contemptible movement was comprised within the smallest space," she wrote her mother; "I believe not more than five or six persons." In scathing terms, she listed the principal culprits: "The illustrious and highly intellectual Richard S. Rodgers, who never had an idea in his life. Nat Silsbee, Jr. — a man of the smallest scope, narrow and stingy to the last degree. George Devereux, a furious demagogue and a most rancorous spirit in all points . . ." But the chief villain, the "first in mischief," was Charles Wentworth Upham, the former-minister-turned-politician, "who has proved himself a liar and a most consummate hypocrite! for he always professed himself the warmest friend." Charles Sumner, having heard of Upham's role in the plot, had remarked, "What, that smooth, smiling, oily man of God!" — so Sophia informed her mother.

Hawthorne was, at first, reluctant to make a public fight to retain a political office, but as the campaign mounted, he decided to respond. On June 16, an anonymous editorial in the Boston Whig paper, the *Atlas*, outlined the charges against him — most of them complaints that Hawthorne had anticipated early in March, and one that was new. The writer, who may have been Upham himself, asked that Hawthorne "explain a piece of mystery as it appears on the pages of the Blue Book. How comes it that his Loco Foco subordinates receive some hundred dollars a year more than their Whig associates?"

In a calm and reasoned letter, written to George Hillard on June 18, Hawthorne responded point by point. His letter was clearly intended for publication, and it appeared a few days later in Boston's *Daily Advertiser*. With an air of injured innocence, and a slightly faulty recall, Hawthorne maintained that he had been a very reluctant office-seeker and that he had applied for the Salem postmastership only at the urgent and repeated requests of "a person who claimed to be the representative of the great majority of the local Democratic party." That Hawthorne should have conveniently forgotten both his active campaign for the office and his irritation with Bancroft was disingenuous, to say the least. (The fact that the issue should have come up at all makes it sound suspiciously as if Conolly, who had been Hawthorne's spy among the Salem Democrats, had brought it to the attention of the Whigs.) Hawthorne was on far surer ground when he responded to the *Atlas'* contention that he had replaced a Whig surveyor. Triumphantly, Hawthorne referred to Nehemiah Brown's membership in the Hickory Club and his reputation as a Democrat among local Whigs and Democrats. As a final bit of incontrovertible proof of his innocence, he referred "to a gentleman now very prominent and active in our local politics, the Rev. Charles Wentworth Upham, who told me, in the presence of David Roberts, Esq., that I need never fear removal under a Whig administration, inasmuch as my appointment had not displaced a Whig." It was, admittedly, a minor drop of venom, but Hawthorne seemed pleased to release it.

As to the charges that he had been an "active politician" for the Democratic Party while in office, Hawthorne answered that he had never taken part in any Democratic convention; had never even walked in a torchlight procession. He once more categorically denied the familiar charge that he had written political articles. His articles for the *Salem Advertiser* had consisted of "a few notices of books, and other miscellaneous paragraphs, perhaps a dozen in all; never a single line of politics." His affiliation with the *Democratic Review* had ended three years before, he contended, and with the exception of his article on Jonathan Cilley, which was clearly a eulogy for a dead friend, nothing else that he had written there could be considered remotely political in character. To the new charge that his Democratic subordinates were more highly paid than the Whig officers, he argued, somewhat evasively, that the payments made were "strictly and necessarily commensurate with the amount of service rendered" and that, in any event, all such salary decisions had been made under the supervision and direction of "Colonel Miller, a Whig, the Deputy Collector, and now the Collector of the port." In a well-calculated swipe at the anonymous editorial writer, Hawthorne claimed that he was happy to answer the charges but would have been happier still if his accuser had "come forward under his own name, and met me, face to face before the public."

Hawthorne's most convinced supporter was gratified. Writing to her mother, Sophia exclaimed, "You never heard such a time about anyone as there has been about Mr. Hawthorne. The whole country is up in arms and will not allow Mr. Hawthorne to be removed." She reported that the removal had been suspended in Washington and that it was likely Hawthorne would retain his office or be given a better one. "Mr. Hawthorne's name is ringing throughout the land," she repeated. "All the latent feeling about him now comes out, and he finds himself very famous." Hawthorne's political ouster had, indeed, become a minor cause célèbre. Prominent Whigs began to see it as a political blunder. The historian William H. Prescott, personally unacquainted with Hawthorne, felt that the publicity was giving the party a bad name nationally. Daniel Webster, writing to Secretary of the Treasury William Meredith, somewhat weakly suggested, "I suppose it will be for the best to leave Mr. Hawthorne where he is, for the present." Edward Everett, president of Harvard, expressed little sympathy for a "gentleman" who would ally himself with the "radical party," but clearly considered Hawthorne's removal "an ill-advised step." Democratic newspapers around the country made whatever political capital they could out of the circumstances. The *New York Evening Post*, William Cullen Bryant's newspaper, branded it "an act of wanton and unmitigated oppression." And the nonpartisan *Boston Transcript*, quoting Talleyrand, called it "something worse than a crime — a blunder." Throughout that uncertain summer, Hawthorne's political future hung in the balance while his enemies took advantage of the temporary lull to mount new charges.

Hawthorne's attitude was distinctly ambivalent; at times, he seemed bent on revenge or, at the least, self-vindication. At other times, he thought himself well rid of the despised political profession. There were moments, however, when he achieved a kind of humorous equanimity. Writing to Longfellow, he commented wryly, "I feel pretty well since my head has been chopt off. It is not so essential a part of the human system as a man is apt to think."

In that steamy midsummer of his forty-fifth year, Hawthorne reached his psychological nadir. Not only did he have to face frustrating political battles and financial anxieties, but his mother became seriously ill. For several days, she lay feeble and unconscious in her upper room in the Mall Street house. During the anxious hours and days of waiting, Sophia and Hawthorne's aunt Priscilla Dike stood watch in the sickroom, relieving Louisa and Ebe, who seemed of little help in the emergency. Hawthorne took charge of his restless children. In the hushed household atmosphere, both Una and Julian displayed a peculiar fascination with their grandmother's illness. They acted out the little sickroom dramas, the pathetic gestures, the solemn inquiries, with a bizarre innocence and a frequent changing of roles. Hawthorne recorded their activities and his own emotions with a kind of dumb awe. Sunday, July 29, 1849:

> At about five o'clock, I went to my mother's chamber, and was shocked to see such an alteration since my last visit, the day before yesterday. I love my mother; but there has been, ever since my boyhood, a sort of coldness of intercourse between us, such as is apt to come between persons of strong feelings, if they are not managed rightly. I did not expect to be much moved at the time — that is to say, not to feel any overpowering emotion struggling, just then — though I knew that I should deeply remember and regret her. Mrs. Dike was in the chamber. Louisa pointed to a chair near the bed; but I was moved to kneel down close by my mother, and take her hand. She knew me, but could only murmur a few indistinct words — among which I understood an injunction to take care of my sisters. Mrs. Dike left the chamber, and then I found the tears slowly gathering in my eyes. I tried to keep them down; but it would not be — I kept filling up, till, for a few moments, I shook with sobs. For a long time, I knelt there, holding her hand; and surely it is the darkest hour I ever lived. Afterwards, I stood by the open window and looked through the crevice of the curtain. The shouts, laughter, and cries of the two children had come up into the chamber from the open air, making a strange contrast with the death-bed scene. And now, through the crevice of the curtain, I saw my little Una of the golden locks, looking very beautiful; and so full

of spirit and life, that she was life itself. And then I looked at my poor dying mother; and seemed to see the whole of human existence at once, standing in the dusty midst of it. Oh what a mockery, if what I saw were all — let the interval between extreme youth and dying age be filled up with what happiness it might! But God would not have made the close so dark and wretched, if there were nothing beyond . . .

At one moment, little Una's voice came up, very clear and distinct, into the chamber — "Yes; — she is going to die." I wish she had said "going to God" which is her idea and usual expression of death; it would have been so hopeful and comforting, uttered in the bright young voice. She must have been repeating or enforcing the words of some elder person who had just spoken.

July 30th, ½ past 10 o'clock . . .

Una takes a strong and strange interest in poor mother's condition, and can hardly be kept out of the chamber — endeavoring to thrust herself into the door, whenever it is opened . . . There is something that almost frightens me about the child — I know not whether elfish or angelic, but, at all events, supernatural. She steps so boldly into the midst of everything, shrinks from nothing, has such a comprehension of everything, seems at times to have but little delicacy, and anon shows that she possesses the finest essence of it . . . In short, I now and then catch an aspect of her, in which I cannot believe her to be my own human child, but a spirit strangely mingled with good and evil, haunting the house where I dwell. The little boy is always the same child, and never varies in his relation to me.

3 o'clock, P.M. Julian is now lying on the couch in the character of sick grandmamma, while Una waits on him as Mrs. Dike. She prompts him in the performance, showing a quite perfect idea of how it should all be. "Now, stretch out your hands to be held." "Will you have some of this jelly?" Julian starts up to take the imaginary jelly. "No; grandmamma lies still." He smacks his lips. "You must not move your lips so hard." "Do you think Una had better come up?" "No!" "You feel so, don't you?" His round, curly head, and rosy face, with a twinkling of a smile upon it, do not look the character very well. Now Una is transformed into grandmamma, and Julian is mamma, taking care of her. She groans and speaks with difficulty, and moves herself feebly and wearisomely — then lies perfectly still, as if in an insensible state . . . It recalls the scene of yesterday to me, with a frightful distinctness; and out of the midst of it, little Una looks at me with a smile of glee. Again, Julian assumes the character. "You're dying now," says Una, "so you must lie still." "I shall walk, if I'm dying," answers Julian, whereupon he gets up, and stumps about the room with heavy steps. Meantime, Una lies down on the couch, and is again grand-

mamma, stretching out her hand, in search of some tender grasp, to assure herself that she is still on the hither side of the grave . . .

In the innocent, heartless games of children, the roles might be exchanged at will; in the fixed reality of life, they could never be altered. The deathbed scene that Una and Julian rehearsed in childish accents took place, in reality, on the following day: Hawthorne's mother died in the late afternoon of July 31. It was a protracted, nineteenth-century death: the warm, stale atmosphere of the sickroom; the clutter of washbasins and pitchers, glasses half-filled with medicines or tepid water; the silent, patient figures of women, watching for signs of the end; a disorder of emotions, hastily taken up, then put aside, like used napkins. Throughout the ordeal, there were the spasms of pain and fitful breathing; then longer spells of silence, broken only by hushed voices and harmless remarks; the insistent droning of the flies. Sophia, in her consistently thorough fashion, described the scene for her mother, transforming the solemn details into the noble passage of a soul into the hereafter:

> My dearest Mother — Mrs. Hawthorne died yesterday afternoon, after four or five days of excessive agony, relieved by intervals of unconsciousness. I am weary, weary, weary, heart and head. I have watched through all the days (not nights) keeping off flies, holding her in my arms as she sat up for breath, and sympathizing far too deeply and vividly with her children and with herself to escape unscathed. My husband came near a brain fever, after seeing her for an hour, and while our hearts were aching with sorrow and care, Mrs. Dike has been like some marble-souled fiend. But of that I cannot speak now or perhaps ever. I hope God will forgive her, but I do not see how He can! Elizabeth and Louisa are desolate beyond all words. We have lost an angel of excellence, and in mind and person an angel — oh, such a loss! . . .
>
> At the last she had no suffering — for eight hours no suffering — but gradually faded as day fades, no differences momentarily; but hourly a change. I thought I could not stay through the final hour, but found myself courageous for Louisa's and Elizabeth's sakes; and her disinterested devoted life exhaled in a sigh, exquisitely painful to hear when we knew it to be the last sigh — but to her not painful.
>
> I am too tired to rest yet. Sophia.
>
> The funeral takes place tomorrow at four o'clock.

ᴄᴗ VI ᴄᴗ

There was little time for grief: Hawthorne was faced with new charges from his political enemies. In the effort to recapture the Custom House, Upham and the local Whigs stepped up their assault, in view of the high-level support for Hawthorne's reinstatement. Throughout the summer, at the meetings of the Whig ward committees and the Zachary Taylor Club (meetings attended by the fickle Horace Conolly), they had mustered the support of such men as former Senator Nathaniel Silsbee and his son, the present mayor of Salem. For the benefit of the secretary of the treasury, they had also prepared a detailed report, a Memorial, outlining their grievances, setting forth the history of their actions, and complaining bitterly of Hawthorne's "personal and literary friends" of both parties who had rushed to his defense, bringing reproach upon the Salem Whigs. It had never been their original intention, so Upham and his colleagues claimed, to remove Hawthorne from office. But it had become clear that the present collector of the port, Ephraim Miller, a nominal Whig who had received his appointment with the support of the Democratic Party, was collaborating with the Democrats to avoid making even the normal minor appointments the Whigs had asked for. Hawthorne, it was evident, was being used to forestall any action whatsoever. "That gentleman was placed as a barrier in our way," the Memorial claimed. "The Collector and his official associates planted themselves, as they thought, securely behind him, and actually made his removal necessary before we could advance a step in obtaining our rightful authority over the Custom House." Although the tone was plaintive, the charge was probably accurate. One by one, they had seen the political plums captured by fast appointments by the outgoing Polk administration. There was some justice in the Whig claim that the dismissal of Hawthorne was the first evidence in Salem politics "that Zachary Taylor and not James K. Polk, is the President of the United States."

Since it had been one of Zachary Taylor's campaign promises that office-holders would be dismissed only because of "malfeasance," the local Whigs were obliged to find more satisfactory grounds for Hawthorne's dismissal than they had managed so far. In their new assault, they fixed on the long-term political practice of squeezing office-holders for "assessments," or kickbacks for the support of the party in power. The Whigs claimed not only that Hawthorne had condoned the old practice, but that he had been involved in an attempt to levy an additional assessment against his own Democratic inspectors. "There is a Democratic newspaper in this city, the Salem Advertiser," the Memorial noted, by way of evidence. "The editor, under the sanction of Mr. Hawthorne, claimed from the Democratic Inspectors, for the support of this paper, an assessment, so much beyond all reason, that three of their number, conferring together, declined to pay it, and proposed a smaller sum." Within a day, the indictment claimed, a notice of dismissal was drawn up — written and signed by Hawthorne himself — that was intended to be given to two of the inspectors. The Memorial acknowledged that the notice of dismissal was subsequently withdrawn — but the clear implication was that it was done so only after the rebellious inspectors had been "worked over into compliant shape by party machinery." The single brave hold-out against this extortion thereafter had not been assigned extra work. His salary was never higher than the lesser-paid Whig members of Hawthorne's staff. As an exercise of good will, the writers of the Memorial expressed doubt that Hawthorne had been "fully aware" of such outright extortion. It was their belief that the surveyor had been, "to a great extent, the abused instrument of others." What the writers of the testimony against Hawthorne deliberately failed to note was that the editor of the *Salem Advertiser* at the time the "extortion" had taken place was none other than Horace L. Conolly, whose name now appeared prominently in the records of the Whig ward committee meetings. It was very likely that Hawthorne's erstwhile friend had supplied the Whigs with the evidence they needed.

Early in his political difficulties, Hawthorne had turned to Horace Mann, as well as to Hillard, for support from the Boston Whigs. When he learned that the local Whigs were submitting new and secret charges to Washington, he asked Mann to obtain a copy of the document. He clearly felt that Mann deserved an explanation, and he did his best to clear himself. But the Salem Whigs had presented him with a well-devised political dilemma: either he had to admit that he had "sanctioned" the move to put pressure on the dismissed inspectors, or he had to acknowledge that he was ignorant of the political activities of the lesser members of his staff. Writing to Mann on August 8, Hawthorne tried to give the appearance of being above the fray. He admitted that he had received instructions to dismiss the temporary inspectors on his staff — but these instructions had come from the Treasury Department itself. There were two such temporary officials, both Democrats and men "with large families and no resources," so he was reluctant to comply with the order. His intention was to suspend the men during the "inactive season" so that they could be reinstated when the work load warranted. But he had written out the formal order for dismissal of the men. His head clerk, Zachariah Burchmore, however, had advised him to take no action but to wait for further word from the Treasury Department, since the dismissal was the responsibility of the collector of the port. Hawthorne, only too happy to oblige, left the matter there.

In the meantime, Hawthorne explained, a friend of the two inspectors had informed them of their possible dismissal. Although he had taken no part in it, Hawthorne suspected the men had been subsequently pressed into paying an assessment. (In his letter to Mann, Hawthorne made no mention of the Whig charge that the extra assessment had been for the *Salem Advertiser*, to which he was a valued contributor.) "I may be mistaken," Hawthorne wrote, "but [my idea] is founded on some observation of the maneuvers of small politicians, and knowing the rigid discipline of Custom Houses as to party-subscriptions." Upham and his colleagues, Hawthorne was convinced, had bullied one of his subordinates into pointing the finger at him and now had "defined and completed the lie." Hawthorne stated that he had two Custom House witnesses to his side of the story: one of them, Zachariah Burchmore, having just been turned out of office, would willingly testify on his behalf. The other was a poor man, in debt, who was hoping to save enough money to go to California. Hawthorne was reluctant to call on him unless it was absolutely necessary.

He was no longer interested in retaining his post. In a bitter moment, he admitted, "My purpose is simply to make such a defense to the Senate as will insure the rejection of my successor, and thus satisfy the public that I was removed on false or insufficient grounds." But even on this point he relented; finding that his successor, Allen Putnam, was a decent enough man, caught in a political bind, Hawthorne did not follow up on his threat. He did, however, cling to one vengeful thought: if Charles Wentworth Upham gave him the opportunity — and even if he did not — he told Mann, "I shall do my best to kill and scalp him in the public prints; and I think I shall succeed." Thoroughly disgusted with his home town and its treacherous politicians, he gave vent to his anger in his letter: "I mean, as soon as possible — that is to say, as soon as I can find a cheap, pleasant and healthy residence — to remove into the country and bid farewell forever to this abominable city; for, now that my mother is gone, I have no longer anything to keep me here."

―――――――

Out of the emotional upheaval of that dismal summer of political recriminations and private grief, Hawthorne fashioned a powerful story of public shame and private guilt. What he had, at first, regarded as a long short story developed into his first major novel, *The Scarlet Letter*, a book that was to be seen, both by Hawthorne's contemporary admirers and his later critics, as an American classic, one of the first in the national literature.

Hawthorne wrote the book as if under compulsion. A family legend, passed on by Julian Hawthorne, has it that Hawthorne had begun work on the book on the day that he had been dismissed from office. The more circumstantial evidence of Sophia's letters to her mother suggests that by early September he was closeted in his study, writing both in the mornings and the afternoons. His intensity made his wife anxious. "He writes immensely," Sophia told Mrs. Peabody later that month. "I am almost frightened about it. But he is well now and looks shining." By mid January 1850, he had completed all but the three final chapters; by that time, too, he had finished his lengthy introductory essay, "The Custom House." Within another nineteen days — on February 3 — the book was completed. Writing to his friend Bridge on the following day, he commented that the book was "positively a h——l f——d story, into which I found it almost impossible to throw any cheering light." And it is true that the book consisted of a series of starkly presented tableaux, centering on the three scenes at the scaffold of the pillory where Hester Prynne is exposed to public shame, where the guilty minister, Arthur Dimmesdale, keeps his silent vigil as an act of repentance, and where, later, following an ambiguous confession of sin, he dies.

An early hint of Hawthorne's story of private sin and penitential shame occurs in an 1836–1837 journal entry. "Insincerity in a man's own heart makes all his enjoyments, all that concerns him, unreal; so that his whole life must seem like a merely dramatic representation," Hawthorne wrote, in anticipation of Dimmesdale's character. An 1838 notation defines the peculiar bondage that links Dimmesdale with the hunchbacked physician, Roger Chillingworth: "The situation of a man in the midst of a crowd, yet as completely in the power of another, life and all, as if they two were in the deepest solitude." An 1847 entry defines both the character of the cuckolded husband and the dramatic crux of *The Scarlet Letter*: "A story of the effects of revenge in diabolizing him who indulges in it." That Hawthorne's imagination had hovered over the possibilities of the story for a decade suggests the peculiar force the ideas held for him.

A good deal earlier, too, he had hit on a fairly well-defined characterization of his feminine protagonist, Hester Prynne. In his story "Endicott and the Red Cross," published in the 1838 *Token*, he had dealt with the harsh justice of the Puritans and the sins of "a young woman with no mean share of beauty, whose doom it was to wear the letter A on the breast of her gown, in the eyes of all the world

and her own children." Moreover, this earlier, unnamed adulteress
was as deft with the needle as his later heroine, having "embroidered the fatal token in scarlet cloth, with golden thread, and the
nicest art of needle-work; so that the capital A might have been
thought to mean Admirable, or any thing rather than Adulteress."

In his allegorical contrast of the dark prison of the self and the
noonday glare of public shame, Hawthorne echoed a number of the
themes of his earlier stories. *The Scarlet Letter* owes a good deal of its
power precisely to the sense of the gathering-in of the obsessive
themes of a decade. The motif of a poisoned human nature had been
sounded in his allegory "Egotism; or, the Bosom-Serpent," and, certainly, Roger Chillingworth exemplifies the unpardonable sinner,
divorced from the warmth and disorder of human affection, coldly
bent on the destruction of another human soul. The difference is
that Chillingworth, with his overpowering need for revenge, is better motivated than Ethan Brand, who remained a clinical and abstract personification of evil.

The image of the dark wood — both an Eden and a haunt of the
devil — was another of Hawthorne's fictional devices that found use
in *The Scarlet Letter*. The symbol of the forest, probably derived from
Spenser's allegory, was not only the dark wood of error, but also the
scene of diabolical encounters, the realm of untamed and indifferent
nature, the antithesis of civilization — even the meager civilization
of Puritan Boston. Hawthorne used the setting in his early witchcraft tale, "The Hollow of the Three Hills," for instance, and in
"Roger Malvin's Burial." In "Young Goodman Brown," it is the
scene of the witches' Sabbath at which Hawthorne's young protagonist acquires his bleak knowledge of the sinfulness of human nature.
Like Goodman Brown, Hester Prynne becomes a secret sharer of the
hidden guilts and shames of others; instinctively, she knows when
she has passed a fellow sinner, even if it be a blushing maid or
a pious old woman. And like Goodman Brown, the Reverend
Dimmesdale, after his encounter with Hester in the forest, has an "obtrusive sense of change." In their forest meeting, Hester proposes
that they return to the Old World and take up a new life together,
but Dimmesdale recants after his momentary agreement, and views
it as a compact with the devil. On his return to the village, the familiar streets, the gable-peaked houses look the same; yet he experiences an unaccountable sense of change. "The minister's own will,"
the author explains, "and Hester's will, and the fate that grew between them, had wrought this transformation." For Dimmesdale,
the change is fearful: he feels a powerful urge to shout blasphemies
at the pious parishioners; he can barely restrain himself from teach-

ing obscenities to a group of children. He is a man on the edge of a breakdown — or, as Sophia would have described it, a man suffering a "brain fever."

In *The Scarlet Letter*, Hawthorne proposed a more extenuating view of human sinfulness than he had outlined in his earlier parables. With that ambiguity which enabled him to maintain contradictory views in precarious balance, Hawthorne presents Chillingworth as having a keen insight into his own depravity, while, at the same time, being aware of the web of circumstances that has brought him and Hester and Dimmesdale to their complex fate. *The Scarlet Letter* is a novel in which character is action. In one of those characteristic interviews through which the plot unfolds, Chillingworth absolves Hester. "By thy first step awry," he tells her, "thou didst plant the germ of evil; but since that moment, it has all been a dark necessity. Ye that have wronged me are not sinful, save in a kind of typical illusion; neither am I fiend-like, who have snatched a fiend's office from his hands. It is our fate."

The "typical" is not a careless adjective; it is Hawthorne's way of specifying the method of his book. *The Scarlet Letter* is relentlessly allegorical; it is full of "types" and "symbols." Hester is "the type of shame," or "the general symbol at which the preacher and moralist might point." Weeds growing above a grave may "typify" the hideous secret of a buried man. The Reverend Dimmesdale, we are told, stares at his image in the mirror, trying to determine the secret of his own character. "He thus typified," Hawthorne notes, "the constant introspection wherewith he tortured, but could not purify himself." It is one of the flaws of the novel — among its considerable virtues — that the characters remain "types" of the guilty heart, and of fallen human nature, serving out their predetermined roles in the allegory. Little Pearl, with her fierce temper, her uncanny insights, and antic nature, is admittedly a tiresome character, but she often achieves a kind of fitful and perverse life: Hawthorne had drawn her more realistic details from his observations of his daughter, Una.

That he had written the book under a kind of compulsion and in a troubled state of mind probably accounts for the overuse Hawthorne made of his basic symbol, the scarlet letter itself. It has its force as the emblem of Hester's shame. As the hidden brand upon Dimmesdale's breast, it is a sign of his complicity. But, under the pressure of inspiration, Hawthorne overworks the device. It becomes an emblem of green nature, woven out of eel grass, by Pearl; it appears again as an omen in the heavens on the night of Dimmesdale's guilty vigil.

It serves, too, as Hawthorne's private symbol. (In Hawthorne's symbology, the scarlet A may stand for Art as well as Adultery.) Hester's needlework is a "type" of art — an embroidery on the dark knowledge of human nature. In the chapter "Hester at her Needle," Hawthorne clearly intends an analogy between his own art and Hester's craft — a luxury "in a land that afforded comparatively little scope for its exercise." Similarly, Hawthorne also sees Dimmesdale as a "type" of the writer. His sermons are intended to convey "the highest truths through the humblest medium of familiar words and images."

There is, in fact, something awesome about the manner in which Hawthorne fuses art and human sinfulness. In one of the protracted interviews between Dimmesdale and Roger Chillingworth, the minister puts off the prying physician by claiming that no power on earth, short of divine mercy, can disclose, "whether by uttered words, or by type or emblem, the secrets that may be buried with a human heart." Although Dimmesdale acknowledges the relief that comes with confession, he still maintains that the revelations of sinful mankind are meant to be published on doomsday, when everyone will "see the dark problem of this life made plain." But it is equally clear that Hawthorne's view was that it was a writer's function to make plain "the dark problem of this life."

There are moments in Dimmesdale's private drama that approach autobiography for Hawthorne. Like many of his characters, Dimmesdale is constantly drawn to the mirror, seeing there phantom images, visions of dead young friends. But what is one to make of Dimmesdale's fleeting glimpse of his mother "turning her face away as she passed by." More important, what is one to make of the author's reproof: "Ghost of a mother — thinnest fantasy of a mother — methinks she might yet have thrown a pitying glance toward her son!" Coming as it does in a passage of dreamy speculation, it has the anguish of a bitter personal regret.

Hawthorne's account of the minister's solitary nights in his study is strictly a more dramatic reprise of Hawthorne's vigils in the dismal chamber at Herbert Street: "Here he [Dimmesdale] had studied and written; here gone through fast and vigil, and come forth half alive; here, striven to pray; here, borne a hundred thousand agonies!" And when the minister, returning from his forest interview with Hester, reflects on his former self, Hawthorne may well have had his own recent experiences in mind: "But he seemed to stand apart, and eye this former self with scornful, pitying, but half-envious curiosity. That self was gone! Another man had returned out of the forest; a wiser one; with a knowledge of hidden mysteries which the simplicity of the former never could have reached. A bitter kind of knowledge that!"

The knowledge that Hawthorne had most recently acquired was the bitter knowledge learned in the dark wood of American politics. If, at first, he had felt the urge for revenge, the need to pillory his enemies, Hawthorne did not mar his book with it. He satisfied himself with only a surprisingly oblique remark about "that stubborn fidelity with which a man's friends — and especially a clergyman's — will sometimes uphold his character; when proofs, clear as mid-day sunshine on the scarlet letter, establish him a false and sin-stained creature of the dust." So much for the Reverend Charles Wentworth Upham.

What Hawthorne had done was to use the marvelous duplicity of art as a form of catharsis. Like Una and Julian rehearsing his mother's deathbed scene, Hawthorne assumed roles at will. There is, undeniably, an analogy between Hester's ordeal on the scaffold and Hawthorne's recent public humiliation. Hester's seemingly haughty attitude before the unruly crowd is only a mask; she suffers in secret agony, wanting to "shriek out with the full power of her lungs, and cast herself from the scaffold . . ." But she finds her only relief in "a stony crust of insensibility." In Arthur Dimmesdale, Hawthorne is the victimized sinner; in Chillingworth, a wronged man and secret avenger. There is more to Chillingworth's bitterness than the dramatic revenge of literary convention; in Hawthorne's characterization, it is a complex and deeply plumbed emotion. Interestingly enough — in light of his political involvements — Hawthorne's identifications are with the guilty; the only innocence in *The Scarlet Letter* is the cruel innocence of little Pearl.

Hawthorne's political ordeal, the death of his mother — and whatever guilt he may have harbored on either score, whether real or imagined — afforded him an understanding of the secret psychological springs of guilt. *The Scarlet Letter* is the book of a changed man and writer. Its deeper insights have little to do with orthodox morality or religion — or the universal or allegorical applications of a moral. The greatness of the book is related to its sometimes fitful characterizations of human nature and the author's almost uncanny intuitions: his realization of the bond between psychological malaise and physical illness, the nearly perfect, if sinister, outlining of the psychological techniques Chillingworth deployed against his victim.

Hawthorne, consciously or unconsciously, immersed himself in

the roles of both Dimmesdale and Chillingworth. (In the "inextricable knot" of his fiction, it is not altogether clear which is the victim
and which the transgressor.) This evenhandedness is revealed in one
of those lapses that an author writing in a calmer, more considered
frame of mind might have caught. "When poor Mr. Dimmesdale was
thinking of his grave," Hawthorne writes at one point, "he questioned with himself whether the grass would ever grow on it, because an accursed thing must there be buried!" He used the same
image once more — this time referring to Chillingworth: "And
whither was he now going? Would he not suddenly sink into the
earth, leaving a barren and blasted spot . . . ?"

In both cases, the imagery relates to the disturbing dream Hawthorne had had years before, the dream of lying down to sleep and
awaking to find the earth blasted and burned beneath him. "And
what was the fire that blasted the spot of earth which I occupied,
while the grass flourished all around?" he had asked in his letter to
Sophia. However universal Hawthorne had intended his fable of the
guilty heart to be, out of some dark necessity it had sent roots down
into his personal life and private dreams.

The Citizen of Somewhere Else

IT IS EITHER very good or very bad — I don't know which," Haw-thorne told the publisher James T. Fields in a rash moment after having decided to hand Fields the incomplete manuscript of *The Scarlet Letter*. Energetic and immensely sociable, Fields was a young junior partner in the notable Boston publishing firm of Ticknor, Reed & Fields. He was also a sometime poet; Hawthorne had first met him in November 1848, when he had engaged Fields to read one of his poems following Daniel Webster's rousing Salem lecture on the Constitution. Approximately a year later, in the winter following Hawthorne's ouster from the Custom House, Fields paid a business call on the author in his Mall Street house. Fields, convinced that Hawthorne must have been writing during his term as surveyor, was eager to secure a book for his firm. "I remember," he recalled in his memoirs, *Yesterdays with Authors*, "that I pressed him to reveal to me what he had been writing. He shook his head and gave me to un-derstand he had produced nothing. At that moment, I caught sight of a bureau or set of drawers near where we were sitting; and imme-diately it occurred to me that hidden away somewhere in that ar-ticle of furniture was a story or stories by the author of 'Twice-told Tales' and I became so positive of it that I charged him vehemently with the fact. He seemed surprised, I thought, but shook his head again." Still unconvinced, but in a hurry to catch a train for Boston, Fields left. No sooner had he started down the cold stairway from Hawthorne's third-floor study than the author called after him. Standing at the head of the stairs, Hawthorne thrust a roll of manu-script at the publisher. "How in Heaven's name did you know this thing was there?" he asked.

Fields read the manuscript on the train. That evening, he wrote Hawthorne a note "all aglow with admiration." He planned to re-turn the following day to make arrangements for publication. It was

Fields's opinion that the story should be elaborated further and published in book form. But Hawthorne, who had been thinking of a volume of two or three long tales and some incidental sketches to be called "Old-Time Legends," was plainly wary. He was still of the same opinion on January 15, when he sent Fields all but the three final chapters of *The Scarlet Letter* and the introductory sketch dealing with his years of service in the Custom House. Hawthorne was apprehensive, to begin with, about the theme of adultery — "a delicate subject to write upon," he noted, "but in the way in which I have treated it, it appears to me there can be no objections on that score." He also had some minor misgivings about his satirical portraits of his Custom House colleagues in the introductory essay. He hoped Fields would read that first. "In the process of writing," he noted, "all political and official turmoil has subsided within me, so that I have not felt inclined to execute justice on any of my enemies."

Only reluctantly did he yield to Fields's enthusiasm. Five days later, he still questioned the wisdom of printing *The Scarlet Letter* as a volume in itself. "Keeping so close to its point as the tale does, and diversified no otherwise than by turning different sides of the same dark idea to the reader's eye," he argued, "it will weary very many people and disgust some." Hawthorne had, quite plainly, conceived of *The Scarlet Letter* as a long tale, and he may well have subscribed to one of Poe's recent dicta that the tale — as distinct from the diffuse novel form — required unity of effect. In his letter of January 20, however, his anxiety was based more on commercial than aesthetic grounds. He worried about pinning his hopes for success on a single gloomy story. "Is it safe, then," he asked, "to stake the fate of the book on this one chance?" It was largely a rhetorical question, since one of his offhand remarks clearly indicated that he had already agreed to the publisher's proposition. "If 'The Scarlet Letter' is to be the title," he suggested to Fields, "would it not be well to print it on the title page in red ink? I am not quite sure about the good taste of so doing, but it would certainly be piquant and appropriate."

On the same day that he wrote Fields, Hawthorne also received a letter from George Hillard, enclosing a check for $500. The money had been contributed, Hillard said, by unnamed friends who "admire your genius and respect your character." Hillard's letter was both generous and tactful: "I know the sensitive edge of your temperament; but do not speak or think of obligation. It is only paying, in a very imperfect measure, the debt we owe you for what you have done for American Literature." Hillard was obviously one of the contributors to the fund, and Longfellow was more than likely another. The poet was always generous — and discreet — in providing money for less successful literary colleagues.

Hawthorne was deeply moved. "I read your letter in the entry of the Post Office," he wrote the lawyer, "and it drew — what my troubles never have — the water to my eyes." He also expressed some personal bitterness. In his letter, Hawthorne acknowledged the extent to which he subscribed to the American credo that success was the option of every ambitious citizen of a new country. Failure, conversely, was the fault of any individual who did not make the most of his opportunities. "It is something else besides pride," he told Hillard, "that teaches me that ill-success in life is really and justly a matter of shame. I am ashamed of it, and I ought to be. The fault of a failure is attributable — in a great degree, at least — to the man who fails." That was the manner in which he would judge other men; the same standard applied to himself. "Nobody has a right to live in this world," he went on, "unless he be strong and able, and applies his ability to good purpose." The money, he told Hillard, "will smooth my path for a long time to come." His circumstances, however, pointed a moral: "The only way in which a man can retain his self-respect, while availing himself of the generosity of his friends, is, by making it an incitement to his utmost exertions, so that he may not need their help again."

Hillard's gesture may well have provided the impetus for Hawthorne's decision to publish *The Scarlet Letter* as a separate volume; it seems to have spurred him on toward completing what he called — in a letter to his friend Bridge — his fourteen-mile-long story, "one end being in press in Boston, while the other was in my head here in Salem." His letter to Bridge was written on February 4, the day after he had finished writing the last chapters. He had read the concluding chapters to Sophia. "It broke her heart," he informed Bridge, "and sent her to bed with a grievous headache, which I look upon as a triumphant success." For Bridge's benefit, he was willing to concede: "Some portions of the book are powerfully written." Only years later, and then in the privacy of his notebook, did he admit that he had been moved, as well. During the reading, he acknowledged, his voice had "swelled and heaved, as if I were tossed up and down on an ocean as it subsides after a storm." But he ascribed that loss of control to the fact that he had been under a strain, having gone through "a great diversity and severity of emotion" for several months during the writing of the book. In retrospect, he boasted, "I think I have never overcome my own adamant in any other instance."

With the book finished, he felt a compelling urge to move — as he informed Bridge. The strain of the past months was beginning to affect him; what he needed was work in a garden or daily walks in the country air or along the seashore. "Here I hardly go out once a week," he admitted, then added, "Do not allude to this matter in your letters to me; as my wife already sermonizes me quite sufficiently on my habits — and I never own up to not feeling perfectly well. Neither do I feel anywise ill, but only a lack of physical vigor and energy which reacts upon the mind. I detest this town so much that I hate to go into the streets or to have the people see me. Anywhere else, I shall at once be entirely another man."

In joining his fortunes with the recently established house of Ticknor, Reed & Fields, Hawthorne had made an alliance with one of the more successful publishers in America. William D. Ticknor, the senior partner, was the son of a prosperous New Hampshire farmer and a cousin of George Ticknor, Harvard professor and historian of Spanish literature. At the age of seventeen, in 1827, Ticknor had moved to Boston, working first in an investment house, then in a bank. In 1832, he ventured into the growing American publishing industry, establishing a short-lived partnership with John Allen and acquiring the stock and assets of the Old Corner Bookstore at 135 Washington Street. Reserved, shy, circumspect, Ticknor developed a reputation for fair-mindedness. Despite the rampant piracy among American and English publishers, Ticknor, in 1842, made a practice of paying royalties to English authors whose works he published. It was a policy that brought to his firm the most eminent and popular English writers of his day: Tennyson, De Quincey, Leigh Hunt, Trollope, Thackeray, and Charles Reade. (Robert Browning was an unprofitable exception; his verse, though published under the Ticknor imprint, was far too obscure for American tastes to be either popular or profitable.) With the advent of James Fields — another enterprising New Hampshire boy, who had begun his career at the age of thirteen — the firm became associated with the rising Boston and Concord writers, publishing the works of Longfellow, Hawthorne, Emerson, Thoreau, Lowell, Whittier, and Holmes. Ticknor held the purse strings; Fields applied the charm. It was Fields — though many years later — who eventually captured the plum of the nineteenth-century publishing industry, the prolific Charles Dickens, whose works had been pirated for decades.

Ebullient, enthusiastic, and a bon vivant, Fields was thirty-one when Hawthorne met him in 1848. The friendship that developed between the two men was to be lifelong. In time, Hawthorne, who admired — and probably envied — Fields's easy sociability and energy, began to rely heavily on the younger man's shrewd judgment in literary and publishing matters. When Hawthorne visited the company's offices at the corner of Washington and School streets, he enjoyed the convivial atmosphere of Fields's green-curtained inner sanctum, with its view of Summer Street glimpsed through the spacious window above a window seat usually piled high with books and manuscripts. There was always the banter of lively conversation and frequent interruptions by visitors. But he also developed an appreciation for the plodding and dutiful Ticknor, who served as a reliable banker and financial manager for Hawthorne. When in need of cash, Hawthorne simply wrote Ticknor for the necessary sums; it gave him, he said, the feeling of being one of "the monied men of Massachusetts." Ticknor's office, at the head of the accounting department in the corner opposite Fields's glamorous retreat, was situated on a platform that allowed him to survey his staff from his desk. The third partner of the firm, John Reed, Jr., remained "a blank," as far as Hawthorne was concerned. "I do not even know him by sight, among your gray-headed or beardless clerks and shopboys," Hawthorne once confessed to Fields.

Both Ticknor and Fields pampered their authors, something Hawthorne appreciated after his sour earlier experiences with most American publishers. Over the years, he grew accustomed to the cigars, the excellent clarets, the special editions of De Quincey and Walter Scott, that Ticknor and Fields thoughtfully sent him. But he never acquired the patrician manner of his friend Longfellow, who struck a hard financial bargain with the publishers when he signed with the firm in 1846. As a natural extension of his contractual rights, Longfellow used the firm as a kind of employment agency, expecting Fields to screen the applicants for domestic service at Craigie House. *"No Irishman need apply,"* he told Fields with the prejudice of a true Yankee. He also expected his publishers to rustle up hard-to-get tickets for Jenny Lind's concert when the Swedish Nightingale made her Boston appearance in 1850. When Longfellow's London publisher sent — by steamer — the proof impressions of a recent portrait intended to illustrate the English edition of his works, the poet did not think it amiss to suggest: "If they are at the Custom House perhaps Mr. Ticknor would like to pass another cheerful and enlivening morning in that handsome edifice!"

As a newly named partner of the firm in 1849, Fields had promised Hawthorne that Ticknor, Reed & Fields would print 2500 copies of any work Hawthorne cared to give them. He was as good as his word. The first edition of *The Scarlet Letter*, published in March 1859, was 2500 copies. A second edition of 2500 copies was issued in April, and an additional 1000 copies in September. The success of the book was due, in part, to the publicity Hawthorne had received as a result of his political ouster. It was also, undoubtedly, the result of Fields's strenuous efforts on behalf of his new author, for Fields was one of the first American publishers to employ modern promotional methods. Even before Hawthorne had decided whether the book was to be a novel or a collection of short stories, Fields had begun announcing the book in the press. He also sent advance sheets to Hawthorne's admirer Evert A. Duyckinck, suggesting that the editor publish extracts from the introductory essay in the *Literary World*, the influential weekly that Duyckinck and his brother George had recently acquired. Fields was sure that Hawthorne's description of the old, gourmandising inspector who could remember a half century of meals, would "raise a roar of laughter thro' N. England." He was equally enthusiastic about *The Scarlet Letter*, giving his opinion that "nothing finer has appeared in this country." He prodded the New York editor, "Do let us try and put that glorious genius where he properly belongs." Fields was indefatigable in cajoling favorable notices of his books from influential critics and editors. He wrote gossipy articles about the Boston literati for publication in New York papers. With a slight amount of exaggeration, he could promise Longfellow, "No family of any respectability shall sleep unapprized of the publication of K[avanagh] on Saturday night. By this hour today New York is glittering with our new show cards."

With the reluctant Hawthorne, Fields mounted a sustained campaign of encouraging the author to write more. "We intend to publish your books à-la-Steam Engine," he told Hawthorne in a cheery letter. As part of his program, Fields suggested a new edition of *Twice-told Tales*; he also plumped for a further volume of Hawthorne's still-uncollected stories. He was receptive to Hawthorne's suggestion for bringing out a collection of children's stories — though postponing it for a season. Fields even made an effort to obtain the copyright from Putnam's for *Mosses from an Old Manse*, but had to wait three years — until 1854 — before he could get it for his company.

Hawthorne was clearly responsive to Field's encouragement. He embarked on a period of literary activity that was unmatched in his later life. In two years' time, he was to add two more major novels — *The House of the Seven Gables* and *The Blithedale Romance* — to the Ticknor, Reed & Fields list. During the same period, the company issued a new edition of *Twice-told Tales*, with Hawthorne's important 1851 preface; a new volume of his previously uncollected stories, *The Snow-Image*; a reprinting of his earlier volumes of children's stories, *True Stories from History and Biography*; and a new children's collection, *A Wonder-Book for Girls and Boys*.

It was from a growing sense of confidence that Hawthorne could write Horatio Bridge about the "only sensible ends" of a literary career: "First, the pleasurable toil of writing; second, the gratification of one's family and friends; and, lastly, the solid cash." He had begun to measure the rewards of success.

The critical response to *The Scarlet Letter* was one of those rewards; the majority of the reviews were full of praise and respect — even when the critics were timorous about the subject of adultery. Duyckinck, in a review in the *Literary World*, spoke of the book in the highest terms. "Nothing is slurred over, superfluous or defective . . ." he stated. "Mr. Hawthorne has, in fine, shown extraordinary power in this volume, great feeling and discrimination, a subtle knowledge of character in its secret springs." Hawthorne, he was convinced, was the only author who could have treated such a theme "without an infusion of George Sand." Another obliging friend of Fields's, the critic E. P. Whipple, writing in *Graham's Magazine*, warned that readers who were familiar with the delicacy of Hawthorne's writings would "hardly be prepared for a novel of so much tragic interest and tragic power, so deep in thought and so condensed in style." Whipple, who was to become Hawthorne's favorite critic, asserted that the book "bears on every page the evidence of a mind thoroughly alive, watching patiently the movements of morbid hearts when stirred by strange experiences." Hawthorne had pierced through "all the externals to the core of things."

George Ripley, the new "literary assistant" for Horace Greeley's *Tribune*, following the failure of Brook Farm, proclaimed *The Scarlet Letter* as "the greatest production of the author . . . sustained with a more vigorous reach of imagination, a more subtle instinct of humanity, and a more imposing splendor of portraiture, than any of his most successful previous works." Comparing Hawthorne with Poe, Ripley found that Hawthorne's tragedies were "always *motived* with a wonderful insight and skill, to which the intellect of Poe was a stranger." (Poe was past responding to such slights; his tarnished, devious, and brilliant literary career had ended the year before, when, after a five-day disappearance, he was located in a Baltimore tavern in a drunken stupor. He died in a hospital four days later.)

It was no small measure of Hawthorne's success that he had written about a scandalous subject in a style that was above reproach, yet there were critics who reproached the author. Anne W. Abbott, in the stodgy *North American Review*, wondered how the "master of such a wizard power over language" could have chosen a subject as revolting as the Scarlet Letter, "to which fine writing seems as inappropriate as fine embroidery." Unconsciously, she had grasped Hawthorne's analogy between sin and art — and had promptly dismissed it. Orestes Brownson, in a lengthy discussion in *Brownson's Quarterly Review*, acknowledged Hawthorne's genius but scolded the author for being "wholly ignorant of Christian asceticism." The critic declared, "There is an unsound state of public morals when the novelist is permitted, without a scorching rebuke, to select such crimes and invest them with all the fascination of genius and all the charms of a highly polished style." In his moralizing, Brownson even managed to outdo the Episcopal bishop, Arthur Cleveland Coxe, who warned Hawthorne about the fatal direction of his literary talents. Why, Coxe asked in a notice in the *Church Review*, had Hawthorne chosen for the subject of his romance "the nauseous amour of a Puritan pastor, with a frail creature of his charge, whose mind is represented as far more debauched than her body?" The bishop complained of the "running undertide of filth" that had become a necessity in popular romances. "Is the French era actually begun in our literature?" he asked.

If, at long last, *The Scarlet Letter* had made Hawthorne a famous author, his Custom House preface had made him infamous in Salem. His acid sketches of the sleepy and parochial politicians of his home town, and his urbane and condescending treatment of his own removal from office, had raised the hackles of local Whigs. The *Salem Register*, on March 21, was suitably indignant at Hawthorne's venting his spite "by small sneers at Salem, and by vilifying some of his former associates, to a degree of which we should have supposed any gentleman . . . incapable." The editors no longer had any lingering doubts about the justification of Hawthorne's removal from office.

Hawthorne wrote Bridge about the brouhaha with dovelike innocence. "As to the Salem people," he told Bridge, "I really thought that I had been exceedingly good-natured in my treatment of them. They certainly do not deserve good usage at my hands after permitting me to be deliberately lied down — not merely once, but at two several attacks — on two false indictments — with hardly a voice being raised on my behalf; and then sending one of the false witnesses to Congress, others to the Legislature, and choosing another as the mayor." His essay, he told Bridge, had caused "the greatest uproar that had happened here since witch times." It was quite probable that he had expressed more of his "infinite contempt" for the people of Salem than he had intended. "If I escape town without being tarred and feathered," he said, "I shall consider it good luck."

Late in March, before the second edition of the book went to press, Hawthorne had reviewed his essay but felt no urge to retract any of his statements. Adding insult to injury, in fact, he wrote a brief preface to the new edition, disclaiming any "enmity, or ill-feeling of any kind, personal or political." He acknowledged that the Custom House essay might have been omitted altogether: "But having undertaken to write it, the [author] conceives that it could not have been done in a better or a kindlier spirit, nor, so far as his abilities availed, with a livelier effect of truth." He was, therefore, republishing it, "without the change of a word."

In effect, he was burning his bridges behind him. "Soon . . ." Hawthorne had written in his original essay, "my old native town will loom upon me through the haze of memory, a mist brooding over and around it; as if it were no portion of the real earth, but an overgrown village in cloud-land, with only imaginary inhabitants to people its wooden houses, and walk its homely lanes." He went on to make a public declaration of independence from his birthplace. "Henceforth," he asserted, "it ceases to be a reality of my life. I am a citizen of somewhere else."

↶ II ↷

Ever since his ouster, Hawthorne had been eager to quit Salem. Through the dreary months following his political defeat, he and Sophia had considered one house or another in one city or another, hoping to find a new home. Much to Sophia's regret, they had missed out on a farm in Manchester. In mid August, Sophia had continued to search, accompanied by old William Manning. Then she and Hawthorne had gone to look at a house in Kittery, Maine, that had been suggested by Horatio Bridge. In September, Sophia visited her friend Caroline Sturgis — Mrs. William Aspinwall Tappan — who was living in Lenox in the Berkshires. The Tappans had leased an estate, Highwood, from Samuel G. Ward, the Boston broker and friend of Emerson. Although at first she thought Lenox too far away from family and friends, she liked the area. In late October, Hawthorne, too, made a trip to Lenox. For a day and a half, accompanied by Ward and Tappan, he investigated the possibilities.

On the Highwood estate there was a small red farmhouse — "as red as the Scarlet Letter," Hawthorne informed his former Custom House colleague Zachariah Burchmore. Located quite near the Tappan house, it was only a story and a half tall, a rabbit warren of small cosy rooms, but it commanded a fine view of the Stockbridge Bowl. In February, by way of her mother, Sophia began making discreet inquiries as to whether the Tappans would agree to rent the house to them. The Tappans, both eager to have Sophia and her husband near them in the Berkshires, offered the farmhouse rent-free. Hawthorne, however, insisted on paying at least a modest rental. The fee that was settled on was a meager $75 for four years. Sophia thought it a great bargain.

But before their move to the Berkshires, Sophia and the children went to Boston to stay with her parents at West Street, and Hawthorne, late in April, journeyed to Portsmouth to visit Bridge and his wife. Writing to Sophia on April 26, Hawthorne complained that the weather had been so foul and rainy en route that he had had to put up at the Rockingham House before proceeding to the naval yard. There, he had been recognized and "immediately lugged into society," much to his dismay. It was with some relief that he reached Bridge's home, "the quietest place imaginable."

Back in Boston by May 1, he was installed in a boardinghouse, probably on West Street, the Peabody home, as usual, being crowded with family and boarders. In his journal during this interim Hawthorne kept meticulously detailed notes of his city experiences. From the back windows of his room, he studied the daily activities of the "better order" of homes: chambermaids hanging out bedclothes from the upper windows; a woman ironing in the basement; and, in between, the genteel life of well-appointed drawing rooms glimpsed through plate-glass windows. If he were a "solitary prisoner," Hawthorne thought, he would find occupation enough in studying just one of the houses for a whole day.

In the evenings, he sometimes frequented Parker's saloon and restaurant on Court Street, noting the clientele — the veteran drinkers and petty court officials, flashy young men from the country, ordering Tom and Jerries, gin cocktails, brandy smashes. One night he attended a dreary performance of *Jack the Giant Killer* in pantomime at the National Theater in a run-down section of Boston. He was more interested in the audience, which he described, with aristocratic fastidiousness, as belonging to the "middling and lower classes" — Hanover Street shopkeepers, mechanics, drunken sailors who stumbled in and out of the boxes, shouting to the performers. He especially observed a young woman taking out her breast to feed an infant, "with so little care of concealment that I saw, and anybody might have seen, the whole breast, and the apex which the infant's little lips compressed. Yet there was nothing indecent in this; but a perfect naturalness." He had enjoyed his evening of "life in the rough."

During his Boston stay, he also sat for a new portrait — this one by Cephas Giovanni Thompson. The sittings took several days, and Hawthorne grew to like the mild-mannered, gently spoken artist with the slight stoop and keen eyes. There were moments when

Thompson became so involved with his work, daubing at the canvas with nervous gestures, that Hawthorne sensed in the painter's excitement the same intensity that he felt when his writing was going well. "I like this painter," Hawthorne noted in his journal; "he seems to reverence his art, and to aim at truth in it." He was less satisfied with the portrait, which, in an early sitting, "looked dimly out from the canvas as from a cloud, with something that I could recognize as my outline; but no strong resemblance as yet." The finished work was stiff and formal, though the artist managed to capture the liveliness of Hawthorne's glance and a certain sensuousness about the lips. Hawthorne complained that there was no such thing as a true portrait: "They are all delusions; and I never saw any two alike, nor hardly, any two that I could recognize, merely by the portraits themselves, as being of the same man. A bust has more reality."

It was in Boston — since he refused to return to Salem — that he arranged for a farewell dinner with his Custom House colleagues, Burchmore and William Pike, at Parker's. It may have been on that occasion, or later, that he had a surprise reunion with his erstwhile friend, relative, and recent political enemy, Horace Conolly. The two men had met, dined, and drunk together as if nothing had occurred between them. It was probably as a result of the meeting that Hawthorne, writing to Burchmore on June 9, gave his friend an odd commission. He wanted Burchmore to ask Conolly if he had been involved in a plot to oust him from the surveyorship soon after he had been appointed to the post. "As it is now merely a matter of curiosity," Hawthorne wrote, "he will, perhaps, have no objection to telling the truth about it. The assigned reason was either that I declined to assist in getting him an office, or that I opposed his being put on appraising jobs."

A week later, Hawthorne was even more surprised to hear from the "ex-Cardinal" himself. Conolly, a complete and casual opportunist, was now hoping to get himself appointed as surveyor at the Salem Custom House, and wrote Hawthorne to enlist his help. Hawthorne answered his letter with stunned amusement. "If you had any chance of getting the Surveyorship for yourself," he told Conolly, "I might take some little trouble to promote it, to reward you for getting me out, and to punish you and your misdeeds generally." In his new-found equanimity, Hawthorne viewed Conolly's double-dealing as a good deed: "If I had stayed four hours longer in the Custom House, I should have rusted utterly away, and never have been heard of more."

Still, the reunion with Conolly was a subject of some amazement to Hawthorne. "Who would have thought of our ever corresponding again," he commented, "and what a meeting that was in Boston! It is almost too incredible to be put into a romance . . . I am a true Christian and the only one I ever met with. You have been slandering and backbiting and stabbing me in the dark for years past, both before and after our breach. You dug me out of office, and did your best to starve me and at the close of all, I find myself eating bread and salt and getting corned with you, and just as kindly as if nothing had happened." If his political downfall had been a bitter experience, he was now able to see it in perspective; Conolly had blessed where he intended to curse. "I don't reckon you among my enemies, nor ever have," Hawthorne assured Conolly with a well-honed malice. "You are a kind of pet serpent, and must be allowed to bite now and then, that being the nature of the critter."

By June 9, when he wrote to Burchmore, Hawthorne was already settled into the little red farmhouse. The move to the Berkshires had not been accomplished without difficulty, however. For the first week or two, Hawthorne, Sophia, and the children had stayed with the Tappans at Highwood while the farmhouse was made livable with new paint and paper on the walls. The Tappans had pressed them to live with them, but neither Hawthorne nor Sophia could be persuaded to remain. No sooner had they settled into the farmhouse than Hawthorne came down with a serious cold and was forced to remain in bed in their tiny upstairs bedroom. Sophia was sure that her husband's illness was the result of his having been "so harassed in spirit." The cold, together with "brain-work and disquiet," had brought about a "tolerable nervous fever," she explained to her mother — an illness similar, it seems, to the one Hawthorne had suffered while his mother was dying. The ailment was serious enough that he was treated with belladonna, which, Sophia claimed, "conquered the enemy." "Mr. Hawthorne," she reported in a later note, "thinks it is *Salem* which he is dragging at his ankles still."

In his letter to Burchmore, Hawthorne had recovered sufficiently to claim that he had "planted vegetables enough to supply all Salem," if he could only bring them to market. He was pleased with his new situation and was already tanned from the summer sun. The children, out of doors all day, were now "brown as berries." His quarters were small and snug, but large enough "for all our occasions." He had not yet been to the village, even though it was only a mile and a half distant. "Neither have I seen a single newspaper (except an anti-slavery paper) since the day I left Boston; and I know no more of what is going on in the world than if I had migrated to the moon."

With her usual energy and cheerfulness, Sophia set about making a nest for her family in what she termed "the smallest of ten-feet houses." She described the rooms in detail for her mother: the wide hall with its fireplace that she had converted into an entrance parlor where she gave the children their Bible lessons in the morning; the parlor on the right with its center table on which there was a nice arrangement of books and the Indian punch bowl and pitcher that had belonged to Hawthorne's father. In one corner she had put the cast of Apollo that Caroline Tappan had given them as a wedding gift, but the intervening years and their several moves had had an effect. The sculpture had suffered a broken neck, and Sophia had tied the head back on with a ribbon. There was a ground-floor "boudoir," where Sophia had placed a couch, covered in "red-patch," to take advantage of the fine view of the deep meadows and the lake. The walls were hung with reproductions of Claude Lorrain and Salvatore Rosa, and on a corner bracket she had put their small bust of Hadrian's lover, Antinoüs, a favorite nineteenth-century subject, considered an emblem of ideal friendship. The upstairs bedroom was admittedly small, but, in Sophia's lyrical fashion, it was a "golden chamber."

Upstairs, too, was Hawthorne's small study, "which can boast of nothing but his presence in the morning and the picture out of the window in the evening." She had put down the old red carpet from his Concord study, and his secretary, which had been "much abused" in the move but was still serviceable. She had had their old ottoman reupholstered in red. Hawthorne, it seems, had developed a taste for the color red in his working arrangements. As Sophia explained in a later letter to her mother, "Mr. Hawthorne said this morning that he would like a study with a soft, thick Turkey carpet upon the floor, and hung round with full crimson curtains so as to hide all rectangles. I hope to see the day when he shall have such a study. But it will not be while it would demand the slightest extravagance, because he is as severe as a stoic about all personal comforts and never in his life allowed himself a luxury."

Whatever his Puritanical inclinations, Hawthorne was not an absolute stranger to luxuries. One of his admirers, Lewis W. Mansfield, a well-to-do writer from Cohoes, in upstate New York, had struck up an epistolary friendship with the author. Early in 1850, Mansfield had sent Hawthorne the manuscript of his allegorical poem, "The Morning Watch," for critical comment, and had paid Hawthorne a fee for his services. Later, having learned of Hawthorne's financial straits, he offered a loan of $1000—an offer Hawthorne had declined, though with gratitude. Now that Hawthorne was established in Lenox, Mansfield sent a gift of a case of champagne. Hawthorne, who was never abstemious of drink, responded warmly. "I have not yet tasted the wine," he wrote Mansfield, "but reserve it for some especially bright and festive occasion. If a man of genius, as has now and then happened, should sit at our humble board, I shall let loose a cork and talk over your book and tell that the poet's wine is sparkling in the goblet." The festive occasion would soon present itself.

Lenox in summer; a dry, stultifying heat. Sophia attempted a flower garden, planting columbines and peonies and tiger lilies that did poorly in the droughtlike conditions. Hawthorne tended his vegetable garden. His journal entries during that first July in the Berkshires were terse; he noted the end of the raspberry season, the fact that the currants were just beginning to ripen; that the chestnuts were coming into late bloom. In the heat of his study, with the windows wide open, he recorded the visits of wasps and bees buzzing about the small room in angry circles — a droning life. With odd precision, he observed the antics of a broody hen looking for a spot to deposit her egg — "her self-important gait; the side-way turn of her head, and cock of her eye, as she pries into one and another nook, croaking all the while — evidently with the idea that the egg in question is the most important thing that has been brought to pass since the world began." His colony of hens — named Snowdrop, Queenie, Fawn, Crown Imperial — exerted a peculiar fascination for the author; he turned philosophical, a rare occurrence among the laconic journal entries of the period. "Language," he wrote, "— human language — after all, is but little better than the croak and cackle of fowls . . . sometimes not so adequate." In the drowsy summer heat of Lenox, he experienced a certain distancing from the human race.

Often during the hot afternoons the family set out for the woods, discovering, as Sophia fancifully described them, "Indian council-chambers, boudoirs and cabinets" in the forest groves. For Sophia, there would always be successions of golden days and rose-colored twilights; distant mountains were inevitably of "the palest azure." There were always happy hours — "oh such happy hours!" — and the air was sure to be fragrant with "the dying breath of clover and sweet-scented grass." Her children were special; for her mother's benefit, she recorded the mysterious conversations of Una and Julian, a pair of minor transcendentalists. "The other afternoon at the lake," she wrote, "when Papa was lying his length along beneath the trees, Una and Julian were playing about, and presently Una said, 'Take care, Julian, do not run upon Papa's head. *His is a real head, for it is full of thought.'* 'Yes,' responded little Prince Rose-red with most unconscious wisdom, 'It is thought that makes his head.' "

Thanks to Hawthorne's reputation, it was not long before he became acquainted with the lively little society of intellectuals, reformers, and writers in the Berkshires. The cultural atmosphere of the rural retreat was not as strenuously idealistic as Concord nor as abrasive as Boston with its host of abolitionists, but it was agreeably relaxed. In Lenox, the novelist and sixty-one-year-old spinster, Catharine Maria Sedgwick, presided over the populous and helpful Sedgwick clan. A moderate feminist, author of books on domestic management and historical romances with bold American heroines, she had acquired an international reputation, and her home was a Mecca for visiting foreigners. The Sedgwicks were particularly attentive to the Hawthornes, and not long after their arrival in Lenox, Sophia reported how the entire family delighted in making others happy and were "as happy as summer days themselves." Hawthorne, rather feebly, described Catharine Sedgwick as "our most truthful novelist, who has made the scenery and life of Berkshire all her own." In Stockbridge, there was David Dudley Field, an eminent jurist and legal writer, a man of confirmed literary tastes, and an ingratiating host, whose house on Main Street, according to Sophia, had "india-rubber rooms that always stretch to accommodate any number of guests." Although not so numerous as the Sedgwick clan, the Field family achieved greater national celebrity. An older brother, Cyrus Field, became famous some years later as the promoter of the transatlantic cable; and Stephen Field, after a brief career as a lawyer in the newly opened territory of California, was appointed to the United States Supreme Court. A fourth, younger brother, the minister Henry Field, achieved more than local notoriety when, in May 1851, he married Henriette Deluzy-Desportes. Mlle. Desportes had been the governess of the children of the Duc de Choiseul-Praslin in 1847, when the duchess was found dead in her rooms under questionable circumstances. The duke died of arsenic poisoning a short while later. That aristocratic scandal had shaken the already precarious regime of Louis Philippe, and the young governess was felt to be deeply implicated in the tragedy. She subsequently moved to New York, changing her name. There, she married Henry Field. In that same year, Field took the pastorate of the Congregational Church in West Springfield. As the wife of an American clergyman, Mrs. Field lived in understandable seclusion, but Hawthorne might possibly have met her during one of her visits to her Stockbridge in-laws. He certainly must have heard of the international scandal that clung to her name, for he seems — unconsciously, perhaps — to have made use of it in creating the figure of Miriam in *The Marble Faun*.

Among the other literary lights of the region were the young satiric poet Dr. Oliver Wendell Holmes, who had a summer residence on the Pittsfield estate left to him by his grandfather, and the popular historian and journalist Joel Tyler Headley, whose *Napoleon and his Marshals* ran to fifty editions during the author's lifetime. (Poe, however, had unkindly dubbed Headley "The Autocrat of all the Quacks.") The prolific English novelist and lecturer George Payne Rainsford James also settled in the Berkshires in 1851. Hawthorne admired, and perhaps envied, James's undeniable literary success, and claimed a certain appreciation for James's historical novels. Sophia, who referred to the writer as "George Prince Regent James," at first claimed that she would hate to be "condemned to read any of James' novels," since she found the author so "unfathomably tedious and monotonous." But she gradually warmed to the hospitable Englishman, who moved into the region with a wife and children and a full-time secretary who assisted him in his literary labors. James, who displayed a vast admiration for Hawthorne, may have been a bit too fervent for Hawthorne's taste, for he was apt to make inopportune visits to the little red farmhouse.

Nearby, too, was the tempestuous English actress Fanny Kemble, a friend of the Sedgwicks, who had bought a house in the Berkshires following her much-publicized divorce from the Georgian planter Pierce Butler. Julian recalled an instance of the actress's dashing style one summer day when he was four. Stopping on horseback at the cottage gate, she swooped up the boy in her arms and galloped wildly off over the Stockbridge hills. Returning, she reined in her black steed and thrust the child out to his father, exclaiming, "Take your boy — Julian the Apostate!" Julian remembered the exhilarating adventure for the rest of his life.

However small their quarters, Hawthorne and Sophia entertained a number of guests and visitors at the little farmhouse. Horatio Bridge spent a few days in mid July, and later in the month there was a surprise visit from John O'Sullivan. The last reports they had had of O'Sullivan were that he was ill of yellow fever in New Orleans and that he had been arrested for his political activities. True to his dictum of Manifest Destiny, O'Sullivan was pushing for the annexation of Cuba and had backed the Cuban insurrectionist, García Lopez. He was to be twice indicted and twice acquitted for violation of the Neutrality Act. At the moment, he was out on bail, awaiting the first trial. A month later he made another visit, boarding in Pittsfield with his new wife, his mother-in-law, and his sister. Sophia was impressed with Mrs. O'Sullivan, a "very prepossessing and lady-like" blue-eyed brunette. Susan O'Sullivan had brought Sophia four jars of peaches she had preserved herself — proof that she was not a "fine lady" incapable of domestic chores. In August, Mother Peabody descended on the Red Shanty for a brief stay. During the early months in Lenox, there were also visits from the critic Edwin Whipple and his wife; and from the Lowells, who were traveling with the Swedish writer and feminist, Fredrika Bremer, on their way to visit Niagara Falls. The novelist had spent what was probably an uncomfortable evening with the Hawthornes. Although she spoke English, Hawthorne found it difficult to understand her accent and so was uncertain in his responses. Remembering the unsatisfactory meeting, Hawthorne confessed, "There must first be a close and unembarrassed contiguity with my companion, or I cannot say one real word. I doubt whether I have ever really talked with half a dozen persons in my life, either men or women."

Despite the parade of visitors — and his usual summer delinquency where writing was concerned — Hawthorne managed to begin work on a new novel. By late August, James T. Fields was pumping him for information about the book. Hawthorne answered, on August 23, "All I can say is that I religiously seclude myself, every morning (much against my will), and remain in retirement till dinner-time, or thereabouts. But the summer is not my natural season for work; and I often find myself gazing at Monument Mountain, broad before my eyes, instead of at the infernal sheet of paper under my hand. However, I make some little progress; and shall continue to lumber along with accelerated velocity; so that I should not much wonder if I were to be ready by November. If not, it can't be helped. I must not pull up my cabbage by the roots, by way of hastening its growth." Hawthorne was premature; he did not finish writing his book until late in January of the following year. Throughout the fall, however, he kept the increasingly eager Fields informed about his erratic progress on the new romance. "The scene of it," he wrote Fields in a later letter, "is in one of those old projecting-storied houses, familiar to my eye in Salem, and the story, horrible to say, is a little less than two hundred years long, though all but thirty or forty pages of it refer to the present time. I think of such titles as 'The House of the Seven Gables' there being that number of gable-ends to the old shanty."

He had quit Salem in bitterness, but his native town had lingered in his mind — a village in cloudland, with "only imaginary inhabitants to people its wooden houses, and walk its homely lanes," as he had written in his Custom House essay. It was in that Salem of his mind, in fact, and in an ancient wooden dwelling patterned after Suzy Ingersoll's weathered and many-gabled house, that Hawthorne situated his imaginary and pathetic couple, Clifford and Hepzibah Pyncheon, shabby-genteel members of a once-proud, now poor Salem family.

In July, during their first summer in Lenox, they were stunned by the news of Margaret Fuller's death. Although there had been a random exchange of letters, they had not seen Margaret since their Concord days. In 1844, Margaret Fuller had settled in New York, working for Greeley's *Tribune*. Two years later, she made a trip abroad, accompanying her friends Marcus and Rebecca Spring and their young son Edward.

In London, she had been introduced to Carlyle and his wife, Jane, and struck up a lively friendship with the exiled Italian patriot, Giuseppe Mazzini, who was running a school there for poor Italian boys. In Paris, she had a long interview with one of her intellectual heroines, George Sand, and her lover Chopin. She had also been introduced to the exiled Polish poet, Adam Mickiewicz, with whom she had formed an intense and immediate friendship. Mickiewicz, with startling bluntness, had told her that the first step of her "deliverance" would be her decision to shed her virginity. Away from America, she had already begun to feel herself on easier, less inhibited terms, with the men she met. "As soon as I reached England," she wrote to her then-unmarried friend Caroline Sturgis, "I found how right we were in supposing there was elsewhere a greater range of interesting character among the men, than with us." Her European experiences had begun to seem like the fulfillment of her restless life. "I find myself in my element in European society," she wrote Emerson. "It does not, indeed, come up to my ideal, but so many of the encumbrances are cleared away that used to weary me in America, that I can enjoy a freer play of faculty and feel, if not like a bird in the air, at least as easy as a fish in water."

Her European experiences had also heightened her awareness of social injustice. Unlike conventional tourists, she was not content to tour only palaces and art museums; she visited prisons, schools for poor workers, mental asylums, bathing and health facilities. As a foreign correspondent, now, for Greeley's newspaper, she had harsh words for her countrymen: "The more I see of the terrible ills which infest the body politic of Europe, the more indignation I feel at the selfishness or stupidity of those in my own country who oppose an examination of these subjects." So, from Manchester, she wrote about the women who worked in the textile mills by day and sat in the "gin-palaces" at night, vacant and staring, "too dull to carouse." In Paris, beneath the surface glitter of Louis Philippe's prosperous bourgeois kingdom, she sensed the repressive censorship that forbade any discussion of the dire poverty that existed in the slums and provinces. She accurately predicted a revolution. "Radical measures of reform" were needed, she informed the readers of the *Tribune* ". . . the time will come before long, when such will be imperatively demanded." In her growing radicalism, she had even begun to outdistance her hero Mazzini, whose approach began to seem limited. "He aims at political emancipation," she wrote in one of her regular columns, "but he sees not, perhaps would deny, the bearing of some events which even now begin to work their way . . . I allude to that of which the cry of Communism, the systems of Fourier, etc. are but forerunners."

Italy had been the true destination of her European trip, and she settled there in 1847, parting company with the Springs. In Florence and Rome, she became acquainted with the circle of English and American intellectuals and artists — the Brownings, and the American sculptors Thomas Crawford and William Wetmore Story, whose studios in Rome she visited. The winter in Rome had been dismal and rainy, but in the spring political events roused her spirits. Revolution was everywhere; there were bloody riots in Berlin and Poland. In Paris, Louis Philippe had been forced to resign; in Vienna, Metternich was dismissed. "It is a time such as I always dreamed of, and for long secretly hoped to see," she wrote her friend William Henry Channing. "I rejoice to be in Europe at this time, and shall return possessed of a great history. Perhaps I shall be called to act." She had begun to think of writing a history of the stirring times she was living through. At the same time, she hinted to Channing that her personal life was troubled: "My private fortunes are dark and tangled; my strength to govern them . . . much diminished."

She had already moved toward the "deliverance" that Mickiewicz had suggested, having struck up a liaison with a young Italian, the Marchese Angelo Ossoli, a member of the conservative Roman nobility, whose family had connections with the papal court. Her American friends — when they later learned the extent of her relationship — could only wonder at her choice. Ossoli, attractive, somewhat foppish, and docile, was eleven years her junior, a young man with no discernible intellectual interests or abilities. In late May 1848, Margaret had left Rome for L'Aquila in the Abruzzi — ostensibly for the necessary seclusion to write her history. But she was pregnant, and her departure from Rome was a timely effort to conceal the fact from her friends. Emerson, in Paris at the time, with the acrid smoke of the revolution still in the air, wrote Margaret, insisting that she return home with him — a move she could scarcely make, since her baby was due in September. "I should like to return with you," she countered, "but I have much to do and learn in Europe yet. I am deeply interested in this public drama, and wish to see it *played out*. Methinks I have *my part*, therein, either as actor or historian." On September 5, she gave birth to a son, whom she and Ossoli later christened Angelo Eugenio Filippo Ossoli. It was not until after her return to Rome — having left the baby in the care of a wetnurse in Rieti — that she informed her friends that she and Ossoli had been secretly married. It was some months later that she wrote Caroline Tappan and her family about the birth of her child. In Rome, most members of the American circle found the account of the marriage dubious.

Rome that winter was an armed city; Pope Pius IX had fled in November, and the Roman republic had been proclaimed. Apparently at Margaret's urging, Ossoli had joined the rebels. When the French laid siege to the city, he was assigned to the barricades. Margaret was appointed directress of the Hospital of the Fate Bene Fratelli during the siege. Separated from her child for months, she was anxious; seeing the wounded in the hospital wards, she confessed, "I forget the great ideas, to sympathize with the poor mothers, who had nursed their precious forms, only to see them all lopped and gashed." After days of relentless bombardment, she asked the American chargé d'affaires, Lewis Cass, Jr. — of whose official neutrality she had been critical — to safeguard her private papers. She intended to stand watch with her husband that night and was fearful that it might be their last evening together. They both survived, but four days later, on July 4 (the irony of the date was not lost on her), the French marched triumphantly into the city and the days of the Roman republic were at an end. She and Ossoli moved to Florence, where they lived in straitened circumstances. Reluctantly, and against the advice of friends, she decided to return to America with her husband and infant.

The voyage, begun on May 17, 1850, in the brig *Elizabeth*, was doomed. Off Gibraltar, the captain, Seth Hasty, died of smallpox and was buried at sea since the ship was forbidden to dock at port. Then Angelino came down with the disease and was critically ill for nine days. The crossing, under the directions of an inexperienced mate, went without incident. But on the evening of July 18, the *Elizabeth* anchored for the night offshore, expecting to reach New York in the morning. The mate, Mr. Bangs, had seriously miscalculated his position, thinking they were off New Jersey when, in fact, they were dangerously close to Fire Island. During the night a storm arose, and by the small hours of the morning the winds reached gale force. Around four o'clock, the *Elizabeth* was driven aground. Carrying a cargo of tons of Carrara marble, as well as a marble replica of one of Hiram Powers' sculptures, the vessel held fast on a sandbar, the stern swinging around to take the waves. Under the relentless pounding, the marble broke through the hold and the ship began to take water. Waves poured over the decks and down the hatches; the few lifeboats were stoved in or floated off in the heavy seas. Through the dark hours till morning, the passengers and crew huddled in the cabins and in the forecastle.

In the first light of dawn, it was clear that the ship was only several hundred yards from shore. Distant figures were gathered on the beach, but, inexplicably, no rescue effort was made. In midmorning, two crewmen and one of the passengers, Horace Sumner, the senator's younger brother, attempted to swim to safety. The seamen managed to reach shore, exhausted, but young Summer was swallowed up in the churning waves. Later, Mrs. Hasty and a crewman managed to survive the waters, clinging to a makeshift raft of planks. Margaret, steadfastly refusing to be separated from her husband and child, resisted any attempt to make a similar effort. She clung to the hope that a rescue boat would be sent out for them. It was not until early afternoon that a boat appeared on the beach. By then, it was too late; the tide had begun to turn and the seas were running too high. Along the beach the scavengers and beach pirates had gathered, lugging off everything of value that managed to reach the shore.

In the final moments, the ship began to break up. Ossoli and Celeste Paolini, their maidservant, were swept overboard into the tangled rigging and were immediately drowned. A steward snatched Angelino in a desperate attempt to save the child by swimming for shore; their bodies were washed up on the beach soon afterward. Margaret, still in her white nightgown, went under in a huge wave as the topmast fell. The cook, who managed to survive the breakup, remembered her last words: "I see nothing but death before me — I shall never reach the shore." Her body and that of her husband were not recovered. Presumably, they had been swept out to sea.

Sophia learned the news from Caroline Tappan, who did not tell her beforehand, but simply handed her the newspaper accounts with a look of foreboding. Writing to her mother, Sophia commented, "I dread to speak of Margaret. Oh, was ever anything so tragical, so dreary, so unspeakably agonizing as the image of Margaret upon that wreck alone, sitting with her hands upon her knees and tempestuous waves breaking over her! But I cannot dwell upon it . . . I wish at least Angelino could have been saved."

In the aftermath of the disaster, Emerson sent Thoreau and Ellery

Channing to the scene, hoping they might find the manuscript of Margaret's history of the Roman republic. A small trunk containing her letters and a few documents was located on the beach. "Mr. Thoreau and Ellery are at Fire Island," Sophia reported, "and Elizabeth Hoar sent Caroline [Tappan] Ellery's letter to Mr. Emerson and Mr. Thoreau's report. Neither Margaret's nor Ossoli's body had been found up to their date. Ellery was drying papers — but not yet had found the book of Italy." The history of the Roman uprising was not recovered.

Before trailing off into vain regrets, Sophia's letter acknowledged the persistent rumors and doubts about Margaret's marriage. "If they were truly bound together, as they seemed to be," she told her mother, "I am glad they died together. But Margaret is such a loss, with her new and deeper experience of life in all its relations — her rich harvest of observation . . ."

ᴄ᷍᷍ III ᷍᷍ᴄ

On August 5, Hawthorne attended a notable literary picnic. His journal entry gives little idea of the importance of the occasion.

> Rode with Fields and wife to Stockbridge, being thereto invited by Mr. Field of S——., in order to ascend Monument Mountain. Found at Mr. F's Dr. Holmes, Mr. Duyckinck of New York. Also Messrs. Cornelius Mathews and Herman Melville. Ascended the Mountain — that is to say, Mrs. Fields and Miss Jenny Field — Messrs. Field and Fields — Dr. Holmes, Messrs. Duyckinck, Mathews, Melville, Mr. Henry Sedgwick and I — and were caught in a shower. Dined at Mr. F's. Afternoon, under guidance of J. T. Headley, the party scrambled through the Ice Glen. Left Stockbridge and arrived at home, about 8:00 P.M.

The Mr. Field of Stockbridge was David Dudley Field, the sociable Stockbridge attorney; the Mr. Fields was Hawthorne's publisher, James T. Fields, who was visiting the region with his new bride, Eliza Willard — "the violet of the season," according to one commentator, referring to her bright blue silk dress. Cornelius Mathews, an officious and self-serving critic and poet, was the chief editorial writer for Evert Duyckinck's *Literary World*. Both Duyckinck and Mathews were the guests of Herman Melville, whom Hawthorne now met for the first time. Melville and his family were staying at Broadhall, a rambling, spacious mansion and boardinghouse on the Pittsfield Road, which belonged to his cousin Robert. Henry Sedgwick was a young graduate of Harvard, a former student of Longfellow's.

The festivities on that memorable day began with the ascent of Monument Mountain near Stockbridge, a site of local legend made famous by William Cullen Bryant's romantic poem, "The Story of the Indian Girl," relating the tragic fate of an Indian maiden who threw herself off a precipice out of thwarted love. The assembled party of eight men and two women journeyed by carriage and wagon as far up the mountain as the road permitted. Then they began the slow climb on foot. A sudden squall, however, overtook the party, and they huddled for shelter under an overhanging cliff. Oliver Wendell Holmes gallantly fashioned an umbrella for the ladies from a leafy branch; iced champagne was passed around in a silver mug. In the fury of the storm, Mathews, not to be denied his literary moment, recited Bryant's poem to an accompaniment of lightning flashes and rolling thunder.

When the rain stopped, the party pushed on to the summit. Melville, the boldest of the group — made bolder by the champagne — climbed out on a projecting ledge to give a demonstration of a sailor hauling in sail. Hawthorne was in a relaxed, if not an effervescent mood. According to Evert Duyckinck, he loosened up to the point of pretending to look "wildly about" for the great carbuncle.

Early in the afternoon, the party returned to Field's house and a feast of turkey, roast beef, and several desserts — all "well-moistened" with wines. The dinner took a leisurely three hours. Holmes, in a roguish mood, twitted Mathews for his literary chauvinism, and began praising both Englishmen and English authors without reservation. Melville joined in the dispute on the side of the American claimants, and Hawthorne — so Duyckinck confided to his wife — looked on placidly. James Fields, recalling the events some twenty-eight years later, remembered that Hawthorne had stoutly defended the Americans.

Late in the day, an additional guest, J. T. Headley suggested the excursion to Ice Glen, a dark and secluded spot where the winter's ice purportedly lingered until midsummer. The women remained at home. The slightly drunken men scrambled around over the slippery, moss-covered rocks, stumbling past fallen and moldering tree trunks. James Fields was equally concerned about scuffing his glossy patent leather shoes and the fate of his two profitable authors; he was expecting new books from both Hawthorne and Holmes. Mathews, eyeing the huffing and puffing publisher, meanly suggested that if he paid his authors 10 percent more on their royalties, he would have less fat to complain of. Hawthorne, even more relaxed than he had been in the morning, entered into the spirit of the affair, calling out in a dramatic and gloomy voice that "certain destruction" awaited the entire troop. After their passage through the dripping glen, the party returned again to Field's home for coffee and more conversation. There they were joined by another of the Stockbridge literary celebrities, Catharine Sedgwick. It was not until late that night that Melville and his party caught the train for Pittsfield and the twelve-mile ride to Broadhall; Hawthorne had left earlier for Lenox.

Neither Hawthorne nor Melville, it appears, left any account of their discussions on that first meeting — if they had had much time for serious talk. Nor, it seems, were any of the other participants aware that something unique — the meeting of two American geniuses, both at the summit of their literary powers — had taken place on that summer day in the Berkshires. James Fields, writing Longfellow a few days later, gave an account of the mere events. "I have just got back to my desk from the Berkshire hills," he wrote, "where we have been tramping over the soil with Hawthorne, dining with Holmes, hunting up the mountains with Headley; and sitting in all manner of dangerous places with Melville, the author of 'Typee.'" As if to console his most favored author, Fields added, "We have had rare times and your name was mentioned over a glass of iced Champagne six thousand feet above Stockbridge." That elevation of Longfellow's name was somewhat magnanimous; Monument Mountain is only 1600 feet above sea level, to say nothing of Stockbridge. The slightly awed Henry Dwight Sedgwick, the only man in the party who could then claim the distinction of never having written a book, remembered only that the various members of the party had "talked prose apparently as unconsciously as *M. Jourdain* himself." Cornelius Mathews, the most prolix of the invited guests, devoted a series of lengthy self-promotional articles to the midcentury literary picnic in the pages of the *Literary World*. Writing under the name "Esteemed Correspondent," he awarded equally florid epithets to the other notables of the group. His employer, Duyckinck, was dubbed "Silver Pen," and Holmes was named "The Town Wit." Melville, as an old salt, was called "New Neptune," and Hawthorne, "Mr. Noble Melancholy." With arch coyness, Mathews spoke of himself as "an earth monster, a perfect Behemoth, the mention of whose name has before now driven three critics crazy and scared a number of small publishers out of a year's growth." Teasingly, he informed his readers, "You would give the world to have an accurate account of so careful a pen as ours of what that picked company of wits and belles had to say to each other over the wine." Then he adamantly stated, "We have sealed a seal, never, never to divulge, no never" what had been discussed.

In his journal notes, Hawthorne was not expansive about his views of Melville when, a few days after the picnic, the writer and his younger brother, along with Duyckinck and Mathews, paid a visit to the red farmhouse. "Gave them a couple of bottles of Mr. Mansfield's champagne, and walked down to the lake with them," he wrote tersely. It is not clear whether he remembered his prophecy to Mansfield that he would serve up the wine when the next genius arrived at his door. Duyckinck, writing to his wife, was impressed with Hawthorne and with his glimpse of the author's domestic life. "Hawthorne," he wrote, "is a fine ghost in a case of iron — a man of genius and he looks it and lives it — he gave us some Heidsieck which a literary friend had presented to him, popping the corks in his nervous way." (Not to be outdone in such literary gestures, as soon as he returned to New York Duyckinck sent a gift of champagne — plus cigars — to his host, Melville.) The new York editor was equally impressed with Sophia's knack for bringing culture and Italian prints to a rural American farmhouse. Sophia, he told his wife, "resembles Margaret Fuller in appearance though more robust than she was" — which was a way of saying that Mrs. Hawthorne was somewhat plain.

In a letter to Horatio Bridge, Hawthorne opened up, to a certain extent, about his feelings concerning Melville. Bridge, like Melville, had done service on the *United States* and was presumably interested in the sea-faring author. "I met Melville, the other day," Hawthorne wrote, "and liked him so much that I have asked him to spend a few days with me before leaving these parts." The two men had evidently hit it off well enough for the privacy-hugging Hawthorne to issue such an invitation. Following the visits of Duyckinck and the Melvilles at the farmhouse, Hawthorne wrote Bridge once more, noting that Melville's longer visit was still in the offing for reasons beyond Hawthorne's control. "My hospitality (what little I have)," he said, "is fully engrossed, just now, by Mrs. Peabody." In his glum way he added, "If I mistake not, you have very kindly feelings for your mother-in-law. You were always more amiable than I — but this is between ourselves."

There is little doubt about what Melville thought of Hawthorne — as a writer. Within two weeks' time, his impressions of the New England author were published in a two-part article, glowing with outrageous praise, in the August 17 and 24 issues of Duyckinck's *Literary World*. Melville's essay, "Hawthorne and His Mosses," is one of the most flattering and extravagant reviews that one American author has ever accorded another. It is a matter of scholarly debate whether Melville wrote his essay before meeting the Salem author or whether — despite the heavy social calendar of early August in the Berkshires — he wrote it hurriedly during Duyckinck's visit, handing it to the editor before his return to New York on August 12. In any event, by August 16, Melville had received his copy of the *Literary World* with the first installment, and complained of one or two printer's errors, asking to see proof, if possible, of the second installment.

Melville's essay began with a number of fictions, the first being that he was "A Virginian Spending His Summer in Vermont" — the byline under which the essay appeared. The second was that his copy of *Mosses from an Old Manse* had been given to him by a luscious (and presumably ripe) young Vermont cousin named Cherry, who had advised him to read it while he loafed away his mornings in the hay mow. (The truth was that the book had been given to him, in mid July, by his elderly Aunt Mary, who was well past the age of ripeness.) It may also have been another of Melville's fictions that he had never met the author of *Mosses*, maintaining, "I never saw the man; and in the chances of a quiet plantation life, remote from his haunts, perhaps never shall." It was on the basis of a purely literary encounter between a Southern gentleman and an admired New England author that Melville offered his tribute.

The whole scenario of the essay is given over to images of bucolic abundance. "Yes, it is that flowery Hawthorne," Cousin Cherry says as she hands the "verdantly-bound" copy of *Mosses* to the author, who accidentally spills his raspberries at the breakfast table when he receives the book. Everything is calculated to heighten the lush seasonableness of the intellectual encounter. Melville had been especially moved by Hawthorne's description of the orchard at the Old Manse and saw it, in allegorical fashion, as "the visible type of the fine mind that had described it." In the stillness of summer afternoons, he, too, had heard the apples falling "out of the mere necessity of perfect ripeness." Having recently made a study of Shakespeare, Melville could hardly have failed to catch the echo of Lear's dictum, "Ripeness is all."

It was Melville's readings in Shakespeare and his bold coupling of Hawthorne's name with the Bard of Avon that raised one of the more debatable points in his essay. The comparison inevitably flustered Hawthorne's conservative admirers. There was a considerable amount of American jingoism in Melville's account of the contemporary literary scene. Much of it sounded suspiciously like afterthoughts the author had had following his dinnertime discussion with Oliver Wendell Holmes. Melville maintained that Shakespeare's reputation was not unapproachable. "There are minds that have gone as far as Shakespeare into the universe," he claimed. "And hardly a mortal man, who at some time or another, has not felt as great thoughts in him as any you will find in Hamlet." But Melville was prepared to go even further. "Let America," he commanded in an exuberant and dubious lowering of critical standards, "first praise mediocrity even, in her own children, before she praises . . . the best excellence in the children of any other land. Let her own authors, I say, have the priority of appreciation." He called for an end to the "leaven of literary flunkeyism toward England."

One of the principal thrusts of Melville's essay was directed toward contradicting the widely accepted notion of Hawthorne as a spinner of pleasant tales and genteel sketches. "For spite of all the Indian-summer sunlight on the hither side of Hawthorne's soul," he informed the readers of the *Literary World*, "the other side — like the dark half of the physical sphere — is shrouded in a blackness, ten times black." It was Melville's feeling that a lingering taint of Calvinism, the Puritan heritage with its sense of original sin, made Hawthorne stand out amongst the puerile and sentimental fiction-writers of his time.

What was astonishing in Melville's essay were the unmistakable sexual implications of his imagery. Florid praise was hardly unusual in the nineteenth century, but even so, the terms of Melville's praise were certainly distinctive. In the first installment, Melville began, mildly enough, by speaking of the "soft ravishments" of Hawthorne's style. Hawthorne, Melville suggested, was a magician who had cast a spell and then "dismissed me with but misty reminiscences, as if I had been dreaming of him." In the next installment, the language became embarrassingly erotic. There, Melville spoke of the "infinite height of loving wonder and admiration" that a reading and rereading of *Mosses* excited in him. In the essay's most extravagant and revealing metaphor, Melville described his response to Hawthorne's potency in a manner that was distinctly feminine and passive. In an odd merger of the agricultural and the physiological, he hinted at sexual climax. "But already," Melville confessed, "I feel that this Hawthorne has dropped germinous seeds into my soul. He expands and deepens down, the more I contemplate him; and further, and further, shoots his strong New England roots into the hot soil of my Southern soul."

Melville's reading of Hawthorne and, certainly, his personal encounters with the author had a dramatic effect on his life and career. At the time, he was engaged in writing a new book, ostensibly a narrative of a whaling voyage. He had already told Duyckinck that the book was nearly finished. That, perhaps, was Melville's optimistic hope, but it was another year before he completed his masterpiece, *Moby-Dick*. It was after his initial meetings with Hawthorne that Melville decided to rewrite and expand his whaling story. The force of Hawthorne's allegorical style, the seductive persuasiveness of the man himself, seemed to release Melville's own creative energies, opening up new possibilities in his concept of writing. His narrative of a whaling voyage became a far more complex and ambitious book than he had originally anticipated.

At about the same time, Melville decided to leave New York and settle in the Berkshires. In September, he bought a farm, which he renamed Arrowhead, and shortly after moved his family — his wife, his son, Malcolm, his mother, and unmarried sisters. Hawthorne, it seems, served as the necessary wizard for this new commitment. Melville had reached a point in his career when time, circumstances — and the right human encounter — pushed him toward greatness.

Throughout his essay on Hawthorne, there is an echoing self-identification. Melville was intent on stating the "parity of ideas" that he sensed existed "between a man like Hawthorne and a man like me." In praising Hawthorne, he was also laying claim to his own admittance to the "brotherhood" of the arts, to his own election to the "new and far better generation" of American writers that he was promoting. Melville clearly had his meeting with Hawthorne in mind when, in one of the most famous passages of his essay, he claimed, "For genius, all over the world, stands hand in hand, and one shock of recognition runs the whole circle round."

There was understandable rejoicing in the Hawthorne household when Melville's anonymous essay appeared in the *Literary World*. Sophia, in particular, was convinced that her husband had at last received his just appraisal. She advised her mother not to "wait an hour to procure the last two numbers of 'The Literary World,' and read a new criticism on Mr. Hawthorne . . . I know you will enjoy the words of this ardent Virginian as I do." Mrs. Peabody's response to her daughter's enthusiasm was a cautionary tale: "I carried the 'Literary World' to Aunt Rawlins. She agreed in the main with the reviewer but thought he had injured the subject by saying too much. 'No man of common-sense,' she said, 'would seriously name Mr. Hawthorne, deserving as he is of respect and admiration, in the same day with Shakespeare . . . to compare any one to Shakespeare argues ignorance, and only injures the friend he is attempting to serve.' So said that lady." Sophia was amused. "Poor Aunty!" she answered, "I really do not believe Shakespeare will be injured by being spoken of in the same paper with Mr. Hawthorne. *But no comparison* is made between them; though there is no reason why a great man may not be compared to another."

With such admiration at home, Hawthorne needed little outside support. "Nevertheless," he conceded in a letter to Duyckinck, "I must own that I have read the articles in the Literary World with very great pleasure. The writer has a truly generous heart; nor do I think it necessary to appropriate the whole magnificence of his encomium, any more than to devour everything on the table when a host of noble hospitality spreads a banquet before me. But he is no common man and, next to deserving his praise, it is good to have beguiled and bewitched such a man into praising me more than I deserve."

There is, at least, the possibility that Hawthorne instinctively associated Melville with the anonymous reviewer of *Mosses*. Duyckinck had sent Hawthorne copies of Melville's recent books, and at the beginning of his August 29 letter to the editor Hawthorne commented that he was reading Melville "with a progressive appreciation of the author." Years before, when he had reviewed *Typee* for the *Salem Advertiser*, Hawthorne had praised the book for being "lightly but vigorously written." He had expressly appreciated Melville's account of the voluptuous native girls climbing aboard the ship in Nukahiva Bay, and he went on to praise Melville's uninhibited outlook: "He has that freedom of view — it would be too harsh to call it laxity of principle — which renders him tolerant of codes of morals that may be little in accordance with our own; a spirit proper enough to a young and adventurous sailor . . ." Now, Hawthorne praised more solid and more mature virtues. "No writer," he told Duyckinck, "ever put the reality before his reader more unflinchingly than he does in 'Redburn' and 'White-Jacket.' 'Mardi' is a rich book, with depths here and there that compel a man to swim for his life. It is so good that one scarcely pardons the writer for not having brooded long over it, so as to make it a great deal better."

Was it coincidence only that Sophia, too, in a note added to her husband's letter, mentioned the unknown reviewer and then Melville in rapid succession. "I cannot speak or think of anything now but the extraordinary review of Mr. Hawthorne in the Literary World," she exclaimed. "The Virginian is the first person who has ever in *print* apprehended Mr. Hawthorne." (It was an uncharacteristic lack of tact on Sophia's part, since Duyckinck had recently written a very favorable essay on her husband.) "Who can he be, so fearless, so rich in heart, of such fine intuition. Is his name altogether hidden?" she asked. Then she proceeded to thank Duyckinck for the Melville books. The unknown Virginian had read Hawthorne stretched out in the barn on the new-mown clover. Was it a mere coincidence that Hawthorne had returned the compliment? "Mr. Hawthorne," Sophia reported, "has read them all on the new hay in the barn — which is a delightful place for the perusal of worthy books."

ぐっ IV ついぐ

Like Nathaniel Hawthorne, Herman Melville had been a boy when his father died. Born August 1, 1819, on Pearl Street in New York City, Melville was twelve when his father, Allan — a failed businessman, harried by debtors — died in a "deranged" state, ranting and spouting the Bible. Melville's Uncle Thomas, another hard-luck businessman, described his brother's condition as "fierce, even *maniacal*" at the time of his death. (When Melville referred to "madness" in his writing, he hardly meant it as an easy metaphor or mere cliché; the term had acquired an awesome meaning in his vocabulary.) Maria Melvill (the family acquired the final *e* after Allan's death), a stolid, somewhat haughty woman of Dutch ancestry, finding herself a widow with eight children, turned to her Gansevoort brothers for help. Like Hawthorne with his Manning uncles, Melville had known the chagrin of living off the charity of more successful relatives.

Neither the Gansevoorts nor the Melvills were among the wealthier citizens of the new Republic, but they could claim historical distinction. Melville's maternal grandfather, General Peter Gansevoort, had been one of the defenders of Fort Stanwix in the American Revolution; Major Thomas Melvill, Allan's father, had been an "Indian" at the Boston Tea Party. Ancient and garrulous, the major lived well into the nineteenth century, wearing his tricornered hat and knee breeches on the Boston streets, an eccentric veteran of another era. He acquired celebrity as "The Last Leaf" of Oliver Wendell Holmes's sentimental poem of that name.

Allan Melvill began his career as an importer of French millinery items, then as the proprietor of a dry-goods store in New York City. He was a traveled man of some culture, having acquired in Paris a library of French books and prints. He was an engaging talker and an opportunist. His frequent business failures seemed to correspond to his own manic cycle of optimism and despair. A portrait of him, painted in Paris in 1810, shows a strikingly featured young man, a bit of a dandy, in a relaxed, lounging pose. His dark hair is close-cropped and curly. There is something peculiarly intense — or, more truthfully, something wayward — about the expression around the eyes. Melville adored his father. But quite early in his life, he seems to have felt the impossibility of ever quite pleasing him or of receiving the same affection his father lavished on his much handsomer brother, Gansevoort. Gansevoort Melville, four years older than Herman, was the darling of both parents: slender, dark-haired, a ready talker, and, in school, always at the head of his class. In family circles, Gansevoort was always "our beloved Gansevoort"; Herman was warmly but condescendingly referred to as "backward in speech and somewhat slow in comprehension," a boy of "a docile and amiable disposition." Despite family encouragement, Gansevoort, who was physically frail and often ill, had only an ineffectual career as a businessman and, later, as a minor diplomat. He died in London at the age of thirty, seemingly in a state of "nervous derangement," like his father. In the pantheon of Herman Melville's seductive fictional men, Allan and Gansevoort were enshrined as the handsome and cultured surrogate fathers and the equally well-favored and envied male companions of Melville's orphaned protagonists.

At the age of thirteen, Herman Melville went to work as a clerk in his uncle Peter Gansevoort's bank in Albany. Then, for several months during the summer of 1834, he worked on his uncle Thomas Melvill's farm in Pittsfield. For a few years, while attending the Albany Classical School, Herman also clerked in his brother Gansevoort's fur and cap store. The financial panic of 1837, however, put Gansevoort out of business. At nineteen, Melville signed on for his first voyage, as cabin boy on the *St. Lawrence*, bound for Liverpool. In 1841, following an unrewarding stint as a schoolteacher in Albany and an equally unrewarding trip to the Midwest, Melville turned, once more to the sea.

This time he made his first cruise on a whaler, the *Acushnet*, which sailed from Fairhaven, Massachusetts, under wintry skies on January 3. It was the voyage that was to initiate his later masterpiece. At Nukahiva, in the Marquesas Islands, Melville and a companion, Richard T. Greene (the ingratiating Toby of *Typee*), jumped ship to live among the remarkably handsome, fierce, and supposedly cannibalistic Typees. For the next year, Melville lived the life of a beachcomber and roustabout sailor, serving on one ship or another, visiting one island or another, becoming involved in a brief mutiny and being imprisoned on Tahiti, until, in August 1843, in Honolulu, he signed aboard the frigate *United States* and made the long fourteen-month voyage home that ended in Boston Harbor in October 1844.

Melville belittled the years of his youthful maritime service, claiming that his real education in life began only after his return home. "From my twenty-fifth year, I date my life," he told Hawthorne in one of his exuberant letters. "Three weeks have scarcely passed, at any time between then and now, that I have not unfolded within myself." Yet it was out of those earlier experiences that he fashioned his first books — *Typee, Omoo, Redburn, White-Jacket* — the novels that brought him popularity.

Like Hawthorne, Melville seemed to be approaching a sense of maturity, a conviction that it was not "experiences" which counted in life, but the deepening of experience; that the fruitful years beyond the self-righteousness of youth lay ahead. It was then that one began to understand the complexities of life, to appreciate the touching awkwardness of human relationships. Hawthorne would express a similar view — though in more optimistic terms — in a letter to Longfellow written a few years later. "Don't you think that the autumn may be the golden age both of the intellect and imagination?" he asked the poet. "You certainly grow richer and deeper at every step of your advance in life. I shall be glad to think that I, too, may improve — that, for instance, there may be something ruddier, warmer, and more genial, in my later fruitage." Melville, typically, found a more ironic metaphor for his sense of his late development — the Egyptian wheat that had recently been found in a mummy case. Planted in English soil, it "grew to greenness, and then fell to mould. So I." Characteristically, he added, "But I feel that I am now come to the inmost leaf of the bulb, and that shortly the flower must fall to mould." He acknowledged that his literary acclaim had come from his maritime adventures. But still, Melville complained, "What 'reputation' H.M. has is horrible. Think of it! to go down to posterity is bad enough, any way; but to go down as a 'man who lived among the cannibals'!"

Becalmed, now, in a houseful of women in rural Pittsfield, far from the ocean, Melville began to reshape his interrupted narrative of a whaling voyage — a book about the rough, hierarchical, society of men in pursuit of a mythical whale, in the midst of an ocean that was both real and cosmological. At home, he seems to have had few opportunities, or little inclination, to discuss his literary ambitions. Melville's wife — the former Elizabeth Shaw, daughter of the eminent chief justice of Massachusetts, Lemuel Shaw, whom Melville married in 1847 — was a stolid and dutiful woman. She regularly transcribed Melville's manuscripts into fair copies, but she does not seem to have been the recipient of Melville's literary confidences. (In later life, after Melville's death, she had less to say about her husband's literary habits and ambitions than did most widows of authors.) In Pittsfield, Melville shut himself up in his upstairs writing room, giving the strictest orders that he was never to be disturbed until early in the afternoon, usually around two-thirty. On more than one occasion, Lizzie Melville worried about the feverish intensity with which Melville approached his work. The history of mental breakdowns among the male members of the Melville family could only have added to her anxieties.

With Hawthorne, however, Melville became expansive. His surviving letters to his fellow author indicate a kind of extravagant release, a flooding of all his pent-up notions about the art of writing, his deepest feelings about the profound human issues that he expected to be the subject of any art worth its name. (Hawthorne's letters to Melville have not survived; according to Julian Hawthorne, Melville many years later claimed that they had all been destroyed.) When the two men were together in the parlor of the Lenox cottage or in the more relaxed privacy of Melville's writing room at Arrowhead (where they could indulge in port and cigars), Melville launched into what he described as his "ontological heroics." In the regular exchange of letters and visits that took place during the fifteen months Hawthorne remained in Lenox, Melville was the aggressive suitor in their literary courtship.

Melville admired men who stood above the common level. His apprenticeship as a writer — and perhaps his life itself — was a search for such men. Having heard Emerson, a "Plato who talks thro' his nose," lecture in Boston in February 1849, Melville confessed that he had been "agreeably disappointed." He had expected the Concord sage to be "full of transcendentalisms, myths and oracular gibberish," but found a man "elevated above mediocrity." He had written Duyckinck on that occasion, "I love all men who *dive*. Any fish can swim near the surface, but it takes a great whale to go down stairs five miles or more; & if he don't attain the bottom, why all the lead in Galena can't fashion the plummet that will." (It was typical of Melville that where other poets pointed their aspiring metaphors skyward, his always plunged deep and down.) Having discovered Hawthorne, Emerson's former Concord neighbor, Melville was even more ready, in his generosity, to concede that Hawthorne's was "a great, deep intellect, which drops down into the universe like a plummet."

He was never a niggling man. He had, no doubt, the sailor's brag and boast — and probably the sailor's easy manner with facts. His youthful experiences had been formed against the wide circumference of the ocean — "the sky above, the sea around, and nothing else!" as he described it in his first book, *Typee*. It was a realm that encouraged abstraction, a taste for expansive thoughts. "Yes, as everyone knows," his Ishmael would claim, "meditation and water are wedded for ever." At sea, there was little sense of the usual relationships, of one set of circumstances conveniently measured against another set of circumstances — the inevitable conditions of civilization. At sea, there were the unending circle of the horizon, the choppy rhythm of the waves, the sun rising, the sun setting, from one day to the next — and, after intervals of weeks, perhaps, a chance encounter with another ship, another floating microcosm.

Hawthorne, by contrast, had lived out his life in the confined world of Salem's streets — a world that stopped short, after all, at Salem's wharves, the commercial edge of the sea. He had lived in the narrow precincts of a New England village like Concord. His life, however reclusive it had been in the past, was bounded by neighbors and newspapers and small-town connections. There was that interesting difference between the two men.

On September 3, 1850, Melville paid a four-day visit to the Red Shanty. Hawthorne's journal entries for the period are taciturn, recording only the dates of his guest's arrival and departure and the fact that on the 4th they had spent the day at Broadhall, Robert Melvill's house, dining there and returning to Lenox at eight in the evening. Throughout the visit, Hawthorne maintained his morning routine of writing. (Evidently with some intensity, since Sophia wrote her sister Mary that she could not put the children in his care "even in the afternoon because he still is mentally engaged when out of his study.") With Hawthorne preoccupied much of the time, Melville was left to his own devices, though the two men took long walks together when Hawthorne was free.

"Mr. Omoo," Sophia called Melville. In a letter written to her mother on the day after his arrival, she launched into one of her extravagant tributes, describing him as "a man with a true warm heart and a soul and an intellect — with life to his fingertips — earnest, sincere and reverent, very tender and *modest* — And I am not sure that he is not a very great man; but I have not quite decided upon my own opinion — I should say, I am not quite sure that I *do not think him* a very great man — for my opinion is, of course, as far as possible from settling the matter." Certainly she found him a good deal more agreeable than James Russell Lowell, who had visited the Hawthornes a few days before. Lowell was much "altered" since his marriage, Sophia thought, and she did not like the change. In contrast to Melville, Lowell was "very unsatisfactory."

Sophia's report on Melville continued in glowing terms: Melville was "tall and erect, with an air free, brave & manly" — she still had not mastered the art of selecting two adjectives when three or four were ready to hand. Robust and heavier than he was in later life, Melville had a ruddy beard and luxuriant hair. Sophia thought his eyes unaccountably small: "He seems to see everything very accurately, and how he can do so with his small eyes, I cannot tell.

They are not keen eyes, either, but quite undistinguished in any way." Melville had, she noted, "an indrawn dim look, but which at the same time makes you feel that he is at that instant taking deepest note of what is before him. It is a strange, lazy glance, but with a power in it quite unique. It does not seem to penetrate through you, but to take you into himself. I saw him look at Una so, yesterday, several times." There were moments when Sophia was a master of the minor but telling detail.

Melville seems to have struck up a warm and confidential intimacy with Sophia during his brief stay. Not long after the visit Sophia, in a letter written probably to her sister Lizzie, announced an important piece of news: "We have discovered who wrote the Review in the Literary World. It was no other than Herman Melville himself!" Melville, whether altogether truthfully or not, had told her he had had "no idea when he wrote it that he should ever see Mr. Hawthorne." He also complained that the article had been "too carelessly written — that he dashed it off in great haste . . ."

In Sophia, Melville had found a very attentive listener on a subject that was dear to her heart. She reported that she and Melville had had a series of "delightful conversations" about her husband, one of which she described, complete with its atmospheric setting. "In the golden light of evening twilight," she and Melville had paid a visit to Highwood. (Hawthorne had not accompanied them.) While Caroline Tappan was putting her baby to bed, the pair had sat on the verandah, looking out over Stockbridge Pond in the glow of the setting sun. "He [Melville] said Mr. Hawthorne was the first person whose physical being appeared to him wholly in harmony with the intellectual and spiritual." The inventory Melville gave her was quite extensive: "He said the sunny haze and the pensiveness, the symmetry of his face, the depth of eyes, 'the gleam — the shadow — and the peace supreme,' all were in exact response to the high calm intellect, the glowing, deep heart . . ." In Sophia's presence, Melville had carried on the discussion with some eloquence, for she reported, "Mr. Melville is a person of great ardor and simplicity. He is all on fire with the subject that interests him. It rings through his frame like a cathedral bell."

The guest, she added, had been tactful enough not to interrupt her husband's work routine. "He generally walked off somewhere — and one morning, he shut himself into the boudoir and read Mr. Emerson's Essays . . . In the afternoon he walked with Mr. Hawthorne. He told me he was naturally a silent man, that he was complained of a great deal on this account; but that he found himself talking to Mr. Hawthorne to a great extent. He said Mr. Hawthorne's great but hospitable silence drew him out — that it was astonishing how *so-*

ciable his silence was. (This, Mr. Emerson used to feel.) He said sometimes they would walk along without talking on either side; but that even then they seemed to be very social."

Sophia was to watch the growing intimacy of the two men with an appreciative eye. Months later, writing to Lizzie, she offered a vivid picture of the two men in conversation — Melville, talkative and aggressive, Hawthorne, quiet but responsive. "Nothing pleases me better," she wrote, "than to sit & hear this growing man dash his tumultuous waves of thought against Mr. Hawthorne's great, genial, comprehending silences." With her taste for the metaphorical, she chose the appropriate analogies — Melville's "tumultuous waves of thought" rolling in against her husband's granitic, landlocked silences. From out of his profound self-possession, Hawthorne would offer "a wonderful smile or one powerful word" that would send back Melville's "foam and fury into a peaceful booming calm — or perchance not into a calm — but a murmuring expostulation." Borrowing a phrase from Emerson, she remarked of Melville, "For there is never a 'mush of concession' in him, yet such a love & reverence & admiration for Mr. Hawthorne as is really beautiful to witness."

What she appreciated in this growing fraternity were the proofs of her husband's greatness. "Without doing anything on his own part," she said of Hawthorne, "except merely *being*, it is astonishing how people make him their innermost Father Confessor."

ᴄﾝ V ᴄﾝ

In Ralph Waldo Emerson's philosophy, love was "the great enchantment of life." In his lecture "Love," Emerson spoke of it as a divine rage, which, seizing on man at an early period in life, works a revolution in his soul and body and bends him to all the civilized virtues. Love, Emerson claimed, "unites [man] to his race, pledges him to the domestic and civic relation, carries him with new sympathy into nature; enhances the power of the senses . . . adds to his character the heroic and even the sacred attributes; establishes marriage; and gives permanence to human society."

Among the virtues of love in the pretty catalogue Emerson set forth in his early lecture, there was nothing that was not fit to be heard by modest young ladies in a female seminary. It was, in fact, to Elizabeth Palmer Peabody, when she was mistress of a school for young girls, that Emerson gave the manuscript copy of his lecture. Lizzie Peabody, who clearly felt safe with the simpler but exalted human affections, had read the lecture to her girls and treasured the manuscript for the rest of her life. Love, it was clear, was a harmless and benevolent emotion.

It was typical of Emerson and his idealizing views that not even the slightest rumble of the physical was allowed to disturb the calm surface of his lecture. Straightaway, he informed his audiences that he intended to leave aside any "lingering adherence to the actual, to facts, and seek to study this sentiment in its ideal manifestation." The birds, the bees — all of rutting nature — were lightly glossed over. In the realm of nature, Emerson saw the power of love as a kind of chemical reaction that displayed itself "in elective affinities, in explosion, in flame, in new products." In the spring, the woods filled up with welcome birdsong; but the passions aroused by the surging tides of spring, Emerson dutifully noted, were best left to poets and the young.

Such were Emerson's views on love; his lecture-essay "Friendship" was more substantial. In that innocent time, friendship, too, was remote from the taint of gross physical implications. But, in an odd way, Emerson was willing to view the friend — whether male or female — as a kind of helpmate to the steady upward progress of the soul. A friend, he claimed, might well be reckoned "the masterpiece of nature" — something, apparently, more definitive than a wife or a lover.

The Concord philosopher found little of value in mere acquaintanceship — friendships that were nothing more than "modish and worldly alliances," involving nothing better than "rides in a curricle and dinners at the best taverns." For Emerson, a friend was an irreconcilable *other* — "a sort of beautiful enemy, untamable, devoutly revered, and not a trivial conveniency to be soon outgrown and cast aside." In friendship, Emerson was as wary of the physical as he was in love. "Why insist on rash personal relations with your friend?" he asked his listeners. "Why go to his house, or know his mother and brother and sisters?" He advised, "Leave this touching and clawing. Let him be to me a spirit. A message, a thought, a sincerity, a glance from him, I want, but not news, nor pottage. I can get politics and chat and neighborly conveniences from cheaper companions." Yet in describing his ideal friend, Emerson became remarkably possessive. "The only joy I have in his being mine," he claimed, "is that the *not mine* is *mine*. I hate, where I looked for a manly furtherance, or at least a manly resistance, to find a mush of concession."

It was an age of such high-minded relationships. A classicizing impulse hung over the entire subject of the affections, providing a sanction for more concealed emotions. The relationships of Socrates and Alcibiades, of Hadrian and Antinoüs, were often invoked — but always in the purest phrases. In both instances, the carnal undersides of the relationship were discreetly ignored. (Melville, on a trip to Rome, was ecstatic over a bas-relief of Antinoüs: "head like moss-rose with curls & buds . . . end of fillet on shoulder . . . hand full of flowers and eyeing them." Antinoüs was transformed into one of his "flowery" males. George William Curtis, fascinated by a head of Antinoüs in the Vatican, "realized the pure deep love he could have inspired.") No doubt some of the sympathetic attitude toward male bonding came from the Hellenizing impulses of the German idealists who dominated the New England mind. But it came from Byron as well. Whatever the scandalous nature of Byron's relationships with women, his comradeship with the Greek soldiers in their fight for independence was sanctified. Byron's death at Missolonghi, in the midst of his Greek "brothers," had glorified the poet for generations of Americans.

The Greek connection colored the age. The doughty Henry Ward Beecher — whose relationship with certain of his female parishioners scandalized his congregation late in his ministry — had in youth a passionate attachment to a young Greek schoolmate, Constantine Fondolaik, a refugee from the Turkish massacres. When Beecher was nineteen, he and the Greek youth signed a mutual compact of brotherly love that reads, poignantly, like a marriage vow: "As formerly we were connected by nothing save voluntary friendship, which could be broken off, so now we are connected by a love which cannot be broken; and we have pledged ourselves before God and his angels to be as written above . . . we have not done this thoughtlessly, but being convinced by *three years'* friendship that we mutually love one another." Fondolaik returned to Greece in 1842 and died there of cholera. But Beecher remembered him always — and in vividly sensual terms. "He was the most beautiful thing I had ever seen," he said years afterward. "He was like a young Greek god. When we boys used to go swimming together, I would climb out on the bank to watch Constantine swim, he was so powerful, so beautiful." One of Beecher's sons was named after the dead youth.

Charles Sumner had an equally intense relationship with Samuel Gridley Howe, who, like Byron, had fought with the Greeks against the Turks. In their relationship, Sumner was a captive adorer. "Bachelors both," he wrote to a friend, "we drive and ride together — and pass our evenings far into the watches of the night in free and warm communion." The two were so constantly together that George Hillard, another of Sumner's friends, could write in jocular fashion, "He is quite in love with Howe and spends so much time with him that I begin to feel the shooting pains of jealousy."

There was something overdependent and morbid about Sumner's attachments to his male friends. When first Howe, then Longfellow, married, Sumner was positively dejected. "Nobody is left with whom I can have sweet sympathy . . ." he complained. "What shall I do these long summer evenings?" Howe had invited Sumner to accompany him and his bride on their European honeymoon, an offer that Sumner, in his dejection, refused. (Much to Julia Ward Howe's relief, quite probably.) But even on his honeymoon, Howe sent ardent letters reassuring Sumner of his continuing devotion. "The torrent of affection which is continually flowing from my heart toward the new object of my love diminishes not by one drop the tide of feeling which swells within my bosom at the thought of thee, dear Sumner," Howe wrote his friend. "I love thee not less because I love her more." The transatlantic condolences became so frequent that Julia Howe, in exasperation, told her husband, "Sumner ought to have been a woman and you to have married her" — a message Howe, in all innocence, relayed to Sumner as another proof of devotion.

Such heady liaisons were not the custom only of male members of nineteenth-century society; women, too, formed equally passionate attachments. The celebrated Boston-born actress Charlotte Cushman had a reputation for such friendships with young, and generally talented, women. In England, her friendship with the actress Matilda Hays was remarked on by Elizabeth Barrett Browning. Cushman and Miss Hays, the poet explained in a letter, "have made vows of celibacy and of eternal attachment to each other — they live together, dress alike." A friend explained to Mrs. Browning that such arrangements were called "Boston marriages." As an actress, Cushman was forceful and bold; she acquired a certain notoriety by playing masculine roles — Romeo, for instance, opposite her sister's Juliet. The *Times* of London, perhaps as a compliment to her acting skill, remarked that "in point of sex," Miss Cushman was "almost amphibious." Fanny Kemble's aggressive acting style gave rise to a similar ambiguity. Melville, who heard Kemble give a formidable reading of Lady Macbeth, doubted that the actress was really a woman and capable of giving birth to a child. "I should be curious to learn the result of a surgical examination of her person in private," he wrote Duyckinck with uncharacteristic sarcasm.

Margaret Fuller, who had had her share of intense feelings toward members of her own sex, was one of the few writers of the period — male or female — to examine the subject with an unembarrassed eye. Although she shunned the physical implications, she did, at least in the privacy of her journals, acknowledge the passionate nature of such involvements. Concerning her own relationship with the beautiful Anna Barker, she wrote, "It is so true that a woman may be in love with a woman and a man with a man . . . It is regulated by the same law as that of love between persons of different sexes, only it is purely intellectual and spiritual, unprofaned by any mixture of lower instincts, undisturbed by any need of consulting temporal interests . . ."

That was putting the best face on it. Like most of her contemporaries, Fuller found sanction for such feelings in history and literature. "Why did Socrates so love Alcibiades?" she queried in her journal. "Why did Koerner love Schneider? How natural is the love of Wallenstein for Max; that of De Staël for De Récamier, mine for _____?" Yet, however high-minded her intentions, she could not altogether escape the sensual. "She loved me, too," Margaret confided in her journal shortly after Anna married Samuel Gray Ward, "though not so much . . . but she loved more tenderly, less passionately. She loved me, for I well remember her suffering when she first could feel my faults . . . how she wished to stay apart and weep the whole day. Then again that night, when she leaned on me and her eyes were such a deep violet blue like the night, as they never were before and we both felt such a strange mystic thrill and knew what we had never known before."

For Margaret Fuller, intelligent and unattractive as she was, the problem was peculiarly "amphibious." In one of her early poems, Margaret imagined herself, not as an attractive girl, but as Ganymede, the beautiful youth whom the lecherous Jove, in the form of an eagle, swooped up into the skies. Margaret, thinking of the stern and demanding Timothy Fuller, must have reasoned that if she had been a handsome boy rather than a plain girl, she might have been all the more quickly swept up into the heaven of a father's love.

In the upper reaches of transcendental thought, it seems, the distinctions between love and friendship, between one sex and another, tended to blur.

As a writer, Melville had an unfailing eye for handsome men. Although there are, at times, decorative women in his fictions — like the obliging Fayaway in *Typee* — Melville's descriptions of attractive men are always instinct with sensual life. The long line of beautiful comrades and heroes in Melville's writings stretches from Marnoo, the Polynesian youth of *Typee*, to the astonishing blond Billy Budd, whose "significant personal beauty" seems to make suitors out of the entire crew of the *Indomitable*. Melville can sometimes be coyly ironic about his eager male suitors. There is a funny moment in *Typee* when Marnoo, with his dark glossy ringlets and cheeks of "feminine softness," spurns the narrator's offer of a seat next to him. In his chagrin, the narrator confesses, "Had the belle of the season, in the pride of her beauty and power, been cut in a place of public resort by some supercilious exquisite, she could not have felt greater indignation than I did at this unexpected slight." By way of comic relief, Melville had a gift for introducing into his masculine world the sentimental conventions of ladies' literature. The comedy works, but it does not altogether disguise the implied yearning.

In *White-Jacket*, Melville describes another of his honorable and unapproachable ideals, Jack Chase, a middle-aged, slightly balding Apollo who recites Camoëns and sponsors Lemsford, the poetry-writing seaman of the *Neversink*. (It was to Chase, his actual companion aboard the *United States*, that Melville later dedicated his *Billy Budd*; "Wherever that great heart may now be / Here on Earth or harbored in Paradise.") Melville's relationship to Chase — both the actual and fictional persona — seems to have prefigured his relationship with Hawthorne.

Considering the heated view of friendship the age encouraged, a "manly resistance" must have been an essential requirement in any intimate masculine relationship. But Melville had had a larger experience of the world than many of his contemporaries. He had visited exotic ports and primitive peoples; he had lived among rough and hardened sailors. He had a broader understanding of the sexual drama than might be guessed at in polite Concord or Pittsfield. He could hardly have avoided the knowledge that sodomy was common among men at sea — and he discreetly hinted as much when he referred, in *White-Jacket*, to the "goggling glances" of old yeomen who might drag his young heroes "down into tarry perdition" in ships' storerooms. He must also have sensed that the brutality and sadism rampant among officers and men on long ocean voyages had strong sexual undercurrents.

As an idealistic youth, Melville perhaps subscribed to the Emersonian view of friendship. As an old man, a neglected author, he occasionally touched on the "sexual feud [that] clogs the aspirant life," in poems that he published at his own expense. In one of these, poignantly titled "After the Pleasure Party," he wrote as a veteran of the wars of the divided self:

> . . . *Nature, in no shallow surge*
> *Against thee either sex may urge.*
> *Why hast thou made us but in halves —*
> *Co-relatives? This makes us slaves.*
> *If these co-relatives never meet*
> *Selfhood itself seems incomplete.*

And such the dicing of blind fate
Few matching halves here meet and mate.

In his headlong friendship with Hawthorne, knowing that it could go nowhere, Melville may well have felt the sharp, hurting edge of its impossibility.

This Infinite Fraternity of Feeling

IN THAT FIRST cold winter in Lenox, Hawthorne settled down to writing *The House of the Seven Gables*. He had begun work on it in August; by October he had even chosen a title. In November, however, he complained of making only slow progress. "I write diligently, but not so rapidly as I hoped," he informed Fields on November 3. "I find the book requires more care and thought than the 'Scarlet Letter' — also I have to wait oftener for a mood. The Scarlet Letter being all in one tone, I had only to get my pitch, and could then go on interminably." A month later, he was stalled again, but this time for a different reason. "I have been in a Slough of Despond for some days past," he wrote Fields on December 9, "having written so fiercely that I came to a stand still. There are points where a writer gets bewildered, and cannot form any judgment of what he has done, nor what to do next."

Fields was decidedly pressing his writer. In October, his firm had begun announcing "a new Romance by the author of 'The Scarlet Letter,'" and by January it was taking orders for a book it did not yet have in manuscript. But Hawthorne's problems came from something more than an overeager publisher. Like any sensitive author, he was attempting to extend his range. In *The House of the Seven Gables* he was trying for a greater variety of mood and a greater precision of detail than he had managed in *The Scarlet Letter*. Many passages of the new book, he reported to Fields, "ought to be finished with the minuteness of a Dutch picture." He was also attempting to situate his narrative in the clear American present, with its railroad cars and omnibuses, rather than in a misty past. Not altogether, of course, for in its broad scope, *The House of the Seven Gables* is the saga of the fictional Pyncheon family; its subject is the dead weight of the past upon the present, symbolized by the ancient curse of Matthew Maule, hanged as a wizard during the Salem witchcraft trials through the too-strenuous efforts of Colonel Pyncheon. Maule's curse, as he steps up to the gallows, pointing his finger toward his accuser — "God will give him blood to drink!" — echoes down the generations of Hawthorne's story. Interestingly, where Hawthorne's contemporaries and later scholars viewed the witchcraft trials as an example of seventeenth-century religious hysteria, Hawthorne, with a modern's foresight, suggested that there was a probable economic motive behind the persecution of Matthew Maule. The rapacious Colonel Pyncheon coveted Maule's property; he had already brought legal action to establish his dubious claim. His religious convictions easily accommodated his more questionable personal motives.

Hawthorne intended his story to point a moral; in a brief preface, he was to spell it out: ". . . the truth, namely, that the wrong-doing of one generation lives into the successive ones, and divesting itself of every temporary advantage, becomes a pure and uncontrollable mischief." In an increasingly commercial and industrial America, where the old republican virtues seemed to be passing from the scene, Hawthorne was prepared to sermonize about "the folly of tumbling down an avalanche of ill-gotten gold, or real estate, on the heads of an unfortunate posterity." But he was content to define the evils without offering suggestions for a cure.

Another of his problems was that he insisted on finding a suitable aesthetic form for his story. In the ambiguous preface, he tried hard to define the differences between the novel proper and the romance — the designation he gave *The House of the Seven Gables*. The novel, Hawthorne stated, aimed at "a very minute fidelity, not merely to the possible, but to the probable and ordinary course of man's experience." His book, on the other hand, was a romance because it attempted "to connect a bygone time with the very Present that is flitting away from us." It dealt with a legend from a misty and gray epoch that had prolonged itself "into our own broad daylight." But what Hawthorne might state in the preface and what he did in the romance itself were not always in agreement. Many of the episodes in the book were finished with novelistic precision: the vivid pictures of Salem street life with its hawkers and pedlars, its political processions; the detailed photographs of the ruined Pyncheon garden with its summerhouse and its scratching hens; the harried train ride to nowhere that Clifford and Hepzibah Pyncheon, two innocents abroad, take in the company of newspaper-reading commuters. Then, perversely, like a sorcerer with a wand, the author speaks of "this visionary and impalpable Now, which, if you once look closely at it, is nothing." Suddenly, the carefully contrived structure of reality dissolves, revealing an abyss. In gloomier moments, Hawthorne confessed to Fields that the book seemed "an absurdity, from beginning to end; but the fact is, in writing a romance, a man is always, or always ought to be, careening on the utmost verge of a precipitous absurdity, and the skill lies in coming as close as possible, without actually tumbling over."

In spite of his difficulties, Hawthorne worked steadily at the book, and by January 12, 1851, he was writing Fields, "My House of Seven Gables is, so to speak, finished; only I am hammering away a little on the roof, and doing a few odd jobs that were left incomplete." By that time, he had also completed a preface for the new edition of *Twice-told Tales*, which was already on the presses for March publication. Like his preface for *The House of the Seven Gables*, the introduction for his collected stories was a curious and self-reflexive performance. It was as if Hawthorne had come to a new vantage point. From the other side of fame, after the publication of *The Scarlet Letter*, he surveyed his earlier career, when he was, he claimed, "the obscurest man of letters in America." His early failure, Hawthorne reflected, was probably due to the fact that his stories were too tame; they created no critical enemies. Looking over his collected tales, he found only "the pale tint of flowers that blossomed in too retired a shade." He went on, "Instead of passion, there is sentiment; and, even in what purport to be pictures of actual life, we have allegory." The stories lacked the depth one ought to expect from the "communications of a solitary mind with itself." Considering his circumscribed life at the time, he confessed, the stories seemed written, rather perversely, in "the style of a man of society." They were, he decided, not altogether successful attempts "to open an intercourse with the world."

His 1851 preface also gave Hawthorne an opportunity to cast a cold, critical eye on his public image as an author. Hawthorne seemed ready to discard that fictional character, the "mild, shy, gentle, melancholic, exceedingly sensitive, and not very forcible man" he had become in the public mind. In a mood of self-depreciation, he admitted he would find it difficult to relinquish that image of himself without shedding "a few tears of tender sensibility." But he was prepared to do so. Perhaps his willingness had been prompted by the novel he was finishing. In *The House of the Seven Gables* Hawthorne was exorcising the spirit of an overly refined and ineffectual man — the exceedingly sensitive and not very forceful Clifford Pyncheon — a character that in certain negative respects bore a resemblance to its author.

It was evidently the final hammering away at *The House of the Seven Gables* that caused Hawthorne to put off a visit to Melville at Arrowhead. Late in January, Hawthorne took the expedient way out by having Sophia write a note expressing his regrets. Melville would have none of it. "That side-blow thro' Mrs. Hawthorne will not do," he blusteringly informed Hawthorne. "I am not to be charmed out of my promised pleasure by any of that lady's syrenisms. *You*, Sir, I hold accountable and the visit (in all its original integrity) must be made." He had already notched the tail feathers of two fowls that were to be served up for Hawthorne and his family. He promised some "excellent Montado Sherry" and some "most potent port." Melville assured his fellow author that Arrowhead was not "any prim nonsensical house"; there would be no formalities. "You may do what you please," he wrote, "— say or say *not* what you please. And if you feel any inclination for that sort of thing — you may spend the period of your visit *in bed*, if you like — every hour of your visit." Otherwise, Melville claimed, "We will have mulled wine with wisdom and buttered toast with story-telling and crack jokes and bottles from morning till night." The countryside lay deep in snow; nevertheless, Melville both promised and threatened to drive down to Lenox in his sleigh and pick up his reluctant guests.

Later, in February, writing to Evert Duyckinck, Melville complained that the visit still had not taken place. He had paid a visit to Lenox two weeks earlier, he noted, and found Hawthorne, "of course, buried in snow; and the delightful scenery about him, all wrapped up and tucked away under a napkin, as it were. He was to have made a day's visit and I had promised myself much pleasure in getting him up in my snug room here, and discussing the Universe with a bottle of brandy and cigars. But he has not been able to come, owing to sickness in his family — or else, he's up to the lips in the *Universe* again."

Hawthorne had given Melville an inscribed copy of the earlier edition of *Twice-told Tales*, and he had been reading the book in the interim. Melville had a better opinion of the early stories than their author did at the moment. "I think they far exceed the 'Mosses,'" Melville told Duyckinck; "— they are, I fancy an earlier vintage from his vine." Where Hawthorne found his tales shallow, Melville took the opposite view. "Some of those sketches are wonderfully subtle," he wrote Duyckinck. "Their deeper meanings are worthy of a Brahmin." In his copy, Melville underscored a number of significant passages. One of them — from "The Gentle Boy" — seemed to have a coincidental echo in the opening line of *Moby-Dick*: "'Friend,' replied the little boy in a sweet though faltering voice, 'they call me Ilbrahim and my home is here.'"

Beneath the surface amiabilities, however, Melville found something insubstantial about Hawthorne the man; maybe his criticism reflected only his sense of something insubstantial in their relationship. "Still there is something lacking — a good deal lacking — to the plump sphericity of the man . . ." he informed Duyckinck. "He doesn't patronize the butcher — he needs roastbeef done rare." And he added, "Nevertheless, for one, I regard Hawthorne (in his books) as evincing a quality of genius, immensely loftier, and more profound, too, than any other American has shown . . . Irving is a grasshopper to him."

Sophia's response to the Lenox winter was blissful; her attitude may have been colored by her realization that she was once again pregnant. The children, she wrote her mother, had lived on "the blue nectared air" all winter. In the mornings, when they clamored to get up, there were "opaline mists" clinging to the mountains. Hawthorne made the fires in the bathroom, and the children, squealing with delight, were bathed and heartily rubbed down. Sophia's account of Una and Julian was typically expansive: "Such clear, unclouded eyes, such superb cheeks, as come in and out of the icy atmosphere! such relish for dry bread, such dewy sleep, such joyful uprisings, such merry gambols under pails of cold water!"

Early in the morning, Hawthorne fed the chickens; after breakfast, he retired to his upstairs study. Sophia gave the children lessons in "French, arithmetic, history and geography" or took up her workbasket. At noon, Hawthorne came downstairs — an event that caused "great rejoicing throughout his kingdom," so Sophia related. At sunset, they dined and then the children were put to bed. She and Hawthorne had the long evenings together. Hawthorne read aloud — that winter from *David Copperfield*, De Quincey, Milton's *Samson Agonistes*. "He reads so wonderfully. Each person is so distinct," Sophia exulted. "It is better than any acting I ever saw on the stage."

On January 27, Sophia reported that *The House of the Seven Gables* had been completed. "Mr. Hawthorne read me the close, last evening," she wrote her mother. "There is unspeakable grace and beauty in the conclusion, throwing back upon the sterner tragedy of the commencement an ethereal light, and a dear home-loveliness and satisfaction." She prophesied, "How you will enjoy the book, its depth of wisdom, its high tone, the flowers of Paradise scattered over all the dark places . . ."

On those wintry mornings, Hawthorne had written in his small, stuffy, second-floor study, wearing the old purple damask dressing gown Sophia had made for him, the gold palm-leaf pattern now badly faded, but the interior lining still a vivid red. His desk was a hinged lap-desk placed open on his library table. It had once belonged to his brother-in-law George Peabody. Sophia had scrubbed off the ink stains and polished the mahogany and made new black velvet covers for the interior. As if documenting an important fact, she proudly reported to her mother, "The House of the Seven Gables has been written upon it."

Julian Hawthorne was also to remember his father's old dressing gown. But he recalled the black ink stains on the inside of the skirt. For many years, Hawthorne had been wiping his pen there, a habit Sophia had tried to break by covering the spot with a large felt butterfly that served as a pen wiper. Julian recalled, too, his father's mahogany writing desk with its bright brass fittings, but he cared little about its familial history. What he remembered was the day his father initiated him into a little mystery — a hidden compartment, beneath the pen tray, that sprang open with a sudden snap, revealing two secret drawers. It was appropriate, perhaps, that Hawthorne should have a writing desk with a secret compartment.

ᶜᵔᵓ II ᶜᵔᵓ

In Clifford Pyncheon, Hawthorne created another of those *messieurs-du-miroir* that populate his fictions. Clifford is a bachelor, a member of an ancient New England family. He is a consumer, a lover of "the Beautiful" — a creature almost too rarefied, too exquisite for life. Clifford has little resiliency, few of the strengths required for dealing with adversity. Hawthorne carefully stages the contrast between the feminine grace of the young Clifford, pictured in a Malbone miniature, and the tremulous, aged wreck that returns from prison, a secretive guest in *The House of the Seven Gables*. The old Clifford is a ruined sensibility, easily moved to womanly tears; so hypersensitive that even the ringing of Hepzibah's shop bell causes him pain. Sitting in his worn damask dressing gown, being read to by a girl, he is the ruin of a once-handsome man. But he is, after all, a man who has survived an ordeal.

It is not without significance that Clifford is presumed guilty of a crime he did not actually commit — the killing of an aged and eccentric uncle, whose death from an apoplectic stroke — the curse of the Pyncheons — is mistaken for murder. From some fatal want of character or an unwarranted sense of guilt, Clifford has allowed himself to be convicted of the crime. His imprisonment has been ably assisted by a grasping cousin, Jaffrey Pyncheon, the iron-willed judge of thirty years later, when the story opens. ("I do not belong to the dreaming class of men," Judge Pyncheon boasts to Hepzibah, in vivid contrast to Clifford.) Hawthorne's confrontation between two types of men — the dreamer and the man of action — is set in motion when Judge Pyncheon secures Clifford's release from prison in hopes of learning the whereabouts of a lost and ancient family deed to land grants in Maine. Despite the book's modern setting, Hawthorne resorted to a number of Gothic and Romantic trappings: ancient curses, lost deeds, secret hiding places operated by means of concealed springs, ghostly melodies played on a harpsichord, presaging a death in the family.

There is a slight edge of disdain in Hawthorne's treatment of his protagonist; he presents Clifford as the dispensable man, someone who performs no visible function in the world, someone whose nature is "selfish in its essence." Hepzibah, with her shabby gentility, her sequestered life, her timorousness that turns to fierce strength on the right occasions, is a far more vital character. (Hawthorne's mother and sisters may have inspired the portrait. The masterly scene of Hepzibah's early morning toilet — the weary sighs from behind a closed door, the sound of drawers being opened and closed jerkily, the tread of footsteps back and forth across an uncarpeted floor, the rustle of silk — was undoubtedly drawn from Hawthorne's morning deductions in a household of women.) Yet Clifford has his affinities to Hawthorne himself; he is, in a sense, the man Hawthorne might have become except for the saving grace of his marriage to Sophia. Hawthorne likens Clifford's spirit to "a flame which we see twinkling among half-extinguished embers," something viewed with impatience "as if it ought either to kindle itself into satisfactory splendor, or be at once extinguished." (Years later, in sadder circumstances, he would revert to the same image in describing his own life as one of "much smoulder and scanty fire.") Yet, if he is scornful of Clifford's childlike petulance, his inability to come to grips with his life and personality, Hawthorne has an extraordinary sensitivity to his protagonist's heartfelt plea — and demand: "I want my happiness . . . Many many years have I waited for it! It is late! It is late! . . ." It is an echo of the complaint lodged by the unhappy man in "The Intelligence Office," who wants his place in life — "my own place! — my true place in the world."

It may be that Hawthorne's meetings with the robust Herman Melville — a widely traveled man still seeking his "place" as an author — had given him a sharper insight into the negative aspects of his own character. Melville seems to have sensed some underlying identification between Clifford and Hawthorne. Gingerly — as if treading on uncertain ground — he praised Hawthorne's characterization but seemed at a loss to explain what it was that he found so moving. "Clifford is full of an awful truth throughout. He is conceived in the finest, truest spirit," he wrote Hawthorne. "He is no caricature. He is Clifford . . ." The remark sheds little light. Melville may have sensed in Clifford the same insubstantiality he complained of in Hawthorne in his letter to Evert Duyckinck.

Ironically, Hawthorne borrowed something from Melville's personal history when he came to the delineation of Holgrave, the symbol of the brash, new, up-and-coming young man of mid-nineteenth-century America. "In his crude, wild and misty philosophy, and the practical experience that counteracted some of its tendencies; in his magnanimous zeal for man's welfare, and his recklessness of whatever the ages had established in man's behalf; in his faith, and in his infidelity, in what he had, and in what he lacked," Holgrave might easily represent some aspects of Herman Melville. Holgrave's latest profession is that of daguerreotypist, making him "the artist," one of the familiars in Hawthorne's gallery of symbolic characters. But for Holgrave this is only the latest in a long line of desultory careers. In one of his sharpest touches, Hawthorne presents Holgrave as the heir of the new democracy, a representative figure "in a country where everything is free to the hand that can grasp it." Hawthorne is admiring and condescending. Holgrave has tried his hand at everything:

> Though now but twenty-two years old (lacking some months, which are years, in such a life), he had already been, first a country school-master; next, a salesman in a country-store; and, either at the same time or afterwards, the political editor of a country newspaper. He had subsequently travelled New England and the middle states as a pedlar, in the employment of a Connecticut manufactory of Cologne water and other essences. In an episodical way, he had studied and practised dentistry, and with very flattering success, especially in many of the factory-towns along our inland streams. As a supernumerary official of some kind or other, aboard a packet-ship, he had visited Europe and found means, before his return to see Italy and part of France and Germany. At a later period he had spent some months in a community of Fourierists. Still more recently, he had been a public lecturer on Mesmerism . . .

With Yankee economy, Hawthorne lifted much of this quixotic history from his own notebooks. Holgrave is the new breed that Hawthorne had encountered on his rural excursions. But the roles of a country schoolmaster, a clerk in a country store, and a lengthy service at sea, would comfortably fit the youthful career of Herman Melville.

It is part of Hawthorne's ambivalence that he sympathizes with Holgrave's antipathy toward the past. "Shall we never, never get rid of this Past!" the young man complains. "It lies upon the Present like a giant's dead body!" Holgrave feels the burden of the past like a personal affliction: "A Dead Man sits on all our judgement-seats; and living judges do but search out and repeat his decisions. We read in Dead Men's books! We laugh at Dead Men's jokes, and cry at Dead Men's pathos! We are sick of Dead Men's diseases, physical and moral . . ." It is one of Hawthorne's more eloquent and bitter indictments of society and its institutions. Yet Hawthorne suspects, too, that Holgrave may be another of those blustering young radicals from whom one expects great things "but of whom, even after much and careful inquiry, we never happen to hear another word." Holgrave, in other words, might well turn out to be another of those self-important bores whom Emerson seemed to collect. Still, Hawthorne is careful to point out that his young radical has kept his integrity. "Homeless as he had been," Hawthorne says of him kindly, "continually changing his whereabout, and therefore responsible neither to public opinion nor to individuals — putting off one exterior, and snatching up another, to be soon shifted for a third — he had never violated the innermost man, but had carried his conscience along with him."

Hepzibah, who has taken the young man in as a boarder in the House of the Seven Gables, has a muddled appreciation for him. She has seen his strange companions — "reformers, temperance-lecturers, and all manner of cross-looking philanthropists, community-men and come-outers"; she has even read an item about him in a penny-paper that accused him of making a speech "full of wild and disorganizing matter." But in her untutored wisdom, she supposes that Holgrave "has a law of his own!" Phoebe, a prissy and conservative young lady, is at first put off by Holgrave's "lack of reverence for what was fixed." But she soon falls in love with him. It is clear that Phoebe, with her chirrupy temperament, her sunny disposition, and incurable optimism, is drawn from Sophia, whom Hawthorne on several occasions addressed as Phoebe in his letters. Phoebe also has Sophia's "gift of practical arrangement," the ability to create a habitable atmosphere anywhere she considered home — and for however brief a period. It is clear from the outset — and from the happy ending that Hawthorne starts preparing for midway through the story — that Phoebe will tame Holgrave. His radical views are verbal and idealistic; he softens rather too quickly to Phoebe's conventional attitudes. It was a persistent tenet of Hawthorne's philosophy that the influence of a good woman — Sophia's influence on himself — was an absolute necessity in a man's life and one of the indispensable foundations of civilized society. But Hawthorne obviously felt a certain nostalgia for Holgrave's unreconstructed nature — as he felt a certain envy of Melville's uninhibited style. The taming of Holgrave is, perhaps, Hawthorne's only admission — a slight and subtle one, if it was conscious at all — that Sophia's high-mindedness, her implacable goodness, had exacted a price.

He had written much of his romance in the heart of winter, when the snow lay deep in Lenox. Oddly — but probably with a corresponding intensity — the setting of the book is fixed at summer solstice. All of the action takes place in midsummer — in the dim, green, leafy midsummer along Pyncheon Street and under the shady boughs of the Pyncheon elm. There are graphic pictures in *The House of the Seven Gables*: Clifford peering out of the arbor to watch the brilliant flashing of the hummingbirds among the scarlet bean blossoms; the Italian organ-grinder with his greedy monkey and his mechanical figures, twirling and dancing to "one identical tune" cranked out on the music box; the noisy political procession that moves up Pyncheon Street, the marchers all "perspiration and weary self-importance" — a commonplace scene viewed close up, but one that takes on grandeur from another vantage point, when all the petty personalities melt into "one great life — one collected body of mankind, with a vast, homogeneous spirit animating it." The scenes in *The House of the Seven Gables* are scenes that Holgrave might have focused on with his unwieldy camera.

It was not merely chance that Hawthorne had fixed on Holgrave's profession as that of a photographer. He developed a conscientious metaphor out of the broad daylight of modern life, the new science of photography, and his own art of writing. When Holgrave tells Phoebe, "In short, I make pictures out of sunshine," Hawthorne is preparing his reader for the aesthetic announcement that promptly follows. "There is a wonderful insight in heaven's broad and simple sunshine," Holgrave claims. "While we give it credit only for depicting the merest surface, it actually brings out the secret character with a truth that no painter would ever venture upon, even could he detect it. There is at least no flattery in my humble line of art." Hawthorne, in short, is announcing that he is an author in search of the "secret character" that lies beneath the surfaces of life and the usual conventions of the novel.

Contemporary readers of *The House of the Seven Gables* found the long episode on the death of Judge Pyncheon impressive. Hawthorne seems to have been determined to make it a tour de force, for it is one of the most sustained and reflective passages of his writing. In describing the judge's rise to public eminence and his growing political ambitions, Hawthorne drew on his own recent and unfortunate political experiences to describe the precise steps — the public acts and the private dinners — by which the judge hoped to achieve his ambition of becoming governor. In sketching out the hypocritical character of the judge, with his prominent charities and calculated smiles, Hawthorne undoubtedly intended to point a finger at his old political enemy, the smiling and unctuous Charles Wentworth Upham. But he may also have had in mind another of the men who had helped to oust him from office, former Senator Nathaniel Silsbee, a much-respected public man, who had died in Salem in July 1850, the month before Hawthorne began work on his novel. Among the fictional achievements of Judge Pyncheon's career is that he has attended splendid banquets as a guest of honor and poured out his eloquence "to ears yet echoing with Webster's mighty organ-tones." Nathaniel Silsbee and Daniel Webster, some years before, had been honored with a well-publicized Whig dinner, a notable event in Salem's civic history, held in a specially constructed pavilion on the Mall, virtually opposite the senator's Pleasant Street mansion. It was another realistic touch added to his fictional portrait of a disagreeable man. (An odd bit of telltale evidence suggests that the character of Judge Pyncheon may have been the victim of some long-buried animus of Hawthorne's toward his Uncle Robert: Judge Pyncheon, too, is an eminent horticulturalist, the producer of "two much-esteemed varieties of the pear.") The chapter, ironically titled "Governor Pyncheon," is undeniably long — Hawthorne was unwilling to cut a good thing short — but it remains a high point in the book and a great set piece in nineteenth-century American writing.

Melville, responding to some personal insight and anticipating later critics, was especially moved by the episode in which Clifford attempts to leap from his upper-story window into the very thick of the political procession — all fluttering banners, pounding drums and shuffling feet — passing in front of the old Pyncheon home. (It adds a note of personal irony to the scene to recall that Hawthorne, professing his political innocence, claimed he had never taken part in such processions because it would have been out of character for him to do so.) The scene was intended to be one of crucial symbolic moments in the life of his weary hermit. Hawthorne carefully analyzes the conflicting emotions that lead to that psychologically ambivalent moment. Clifford, in a seizure of temporary madness, is "impelled by the species of terror, that sometimes urges its victim over the very precipice which he shrinks from, or by a natural magnetism, tending towards the great center of humanity . . ." In one of his perfect strokes, Hawthorne underscores the maddening complexity of human motives, adding, "Both impulses might have wrought on him at once."

There is another great dramatic chapter that is meant, in all prob-

ability, to contrast with the static nature of many of the episodes in
The House of the Seven Gables. In his chapter "The Flight of Two
Owls," Hawthorne sends his pathetic principals on an aimless excursion into the mainstream of contemporary life. Leaving the time-
haunted stillness of the ruined Pyncheon garden, Hepzibah and Clifford, in a blustering east wind and rain, struggle to the railroad station, where they buy tickets to nowhere in particular. Here, Hawthorne introduces the restless modern note of speed and illusionary
progress. His two "strangely enfranchised prisoners" seem bent on
making their escape in an exhilaration of movement:

> Meanwhile, looking from the window, they could see the world rac-
> ing past them. At one moment, they were rattling through a soli-
> tude — the next, a village had grown up around them — a few
> breaths more, and it had vanished, as if swallowed by an earth-
> quake. The spires of the meeting-houses seemed set adrift from
> their foundations; the broadbased hills glided away. Everything
> was unfixed from its age-long rest, and moving at whirlwind speed
> in a direction opposite to their own.

The description serves as an overture to Clifford's apparently abrupt
adoption of the modern philosophy of speed and change and techno-
logical progress. For the benefit of his fellow passengers, who eye
him suspiciously, he extols the new "nomadic" life the railroad will
make possible. Why should a man, Clifford asks, "make himself a
prisoner for life in brick and stone, and old worm-eaten timber,
when he may just as easily dwell, in one sense, nowhere — in a better sense, wherever the fit and beautiful shall offer him a home?" In
his mind, the House of the Seven Gables is a symbol of the poisonous past. It is the house of past decisions, past misdeeds, which
goes on exacting tribute from the living. The past — even the architectural past — is a monstrous inheritance: "A man will commit almost any wrong — he will heap up an immense pile of wickedness,
as hard as granite, and which will weigh as heavily upon his soul, to
eternal ages — only to build a great, gloomy, dark-chambered mansion, for himself to die in, and for his posterity to be miserable in."
    Clifford becomes a spokesman, though a somewhat rattled one,
for immediacy, for the escape from the past, from history — if only
from the small tyrannies of family history. His views are Holgrave's
views, but more highly colored, inspired by a kind of lyrical dot-
tiness. He expounds on the virtues of electricity, of mesmerism, the
railroad. Speaking of the burdens of the past — architectural, insti-
tutional, familial — he prophesies, "Within the lifetime of the child
already born all this will be done away. The world is growing too

ethereal and spiritual to bear these enormities a great while longer." It is typical of Hawthorne's method that he exploits such ideas and then punctures them with the grim common sense of a fellow passenger who pronounces Clifford's notions "All a humbug!" When Clifford offers his explanation of human progress as an "ascending spiral curve," there is the slight suspicion that Hawthorne would like to deal in the transcendental metaphysics that came so readily to his former Concord neighbors — Emerson, Thoreau, Bronson Alcott. But he is wary of such views; he knows that society — American society — will increasingly belong to the Judge Pyncheons of the world. Hawthorne's distrust of the metaphysical is evident at the end of Hepzibah and Clifford's wayward journey. Having no place to go, the pathetic couple simply get off at the next stop. There, Clifford, losing all his false confidence, quiveringly places himself in Hepzibah's hands. "You must take the lead now, Hepzibah," he tells her. "Do with me as you will!"

As a writer, Hawthorne had made the useful discovery that in fiction he could have it both ways: he could be both the participant and the critic; he could fling himself into the swift current of life and, at the same time, be the cool and dispassionate observer standing on the shore.

ᜒ III ᜒ

Hawthorne's second daughter, Rose, was born on May 20, 1851, at about three in the morning. The baby, so Hawthorne wrote his sister Louisa, had reddish hair, the shade of Una's, and was a "very promising child — kicking valiantly and crying most obstreperously." At first, Sophia had not informed her mother of the impending birth because Mrs. Peabody was seriously ill. But in the spring Sophia told her family. Father Peabody made the trip to Lenox for the confinement and presided over the birth scene with an imperturbability Hawthorne found "heroic and sublime and, at the same time, almost laughable."

With each new child — Rose was to be the last addition to the family — Hawthorne turned more reflective and sometimes a bit somber. In one of those striking coincidences of life, Hawthorne's family virtually recapitulated his own childhood situation: a solitary boy with one sister two years older and another four years (in this case, five) younger. Elizabeth Peabody maintained that Hawthorne had planned it that way. Sophia had told her that her husband "proposed they should have but three children, and that there should be two and a half years between the first two, and five years between the second and third." Evidently approving of her brother-in-law's self control, Lizzie also recalled Sophia's contention that "Mr. Hawthorne's passions were under his feet."

Five days after Rose's birth, Hawthorne wrote Lizzie Peabody in the perverse manner he sometimes adopted with his sister-in-law. He seemed to take pleasure in mocking the sentimental pieties that Lizzie held dear. Sophia and the new baby, he reported, were "getting on bravely." Sophia could gaze at the baby a dozen times a day and continually find "new beauties." But as for himself, he confessed, he had yet to discover even "the *first* beauty." Hawthorne found it difficult to believe that any squawling newborn child could be attractive. "But I think I never have had any natural partiality for my children," he explained to Lizzie. "I love them according to their deserts; they have to prove their claim to all the affection they get; and I believe I could love other people's children better than mine, if I felt that they deserved it more. Perhaps, however, I should not be quite a fair judge on which side the merit lay." His attitude, no doubt, was considered outrageous by Lizzie, who had very exalted views on motherhood, childhood, and the sweet innocence of youth.

Still, in a more solemn mood, Hawthorne was willing to concede that he felt a "more decided drawing of the heart" toward this newest child. "She is my last and latest; my autumnal flower," he added, "and will be still in her gayest bloom when I shall be most decidedly an old man — the daughter of my age, if age and decrepitude are really to be my lot."

For Lizzie's benefit, too, he provided a less than exalted view of the visiting Nathaniel Peabody, who was in his dotage. "Your father as I see him here," he wrote, "presents as comfortable an aspect of old age as I can possibly imagine. He does not appear to suffer any disquietude from your mother's precarious condition; what is not present to his perceptions has no existence for him. The children hang about him continually, and find him an excellent playmate; merely a playmate, however, for he is the most heedless and venturesome of the three." Father Peabody, in other words, was an additional child and something of a bother. Hawthorne was clearly becoming concerned about the length of his stay. "I do not believe he has any uneasy desire to leave us," Hawthorne commented drily, "but rather dreads returning to the anxieties which he has left behind him."

A good deal of Hawthorne's irritation may have come from the fact that the Lenox cottage was too small for extended family visits. "The most inconvenient and wretched little hovel that I ever put my head in," he complained in a letter to Louisa. (Louisa was well aware of how modest the cottage was; she had paid a brief visit in midwinter, and had annoyed her brother by absent-mindedly taking his copy of De Quincey when she returned to Salem.) But the sharp edge of his irritation was probably directed at Lizzie herself. Unfortunately, she was once again at large in life — and in those circumstances she was always ready to meddle and give advice. Lizzie had come through a series of recent defeats that would have sunk a mind less buoyant than her own. She had returned the publication of the unsuccessful *Dial* to Emerson; her own brave publishing venture, *Aesthetic Papers*, had failed ignominiously for lack of support. She had recently taken up a new method of studying languages, promoted by a poor immigrant Hungarian, Dr. Charles Kraitsir. For a time, Lizzie had taught in Kraitsir's school in Boston. With her usual wholeheartedness, Lizzie became involved in Kraitsir's private life. He had an insane wife, whom he had left behind in Philadelphia, and Lizzie had gone there to reason with the disturbed woman, who was creating a public scandal. (Sophia, writing to her mother, advised that Kraitsir would have to prove that his wife was "insane and if not insane an altogether worthless and wicked woman . . . Everybody seems to think Dr. Kraitsir very dilatory, weak, even *craven* not to justify himself and Elizabeth by the revelation of the whole.") Mrs. Kraitsir was eventually institutionalized, and Dr. Kraitsir returned to Hungary on funds solicited by Lizzie. Once again at large, she took up the theories of the Polish general, Josef Bem, who had devised a system of teaching history by means of complicated, color-coded charts, listing all the significant events in the history of the world. In November 1850, she had visited Lenox, after lecturing at Great Barrington. Julian Hawthorne recalled squirming through one of Aunt Lizzie's demonstrations of the Bem method; he was convinced that his complete inability to remember historic events was the result of that childhood lesson.

But it was probably Lizzie's renewed enthusiasm for spiritualism that caused the most concern to Hawthorne. To be sure, Lizzie did not write to Hawthorne on the subject, but she did confide to Sophia her recent experiences at séances in Boston. Spirit-rappings had informed her that Una had mediumistic gifts, and when she had asked if Hawthorne would consent to her being used, the rappings had told her yes. But Hawthorne, who already sensed another-worldly quality in his eldest daughter that he found disturbing, was not pleased. Furthermore, he had a real distaste for any spiritualistic experiments as far as his family was concerned. Lizzie, nonetheless, assured Sophia that her own intercourse with the dead spirits had been very congenial. The spirits had "said nothing absurd or disagreeable and seem to be very lovely to me," she wrote. Hawthorne ought not to be the least worried about Una's suddenly becoming a medium; it would take some patience to develop the talent in the first place. In Elizabeth's warm and woolly view of things, critical objections, such as Hawthorne's complete distrust of any such adventure, were no sooner raised than they were dismissed. "I do not wonder that Hawthorne will not let Una be tried," Lizzie rattled on. "I should feel just so. But should it ever come of itself, the purity of the medium would be a fine chance to take an observation, and I should treat it to Una as if it were not at all *strange* — only rather curious. Then it will not agitate her."

Sophia could take her sister with a good deal more equanimity than her husband; she understood the always lofty nature of Lizzie's meddling. In a family letter Sophia, in fact, rose to one of the great eulogies of Lizzie Peabody's life. Writing to her mother during the winter, she had pointedly asked about a new recipient of the Peabody family's charity. "Who, I pray, is Dwight Currier?" Sophia asked. "Is he one of the many lame, halt, forlorn, poverty-stricken mortals whom you and Elizabeth, in the infinite scope of your pity, sympathy, and hospitality, take in from the highways, because they have no roof to cover them?" In the midst of her own more secluded life, her strictly family concerns, Sophia had had a vision of Elizabeth's generosity of spirit. "As I sit and look on these mountains," Sophia wrote, "so grand and flowing and the illimitable, aerial blue, beyond and over, I seem to realize with peculiar force that bountiful, fathomless heart of Elizabeth, forever disappointed, but forever believing; sorely rebuffed, yet never bitter; robbed day by day, yet giving again, from an endless store; more sweet, more tender, more serene, as the hours pass over her, though they may drop gall instead of flowers upon this unguarded heart."

But Lizzie in the mind — Lizzie in the abstract and in absentia — was one thing. Lizzie in the cramped quarters of the Lenox cottage was quite another. For whatever reasons — undoubtedly overcrowding but probably a coolness on Hawthorne's part — Sophia felt it necessary to apologize for the "pitiful hospitality" Lizzie had received when she came to pick up Father Peabody at the end of his overlong stay. "You not only had no bed to sleep on, and no room to sleep in, but nothing to eat, besides sewing all the time, and washing your own clothes! I was very unhappy about it all, but thought I would not add to the trouble by complaining as I did not see how I could remedy the matter." The recent spate of family visits had quite evidently moved Sophia to some new resolutions. "I never intend to have a guest again for so long as father stayed, on Mr. Hawthorne's account," she told Lizzie. "It fairly destroys both his artistic and his domestic life. He has no other life — never visiting and having nothing to do with the public. I do not know as any one but myself can estimate the cost to him of having a stranger in our courts; especially in these narrow ones. A week or so does very well, but months will not do at all . . . You know he has but just stepped over the threshold of a hermitage. He is but just not a hermit still." Neither Phoebe nor Hepzibah could have been more solicitous of Clifford's welfare.

"How slowly I have made my way in life!" Hawthorne had written Horatio Bridge on March 15, a few weeks before the publication of *The House of the Seven Gables.* "How much is still to be done! How little worth — outwardly speaking — is all that I have achieved. The bubble reputation is as much a bubble in literature as in war, and I should not be one whit the happier if mine were world-wide and time-long than I was when nobody but yourself had faith in me."

It was Hawthorne's opinion that *The House of the Seven Gables* was a better book than *The Scarlet Letter,* and he told Bridge so, adding, "But I should not wonder if I had refined upon the principal character a little too much for popular appreciation; nor if the romance of the book should be found somewhat at odds with the humble and familiar scenery in which I invest it. But I feel that portions of it are as good as anything I can hope to write, and the publisher speaks encouragingly of its success."

When Bridge failed to make any mention of the new book, Hawthorne frankly courted his opinion. "Did you feel shy of expressing an unfavorable opinion?" he wrote Bridge in July. "It would not have hurt me in the least, though I am always glad to please you; but I rather think that I have reached that stage when I do not care, very essentially one way or the other, for anybody's opinion on any one production. On this last romance, for instance, I have heard and seen such diversity of judgment that I should be altogether bewildered if I attempted to strike a balance."

The book had done well, as Fields had predicted. Two printings were issued in April, with another following in May and a fourth in September, making a total of 6710 copies — 710 more than *The Scarlet Letter* in its first year. Hawthorne's royalties were 15 percent of the $1.00 price of the book. The book's success brought him an unexpected problem. In his preface, Hawthorne had disclaimed any relationship between his fictional characters and the residents of Salem. But in choosing the Pyncheon name, he had unconsciously hit on an ancient and supposedly honorable Salem family. A Peter Oliver, Esquire, of Boston complained that the book sullied the reputation of his grandfather, Judge Pynchon, a respectable figure of Revolutionary times. A Reverend Thomas Pynchon of Stockbridge wrote

Hawthorne that his romance held up "the good name of our Ancestors to the derision and contempt of our countrymen." He insisted that in any further printings the name be changed. Hawthorne, writing to Fields, railed at the "Pyncheon jackasses" and suggested that his entire correspondence with the angry descendants be published "in a style corresponding with that of my other works." Later, he sent a disclaimer that he hoped would be added to the preface of a later edition. It arrived too late for the third printing in May and, although Fields had promised it would be used, it never appeared.

After the popular success of *The Scarlet Letter*, the reviews for *The House of the Seven Gables* were less bewildering than they were perfunctory. Most critics found the book more congenial and true to life, though some complained that it was less dramatic than its predecessor. In some respects, it suffered from the "second-book" syndrome. The anonymous reviewer in the *Christian Examiner* found it pleasant but complained that "its plot is more complex, the characterization more exaggerated, and the artistic execution less perfect." That view was seconded in the *Southern Quarterly Review*, which thought it "less ambitious in plan and manner" than *The Scarlet Letter*, but "a more truthful book." Nearly all of the reviewers fastened on Phoebe as affording some welcome sunshine in a gloomy chronicle; Hawthorne had accurately tailored his character to the sentimental taste of the time. All the critics praised his characterization of Hepzibah.

Hawthorne particularly appreciated E. P. Whipple's even-handed treatment in *Graham's Magazine*. Whipple thought the first hundred pages of the book were best: "The mental nerve which characterizes the first part, slips occasionally into mental nervousness as the author proceeds" — an odd judgment, considering that all the great set pieces fall within the latter segment of the book. He also considered Clifford a failed character, since it was impossible to like him; moveover, Clifford occupied too much space in the narrative. (Whipple's opinions must have reinforced Hawthorne's feeling that he had overdrawn his principal character.) Despite the criticisms, Whipple claimed it was Hawthorne's "greatest work" and one that would command "immediate popularity and permanent fame." It came close to being "the deepest work of imagination ever produced on the American continent." Hawthorne, referring to the review in a letter to Fields, said that Whipple had "helped me to see my book. Much of the censure I recognize as just. I wish I could feel the praise to be so fully deserved."

If Hawthorne considered himself indifferent to praise or blame, he nevertheless cherished a letter from James Russell Lowell, who wrote him enthusiastically, "I thought I could not forgive you if you

Above left: Jones Very, the Salem poet. *Above right:* Ralph Waldo Emerson. Portrait sketch in crayon by Eastman Johnson, 1846. *Left:* Margaret Fuller. Engraving by Frederick T. Stuart. *Below left:* Henry David Thoreau. Crayon portrait by Samuel Worcester Rowse, 1854. *Below right:* A. Bronson Alcott.

Hawthorne at forty-six. Oil portrait by Cephas Giovanni Thompson, 1850.

Herman Melville in his late twenties. Oil portrait by Asa W. Twitchell, ca. 1847.

Hawthorne as a public man. Oil portrait
by G. P. A. Healy, 1853.

Franklin Pierce. Daguerreotype, ca. 1847.

Daniel Webster.

Horatio Bridge. Nineteenth-century oil by an unknown artist.

Charles Sumner, photographed by Southworth and Hawes, 1850.

Horace Mann. Undated photograph by Southworth and Hawes.

James T. Fields, Hawthorne, and William D. Ticknor. Photograph by
J. W. Black, 1863.

Mrs. Franklin Pierce and Benny.
Undated daguerreotype.

Elizabeth Barrett Browning and "Pen,"
photographed in Rome, 1860.

Una and Julian Hawthorne in a daguerreotype by an unknown photographer.

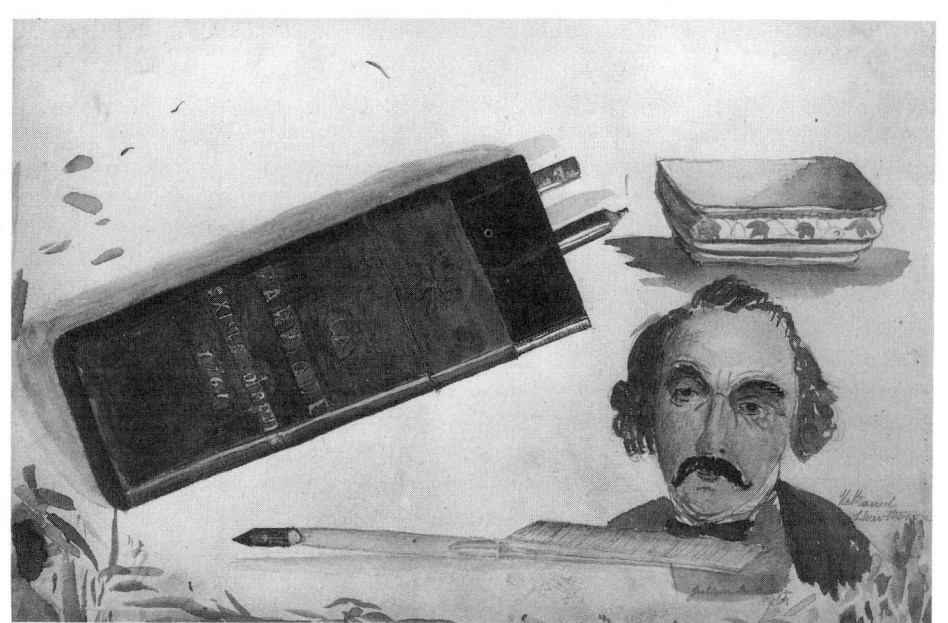

1859 sketch of Hawthorne, probably by his son, Julian, from a sketchbook in the collection of the Bancroft Library, University of California at Berkeley.

Group photograph by Philip Henry Delamotte, taken in the garden of R. H. Spiers, Oxford, England, September 4, 1856. Left to right: Sophia Hawthorne, Mrs. Spiers, R. Phené Spiers, Fanny Hall, Mr. Addison, Mr. Spiers(?), Mrs. S. C. Hall, Mr. S. C. Hall(?), and Hawthorne.

The Wayside, Concord, Massachusetts. Hawthorne and Sophia are
standing in the foreground.

The "Brady" photograph, probably taken by
Alexander Gardner in the Brady studio,
Washington, D.C., 1862.

wrote anything better than 'The Scarlet Letter,' but I cannot help believing it a great triumph that you should have been able to deepen and widen the impression made by such a book as that. It seems to me that the 'House' is the most valuable contribution to New England history that has been made." Hawthorne also boasted, in a letter to Louisa, that Fanny Kemble — then in London — had written him that pirated editions of both his romances were producing "a greater sensation than any book since 'Jane Eyre.'"

Despite his usual summer doldrums and the presence of family visitors, Hawthorne managed to comply with Fields's stepped-up publication program. He completed a new series of children's stories, *A Wonder-Book*, in a concentrated period of writing between early June and mid July. He also began gathering his more recent stories for a new collected edition. Sending the final manuscript pages of *A Wonder-Book* to Fields on July 15, he heaved a sigh of relief: "I am going to begin to enjoy the summer now and to read foolish novels, if I can get any, and smoke cigars and think of nothing at all — which is equivalent to thinking of all manner of things."

ᘓ IV ᘏ

Throughout the spring and summer, Herman Melville, busily revising his story of the white whale, pursued his acquaintance with the Hawthornes. In her terse diary entries, Sophia recorded his random visits. On March 12, she reported, "At dusk, arrived Herman Melville from Pittsfield. He was entertained with Champagne foam — manufactured of beaten eggs, loaf sugar and champagne — bread and butter and cheese. He invited us all to go and spend tomorrow at his house. My husband concluded to go with Una." On the following day, in the midst of a snowstorm, Hawthorne and Una drove off to Arrowhead for a two-day visit. Hawthorne made no further entries in his journal, but while at Arrowhead he penned a brief note to Duyckinck: "I write to you from the house of our friend Herman Melville, and have only to glance my eye aside to obtain a fine snow-covered prospect of Graylock." Before leaving, he presented Melville with a gift, a four-volume narrative of shipwrecks and maritime disasters, *The Mariner's Chronicle*, which had been given to him by his uncle years before.

Sophia noted another visit on April 11. It had been a busy day, with a visit from John O'Sullivan, who stayed for supper. "Mr. Melville came and brought bedstead and clock," she reported. The extra bed may have been borrowed in anticipation of her father's coming visit. That evening, Hawthorne gave Melville a copy of *The House of the Seven Gables*, inscribing it simply "Herman Melville, from Nath'l

Hawthorne." Perhaps from some instinctive sense of the occasion, Sophia added the date in her own hand: "April 11th, 1851, Friday evening."

She was evidently on familiar enough terms with Melville to ask if he would look in the Pittsfield shops for a pair of shoes for Julian. Melville, writing to Hawthorne a few days later, reported that his "metropolitan pride" had been wounded by his failure to find any suitable shoes. He asked if Sophia would be satisfied with "a pair of *bootees.*" The chief business of his letter, however, was a private review of Hawthorne's book:

> "The House of the Seven Gables: A Romance. By Nathaniel Hawthorne. One volume, 16.mo.p.p.,344." The contents of this book do not belie its rich, clustering, romantic title. With great enjoyment we spent almost an hour in each separate gable . . . It has delighted us; it has piqued a re-perusal; it has robbed us of a day, and made us a present of a whole year of thoughtfulness; it has bred great exhilaration and exultation with the remembrance that the architect of the Gables resides only six miles off, and not three thousand miles away, in England, say. We think the book, for pleasantness of running interest, surpasses the other works of the author. The curtains are more drawn; the sun comes in more; genialities peep out more.

Melville, then designating the scene of Clifford's near-leap into the passing parade and the episode of Pyncheon's death as among the "deeper passages" of the book, went on to give a more serious assessment:

> There is a certain tragic phase of humanity which, in our opinion, was never more powerfully embodied than by Hawthorne. We mean the tragicalness of human thought in its own unbiassed, native, and profounder workings. We think that into no recorded mind has the intense feeling of the visible truth ever entered more deeply than into this man's. By visible truth we mean the apprehension of the absolute condition of present things as they strike the eye of the man who fears them not, though they do their worst to him . . .
>
> There is the grand truth about Nathaniel Hawthorne. He says NO! in thunder; but the devil himself cannot make him say *yes.* For all men who say *yes,* lie; and all men who say *no* — why, they are in the happy condition of judicious, unincumbered travellers in Europe; they cross the frontiers into Eternity with nothing but a carpetbag — that is to say, the *Ego.* Whereas those *yes*-gentry, they travel with heaps of baggage, and, damn them! they will never get through the Custom House. What's the reason, Mr. Hawthorne, that

in the last stages of metaphysics a fellow always falls to *swearing* so? I could rip an hour.

Clearly, in Melville's mind, he and Hawthorne had established the companionship of two nay-sayers among the niggling, business-minded "yes-gentry" of the period. In Hawthorne, Melville had found the ideal companion — father, brother, inspired mentor, intelligent audience. He was eager to make the most of the advantage. "Walk down one of these mornings and see me," he added. "No nonsense, come."

How much Hawthorne's understanding and attention meant to Melville, at this phase of his career, is evident in his letters, extravagant, given to easy hyperbole, full of self-mockery and self-justification. They are the letters of a man who has found release but who still feels it necessary to explain himself.

Early in June 1851, Melville reported on the progress of his book. As usual, in his letters (to Hawthorne and to others), he began in a vein of rough camaraderie:

> My dear Hawthorne, I should have been rumblng down to you in my pine-board chariot a long time ago, were it not that for some weeks past I have been more busy than you can well imagine — out of doors — building and patching and tinkering away in all directions. Besides, I had my crops to get in . . . I work myself; and at night my bodily sensations are akin to those I have so often felt before, when a hired man, doing my day's work from sun to sun . . . I am told, my fellow-man, that there is an aristocracy of the brain. Some men have boldly advocated and asserted it. Schiller seems to have done so, though I don't know much about him . . .

It was typical of Melville that, though he was attempting to establish the bond of initimacy between Hawthorne and himself in that "aristocracy of the intellect," he also felt the need to undermine his effort. In the next breath, he asserted that Hawthorne, recognizing his "ruthless democracy," would no doubt feel a need to recoil. "It is but nature to be shy of a mortal who boldly declares that a thief in jail is as honorable a personage as Gen. George Washington. This is ludicrous. But Truth is the silliest thing under the sun. Try to get a living by the Truth — and go to the Soup Societies."

He had, he acknowledged, come to an impasse with his book, part of which was in the hands of a New York printer. He was planning to go to New York in a week or so and there bury himself in a third-floor room, where he could make a concentrated effort on his "whale" as it went through the press. *"That* is the only way I can finish it now — I am so pulled hither and thither by circumstances." In a moment of self-pity, he noted, "The calm, the coolness, the silent grass-growing mood in which a man *ought* always to compose — that, I fear, can seldom be mine." It was an astonishing metaphor and one that he must have known intuitively Hawthorne would appreciate — the image of the slow and imperceptible growth of creation. Hawthorne had used similar terms in speaking of the art of writing. (Though in moments of darker imagination, Hawthorne would also write of blasted spots of earth where grass would not grow.)

"Dollars damn me . . ." Melville complained. "What I feel most moved to write, that is banned — it will not pay. Yet, altogether, write the *other* way I cannot. So the product is a final hash, and all my books are botches." It was a rainy morning, he acknowledged, and therefore he was writing "a little bluely." He also became increasingly personal. "I talk all about myself, and this is selfishness and egotism," he noted. "Granted. But how help it? I am writing to you; I know little about you, but something about myself. So I write about myself — at least, to you." It was clearly an invitation for Hawthorne to respond in like manner, but Melville quite probably understood that Hawthorne's essential reserve would never melt to the point of intimacy. He seems to have pulled back, worried that he had gone too far. "Don't trouble yourself, though, about writing," he said straightaway, "and don't trouble yourself about visiting; and when you *do* visit; don't trouble yourself about talking. I will do all the writing and visiting and talking myself."

He had recently been reading Hawthorne's story "The Unpardonable Sin" and suggested that Hawthorne's somber tale must have given the timid American readership "many a shake and tremor." He wrote, "It is a frightful poetical creed that the cultivation of the brain eats out the heart . . . I stand for the heart. To the dogs with the head!"

He then launched into a cogent and droll religious discussion: "The reason the mass of men fear God, and *at bottom dislike* Him, is because they rather distrust His heart, and fancy Him all brain like a watch. (You perceive I employ a capital initial in the pronoun referring to the Deity: don't you think there is a slight dash of flunkeyism in that usage?)" In his tenuous relations with the Almighty, Melville was never a mere genuflecting suitor or servant.

At the close of his long letter, Melville reverted once again to his grass-growing metaphor. He had been reading Goethe and had come across the German sage's admonition *"Live in the all."* Such transcendental exhortations aroused Melville's suspicions, and he attempted to both explain the phrase and explain it away. "That is to say," he informed Hawthorne, "your separate identity is but a wretched one — good; but get out of yourself, spread and expand yourself, and bring to yourself the tinglings of life that are felt in the flowers and the woods, that are felt in the planets Saturn and Venus and the Fixed Stars." Still, it was nonsense, Melville exclaimed, to tell someone with a raging toothache to go and live in the all. "As with all great genius," Melville confessed, "there is an immense deal of flummery in Goethe, and in proportion to my own contact with him, a monstrous deal of it in me.

"P.S. 'Amen!' saith Hawthorne," Melville added in a self-deprecating postscript.

But he could not quite let go of the subject; he nagged at Hawthorne for a bit of corroboration. "This 'all' feeling, though, there is some truth in," he asserted. "You must often have felt it, lying on the grass on a warm summer's day. Your legs seem to send out shoots into the earth. Your hair feels like leaves upon your head. This is the *all* feeling."

———

Throughout the summer, Melville's letters to Hawthorne became increasingly confidential and increasingly laced with references to and borrowed phrases from his novel in progress, as if the book and his association with Hawthorne were intimately connected. At the end of June, just back from the "babylonish brick-kiln of New York," where he had been unable to finish his book, he threatened to pay a visit to Lenox. "Have ready a bottle of brandy," he told Hawthorne, "because I always feel like drinking that heroic drink when we talk ontological heroics together." He asked, "Shall I send you a fin of the *Whale* by way of a specimen mouthful? The tail is not yet cooked — though the hell-fire in which the whole book is broiled might not unreasonably have cooked it all ere this." Was it merely coincidence that Hawthorne, writing to Horatio Bridge, had called *The Scarlet Letter* a "positively hell-fired story"? Or had he also made the same remark to Melville? Melville insisted on the infernal connection. He told Hawthorne: "This is the book's motto (the secret one) — *Ego non baptiso te in nomine* — but make out the rest yourself." The blessing that Captain Ahab pronounces over the harpoon, baptized with the blood of the pagan harpooners, is not in the name of the Father but of the devil — *sed in nomine Diaboli*. Hawthorne, who had his own diabolical associations with the art of writing, was sure to understand the allusion.

In mid July, Melville wrote Hawthorne "not a letter, or even a note — but only a passing word said to you over your garden gate."

It was a response to a letter from Hawthorne, an "easy-flowing, long letter," now lost. Melville reported that he had been busy with haying and other chores, but promised, "I shall roll down to you, my good fellow, seeing we — that is, you and I — must hit upon some little bit of vagabondism before Autumn comes. Graylock — we must go and vagabondize there. But ere we start, we must dig a deep hole and bury all the Blue Devils, there to abide till the Last Day." He signed off with a "Goodbye," but in place of a signature he marked an X.

The X was the mark that Queequeg, the tattooed savage prince and harpooner, made when, out of affection and trust for his new-found friend, Ishmael, he signed aboard the ill-fated *Pequod*. Melville's couple — the savage and the common sailor — have enjoyed a tender and comic "honeymoon" in a New Bedford boardinghouse. Sharing the same bed, Ishmael wakes to find himself locked in Queequeg's "bridegroom clasp." In the privacy of their room, the two indulge in warm comradeship and intimate conversation. "How it is I know not," Ishmael explains, "but there is no place like a bed for confidential disclosures between friends. Man and wife, they say, there open the very bottom of their souls to each other; and some old couples often lie and chat over old times till nearly morning. Thus, then, in our hearts' honeymoon, lay I and Queequeg — a cosy, loving pair."

Oddly, in *Moby-Dick*, Melville put himself into the role of his narrator, Ishmael. But in his half-bantering, half-pleading letters to Hawthorne, he cast himself as the other member of his "cosy, loving pair" — as Queequeg, the exemplary and affectionate savage.

Hawthorne's response to Melville's overtures was measured and restrained. Fastidious, slow to open up, he was evidently cordial but cautious about the relationship. In his newly completed *A Wonder-Book*, discussing the various literary lights of the Berkshire region, Hawthorne made a passing reference to his new admirer. "On the hither side of Pittsfield," his narrator, Eustace Bright, remarks, "sits Herman Melville, shaping out the gigantic conception of his 'White Whale' while the gigantic shape of Graylock looms upon him from his study-window." It was a friendly puff for Melville's forthcoming book. In his letters to others, Hawthorne spoke well of his neighbor and fellow writer. Writing to George William Curtis, praising Curtis' travel book, *Nile Notes of a Howadji*, Hawthorne commented, "Herman Melville (whom you praise in your book) lives about six miles off, and is an admirable fellow, and has some excellent old port and sherry wine." In writing to Evert Duyckinck, he mentioned that he might make a trip to New York: "Melville and I talk of making an excursion thither, at some indefinite period; but I must first go to Boston and Salem." The proposed trip never took place, but Hawthorne must have thought of his Pittsfield neighbor as an agreeable traveling companion.

In his letter to Duyckinck, Hawthorne seemed much more animated about his mounting dissatisfaction with his rural retreat. "I have nearly come to the conclusion," he told Duyckinck, "that summer is the worst time to be in the country, it being impossible to ramble about in the hot sun." Rather queerly, he argued that in the city, at least, there was always a shady side of the street and awnings on the sunny side — "not to speak of iced creams and all kinds of iced liquors, which are greatly preferable to the lukewarm basin of a brook, with its tadpoles and insects mingling in your draught." There was a perverse side to Hawthorne's nature that he liked to exercise on occasion for comic effect.

Ever since the birth of Rose, Sophia had been planning, as soon as the infant was old enough, to make a family visit. Mother and Father Peabody were living in West Newton, not far from the Horace Manns. Late in July, Lizzie Peabody stopped in Lenox to accompany Sophia on the trip east. On July 28, the day that Sophia, Una, baby Rose, and Lizzie left the Red Shanty, Hawthorne started a diary. He was to title it, wistfully, "Twenty Days with Julian & Little Bunny. By Papa." The bunny was Julian's pet rabbit, variously named Spring and Hindlegs. In the beginning, Hawthorne felt a special animosity toward the creature, which was allowed to run free through the downstairs rooms. "I am strongly tempted of the Evil One to murder him privately," he confessed on the very first day. In time, he rather warmed to "Bunny." It was a brief affection; the poor animal, passed back and forth between Julian and the neighboring Tappan children, alternately squeezed and neglected, died of a shivering fit and was duly buried in the garden. Julian, who attributed all misfortunes to the Giant Despair, was convinced that the giant was responsible for Bunny's death and declared the act "more wickeder" than anything the giant had yet done, including the making of "cow-mud," a rural hazard that Julian frequently encountered in the roads and pastures of Lenox.

As usual during his periods of enforced bachelorhood, Hawthorne was quick to complain in his journal. The weather turned "chill and sulky"; he immediately came down with a cold. There was a series of unexpected visits by unwanted guests. Hawthorne, without a wife, grudgingly entertained them — or at least gave the impression in his journal that his efforts had been grudging. There were two boring encounters with G. P. R. James; on the first, the English novelist insisted on talking about *The House of the Seven Gables* to the author's face; on the second, James, out with his family for a drive that was interrupted by a violent thunderstorm, had stopped at the little farmhouse for shelter, Hawthorne had been hard pressed to entertain such an invasion, which included James's wife, his three children, and a maidservant. (He was glad that Mrs. James was so terrified of the thunder and lightning that it kept her preoccupied throughout the visit.) On another day, a young Quaker woman, Elizabeth Lloyd, appeared at his doorstep, wanting to meet the celebrated author. That encounter had not gone badly, though Julian had clambered over his father's knees "like a great, awkward, overgrown baby." Miss Lloyd had sensibly and comfortably confined her admiration to one or two discreet compliments, and the remainder of their talk turned to such literary figures as G. P. R. James and Herman Melville and her particular friend, John Greenleaf Whittier.

His stint as full-time baby-sitter and companion for his son was not a period of unalloyed pleasure. Julian, during one of their early walks, had been promptly stung by a wasp, which caused his leg to swell badly. There was, too, a bed-wetting accident. And from the moment of his mother's departure, the child had started a constant babble of talk and questioning that his father found annoying. But for Sophia's benefit, Hawthorne recorded much of it. He had hoped to do some reading, stretched out under an apple tree, having borrowed *Pendennis* from the Tappans. But unfortunately, Julian, astride one of the boughs above him, began a long, rambling monologue about how he proposed to live in a tree forever, making a nest for himself; how he next intended to become a bird and fly to West Newton to bring his mother back; how he would also fly to the post office to pick up the mail. It was more than "mortal father ought to be expected to endure," Hawthorne wrote reproachfully. "He does put me almost beside my propriety: never quitting me, and continually thrusting his word between every sentence of all my reading, and smashing every attempt at reflection into a thousand fragments." It was only after Julian was put to bed in the evening that he had peace.

It was another index of his irritation that his complaints about the Berkshire weather were so vehement: "This is a horrible, horrible, most hor-r-ible climate; one knows not, for ten minutes together, whether he is too cool or too warm; but he is always one or the other . . . I detest it! I detest it!! I detest it!!! I hate Berkshire with my whole soul, and would joyfully see its mountains laid flat."

What he longed for was a breath of salt sea air. He wrote his old

Salem friend William Pike to look for a suitable house — without too much land — though not in Salem itself. "I hope Providence has no intention of ever requiring me to live within its limits again," he stated. Pike had suggested a house at Marblehead Neck, but Hawthorne had some curious — though characteristic — objections. In the winter, he felt, it would be a "very bleak and dreary abode." Chiefly it was a question of neighbors — and the lack of them — that troubled him. "The society in summer would not be very eligible for people of our means and habits — consisting, as it would, entirely of Boston aristocrats and capitalists; so that three fourths of the year, we should be in total solitude, and the remaining fourth, should be bothered with all the nonsense of fashionable life." Hawthorne's views about the sins of capitalist wealth handed down from one generation to another, expressed in *The House of the Seven Gables*, were more than literary speculations. They were drawn from his own convictions about growing trends in American society. His letter may also indicate that living in cramped quarters, too close to the far wealthier Tappans, had become a trying situation.

Yet at the same time that he was pressing Pike to look for a house on the coast, he told a neighbor, Charles Sedgwick, of his plans to rent Fanny Kemble's nearby farmhouse in the fall. He was also writing to James Fields that he was, unhappily, resigned to staying in Lenox. "To tell you a secret," he wrote Fields, "I am sick to death of Berkshire, and hate to think of spending another winter here. But I must. The air and climate do not agree with my health at all; and for the first time since I was a boy, I have felt languid and dispirited, during almost my whole residence here. Oh that Providence would build me the merest little shanty, and mark me out a rood or two of garden-ground near the sea-coast."

Under the circumstances, Hawthorne must have welcomed Herman Melville's random visits during Sophia's absence. One afternoon, returning with Julian from his routine walk to the village post office, Hawthorne sat down in a wooded area called Love Grove to read his newspapers. Melville, riding past on horseback, saluted him in Spanish. It was only after the second greeting that Hawthorne looked up and identified the "cavalier." With Julian put in the saddle, the two men had walked and talked their way to the red farmhouse. Melville was invited to tea and stayed through supper — and beyond. It was August 1, Melville's thirty-second birthday. According to Hawthorne's account, he and Melville had sat up late, talking "about time and eternity, things of this world and of the next, and books and publishers and all possible matters." Purely for Sophia, Hawthorne added, "And if truth must be known, we smoked cigars even within the sacred precincts of the sitting-room." In the course of his visit, Melville mentioned that the Duyckinck brothers, Evert and George, would be arriving in the Berkshires; both Hawthorne and Julian were cordially invited to spend a night at Arrowhead.

Around noon on August 8, Melville and the two brothers drove up to the little farmhouse in a barouche and pair. It was a cause of some consternation to Hawthorne, who would have preferred to give his guests dinner but found to his embarrassment that there was nothing in the house to offer them. He did, however, break out the last bottle of Mansfield's champagne. Fortunately, Melville had packed a supply of sandwiches and gingerbread, and a picnic was proposed. The little group drove off to lunch under the trees along the road, where they talked of literature and puffed on cigars. Next, it was suggested that they pay an afternoon visit to the Shaker settlement near Hancock, three miles away.

Melville may have proposed the excursion; he had a deep curiosity about the sect. Hawthorne's interest in the Shakers was long-standing, but over the years he had grown markedly colder in his evaluation of the sect. He had first encountered them at the Canterbury, New Hampshire, settlement that he visited with his Uncle Sam in 1831. Then he had even jokingly suggested that he might join the celibate religious group. During his Concord stay, he had made an excursion with Emerson to the nearby Harvard community, a visit that had been so lacking in incident, he had scarcely commented on it in his notebook.

Hawthorne's tour of the Hancock settlement, however, produced a violent reaction. Touring the large brick residence with its polished wood floors and its plastered walls as smooth as marble, Hawthorne found everything so neat, "it was a pain and constraint to look at it; especially as it did not imply any real delicacy or moral purity in the occupants of the house." He was dismayed to see that men and women shared only the meagerest of washing facilities — a sink and wash basin, for both sexes, in the entry room that separated the men's and women's apartments. Visiting the men's dormitories, he was shocked to discover that the narrow cots, barely large enough for one person, were, in fact, used by two men. Whether this revived distasteful memories of having to sleep with his Uncle Robert is not clear, but Hawthorne's response was blunt. "The fact shows that all their miserable pretense of cleanliness and neatness is the thinnest superficiality," he argued in his notebook, "and that the Shakers are and must needs be a filthy set." The tirade mounted in intensity. "And their utter and systematic lack of privacy," he went on, "their close conjunction of man with man, and supervision of one man over another — it is hateful and disgusting to think of; and the sooner the sect is extinct, the better — a consummation which, I am happy to hear, is thought to be not a great many years distant."

His judgment of the Hancock Shakers was unusually harsh. It is one of the rare outbursts of spleen in his notebooks. Part of it may have been psychological; Hawthorne seems to have had a distinct aversion to physical contact. ("He hates to be touched more than anyone I ever knew," Sophia recalled on one occasion.) But there could have been other causes. Beneath the ordered surface of the community life, he may have sensed an actual lowering of morale and a decline in standards. For several years the Hancock community had been split by theological disputes, and there had been a gradual erosion of the population, particularly among the male members. It is also possible that Hawthorne's own celibacy at the moment contributed to his irritation with the Shaker's celibate style of living. As the little troop of male visitors made its way through the neat workshops and trim grounds, Hawthorne noticed that the women and young girls, supposedly intent on their work, were slyly looking them over. What distressed him particularly about the community was that none of the men had "a jolly aspect" and all the women looked pale and unhealthy. "They are certainly the most singular and bedevilled set of people that ever existed in a civilized land," he confided to his journal, "and one of these days, when their sect and system shall have passed away, a History of the Shakers will be a very curious book."

Hawthorne's distaste for the Shaker way of life may also have reflected his own hardening and negative views about communal experiments. He was turning over in his mind the subject of a new romance and had borrowed several volumes of Fourier from Caroline Tappan. His next novel, though intended to be a purely fictional account, would be based on his personal experience at Brook Farm. It was to form a "very curious book" in the canon of his own writings.

Shortly after Sophia's return to Lenox, Hawthorne found himself in the middle of a disagreement with his landlords, the Tappans. Having paid a modest rental for the little Red Shanty, Hawthorne was convinced — partly from his experience at the Old Manse — that the produce of the apple orchard on the property was his. Caroline Tappan, however — at least in the second year of their residence — decided otherwise, and in a highhanded fashion chose to make an issue of it. Highwood was within sight of the cottage, and when Caroline spied the Hawthornes' maidservant carrying a basket of apples, she had questioned the girl sharply about how she had come by them. She had followed this up with a note to Sophia.

There was a certain opportunistic side to Hawthorne where money matters were concerned, and although he had paid little for the rental of the cottage, he saw no reason to give up any economic advantage to be had from the orchard. Moreover, in his anticapitalistic mood, he perhaps felt a certain resentment at being the recipient of any implied charity from the more affluent Tappans. The little affair of the apple orchard brought out his haughtiest manner, though in writing to Caroline Tappan he was civilized but firm. Since "questions of disputed boundary" were ticklish affairs, he wrote his landlady on September 5, he took it on himself to handle the "diplomatic correspondence." "In the first place, permit me to notice the question which you put to Sophia, whether she would not prefer to receive kindness rather than assume rights. I do not know what would be her reply; but for myself in view of the infirmities of human nature in general . . . I infinitely prefer a small right to a great favor." It was for this reason he had insisted on paying his rental; the "little difficulty" they now found themselves in only confirmed him in his judgment. He insisted on his orchard rights. "What is a garden without its currant bushes and fruit trees?" he asked. "Last year no question of this nature was raised; our right seemed to be tacitly conceded, and if you claimed or exercised any manorial privileges, it never came to my knowledge."

If the manner of his letter was courtly, Hawthorne's irritation must have been plainly evident to Caroline Tappan and her husband. He made it clear in his dramatization of the affair with the servant-girl, Mary Beekman. "You stop her," Hawthorne stated in his account, "look at the contents of her basket, and inquire as to its destination . . . You conduct this examination in such a mode, as to make it evident to our servant-girl that you consider Sophia and Mrs. Peters [the Hawthornes' black cook] as combining in a depredation on your property." However, he was circumspect enough not to push the affair to an irreconcilable break. In time, the little dispute over the garden rights was settled by generous letters between the two husbands, although Caroline remained "at war," according to Sophia. The question still hung fire in mid September, when Hawthorne finally made his journey to Salem. It seems to have prompted him to take action about moving from the Berkshires.

Hawthorne had been unable to stop over in Boston as he had planned. President Millard Fillmore, who had only the year before succeeded to the office on the death of Zachary Taylor, was making an official visit to Boston. The influx of tourists and visitors was so great that there were no rooms to be had. Hawthorne had therefore stopped off in West Newton to stay with Horace Mann's family. Mann, who had recently been elected to Congress as a member of the Free-Soil Party, was planning to take his family to Washington for the coming congressional session. On September 19, Hawthorne wrote Sophia, "Talking with Mary last night, I explained our troubles to her, and our wish to get away from Lenox, and she renewed the old proposition about our taking this house for the winter." Hawthorne welcomed the suggestion. With the bluntness that characterized his attitude to his in-laws, he explained to Sophia, "The great objection to it, when first talked of, was that we, or I, did not wish to have the care and responsibility of your father and mother." Since Mr. and Mrs. Peabody were living elsewhere in West Newton, there no longer seemed to be any obstacle. Renting the Manns' house for the winter struck him as "one of those unexpected, but easy and natural solutions" to their problem.

Late in October, Ellery Channing, who had roomed with William Tappan in New York during his *Tribune* days, paid an extended visit to Lenox. In his calls on the various households — the Sedgwicks', the Tappans', and the Hawthornes' — he sensed that Hawthorne's dispute with Caroline and her husband had somewhat clouded the air. Writing to Ellen (asking her to burn his letter), Channing gave a caustic picture of the Hawthorne ménage. Berkshire society, he informed her on October 30, was critical.

> Hawthorne has perceived it. His ways not the ways of the world have attracted the attention of the people; his habit of not calling on people, & his having written some books have made him a lion. I do not know that he has felt this, but I think he has felt his lack of society. I do not know that he is absolutely discontented but he seems rather dry & out of spirits . . . He thinks a good deal of coming to Concord, and possibly to buy a place. Such a plan I would not encourage. Assuredly he would get tired of his purchase & then he would be obliged all his days to think of selling or again go to work moving. He always I believe finds fault with the people among whom he settles not at the best a good beginning to make.

His observations about Sophia and the children were even more pointed:

> I should think Sophia could not realize his ideal at all. She is by no means prepossessing and has not added to her beauty by time. And she has none of the means whereby elegance & refinement may be shed over the humblest apartment. Her children brought up in the worst way for visitors, by themselves, & never having been to school, have of course nothing but bad manners. They break in when not required, & are not in fact either handsome or attractive.

> But how could the parents help this. I have formed a very different
> opinion of the H's this visit from any I ever had before, and H. has
> greatly altered.

Channing's acerb little picture of the Hawthorne household had its
accuracies, but it was also colored by his mood and his notorious
distaste for children — other people's no less than his own. But he
had clearly understood that for the Hawthornes life in Lenox had
turned disagreeable.

In mid November, Melville's masterpiece, *Moby-Dick*, was published
by Harper & Brothers, in New York. With characteristic generosity,
Melville had made a grand gesture in his dedication: "In token of
my admiration for his genius, this book is inscribed to Nathaniel
Hawthorne." Hawthorne wrote Melville an obviously grateful and
enthusiastic letter in response, but it is impossible to determine the
degree of his praise, since his letter was lost or destroyed. In a later
letter to Evert Duyckinck, however, there is some inkling of Hawthorne's high estimation: "What a book Melville has written! It
gives me an idea of much greater power than his preceding ones. It
hardly seemed to me that the reviewer of it, in the *Literary World*,
did justice to its best points."

To a certain extent, one can gauge Hawthorne's appraisal by the
terms of Melville's response, written in mid November. It was one of
Melville's lengthiest and most affectionate — if not adoring — letters. He wrote:

> My Dear Hawthorne, People think that if a man has undergone any
> hardship, he should have a reward; but for my part, if I have done
> the hardest possible day's work, and then come to sit down in a
> corner and eat my supper comfortably — why, then I don't think I
> deserve any reward for my hard day's work . . . So your joy-giving
> and exultation-breeding letter is not my reward for my ditcher's
> work with that book, but is the good goddess's bonus over and
> above what was stipulated for . . . I say your appreciation is my
> glorious gratuity. In my proud, humble way — a shepherd-king — I
> was lord of a little vale in the solitary Crimea; but you have now
> given me the crown of India.

He had received the letter the night before on the road to a neighbor's house and had read it there: "Had I been at home, I would
have sat down at once and answered it. In me divine magnanimities
are spontaneous and instantaneous — catch them while you can.
The world goes round, and the other side comes up. So now I can't

write what I felt." Nevertheless, he managed to recapture his feelings well enough to write one of the most extraordinarily intimate letters one author ever sent another. He claimed an intimacy, however, that Hawthorne, in his reticent manner, could not fully appreciate.

> But I felt pantheistic then [Melville wrote] — your heart beat in my ribs and mine in yours, and both in God's. A sense of unspeakable security is in me this moment, on account of your having understood the book. I have written a wicked book, and feel spotless as a lamb. Ineffable socialities are in me. I would sit down and dine with you and all the gods in old Rome's Pantheon. It is a strange feeling — no hopefulness is in it, no despair. Content — that is it; and irresponsibility; but without licentious inclination. I speak now of my profoundest sense of being, not of an incidental feeling.
>
> Whence come you Hawthorne? By what right do you drink from my flagon of life? And when I put it to my lips — lo, they are yours not mine. I feel that the Godhead is broken up like the bread at the Supper, and that we are the pieces. Hence this infinite fraternity of feeling.

Characteristically, Melville now pulled back. "You did not care a penny for the book," he charged. "But, now and then as you read, you understood the pervading thought that impelled the book — and that you praised. Was it not so? You were archangel enough to despise the imperfect body, and embrace the soul. Once you hugged the ugly Socrates because you saw the flame in the mouth, and heard the rushing of the demon — the familiar — and recognized the sound; for you have heard it in your own solitudes."

Each rush of feeling was accompanied by a dialectical caution: "My dear Hawthorne," he wrote, "the atmospheric skepticisms steal into me now, and make me doubtful of my sanity in writing you thus." Still, Melville couldn't resist another extravagant compliment: "Lord, when shall we be done changing? Ah! it's a long stage, and no inn in sight, and night coming, and the body cold. But with you for a passenger, I am content and can be happy. I shall leave the world, I feel, with more satisfaction for having come to know you. Knowing you persuades me more than the Bible of our immortality."

Then, another retrenchment. Melville apologized: "What a pity, that for your plain, bluff letter, you should get such gibberish!" He signed the letter hastily, but, unable to close, added a lengthy postscript. "The divine magnet is on you, and my magnet responds," he told Hawthorne. "Which is the biggest? A foolish question — they are *One*."

"Don't think that by writing me a letter," he added in a further postscript, "you shall always be bored with an immediate reply to it — and so keep both of us delving over a writing-desk eternally. No such thing! I sh'n't always answer your letters, and you may do just as you please."

—————

On a slate-gray day, in late November, the Hawthornes left Lenox for West Newton. Their trunks and belongings had been piled into an old farm wagon, and they took the gloomy road over frozen ground to the Pittsfield station. The snow had begun to fall as they left, increasing in intensity, turning into dismal sleet.

All that Julian Hawthorne remembered of their departure was the sad sight of the household cats, now abandoned, watching as the wagon lumbered down the road. That, and the pleasure of riding in the last car of the train and seeing the tracks converge behind them.

Part Four

*Given from under my Hand and Seal of Office at Liverpool,
the 13ᵗʰ day of March
and year one thousand eight hundred and fifty- five*

Nath¹ Hawthorne

The Metal Hardens

THE BLUSTERY SNOWSTORM that figures prominently in the early pages of *The Blithedale Romance* is not the dreary one that accompanied the family move from Lenox to West Newton. But, like many circumstances in the novel, it was derived from Hawthorne's personal experience. The unseasonable April snowfall that dampens the spirits of Miles Coverdale as he journeys to Blithedale is the same disagreeable storm Hawthorne had faced, on an April day in 1841, when he moved to Brook Farm from his bachelor quarters in Boston. As a writer, he was drawing more heavily on the personal present than on a misty, historical past.

He had been ruminating about the new book for months. It was at Lenox, for instance, that he had determined on the subject; he also seems to have decided to give his fictional narrative a solid grounding in fact. On July 24, he had written William Pike, "When I write another romance, I shall take the Community for a subject, and shall give some of my experiences and observations at Brook Farm." But it was not until after his move to West Newton that he began work on *The Blithedale Romance*. On November 23, two days after settling into the Mann house, Hawthorne wrote to John Sullivan Dwight, the former Brook Farmer, who had asked for a contribution to *Sartain's Union Magazine*, which he was editing. Hawthorne offered him the only piece he had on hand, "Feathertop," a long short story, written during his final days at Lenox. He asked a steep price for it — $100 — and commented that he would not be able to send anything else since he was about to "engage in a longer work."

Another fictional circumstance in *The Blithedale Romance* indicates Hawthorne's reliance on personal experience. When Miles Coverdale arrives at his polar utopia, he comes down with a cold that keeps him in bed for several days. Hawthorne had had just such an experience after his arrival at Brook Farm. With the economy and taut construction that characterizes *The Blithedale Romance*, Hawthorne used that slight autobiographical incident as a device for establishing differences of character in two of his principals, both of whom nurse his narrator-hero back to health: Zenobia, the most exotic of Hawthorne's female characters, and Hollingsworth, the fanatical reformer.

Still, it must have struck Hawthorne with the force of déjà vu that no sooner had he begun writing about the affairs of Miles Coverdale than he became ill himself — with influenza. Virtually the whole family was stricken. On Christmas Day, Sophia wrote to Louisa Hawthorne, complaining that their new quarters had been "a perfect hospital" for days. She and Una were the most seriously affected; Hawthorne, Julian, and the cook slightly less so. Louisa had been planning a visit to West Newton, but with her usual dithering and delays, she had written to say she would not be able to come until mid January. Sophia confessed that, under the circumstances, it was just as well.

The family's ill health may have been caused by domestic progress. The Mann house had a new coal furnace that regularly sent up blasts of dry heat through the hot-air registers. In his notebook, Hawthorne jotted down a wry suggestion for a story about a man "building a house and locating it over the pit of Acheron." It was in that almost-infernal atmosphere that Hawthorne completed *The Blithedale Romance*; it was to take him five months of steady writing.

Amid the other items of news that Sophia communicated to Louisa was the information that the popular feminist writer Grace Greenwood had paid them a visit of two or three days. It could hardly have been a pleasure for Hawthorne. Grace Greenwood, under her real name, Sara Jane Clarke, was a friend of Lizzie Peabody's; Hawthorne found her an affected young woman and a self-advertising writer. Sophia was also pleased to relay the information that her husband's books were as readily published in France as in England; James Fields, then in Paris, had written them to that effect. Fields had also met Robert Browning, who claimed that Hawthorne was "the finest genius that has appeared in English literature for many years."

In a postscript, Hawthorne added a sentence to inform Louisa that a new collection of his tales had just been published, "but you shall not have a copy till you come for it." Louisa would have had a special interest in *The Snow-Image, and Other Twice-told Tales*, published that month, since she had hunted down some of the old, previously uncollected, stories for the volume. With peremptory optimism, Sophia added a second postscript, noting that 1000 copies had already been sold and that Mr. Ticknor had informed them there were not enough bound copies to meet the demand.

The Snow-Image was not a substantial collection, although it included one or two of Hawthorne's early masterpieces, among them "My Kinsman, Major Molineux," and "The Wives of the Dead." Hawthorne, busy during the summer with writing *A Wonder-Book*, had not taken his usual editorial pains with the makeup of the collection; it consisted largely of leftover tales and sketches gathered by Louisa and James Fields. And despite the initial flurry of interest, it was not a popular success; Hawthorne realized only $172.50 in royalties from the first edition, and a second printing was not called for until a year later.

As with his earlier collections, Hawthorne wrote a preface — this one a tribute in the form of a personal letter to his old friend Horatio Bridge, acknowledging Bridge's encouragement of his literary career and recalling the long, faraway days when they had stood together on the banks of the Androscoggin, watching the great logs tumbling downstream, and the afternoons they had spent shooting pigeons and gray squirrels in the woods.

In more general terms, Hawthorne took note of critics who complained that his prefaces were too personal, too revealing of the author. His introductions, he responded, dealt only with the author's "external habits, his abode, his casual associates, and other matters entirely upon the surface," and hid more than they ever revealed. "You must make quite another kind of inquest," he cautioned, "and look through the whole range of [the author's] fictitious characters, good and evil, in order to detect any of his essential traits." It was both a boast and an invitation to the curious.

He also promised that this would be the last collection of "musty and mouse-nibbled leaves of old periodicals" that he would foist on his readers. He was clearly ambivalent about his earlier writings — too conscious of their faults and, at the same time, too aware that they came up to the standards of his most recent stories. "The ripened autumnal fruit tastes but little better than the early windfalls," he confessed. "It would, indeed, be mortifying to believe that the summertime of life has passed away, without any greater progress and improvement than is indicated here."

It was also clear that he was dissatisfied with the short story as a fictional form. When John Sartain, following up on Dwight's inquiry, wrote about "Feathertop" and the possibility of Hawthorne's becoming a regular contributor to his magazine, Hawthorne was openly discouraging. "These magazine stories," he told the pub-

lisher, "make a great draft upon an author's time and thoughts —
much greater, in proportion both to the bulk of the matter and the
compensation — than a long romance." He correctly judged that
Sartain would not want to pay the asking fee for "Feathertop" — "I
myself would not pay it, were I in the chair editorial," he said — but
he stuck to his price. (Sartain backed off, and Hawthorne sold it to
Rufus W. Griswold, then editor of the *International Monthly Magazine*, where it appeared in two installments in the February and
March 1852 numbers.) Commenting on his asking fee, Hawthorne
claimed point blank that he "would not write another for the same
price," and, in fact, "Feathertop," a "grotesque" story of an empty-
headed scarecrow that manages to pass itself off as a fine gentleman, a desirable suitor, and a public figure of sorts (at least until he
catches a demolishing glimpse of himself in a mirror), was the last
adult tale Hawthorne was to write.

As one of her last acts of the old year, Sophia, on December 29,
wrote Herman Melville a letter full of glowing praise for *Moby-Dick*.
Sophia's letter has not survived, but Melville's response, written
with the exaggerated courtesy he was apt to employ with the opposite sex, gives an indication of its content. Replying on January 8
and using his finest Bath stationery, "gilt-edged and stamped," Melville exclaimed, "It really amazed me that you should find any satisfaction in that book. It is true that some *men* have said they were
pleased with it, but you are the only *woman* — for as a general
thing, women have small taste for the sea." Sophia had evidently
commented upon some allegorical implications of the book. Melville
was inclined to attribute this to Sophia's own "spiritualizing nature," her ability to "see more things than other people, and by the
same process, refine all you see." He confessed, "At any rate, your
allusion for example to the 'Spirit Spout,' first showed to me that
there was a subtle significance in that thing — but I did not, in that
case, *mean* it. I had some vague idea while writing it, that the whole
book was susceptible of an allegoric construction, & also that *parts*
of it were — but the specialty of many of the particular subordinate
allegories, were revealed to me after reading Mr. Hawthorne's letter, which, without citing any particular examples, yet intimated the
part-&-parcel allegoricalness of the whole." There was, obviously, a
good deal of the tongue in cheek in Melville's disclaimer.

In his teasing vein, Melville asked, "And does Mr. Hawthorne continue his series of calls upon all his neighbors within a radius of ten
miles? Shall I send him ten packs of visiting cards? And a box of kid
gloves? and the latest style of Parisian handkerchief? — He goes

into society too much altogether — seven evenings out, a week, should content any reasonable man."

As Melville was well aware, Hawthorne was scarcely the socializing sort. Threatened with visits of family and friends — Louisa was expected to arrive shortly, and G. P. R. James — he was not inclined to socialize more than was necessary. He was also particularly eager to find a new home. Only a few weeks after arriving in West Newton, he wrote Ellery Channing about possibilities in Concord. Channing promptly invited him to pay a visit. "Nobody at home," he assured Hawthorne on December 13," and a prospect of strong waters. It is so damned near where you live that perhaps you would like to leave home." The implication of the latter remark, perhaps, was that Hawthorne, staying in the home of the teetotaling Horace Mann, might find it uncomfortable to indulge in drink. (Rather perversely, Hawthorne, writing in that temple of temperance, would include a lengthy eulogy to the pleasures of drinking in his new book, stating baldly, "The temperance-men may preach till doom's day; and still this cold and barren world will look warmer, kindlier, mellower through the medium of a toper's glass . . .")

Channing pointedly encouraged the visit: "I have got a good cook, and some wood, and you can have whole days, as I never dine before five." As an extra inducement he added, "Emerson is gone, and nobody here to bore you. The skating is damned good . . . Pipes and old tobac no end." When Hawthorne declined a few days later, Channing made a show of disappointment and mild irritation. "But as you are sweating Romances," he conceded, "and have got that execrable bore, a small family, it is all right. I am glad *now* you did not come. I was afraid you would be disappointed if you had." Channing was not optimistic about Hawthorne's resettling in Concord nor about his idea of buying Bronson Alcott's house, Hillside, which had come up for sale. "For my own part," Channing told Hawthorne, "I would infinitely rather settle on the icy peak of Mt. Ararat than in this village. It is absolutely the worst spot in the world. There are so many things against it, that it would be useless to enumerate the first. Among the others, day before yesterday, at six A.M., the thermometer was ten degrees below nothing." About Hillside, he added, "I have never lived in Alcott's place; but I judge the thermometer there goes as low as anywhere else in this country." Channing's discouraging letter had no marked effect on Hawthorne's decision. By the time he had finished his manuscript and written the preface, on May 1, he had bought the Alcott house and nine acres for $1500, and was preparing to move by the end of the month.

On May 2, 1852, Hawthorne sent the manuscript for *The Blithedale*

Romance to E. P. Whipple, whose opinion he wanted. "Behold, a huge bundle of scribble," he wrote, "which you have thoughtlessly promised to look over! If you find it beyond your powers, hand it over to Ticknor at once, and let him send it to the Devil . . . Nobody has yet read it, except my wife; and her sympathy, though very gratifying, is a little too unreserved to afford me the advantages of criticism." But he warned Whipple, "After all, should you spy ever so many defects, I cannot promise to amend them; the metal hardens very soon after I pour it out of my melting-pot into the mould."

On May 16, he wrote Louisa that his book was in press. By then, he had urgent reasons for wanting to make a swift move to Concord. "The whole family of Manns, great and little, have come home," he reported to his sister, "and you may readily conceive that we are anxious to get away." Considering that the subject of his new novel involved the troublesome breed of reformers, it may easily have crossed Hawthorne's mind that in fleeing the home of one zealous reformer, he was moving into the vacated nest of another.

ᵔᕤ II ᕤᵔ

In his preface to *The Blithedale Romance*, Hawthorne attempted to discount any overt connection between the events of his novel and his experiences at Brook Farm. He willingly admitted that his stay in the West Roxbury community was, "certainly, the most romantic episode" of his own life — "essentially a daydream, and yet a fact" — but he maintained that he had not patterned his narrative on his life there. Brook Farm merely provided his imaginary story with a convenient "foothold between fiction and reality." Nor, he claimed, did he intend his romance to "illustrate a theory, or elicit a conclusion, favorable or otherwise" with respect to experiments in socialism.

Mindful of his previous difficulties with the descendants of the Pyncheon family, Hawthorne made a careful effort to dissociate his fictional characters from real-life acquaintances. In a somewhat disingenuous passage, he claimed that his fictional characters had so few "amiable qualities" that it would be wrong to suppose their author intended them to refer to real persons: "Had he attempted it, they would at least have recognized the touches of a friendly pencil." In his suavest manner, he analyzed his four principals: "The self-concentrated Philanthropist; the high-spirited Woman, bruising herself against the narrow limitations of her sex; the weakly Maiden, whose tremulous nerves endow her with Sibylline attributes; the minor Poet, beginning life with strenuous aspirations, which die out with his youthful fervor — all these might have been looked for at Brook Farm, but, by some accident, never made their appearance there." That he should take such pains to distinguish the context of his novel from his private history indicates his awareness that he was treading dangerously close to the actual.

In his new novel, Hawthorne dispensed with much of the heavy machinery of allegory that had encumbered a good deal of his earlier fiction. And, despite the trafficking in spiritualism and séances, there are fewer Gothic devices — no ancestral portraits, no family curses — in *The Blithedale Romance*. It is of some interest, considering the intersecting careers of Melville and Hawthorne, that at the moment when Melville (with Hawthorne as exemplar) was becoming openly allegorical, Hawthorne should have been pursuing the fictional possibilities of the actual.

The Blithedale Romance is a novel of disclosures — of the narrator's slowly unfolding discovery of the secret relationships between Zenobia and Priscilla, between Hollingsworth and Zenobia and Westervelt, the handsome, diabolical catalyst of the tragic action of the story — and his own painful confession of his ineffectual love for Priscilla. The too-conventional plotting-out of unhappy and unrequited love affairs is fortunately fleshed out with a good deal more by way of interpretation. For this novel, Hawthorne had hit on the useful device of the first-person narrator. Moreover, it was better for his purposes that his inexperienced narrator-hero, Miles Coverdale — as distinct from his creator — was a somewhat obtuse and stumbling observer. In his earlier novels, Hawthorne had been the omniscient author. His use of the first-person narrative may have been suggested by the autobiographical material he used in the course of his story, or it may have been sparked by the power of Melville's *Moby-Dick*, with its opening salute: "Call me Ishmael." It was not, to be sure, an original device with either Hawthorne or Melville, but Hawthorne used it in a distinctly modern fashion as a method of distancing himself from his fictional narrator and at the same time making full use of the self-reflecting ironies of his hero's ineffectiveness. At times, Hawthorne may be almost too bright and too clever. Coverdale, for example, sees himself in the role of the chorus in a classical drama, "set aloof from the possibility of personal concernment." In lofty fashion, he goes on, "Destiny, it may be — the most skilful of stage managers — seldom chooses to arrange its scenes, and carry forward its drama, without securing the presence of at least one calm observer. It is his office to give applause, when due, and sometimes an inevitable tear . . ." The tone is pompous — intentionally so, for Coverdale is deeply implicated in the drama.

On a different level, *The Blithedale Romance* is an autopsy report on the rationalized morals, the disguised motivations of a little community of high-minded individuals bent on creating a social utopia. *Blithedale*, in fact, is the intelligent man's guide to the reformist temperament; a cruel portrait of the moral evasions, the self-deception and self-righteousness of those who set themselves up as the arbiters of morals, of those who appoint themselves the directors of society, managing the lives of others — for their own good, of course. Like his author, Miles Coverdale is aware of the acerbity of intellectual relationships. Describing the blind adoration Priscilla showers upon Hollingsworth, Coverdale sees, immediately, that Hollingsworth prefers such unconditional faith to the "intellectual approbation" of his peers. The latter, Hawthorne caustically notes, "always involves a possible reserve of latent censure." He was perfectly conscious of the careful misjudgments, the praise tinctured by envy, the inspired backbiting, that inevitably make up the life of the intellectual professions.

Hollingsworth — aptly described as "a tolerably educated bear" — is the arch offender. He has little faith in the Blithedale enterprise. "I see through the system," he claims. "It is full of defects — irremediable and damning ones!" Hollingsworth has his own form of monolithic hypocrisy: with the help of Zenobia's money, he intends — at the right moment — to take over Blithedale and establish his own system of reform, a colony for the rehabilitation of prisoners. In his ambition, he is quite willing to use anyone — Priscilla, Zenobia, even Coverdale — to achieve his purposes. Coverdale observes that the besetting sin of a philanthropist like Hollingsworth is "a moral obliquity." "At some point of his course," Coverdale speculates, "I know not exactly when nor where — he is tempted to palter with the right, and can scarcely forbear persuading himself that the importance of his public ends renders it allowable to throw aside his private conscience." Hawthorne has an instinct for such "obliquities" in human nature. He nails down the condescension the reformers feel toward a rude farmer like Silas Foster — the one member of the community who stands for the reality principle. Even while sitting down to their common meals, in a supposedly classless society of brothers and sisters, Blithedale's intellectual reformers are self-conscious about their "superior cultivation and refinement." Even Coverdale's motives are suspect; he is forced to acknowledge that in strenuously trying to prove himself Foster's equal, he is most guilty of "secretly putting weight upon some imaginary social advantage." He notes, "The poor, proud man should look at both sides of sympathy like this."

Hawthorne's view of the female reformer — Zenobia, principally — is equally critical. He takes the masculine view that women are moved to such unsuitable efforts only after some unhappiness in their private lives, and in veiled fashion implies that reformist sympathies in women are a sublimation for unachieved sexual satisfactions. Hollingsworth, on the other hand, is the outright male chauvinist; women reformers are "petticoated monstrosities." He voices the conventional masculine attitude that, though woman is "the most admirable handiwork of God," she is so "in her true place and character" — that being "at a man's side." Coverdale sees this view as making woman "the gentle parasite, the soft reflection of a more powerful existence." Although he does not subscribe to this view, Coverdale has his own strictures about the female reformer. As an observer of Lizzie Peabody and Margaret Fuller, Hawthorne detected a certain ruthlessness in women obsessed with a cause. "A female reformer, in her attacks upon society," he has Coverdale state, "has an instinctive sense of where the life lies, and is inclined to aim directly at that spot. Especially, the relation between the sexes is naturally among the earliest to attract her notice."

He was probably indulging in a bit of slyness; one of the minor ironies of *Blithedale* is that it, too, is about the "relation between the sexes." At times, the book comes close to being a tract on the subject. Men, Hawthorne suggests (though he makes a significant exception of Hollingsworth), are far too callous to be good Christians; they have "a natural indifference, if not an absolutely hostile feeling, towards those whom disease, or weakness, or calamity of any kind, causes to falter and faint amid the rude jostle of our selfish existence." Only the example of women and the "education of Christianity" manage to soften this "ugly characteristic" of the male sex. In one of the more forthright statements on the battle of the sexes, Hawthorne, through Zenobia, gives the woman's view of men in love. (Educated by years of Sophia's principled views, Hawthorne seems to have genuinely agreed with it.) Zenobia observes that the too-simple and too-innocent Priscilla is the perfect example of what men have made of women through the centuries. A man, Zenobia contends, "is never content, unless he can degrade himself by stooping towards what he loves. In denying us our rights, he betrays even more blindness to his own interests, than profligate disregard of ours." Throughout his narrative, Hawthorne hints at the confluence of sex and politics in his utopian community. *The Blithedale Romance*, in fact, is a book about sexual politics.

Women, as well as men, come in for their share of praise and blame. Coverdale, for example, is highly critical of the cult of "personal worship" women lavish on their "saints and heroes." "It often requires," he notes, "but one smile out of the hero's eyes into the girl's or woman's heart, to transform this devotion from a sentiment of the highest approval and confidence, into passionate love." Yet when Zenobia spurns the friendly overtures of Priscilla, Coverdale observes, "But women are always more cautious, in their casual hospitalities than men." Hawthorne was, in fact, ambivalent about the unquestioned admiration that young women and girls expended on the heroines of their sex; it was the kind of idolatry he had witnessed among the girlish admirers of Margaret Fuller. Still, Coverdale pontificates, "There is nothing parallel to this, I believe — nothing so foolishly disinterested, and hardly anything so beautiful — in the masculine nature, at whatever epoch of life. It is to a woman — and woman's intuition — that Hawthorne gives one of the sharpest insights into the egotism of humanitarian impulses. "It is all self!" Zenobia laments in the extremity of her disillusionment with Hollingsworth. "Nothing else; nothing but self, self, self!"

Oddly, it is in the analyses of women's psychological attitudes that Hawthorne succeeds best in making *The Blithedale Romance* something more than a tract on the subjects of woman's rights and the battle of the sexes. At one point, Zenobia delivers one of Hawthorne's bitterest comments on the destiny of women in American society. "Did you ever see a happy woman in your life?" Zenobia asks Coverdale. "Of course, I do not mean a girl — like Priscilla, and a thousand others, for they are all alike, while on the sunny side of experience — but a grown woman. How can she be happy, after discovering that fate has assigned her but one single event, which she must contrive to make the substance of her whole life? A man has his choice of innumerable events."

Hawthorne's blunt indictment of the male-dominant society of the nineteenth century could easily have been written by one of the professed champions of women's rights.

There is a persistent thread of subliminal eroticism running through *The Blithedale Romance*. At times, it is presented in a curiously ambiguous form. Coverdale recognizes that a society aspiring "towards the millennium of love" may give rise to unconventional modes and manners. "While inclining us to the soft affections of the Golden Age," he observes of the Blithedale community, "it seemed to authorize any individual, of either sex, to fall in love with any other, regardless of what would elsewhere be judged suitable and prudent. Accordingly, the tender passion was very rife among us." On the surface, it would appear, the author was discussing purely heterosexual attachments, but the vagueness of the terminology — "it seemed to authorize any individual, of either sex, to fall in love with any other, regardless . . ." — offers a discreet hint that "the tender passion" might encompass less conventional forms as well. The passage represents one of the few moments — there is another reference later in *The Blithedale Romance* — when Hawthorne, in guarded fashion, hints at possibly homosexual attachments. But where Melville (who thought a sculpture of Antinoüs more beautiful than the Venus de Milo) lingers over his descriptions of attractive heroes with a distinct sensuality and yearning, Hawthorne's vision is cool and fastidious. Hawthorne frequently remarks on the physical attractions of his male characters: Westervelt, for example, is described as "a tall and well-developed figure, and as handsome a man as I ever beheld." But there is always something confident and primly self-aware in Hawthorne's mentions of handsome men; they are himself in other circumstances.

It is women of all ages who exercise a fascination for Hawthorne. He is attracted to women's essential otherness. "There is hardly another sight in the world so pretty," Coverdale observes, "as that of young girls, almost women grown, at play." It is a vision that haunts Hawthorne's novels and short stories. "Girls are incomparably wilder and more effervescent than boys," Coverdale continues, "more untameable, and regardless of rule and limit, with an evershifting variety, breaking continually into new modes of fun." Coverdale's summary judgment is drawn from Hawthorne's experience as a father: "A man, however stern, however wise, can never sway and guide a female child."

In *The Blithedale Romance* Zenobia bears the full brunt of Hawthorne's sexual interest. She represents one of the persistent, exotic, almost Oriental, and occasionally dangerous, dark women (Hester, Beatrice Rappaccini, Miriam in *The Marble Faun*) who inhabit Hawthorne's fictional territory as counterweights to more conventional good women (Phoebe, Priscilla, Hilda). From the moment of her entrance, slightly *déshabillée* (Coverdale catches a glimpse of her white shoulder beneath her neckerchief), Zenobia exercises a persistent sensual fascination. "It struck me as a great piece of good fortune," Coverdale admits, "that there should be just that glimpse."

Zenobia is a woman "just on the hither verge of her richest maturity," as Coverdale describes her — an Eve in the chilly Blithedale paradise. With her rich, dark, glossy hair, ornamented with an exotic flower that she changes every day, she is a woman built on the capacious plan, lacking, perhaps, delicacy and softness. Zenobia is accustomed to the society of men; when Coverdale makes an oblique reference to Eden, she banteringly tells him that figs are out of season and that she could hardly take up "the garb of Eden" until after May Day. She is a woman, as Hawthorne admiringly describes her, who scorns "the petty restraints which take the life and color out of other women's conversation."

During Coverdale's illness, Zenobia makes him gruel. (It is one of the nicer touches, indicating the asperity of the invalid, that Coverdale complains the gruel is not very good.) During his half-delirium, with an intuition that comes with illness or asceticism, Coverdale senses that Zenobia has previously been married, though he knows little of her former history. There is a bloom to her that he otherwise cannot account for; he thinks of her as "a woman to whom wedlock had thrown wide the gates of mystery." In a rather sentimental but nevertheless sexual metaphor, Hawthorne has Coverdale exclaim, "Zenobia is a wife! Zenobia has lived, and loved. There is no folded petal, no latent dew drop in this perfectly developed rose!" He is deft, too, at depicting the minor episodes of masculine vanity. "A bachelor," Coverdale muses, "always feels himself defrauded, when he knows or suspects, that any woman of his acquaintance has given herself away."

With the frankness of an experienced woman, Zenobia turns to Coverdale with frosty amusement. "I have been exposed to a great deal of eye-shot in the few years of my mixing in the world," she tells him, "but never, I think, to precisely such glances as you are in the habit of favoring me with. I seem to interest you very much, and yet — or else a woman's instinct is for once deceived — I cannot reckon you as an admirer. What are you seeking to discover in me?"

"The mystery of your life," Coverdale answers. "And you will never tell me . . ."

At times, the eroticism of *The Blithedale Romance* takes a strange psychological turn. There is, for instance, the matter of the little silk purses that the virginal Priscilla makes. "Their peculiar excellence," Coverdale explains, "besides the great delicacy and beauty of the manufacture, lay in the almost impossibility that any uninitiated person should discover the aperture; although to a practised touch, they would open as wide as charity or prodigality might wish. I wondered if it were not a symbol of Priscilla's own mystery." In another passage, Coverdale asserts that it would be a kind of sacrilege for him to try to probe into Priscilla's "maidenly mystery." But he adds, "I could not resist the impulse to take just one peep beneath her folded petals."

But however important the relationship between the sexes is to the novel, the critical confrontation in *The Blithedale Romance* is between two men, Coverdale and Hollingsworth, and it, too, has sexual implications. Physically, Hollingsworth has the brawny figure of a blacksmith — one of his earlier professions; he is, as well, an orator of compelling force. Yet it is Hollingsworth who nurses Coverdale back to health with a devotion that is almost feminine. Despite his uncouth personality, Hollingsworth has "a tenderness in his voice, eyes, mouth, in his gesture, and in every indescribable manifestation, which few men could resist, and no woman." There is, Coverdale reveals, "something of the woman moulded into the great, stalwart frame of Hollingsworth; nor was he ashamed of it, as men often are of what is best in them." As a nursemaid, Hollingsworth is far more effective than Zenobia.

Coverdale's loyalty and affection tempers his distaste for Hollingsworth's methods in using both Priscilla and Zenobia in his underhanded scheme for taking over the Blithedale experiment. Hollingsworth, in his attempt to enlist Coverdale in his cause, presumes upon Coverdale's physical susceptibility. "There is not the man in this wide world whom I can love as I could you," Hollingsworth seductively tells Coverdale. "Do not forsake me!" The weight of the announcement, led up to by an intimate exchange between the two men, hints at something more than an easy euphemism. The subtle implication is that Hollingsworth is quite prepared to use his personal charisma as a weapon in dealing with both sexes. Coverdale concedes that if, at that moment, he had merely touched Hollingsworth's extended hand, he would have been so overpowered by Hollingsworth's "magnetism" that he would never have resisted.

Instead, however, he gives a flat no to the suggestion that he join the cause. "I never said the word — and certainly can never have it to say, hereafter — that cost me a thousandth part so hard an effort as did that one syllable . . ." Coverdale confesses. "It seemed to me that it struck him, too, like a bullet. A ghastly paleness — always so terrific on a swarthy face — overspread his features." Coverdale, like his creator, is a man who can say No! in thunder.

Hawthorne's contemporaries — and his later commentators — reading *The Blithedale Romance* as a roman à clef — found fertile ground for identifying the character of Hollingsworth. Spellbinding orators and politicians of the time offered possibilities: Orestes Brownson, certainly, and Albert Brisbane, the promoter of Fourierism, both had associations with Brook Farm. Daniel Webster, William Lloyd Garrison, Wendell Phillips were commanding orators. Hawthorne, in his direct and indirect experiences with these men, may have borrowed elements for his characterization. But there was a recent relationship in Hawthorne's life with a man of "about thirty years old" that could have provided the deeper psychological motivation for the character of Hollingsworth. Had Hawthorne — consciously or unconsciously — sensed the sexual urgency behind Melville's courtship? Had he sensed, as well, a certain responsiveness in his own attitude? Some recent experience, it would seem, had allowed him to plumb the relationship between Hollingsworth and Coverdale, making it more than a confrontation of types, a war of social ideologies.

Yet it would be wrong to bring the full weight of Hawthorne's friendship with Melville to bear upon his characterization of Coverdale and Hollingsworth. The relationship of the two men, in one sense, is an extension of the psychological intimacy of Dimmesdale and Chillingworth in *The Scarlet Letter*. (Even the paired names — Dimmesdale and Chillingworth, Coverdale and Hollingsworth — suggest an echoing parallel.) And the device of a four-sided relationship — two men, two women, with the introduction of an evil masculine catalyst — was one that had been carried over from *The House of the Seven Gables* and would be used again in *The Marble Faun*. There was an obsessive side to Hawthorne's fictional situations. It is also noteworthy that Melville, in his next-published book, *Pierre*, should adopt a similar quadrangle of friends and lovers. Melville, however, pushed the sexual implications of his story to the suggestion of incest between Pierre and his illegitimate half sister, Isabel — a boldness that was beyond the more reticent Hawthorne. Was it out of some sly impulse that Melville, in a letter to Sophia, blandly described his novel in progress as a "rural bowl of milk"?

Despite all his disclaimers that his fictional characters had not been drawn from life, Hawthorne's public searched for the models. This was particularly the case with Zenobia, whom the majority of his readers and critics identified with Margaret Fuller. Certainly, the exceedingly plain Margaret was not the model for Zenobia's voluptuous beauty. But there, Hawthorne may have had recourse to Almira Barlow, the beautiful and popular boarder at Brook Farm. As a means of throwing his readers off guard, Hawthorne resorted to the novel device of introducing Margaret Fuller's name into his narrative. While recuperating, Coverdale receives a letter from the bluestocking writer. Mergers of fictional situations and actual names, including mentions of Emerson, *The Dial*, Carlyle's *Essays*, are among the strategies Hawthorne uses to give a contemporaneous texture to his story. In an even more clever move, Hawthorne attributes to Priscilla — just at the moment she is handing Coverdale the letter from Margaret Fuller — physical characteristics that were clearly identified with Margaret; a slight curving of the shoulders, the habit of squinting when she was engaged in earnest conversation. For Hawthorne, the carefully staged coincidence was meant to serve two purposes — as a preliminary hint of Priscilla's mediumistic tendencies and as a ruse for throwing his readers off the scent. It also allowed him to pay tribute to Margaret Fuller in passing, describing her as "a friend of mine, one of the most gifted women of the age."

But Hawthorne was too clever. His tactics only reinforced the analogy: the spirit of Margaret Fuller hovers over his characterization of Zenobia with an insistence that is hard to miss. Zenobia's intellectual brilliance, her attractiveness to timorous girls, her considerable conversational abilities — and the fact that in Coverdale's view, Zenobia was more successful as an advocate of women's rights in person and in conversation than she was as a writer — all suggest that she was modeled after Margaret Fuller. Then, too, Coverdale's speculations about the liaison or shadowy marriage of Zenobia and Westervelt could only have recalled the rumors, among the New England literary set, of Margaret Fuller's relationship with the Marchese Ossoli.

In his novel, Hawthorne helped himself to passages from his notebooks dealing with his experiences at Brook Farm, as well as descriptive episodes relating to other periods in his life. It is a measure of Hawthorne's genius — and the diffidence that marked his talent — that he could have incorporated such scattered factual material so successfully into a tightly constructed narrative. *The Blithedale Romance* is the one novel in the Hawthorne canon in which fact and fiction live together in the easiest terms. Coverdale's lengthy stay in Boston, following his break with Hollingsworth, is drawn almost entirely from Hawthorne's sojourn there, following his ouster from the Salem Custom House. The setting of his meeting with Old Moodie in a Boston grog shop is drawn from his notes of visits to Parker's saloon on Court Street. For his description of Zenobia's suicide, Hawthorne turned to his account of the grim July night in 1845, when he and Ellery Channing probed the dark Concord River for the body of Martha Hunt. But the suicide of Zenobia and the recent, highly publicized drowning of Margaret Fuller were too coincidental for any informed reader to ignore.

There is at least one item of telling circumstantial evidence which suggests that Hawthorne, perhaps unconsciously, connected the fate of Zenobia with the death of Margaret Fuller. Published accounts of the disaster off Fire Island included the listings of the unfortunate victims besides Margaret and her family. Among those names was the uncommon one of Henry Westervelt.

———

The Blithedale Romance was not a critical success and it had only a short-lived popularity. Ticknor, Reed & Fields issued a first printing of 5090 on July 14, and a second impression of 2350 in August. But after that seemingly auspicious beginning there were no further printings of the book until three years later, and then only a meager 536 copies.

Many of Hawthorne's critics — then and later — felt that Hawthorne had overstepped the bounds of his imaginative talents in taking a contemporary theme and working so close to actuality. Only E. P. Whipple, in *Graham's Magazine,* gave the book unqualified praise as "the most perfect in execution of any of Hawthorne's works, and as a work of art, hardly equalled by anything else which the country has produced." The praise, however, may have been compromised by the fact that the critic had read the book in manuscript and had quite probably offered suggestions that Hawthorne had taken before publication. Whipple appears to have felt that the ending — with Coverdale at Zenobia's graveside — was too abrupt. Hawthorne softened the effect by adding a page or two of Coverdale's later reflections. Whipple's only demurrer was that the book had "a certain morbid tint." The same complaint was made by the reviewer for the *Southern Quarterly Review,* who found the suicide of Zenobia unacceptable — in fact, declared that it was "equally shocking and unnecessary" and suggested that the author should have converted Zenobia to marriage, "the best remedy for such a case."

Orestes Brownson, writing in his *Quarterly,* complained that the suicide of a woman like Zenobia was highly unlikely, "an exceedingly bungling way" for an author to dispose of an unmanageable character. He recommended "a fever, the consumption, the plague, the cholera, the cholic" as reasonable alternatives. Where some critics felt Hawthorne had been harsh on his philanthropists and reformers, Brownson was of the opinion that the author had exhibited "too much tenderness for experiments like that of Brook Farm." Still, he felt *The Blithedale Romance* was a useful antidote for curing "the young and enthusiastic of their socialistic tendencies and dreams of world reform." Brownson performed the unusual service of identifying himself completely with the rude male chauvinism of Hollingsworth's views. He even improved on them by insisting that women in general were "less capable of love, and less steady in it, than man. All the pretty things said of woman's love in novels and romances are mere moonshine."

Even Hawthorne's publisher was dismayed by the book. In London, that spring, James Fields had sold the English rights to Chapman and Hall, for £200. Hawthorne, in gratitude, had written him, on June 17, that it was "just £150 more than I expected to receive." When Fields returned to Boston, however, he was plainly disappointed with both the grim tone of the book and its poor sales. Writing one of Hawthorne's most fervent admirers, the London literary hostess Mary Russell Mitford, Fields complained, "I hope Hawthorne will give us no more Blithedales."

☙ III ❧

In the first week of June 1852, in sweltering heat, the Democratic Party convened in Baltimore to choose a presidential candidate. Like their rivals, the Whigs, the Democrats were fragmented by contending factions, liberals against conservatives, Northerners versus Southerners. Both parties had suffered erosion through the bolting of antislavery proponents and the formation of the Free-Soil Party. The Compromise of 1850 and its follow-up, the Fugitive Slave Law, which required that runaway slaves be remanded to their owners, were crucial issues in the selection of a nominee. The Democratic Party, split between its liberal-radical and conservative wings, the Barnburners and the Hunkers, faced a welter of candidates and a convention that would inevitably be thrown into prolonged voting and political in-fighting. Stephen Douglas, James Buchanan, Lewis Cass, and General William O. Butler, each with his modicum of support and broad opposition, were considered the front runners. In such a situation, a dark horse candidate, agreeable to all or most factions, was an attractive possibility.

Hawthorne's college friend Franklin Pierce was early named as a possible contender. Pierce had in his favor the successful management of the New Hampshire Democratic Party; it had won handily in the recent state elections. He had also served honorably, if not gloriously, as a brigadier general in the Mexican War. This was considered an asset if, as many suspected, the Whigs — meeting in Baltimore in mid June — should choose General Winfield Scott as their candidate. Pierce was a loyal Democrat; he was, in fact, considered a "dictator" for suppressing a Free-Soil insurrection in his state party. He was also a strict constructionist in interpreting the Constitution. For all his political ambitions and opportunism, Pierce was a genuine believer in the Union — and in the compromises necessary to maintain it. His parochial effectiveness was enhanced by his earlier record as a senator in Washington, which had been unremarkable enough to make him few enemies on the national front.

A shrewd politician, Pierce realized that his chances were slim; that he would have to proceed without false moves. Accordingly, he took the first step of all weak political candidates: he wrote a letter — for publication — stating that he did not seek the nomination and that he would find it "repugnant" if his name were put forward in Baltimore. As a result, he was chosen the favorite-son candidate of New Hampshire. His political supporters, testing the ground in late spring, reported that the "ultra men of the South" found nothing objectionable in Pierce's candidacy and that so far "no mistake has yet been committed" in the management of his campaign. When the New Hampshire delegates left for Baltimore in June, Pierce clarified his position to the extent of saying that his name should not be placed in nomination "until all efforts to harmonize upon one of the candidates already prominently before the public shall have failed."

As a noncandidate from a small state, Pierce could afford to soft-pedal the divisive issues of the 1850 Compromise and the Fugitive Slave Law. Yet locally — particularly in a two-and-a-half-hour speech made on New Year's Day — he forthrightly supported the Compromise as a necessary step. He harked back to the inability of the Founding Fathers to eliminate "involuntary servitude" when they framed the Constitution. Heckled about the Fugitive Slave Law, he maintained that since it was now the law of the land, he had no choice but to obey it.

Nationally, Pierce was to be a good deal more evasive about the issues. Late in May, Robert G. Scott, the editor of the *Enquirer* of Richmond, Virginia, sent a questionnaire to all the Democratic candidates. He asked each of the candidates whether, as President, he would sustain the Compromise; whether he would do everything in his power to prevent any change in the Fugitive Slave Law; whether he would veto any law that sought to change it. Stephen Douglas, who answered the questionnaire, nonetheless clearly recognized it was a preconvention ploy to "ketch & kill off all *Northern Men* and then abandon them." The replies were published in New York in the *Herald* on May 30, two days before the convention opened. Only Pierce and William Butler failed to respond in time.

Pierce shrewdly delayed his answer so that it arrived in Baltimore on the eve of the convention. Nor did he reply directly to Scott. Instead, he sent his answers to one of his principal supporters, Major Folliot Lally, an old army associate who was serving as a delegate to the convention. The general tone of his replies, couched in diplomatic and woolly terms, was conciliatory to the South. "I believe there will be no disposition on the part of the South to press resolutions unnecessarily offensive to the sentiments of the North," he maintained. "But can we say as much on our side?" If Pierce was willing to jettison anyone in his bid for support, it would clearly be the radical abolitionists and Free-Soilers.

For five steamy days and nights, the balloting continued in the Baltimore convention hall. On the thirty-first ballot, Douglas' strength peaked and then declined when support swung to Cass in an effort to head off the Douglas candidacy. Buchanan's supporters were mustering their forces; Pierce's name had not even been placed in nomination.

Pierce waited patiently for word from the deadlocked convention. On the evening of June 5, as he and his wife were riding back to Boston from a pleasant carriage ride to Mount Auburn, they were met by a friend, Colonel Barnes, who had sped out on horseback to intercept them. Word had come by telegraph that Pierce had been nominated on the forty-ninth ballot.

On the day of Franklin Pierce's nomination, the Hawthornes moved into their new home in Concord. Hawthorne had first seen Hillside in frigid winter weather when Concord was deep in snow. He thought of it then as a menagerie for cattle rather than a human habitation. The original structure was an old farmhouse that had been subjected to several random additions. It stood directly on the old Lexington Road, fronting a steep hill crowned with pines and acacias. Another plot of land, approximately eight acres deeded to Emerson, which Hawthorne later acquired, stood across the street. Mrs. Alcott had bought Hillside in 1845 with family money and some financial assistance from Emerson. Alcott, in a state of angry depression following the failure of his communal living experiment, Fruitlands, had refused to concern himself with matters of property or labor. Full of grievances, he blamed the world for its lack of appreciation for his philanthropic efforts, and he considered his hard-pressed family an obstacle to his utopian ambitions. He seems to have indulged in some marital recriminations as well. According to Mother Peabody, the visiting English reformer, Samuel Bower (who had unsuccessfully tried to promote nudism at Fruitlands), had told her Alcott considered himself "a Shaker in principle," maintaining that he "had long since been divorced from his wife by the high court of *his* work and that she was no longer anything to him!" Alcott had told Bower that if it were not for the children, he would have joined the Shakers at once.

During his tenancy at Hillside, however, Alcott had concerned himself to the point of terracing the grounds behind the house, cultivating a vegetable garden, and adding to the chaotic jumble of the farmhouse by cutting an outbuilding in half to make a study on the west side of Hillside and a kitchen on the east side. But in their usual hand-to-mouth fashion, the Alcotts had vacated the house in 1848, moving to Boston. Mrs. Alcott had refused to spend another winter there.

Whatever his initial impressions, Hawthorne was optimistic about the possibilities of the place. Writing to Duyckinck, he described it as a bargain with advantages. "It is no very splendid mansion . . ." he said, "but Mr. Alcott, the Orphic Sayer, of whom I bought it had wasted a good deal of money in fitting it up to suit his own taste — all which improvements I get for little or nothing. Having been much neglected, the place is the raggedest in the world, but it will make, sooner or later, a comfortable and sufficiently pleasant home." He had promptly rebaptized it the Wayside, since it stood close — "too nigh, indeed" — to the road.

It was not until three days after his move, when he went to the village post office, that Hawthorne learned of Pierce's nomination. On the following day, June 9, he wrote Pierce that he had been confident of his victory. "I hardly know whether to congratulate you," he added, "for it would be absurd to suppose that the great office to which you are destined will ever afford you one happy or comfortable moment — and yet it is an end worthy of all ambition, as the highest success that the whole world offers to a statesman."

If Pierce had not already considered the possibility of Hawthorne's writing his campaign biography, Hawthorne, with a politician's adroitness, promptly announced both his availability for the task and his reluctance to perform it.

> It has occurred to me [he told his old friend] that you might have some thoughts of getting me to write the necessary biography. Whatever service I can do you, I need not say, would be at your command; but I do not believe that I should succeed in this matter so well as many other men. It needs long thought with me, in order to produce anything good, and, after all, my style and qualities as a writer, are certainly not those of the broadest popularity . . . I should write a better life of you after your term of office and life itself were over, than on the eve of an election. I say this with perfect frankness; and (supposing you have ever had the subject in your thoughts) submit my honest opinion to your consideration.

Although he claimed his house was hardly fit to entertain a future President, he and Sophia cordially invited Pierce to visit them in

Concord. "We promise to treat you just as simply as if you were a mere country lawyer," he jibed.

Despite his reluctance, Hawthorne acted like a man suspiciously eager for the job. He let Pierce know he was going to Boston on the following day and would remain there for the rest of the week, "being engaged to sit for a portrait." "By the by," he quipped, "I suppose we shall soon see numberless engravings of your face." In a postscript, he added that in Boston he could be reached through his publishers or at the America House.

The request for Hawthorne's portrait had come by way of Grace Greenwood. She was a friend of Charlotte Cushman, who, retiring from the stage and planning a lengthy stay abroad, wanted likenesses of some of her famous countrymen, including Hawthorne and Longfellow. Hawthorne, in his reply to Grace Greenwood's letter, said he had hoped never to sit for another portrait and jokingly wished that his reputation had come earlier "so that my face might have been in request, while it had the grace of youth, at least." But he agreed to sit for Mrs. Daniel Steele, the Boston miniaturist and portrait painter. ". . . After the impression of her own face, which Miss Cushman has indelibly stamped on my remembrance," he claimed, "she has a right to do just what she pleases with mine."

Franklin Pierce was eager to have Hawthorne write his official campaign biography. By June 17, when Hawthorne wrote to James Fields, still abroad in London, the affair had been settled. (The biography was to be published by Ticknor, Reed & Fields.) Hawthorne, in writing the news, acknowledged that he and Pierce had been "intimate through life." "He wishes me to write his biography, and I have consented to do so — somewhat reluctantly, however — for Pierce has now reached that altitude when a man, careful of his personal dignity, will begin to think of cutting his acquaintance." It was a very curious view to take of a friend, and a more curious one toward an assignment that he had, in great part, sponsored for himself. "But I seek nothing from him," Hawthorne claimed, "and therefore need not be ashamed to tell the truth of an old friend." Throughout the writing of the biography and the ensuing political campaign, he was to maintain that he had no ambitions for a political career himself.

He was under no illusions about the results of his actions. Associating himself with Franklin Pierce was certain to give him a bad name in the more liberal circles of Concord and Boston. Within his own family, politics had begun to have a divisive effect, though it involved only his Peabody relatives and may not have troubled him greatly. It proved to be more distressing to Sophia.

Horace Mann and Daniel Webster, in recent years, had developed a fierce enmity toward one another and in their public addresses had traded insults. Mother Peabody was sure of the integrity of her son-in-law, who in 1852 was running for governor of Massachusetts on the Free-Soil ticket. She was equally convinced of Webster's iniquities. In spite of his "fine sentences and sophisticated reasoning," she claimed Webster was "dishonest, low-minded, immoral, irreligious, devoted to his own aggrandizement." It was a "known fact" that the Great Defender was "unchaste, keeping not one only, but many colored mistresses." It had probably not helped matters either that Webster, embittered and ill following his defeat at the Baltimore convention, had retired to his Marshfield home and steadfastly refused to endorse the Whig candidate, General Winfield Scott. Instead, Webster had privately advised his friends to vote for his New Hampshire neighbor and friend, Franklin Pierce.

Sophia, responding to one of Mann's published speeches, which her mother had pointedly sent her, replied that she had found it "admirable" but regretted that Mann had "stooped from the dignity of parliamentary debate to fling innuendos at General Pierce and trample on Mr. Webster." She suggested, "Why not let God take care of Mr. Webster and punish him in his own way? As for General Pierce, he cannot be hurt by innuendos. They only hurt Mr. Mann." In family circles, when it was learned that Hawthorne was writing the campaign biography, there had been some amazement. Horace Mann — in a rare moment of wit — remarked that if Hawthorne succeeded in making a hero out of such a lackluster figure as Pierce, it would be "the greatest work of fiction he ever wrote."

Aware of the difficulties facing him, Hawthorne had promptly set about acquiring information from Pierce's political associates. He also asked Pierce to send him copies of speeches and committee reports that might be useful in dealing with his Washington career. Some of Pierce's military cronies — Colonel T. J. Whipple and General Solomon McNeill — stopped at the Wayside to add whatever useful information they could. Hawthorne stressed his need for a lengthy interview with Pierce before the biography took final shape. In reviewing Pierce's congressional career, he was concerned about the modesty of the candidate's political record. "Instead of thrusting yourself forward on all good or bad occasions," he wrote Pierce, "it always required a case of necessity to bring you out; and having done the needful with as little noise as possible, you withdrew into the background." Hawthorne's assessment may well have been a compliment of sorts; it was also the complaint of a writer faced with material that was not very promising.

There was, however, a dramatic and unavoidable issue in the campaign that Hawthorne had to face head on. He wrote Pierce:

> I am sensible of a very difficult and delicate part of my task in your connection with the great subject of variance between the North and the South. There is no way, however, open to my perception — no course either of true policy, or worthy either of you or your biographer — save to meet the question with perfect candor and frankness, and to state what has been your action, and what your position . . . I suppose I shall see my way clearer, when I actually approach these knotty points; but at all events they are not to be shirked nor blinked.

It was all the more difficult an issue, since Hawthorne held slightly different opinions on the matter from those of Franklin Pierce — a fact that Hawthorne's detractors failed to recognize. It was clearly Pierce's view that the radical abolitionists were responsible for the climate of violence and agitation that was dividing the country and threatening the Union. It is not certain that Hawthorne, at that moment, felt the Union was endangered. Like Pierce, he found the abolitionists a meddlesome breed, but he was not in sympathy with the provisions of the Fugitive Slave Law. He had been glad to see Charles Sumner win his bitterly contested seat in the U.S. Senate as the choice of a coalition of Free-Soilers and liberal Democrats, and had told Longfellow so. "Not that I ever did, nor ever shall, feel any pre-eminent ardor for the cause which he advocates," he conceded in his letter to Longfellow, "nor could ever have been moved, as you were, to dedicate poetry — or prose either — to its advancement. There are a hundred modes of philanthropy in which I could blaze with intenser zeal. This Fugitive Law is the only thing that could have blown me into any respectable degree of warmth on this great subject of the day — if it really be the great subject — a point which another age can determine better than ours." Fanny Longfellow, forwarding Hawthorne's remarks to the newly elected senator, gave them a rosier tint than may have been warranted. "His sympathies are absorbed by the sufferings of his own race, but a large heart can hold all," she commented.

In the spring of 1851, Hawthorne had backed up his opinions by lending his name to a Free-Soil petition, not out of wholehearted agreement with the abolitionists, but because of his distaste for the Fugitive Slave Law. Hawthorne had frankly outlined his motives in a letter to his Salem friend Zachariah Burchmore, a conservative

Democrat and party man who had held out against any compromise with the Free-Soil forces. Hawthorne conceded that Burchmore probably had taken the right stand, "if there should be any right side up in the case." He continued, "As for myself, being entirely out of political life, I act upon other considerations. I have not, as you suggest, the slightest sympathy for the slaves; or, at least, not half so much as for the laboring whites, who, I believe, as a general thing, are ten times worse off than the Southern negroes." Throughout his political life, Hawthorne remained frankly ambivalent on the Negro question. "Still," he told Burchmore, "whenever I am absolutely cornered, I shall go for New England rather than the South — and the Fugitive Law cornered me." Interestingly, Hawthorne's next remark makes it clear that prior to Pierce's nomination, he had been giving some passing thought to political office and was quite prepared to accept the consequences of his recent action. "Of course, I knew what I was doing when I signed the Free-Soil document," he told Burchmore, "and bade farewell to all ideas of foreign consulships, or other official stations; so that I doubt whether you and I ever go to Rio together. Perhaps you may go alone, if you wish it. I don't care a d—— for office."

Throughout late June and early July of 1852, Hawthorne, in his letters to Pierce, complained of the lack of material and urged Pierce to tell his friends to make haste so that he could begin in earnest. By July 24, writing to Ticknor, he claimed he had the necessary information in hand. He was planning to begin work on the following day "and shall not show my face till it is finished." Writing to Pierce three days later, Hawthorne was in an expansive mood. "I am taking your life as fast as I can — murdering and mangling you. God forgive me; as I hope you will. I want to know whether you have any objection to my including portions of your military journal in the biography. There are occasional references to individuals which it would not be advisable to print, but parts of the manuscript, I think, would have much interest with the public, and be creditable to you."

His work on the biography, however, was soon cut short by a family tragedy. Since their move to Concord, both Hawthorne and Sophia had been encouraging his sister Louisa to pay a visit. The house was still not in order, Hawthorne admitted, but they could make her comfortable. He was afraid that if she did not come soon, something might intervene "to prevent your coming this summer." He listed the scheduled trains from Boston and asked her to arrange things so that she could have "a good long visit."

In her desultory way, Louisa put off the trip. First, there was the illness of Robert Manning's widow, which kept her in Salem. Then, in mid July, Sophia received a note from her — from the Columbian Hotel in Saratoga Springs — announcing that she had suddenly agreed to accompany Uncle John Dike on a trip to the spa, where he planned to take the prescribed course of waters. They might possibly return home by way of New York City, traveling down the Hudson — "but I hardly think we shall," Louisa added.

On July 28, in midafternoon, the steamboat *Henry Clay*, over the protests of the passengers, was racing the rival steamer, the *Armenia*. Just off the Palisades, near Fort Lee, New Jersey, fire broke out amidships. Passengers on the promenade deck were not aware of what had happened until the lower deck was well aflame. Terrified women and children jumped overboard or clung to the railings until, exhausted, they dropped off into the water. The ship was speedily run aground, where it broke in two. Some sixty passengers were drowned or burned to death. John Dike was rescued. Louisa had been reading *Pilgrim's Progress* in her cabin; Dike had visited her only minutes before the fire broke out, just after he returned to the upper deck. In the first reports of the disaster, Louisa's name was not listed among the victims; her body was not recovered and identified until the following Saturday.

At the request of the family, William Pike brought the news to Hawthorne at Concord. It was seven o'clock on the morning of the 30th when Sophia, hearing the railroad coach stop, looked out the bedroom window and saw Pike step out. By the time she came downstairs, Hawthorne was standing at the door, stunned by the news. Julian remembered his father with "an expression of darkness and suffering on his face such as his children had never seen there before." Hawthorne turned and shut himself up in his study.

Pike was asked to write a brief note to Pierce, explaining that the biography would have to be put aside for the moment. Sophia penned a hurried letter to her mother, pointedly advising, "If Elizabeth (my sister) has gone to Brattleboro, I wish you would write her of this and tell her she had better not stop here on her way back as she intended." While trying to comfort the children, she had a happy thought of Louisa together with her mother in heaven. In time, that idea was to give her a sense of "positive bliss." "If there is anything immortal in life, it is the home relations," she later wrote her mother with the Peabody talent for finding consolation in every circumstance, "and heaven would be no heaven without them. God has never knit my soul with my husband's soul for such a paltry moment as this human life."

For Hawthorne, Louisa's sudden death could hardly have given rise to uplifting thoughts. Pictures of the unassuming Louisa in the final, terror-stricken moments must have been fixed in his mind. The death of Margaret Fuller, whose body had been washed out to sea, was still fresh in Hawthorne's thoughts. The grim physiological details of Martha Hunt's suicide had stamped themselves in his memory — the clenched fists, the remorseless stiffness of the body, the fearful condition of the dead girl's face when she was pulled from the river. He had written the scene only recently, fixing it with such permanence as prose allowed. It had been a rehearsal for a nearer, actual tragedy. Sophia, who had similar thoughts, tried to put them from her mind. "I have not the courage to ask whether she was burnt before she was drowned," she wrote her mother. She chose to believe that the breast pin Louisa had been wearing at the time, which was sent to Una as a remembrance of her aunt, had been "blackened and stained with salt water."

Hawthorne traveled to Salem but mercifully arrived too late for the burial services. Sophia, writing to her family on the day after her husband's return, August 5, was grateful for the fact. "It would have been so painful to him to go through any ceremony, and to hear all the Calvinistic talk . . ." Ebe Hawthorne had not returned with him, as they both had hoped, but had decided to return to Beverly, where she had been living since her mother's death.

Emerson had learned of the tragedy in the newspapers. He had been hoping, he said in a brief note to Sophia, that the reports of Louisa's death had been mistaken. "But who knows which is the shortest & most excellent way out of the calamities of the present world?" he asked, serenely. It was meant as consolation.

⌐ IV ⌐

The writing of Franklin Pierce's campaign biography added much to Hawthorne's political experience. It was a sad education; at midcentury, American politics had turned increasingly bitter and rancorous. Early in the campaign, Whig papers began asking insidious questions about Pierce's courage under fire during the Mexican War. It was also rumored that Pierce was an alcoholic. The difficulty in responding to such charges — American politics being a matter of black-and-white assertions — was that the slanders and libels were grounded in circumstantial details, the complications of reality. Attempts to explain and explicate seemed only further to compromise the candidate.

Pierce's record in the Mexican War had been neither dashing nor glorious; he was, in effect, one of numerous officers who had done honorable but undistinguished service in a controversial war. Through illness and the assignments given him by his superiors, he had seldom taken part in the major battles, which had brought glory to Generals Taylor and Winfield Scott. The charge of cowardice leveled against him was grounded in an unfortunate accident during the Battle of Contreras. An unexpected barrage of artillery had caused Pierce's nervous mount to rear up suddenly. Thrust hard in the groin and pelvis by the pommel of his saddle — an excruciating pain — Pierce had blacked out; his horse stumbled and went down. A call went out for Major Truman Ransom, Pierce's aide and friend, to take command, but Ransom was too distant to hear. Another officer, George W. Morgan, unaware of the circumstances, had shouted to Ransom with loud and angry disgust, "Take command of the Brigade, General Pierce is a damned coward." Later, Morgan publicly retracted his statement, but it did not put an end to the stories. Although badly injured and with a wrenched knee sustained in the fall of his horse, Pierce had insisted on taking command of his brigade during the Battle of Churubusco. There, his knee had given out on him, but he lay on the ground within range of enemy fire, bitterly refusing any attempt by his men to remove him to safer quarters. In the last major battle of the war, that of Chapultepec, Pierce was ingloriously laid up with a severe case of diarrhea — a common and frequently fatal ailment during much of the Mexican campaign. Pierce's military experiences had been mostly unfortunate, a fact that Hawthorne tried to mitigate by quoting segments of the general's journal, relating the hardships of those engagements in which he had taken part.

The charges of Pierce's alcoholism, too, had some basis in fact. Hawthorne, well aware of Pierce's dissipations during their college years, stressed the incident of Pierce's strenuous effort to bring up his grades as an example of his friend's will power and perseverance. Although in the course of his later career Pierce had reformed and embraced the temperance cause, rumors of his drunkenness dogged his public life.

It was late in the campaign that a slanderous story began to make the rounds. It was said that Pierce had been involved in an argument with a fellow officer during a card game. The officer, so the story went, had struck Pierce, and Pierce had taken it without a murmur. Pierce had, in fact, had an argument with a fellow officer, John Magruder, but they had never come to blows. The canard, first printed in September in a Baltimore paper, the *Old Defender*, incensed Sophia. Writing defensively to her mother — and the less than sympathetic Peabody family in general — she deplored the slander: "This story, fabricated out of nothing but malice, was meant to injure in two ways, by proving [Pierce] a gambler and also pusillanimous." She was happy to report that Pierce had just received a warm and friendly letter from the officer in question, then living in California. It was full of "the highest admiration and respect," as well as congratulations for Pierce. She was sure the letter, which was being sent to Baltimore for publication, would refute all the malicious charges.

On August 27, despite his grief and the mounting pressures of the campaign, Hawthorne managed to finish his manuscript and send it to his publishers. Pierce, who had been receiving installments during the writing of the book, was evidently pleased with it; his political supporters — like the wealthy New York banker Augustus Schell, who ordered 500 copies for distribution in his state — hoped the biography would counteract the Whig charges and strengthen the candidate's appeal to the public at large. In his letters to his publishers, Hawthorne was unusually enthusiastic and demanding. Having seen the firm's advance announcements of the book, he told Ticknor, "I think you must blaze away a little harder in your advertisement. Say, for instance, 'The Life of Franklin Pierce by Nath'l H——, drawn up from original sources, with extracts from the General's Military Journal' . . . Go it strong, at any rate. We are politicians now; and you must not expect to conduct yourself like a gentlemanly publisher."

Writing to Horatio Bridge, Hawthorne gave the impression of being far more modest about the book. He owned that he had been "terribly reluctant" to write the biography, that he had tried to convince Pierce "both by letter and *viva voce* — that I could not perform it so well as many others; but he thought differently; and, of course, after a friendship of thirty years, it was impossible to refuse my best efforts in his behalf at the great pinch of his life." He felt he had acquitted himself well enough: other writers might have made larger claims for Pierce, but he had "secured all the credit possible for him without spoiling all by asserting too much."

It is clear from his pre-election letter to Bridge that he had changed his mind about accepting a political reward for his services. He had, in fact, been giving serious thought to very specific possibilities. He told Bridge that before undertaking the book, "I made an inward resolution that I would accept no office from him; but to say the truth, I doubt whether it would not be rather folly than heroism to adhere to this purpose in case he should offer me anything particularly good. We shall see. A foreign mission I could not afford to take. The consulship at Liverpool, I might; and he could not do a better thing, either for me or the credit of his administration than to make the appointment." Hawthorne was hardly immune to normal human vanity, and, as Sophia would later gladly report to her family, the Liverpool consulship was "second in dignity to the Embassy to London." Moreover, Hawthorne's recent books had brought him a growing reputation in England, and he was being encouraged to visit there. "Just at this time," he boasted to Bridge, "I rather think your friend stands foremost there, as an American fiction-monger." An appointment to England as an honored public official, stationed there with his family at the government's expense, would be particularly appropriate; the Liverpool assignment, he conceded to Bridge, "would make all straight." The principal considerations, however, were undoubtedly financial, for the Liverpool consulate was deemed the most lucrative in the foreign service. Aside from the official salary (out of which clerks' salaries and office rent had to be paid), the consul received "emoluments" — a percentage on all American shipping in the busy English port. The prospect of clearing $5000 to $7000 a year during a four-year term was particularly attractive.

His glowing personal prospects were evidently caught up in the high excitement and political drama of the campaign itself. In his letter to Bridge, he commented on Pierce, "What luck that fellow has! . . . I have come seriously to the conclusion that he has in him many of the chief elements of a great ruler. His talents are administrative; he has a subtle faculty for making affairs roll onward according to his will, and of influencing their course without showing any trace of his action." It was a thorough overestimation of his friend, for Pierce, in his administration, was to be continually at the mercy of events rather than the master of them. "There are scores of men in the country that seem brighter than he is," Hawthorne added, "but Frank has the directing mind . . . Such is my idea of him, after many an hour of reflection on his character while making the best of his poor little biography. He is deep, deep, deep. But what luck withal! Nothing can ruin him." Still, Hawthorne was not sanguine about the outcome of the election in Massachusetts. "There is hardly a spark of enthusiasm in either party," he said, "but what there is, so far as I can judge, is on the side of Scott. The prospect is none of the brightest, either in New York, Ohio, or Pennsylvania, and unless he gets one of them, he goes to the wall."

Pierce, he noted,

> does not appear to admit the possibility of failure; but I doubt whether in a position like his, a man can ever form a reliable judg-

ment of the prospect before him. Should he fail, what an extinction it will be. He is now in the intensest blaze of celebrity. His portrait is everywhere . . . He is playing a terrible game, and for a tremendous stake; on one side, power, the broadest popularity, and a place in history; on the other (for I doubt whether it would not prove a knock-down blow) insanity, or death and a forgotten grave. He says, however, that he should bear defeat with equanimity. Perhaps he might, but I think he is not aware of the intense excitement in which he lives. He seems calm, but his hair is whitening, I assure you.

In a final attempt to summarize his emotions, Hawthorne confided, "I love him, and, oddly enough, there is a kind of pitying sentiment mixed up with my affection for him just now."

Having finished the biography, Hawthorne planned to escape from Concord and take a vacation on the Isle of Shoals. But first there was to be a reunion with Pierce and his Bowdoin classmates at Brunswick. His alma mater was celebrating its semicentennial year. Fortunately, heavy rains delayed his arrival until after the official program, in which he was the subject of a number of tributes and poems. Hawthorne, seeing his former classmates, found himself confronting his own middle age. "All my contemporaries have grown the funniest old men in the world," he wrote Sophia. "Am I a funny old man?" he asked plaintively.

ᘓ V ᘏ

Throughout that season of anxious expectations, Hawthorne was in touch with Herman Melville. In mid July, he sent the Pittsfield author a copy of his just-published *Blithedale Romance* and a note inviting him to pay a visit to Concord. Melville, having just returned from a trip to Martha's Vineyard and Nantucket, begged off. He relayed to Hawthorne, however, the unusual circumstance that on his trip he had encountered no less than three people who had just bought Hawthorne's book and that as soon as he arrived home he was told that it had just come by mail. "This name of 'Hawthorne' seems to be ubiquitous," he claimed. Although he had not had time to get very far into *Blithedale*, he was surprised to find the material "richer" than he had expected. Like Brownson, Melville saw the book as "an antidote to the mooniness of some dreamers — who are merely dreamers." And he added, "Yet who the devil aint a dreamer?"

The two writers seemed to be in some parallel phase; within a month Melville reciprocated by sending Hawthorne his new novel, *Pierre*, the hero of which, like Coverdale in *The Blithedale Romance*, was a minor author. Hawthorne's response to the latest of Melville's books has not survived; Melville's critics, though, were savage, pronouncing it "the craziest fiction extant" and suggesting that the author be placed in a lunatic ward at the earliest possible date. Melville's career had begun its slide into a long and lonely obscurity.

With the book, Melville also sent a lengthy and involved letter in which, oddly, he offered Hawthorne the idea for a story he had heard in Nantucket. The tale had been told to him by a New Bedford lawyer who had handled the case and supplied a documentary journal of it. It concerned a young woman, Agatha Hatch Robertson, who had been deserted by the sailor she had married. The story seemed so reminiscent of Hawthorne's early tale "Wakefield," in which a husband leaves his wife but secretly lives nearby for twenty years, that Melville, after turning over the possibilities in his own mind, decided Hawthorne was the person to write it. "I do not, therefore, My Dear Hawthorne, at all imagine that you will think I am so silly as to flatter myself I am giving you anything of my own. I am but restoring to you your own property."

Still, it was more than the offer of an idea for a story, for Melville went on to describe, in pertinent detail, the many ways in which he would himself handle the particulars of the tale. It was almost as if he were suggesting a collaboration. That it was more than a passing gesture seems clear from a letter he wrote Hawthorne in October, filled with additional suggestions. The Agatha story was clearly something he had been keeping in mind. When, finally, Melville visited Concord a month later, Hawthorne relinquished the story entirely and, in his turn, suggested Melville write it, but offered the suggestion that he set the tale in the Isle of Shoals. A day or two later, Melville wrote saying he would take Hawthorne's advice. "I wish I had come to this determination at Concord," he confessed, "for then we might have more fully and closely talked over the story, and so struck out new light . . . I invoke your blessing upon my endeavors." Despite the slow waltz of collaboration between the authors, however, the Agatha story was never written.

On a warm Sunday afternoon in late October — the 24th — Sophia and Hawthorne, Una and Julian had gone up to the woods on the steep hill behind the Wayside. It was an afternoon of delicious calm, with a blue haze at the horizon, one of those late fall days when Hawthorne tended to feel a sense of poignancy in the midst of nature and, strangely, a sense of warmth and security that he never experienced in the full tide of summer. Hawthorne was stretched out, in silence, on a carpet of dried pine needles. Sophia and the children were making wreaths of red and russet oak leaves. They had learned that day of the death of Daniel Webster — the "Great Daniel," as Sophia referred to him — who had died at his farm in Marshfield at three that morning.

To the very last — probably as a matter of conviction, possibly from bitterness — Webster had held out against endorsing the candidacy of General Scott, despite the pleas of Whig politicians. He was convinced that Scott's nomination would mean the demise of the party — and he would be proven right. In his final years, Webster had been pilloried by men like Horace Mann and Charles Sumner, who regarded his March 7 speech as a betrayal of principle; his defeat at the Baltimore convention was seen as a kind of divine retribution. In his last days, when one of the more presumptuous party politicians argued that Webster should endorse Scott, that he should think of his "future fame," the old lion had roused himself to exclaim: "I have no future on earth; my past is my future."

Toward evening on that autumnal Sunday of Webster's death, the Hawthornes were joined by their neighbor Edmund Hosmer, Emerson's Arcadian farmer. Knowing the family's political sympathies, Hosmer began discoursing on the country's great men. He could recall old John Adams, who, at eighty-three, when Hosmer had sat next to him at church on Sundays, was still "a perfect beauty," with cheeks as "unwrinkled as a girl's, and as fair and white." Mindful of Webster's tarnished reputation, Hosmer praised the statesman's speeches and his formidable public letters. He was glad, he said, that Webster had died "in the fullness of his power of mind, and not sunken in the socket." Sophia felt that Webster's death was an "immense loss."

In writing to her unreconciled mother and family, Sophia launched into one of her lengthy private eulogies for a public man. "I should be grieved to hear that he died of a broken heart," she told her mother, "and there is no sign of such a thing in the calm, grand death of which we hear." She was conscious of Webster's faults: "It blinds me with tears of profoundest sorrow to see that Ambition could make him stoop. He made that fatal mistake which so many make; he did evil that good might come of it." But she felt it was niggling to reduce a great man to his mistakes and failings; she was glad that God would be Webster's judge. "It will take an aeon to compose another such man as Webster," she claimed with her usual generosity. "I do not believe so great a man is to be found here or in Europe now." Her final bit of counsel to her family was this: "Let us freely, and with generous awe, admire greatness, and with tenderness, not pride, mourn over a vast soul in eclipse, passing into the unknown world . . ."

Another architect of political compromise, Henry Clay, had died barely three months before. With Webster's death, the old politics of accommodation and expansive patriotism was passing out of American political life.

VI

On November 4, 1852, Franklin Pierce was elected the fourteenth President of the United States. He won by a large electoral vote, carrying all but four states. (Massachusetts, as Hawthorne had expected, had gone for Scott.) But despite the electoral landslide, the popular vote was not impressive. Pierce was well aware that he presided over a divided party and a nation that was increasingly split over the slavery issue. In selecting a new cabinet, Pierce was exceedingly cautious. For a time, he even considered so radical a figure as John Dix, a rabid "Barnburner," but his final choices were evenly divided between conservatives and moderates, with ample recognition of the South. It was clearly as a conciliatory gesture that Pierce chose Jefferson Davis as his secretary of war.

Whatever his efforts, Pierce's term of office was to be plagued by unhappiness and dissension; the tone of his administration seemed to be set by his private misfortunes. On January 6, Pierce, his wife, and their only son, Benjamin, took a morning train from Boston to Concord, New Hampshire. Not far out of Boston, the car in which they were riding toppled over and fell down an embankment into a field. Pierce and his wife, though badly shaken up, were unharmed, but eleven-year-old Benny was killed instantly. Mrs. Pierce, a woman of neurotic temperament and rigorous Calvinist beliefs, was distraught. For days after the tragedy, the unhappy couple kept themselves in seclusion, trying to fathom the mystery of God's purposes. Mrs. Pierce, as a form of cruel consolation, came to believe that Benny, to whom she had been absolutely devoted, had been taken from them because he would have been an interference in the great responsibilities her husband now faced. Franklin Pierce, who had never felt the required "grace" of Calvinist theology, regarded his son's death as a punishment for his sins. Knowing as he did that he had deliberately misled his wife into believing he had been pressed into the presidential campaign against his wishes did not help assuage Pierce's sense of guilt. She had not wanted him to run for the office. When she learned the truth, a few days before the inauguration, while she and Pierce were staying at a Baltimore hotel, she evidently gave vent to her emotions. Unwilling or unable to attend the inauguration ceremonies, she did not accompany her husband to Washington, and, in fact, Jane Pierce was never to be an effective hostess at the White House. A woman of timorous habits that were intensified by her grief, she became more and more secluded after the tragedy. She attended official functions only rarely; much of the time she stayed in her room, writing notes to her dead son.

From the moment the election was decided, Hawthorne found himself caught up in questions of political patronage. As a close friend of the President-elect, he was besieged by hopeful office-seekers — friends, acquaintances, comparative strangers. Zachariah Burchmore immediately sought his assistance in getting the position of naval officer at the Salem Custom House. Unfortunately, Burchmore, a hard-drinking and contentious man, began bucking the local Democrats, working against the appointment of another of Hawthorne's acquaintances, Dr. George Loring, who was seeking the post of collector. Hawthorne, well aware of Burchmore's bullheadedness and suspecting that the local politicians would prefer to get rid of Burchmore altogether, suggested that he patch up his differences and withdraw his claims for the naval office in exchange for a post in the Boston Custom House — a move that he felt sure Loring would support. He did not want to become too deeply involved in the political maneuvering; as early as December, he specifically warned Burchmore: "Do not let my name be mixed up with the above business." Increasingly, Hawthorne found himself in the middle, reassuring Loring of his good will, reproaching Burchmore for not accepting his earlier advice, and urging him to take "all possible means of reconciling your differences, even now." Bluntly, he told Burchmore, "You have the vice of all veteran politicians, that of mistrusting all persons with whom you have politicial dealings." In the end, he found it necessary to hand Burchmore over to his Custom House crony, William Pike. He wrote Pike that Burchmore was "a poor, miserable, broken, drunken, disagreeable loafer, contemptible as an enemy, and only troublesome to his friends; and for these very reasons, I throw him upon your generosity. Help him, or he sinks." Pike, too, was seeking political advancement. With Hawthorne's appointment to the Liverpool consulate seemingly assured, Pike hoped to be given some subsidiary office in England.

Hawthorne did whatever was possible, urging positions for those he felt deserving, discouraging petitioners who seemed to be asking for too much. The claims on his time and patience mounted. The literary critic and editor Charles Wilkins Webber wanted to be appointed chargé d'affaires in Bolivia; a distant cousin, Haley Barstow, was pressing him to be made "first assistant" at Liverpool ("God deliver me from such assistance!" Hawthorne prayed); even his ancient Uncle William was seeking a plum in the Salem Custom House, and was eventually awarded the newly created post of superintendent of repairs — a lofty title for the position of janitor. At one point, Hawthorne was forced to hold back on his letters of recommendation. "There is so much of my paper now in the President's hands," he explained, "that (as the note-shavers say) I am afraid it will be going at a discount."

His strategies for office-seeking and office-holding were summed up in his dealings with Richard H. Stoddard, a young poet and admirer who had visited him in Concord the previous summer. At first, Hawthorne had considered taking the young man abroad as his secretary. But writing to Fields, Hawthorne confessed that he had thought better of it. Stoddard, he felt, "has not the requisites for such a position. He ought to have all the diplomatic and courtly qualities that are deficient in me — and you may imagine what an enormous amount that is." He wrote to Stoddard and advised him to seek some post that had a "literary fragrance" about it — the librarianship in some Washington department. "Are you fond of brandy?" Hawthorne asked, then proceeded to warn the young man that public men were "inveterate guzzlers; and love a man that can stand up to them in that particular. It would never do to let them see you corned, however . . . You will find them a new class; and very unlike poets." Hawthorne complained, "I have had as many office-seekers knocking at my door, for three months past, as if I were a prime minister, so that I have made a good many scientific observations in respect to them." He offered the young hopeful one piece of advice in particular: "When applying for office, if you are conscious of any deficiencies (moral, intellectual, or educational, whatever else) keep them to yourself, and let those find them out whose business it may be. For example, supposing the office of Translator to the State Department to be tendered you, accept it boldly, without hinting that your acquaintance with foreign languages may not be the most familiar. If this unimportant fact be discovered afterwards, you can be transferred to some more suitable post. The business is, to establish yourself, somehow and anywhere." It was not the advice of a dreamer.

Hawthorne made a persistent effort, too, to aid Herman Melville, who unfortunately had never pursued any vital political ties. Moreover, Melville's caustic treatment of the navy (and the clergy) in his early books was not likely to create friends in establishment circles. Hawthorne spoke to both Pierce and the new secretary of state, William Marcy, on the author's behalf. (It may also have been for Melville's benefit that he asked Ticknor to inquire of Pierce, who was in Boston in mid February, whether he planned to remove young Lewis Cass, Jr., as chargé d'affaires at Rome. "The fact is, I have a friend who wishes to apply for it, in case Cass is to be removed," he told Ticknor.) But despite Hawthorne's efforts, neither the consulship at Honolulu nor a post in Antwerp — two of the several possibilities — was offered to the author. Melville's family, including the influential Judge Lemuel Shaw, were no more successful than Hawthorne.

With Charlotte Bridge, Hawthorne found himself in another touchy situation. Since 1851, Horatio Bridge had been serving as purser on the U.S.S. *Portsmouth*, cruising in the Pacific. Charlotte Bridge was pressing Hawthorne to have her husband promoted to some important administrative post. Hawthorne may have been in a quandary, since one of the suitable positions for Bridge would have been the consulship at Honolulu, a prize that Melville had also been seeking. Writing to Charlotte Bridge in May, Hawthorne assured her that Pierce had a "genuine affection" for her husband. He remarked that Pierce's friendship tended to be more sentimental than practical, but that he would not make any appointments on the grounds of friendship alone. "My only hope of [Horatio's] obtaining the Honolulu consulship was based on the idea that, by some peculiar turn of affairs, the President's views of policy might be brought to coincide with his personal partialities." In a moment of abrupt candor, Hawthorne added, "He is a very remarkable man — seemingly impulsive, and often apparently governed by his impulses, but always in such a way that his pre-determined ends are forwarded thereby. I never knew nor heard of a man at once so warm and so cold, so subtile and so true, as Franklin Pierce." It was a remarkable portrait of his friend and benefactor — a portrait sharpened by an edge of unkindness, perhaps, but no less valid for that. After the exhilaration of the election campaign, Hawthorne had begun to see his friend in the hard light of political reality.

Despite the upheavals in his life, the pressures of office-seekers (his own appointment was not voted until March 26), Hawthorne had been attempting to write a sequel to his earlier collection of children's stories. *Tanglewood Tales* was the only literary work he could countenance during a time of increased social obligations and family pressures. Hawthorne seems to have had a genuine enthusiasm for the task. In his letter to Stoddard, he remarked that he had just completed his retelling of the six classical myths that made up the new volume. "I never did anything else so well as these old baby stories," he claimed.

It was ostensibly because of the pressures of writing that Hawthorne declined, on January 3, James Russell Lowell's invitation to a dinner in Boston given for the visiting William Makepeace Thackeray. "I am a terribly heavy guest," Hawthorne responded, "and it is a matter of conscience with me not to inflict myself on you for two days and a night. Then, too, I am trying hard to write something amidst innumerable interruptions and botherations." Aside from the legitimate excuses, Hawthorne exhibited a certain reluctance about meeting the popular English celebrity. In his note, Hawthorne conceded, "There is a lion in the way. I enjoy Thackeray's books above all things, but it is quite a nonsequitur that I should therefore seek his society." In spite of his busy schedule, he nevertheless managed to keep several Boston appointments throughout January and early February, sitting for a new portrait commissioned by Franklin Pierce. In a studio at the corner of West and Washington streets, Hawthorne sat for the Parisian-trained artist, George P. A. Healy, who had recently completed a portrait of the President-elect. While Healy's wife entertained by reading aloud one of Bulwer-Lytton's popular historical novels, Healy studied his subject, impressed by the dark gray eyes, bright with intelligence, and the expansive brow that gave Hawthorne the appearance of some poetical version of Daniel Webster. He was amused to discover that the celebrated author was as timid as any maiden who had ever sat for him. The portrait, which remained in the Pierce family for years, portrayed the shy author, however, as a man of affairs, alert and lean, wearing the unmistakable uniform of the midcentury public man — frock coat, wing collar, and black cravat. Sophia, who brought the children to the studio for the final sitting on February 9, was not altogether satisfied; she thought the likeness was "wonderful, and the whole style spirited and lifelike," but felt the artist hadn't revealed "the depth and sunniness" of her husband's eyes. At her suggestion, Healy "deepened" the eyes, claiming to be grateful for the advice.

Among the "domestic and external" reasons that made it impossible for Hawthorne to attend the Thackeray dinner, there had been a quite legitimate one — the serious illness of his mother-in-law. Since December, Mrs. Peabody had been under a doctor's care in West Newton. Lizzie had been called home from Pennsylvania; Mary was within reach. It was likely that Sophia would be sent for.

For six weeks, breathing only with great difficulty, Mother Peabody had been forced to sit erect, falling off to sleep only when exhausted. Until her last moments, she had insisted that Sophia not be called, because of the children. When the end came, on the afternoon of January 11, Sophia was not on hand. Lizzie, writing that evening, provided a detailed picture of her mother's death:

> At the last moment, Mary was lying round the head of the bed, supporting her, with the intervention of some pillows . . . I laid down on the other bed so that I could see her, and father sat in the rocking chair. So long a time passed without a sound that father rose and went to look, and then I; and (as I said) it was a quarter of an hour. She breathed very gently the first part of the time. We all felt so thankful when it seemed that she had indeed fled without a sigh, when we had been dreading a final struggle between her tenacious life and the death angel. But, no; *her life went out into the free spaces,* and here she lies, for I am sitting by her bedside, this first night. Mary Mann has gone home; father has gone to bed. We are all at peace — peace — peace. This sentiment in me shuts out all realization that the only being in the wide world whose affection for me knew no limit, has gone out of it . . .

For Sophia and Mary, no less than Lizzie, it was the end of an irreplaceable relationship. And the end of that seemingly endless dialogue, the long chain of comforting, moralizing, hortatory letters on domestic affairs, literary matters, public events, spiritual certainties, that Mother Peabody had kept up with each of her daughters for more than a quarter of a century.

Our Old Home

ON JULY 6, 1853, the *Niagara*, a paddle-wheel steamer of the Cunard Line, under the direction of Captain John Leitch, steamed out of Boston Harbor. The air reverberated with a lengthy cannonade, a salute to the new American consul to Liverpool, who was on board. Also on board was the British minister to Washington, John F. Crampton, on his way to Halifax, Nova Scotia, where the *Niagara* would put in before its Atlantic crossing. Hawthorne, Sophia, and the excited children stood on the afterdeck, waving farewell to Dr. Peabody and James Fields, who had come to see them off. Sophia was comforted by seeing that Mr. Fields had taken her father in hand and was engaging him in conversation. She was pleased to note her father smiling as the ship pulled away from the dock.

There would be more than enough companionship on the eleven-day crossing — at least for Sophia. Among the other passengers was William Ticknor, who was accompanying them to England, and the Hawthornes' two maids, Ellen and Mary Herne, who had agreed to make the trip, with the provision that they would be able to pay a lengthy visit to their parents in Ireland. Also on board was William Silsbee, a friend of the Peabody family, who looked "so thin and pale" that Sophia feared for his health. Silsbee's traveling companion, O. W. Wight, was something of a bother: throughout the voyage he insisted on airing his transcendental views, until even the usually patient Sophia wanted to "fling him to the fishes, to baptize him in realities."

Sophia was already primed to admire English civility, and was immediately taken with the British minister, who was eager to meet her husband, and with an obliging young Englishman, Field Talfourd, whom she at first mistook for Crampton's attaché. Talfourd, later to become a notable artist and portraitist, was returning to

England after an American tour. A proficient conversationalist, an admirable playmate for her children, and an expert at gymnastics who very obligingly climbed the rigging to display his skill, Talfourd was a species of young man Sophia had never come across in America. "It seems to require more leisure and a deeper culture than we Americans have yet, to produce such a lovely flower," she commented.

The first day of the voyage had been one of unrelenting sunshine and intolerable heat. The calm was extraordinary; according to Sophia, the ocean was "a vast pearl, almost white with peace." Much to the relief of the passengers, an awning was soon spread out over the sterndeck. Hawthorne and the children, standing in the shade, watched the churning wake. Catching sight of a distant, blue point of land, Julian said with a sneer, "That, I suppose, is the end of America! I do not think America reaches very far!" In a boisterous mood, the two children chanted a made-up song, "Go away, tiresome old land." Hawthorne, roused from his own thoughts, turned grave. He told the youngsters to be quiet, saying they should "view with regret, the disappearance of the land that we might never see again."

The months before their July departure had been hectic and full. After the official confirmation by the Senate, Hawthorne had been swamped with letters of congratulation — among the first, a note from Charles Sumner, written from the Senate chamber: " 'Good!' 'Good!' I exclaimed aloud on the floor of the Senate as your nomination was announced . . . 'Good!' 'Good!' I now write to you on its confirmation. Nothing could be more grateful to me." Sophia happily reported the compliment to her family, adding, "So from all sides Mr. Hawthorne seems chosen by acclamation." On April 14, in a black rain, Hawthorne set out for Washington, accompanied by his obliging publisher, William Ticknor. Aside from paying an official and friendly visit to the new President, Hawthorne had matters of political patronage to discuss, among them possible appointments for Melville and Bridge.

Pierce was cordial, but pressed by business. Washington was a malarial city, and the President had been ailing throughout the spring, which gave rise to exaggerated reports about his health. (The administration paper, the *Union*, eventually felt it necessary to deny the rumors.) Then, too, during Hawthorne's visit, the vice-president, William R. King, who had been too ill even to attend the inauguration ceremonies, had died, creating another burden on the President. With Mrs. Pierce in mourning, and her friend, Mrs. Abby

Means, serving as official hostess at White House functions, Pierce's administration had begun on a gloomy note. In his grief and personal guilt, Pierce, like his wife, was attempting to find solace in religion. It did not liven the atmosphere.

There were other, more political problems facing the nation's fourteenth president. Pierce's cabinet nominations, by which he attempted to please all factions, had satisfied very few. In the midst of party squabbles, he was faced with international crises for which neither he nor his poorly assembled cabinet was prepared. Pierce's frankly expansionist policies, set forth in his inaugural address, had prompted a reaction from the English, who became suspiciously active in Central American politics and in Canada. Most immediately, Pierce was faced with the threatening presence of the British fleet in Canadian waters. He had been in hopes of arranging a fishing treaty with the more amenable Canadian government to secure the rights of American fishermen in Canadian territorial waters. The sudden appearance of British warships in the area created a nearly explosive situation. (It was quite likely that Crampton's trip to Halifax aboard the *Niagara* was intended to caution the British admiral about official American views.)

Given the circumstances, it was perhaps understandable that Pierce failed to give Hawthorne as warm a welcome as he may have expected. Hawthorne had a lengthy private meeting with the President and was invited to tea one evening at the White House. He also made an excursion to Mount Vernon, accompanying Mrs. Pierce on one of her rare public outings. For personal or political reasons that are not now clear, Pierce had even asked Hawthorne to prolong his stay by several days. William Ticknor sensed some dissatisfaction on Hawthorne's part, but attributed it to the author's being forced to play the celebrity. Hawthorne, Ticknor wrote his wife, "is quite a lion here. Much attention is shown, and yet it annoys him very much."

Ticknor found the protracted stay tiresome, but he did not want to leave his friend behind. He was gathering some distinct impressions of the political scene. Following a dinner with Stephen Douglas and other politicians, he wrote his wife that he was convinced "old party lines in every section of the country are breaking up and . . . there is a spirit abroad which is to revolutionize the politics of the country. Whether it will be for the best good of the Nation is a question of great importance — but the tide is rolling on . . . I have learnt more of political intrigue and management, since I have been here, than I ever dreamed of." Hawthorne was to benefit from the political maneuvering. In addition to his Liverpool consulship, he also secured the emoluments from the vacant consulship at Manchester, adding another $3000 to his official salary. "It is very queer," he wrote Sophia, "how much I have done for other people and myself since my arrival here."

Despite the lionizing and the success, Hawthorne felt neglected when he left Washington and Pierce. It rankled him that the President, currying favor with influential Southerners, had particularly courted George N. Sanders, a Kentuckian and agent for the Hudson Bay Company and more recently the publisher of the *Democratic Review*. Sanders had used O'Sullivan's old magazine to support Pierce's candidacy, callously misrepresenting the views of rivals like Douglas.

In retrospect, Hawthorne's response to his Washington trip was remarkably bitter and ungrateful. "Frank was as free and kind, in our personal interviews, as ever he was in our college days," he later wrote Horatio Bridge, "but his public attentions to me were few and by no means distinguished — only inviting me once to tea, and once to go to a Methodist meeting with him; while such people as George Sanders &c were invited to dinner and made much of. To confess the truth, I did not in the least regret being almost shut out of the White House; for of all dismally dull and heavy domestic circles, poor Frank's is certainly the most intolerable." Hawthorne was particularly harsh on sad, neurotic Jane Pierce, wishing that his friend had a better wife or none at all. "It is too bad that the nation should be compelled to see such a death's head in the pre-eminent place among American women," he remarked, unkindly.

For Sophia, the most troublesome worry about their proposed four-year stay in England had been her father. Hawthorne undoubtedly was grateful that his foreign appointment would relieve him of the burden of taking in his father-in-law. Dr. Peabody, however, would be staying at the Wayside with his son, Nathaniel Cranch Peabody, and his family. Well before her departure for Liverpool, Sophia had tried to allay Dr. Peabody's fears about their absence. "There is really no *distance* now," she had written her father. "I do not feel as if Liverpool were far off . . . I can write to you by every steamer, and you will know exactly about us, as if you were in Newton and we in Concord. And soon the telegraph will take news by lightning from the old to the new world."

As if to keep her promise, she wrote her father from the deck of the *Niagara* so that the letter could be mailed from Halifax. She reported happily on a delightful interview with the British minister. Mr. Crampton was a man of "great simplicity and charm of manner" and she had learned he was an "exquisite amateur artist." Captain Leitch was one of the most able captains on the Cunard Line, and she and Mr. Hawthorne had seats of honor at his table. As if to calm her father's fears of the effects of the sea voyage and her health, she concluded exuberantly, "It is glorious, glorious — this blue surrounding sea, and no land."

Except for a rough thirty-six-hour gale off the coast of Ireland, it was to be a mild crossing, and on July 17, the *Niagara* put down anchor in the Mersey River at Liverpool. At first, the family stayed at the Waterloo Hotel, but Hawthorne considered it a very mean establishment and was not satisfied. Sophia, however, admired the manner in which the proprietor, Mr. Lynn, conscious of the honor of having the United States consul under his roof, held the soup plates while she poured. Within a few days, they moved to a comfortable boardinghouse, Mrs. Blodget's, at 133 Duke Street, where the food was heartier and more plentiful. Mrs. Blodget was a buxom and respectable English widow, no taller than five feet, four inches, amply endowed with chins, who catered to Yankee captains. The Hawthornes felt strangely at home.

ᥳᐠ II ᥤᥕ

From the notebooks of the United States consul at Liverpool:

Liverpool, August 4th, 1853: . . . I began my services (such as they are) on Monday last, August 1st; and here I sit in my private room at the Consulate, while the Vice-Consul and clerk are carrying on affairs in the outer office . . . The pleasantest incident of the morning is when Mr. Pearce (the vice-consul or head-clerk) makes his appearance with the account-books, containing the receipts and expenditures of the preceding day, and deposits on my desk a little rouleau of the Queen's coin, wrapt up in a piece of paper . . . This forenoon, thus far, I have had two calls, not of business — one from an American captain, Foster, and his son, a boy — another from Mr. H[enry] A. B[right], whom I met in America, and who has shown us great attention here. He has arranged for us to go to the Theatre with his family this evening . . .

At two o'clock, I went over to the Royal Rock Hotel, about fifteen or twenty minutes steaming from this side of the river. We are going there on Saturday to reside for a while . . .

August 10th: . . . Visitors this morning, Mr. Ogden of Chicago, or somewhere in the western States, who arrived in England a fortnight or thereabouts ago, and who called on me at that time. He has since been in Scotland, and is now going to London and the Continent; secondly, the Captain of the Collins's steamer, *Pacific*, which sails today; thirdly an American shipmaster, who complained that he had never, in his heretofore voyages, been able to get a sight of the American Consul.

Mr. Pearce's customary matutinal visit was unusually agreeable today; inasmuch as he laid on my desk nineteen gold sovereigns, and thirteen shillings. It being the day of the steamers' departure, an unusual number of invoice certificates had been required — my signature to each of which brings me two dollars. The autograph of a living author has seldom been so much in request at so respectable a price . . .

August 15th: — Many scenes which I should have liked to record have occurred; but the pressure of business has prevented me from recording them from day to day . . .

On Friday, at 7 P.M., I went to dine with the Mayor. It was a dinner given to the Judges and the Grand Jury . . . The dinner was at the Town-Hall; and the rooms, and the whole affair, were all in the most splendid style . . . The rooms were beautiful, gorgeously painted and gilded, gorgeously lighted . . . the plate gorgeous, the dinner gorgeous, in the English fashion . . . After the removal of the cloth, the Mayor gave various toasts . . . and by-and-by came a toast to the United States and me as their representative. Hereupon, either "Hail Columbia" or "Yankee Doodle," or some other of our national tunes (but Heaven knows which) was played; and at the conclusion — being cornered and with no alternative — I got upon my legs and made a response. They received me and listened to my nonsense with a good deal of rapping . . . My speech was not more than two or three inches long . . .

August 22nd: — A Captain Auld, an American, having died here yesterday, I went with my clerk and an American shipmaster, to take inventory of his effects. His boarding-house was in a mean street . . . the class of boarding house frequented by mates of vessels, and inferior to those generally patronized by masters . . . The chattels of the dead man were contained in two trunks, a chest, a sail-cloth bag, and a barrel, and consisted of clothing, suggesting a thickset, middle-sized man; papers relative to ships and business; a spyglass, a loaded iron pistol, some books on navigation . . . some little plaster images, that he had probably bought for his children; a cotton umbrella; and other trumpery of no great value. In one of the trunks we found about twenty pounds' worth of English and American gold and silver . . . As his executor, I shall pay his landlady and nurse; and for the rest of the expenses, a subscription must be made (according to custom in such cases), among the shipmasters, headed by myself . . .

August 24th: . . . In the afternoon, at three o'clock, I attended the funeral of Captain Auld. Being ushered into the dining-room of his boarding-house, I found brandy, gin, and wine set out on a tray, together with some little spice-cakes . . . After waiting the better part of an hour, nobody else appeared, although several ship-masters had promised to attend. Hereupon, the undertaker was anxious to set forth; but the landlady (who was arrayed in shining black silk) thought it a shame that the poor man should be buried with such a small attendance. So we waited a little longer; during which interval, I heard the landlady's daughter sobbing and wailing in the entry . . .

September 1st: — Today we leave the Rock Ferry Hotel, where we have spent nearly four weeks. It is a comfortable place; and we have been well-victualled and kindly treated. We have occupied a large parlor, extending through the whole breadth of the house, and with a projecting window looking towards Liverpool, and adown the intervening river . . . The river would be a pleasanter object, if it were blue and transparent, instead of such a mud-puddly hue . . . Nevertheless, the parlor-window had given us a pretty good idea of the nautical business of Liverpool . . . the little black steamers, puffing unquietly along . . .

September 2nd: — We got into our new house in Rock Park yesterday. It is quite a good house, with three apartments, besides kitchen and pantry on the lower floor; and three stories high, with four good chambers in each story . . . It was a dismal, rainy day, yesterday; and we had a coal fire in the sitting-room; beside which I sat, last evening, as twilight came on, and thought rather sadly how many times we have changed our home, since we were married . . .

September 12th — On Saturday, a young man [George Ruggles] was found wandering about in West Derby (a suburb of Liverpool) in a state of insanity; and being taken before a magistrate, he proved to be an American. As he seemed to be in a respectable station of life, the magistrate sent the master of the workhouse to me in order to find out whether I would take the responsibility of his expense, rather than have him put in the workhouse . . . I decided to put him into the insane hospital, where he now accordingly is . . .

September 14th: . . . In a few minutes, the Governor [of the asylum] came in, a middle-aged man, tall and thin, for an Englishman, kindly and agreeable enough in aspect . . . I should not judge from his conversation that he was an educated man, or that he had any scientific acquaintance with the subject of insanity. He said that Mr. Ruggles was still quite uncommunicative, and not in a very promising state . . . that it would not be safe, at present, to send him home to America, without an attendant — and this was about all. But on returning home, I learned from my wife (who had had a call from Mrs. Blodget) that Mrs. B. knew Mr. Ruggles and his mother, who has recently been remarried to a younger husband and is now somewhere in Italy . . .

September 22nd: — Some days ago, an American captain came to the office and told how he had shot one of his crew, shortly after sailing from New Orleans, and while the ship was still in the river. As he described the event, he was in peril of his life from this man, who was an Irishman; and he only fired his pistol, when the man was coming upon him with a knife in one hand . . . Two or three days since . . . two of the sailors came before me, and gave their account of the matter; and it looked very different from that of the captain. According to them, the man had no idea of attacking the captain, and was so drunk that he could not keep himself upright, without assistance. One of these two men was actually holding him up, when the captain fired two barrels of his pistol, one immediately after the other, and lodged two balls in the pit of his stomach. The man immediately sank down, saying, "Jack, I'm killed" — and died very shortly . . . In my opinion it is little short of murder, if at all; but then what would be murder on shore is almost a natural occurrence, when done in such a hell on earth as one of these ships, in the first hours of her voyage. The men are then all drunk, some of them often in delirium tremens; and the captain feels no safety for his life, except in making himself as terrible as a fiend . . .

October 8th: — Coming to my office, two or three mornings ago, I found Mrs. Eaton, the mother of Mr. Ruggles, the insane young man whom I had taken charge of. She is a lady of fifty or thereabouts, and not very remarkable anyway, nor particularly ladylike. However, she was just come off a rapid journey, having come from Naples, without taking rest, since my letter reached her, together with three small children. A son of about twenty had come with her to the Consulate. [The "son" was, in fact, her new husband.] She was, of course, infinitely grieved about the young man's insanity, and had two or three bursts of tears . . . She said he was the hope of her life — the best, purest, most innocent child that ever was, and wholly free from every kind of vice — (at which I could not but smile, knowing that the young gentleman had been in company with a lady, two nights, at a hotel here, and, from the items of his bill, had had a particularly jolly time) — but it appears that he had a previous attack of insanity, lasting three months, about three years ago . . .

October 19th: — I have [had] a good many visitors at the consulate from the United States, within a short time — among others, Mr. D. D. Barnard, our late minister to Berlin, returning homeward today by the *Arctic*; Mr. Sickles, Secretary of Legation to London, a fine-looking, gentlemanly, intelligent young man, but, so I am told, very dissolute, and with some remarkably dark stains in his character. Unless belied, he has been kept by a prostitute, within a few years, and is now married to a woman whom he seduced . . . Be that as it may, in aspect and address he does us credit . . . With him came Judge Douglas, the chosen man of Young America. He is very short — extremely short — but has an uncommonly good head, and uncommon dignity of manner, without seeming to aim at it, being free and simple in manners. I judge him to be a very able man, with the Western sociability and free fellowship. When I saw him in Washington, he had on a very dirty shirt-collar. I believe it was clean, yesterday . . .

November 14th: — There is a heavy, dun fog on the river, and over the city, today; the very gloomiest atmosphere that ever I was acquainted with. On the river, the steamboats strike gongs or ring bells, to give warning of their approach. There are lamps burning in the counting-rooms and entries of the warehouses, and they gleam distinctly through the windows.

As a representative of the United States government in England, Hawthorne was confronted by odder aspects of the American character than he had ever noticed in the smallest rural tavern back home. What especially amused him were the eternally optimistic American types, convinced of some legitimate claim against ancestral English estates, who showed up at the consulate demanding his assistance. There seemed to be a "peculiar insanity" buried deep in the Anglo-American heart. "After all these bloody wars and vindictive animosities," Hawthorne reflected, "we have still an unspeakable yearning towards England." In other instances, Hawthorne was cast in a thoroughly unfamiliar role. A New Orleans clergyman, the Reverend Dr. Richards, arrived at the consulate, destitute after a week spent in a Liverpool brothel, and shaking from delirium tremens. "I wish you could have heard the lecture I gave him," Hawthorne wrote Ticknor, who was back in Boston. "He shook in his shoes, I can tell you. Not knowing whether I should ever have another opportunity of preaching to a Doctor of Divinity (an orthodox man, too) I laid it on without mercy." As usual with the unfortunate cases he had to deal with, Hawthorne advanced the money for the shaken clergyman to return home on the next ship. In the privacy of his journal, Hawthorne concluded, "In my opinion, he has incurred sin no further than as a madman may."

Among the sadder duties of his office were the cases like that of Captain Auld, dying in a foreign port — as Hawthorne's father had died — among strangers, with no one to mourn him and little to commemorate the man and his life except a bundle of useless clothes and a few personal items. In such cases he wrote letters to the family, relaying the sorry news that a husband or a son had died and been buried "in the Cemetery of Saint James in this city," adding his cool condolences: "I beg leave to assure you of my heartfelt sympathy in this sad bereavement." There were the minor tragedies like that of the insane young man — disordered, abandoned lives — for whom he could do little more than contact the family.

And there were the continuing, brutal cases of mistreated sailors that were brought to his attention. Month by month, Hawthorne wrote them up in his journal and sent official dispatches to the State Department. They formed a dossier of intolerable abuses: crewmen murdered in cold blood by sadistic or terrified captains or mates; cooks who had their noses broken or lamp oil forced down their throats; sailors who had been beaten or flogged for minor offenses. Many of the men had been shanghaied in American ports and had no experience at sea; others were foreign-born, having signed on American vessels for the return passage to Liverpool. Unless the crime had occurred in English waters, the English courts would not handle the case. If it had occurred at sea and was within the jurisdiction of American law, a foreign-born sailor could never be induced to make the return trip to the United States in order to press charges. Even where prosecution was possible, Hawthorne could never be sure that the American witnesses whose depositions he took would return to America for the trial. The only effective measures he seemed able to take were to secure the discharges of the abused men and see that the captains paid them their due wages. It was common practice among captains who brutally mistreated their crewmen to charge them with incompetence and refuse to pay.

After months and years of sending official reports that had little effect, Hawthorne took the unusual step of enlisting the aid of Charles Sumner, hardly a friend of the administration, to push for corrective legislation. In a move that his superiors could have regarded as insubordination, Hawthorne wrote the senator on May 23, 1855. It was one of his lengthiest and most straightforward statements on the problem:

> For some time past I have been thinking of asking you to interest yourself in bringing the condition of our mercantile marine before Congress. Matters are really in a very terrible state between shipmasters and seamen; and having been thrust by Providence (and Pierce) into this consulate, I ought not to leave it without an attempt to do some little good. Everyday, some miserable cruelty and wrong is brought under my notice . . . In three instances, which came before me, sailors had been shot dead by their officers; and the most perplexing part of the matter, is that all the bloodshed and cruelty seems to be strangely justifiable, and almost inevitable under the circumstances. It certainly is not the fault, so much as it

is the fate, of our shipmasters to do these abominable deeds. They are involved in a wrong system, which renders it impossible for them to do right; and they themselves become morally deteriorated by it and continually grow worse and worse. As for the seamen, they are no better than pirates. The truth is, we have no seamen of our own, our ships being manned almost entirely by the offscourings of the British merchant service, and by Germans and other foreigners whom the shipping-masters entrap. I should like to know what is to become of us at sea, in case of a war — but *that* you don't care about.

Hawthorne was well aware of the egoism that was inextricably woven into the zeal of a reformer — that, after all, had been one of the profounder insights of *The Blithedale Romance*. It was odd, therefore — and certainly a lapse of tact on his part — that in trying to enlist Sumner's aid, he should have made so little of the senator's commitment to the antislavery cause. "If you will let slavery alone for a little while," Hawthorne lectured the senator, "and attend to this business (where much good may, and no harm can possibly be done) I think you will be doing our country a vast service. The shipping-masters in the American ports seem to be at the bottom, or near the bottom, of the mischief . . . [They] should be annihilated at once — no slave drivers are so wicked as they, and there is nothing in slavery so bad as the system with which they are connected."

His letter had no appreciable effect on Sumner, who did not involve himself with the rampant abuses of the American merchant marine. Hawthorne seems to have donned blinkers in pressing for his own brand of reform.

Early in his diplomatic career, Hawthorne was faced with a political embarrassment. On December 24, 1853, the ship *San Francisco*, carrying United States troops, was wrecked in the Atlantic. A passing ship, the *Antarctic*, managed to rescue some 180 passengers and crew members and bring them to Liverpool. Hawthorne was asked to arrange passage back home for the refugees. As consul, he had no authority to do so, but he answered that he would immediately contact the American minister in London, James Buchanan, for instructions. In the meantime, on his own, Hawthorne had arranged to pay for clothing and provisions for the disaster victims. He also conferred with several American shipmasters, and by the following day, he had four propositions in hand waiting for Buchanan's response. Buchanan answered that he had no authority either, but he instructed the firm of Baring Brothers to open a line of credit for Hawthorne's use.

Soon after the episode, American newspapers circulated reports that Hawthorne had refused to assist the *San Francisco* victims, giving an altered version of the story, in which Buchanan, who ostensibly had presidential ambitions, was being touted as the hero. The *Portsmouth Journal of Literature & Politics* pointedly asked, "Should not Mr. Hawthorne have a 'scarlet letter' branded on his own forehead?"

Hawthorne was reluctant to answer the charges openly — partly, it seems, because he did not know the extent to which the false story was being circulated at home. But he wrote an explanatory letter and sent it to William Ticknor. He suggested that Ticknor consult with Hillard before deciding to publish, and asked that the letter be published only if absolutely necessary. "I hate nothing worse than to be defending myself in newspapers," he said. "An officeholder's credit, like a woman's chastity," he quipped, "suffers from being talked about, even though the defense be perfectly successful."

In his official letter, Hawthorne made it clear that he had received little advice or assistance from Buchanan. "I do not question the propriety of Mr. Buchanan's conduct," he stated, "and am bound to presume that he could estimate the extent of his official powers better than I could do it for him." But, writing Ticknor, he complained that he took it hard that he should be "slandered" because of the *San Francisco* affair, "when everybody else has been so egregiously and extravagantly lauded. I really think I deserve a gold medal and a dinner as well as any other man."

The letter to Ticknor was purely precautionary, and Hawthorne later was grateful he had made no public statement against his immediate superior. He was to meet Buchanan at the end of April, when the American minister was in Liverpool awaiting the arrival of his niece, Harriet Lane. Writing to Ticknor on April 30, Hawthorne mentioned, "I had the old fellow to dine with me, and liked him better than I expected; so I hope you have not found it necessary to publish my letter on the *San Francisco* business; for though I made it bear lightly on him, it would undoubtedly have provoked a feud between us. But he takes his wine like a true man, loves a good cigar, and is doubtless as honest as nine diplomatists out of ten." A few days later, he again expressed his relief that his defense had not been published, "for it is humiliating to be compelled to stand before the public in an attitude of defense. And besides I should have made several enemies — which it is not desirable to do except in a case of necessity. But somebody must have lied most damnably." He had begun to acquire the prudence necessary for dealing with political life and presidential aspirants.

Hawthorne and Buchanan were to have several meetings, in

Liverpool and London, during Hawthorne's term as consul. Buchanan, knowing that Hawthorne was an intimate friend of Pierce's, was understandably cautious. He had been bitterly disappointed in his bid for the presidency and had only reluctantly accepted a post in the Pierce administration. He had extracted a firm promise from Pierce that he would have a free hand in dealing with the tangled relationships between the United States and England. Although this should have been the prerogative of Secretary of State William Marcy, Pierce had agreed to the condition. But very shortly after the Senate confirmation, Buchanan found that Pierce had reneged on his promise, turning over to Marcy the negotiations for the Canadian fishing treaty. Buchanan felt his position had been severely compromised but decided it was poor strategy to resign a commission he had only just accepted. He was, naturally, circumspect in dealing with Pierce and his friends.

Hawthorne's agreeable impressions of the man were slightly tainted by his suspicions of the politician. He liked the sixty-four-year-old bachelor's "good sense and plainness of speech," and thought him an impressive figure with a certain rustic dignity except for his habit of squinting one eye, the result of a physical defect. Yet he wondered if Buchanan might not be as "crafty as other diplomatists are said to be." In one of their early interviews Buchanan had told him he planned to retire from politics to write his memoirs. When Hawthorne suggested that the public might not allow him to, Buchanan stated firmly that he would not run for the office again. "He acknowledged that he should have been glad of the nomination for the Presidency in 1852," Hawthorne noted, "but that it was now too late, and that he was too old." Privately, Hawthorne questioned the motive behind Buchanan's assertion: "I wonder whether he can have had any object in saying all this to me. He might see that it would be perfectly natural for me to tell it to General Pierce. But it is a very vulgar idea — this of seeing craft and subtlety, where there is a plain and honest aspect."

They were to have an extended political discussion in the minister's somewhat shabby Harley Street residence in London — and there, there was no further talk of Buchanan's retirement. But Buchanan opened up in his views of the administration, maintaining that if Pierce had taken his early advice, he would have had a "perfectly quiet and successful term of office." He had, he said, advised Pierce to form "a perfectly homogeneous cabinet of Union men, and to satisfy the extremes of the party by a fair distribution of minor offices." Pierce, he felt, had made a mistake in assembling a cabinet of extreme men of both sides and distributing the minor offices among the moderates. This was an obvious misreading of Pierce's political maneuverings, and Hawthorne, in his notes on the meeting, accurately queried, "But the anti-slavery people, surely, had no representative in the cabinet." Even at its highest levels, American politics was, at best, an unskilled profession.

Like many of his predecessors in office, Hawthorne took advantage of his position to do some minor smuggling, sending and receiving his private letters by way of diplomatic courier to avoid the expense of overseas mail. He performed the same service for friends like Longfellow and Ticknor, who sent their letters to English friends by diplomatic pouch. More profitably, he engaged — as did most ministers and foreign-service appointees — in sending dutiable merchandise in small quantities by the same route. Cigars, taxable jewelry, and silver were regularly shipped to and from the United States and between American legations. At times, Hawthorne warned Fields and Ticknor that their gifts should be kept to moderate-sized packages; otherwise the customs officials inspected the diplomatic mail and he was forced to pay the required fees.

A letter from Hawthorne to Buchanan, dated November 18, 1854, is one of the minor items of evidence of the trade among American diplomats. In it, Hawthorne advised Buchanan that two cases of guns for General Webb had been sent. The self-styled "General" was James Watson Webb, who years before had precipitated the duel in which Jonathan Cilley was killed. Webb, in London, covering the Crimean War for his paper, the *Courier and Enquirer*, was accorded the same diplomatic privileges extended to any American dignitary. For Hawthorne, politics had created a strange bedfellow.

↶ III ↷

Despite his growing literary reputation, Hawthorne did not take advantage of his position to meet the celebrated English writers of his time. His notebooks are studded with gossip about such figures as Dickens, but it is often information learned secondhand, at minor affairs and in provincial salons. At a banquet, for instance, he was told that Dickens was a born plebeian who aspired to "aristocratic society." This characterization was contradicted later, in conversation with other English acquaintances. "Speaking of Dickens last evening," Hawthorne wrote in his journal after a dinner conversation, "Mrs. Milnes mentioned his domestic tastes, how he preferred home enjoyments to all others, and did not willingly go much into society . . . There is a great variety of testimony, various and variant, as to the character of Dickens. I must see him before I finally leave England." His resolution came to nothing; Hawthorne made no attempt to call on the English novelist.

About the equally popular and famous Tennyson, Hawthorne might state, "I should be glad to smoke a cigar with him," but, catching sight of the poet in the picture galleries of the Manchester Exhibition of 1857, he was too shy to allow any introduction. He stared in fascination at the poet laureate, a middle-sized, slouching man in a buttoned-up frock coat and wide hat, with long, tangled, unkempt hair and a none-too-clean collar. Tennyson, accompanied by a friend, moved rapidly through the gallery, inspecting the paintings, entirely oblivious of the crowd.

Knowing of Sophia's fondness for the poet, Hawthorne searched her out in the music galleries, bringing her back in time to catch a final glimpse of the great man. In his notebooks, Hawthorne described the poet's passage. He caught the intonation of Tennyson's bass voice — "not of a resounding depth; a voice rather broken, as it were, and ragged about the edges, but pleasant to the ear." He also noted Tennyson's curious gait as he left the gallery, "shuffling along the floor with short irregular steps . . . as if he were walking in slippers too loose for him." He observed, "In his whole presence, I was indescribably sensible of a morbid painfulness in him, a something not to be meddled with." And he concluded, "He might well enough pass for a madman at any time."

Hawthorne was far more agreeable to meeting the lesser stars of the English literary firmament. Ticknor encouraged him to visit Charles Reade, but the popular English author did not make a strong impression. "I like his books better than himself; not that I saw any fault in him either. I tell you this because you particularly wished me to see him," Hawthorne wrote Ticknor. On a later occasion, after having read *Never Too Late to Mend*, he regretted that he hadn't got to know Reade better. Hawthorne's meeting with the poet Coventry Patmore was more satisfactory. Patmore's "An Angel in the House" was a favorite of his and Sophia's. Hawthorne, whose taste in poetry verged on the sentimental at best, considered it "a poem for happy married people to read together." Patmore, shy and younger than Hawthorne expected, was very glad to learn of his reputation in America. Hawthorne also visited the aged Leigh Hunt, survivor and friend of Shelley and Byron, who was living in a "shabby little house" in Hammersmith. Hawthorne concluded that Hunt was a man with a taste for beautiful things that were denied him in his pitiful old age; his cottage door had been opened by a "slatternly maid-servant," and Hawthorne had been ushered into a dreary parlor — "a very forlorn room, with poor paper-hangings and carpet, few books, no pictures that I remember, and an awful lack of upholstery."

At the Reform Club, one April evening in 1856, he dined with Dr. Charles Mackay, a popular songwriter, and Douglas Jerrold, the London playwright, critic, and contributor to *Punch*. The several-course meal had been accompanied by the proper wines — a Château Margaux, a Chambertin, a Clos Vougeot — and the three had had a lively literary discussion of Bulwer-Lytton, Dickens, and the success of Thackeray's recent visit to America. Hawthorne took a liking to Jerrold, sensing that he had a warm heart under "a very thin crust of outward acerbity." But when the discussion turned to such American authors as Emerson, Longfellow, and Thoreau, Hawthorne had tactlessly remarked that Jerrold's viewpoint was, perhaps, too "acrid" for him to appreciate Thoreau. Jerrold, distinctly wounded, retreated into a glum silence. Hawthorne thought he had repaired the damage, midway through the second bottle of Burgundy, by stating that the playwright was as "genial" as the glass of wine he held in his hand. Following the meal, the three men, glowing warmly, set off for the Haymarket Theatre, where they took in the performance of a troupe of Spanish dancers. According to Mackay, however, Jerrold did not forgive the slight. Instead, he claimed that Hawthorne was one of the "heaviest and most awkward of persons" he had ever met. "But he means well," Jerrold remarked, "as all clumsy people do."

Throughout his English residence, Hawthorne was to meet a number of literary women, but not the pre-eminent one, George Eliot. An early biographer of Hawthorne, Moncure Conway, maintained that Hawthorne's failure to meet Thackeray, Dickens, and Eliot could be attributed to Hawthorne's "hereditary prejudices" against the condescending airs of many Englishmen toward Americans. Later, in an article, Conway claimed that Hawthorne had tried to arrange a meeting with Eliot through several English hostesses, but none of these was on "visiting terms" with the novelist, presumably because of her adulterous relationship with George Henry Lewes. That explanation, though, may have been somewhat after the fact. Eliot's great success did not begin until the publication of her first novel, *Adam Bede*, in February 1859 (when the Hawthornes were in Italy), and even then her nom de plume was intended to screen her identity and was still a jealously guarded secret. By February 1860, after his return to England, Hawthorne was clearly aware that Eliot's name was Mary Ann Evans. At a dinner party in Coventry, he met Mr. and Mrs. Charles Bray, dedicated friends of Eliot. (Charles Bray was a writer and publisher with extensive literary connections; Emerson had stayed at his home, Rosehill, on his last trip to England.) Hawthorne, so Mrs. Bray reported, had "talked exclusively about Miss Evans, asking questions of all kinds about her." That the Brays, who certainly were on "visiting terms" with Eliot, did not arrange a meeting was perhaps due to Eliot's hurrying to complete her second novel, *The Mill on the Floss*, before leaving herself for an extended trip to Italy with Lewes.

Hawthorne did, however, call on Harriet Martineau, aging and fearless and very deaf. The fifty-two-year-old abolitionist, political economist, and atheist — "There is no God and Harriet is His prophet," Douglas Jerrold had quipped — had kept up a "lively and sensible" babble of conversation. She used an enormous ear trumpet, which she swung round to each of her visitors. "If you have any little remark to make," Hawthorne observed, "you drop it in." Chiefly, Harriet Martineau had talked about herself and her affairs, and the talk had been cheerful, free from morbid thoughts. "And this woman is an Atheist," Hawthorne commented in his notebook, "and thinks, I believe, that the principle of life will become extinct when her great, fat, well-to-do body is laid in the grave! I will not think so, were it only for her sake."

At a brilliant London dinner party, at which he and Jenny Lind were the guests of honor, in midsummer of 1856, Hawthorne met Geraldine Jewsbury, the English novelist and a dedicated friend of Charlotte Cushman's. She and Hawthorne discussed Emerson, whom she had met in England. Hawthorne, who had never read any of her books, found the spirited, redheaded feminist "very conversable." Later in the evening, Jenny Lind made it known that she wished to meet the famous American author. Hawthorne, seated next to her on the sofa, received compliments on *The Scarlet Letter*. He did his best to reciprocate, considering that he had never heard the prima donna sing and had never greatly cared to. Jenny Lind had discoursed on the "unwholesome modes of life" she had seen in America and the poor health of its women. Hawthorne thought she looked "wan and worn enough to be an American herself." He boasted wryly, "Leaving out the illustrious Jenny, I suspect that I was myself the greatest lion of the evening; for a good many persons sought the felicity of knowing me, and had little or nothing to say when that honor and happiness was conferred upon them."

Midway in his English stay, Hawthorne had also, unfortunately, met another woman writer — this one, an American, Delia Salter Bacon, who claimed kinship with the great Francis Bacon and was a monomaniac on the subject of the authorship of Shakespeare's plays. She was convinced they had been written by an Elizabethan cabal that had included her famous ancestor as well as Sir Walter

Raleigh and Edmund Spenser. The evidence, she claimed, would be found in Shakespeare's tomb, if she could ever persuade the English authorities to open it. A neurotic spinster who had quarreled with her American family, she lived in near-poverty in England. Peppery and blunt in her manner, she once commanded Hawthorne by letter, "Don't call me *Miss Bacon*. I don't know who it means when I see that name. I have forgotten all about it."

Hawthorne cared nothing for her theories, but he was impressed by some of her interpretations of Shakespeare's plays. Touched by her intensity and dedication, he put up money toward the English publication of her book, *The Philosophy of the Plays of Shakspere Unfolded*, the crowning project of her obsessed life. He also persuaded Ticknor to publish it in America. Having agreed to write a preface for the volume, he was pestered with her instructions. "It is no use trying to reason with this preposterous woman," Hawthorne wrote an English friend who was also involved. "I shall not pay the slightest regard to her notions about an Introduction, but shall write such a Preface as seems to me good, and give the book up to its destiny. No doubt, she will impute its failure to her not being permitted to have her own way. So be it." When he finally produced his introduction, Delia Bacon cut large portions of it, argued that he was not supportive enough, and advised him to try again. By the time the book appeared, the two were not on speaking terms. Hawthorne had been correct in his assessment; the book was an utter failure. The distraught author, living in retirement in Stratford-on-Avon, still besieging authorities to open Shakespeare's tomb — but far less certain of her theories — went insane. Hawthorne, the most available American she knew, found himself responsible for her care and maintenance, until a nephew, returning from China, took her to America, where she died. Delia Bacon, whose claims on her English heritage were entirely literary, was another of the dreaming American innocents abroad who figured in Hawthorne's consular experiences. He was to use her pathetic story in "Recollections of a Gifted Woman," one of the segments of *Our Old Home*, the later, purified, and polite version of his experiences drawn from his notebooks.

That Hawthorne was being lionized was evident by the attentions of Richard Monckton Milnes, a minor writer but the most eminent literary host of his time. In his London home, Milnes, later Lord Houghton, gave literary breakfasts that became an institution for decades. At these social events one was sure to find the most celebrated and glamorous figures of the period. Poets, actors, explorers, and politicians mingled at his table. Milnes's library was famous for its rare volumes. Less well known was the collection of erotica he had begun to amass; it was to become the most extensive in England. Hawthorne had first met Milnes at a dinner party in Liverpool and had found the forty-five-year-old Englishman agreeable and kindly, with an affability that was somehow reminiscent of Longfellow's. Mrs. Milnes, a daughter of Lord Crewes, was equally charming; Hawthorne maintained she was "of noble blood, and therefore less snobbish than most English ladies."

Milnes had a keen interest in American writers. (In later years, he cultivated Henry Adams and Henry James as assiduously as he had Hawthorne. James referred to him, kindly, as a "bird of paradox.") His taste in American literature was well in advance of American critics. Not long after *Leaves of Grass* was published, Milnes queried Hawthorne about its author. (Unfortunately, no response from Hawthorne has survived, so it is not clear whether he was even aware of Walt Whitman.) Early in the relationship of the two men, Milnes asked for half a dozen books by good American authors he might not have heard of. Hawthorne, writing to Ticknor, suggested that he send Thoreau's *Walden* and *A Week on the Concord and Merrimack Rivers*, as well as Julia Ward Howe's *Passion Flowers* and Lewis Mansfield's *Up-Country Letters*. Other books to be sent to Milnes, Hawthorne wrote Ticknor, "must not be merely good, but must be original, with American characteristics, and not generally known in England." He discounted anything by Whittier, saying, "I like the man, but have no high opinion either of his poetry or prose." He added, "Send Lowell's 'Biglow Papers.' He is very little known in England, and I take that to be the best thing he has written."

Writing to Milnes about his selection, Hawthorne recommended *Passion Flowers* highly, commenting that the poems were "by a very beautiful woman (the wife of Dr. Howe, the philanthropist of blind people) and are certainly more passionate than most husbands would find agreeable. I think we have produced no better poetry than some of her verses." He noted that the two Thoreau volumes were by "a very remarkable man; but I hardly hope you will read his books, unless for the observation of nature contained in them — which is wonderfully accurate. I sometimes fancy it a characteristic of American books that it generally requires an effort to read them; there is hardly ever one that carries the reader away with it . . . Please not to quote this as my opinion."

Milnes, evidently impressed with Thoreau, asked for more information about the Concord writer. Hawthorne responded with another of his surgical dissections of his neighbor:

> I have known Thoreau a good many years [he wrote Milnes], but it would be quite impossible to comprise him within this little sheet of note-paper. He is an excellent scholar, and a man of most various capacity; insomuch that he could make his part good in any way of life, from the most barbarous to the most civilized. But there is more of the Indian in him, I think, than of any other kind of man. He despises the world, and all that it has to offer, and, like other humorists, is an intolerable bore. I shall cause it to be known to him that you sat up till two o'clock, reading his book; and he will pretend that it is of no consequence, but will never forget it.

Having delivered that judgment, Hawthorne went on to temper it with an endorsement of his fellow writer:

> I ought not to forbear saying that he is an upright, conscientious, and courageous man, of whom it is impossible to conceive anything but the highest integrity . . . I wish anything could be done to make his books known to the English public, for certainly they deserve it, being the work of a true man and full of true thought . . . You must not think that he is a particular friend of mine [Hawthorne cautioned]. I do not speak with quite this freedom of my friends. We have never been intimate, though my home is near his residence.

It was not until a bright Friday morning in midsummer of 1856, during a visit to London, that Hawthorne attended his first breakfast in Upper Brook Street. Among the guests, he encountered two Americans of his acquaintance, the Boston historian George Ticknor (a cousin of the publisher) and the Harvard professor John G. Palfrey. Much to his regret, however, the pair had monopolized the table talk, leaving in silence another of the guests, the historian Macaulay, a writer Hawthorne much admired. Also present were the mother and sister of Florence Nightingale. In his notebooks, Hawthorne admitted that he had "liked greatly the manners of almost all," feeling that it was "doubtless owing to their being all people either of high rank, or remarkable intellect, or both. An Englishman can hardly be a gentleman, unless he enjoy one or the other of these advantages." The best way to ensure an Englishman's good manners, he maintained, was to make him a lord.

For Sophia's benefit, Hawthorne especially observed Elizabeth Barrett Browning, describing her as "of that quickly appreciative and responsive order of women, with whom I can talk more freely than with any men." He observed, "She is a small, delicate woman, with ringlets of black . . . . a pleasant, intelligent, sensitive face, and a low, agreeable voice." At table, he and the poet conversed at length about spiritualism, which interested her immensely but which her husband completely rejected. They also discussed Delia Bacon. Much to Mrs. Browning's horror, Hawthorne outlined the lady's theories about the Bard. "We talked, too," Hawthorne noted, "of Margaret Fuller, who spent her last night in Italy with the Brownings; and of William Story, with whom they have been intimate and who, Mrs. Browning says, is much stirred up about spiritualism." In his notebook, Hawthorne was gently disapproving of her interest in the occult: "Really, I cannot help wondering that so fine a spirit as hers should not reject the matter."

In the library after the meal, Hawthorne was introduced to Robert Browning, whom he found "very simple and agreeable in manner, gently impulsive, talking as if his heart were uppermost." Browning, genuinely pleased at meeting the American author, spoke of his appreciation of Hawthorne's novels — "and (which has not often happened to me) mentioned that 'The Blithedale Romance' was the one he most admired." Hawthorne asked, "I wonder why."

Hawthorne was to form two abiding friendships with Englishmen, both men with literary interests. The first was Henry Arthur Bright, the son of a Liverpool merchant and shipping magnate, owner of the *Great Britain,* the largest steamer of its time. Hawthorne had first met Bright in Concord in September 1852, when the young Englishman and two traveling companions arrived, "fortified" with a letter from Longfellow and brought by Emerson to the Wayside. Tall, thin as a reed, nearsighted, with a prominent nose and a deeply cleft chin, Bright was twenty-two years old, a Cambridge student and disputatious. The first meeting had not been promising. Writing to a friend, Bright complained, "He received us with the most frigid manner, but asked us into his house, and that was nearly all he said, except in answer to a question . . . Emerson was much amused." The Concord philosopher had helpfully forewarned the English visitors that Hawthorne hardly ever unbent; that talking with him was like talking to a girl, "were it not that every now and then in his conversation, as in his books, you feel that there is some bitter fairy, which is biting him all the time, and which he is unable to conceal."

In Liverpool, Bright had promptly renewed the acquaintance. At first, Hawthorne deferentially addressed the younger man as "Mr. Bright," but their frequent meetings soon became unusually heated and lively. The two men engaged in free-for-all discussions in which Hawthorne, irritated by some display of English snobbishness and class-consciousness, would assume a scornful democratic air. Bright was an intrepid adversary. Julian, who developed an easygoing loyalty toward the Englishman, described the typical exchanges between his father and Bright: "Hawthorne would launch at him such appalling and unsparing home truths of democracy and republicanism as would utterly have shocked and smothered any other subject of her Majesty, but they only served to make Mr. Bright laugh and declare that it was impossible anybody should seriously entertain such opinions."

Their disagreements extended into literature as well, for Bright was a minor critic and a contributor to the *Westminster Review*, a champion of Tennyson as the greatest English writer of the time — an opinion Hawthorne did not altogether share. With the candor of genuine friendship, Hawthorne was especially critical of an essay Bright wrote on De Quincey. He was convinced that only Americans properly appreciated the English essayist and that Bright's article had been too lukewarm in its praise. "Here comes De Quincey, begging at your door," he complained, "a poor old man of genius, to whom the world is in arrears for half-a-century's revenue of fame! You examine his title deeds, find them authentic, and send him away with the benefaction of half-a-crown!"

From virtually the moment of the Hawthornes' arrival in Liverpool, young Bright had taken them up, arranging theater parties and excursions, introducing them to his extensive upper-class connections, and inviting them to his home, Sandheys, outside Liverpool. The Hawthornes met his aunt, Mrs. Heywood, a vivacious and fashionable hostess who maintained a London house near Hyde Park in season, and for the remainder of the year lived at Norris Green near Liverpool. It was at the Heywoods' that Hawthorne had met Monckton Milnes and his wife.

Sophia could hardly ignore young Bright's devotion to her husband or his attentions to her. An avid gardener, with the English love of flowers, he brought her bouquets of moss roses. Sophia enjoyed talking with him. "He can really converse," she informed her family. She was especially delighted by his accounts of his American trip. "Boston," he told her, "is the Mecca of English Unitarians; Dr. Channing, their patron saint." A Unitarian with liberal and reformist tendencies, Bright had refused to subscribe to the Thirty-nine Articles of the Church of England, a condition for taking the degree at Cambridge. It was not until 1857, when restrictions were lifted, that he and his cousin, James Heywood, became the first Nonconformists to take their degrees from the university.

Francis Bennoch, Hawthorne's other English friend, was a man of a thoroughly different stamp — an Englishman of conservative sympathies, so confident of his politics that he had no need to argue with the American consul. A London wool merchant, head of the prospering firm of Bennoch, Twentyman and Rigg, he was a man of

Dickensian proportions, stalwart and still handsome when Hawthorne met him. A Scot by birth, he entertained a wide acquaintance of literary friends at his suburban Blackheath home. (Bennoch, too, had been an unfortunate partner in Delia Bacon's publishing schemes.) A man of sentiment, he was easily moved to tears. Hawthorne's friendship with him was clinched one gloomy day in Liverpool when Bennoch, visiting at Rock Ferry, watched Hawthorne diffidently prodding the coals in the fireplace. "Give me the poker, my dear sir!" Bennoch exclaimed, "and I'll give you a lesson." With two or three well-aimed thrusts, he stoked up a bright flame. "That's the way to get warmth out of an English fire," he counseled Hawthorne, "and that's the way to get warmth out of an English heart, too! Treat us like that, my dear sir, and you'll find us all good fellows!"

Bennoch was a man of uncompromising loyalties. Some years after Hawthorne's death, he attended a London dinner at which a guest, in the course of an afterdinner speech, referred to Hawthorne, claiming that he had been present on an occasion when Hawthorne had disgraced himself by becoming drunk at an English table. He also passed on the slander that it was on a drinking spree with Franklin Pierce that Hawthorne had died. As soon as the speech was over, Bennoch, indignant over the slur, stood up and declared that he had been present on the occasion referred to and, in fact, had been sitting next to Hawthorne. He announced that he had seen Hawthorne drink wine on a number of occasions and that he had "a head of iron" and drank no more than any Englishman usually had with his dinner. In conclusion, he asserted that the statement "which the gentleman has just made to you, and which I am willing to believe he merely repeated upon hearsay, is a lie from beginning to end. Whoever repeats it, tells a lie; and whoever repeats it after hearing what I have said, tells a lie knowing it to be such." With that firm assertion, Bennoch sat down.

During his term as consul, Hawthorne attended a wide range of social functions — dinners at the lord mayor's, the dedication of a new library, the ceremonies for the *Great Britain*'s maiden voyage to Australia. In his notebooks, he left careful and precise portraits of the English upper classes at the height of their powers. He attended civic banquets by the score and, as the duly appointed American representative — sometimes flushed with wine — stood up to make the necessary and graceful acceptance speeches. Early in his consular career, he might write his friend Bridge, who had just returned to the United States and was hoping for an appointment in Washington, that, though he liked his office well enough, he found the social obligations "irksome to me beyond expression." Yet on occasion he could be boastful. "Tell the President," he wrote Bridge, "that I was a guest at a public entertainment the other day, where his health was drunk, standing, immediately after those of the Queen and the royal family. When the rest of the party sat down, I remained on my legs and returned thanks in a very pretty speech, which was received with more cheering and applause than any other during the dinner. I had missed no opportunity of gulping down champagne, and so had got myself into that state of [illegible] which (as you and he know) is best adapted to bring out my heroic qualities."

Hawthorne was to be a quite visible American official during his term of office, and he was to develop some ideas about the consular role. "One great part of a Consul's duty . . ." he was to remark in *Our Old Home*, "should consist in building up for himself a recognized position in the society where he resides so that his local influence might be felt in behalf of his own country." Yet Hawthorne felt that the American government, with its frequent changes of administration, seldom promoted this consular ideal. "The position," he said frankly, "is totally beyond the attainment of an American; there today, bristling all over with the porcupine-quills of our Republic, and gone tomorrow . . ." He claimed, "Our country wrongs itself by permitting such a system of unsuitable appointments, and, still more, of removals for no cause, just when the incumbent might be beginning to ripen into usefulness."

Hawthorne was scarcely an Anglophile; his reference to the bristling American, critical of other nationalities, was well placed. The evidence of his notebooks is that he himself frequently was the porcupine in question. He observed and recorded the mean life of the blackened Liverpool streets, as well as the glittering affairs of the privileged classes. His notes on English society, of the world of official power and wealth, from the royal family down to David Salomons, lord mayor of London — whom he pronounced "a hard-featured Jew enough" — were often tart and prejudiced. (His fierce, Massachusetts-bred anti-Semitism was particularly virulent on the subject of the lord mayor's brother, whom he described as exemplifying "every old prophet and every old clothesman that ever the tribes produced," and, evidently, a figure of such potency that he "must have been circumcised as much [as] ten times over." The mayor's sister-in-law, however, a "miraculous Jewess," with hair that was "a wonderful deep raven black, black as night, black as death," was to serve in part as the model for his exotic heroine, Miriam, in *The Marble Faun*.)

Living in England during the Crimean War, when Russia was testing the strength of England's global authority, Hawthorne was characteristically ambivalent. "The English are a most intolerable people," he wrote in his notebooks; "nobody is permitted nowadays to have any opinion but the prevalent one. There seems to be very little difference between their educated and ignorant classes in this respect." But confronted with the public response to Crimea, he had to acknowledge it was more acceptable than the American attitude toward the recent Mexican campaign. "It is rather agreeable . . ." he noted, "to observe how all Englishmen pull together . . . And then what a hearty meed of honor they award to their soldiers . . . Whereas, in America, when our soldiers fought as good battles in the Mexican war, with as great proportionate loss, and far more valuable triumphs, the country seemed rather ashamed than proud of them."

Writing to Longfellow in October 1854, at the height of the English war fervor, Hawthorne even exhibited a kind of perverse disloyalty: "For my part, what few sympathies I have are with the Russians; for they are fighting our battle, and unless they win it, we may have to fight it over again. I must confess, I feel like a traitor and a spy among these Englishmen." At times, he was even intolerant. When a report of the fall of Sebastopol proved false and there was bitter public resentment, Hawthorne confided to his journal, "I am glad of it. In spite of his natural sympathies, it is impossible for a true American to be otherwise than glad. Success makes an Englishman intolerable . . . I shall never love England till she sues to us for help." The mood survived even after the war, when he wrote to Emerson to congratulate him on his book *English Traits*, remarking, "These are the truest pages that have yet been written about this country." But buried among the praises there was a complaint: "I am afraid it will please the English only too well; for you give them credit for the possession, in very large measure, of all the qualities that they value, or pride themselves upon; and they never will comprehend that what you deny is far greater and higher than what you concede . . . But perhaps I am no fair judge of Englishmen, just now."

The detailed nature of his notebook observations, his sometimes bitter, sometimes jocular opinions, might be accounted for by his having no regular outlet for his true vocation, writing. During the four years of his consulship, his official duties and his frame of mind provided neither the leisure nor the inclination for writing fiction. "Mr. Hawthorne goes from us at nine," Sophia explained in a letter to her sister, "and we do not see him again till five!!! . . . With Mr. Hawthorne's present constant devotion to the duties of his office, he could no more write a syllable than he could build a cathedral."

The carefulness of his descriptions, the brisk little portrait-vignettes, suggest that Hawthorne hoped his English notes would provide, at some later date, the background material for a novel. He also seems to have courted the idea that his sketches of English places and people might be published on their own. During his English sojourn, he hinted as much to Ticknor and Fields. His notebooks, he told Ticknor, "could easily make up a couple of nice volumes . . . but unluckily, they would be much too good and true to bear publication. It would bring a terrible hornet's nest about my ears."

The manuscript volumes of his English notebooks cover more than four years of his service as American consul and comprise some 300,000 words. Written in an easy, confidential manner, they have a more personal style than the public performance of *Our Old Home*. The fact that, despite his busy schedule, he persisted in recording his observations suggests that Hawthorne had clung to his bit of daily writing as a substitution for the fictions he could no longer entertain. His English notebooks — and his later journals of his experiences in France and Italy — were, in themselves, a distinguished literary performance.

༺ IV ༻

English life and English customs enthralled Sophia. At first, she shunned many of the social functions of her husband's office — probably out of shyness. She used as the excuse that she had not yet had time to have a proper ball gown made. Then, when she had one, a "superb brocade, pale-tinted, low-necked and short-sleeved," she had proudly and quietly looked in on Rose before leaving for a formal dinner. The baby had cried at the sight of her mother in all her uncustomary finery.

Sophia sent such news items to Father Peabody; he, as well as Lizzie and Mary, were now the recipients of her lengthy correspondence. In her letters — and in her own carefully kept travel diaries — Sophia recounted their heavy social life, the parties attended, the people she met. She ticked off the dinners and luncheons at Sandheys, the Bright estate, and at Norris Green, where the Heywoods lived. ("[Mrs. Heywood] is a sister of the present Chancellor of the Exchequer, W. E. Gladstone.") There were visits to the Rathbones, at Green Bank ("Mr. William Rathbone is a millionaire. His wife is a cordial and excellent lady"), and dinners at the home of Mr. and Mrs. Charles Holland, at Liscard Vale ("Mr. Hawthorne as chief guest took Mrs. Holland, and sat at her right hand"). She described the radiance of the chandelier-lighted salons, the service at meals from silver and finest porcelain to sparkling crystal, the alacrity and imperturbable poise of the servants in black breeches and white silk hose ("Not the autocrat of all the Russias feels grander than these livery servants"). She admired the English custom of allowing the children to troop in at dessert, "looking so pretty in full dress." At times, with the finicking detail of a historian of the dinner table, she itemized the menu of an elaborate meal:

> A boiled turkey was before Mrs. Holland, and a roasted goose before Mr. Holland; and in the intermediate spaces, cutlets, fricassees, ragoûts, tongue, chicken-pies and many things whose names I did not know; and on a side table a boiled round of beef as large as the dome of St. Peter's. The pastry of the chicken pie was very elaborate sculpture . . . Grouse and pheasants are always served with the sweets in England, and grouse and pheasants then appeared at either end of the table . . . The wines were port, sherry, Madeira, claret, hock and champagne . . . [I] refused the five first, but the champagne was poured into my glass without any question.

For the Hollands' dinner party, she had worn her brocade and a Parisian wreath of artificial blackberry vine, with black, red, and green fruit of such "cunning workmanship" that Julian was positive they were good to eat. Invariably, her husband was always the handsomest man present, though at first Hawthorne refused to wear the white muslin cravat then in fashion, and held to his old black silk stock. "They look at him as much as they can, covertly . . ." she noted, "as if they wanted to assure themselves that he really were so wondrous handsome. He does not observe this; but it is nuts to me, and *I* observe it . . . I always thought he was born for a palace."

On moving to Rock Ferry, they were able to entertain at home, though not extravagantly. Mr. Bright had spent Thanksgiving with them, their first in England. And he had remained overnight, since "his mamma does not wish him to cross the river in the dark." She had unfortunately missed a visit from Mr. James Martineau and Mrs. Gaskell, who had come to call on a December afternoon; she had gone to Liverpool to buy a silver pen with pearl handle that was to be Father Peabody's Christmas present. On Christmas Night, they had heard the pealing of the church bells, which began at midnight and did not stop until morning. After Christmas, on December 29, they entertained Charlotte Cushman. Sophia thought her famous face had rather a "peculiar square form," but found her "most amiable in expression and so very untheatrical in manner and bearing that I should never suspect her to be an actress. She has left the stage now two years and retires upon the fortune she has made." (It was only one of the several retirements and profitable farewell performances in the actress's career.)

Her tone was less positive when she described the pace of English life. "No one hurries in England," she claimed. "They are not go ahead people like Americans." And in spite of her appreciation of English society, she was conscious of its real faults; it was all "stereotyped, crystallized, with the repose and quiet in it of an immovable condition of caste." Much as she enjoyed the great country houses, the refined manners, the extravagant entertainments, she was conscious of another England. "Provided that the lowest orders could be redeemed from the brutal misery in which they are plunged, there could be a little more enjoyment in contemplating and mingling with the higher," she wrote. Yet it seemed "as if everything must be turned upside down rather than for one moment more to tolerate such suffering, such bestiality. There have been one or two individual cases that went before the courts of London that really make it almost wicked ever to smile again." The Crimean War had stalled most attempts at remedial legislation: "Yet reforms on every point in social life are going on here, or *moving*, to go on. Nothing seems to escape some eye that has suddenly opened." The abuse of President Pierce at home gave her an appreciation of the civility of English politics: "I wish our Senators had as good manners as the noble lords of Parliament. But we are perfect savages in manners as yet, and have no self-control, nor reverence." She did not, however, admire the Church of England, which she claimed was in "the merest petrifaction now . . . fat, lazy, cold, timid and selfish."

The main burden of her letters, however, was the activities of her husband and family. They had received an invitation from the wife of the interim consul at London, Mrs. George Sanders, to bring the children to see the queen open Parliament, but Mr. Hawthorne was so involved with the shipwrecked victims of the *San Francisco* and with trials in court that he could not accept. Lord Dufferin had urgently invited her husband to visit his country seat in Ireland, but Mr. Hawthorne had declined: " 'Flummery' Mr. Hawthorne calls it." Sophia was only too happy to relay some example of her husband's wit in his official capacities. Hawthorne had attended a dinner at Richmond Hill at which Mr. Buchanan had been present. In the course of the evening, a recent public letter of the queen's had been discussed, and Buchanan, in front of the entire company, had asked Hawthorne what he thought of it. "Mr. Hawthorne replied that it showed very kind feeling. 'No,' persisted the wicked Ambassador; 'but what do you think of the *style?*' Mr. Hawthorne was equal to him, or rather conquered him, however, for he said, 'The Queen has a perfect right to do what she pleases with her *own English!*' "

From Rhyl, a seaside resort in North Wales, where Hawthorne had sent her and the children for a summer vacation, Sophia could write her father of the shortcomings of English lodgings. They were reduced "to German silver and the most ordinary table service — with no napkins. Ever since our marriage we have always eaten off the finest French china and had all things pretty and tasteful; because, you know, I would never have *second-best* services, considering my husband to be my most illustrious guest. But now!" Hawthorne had come for a weekend visit, accompanied by John O'Sullivan, who had been appointed to a diplomatic post in Portugal. "It is really laughable to think of the appointments of the table at which the Ambassador to Lisbon and the American Consul sat down last Saturday, when they honored me with their presence. And we did laugh, for it was of no consequence, and the great bow window of our parlor looked out upon the sea. We did not come here to see French china and pure silver forks and spoons, but to walk on the beach, bathe in the ocean, and drive to magnificent old castles — and get rid of whooping cough."

Sophia had, in fact, painted a too-glowing portrait of consular life. The Peabody family got the impression that the Hawthornes were living in luxury. Based on exaggerated reports of American shipping, Lizzie and Dr. Peabody concluded that the American consul was becoming an exceedingly wealthy man. If he was so ready to give charity to stranded Americans and to derelict seamen — as Sophia often reported — perhaps he might provide support for Sophia's aged father. Sophia tried to counter such impressions. She wrote her father with a directness that suggests the requests had become pointed: "But, oh, no, dear father, we do not 'live in grand style,' neither do we intend to have much company. We could not afford it." The week before, Lizzie had written her that she had heard that 10,000 American ships docked in Liverpool each year, and she calculated that, at $4.00 a ship, Mr. Hawthorne was receiving $40,000 a year. "So very far is this from the truth," Sophia wrote, "that it really is *funny* and melancholy at the same time. Instead of 10,000 ships, not quite 700 arrive yearly from the United States to Liverpool." A good part of her husband's income had to be saved, "or we should returned ruined, not benefited by the office." In response to such exaggerated projections, she wrote Lizzie, "I wish you could be undeceived about the income of this Consulate. I only wish we could be pelted within an inch of our lives with a hailstorm of sovereigns, so as to satisfy every one's most gorgeous hopes . . ." Living economically, she acknowledged, they might save $5000 a year. "I have only room to put in the truest, warmest sympathy with all your efforts and trials," she wrote, "and the wish I could lift you up out of all, and sorrow that I cannot. Mr. Hawthorne has relations and personal friends who look to him, I think, with great desires. I can demand nothing for mine."

During the years of Hawthorne's consulship, William Ticknor served as Hawthorne's unofficial banker. Before leaving for Liverpool, Hawthorne had informed Ticknor that his sister Ebe was entitled to draw up to $200 annually from his account if she was in need of money; also, from time to time he instructed his publisher to pay out small sums to his Uncle William. One of the first obligations Hawthorne repaid, during his term as consul, was the $500 Hillard and his anonymous friends had given him at the time of his ouster from the Salem surveyorship. In December 1853, Hawthorne wrote Hillard with gratitude and relief that he could now repay the loan. It was his "creed," he said "that a man has no claim upon his fellow creatures, beyond bread and water, and a grave, unless he can win it by his own strength and skill." Sophia had been truthful when she told her father that Hawthorne had certain obligations to his friends. Early in 1854, he wrote Ticknor to make available to Horatio Bridge a sum of $3000, which Bridge would need for a period of several months. "My relations with Bridge are of such a nature," he wrote, "that I would lend him every cent I had, even if I were certain of never getting it back again." He was less sanguine about a loan to O'Sullivan, who had asked for a similar amount. "I have determined to buy some real estate in New York," Hawthorne informed Ticknor, "not that I want it, but because I must either buy the property, or lend $3000 to O'Sullivan, who never would be able to pay me. He says this property will be a very good investment and pays much more than the interest of the money." The transaction, however, would have to be kept secret, since the property belonged to O'Sullivan's wife. Ticknor advised against it, but Hawthorne responded, "When the friend of half a lifetime asks me to assist him, and when I have perfect confidence in his honor, what is to be done? Shall I prove myself to be one of those persons who have every quality desirable in friendship, except that they invariably fail you in the pinch?"

Other claims against his small fortune were encountered in the line of his official duties. A Captain Gibson was unable to pay his draft against his passage home, and the Cunard agents had applied to Hawthorne; Ticknor was instructed to pay the necessary £30. The American consul in Beirut, Henry Wood, arriving in Liverpool, was short of funds, and Hawthorne had paid the passage to America; Ticknor was asked to forward the due-bill to Wood in New Hampshire. The Reverend Dr. Richards' week in the Liverpool brothel had been costly for Hawthorne; the minister never repaid the money Hawthorne had put out on his account. Ticknor was asked to write the minister's brother. Hawthorne's contribution to the publication of Delia Bacon's *Philosophy of the Plays of Shakspere Unfolded* had similarly proved to be a charitable act. It was understandable that he would complain to Ticknor, "It is marvelous what a difficulty a man finds in keeping his money, the instant he is known to have any. Friends and strangers settle on my poor little pile of gold like flies on a lump of sugar. You must save what you can for me."

What particularly distressed Hawthorne was that Congress was on the verge of revising the salary provisions of the diplomatic corps. It was a near-certainty that they would establish a fixed salary for consuls and rescind the extra fees Hawthorne had been receiving from both the Liverpool and Manchester consulates. The fate of the bill became a factor in Hawthorne's decision whether to remain in office for the full four-year term or resign prematurely. Throughout the spring of 1854, he wrote complaining letters to Bridge, hoping that his friend would convey his views to the President. "It is impossible," he told Bridge, "especially for a man with a family and keeping any kind of establishment, not to spend a vast deal of money here." The dignity of the office unfortunately put the holder "on a level with the highest society, and compels him to associate on equal terms with men who spend more than my whole income on the mere entertainments and other trimmings and embroidery of their lives." Even taking his income at $15,000 a year, "it would be the easiest thing in the world for me to run into debt." The salaries for his three clerks, as well as other bills, had to be paid out of that amount. The American public, he was convinced, would grumble even at a consular salary of $6000 a year. "But with that salary," he said, "the office may go to [Hell] so far as I am concerned . . . I beg and pray therefore that Pierce will . . . not let Mr. Dudley Mann shave off so much as a half-penny of my official emoluments."

But when the consular bill passed, early in 1855, Hawthorne reconsidered. His predecessor had held on to the position for fully five months into the new administration — with Pierce's approval. In an intemperate moment, Hawthorne expressed his irritation to Bridge: ". . . That little bit of Presidential courtesy took at least six thousand dollars out of my pocket. I have no objections to Frank's being as civil as he pleases, but I wish he would do it at his own expense rather than mine." He would have preferred to remain in office for two more years, so he told Ticknor early in January: "I have not seen half enough of England, and there is the germ of a new romance in my mind, which will be all the better for ripening slowly. Besides, America is now wholly given over to a d——d mob of scribbling women, and I should have no chance of success while the public taste is occupied with their trash — and should be ashamed of myself if I did succeed." His new plan was to resign prospectively, before the new law took effect in January 1856. It was a shrewd move, one that would allow him to continue to receive the perquisites of his two consulates for several months longer. Writing to Ticknor again in April, he summed up his financial prospects: "It looks now as if I should nearly or quite make up the $20,000 (including my investments with O'Sullivan and Bridge) before July, and if the President adheres to his purpose of keeping the old system in force, the subsequent months can hardly fail to give me five or six thousand more. If so, I shall be well enough satisfied." But it was to Bridge that he revealed the cause of his discontent: "I shall have about as much money as will be good for me. Enough to educate Julian, and portion off the girls in a moderate way, that is, reckoning my pen as good for something. And, if I die, or am brainstricken, my family will not be beggars, the dread of which has often troubled me in times past."

Hawthorne seldom wrote to Pierce. As he bluntly explained to Bridge, "It is my instinct to turn the cold shoulder on persons in his position." He did not want to give the impression that he was currying favor or going over the heads of his superior officers in the State Department. But having made up his mind about the future, he wrote Pierce a long and objective letter on the subject of consular finances and the impossibility of performing the job under the new law. "For Heaven's sake," he advised, "do not let the next session pass without having this matter amended." Otherwise, he maintained, Pierce would have to appoint as his successor in the office "either a rich man or a rogue — no poor, honest, and capable man, will think of holding it."

In a brief personal note, he added, "I am sure, my dear General, that you will not impute it to any forgetfulness or lack of affection, that I so seldom write you, but to tell you the truth, it is not quite so easy to write to the President of the United States as it used to be to write to Frank Pierce. By and by, we shall be on the old terms again, and for my part, I don't care how soon."

Considering the charity Hawthorne expended on stray Americans in Liverpool, it was strange that he so belatedly concerned himself with Sophia's relatives. It was not, apparently, until the fall of 1854, when Dr. Peabody was seriously ill, that he began sending money for his father-in-law's maintenance. Sophia, responding to one of her father's letters of thanks, was pleased. "It was delightful to see your handwriting this week," she answered, "written with the same firmness as ever. It gives me an unspeakable satisfaction to know that the drafts Mr. Hawthorne sent contribute to your ease, and supply you with embellishments and luxuries, which in sickness are necessaries. I only wish I could put my strength into your limbs . . . Mr. Hawthorne has wished, you see, to prevent your having any anxiety about little wants. It will be all right for the present, and the future, too."

Hawthorne obviously suspected that Dr. Peabody would not survive the illness, and he carefully watched for the arrival of Peabody family letters. He was concerned about Sophia's reactions and her precarious health, and at some point he began intercepting Lizzie Peabody's letters. When, in January 1855, a series of them arrived, including one that brought the expected news, Hawthorne wrote his sister-in-law from the consulate before telling Sophia. "I have just received your letter with the intelligence of your father's death," he wrote Lizzie. "I hope and think, that Sophia will receive it quietly. Your letters (by the same steamer, but received the day before yesterday) have been a very fit preparation for it. The steamer sails so early tomorrow, that she will not probably be able to write further." During his stay abroad Hawthorne had paid out certain sums of money on Elizabeth's behalf. He now informed her that he had intended to send her father a draft for the same amount. "I now request that you will apply the sum in question to defray any funeral or other expenses, and consider it as contributed by Sophia. I think she has written about this in a former letter." Under the circumstances, it was a thrifty gesture rather than a generous one.

Sophia, when she wrote Lizzie, was more caught up by her husband's perfect tact than concerned with her own grief. "If anything could have softened a blow," she told Lizzie, "it would have been the divine way in which my husband told me. If a seraph *can* look more radiant with love — a flaming love, veiled with most tender, sorrowing sympathy, than he did, I am sure I cannot conceive it." She also took a marvelously benign view of Hawthorne's attitude toward Dr. Peabody. Her father's "sincerity, his childlike guilelessness, his good sense and rectitude, his unaffected piety — all and each of his qualities made him interesting and never tedious to my husband. I really do not believe that any one else ever listened to his stories and his conversation with love and interest excepting him."

Lizzie did not take so rosy a view. She seems to have been put off by her brother-in-law's reluctant charity. As the months wore on, she also became increasingly disturbed by her inability to communicate with her sister without Hawthorne's intervention. Within a month, she repaid Hawthorne through Ticknor — a matter that the Boston publisher communicated to Liverpool. Hawthorne responded, "I don't want this money here; and if E. P. Peabody has really paid it over to you, please to add the sum to my balance. It was money which I paid on her behalf here in England, and I did not look to have it refunded, but am perfectly willing, since she chooses to do so."

☙ V ❧

Since arriving in England, Hawthorne had worried about the effect of the English climate, especially the raw, damp Liverpool winters, on Sophia's health. Sophia had consulted a Dr. Drysdale, who recommended an occasional change of scenery. For two summers, Hawthorne arranged for extensive visits for his wife and children on the Isle of Man and at Rhyl, then at Leamington Spa in Warwick. But following her father's death, Sophia was troubled by a persistent cough, and Hawthorne was fearful that her lungs were affected. To make matters worse, Lizzie began bombarding them with letters, anxious about Sophia's condition. "If I were easily alarmed," Sophia wrote her sister, "I think I should go off in a rapid consumption after reading your last two letters. But I assure you there is a good stock of life in me yet and that I have also the identical constitution of mother, or I should have been under the sod . . . very long ago." She promised that if it became necessary, she would consult Dr. James Garth Wilkinson, a noted London specialist and Swedenborgian scholar, the lifelong friend of the elder Henry James and an acquaintance of the visiting Sarah Ann Clarke. It may well have been at this juncture that Lizzie began threatening to hurry to England, an idea that Hawthorne positively discouraged in an undated note. "Dear E.," Hawthorne wrote bluntly, "I hope you will not keep up any discussion in respect to [this] plan of coming over to be with Sophia. She is very clear in her decision, and acts upon grounds which I feel to be right and reasonable."

At first, Hawthorne had considered resigning his consulship and spending a year or two in Italy. Then Franklin Pierce helpfully suggested a diplomatic post in Lisbon, an offer that Hawthorne declined because the money did not seem good enough. Instead, he decided to send Sophia and the two girls to spend the winter with O'Sullivan and his family at the Portuguese court. Julian would remain with him in Liverpool. Sophia's visit to Dr. Wilkinson in September only confirmed him in his decision. Hawthorne, reporting to Ticknor on Sophia's condition, noted that it was "not worse, nor better." Wilkinson had assured him that Sophia's lungs were not dangerously affected, but he had advised that she quit England for the winter.

Sophia was plainly reluctant. Remaining in London while Hawthorne returned to Liverpool for a few days, she wrote him a cheery letter detailing her sightseeing activities with the children. In the midst of it, she apologized for having complained about the forthcoming trip to Portugal. "Since I must go away," she wrote, "I ought not to have said a word; but thou must ascribe what I said and say to infinite love of thee only . . . I could not be happy as you well know if you made any sacrifice for me; and as our interests are indissoluble, it would be my sacrifice too. So I will be good, and not distress thee with more regrets. I once thought that no power on earth should ever induce me to live without thee, and especially thought an ocean should never roll between us. But I am overpowered by necessity."

Before Sophia's departure, there were two weeks of social visits and more sightseeing in London. Hawthorne was determined to make the most of their time together. They visited the Crystal Palace, which, after the famous Exposition of 1851, had been reconstructed at Sydenham. "A gigantic toy for the English people to play with," Hawthorne commented gruffly in his notebook. There were visits to the Houses of Parliament and to Westminster Abbey. Julian had insisted on visiting the Surrey Zoological Gardens, which Hawthorne found a "rather poor place of suburban amusement." The menagerie was scanty at best — one or two giraffes, some camels, a polar bear, and a surplus of lions. The gardens advertised nightly representations of famous battles — among them, the current siege of Sebastopol. In hard daylight, the siege looked improbable and seedy; the Bay of Balaclava, Hawthorne noted caustically, had been reconstructed in a duck pond. He was clearly in a bad mood, but Julian thought the gardens a "delightful place."

On October 7, a showery Sunday, the family took the train for Southampton, arriving in the afternoon and putting up in the Castle Hotel. Monday was a day of alternating sunshine and rain. Around noon, they boarded the steamer *Madrid*. Hawthorne inspected the tiny staterooms — the ship accommodated some seventy passengers — and then they went on deck to wait through the "irksome and dreary hour or two" before departure. Hawthorne studied the passengers, chiefly Portuguese ("undersized, dark, moustachioed people, smoking cigars"), with a fair representation of British. He made a point of introducing Sophia to the captain, "recommending her to his especial care, as she was unattended by any gentleman." Then he and Sophia said their hurried good-byes on deck, in order to cut short the "parting scene." Hawthorne and Julian returned to the hotel for dinner and afterward took the train for Worcester, where they stayed overnight.

"My wife behaved heroically," Hawthorne noted in his journal. "Una was cheerful and Rosebud seemed only anxious to get off . . . Julian bore the separation from his mother well, but took occasion to remind me that he had now no one but myself to depend upon, and therefore suggested that I should be very kind to him."

It was dark when they arrived in Liverpool on the evening of the 9th. They had difficulty in finding a cab to take them to Mrs. Blodget's, where Hawthorne and Julian would spend the months while Sophia was away. Sebastopol had fallen, and despite a pelting rainstorm, the streets were crowded with people celebrating the victory. The glare of the gaslight illuminations colored the night sky.

It was to be a winter of discontent. As consul, he took the depositions sworn to in the consulate office. The inventory of brutalities continued: a sailor from the *Assyria*, in the North Hospital, had died from a beating; the crew of the *William Tapscott*, lying at anchor in the Mersey, reported on the death of a seaman, stabbed before the ship had left New York; a crewman from the *Albert Gallatin* had fallen to his death from the topsail yard after he was kicked by the second mate.

During Sophia's absence, Hawthorne tried to keep himself busy, dined out frequently. He took excursions, sometimes with Julian, in hopes of easing his loneliness. He regularly maintained his journal entries. At Christmas, he noted, the markets were gaily decorated. In the butcher shops there were "fat sheep, with their woolly heads and tails still on, and stars and other devices ingeniously wrought on the quarters; fat pigs, adorned with flowers, like corpses of virgins; hares, wild fowl, geese, ducks, turkeys; and green boughs and banners suspended about the stalls." Despite the festive abundance, it was a gloomy time. Mrs. Blodget's boardinghouse was festive with bunches of mistletoe, and the lively servant-girls had demanded kisses from all the Yankee captains. Only Hawthorne, in his aloofness, had been exempted. Long before the day dawned, lying awake in bed, he had heard music in the streets — and a woman's powerful voice, singing a Christmas hymn. "Before bedtime," he commented, "I presume one half of England, at a moderate calculation, was the worse for liquor." On New Year's Eve, he stayed up until midnight, when the front door was opened to admit the New Year, but he did not wait until the old year was let out the back door. He was not in a mood for celebration. He went upstairs, "sad and lonely," and stepping into Julian's little room, wished his sleeping son a Happy New Year.

He was neither eating nor sleeping well, he reported in his journal.

> I have suffered woefully from low spirits for some time past; and this has not often been the case since I grew to be a man, even in the least auspicious periods of my life. My desolate, bachelor condition, I suppose, is the cause . . . I sleep ill, lying awake late at night to think sad thoughts, and to imagine somber things, and awakening before light with the same thoughts and fancies still in my mind. My heart sinks always as I ascend the stairs to my office, from a dim augury of ill news that I may perhaps hear — of black-sealed letters — or some such horrors. Nothing gives me any joy. I have learned what the bitterness of exile is . . . Life seems so purposeless as not to be worth the trouble of carrying it on any further.

A visit to the West Derby workhouse with Mrs. Heywood only compounded his dissatisfaction. A six-year-old child, with runny eyes and a mouth covered with scurvy sores, hovered around him, plucking at his coat, wanting to be picked up. Somewhat squeamishly, he carried the child for a bit — not knowing whether it was a girl or a boy — then set it down; but the urchin had clung to his fingers, following along. He was touched, but nonetheless glad that he was wearing gloves. "It was a foundling," he wrote, "and out of all human kind, it chose me to be its father! . . . I wish I had not touched the imp; and yet I never should have forgiven myself if I had repelled its advances."

A trip to London and the convivial society of Bennoch and his friends did not improve his mood. He wrote Sophia in a teasing vein, saying he had had "a strange run of luck as regards actresses, having made friends with the three most prominent ones since I came to London." Two of them were English actresses, Helen Faucit and Isabella Glyn, whom he met through Bennoch. The third was their old friend Charlotte Cushman, whom he had encountered on the Strand.

Visits to the National Gallery and the British Museum only proved tiresome; he felt the heavy weight of the past. "It quite crushes a person to see so much at once," he wrote in his notebook, "and I wandered from hall to hall, with a weary and heavy heart, wishing (Heaven forgive me!) that the Elgin marbles and the frieze of the Parthenon were all burnt into lime." It was a revival of his holocaustal fantasy, in which life's follies, ambitions, honors, and high arts were consigned to the flames. Like Holgrave, Hawthorne complained, "The present is burthened too much with the past. We

have not time, in our earthly existence, to appreciate what is warm
with life, and immediately around us; yet we heap up these old
shells . . ." At times, his mind seemed to verge on anarchy.

Sophia's letters to her husband and son were purposely cheerful.
Her life in the parochial little court at Lisbon was an exciting round
of social visits and state occasions. She described the brilliant palace soirées of the fledgling king, Pedro V, just succeeded to the
throne at eighteen, studious and somewhat grave, with the exaggerated Portuguese sense of seriousness and punctilio. His father, the
king regent, Fernando II — like Queen Victoria's Albert, another of
the Saxe-Coburg princes married off into the royal households of
Europe — was an admirer of *The Scarlet Letter* and a bit of a
charmer. At Sophia's urging, Hawthorne sent an expensively bound
set of his works to the urbane Dom Fernando, whose taste and time
were usually occupied with women or the construction of architectural follies like the extravagant Pena Palace.

That Sophia's health was greatly improved, Hawthorne inferred
from the frequent references to her attendance at ballets and operas,
in the company of the high-living O'Sullivans. The American minister and his family were prime examples of American affluence. The
minister's residence, the Pateo de Geraldes, was staffed by ten servants, and O'Sullivan, not to be outdone by the Portuguese craze for
magnificent carriages, had a luxurious one lined with blue damask
and drawn by black Andalusian steeds. For Julian's benefit, Sophia
reported on the "pretty" speeches and flattering attentions of the
lively regent while the young king stood nearby, "sad, but with an
amiable shadow-smile on his face, and an expression of constraint."
She also included comic portraits of such court figures as the
Duchess of Palmella, "as big as a center table," whose small features, "in the midst of an acre of cheeks and chins, look as if they
had lost themselves in a vast plain."

Hawthorne attempted to make his own letters newsy; he was
being pestered by Mrs. O'Hara, the mother of an indigent young
Irishman whom Sophia had taken under her wing. "But I remained
as obdurate as a paving-stone," he wrote his wife, "knowing that if I
yielded this once, she would expect me to supply her with the means
of keeping drunk as long as I stay in Liverpool." He was amused —
and a bit saddened — by Una's letters, he said. They made him
"smile, and sigh too; they are such letters as a girl of fifteen would
write, with a vein of sentiment continually cropping up, as the geol-
ogists say, through the surface." Their religious tone startled him,
however, and he suspected his daughter might follow O'Sullivan's
wife into "that musty old Church of England . . . This looks very
probable to me, but thou wilt know best how it is." He reported

regularly on Julian. Now that there was a war scare between England and the United States over the Crampton affair, Julian had been arming himself: "He insists on buckling his sword the moment he is dressed, and never lays it aside till he is ready to go to bed."

The Crampton affair was only the latest item in the gradually worsening relationship between England and the United States during the Pierce administration. Crampton — whom Sophia had found so agreeable and cultured aboard the *Niagara* — had been guilty of recruiting soldiers for the Crimean War in the western hemisphere, and Pierce's administration considered this a clear violation of hemispheric neutrality. After the British government ignored repeated requests that the minister be recalled, Pierce had declared Crampton persona non grata. Hawthorne, in his letters to Sophia, seemed to welcome the prospect of hostilities. He might be expelled from England; then he could join his wife in Madeira, where Sophia and the girls, accompanying the O'Sullivans, were vacationing in the early spring of 1856.

Chiefly, however, his letters to Sophia shuttled between ardent professions of love and self-pitying complaints about his loneliness:

> Thy letter, my own most beloved . . . revived me at once out of a state of half-torpor, half misery — just as much of each as could co-exist with the other. Do not think that I am always in that state; but one thing, dearest, I have been most thoroughly taught by this separation — that is, the absolute necessity of expression. I must tell thee I love thee. I must be told that thou lovest me . . . Dost thou ever feel, at one and the same moment, the impossibility of doing without me, and also the impossibility of having me? I know not how it is that my strong wishes do not bring thee here bodily, while I am writing these words.

On March 19, learning that the weather in Madeira was bad and that Sophia had been ill, he remarked, "It was a most foolish project of O'Sullivan's (as all his projects are) to lead thee from his comfortable fireside, to that comfortless Madeira. And thou sayest, or Una says, that the rainy season is just commencing there, and that this month and the next are the two worst months of the year!" It moved him to one of his strongest assertions: "Thou *never* again shalt go away anywhere without me. My two arms shall be thy tropics and my breast thy equator; and from henceforth forever, I will keep thee a great deal too warm."

∽ VI ∾

It was more than the separation from his wife that was causing Hawthorne's malaise during the winter of 1855 and well into the following spring. From the perspective of England — and the civility of English politics — he had begun to study the increasingly violent politics of America, and he was dismayed. As early as the *San Francisco* affair, he had expressed his disgust to Horatio Bridge. "It sickens me to look back to America," he wrote. "I am sick to death of the continual fuss, and tumult, and excitement, and bad blood, which we keep up about political topics. If it were not for my children, I should probably never return, but after quitting office, should go to Italy and live and die there . . . In my opinion, we are the most miserable people on earth."

His possible expatriation was a subject on which he blew hot and cold. For the remainder of his stay abroad, it was a continuing theme in his letters to Bridge and to William Ticknor. His ambivalence was also clear in his letters to Longfellow, whom he encouraged to make a visit to England, now that Longfellow had retired from Harvard. "America is a good land for young people," he wrote the poet, "but not for those who are past their prime. It is impossible to grow old comfortably there; for nothing keeps one in countenance. For my part, I have no love for England nor Englishmen, and I do love my own country; but for all that, the honest truth is, I care little whether I ever set eyes on it again . . . I have had enough of progress — now I want to stand stock still . . ."

His angriest and most anxious thoughts were spent on the fate of his friend Franklin Pierce. There had been several unfortunate incidents in Pierce's presidency, and, in scathing terms, the press had made much of them. Coming out of the Capitol rotunda one day, Pierce had been accosted by a very drunk young man who offered him a drink from his bottle. Pierce had immediately stiffened and refused, then walked away. The man had thrown an egg at the retreating President. Pierce, turning round, ordered him arrested. The next morning, sobering up in jail, the youth had attempted suicide. Although Pierce, thinking better of his action, had sent someone to withdraw charges soon after the arrest, it had not dispelled the ugly talk. On another occasion, at a White House reception, Pierce, while receiving his guests, resolutely and ill-advisedly turned his back on his arch political rival, Senator John P. Hale of New Hampshire, who had made a recent and savage personal attack on Pierce and his domestic and foreign policies. It was a breach of statesmanship that scandalized Washington society.

Pierce's real problems, however, were more critical and centered on the irreversible crisis of the slavery issue. The Kansas-Nebraska Act, sponsored by Stephen Douglas and endorsed by the administration, had been intended as a compromise measure meant to defuse an explosive situation. The act established a provisional government and left the decision over free soil or slavery up to the votes of the settlers; it required a population of 93,240 before statehood was conferred on the territory. The legislation merely created in Kansas a stage for bloody riots and massacres between proslavery and abolitionist elements, with the provisional government unable to exercise control. Proslavery terrorists conducted murderous raids from across the Missouri border; supposedly neutral agencies, like the New England Emigrant Aid Company, an abolitionist group, secretly armed the free-soil settlers with rifles, while officially claiming innocence. For two years after the passage of the act, in 1854, "Bleeding Kansas," was a national issue. Pierce and Douglas (who had his own presidential ambitions) found themselves denounced on both sides.

On May 19, 1856, approximately the second anniversary of the Kansas-Nebraska Act, in a speech that had been well advertised in advance, Charles Sumner stood up on the floor of the Senate before a packed house and began an impassioned harangue, titled "The Crime Against Kansas." On the first day, his speech wound through three hours of quotations from classical Latin writers, Dante, and Milton, and erudite references from history. It was resumed again on the 20th. It was — and was intended to be — one of the great moments in Sumner's carefully managed career. He called on the Senate to "redress a great transgression"; the crime, as he specified it, was "the rape of a virgin territory, compelling it to the hateful embrace of slavery." In the course of his address, he pronounced the Kansas-Nebraska Act a "swindle" for greedy railroad and slaveholding interests — not altogether inaccurately. But there was a certain amount of casuistry in Sumner's position; merely taking the word of the secretary of the New England Emigrant Aid Company, he ridiculed the notion that the society had any responsibility for the violence in the territory, declaring it had "supplied no arms of any kind to anybody." Few of Sumner's political foes escaped his personal, heavy-handed attacks. The elderly South Carolina senator, Andrew P. Butler, was caricatured as a Don Quixote who had embraced "the harlot, Slavery," and Stephen Douglas as "the squire of Slavery, its very Sancho Panza, ready to do all its humiliating offices." In his rebuttals, Sumner was particularly virulent in his attacks on Douglas, referring to "the perpetual stench of offensive personality" and to "the noisome, squat and nameless animal" that Douglas seemed to be taking as his model.

Two days later, while Sumner was bent over his Senate desk, Congressman Preston Brooks of South Carolina, a nephew of Senator Butler, came up from behind Sumner and with a gold-headed cane began beating him on the head and shoulders with such force that the cane broke. Stunned and bleeding, Sumner wrenched himself free from the desk, stumbling along the aisle while blows rained down upon him. He was beaten insensible. His colleagues and enemies looked on in disbelief or approval. The news of the attack shocked and outraged the North; it was a subject of editorials and sermons for months. Sumner was to be absent from the Senate for a period of nearly three years, recuperating from effects that were both psychological and physical. His Southern opponents claimed he was malingering for effect.

The brutal attack on Sumner was followed, on May 24, by John Brown's insanely murderous Pottawatomie raid in Kansas, in which three men and two boys — poor whites and illiterates — were dragged from their house, shot, and hacked to death with broadswords. Brown, with the self-righteousness of a fanatic, later claimed that the raid, conducted in retaliation for the murder of five free-soil settlers, had been "decreed by Almighty God, ordained from Eternity."

From England, Hawthorne viewed the multiplying atrocities, the growing violence of American politics, with dismay. Still, he evidently felt that Sumner, whose scorn for political enemies could be bludgeoning, had invited the attack by stirring up the hatred of his opponents. Writing to Ticknor, he conveniently blamed the victim, suggesting that if Sumner had concerned himself with the scandalous abuses in the American merchant marine, as he had advised, "he would have done good service to his country and have escaped Brooks's cudgel."

Hawthorne was patently more sympathetic toward Pierce. At the beginning of the Kansas controversy, he had even chastised Bridge for being disgruntled, possibly because Pierce had been so tardy in offering him an administrative post. (Bridge's feelings were probably soothed, later in the year, when he was appointed chief of the Bureau of Provisions and Clothing in the Navy Department, with the rank of paymaster general. He held the post for fifteen years.) "I am sorry to perceive the tone in which you speak of Pierce," Hawthorne wrote Bridge. "He has bitter enemies enough — do not let him have a soured and suspicious friend — at least not in you; for it would go far nearer his heart than all the abuse which half the nation is heaping on him." In what was to become a refrain in his letters, he added, "I wish you would send me the most minute particulars about Pierce — how he looks and behaves when you meet him, how his health and spirits are — (whether he has any secret bad habits) — and above all, what the public really thinks of him — a point which I am utterly unable to get at through the newspapers.

Give him my best regards, and ask him whether he finds his post any more comfortable than I prophesied it would be."

A short time later, Hawthorne even suggested a bit of Machiavellian strategy, encouraging Bridge to remain in Washington for Pierce's sake:

> I feel a sorrowful sympathy for the poor fellow (for God's sake don't show him this!) and hate to have him left without one true friend, or one man who will speak a single word of truth for him. There is no truer man in the world than yourself, and unless you have let him see a coolness on your part, he will feel the utmost satisfaction in having you near him. You will soon find, if I mistake not, that you can exercise a pretty important influence over his mind . . . Of course it requires a good deal of tact to fill such an office as I suggest, but upon my honor, so far as actual power goes, I would as lief have it as that of Secretary of State.

To Pierce himself, Hawthorne wrote a brief word of encouragement in the course of his letter about consular finances. "What a storm you have had to face!" he told his friend. "And how like a man you have faced it! I long to talk over all these matters with you by the fireside, after the events of your government shall have become history."

In the summer of 1856, the Pierce administration did in fact pass into history. During the first week in June, the Democrats convened in Cincinnati, the first national political convention to be held in the Midwest. Neither Pierce nor the aspiring Stephen Douglas received the nomination. The Democrats chose James Buchanan, who had wisely sat out such controversial issues as the Kansas-Nebraska Act within the safe retreat of the London embassy. "I am sorry Frank has not the nomination if he wished it," Hawthorne wrote Bridge when he learned the news. "Otherwise I am glad he is out of the scrape."

His air of confidence, at the moment, was probably the result of his wife's return to England. Sophia, he was happy to report to Bridge, was "in much better health than I expected to see her . . . She thinks, with great certainty, that she can safely spend another winter in England, and, if so, I shall not resign until the next Administration comes in."

It was over the vexing question of American politics, as well as family affairs, that Hawthorne had a near-break with Lizzie Peabody. The trouble had begun, inevitably, over the settlement of money matters following the death of Dr. Peabody. Writing to his sister-in-law in April 1855, Hawthorne adopted a tone that was tactless and, in some respects, cruel. To anyone less insensitive to rebuffs than Lizzie, the letter would certainly have been final; but Lizzie had a doggedness in pursuing an issue or a cause that could never be put off. "Dear E.," Hawthorne wrote, "I have just received yours; and am glad, on the whole, that you take mine just in the way you do; for, after all, it is not my business to present you with your own portrait, true or false." After the mild beginning, Hawthorne got down to the particulars:

> I shall not let Sophia have your letter to her, because she has had trouble enough about the matter of the Galpin money, and because I fully believe that her first view of it was right. I sometimes feel as if I ought to vindicate her (which would be so easily done) as to all those accusations of neglecting her father and family, which you both hint and express; and also to endeavor to enlighten you as to the relation between husband and wife, and show you that she fully comprehends it in the highest sense. But the conjugal relation is one which God never meant you to share, and which, therefore, He apparently did not give you the instinct to understand; so there my labor would be lost . . .
>
> You *did* make the suggestion about my borrowing the money to set your brother up in life! *What* a memory! Perhaps you write in your sleep?
>
> I did not mean to close all correspondence forever, but only on that particular subject. I hope, in whatever years we may have left, to exchange many letters, and see you many times, for there are few people whose society is so pleasant to me. I never in my life was angry with you; and if you will only allow me to think of you just as I please (or rather just as I cannot help) I really think we shall find great comfort in one another. Upon my honor, I consider myself the one person in the world who does justice to your character!! — an assertion at which you will probably laugh outright . . .

The difficulties had not ended there. As the slavery question became a more and more agitating issue in American life, it spilled over into Lizzie's letters to Sophia — usually in the form of lectures. Sophia remonstrated, "Your letters to me would be far more appropriate to a slaveholder . . . I do not see how they apply to me at all." Frustrated, Lizzie attempted to proselytize her niece. There, Sophia was adamant: "I do wish, dear Elizabeth, you would write all your slavery experiences to me and not refer to the subject to Una. For the consequence is I have to suppress your letters to her and she is disappointed. What is the virtue or the use of forcing the subject upon the poor child?"

When Lizzie sent Sophia a manuscript she had written on the slavery issue, Hawthorne exercised censorship, returning it to his sister-in-law.

I do not choose to bother Sophia with it [he wrote Lizzie], and yet should think it a pity to burn so much of your thought and feeling. You had better publish it. I speak trustingly, though not knowingly, of its merits; for to tell you the truth, I have read only the first line or two, not expecting much benefit even were I to get the whole by heart. No doubt it seems the truest of truth to you; but I do assure you that, like every other Abolitionist, you look at matters with an awful squint, which distorts everything within your line of vision; and it is queer, though natural, that you think everybody squints except yourselves. Perhaps they do; but certainly *you* do.

Not to be put off, Lizzie returned the pamphlet, directing it once again to Sophia. Hawthorne wrote, in stunned amusement at her persistence, that he had read the pamphlet, supposing it to be new, and then discovered that it was the one he had sent back. "Upon my word, it is not very good; not worthy of being sent three times across the ocean; not so good as I supposed you would always write, on a subject in which your mind and heart were interested. However, since you make a point of it, I will give it to Sophia, and will tell her all about its rejection and return." He then took up one of Lizzie's apparent complaints: "As you have suggested dropping your correspondence to Sophia, I hope you will take in good part some remarks which I have often thought of making on that subject. I entirely differ from you in the idea that such correspondence is essential to her peace of mind; not but what she loves you deeply and sincerely . . . But it is a solemn truth that I never in my life knew her to receive a letter from you without turning pale."

Late in August 1856, Hawthorne and Sophia, accompanied by Francis Bennoch, paid a six-day visit to Oxford. At the station, they were met by Samuel Carter Hall, a literary man, one of Bennoch's acquaintances, who was rumored to be the model for Dickens' Mr. Pecksniff. Hawthorne, who had met him earlier (it was at Hall's home that he had been introduced to Jenny Lind), felt there was too much "butter and treacle" in Hall's flattering praises. But he enjoyed Hall's buxom wife and their adopted daughter, Fanny, who also formed part of the convivial little party. They were all the guests of the hospitable former mayor of Oxford, Richard James Spiers, a dapper and congenial host, a collector of art, and the father of thirteen or fourteen children — Hawthorne was never quite sure of the count. Hawthorne admired Spiers's sociability and his largesse; with a touch of condescension, he suspected that Spiers's "smartness" — which he considered uncharacteristic of the English — was the result of his rumored earlier career as a hairdresser. Under the guidance of Spiers, his durable wife, and a Mr. Addison, a devoted Puseyite with whom Hall agreeably quarreled about the popish tendencies of the Oxford Movement, the guests visited New College and Balliol, Christ Church (where they caught a glimpse of the redoubtable Dr. Pusey himself) and the picture gallery of the Bodleian Library. There was a notable excursion to Blenheim-Park, where Hawthorne admired the perfect Eden of the gardens, with lawns and glades like "the memory of places where one has wandered, when first in love." It was a day of splendid sunshine; Hawthorne declared that it would have been impossible to pick a finer one out of a hundred years. And there was a lively dinner party aboard a barge on the Isis — cold ham and pigeon pie, served with sherry and port and shandygaff, a local specialty. The only misfortune in the otherwise idyllic sojourn was that the constant round of large dinner parties and noisy sightseeing excursions brought on a recurrence of Sophia's headaches, and she was forced to remain in her room or retire early.

On the morning of their departure, September 4, the Hawthornes' visit was commemorated by the "famous photographist" Philip Henry Delamotte, who breakfasted with the company. At Spiers's request, Delamotte had artfully arranged the group of nine — Mr. and Mrs. Spiers and their eldest son, Mr. and Mrs. Hall and Fanny, Mr. Addison, Sophia and Hawthorne — beneath a large tree against the dappled garden wall. In the "twinkling of an eye," Hawthorne noted, Delamotte recorded the little frieze of figures, croquet mallets in hand, a parasol raised against the sun, in one of the less transitory moments out of time. Hawthorne, standing aloof and handsome near a rose trellis, was captured in a reflective mood. Sophia, however, had an aversion to being photographed. ("I have no features," she once explained, "and the sun is dismally perplexed to know what to do with my face.") At the decisive moment, she deliberately turned her head, causing a blur; Mrs. Hall had resolutely turned her back. "But all the rest of us were caught to the life," Hawthorne declared. He was "a little startled" at recognizing himself, so apart from himself, fixed permanently in that casual moment.

In mid September, Hawthorne took the precaution of establishing his family at Southport, a beach resort some twenty miles north of Liverpool. Having visited the area beforehand, he studied the local newspaper and learned that it was a none-too-fashionable spa with the names of only two or three baronets finding their way into the weekly visitors' reports. Southport looked out over the Irish Sea; Hawthorne's impression was of an interminable stretch of beach and innumerable "bathing-machines," as he called them — donkey-drawn cabins that transported the bathers across what seemed miles of flat sand to the shallow water. Each evening around seven o'clock, townspeople and tourists strolled along the promenade, buttoning themselves up against the chilling blasts of salt air. In time, Hawthorne decided that Southport was "as stupid a place as ever I lived in." But it was within commuting distance of the consulate, and it provided an escape from the unwholesome atmosphere of Liverpool.

The move to Southport was responsible for a delay in the visit of Herman Melville. Melville, who had been in ill health (it seems to have been partly a psychological complaint), was on his way to the Mediterranean and Constantinople. Having arrived in Liverpool in a driving rain on a Saturday — November 8 — he put himself up at the White Bear Hotel. He was in an amiable frame of mind, for he struck up an easy acquaintance with an "agreeable young Scotchman" who was sailing for the East on the steamer *Damascus* on the following Monday. In his diary Melville reported, "Wanted me to accompany him. Sorry that circumstances prevented me."

Melville had only Hawthorne's Rock Ferry address. The following day, Sunday, was still rainy, but he was eager to meet with Hawthorne, and in the afternoon he took the ferry across the Mersey, only to discover that Hawthorne had moved. Under the circumstances, there was little to be done except wait until Monday, when the American consulate would be open, and hope that he could connect with Hawthorne there.

Their meeting on the afternoon of the 10th was momentarily a bit stiff. Hawthorne, recounting it in his notebook, explained his own reserve. Melville, he said, looked "much the same as he used to do (a little paler, and perhaps a little sadder) in a rough outside coat, and with his characteristic gravity and reserve of manner . . . I felt rather awkward at first; because this is the first time I have met him since my ineffectual attempt to get him a consular appointment from General Pierce. However, I failed only from real lack of power to serve him; so there was no reason to be ashamed, and we soon found ourselves on pretty much our former terms of sociability and confidence."

If Hawthorne mentioned to Melville another attempt he had made on his behalf, he did not record it. Two years before, Commodore Matthew Perry, fresh from his successful treaty negotiations with the Japanese, had stopped at the Liverpool consulate. Perry, planning to publish an account of his expedition, had fixed on Hawthorne as the man to help him prepare the material for publication, but realized that Hawthorne's official duties would scarcely allow it. Instead, he asked for recommendations. Hawthorne had first mentioned Melville — and one or two other possibilities. But Perry, who was familiar with contemporary writers, "did not grasp very cordially" at any of the names Hawthorne suggested.

Melville, Hawthorne reported, "has not been well, of late; he has been affected with neuralgic complaints in his head and limbs, and no doubt has suffered from too constant literary occupation, pursued without much success, latterly; and his writings, for a long while past, have indicated a morbid state of mind." He invited the writer to stay with his family in Southport during his time in Liverpool. Melville accepted, but kept the visit to two days only. On the afternoon of the 11th, the pair took the train to Southport, where Sophia and the children were waiting tea. In his pocket diary, Melville noted that Julian had grown into "a fine lad" and that Una was "taller than her mother." He also noted that Sophia seemed in poor health. Hawthorne, in an overnice passage in his notebooks, expressed surprise at the small amount of luggage Melville brought with him — "the least little bit of a bundle, which, he told me, contained a night-shirt and a tooth-brush." Melville, he suggested, had "very gentlemanly instincts in every respect, save that he is a little heterodox in the matter of clean linen."

On the following day, a day of bright sunshine but blustering winds, the two men took a long walk along the shore, then settled down to talk in a hollow among the dunes. Hawthorne commented:

> Melville, as he always does, began to reason of Providence and futurity, and of everything that lies beyond human ken, and informed me that he had "pretty much made up his mind to be annihilated"; but still he does not seem to rest in that anticipation; and, I think, will never rest until he gets hold of a definite belief. It is strange how he persists — and has persisted ever since I knew him, and probably long before — in wandering to-and-fro over these deserts, as dismal and monotonous as the sand hills amid which we were sitting. He can neither believe, nor be comfortable in his unbelief; and he is too honest and courageous not to try to do one or the other. If he were a religious man, he would be one of the most truly religious and reverential; he has a very high and noble nature, and better worth immortality than most of us.

Throughout the remainder of Melville's Liverpool stay (he and Hawthorne returned to the city on the 13th), the two men continued to meet. Hawthorne introduced Melville to Henry Bright, who took the visiting author to lunch at his club. On November 14, Melville's passport — "Good for Constantinople (via Malta & Gibraltar) Egypt & a tour about the Continent" — was duly endorsed by the American consul at Liverpool. On the 15th, "a fitful and uncertain day," Hawthorne and Melville made a pleasurable journey to nearby Chester, one of Hawthorne's favorite tourist excursions. After the sightseeing, they sat down "in a small snuggery, behind the bar" and smoked cigars and drank stout, talking with the landlord. That evening, Hawthorne, leaving his friend on a Liverpool street corner, took the train to Southport.

Melville's departure on the steamer *Egyptian* was delayed, however. Hawthorne saw him once more on Monday: "He said that he already felt much better than in America; but observed that he did not anticipate much pleasure in his rambles, for that the spirit of adventure is gone out of him. He certainly is much overshadowed since I saw him last; but I hope he will brighten as he goes onward." On the following day, Melville sailed, leaving behind a trunk and taking only a carpetbag. "This is the next best thing to going naked," Hawthorne mused.

⌒ VII ⌒

On February 13, 1857, Hawthorne sent his official letter of resignation to President-elect James Buchanan, requesting permission to quit his post as of August 31. Since Buchanan would not take office until March 4, he sent the resignation under cover of a letter to Horatio Bridge. "It will be a great relief to me to find myself a private citizen again," he told Bridge, "and I think the old literary instincts and habits will begin to revive in due season."

He had a specific request to make of Bridge, regarding O'Sullivan, who would undoubtedly lose his post if Buchanan appointed General Lewis Cass as his new secretary of state, since O'Sullivan and Cass were political adversaries of long standing. "I wish you would see Pierce," Hawthorne wrote, "and beg him, from me, to say one word to Buchanan in reference to O'Sullivan. He has spent more than his income during all the time that he has been at Lisbon . . . If turned out now, he is irremediably ruined."

Hawthorne promised, "I shall endeavor to do some good to my country, after quitting office, by taking measures to make the public and the government aware of the terrible state of our mercantile marine . . . Meanwhile, I suffer considerable odium here in England (and so will my successor, and all others, until Congress takes hold of the matter) for crimes and cruelties which I have no power to prevent or to bring to punishment . . ." Hawthorne did not wait until he left office. On the day he tendered his resignation, he also sent an official dispatch to William Marcy, once more outlining the drastic nature of the problems, making specific suggestions, and recommending that "a competent commission of enquiry" be instituted. "Something must be done," he warned, "as our national character & commerce are suffering great damage." Throughout the spring and summer, he stepped up his reports on the atrocities that came to his attention.

As he predicted, the problem did not blow over, and the new Buchanan administration was faced with it in far more public terms. The subject came up for debate in Parliament, and Lord John Russell denounced the American government. Hawthorne was not unaware of the convenient political uses the humanitarian debate had served. "Nobody," he commented later, "is so humane as John Bull, when his benevolent propensities are to be gratified by finding fault with his neighbor." But on this occasion, he was in agreement with the British critics. When Lord Napier, British minister in Washington, lodged a formal protest with the State Department, General Cass, in an official reply, answered that the reports of abuses had been largely exaggerated and that present American laws were adequate to deal with the problem. Furthermore, he intimated that the interference of the British minister was uncalled for.

Hawthorne felt that Cass's reply exhibited "a perfectly astounding ignorance of the subject." But he was more concerned with the secretary of state's contention that American consuls, particularly in British ports, may have been "delinquent in the discharge of their duty." On June 17, he sent Cass one of his most pointed dispatches. Referring to Cass's letter, which had been published in the English newspapers, Hawthorne began in a conciliatory tone: "In making some remarks upon that letter it is hardly necessary to say that I do not presume to interfere in a discussion between the Head of the Department, in which I am a subordinate officer, and the Minister of a foreign power. But, as the above-mentioned letter has been made public property, there is as much propriety in my referring to it as to any other matter of public importance bearing especial reference to my own official duties." Responding to Cass's claim that the existing laws were adequate, he argued, "I believe that no man, practically connected with our commercial navy, whether as owner, officer, or seaman, would affirm that the present marine laws of the United States are such as the present condition of our nautical affairs imperatively demands. These laws may have been wise and effectual for the welfare of all concerned at the period of their enactment. But they had in view a state of things which has entirely passed away." The old laws were based on the presumption that American sailors manned American ships, Hawthorne argued. He wrote, "It is not an exaggeration to say that the United States have no seamen. Even the officers from the mate downward are usually foreigners, and of a very poor class; being the rejected mates and other subordinates of the British commercial navy." It was an old argument, and one he had repeated often enough in the past, but now he had to spell it out again — this time for a new secretary of state.

Hawthorne made it plain that he was not laying the blame at the doorstep of the new administration, which had inherited the problem. The only efficient remedy, he maintained, was to have American vessels manned by American crews, but until that could be effected, it was "most desirable that the Government should at least recognize the evils that exist, and do its utmost to alleviate them."

In a final paragraph, Hawthorne took up the question of his own involvement. "Now it is undeniable," he wrote, "that outrages on board of our ships have actually occurred . . . Most of them, moreover, in the trade between America and England, have come under my own consular supervision and been fully investigated by me." Hawthorne then, officially and effectively, called Cass's bluff: "If I have possessed the power to punish those offences, and, whether through sluggishness, or fear, or favor, have failed to exercise it, then I am guilty of a great crime, which ought to be visited with a severity and ignominy commensurate with its evil consequences . . . If I am innocent — if I have done my utmost, as an executive officer, under a defective law, to the defects of which I have repeatedly called the attention of my superiors — then unquestionably, the Secretary has wronged me by a suggestion pointing so directly at myself."

It was not until September that Hawthorne was favored with a reply from Cass — and it was bland and equivocating. "The note to Lord Napier . . ." Cass answered, as if the publication were the real cause of complaint, "was correctly published in the English journals, but without the previous knowledge or consent of this Department." He continued, "You seem to suppose that some of its expressions may have been intended to charge you with delinquency in your official duties towards seamen. No such intention, however, was entertained; and now that you are about to retire from your position, I am happy to bear testimony to the prudent and efficient manner in which you have discharged your duties." It was a wonderfully halfhearted tribute, intended perhaps to buy off a troublesome subordinate who might better have spent his remaining months in office in some other way than the embarrassment of his superior officer.

Cass, in a marvelous display of diplomatic skill, set aside Hawthorne's claim that the present laws were inadequate; then, seizing on the explanation, or bait, Hawthorne had provided — the fact that the United States had no native-born merchant marine — he effectively erased that as well. "What you say with regard to the evils that afflict our commercial marine, it is not now necessary to consider," Cass reminded the departing American consul, "but you quite misapprehend my views if you suppose that I am insensible to the magnitude of these evils, or could have ever intended to deny their existence . . . While, therefore, our statutes may be, and probably are, as well adapted to their objects as those of any other country, it is none the less true that our merchant service suffers constantly from the want of American seamen. How this want can be supplied, is a question to which, in my note to Lord Napier, it was not my purpose to reply."

The secretary of state's answer, it was clear, was tempered to admit very little if Hawthorne should have the bad grace to make it public.

Although he held on to his office — and his emoluments — until August, Hawthorne traveled extensively in England during the final months of his tenure, leaving the day-to-day consular business in the hands of his efficient clerks. Throughout the spring and summer, he and Sophia made brief excursions — sometimes taking Julian, but leaving the girls with a governess at Southport — and returning to Liverpool when consular duties required. Early in April, they toured York and its environs, visiting Bolton Priory and the cathedral, where they attended mass on Easter Sunday. Hawthorne, "almost congealed with cold," found the service too long and the sermon dreary. In midmonth, he was forced to return to Liverpool for the laying of the cornerstone of Browne's Free Library. As both the political and literary representative of the United States government, he was obliged to attend the ceremonial banquet and to make a speech. His address, he noted with ironic satisfaction in his notebooks, was "better cheered than any other; especially one passage, where I made a colossus of poor little Mr. Browne, at which the audience grew so tumultuous in their applause, that they drowned my figure of speech before it was half out of my mouth."

In the kinder weather of May, he, Julian, and Sophia toured Lincoln, Nottingham, and Derby. The highlight of the excursion was a visit to Newstead Abbey, the former home of Lord Byron, which the poet had sold to a friend, Colonel Wildman. Touring the abbey, they were shown Byron's bedroom, kept as he had left it, and the skull that the poet had morbidly used as a drinking goblet. Coursing through the extensive grounds, they saw the famous beech tree on which Byron had carved his name and that of his half sister, Augusta Leigh. (An elderly gardener told them that P. T. Barnum had offered the colonel £500 for just the piece of the tree with the inscription and that the colonel had replied that £5000 would not be enough and that Barnum ought to be flogged for suggesting it.) They were also shown the burial monument erected for Byron's favorite Newfoundland dog — "larger than most Christians get," Hawthorne commented. At the local inn, the landlady chattered on with stories and gossip about Byron's daughter, Ada Lady Lovelace, an inveterate gambler, who had made a mournful visit to the abbey shortly before her death. Hawthorne had occasion to remember her elderly husband, Lord Lovelace, who had called at the Liverpool consulate one day, asking Hawthorne's help in tracing one of his wild and dissolute young sons. It was suspected that he had gone to sea, perhaps to America.

In July, they toured Scotland, spending their wedding anniversary in Edinburgh. "As our union has turned out to the utmost satisfaction of both parties, after fifteen years' trial," Hawthorne wrote in his journal, he gave his wife "a golden-backed and blue-bodied Cairn Gorm beetle." They visited Abbotsford, home of his literary hero, Sir Walter Scott, which Hawthorne had seen before on an earlier excursion, alone. Although Hawthorne might write, "I do abhor this mode of making pilgrimage to the shrines of departed great men; there is certainly something wrong in it, for it seldom, or never produces (in me, at least) the right feeling," he had been oddly moved at the sight of the worn cuff of Scott's old green writing coat.

During August, the family settled in Manchester, with Hawthorne commuting several times a week to Liverpool while awaiting his successor. They regularly attended the huge Manchester Arts Exhibition, and Hawthorne diligently made his way through the seeming acres of old master paintings, finding little satisfaction in the Raphaels and Correggios, preferring the infinite care expended on minute details in the paintings of the Dutch School. It was at the exhibition, accompanied by Alexander Ireland, publisher of the *Manchester Examiner*, that Hawthorne had caught his furtive glimpse of Tennyson.

Hawthorne had met Ireland earlier, through Francis Bennoch. The Manchester journalist had, years before, befriended Emerson and introduced him to Carlyle. He was one of the few men Hawthorne had encountered in England who had read Thoreau's books; he had also spoken well of Margaret Fuller, having been a subscriber to *The Dial*. Hawthorne's discussions with the Scots journalist prompted one of his sharper, more personally revealing observations on English politics. Ireland, he admitted, was a sensible man and he had the liberal's usual openness to new trends and ideas. Hawthorne, however, commented in his notebook, "On the whole, I think the illiberals, the conservatives, the men who despise and hate new things and new thoughts, are the best worth knowing. The others, with all their zeal for novelty, do not seem to originate anything; and one feels, as it were, a little disgusted to find them setting forth their poor little views of progress, especially if one happens to have been a Brook Farmer."

Throughout his English travels, Hawthorne had been keeping extensive notes. "Everything that I see in my travels goes down into my journal," he wrote Ticknor, "and I have now hundreds of pages, which I would publish if the least of them were not too spicy. But Mrs. Hawthorne altogether excels me as a writer of travels. Her descriptions are the most perfect pictures that ever were put on paper; it is a pity they cannot be published; but neither she nor I would like to see her name on your list of female authors."

In one of his softer moments in a letter to Lizzie Peabody, Hawthorne repeated his praise of his wife's travel notes. He and Sophia, he mentioned, had never had a better time in their lives than during their recent tours in England and Scotland. "Between us, we might write an immense book of travels," he informed Lizzie. "I have six or seven volumes of Journal, written during my residence in England; but unfortunately, it is written with so free and truth-telling a pen that I never shall dare to publish it. Perhaps parts of it shall be read to you some winter evening, after we get home; but I entirely yield the palm to Sophia, on the score of feelings and accuracy of description."

Hawthorne's successor as consul, Beverley Tucker, did not reach England until October, and the illness of his indispensable clerk-accountant, Mr. Wilding, kept Hawthorne at his consular duties longer than he had planned. During this period, Sophia and the children were living in Leamington, accompanied by a young American woman, Ada Shepard, a former student of Horace Mann's at Antioch College. Hawthorne had hired her as governess for his children during the tour of France and Italy they planned to make before the return to America. Hawthorne had tried English governesses, so he wrote Ticknor, and found them "ignorant and inefficient"; besides, Ada Shepard had agreed to work for no salary, only for her expenses.

It was not until November that the Hawthornes moved to London for a brief round of sightseeing before departure. By mid December, however, they were still in London; the children had come down with the measles and were put under the care of Dr. Wilkinson. It was only after the new year that the family and the new governess were finally able to set off for the Continent.

While in London, they encountered Edward Augustus Silsbee, a cousin of Mary Silsbee Sparks and, at the young age of thirty-one, a retired Salem sea captain. Silsbee, who had returned to London from an extensive tour of Europe, was a man with a very decided artistic bent. He kept up such a continual banter about his experiences abroad that Hawthorne gratefully left him to Sophia. He thought the young man eminently talented, sensitive, and right-minded — and "such a bore as only a sensible man can be." Yet when Silsbee handed him a manuscript describing his experiences in Berlin, Hawthorne found it a commendable piece of work. On a later evening, Silsbee, who had been invited to an oyster supper, proceeded to read aloud his letters on the subject of art, with descriptions of Venice and other Continental cities. The captive audience consisted of Hawthorne, Una, and Miss Shepard. Sophia — in self-defense, perhaps — had caught cold and was forced to remain in bed. Hawthorne had found the letters genuinely admirable and advised Silsbee to work them up into a series of lectures for home consumption.

Silsbee had also insisted on serving as the guide for a family visit to the Crystal Palace, much to Hawthorne's regret, for he found it impossible to follow his own inclinations, much less his own thoughts — what with Silsbee's enlightened, incessant stream of talk. On this occasion, Hawthorne took a far more perceptive view of the Crystal Palace itself, acknowledging it as the precursor for some new "architectural order, of which we have as yet little or no idea" — one that would use glass as a building material rather than brick or stone. "It will have its own rules and its own results," he commented in his journal. He even conceded that the sprawling glass palace was "positively a very beautiful object." In the course of their visits through the interminable and cluttered exhibits, Sophia lost her sable boa. Silsbee, a perennial bachelor, overly attentive and fussing where older, married, women were concerned, hurried off in such a thorough search for the article that Hawthorne had to go in search of Silsbee.

The aesthetic Captain Silsbee seems to have made no mark on Hawthorne's fiction, but some thirty years later, he was to serve as the inspiration for a notable tale by another American writer. Silsbee's all-consuming passion in life was the poet Shelley; he became an avid collector of Shelley manuscripts, relics, and memorabilia, some of which he generously donated to the Bodleian and Harvard

University libraries. Later in his life, settled in Florence, he succeeded in ingratiating himself with Byron's ancient mistress, Mary Jane "Claire" Clairmont, who lived in the Via Romana under the care of an elderly niece. Silsbee had even gone so far as to board with the old woman in hopes of wheedling out of her a valuable collection of Shelley and Byron papers. A local story had it that when Claire Clairmont died, the manuscripts became the property of the spinster niece, who promptly offered them to the captain if he would marry her. Silsbee, so the story went, hurriedly took flight. Henry James, who heard the anecdote during one of his Italian sojourns, used it as the basis for his masterly tale "The Aspern Papers."

During his last weeks in England, Hawthorne was saddened by the news that Francis Bennoch's firm had gone into bankruptcy due to the speculations of his partners. In the winter gloom of London, he had had a farewell visit with the English merchant. "He keeps up a manly courage and aspect of cheerfulness," Hawthorne noted in his journal, "but it is easy to see that he is a very different man from the joyous one whom I knew a few months since . . ." Reporting to Ticknor on the meeting a few days later, he said that he had advised Bennoch to move to America, where he had a better chance of starting over again and could count on the help of friends. As he explained to his publisher, "It almost is a hopeless business for a ruined man ever to recover himself in England." Bennoch had asked him to relay a message to both Ticknor and Fields that he was "not dead yet, though beaten down."

It was to his other English friend, Henry Bright, that Hawthorne entrusted his precious English notebooks. In Liverpool, he had carefully packaged and sealed them, sending them with a mildly bemused note. "Here are these journals," he wrote Bright. "If unreclaimed by myself, or by my heirs or assignees, I consent to your breaking the seals in the year 1900 — not a day sooner. By that time, probably, England will be a minor Republic, under the protection of the United States. If my countrymen of that day partake of the least of my feelings, they will treat you generously. Your friend, Nathaniel Hawthorne."

The Buried Past

IT WAS A BLEAK and wintry January 5 when the Hawthornes took the train to Folkestone. There, they did not bother to explore the town for a parting glimpse of England, but remained in the railroad station until departure time for the channel steamer. During the rough, two-and-a-half-hour crossing, they stayed belowdeck, where Hawthorne, not troubled by seasickness, observed a number of his fellow passengers "stretched on sofas, in a state of placid wretchedness." At Boulogne, their luggage having been forwarded to Paris, they took the train to Amiens, where they planned to spend a day visiting the cathedral. It was a disagreeable, cold journey even with footwarmers placed in the carriages. The frost was so thick on the windows that Hawthorne had to rub it away to get a look at bare, brown fields streaked with snow. "My impression of France," he confided to his journal, "will always be, that it is an Arctic region."

They did not arrive in Paris until the evening of the 6th, when they took a suite of rooms at the Hôtel du Louvre. In his journal that night, Hawthorne recorded his grudging appreciation of French cuisine, sampled in the hotel restaurant. "All the dishes were very delicate," he noted, "and a vast change from the simple English system, with its joints, shoulders, beef-steaks and chops." But his Puritan prejudices tempered even that concession: "I doubt whether English cookery, for the very reason that it is so gross, is not better for man's moral and spiritual nature, than French. In the former case, you know that you are gratifying your coarsest animal needs and propensities, and are duly ashamed of it; but, in dealing with these French delicacies, you delude yourself into the idea that you are cultivating your taste while filling your belly." It would take time before the rigidities of Salem thawed to the seductions of Continental culture.

In the meantime, a succession of cold days must have suitably dampened the pleasures of their visit; Hawthorne, crossing the Seine, probably took some satisfaction from the large chunks of ice floating down the river. The Hôtel du Louvre, it appeared, was admirably situated for the family's daily excursions into the dangers of French culture. The Louvre and the Palais Royal were across the street, the Tuileries not far distant. The Place de la Concorde and the Champs Elysées were within easy walking distance. Although Sophia had an inexhaustible enthusiasm for visiting the Louvre, Hawthorne soon tired of the salons of paintings by the great masters, the halls of Egyptian and Greek antiquities. He felt the burden of the past.

Yet, coming upon a room full of the carefully preserved relics of emperors and tyrants, he indulged in an odd — and old — fantasy: the great halls of the Louvre were filled with returned Childerics and Charleses, Bourbons and Capets, "snatching with ghostly hands at scepters, swords, armour, mantles." Like many creative men of the nineteenth century, Hawthorne was fascinated by Napoleon, that "great boulder in history." He studied the emperor's relics with peculiar fascination — "his coat, his cocked hats, his camp-desk, his field bed, his knives, forks and plates, and even a lock of his hair." With a kind of Proustian awareness of the power of objects to preserve some fleeting human reference out of the flux of history, he wrote in his journal, "I must let it all go. These things cannot be reproduced by pen and ink." There were moments, it seemed, when the sense of the past went beyond the reach of prose.

Paris had its splendors, whatever the temperature. With its throngs of soldiers and priests, its colorful gendarmes in cocked hats, Zouaves in turbans and bronzed faces, it was far more picturesque than London. Paris, Hawthorne admitted, "puts London to the blush." He confessed, "I never knew what a palace was, till I had a glimpse of the Louvre and the Tuileries." He was not sympathetic toward the French themselves, conceding in his notebooks that "their eyes do not win me, nor do their glances melt and mingle with mine." But he was forced to admit that the French "do grand and beautiful things, in the architectural way." He was told that the present, and greatly despised emperor, Napoleon III — "our neighbor across the way" — was responsible for much of the architectural splendor, the long vistas, and the stately edifices. Louis Napoleon, he was informed, had been longer in power than his famous uncle. That fact brought home to Hawthorne the relative nature of greatness, the weight a legend accrued in time. "We, who look back upon [the first Napoleon] as one of the eternal facts of the past . . . cannot well estimate how momentary and unsubstantial the Great Captain may have appeared, to those who beheld his rise out of obscurity."

Not long after their arrival in Paris, they had a visit from Maria Mitchell, the thirty-nine-year-old American astronomer from Nantucket, whose discovery of a new comet, in 1847, had brought her fame and honors. Hawthorne had first met her at the consulate in Liverpool, when she arrived with a letter of introduction. Maria Mitchell was hoping to travel with them to Rome; there were stages of the journey that would be dangerous for a woman traveling alone. Hawthorne was glad to be of service; he found her a "simple, strong, healthy-humored woman," who would be no burden. While in Paris, Hawthorne paid a courtesy call on the American minister, Judge John Mason, in the Rue de Beaujon. Mason, large and red-faced, received him in his morning gown and without getting up from his chair. Hawthorne suspected he suffered from gout. Though he described the minister as "a fat-brained, good-hearted, sensible old man," Hawthorne wondered whether there was any good reason why Uncle Sam should pay him "seventeen thousand dollars a year for sleeping in the dignified post of Ambassador to France. The true ground of complaint is, that, whether he slept or waked, the result would be the same." He had a better opinion of the American consul, Henry Spencer, a "gentlemanly, courteous, cool man of the world," whom he visited in his tiny office in the Rue Caumartin. Spencer, who had spent much time in Italy, advised him to take the steamer from Marseilles to Civitavecchia, rather than Leghorn, and then travel by carriage to Rome.

The journey southward, begun on the 13th, was uneventful. They stopped overnight in Lyons at the huge and musty Hôtel de Provence, then proceeded on to Marseilles, which they reached at eleven o'clock the following evening, putting up at the Hôtel d'Angleterre. The next morning, after a "wretched breakfast," Hawthorne, Julian, and Ada Shepard walked out to a park thronged with people who seemed to be astir with excited conversation. It was only later, at the telegraph office, that Hawthorne learned an assassination attempt had been made on the emperor's life and that several members of his entourage had been killed or wounded, but that Louis Napoleon had escaped injury. From studying the sturdy Marseilles citizenry catching the wintry sunlight in the park, it was Hawthorne's impression that the assassination attempt was more an item of gossip than a matter of vital concern.

On January 17, they embarked for Italy on the steamer *Calabrese*, a clean and comfortable little vessel that belied the reports they had had of it. The pitch and roll of the ship on choppy seas had sent them all to bed early. The voyage lasted three days, with stops at

Genoa and Leghorn. In Genoa, Hawthorne was amazed by the profligate use of colored marbles in the Cathedral of San Lorenzo. "I used to try to imagine how splendidly the English Cathedrals must have looked in their primeval glory, before the Reformation . . ." Hawthorne confessed in his notebook, "but I never imagined anything at all approaching what my eyes now beheld; this sheen of polished and variegated marble, covering every inch of the walls; this glow of brilliant frescos all over the roof, and up within the domes." He gave it all up as indescribable. Leghorn he found inexpressibly dull, except for the tomb of Smollett, a slender white marble obelisk, which he searched out in the little cemetery next to the English Chapel. That evening, a night of glittering stars and "bright young moonlight," Maria Mitchell had stood on deck with the children, giving them a lesson in astronomy. Julian, pointing out a constellation to this father, misnamed its most famous part "O'Brien's belt"; the phrase became a family joke.

The journey from Civitavecchia to Rome had its anxieties. Rail service had not yet been instituted, and one had to make the trip by carriage along narrow and treacherous roads, in a countryside infested with bandits. They had heard rumors of a Nova Scotian bishop who had been robbed only a few days before. The rough, twelve-hour trip, in a small, crowded carriage, passed without incident. As a precaution, they had hidden money in boots and boxes, and even in an old umbrella. The children took the slow, jolting ride through decaying villages and lonely outposts with a sense of high excitement. The fact that they were following, by a few miles, an armed mailcoach may have been fortunate. Julian remembered the ominous silhouettes of two horsemen atop a hill, surveying them as they passed.

There was little comfort at the end of their worrisome journey. At the gates of Rome, weary of traveling, Hawthorne "perpetrated unheard of briberies" on the Italian customs officials before they were allowed to enter the city. They put up in the only lodgings they were able to find, Spillman's Hotel. The rooms were frigid, the food poor. "And this is sunny Italy, and genial Rome!" Hawthorne commented in his journal.

Fortunately, the family moved into new lodgings — a suite of rooms in the Palazzo Larazani at 37 Via Porta Pinciana — within a few days. The quarters, spacious but hardly elegant, were impossible to heat in the rainy, damp weather that plagued their first weeks in Rome. Much of the time the family spent shivering before meager fires, their misery relieved by short excursions of sightseeing.

On February 4, on his way to St. Peter's, Hawthorne encountered an old American acquaintance, the painter Cephas Thompson. The Boston artist was one of the growing host of expatriated painters and sculptors who, disappointed with the opportunities at home, had flocked to Rome and Florence to pursue their careers. The Thompson family, which included two young sons and a daughter, was a godsend for the Hawthorne children. It was with eleven-year-old Edward Thompson that Julian, a few months older, began exploring the city and collecting shell specimens along the banks of the Tiber. The two boys had a scientific bent, spending hours inspecting insects and butterflies under a ten-shilling microscope Hawthorne had bought for his son.

New quarters and the closeness of American friends, however, did little to improve Hawthorne's temperament during the early weeks of his Roman holiday. Very shortly after his arrival, he came down with a bout of influenza. He spent much of his time in his room, sitting before a small fire, swaddled in as much clothing as he could put on, with his thickest greatcoat on top of that. Maria Mitchell, who had taken an apartment nearby, thought Hawthorne too taciturn and too inactive. She and Sophia toured Rome like a pair of eager sisters, but Hawthorne, who had "a horror of sight-seeing," seldom joined them. The American astronomer recalled the seemingly disconsolate author, sitting by an open fire "with his feet thrust into the coals, and an open volume of Thackeray upon his knees. He said that Thackeray was the greatest living novelist. I sometimes suspected that the volume of Thackeray was kept as a foil, that he might not be talked to." She also thought that Sophia was too worshipful of her husband.

For an hour or two at midday, Hawthorne ventured out into the bright, winter-cold streets of Rome. It was a city far different from the sunny fictions of the travel books. For comfort and consolation — and warmth — Hawthorne frequently visited St. Peter's, where, so he fancied, the heat of the summer past had been entrapped behind the padded leather curtains that hung over the entrances. Outside, pools of ice had formed near the fountains. When Rosebud went sliding on them, he followed after. "If my wits had not been too much congealed, and my fingers too numb," Hawthorne complained grumpily, "I should like to have kept a minute journal of my feelings and impressions, during the past fortnight; it would have shown up modern Rome in an aspect in which it has never yet been depicted." Actually, he was keeping two notebooks, one of them a small diary in which he recorded his activities and expenses. From this he worked up the more descriptive passages of the journal, adding the sometimes irritable reflections in which he took revenge on the unobliging city.

The Roman Carnival, which began early in February, did little to arouse his enthusiasm. It seemed a mindless festival — streets thronged with merrymakers and children, avenues crowded with carriages passing and repassing, the riders tossing bouquets of wilted flowers or pelting each other with handfuls of lime and confetti that stuck to one's clothing in the damp weather. "Really, it was great nonsense," Hawthorne commented after one excursion along the route of merrymaking. "There were some queer shapes and faces . . . clowns, harlequins, apes' snouts, young men in feminine guise, and *vice versa*, and several samples of Italian costume . . . Either the masques were not very funny, or I was in no funny mood." He tried, nonetheless, to enter into the spirit of the moment, riding with Sophia, Julian, and Rose along the Corso and dutifully submitting to the bombardments of confetti. The children enjoyed themselves immensely; little Rose had garnered several bouquets. "Only the young ought to write descriptions of such scenes," Hawthorne decided. "My cold criticism chills the life out of it."

A sombering presence seemed to hover over the tawdry licentiousness of the parade. A patrol of papal dragoons was stationed along the Corso. In the Piazza del Popolo, detachments of French troops stood guard near stacks of muskets. It was a precautionary measure against the unruly Roman population, which, ten years before — when Margaret Fuller had been in Rome — had turned against the vacillating Pope Pius IX and driven him from the city. The revolution, a thing of the uneasy past, had been put down with the aid of Napoleon III's army, and the pope had been restored to power. French troops were still everywhere in the city. The streets rang with their military drills and the music of their military bands. In the midst of the revelry, they were a reminder of overriding power. "If the chained tiger-cat (meaning thereby the Roman populace) had but shown the tip of his claws," Hawthorne wrote in his journal, "the bullets would have been flying along the street. But the tiger-cat is a very harmless brute."

He was conscious of missing much; in his walks, he felt he was passing history, unobserving. The heaps of rubbish sprawling at the ground-floor level of the magnificent palaces disturbed his fastidious nature; he found it impossible, he complained, to "get down upon paper the dreariness and ugliness, nastiness, discomfort, shabbiness, un-home-likeness, of a Roman street." But he admired, at the end of the thoroughfares, the sudden access to broad piazzas and tiny squares and the innumerable fountains that seemed to spurt up, trickle down, squander themselves in even the meanest quarters — an endless water fantasy, gushing up everywhere in the ancient city. Gradually, his old ruminative tendencies returned; he began making observations on local habits, national differences. He was glad, on the whole, that he had seen the cathedrals of England — gray ruins, ivy-covered, bathed in soft and warming light — before confronting the less romantic antiquities of the Eternal City. "Whatever beauty there may be in a Roman ruin," he wrote, "is the remnant of what was beautiful originally, whereas an English ruin is more beautiful, often, in its decay than ever it was in its primal strength. If we ever build such noble structures as these Roman ones, we can have just as good ruins after two thousand years, in the United States; but we never can have a Furness Abbey or a Kenilworth."

⌐ II ⌐

As the weather thawed, Hawthorne's prejudices softened. He settled into the circumscribed life of the city's little Anglo-American colony. He and Sophia were soon on friendly terms with William Wetmore Story, living in ducal style in his apartments in the Palazzo Barberini. Story, whom Hawthorne had known as a young man in America, had passed up a brilliant career as a lawyer to become an artist. Now thirty-nine, a man of too many talents but lacking the essential genius, he had not yet become the most celebrated American sculptor of his generation, patronized by European princes and affluent Yankee businessmen. That time was to come in a very few years, when, under the patronage of Pius IX, his marble production, the seated *Cleopatra*, became the overnight sensation in the great London Exhibition of 1862. Hawthorne was to contribute measurably to Story's success through his high praise of the statue in his popular romance, *The Marble Faun*, published in 1860.

From the beginning of Story's Roman residence, his salon in the Palazzo Barberini became the gathering place for American tourists and aspiring American artists. (In the earlier years, Story and his wife, Emelyn, had befriended Margaret Fuller.) A congenial host and affable storyteller, he entertained on the grand scale, to the envy of his less fortunate colleagues. He had a reputation as a man of well-rounded cultural attainments. Hawthorne frankly admired his versatility. "His perplexing variety of talents and accomplishments — a poet, a prose-writer, a lawyer, a painter, a sculptor — seems now to be concentrating itself into this latter vocation," he observed, "and I cannot see why he should not achieve something very good."

What Hawthorne fastened upon among Story's gifts was the sculptor's habit of fixing on a dramatic subject and investing it with a wealth of historic detail in terms of dress and ornament and furniture. Story, in default of a fierce imagination, had the stage designer's gift for the theatrical moment — décor as the setting for emotion. His was essentially a narrative talent — the storyteller's art — one that Hawthorne fully appreciated. Few works of sculpture so impressed Hawthorne as the clay model of *Cleopatra*, which he had seen in an early stage in Story's Via Sistina studio. In his journal, Hawthorne described it as "a grand subject." Story, he claimed, was "sensible of something deeper in his art than merely to make beautiful nudities and baptize them by classic names." But in *The Marble Faun*, attributing the statue to his fictional sculptor, Kenyon, what Hawthorne praised was the dead historical detail — the Egyptian costume, the Egyptian headdress, the "full Nubian lips, and other characteristics of the Egyptian physiognomy" — which Story had industriously copied from "coins, drawings, painted mummy-cases, and whatever other tokens have been dug out of [Egypt's] pyramids, graves, and catacombs." In his prose, Hawthorne managed to invest Story's frozen *Cleopatra* with a spark of animation, describing it as "fierce, voluptuous, passionate, tender, wicked, terrible, and full of poisonous and rapturous enchantment."

Hawthorne and Sophia were frequent guests at the Barberini Palace, attending the Storys' intimate breakfasts and the more lavish evening receptions at which one found a mixture of Roman patrons and Story's American and English admirers. The vast rambling palace was still the residence of the Barberini dukes and cardinals and their armies of retainers. Hawthorne often stopped in the family's picture galleries. It was there that he was struck with admiration for the Guido Reni picture purported to be the portrait of Beatrice Cenci — "the most profoundly wrought picture in the world," he claimed; "no artist did it, or could do it again. Guido may have held the brush, but he painted better than he knew." Hawthorne's Puritan morals were engagingly shocked by the lasciviousness of Raphael's *La Fornarina* — "with a deep, bright glow in her face, naked below the navel, and well pleased to be so for the sake of your admiration — ready for any extent of nudity, for love or money — the brazen trollop that she is. Raphael must have been capable of great sensuality . . ."

Nudity in painting and sculpture was a continuing complaint in Hawthorne's Roman journal. After a visit to the studio of Edward S. Bartholomew, where he encountered a nude *Eve*, he criticized the "awful volume of thighs and calves" in Bartholomew's sculpture. "I do not altogether see the necessity of ever sculpturing another nakedness," he wrote in his journal. "Man is no longer a naked animal; his clothes are as natural to him as his skin, and sculptors have no more right to undress him than to flay him."

He was to make the same point with Anna Jameson, the noted English art historian, to whom he was introduced by Story. In her sixties, a "shortish, round and massive personage," with a black skullcap on her nearly white head, Mrs. Jameson had the vitality that a serious commitment brings to old age. She was full of young and peppery opinions, claimed she could read any picture "like the page of a book," and made it plain that she felt amateurs — in which category Hawthorne placed himself — were unlikely to know "one single, simplest thing about art." She insisted on taking Hawthorne sightseeing, and during a carriage ride beyond the gates of the city, along the Appian Way, she expressed her low opinion of American sculptors — with the presumed exception of Story. She felt they had "no high aims" and were merely "desecrating the marble" with their small ambitions. Hawthorne thought she was right, but argued that English sculptors seemed little better. The two had a lively dispute about nudity and costume in sculpture, Hawthorne claiming that the test of a sculptor's genius would be to make the viewer sense the beauty and grace of the body beneath the clothing. Mrs. Jameson, however, "decidedly objected to buttons, breeches, and all other items of modern costume." Hawthorne, conceding that they did "degrade the marble, and make high sculpture utterly impossible," cavalierly added, "Then let the art perish, as one that the world has done with, as it has done with many other beautiful things . . ."

In the self-protective little Roman colony of American artists, the life of art seemed viable in a way that was not possible at home. Hawthorne's Italian notes devoted a good deal of attention to the painters and sculptors he met. He had hardly been installed in the Palazzo Larazani when Maria Louisa Lander, an ambitious sculptor from his home town, Salem, paid a first social call. Sensing an opportunity, the young woman, who had come to Rome to study under Thomas Crawford, assiduously cultivated Hawthorne and his wife. When Hawthorne and Sophia visited her in her studio on February 6, Miss Lander promptly asked Hawthorne to sit for a portrait bust. Without too much hesitation, he agreed. At his first sitting, on February 15, he was asked not to look at the results and did not, though he had a vague impression of a familiar "heavy-browed physiognomy." Throughout February, March, and into the first week of April, Hawthorne gave the sculptor at least fifteen sittings, spending an hour or two in a large, high, dusty, and sparsely furnished studio room that had once been part of a suite belonging to the great Canova. A close friendship between the Hawthornes and Louisa Lander seemed to be burgeoning. The sculptor was invited to tea and dinner at the Palazzo Larazani, often in the company of Maria Mitchell. Hawthorne and Sophia accompanied her on sightseeing visits to the Colosseum and the Vatican sculpture galleries.

While Louisa Lander roughed out his features in clay, Hawthorne began taking her "portrait" as well — one that he would draw on for the character of Hilda in *The Marble Faun*. Hawthorne was intrigued by the young woman's picturesque studio costume, "a sort of pea-jacket, buttoned across her breast, and a little foraging-cap, just covering the top of her head." He seems to have had, too, a more generous estimate of women sculptors than women writers, granting that the Salem artist "appears to have genuine talent, and spirit and independence enough to give it fair play." It impressed him to see a young woman "living in almost perfect independence, thousands of miles from her New England home, going fearlessly about these mysterious streets, by night as well as by day, with no household ties, no rule or law but that within her." Hawthorne had been highly appreciative of the sculptor's *Virginia Dare*, a remarkably stiff, remarkably full-breasted nude, whose pelvis was strategically draped with fishnetting. At first, he had been pleased with Lander's portrait bust of him. Writing to Ticknor after it was completed, Hawthorne acknowedged that Sophia was "delighted with it," and that it had received high praise from the artists in the American colony. Fredrika Bremer, who was living in Rome, had also pronounced it "the finest modelled bust she ever saw." Since Louisa Lander was planning to make a brief trip to America, Hawthorne asked both Ticknor and Fields to do whatever they could "to bring Miss Lander's name favorably before the public."

On April 13, Hawthorne noted in his pocket diary that he paid Louisa Lander twenty scudi and that the sculptor had called at the Palazzo Larazani "after all but me had gone to bed." On the 15th, the Salem sculptor dined with the Hawthornes, "her farewell visit before returning to America." A month later, he noted another payment of 100 scudi for the bust while it was being translated into marble.

Ebe Hawthorne, who saw a photograph of the clay model when the sculptor called on her in Salem, was not altogether convinced of the likeness. "It looked grand, but very old," she wrote Una. "But she says that the bust will not look old." Hawthorne was to take a less than favorable view of the completed marble. According to Julian, a passable likeness had been turned into something that looked like a "combination of Daniel Webster and George Washington" when a friend of the sculptor's ordered the Italian workmen to make changes in the features. Both Louisa Lander and Hawthorne were away from Rome at the time.

In *The Marble Faun*, Hawthorne also drew on his observations of another feminine compatriot, the sculptor Harriet Hosmer, for his literary portrait of an American artist in Rome. Hosmer shared a studio with the renowned Royal Academician John Gibson, under whom she had studied. She had acquired a sizable reputation and a fair amount of patronage for her playful fountain sculptures of Cupids riding dolphins and a whole breed of ponderous classical and historical heroines. She had been the only American sculptor to receive a commission from the Roman Catholic Church — a funerary monument for a pious sixteen-year-old girl, Mlle. Falconnet. Hawthorne admired the monument in the church of S. Andrea della Fratte, but he was less impressed with Hosmer's treatment of Beatrice Cenci, a sculpture that had received an inordinate amount of praise from the American colony.

Both Hawthorne and Sophia liked the frank and pleasant little artist, who had an air of efficiency and briskness and a taste for masculine attire, dressing in a practical man's smock of plum-colored broadcloth, with a man's shirt front, collar, and cravat. When she had first come to Rome in 1852, Hosmer had been a protégée of Charlotte Cushman. Not long after their arrival on the scene — and their establishment of a cosy ménage on the Corso that included Matilda Hays and Grace Greenwood — William Wetmore Story dubbed the group the "harem (scarem)." Writing to his friend Lowell, he described "Hatty" Hosmer as "very wilful, and too independent by half" and reported on the commotion she had caused by riding horseback unattended, contrary to sedate Roman custom. "The police interfered and countermanded the riding alone," Story gossiped, "on account of the row it made in the streets, and I believe *that* is over, but I cannot affirm." He added, "The Cushman sings savage ballads in a hoarse, manny voice, and requests people recitatively to forget her not. I'm sure I shall not."

On a visit to Hosmer's studio, Hawthorne had an opportunity to study Gibson's sculptures, particularly his famed "tinted Venus," a neoclassical version of the goddess, stained with soft color to give it a natural effect. Hawthorne felt the coloring gave the marble too palpable and too sensual an effect; he found it disturbing. (Told that the sculptor tinted his figures with tobacco juice, Hawthorne quipped that if Gibson sent one of his Cupids to America he "need not trouble himself to stain it beforehand"). Early in his stay in Rome, at a dinner party, Hawthorne had sat next to the aged bachelor and found him agreeable and self-possessed. Hawthorne sensed that Gibson had "doubtless spent a calm life among his clay and marble, meddling little with the world, and entangling himself with no cares beyond his studio." His intuition was accurate enough. Gibson was a man of thoroughly conservative and peace-loving disposition. A decade before, during the uprising against the pope, frightened by the unruly Roman populace and the advancing armies of Napoleon III sent to quell the revolution, he had fled the city and his studio full of sculptures, waiting until the pope was restored under the protection of the French. The Romans, he felt, had proved themselves "unworthy of liberty."

At dinner, Hawthorne and Gibson had discussed the pre-Raphaelite painters of England, whom Gibson dismissed out of hand. "The difference between the pre-Raphaelites and himself is deep and genuine," Hawthorne noted, "they being literalists and realists, in a certain sense, and he a pagan idealist." Hawthorne thought the pre-Raphaelites had hold of "the best end of the matter."

Hawthorne also visited the forlorn studio of Thomas Crawford, who had died the previous October, at the height of his success. Crawford's commissions from the American government for the door reliefs and the dome sculpture of Liberty for the Capitol in Washington had been one of the great coups in American culture. At the time of Hawthorne's visit, Crawford's widow, Louisa, one of the beautiful Ward sisters, was in America arranging details for the completion of the projects.

The studio in the Villa Negroni was a vast stretch of airy, light-filled rooms, in which artisans were still busy chipping away at the marble versions of the original clay models. Hawthorne passed extravagant figural groups, an equestrian statue of Washington on a rearing horse, life-sized sculptures of Jefferson and Patrick Henry. In room after room, emblems of republican virtue consorted with allegorical groups of naked girls and boys, Adams and Eves, Floras with exposed breasts and garlands of posies. It was as if the cluttered fantasies of a mind, now stopped, had been crowded into the dusty rooms. Louisa Lander had told Hawthorne that not long before his death, Crawford had assured her he had "fifteen years of good work still in him." Hawthorne was not altogether satisfied by Crawford's reputation; he considered most of the sculptures "common-places in marble and plaster, such as we should not tolerate on a printed page." He thought it a pity, however, that Crawford had not lived to see all his plaster models translated into gleaming marble. "There is almost as much difference as between flesh and spirit" was his comparison.

Through the warming Roman springtime, Hawthorne busied himself with visits to artists' studios, meeting the resident sculptors and painters: the congenial Maine sculptor Benjamin Paul Akers; the brisk young painter Luther Terry, who later married Crawford's widow; the Boston landscapist George Loring Brown; and Hamilton Gibbs Wilde. A certain chauvinism crept into Hawthorne's estimates of his countrymen. He thought Brown's landscapes preferable to those of Claude; Wilde's Italian sunsets and glimpses of New England woods were "miracles of color." Yet beneath the buzz and hum of the gregarious Roman art colony, he detected something else — the irritability of the creative life:

> I suppose there is a class-feeling among the artists who reside here, and they create a sort of atmosphere among themselves, which they do not find anywhere else, and which is comfortable for them to live in. Nevertheless, they are not generous nor gracious critics of one another; and I hardly remember any full-breathed and whole-souled praise from sculptor to sculptor, or from painter to painter. They dread one another's ill word, and scrupulously exchange little attentions for fear of giving offence; they pine, I suspect, at the sight of another's success, and would willingly keep a rich stranger from the door of any studio save their own. Their public is so much more limited than that of the literary men, that they have the better excuse for these petty jealousies.

One day late in March, Hawthorne paid a visit to the studio of Joseph Mozier, an American businessman-turned-sculptor, who was enjoying a modest vogue. Hawthorne thought his *Pocahontas* and *Prodigal Son* showed ability, but he felt Mozier had rather ordinary capacities. He was not a really creative artist and might still be, for lack of refinement, "a country shopkeeper." Louisa Lander, who was a fund of disagreeable gossip, told him that Mozier had stolen — "adopted," as Hawthorne preferred to put it — the idea for his *Prodigal Son* from a student at the French Academy. Hawthorne, feeling that Mozier lacked originality, was inclined to believe the charge.

His real interest in Mozier lay in what the American sculptor told him about the last days of Margaret Fuller in Italy. Mozier and his wife, living in Florence, had taken in the ailing Margaret, her husband, and infant son. Mozier claimed that Ossoli, the handsomest man he ever met, was "entirely ignorant even of his own language, scarcely able to read at all, destitute of manners; in short, half an idiot, and without any pretensions to be a gentleman." At Margaret's request, Mozier had tried to give Ossoli instructions in sculpture, but after months of labor, all he could produce was a copy of a human foot — with the great toe on the wrong side. In his notebook, Hawthorne wrote at length about the unlikely couple:

> He [Ossoli] could not possibly have had the least appreciation of Margaret; and the wonder is, what attraction she found in this boor, this hymen without the intellectual spark — she that had always shown such a cruel and bitter scorn of intellectual deficiency. As from her towards him, I do not understand what feeling there could have been, except it were purely sensual; as from him towards her, there could hardly have been even this, for she had not the charm of womanhood. But she was a woman anxious to try all things, and fill up her experience in all directions; she had a strong and coarse nature, too, which she had done her utmost to refine, with infinite pains, but which of course could only be superficially changed. The solution of the riddle lies in this direction . . . for — at least this is my own experience — Margaret has not left, in the hearts and minds of those who knew her, any deep witness for her integrity and purity. She was a great humbug; of course with much talent, and, much moral reality, or else she could not have been so great a humbug. But she had stuck herself full of borrowed qualities, which she chose to provide herself with, but which had no root in her.

Fed by Mozier's information, Hawthorne went on to demolish — with some satisfaction, it appears — the last hope of some final literary testimony of Margaret Fuller's genius, the rumored history of the Roman republic that was thought to have been lost in the shipwreck off Fire Island. Mozier, Hawthorne reported in his notebook, assured him that "Margaret had quite lost all power of literary production" before she left Rome. To Mozier's certain knowledge, Hawthorne related, "she had no important manuscripts with her when she sailed (she having shown him all she had, with a view to his procuring their publication in America); and the History of the Roman Revolution about which there was so much lamentation . . . never had existence." Hawthorne's savage observations did not end even there:

> Thus there appears to have been a total collapse in poor Margaret, morally and intellectually; and tragic as her catastrophe was, Providence was, after all, kind in putting her and her clownish husband, and their child, on board that fated ship. There never was such a tragedy as her whole story; the sadder and sterner, because so much of the ridiculous was mixed up with it, and because she could bear anything better than to be ridiculous. It was such an awful joke, that she should have resolved — in all sincerity, no doubt — to make herself the greatest, wisest, best woman of the age; and, to

that end, she set to work on her strong, heavy, unpliable, and, in many respects, defective and evil nature, and adorned it with a mosaic of admirable qualities, such as she chose to possess; putting in here a splendid talent, and there a moral excellence, and polishing each separate piece, and the whole together, till it seemed to shine afar and dazzle all who saw it. She took credit to herself for having been her own Redeemer, if not her own Creator; and, indeed, she was far more a work of art than any of Mozier's statues. But she was not working on an inanimate substance, like marble or clay; there was something within her that she could not possibly have come at, to recreate and refine it; and, by and by, this rude old potency bestirred itself, and undid all her labor in the twinkling of an eye. On the whole, I do not know but I like her the better for it — the better, because she proved herself a very woman, after all, and fell as the weakest of her sisters might.

Considering the far more lenient charity of Hawthorne's fictional view of sinners and sinful human nature, his assessment of Margaret Fuller was the sharpest and most critical judgment he ever made on the human clay. A kind of wrath, a secret animus, surges up in his reflections on a woman who had, at least, passed for a friend and colleague. It was as if his buried animosities, his long-held prejudices against literary women and meddling reformers, and his fears about the seductions of Rome itself, had surfaced for the brief moment in which he recounted his interview with Mozier.

It had always been a suspicion among Margaret Fuller's friends that her marriage — if, in fact, she had been married — had taken place after the birth of her son. Hawthorne, all too believing in the sinfulness of human nature, readily accepted this version. His portrait of Margaret Fuller was drawn from life — the life as he sensed it, abetted by the disagreeable Mr. Mozier. (It was merely another irony that the details had been supplied by a man of small talent and large prejudices, a discredited witness, a possible "plagiarist"; but then the mean-spirited often have a better grasp of the truth than the blandly congenial.) Whatever Hawthorne's own, bitter, masculine prejudices, whatever the truths he managed to incorporate into his extraordinary prose recollection, he had, in spite of himself, sketched out the portrait of a difficult and vital woman — a woman more vivid and unkind, more instinct with life and passion, than he had ever quite created among his fictional heroines. It was also a portrait that was far more incisive in its realization of tragic human nature than any his sculptor-friends had managed to produce among the immaculate, white, attitudinizing slave girls and Indian maidens that populated the studios of Rome.

⌒ III ⌒

With his Murray's Handbook, that "highly essential nuisance,"
Hawthorne trudged about Rome like a dutiful American tourist,
visiting famous cathedrals and interminable picture galleries; he
spent afternoons in bosky Roman gardens. He grew weary of the old
masters, the endless array of immovable saints, infant Jesuses, and
plump Venuses, each one very much like the last. The Sistine Chapel
impressed him; he appreciated the power of Michelangelo and was
willing to concede that perhaps "the greatest pictorial miracles,
ever yet achieved, have been wrought upon the walls and ceiling of
the Sistine Chapel." But he favored the Vatican sculpture galleries,
which he visited on several occasions with Sophia and Louisa Lander. He felt the peculiar force of *Laocoön*, "an immortal agony, with
a strange calmness diffused through it, so that it resembles the vast
rage of the sea"; he had seen the *Apollo Belvedere*, caught for a moment in a sudden flood of light, "ethereal and godlike." In his journal, he commented that he had not had "so good a day as this
(among works of art) since we came to Rome." He had begun to
sense the antitheses of Rome: a city of architectural splendors and
sunless streets running with human filth; a city of the highest artistic aspirations and pestilential fleas. (At tea one afternoon, he noticed that even the dainty Fredrika Bremer, that "funniest little old
fairy" with an overweening nose, was scratching herself unself-
consciously.) It was a city full of dubious relics and miracles: the
table on which the Last Supper had been served; the staircase to
Pontius Pilate's house; a miraculous spring that gushed out of the
stone walls of the dank prison where St. Peter had been held
(Hawthorne, sampling the water, found it brackish and unpalat-
able); the imprint of the Savior's feet in stone, supposedly left after
He appeared to St. Peter in a vision. (On checking his Murray's,
Hawthorne was "mortified" but delighted to find that his expert
guide, Mrs. Jameson, had misled him; the imprint she showed him
was only a facsimile, the "original" being stored in the nearby Basil-
ica of San Sebastiano. Hawthorne had noticed suspicious chisel
marks; he also concluded that the feet were hardly beautiful enough
to belong to "the bearer of the best of glad tidings.")

He had even witnessed sights that might have been taken for miracles. Visiting a Capuchin chapel in the midst of a funeral service,
he had seen an aged monk laid out on his bier, a short, paunchy
man whose face had an unnatural flush that suggested he had died
of apoplexy. Sophia thought the dead man's bushy eyebrows had
suddenly contorted. Staring at him, they saw blood oozing from his

nostrils. "It was about as queer a thing as I ever witnessed," Hawthorne commented. "We soon came away and left him lying there; a sight which I shall never forget."

At St. Peter's, he and Sophia had waited a half hour to catch a glimpse of the tardy Pius IX, arriving for a prayer service in his white silk robe and embroidered cape, scarlet slippers on his feet. Hawthorne was glad to have that essential bit of tourism out of the way. He was far more moved by the sight of the confessionals at St. Peter's: "If I had had a murder on my conscience or any other great sin, I think I should have been inclined to kneel down there, and pour it into the safe secrecy of the confessional. What an institution that is! Man needs it so, that it seems as if God must have ordained it. This popish religion certainly does apply itself most closely and comfortably to human occasions." His Yankee prejudices were thawing, but it seems odd that he had imagined himself guilty of murder rather than of more plausible sins, like adultery or coveting one's neighbor's wife.

On a brilliant May afternoon, he and Sophia and the obliging Storys had driven out beyond the Lateran Gate to the broad campagna, to inspect a recent archeological find — the catacombs of St. Callixtus. The excavations were a favorite tourist attraction, and the roadside was cluttered with carriages and visitors. They had had to wait their turn to descend the long flights of stairs into the tomb, where they inspected the burial chambers with their festive decorations now exposed to light after centuries of darkness. In one, Hawthorne had measured a thigh bone against his own. He had a distinct sense of buried history forever reasserting itself. "You cannot dig six feet downward anywhere into the soil — deep enough to hollow out a grave — without finding some precious relic of the past," he commented; "only they lose somewhat of their value, when you think that you can almost spurn them out of the ground with your foot." In Rome, even the past was profligate; the fields of Concord, by contrast, yielded up only a meager arrowhead or two.

The visit to the catacombs triggered some solemn thoughts. In "The Celestial Rail-road," Hawthorne had conjured up the queer image of death arriving like a sudden interruption of the pleasures of Vanity Fair; people disappeared like ephemeral soap bubbles, never to be seen or heard from again. His afternoon in the green campagna stirred up his old quarrel with the physiology of death. The ancient practice of burial was, perhaps, the preferable one: "But Nature has made it very difficult for us to do anything pleasant and satisfactory with a dead body . . . A person of delicacy hates to think of leaving such a burthen as his decaying mortality, to be disposed of by his friends; but . . . how delightful it would be and how helpful towards our faith in a blessed futurity, if the dying could disappear like vanishing bubbles."

At a party in England, Hawthorne had heard from a dinner companion the strange tale of a footprint — a bloody footprint — that had been left by one of the martyrs of Queen Mary's time on a flagstone at the foot of a great staircase in a Lancashire manor house. It was a story quite different from Mrs. Jameson's account of the footstep of Jesus Christ on the road to Rome, and it had been told to him by Mrs. Peter Ainsworth, the owner of the ancestral mansion, Smithills Hall. She had invited him to see the phenomenon for himself. When he visited the Ainsworths on August 1855, Hawthorne decided that the famous footprint was really a discoloration in the stone and pronounced the story "all a humbug." But he felt the legend was "a good one." In time his interest in the Smithills legend became merged with another theme he had been ruminating about as the subject of a romance — an American claimant, such as he met in his consular offices, who returns to England with hopes of recovering a family fortune. In Rome, in the warming spring of 1858, Hawthorne settled down to his subject, and between April 1 and May 19, wrote out some eighty-eight pages of copybook manuscript, before giving it up as an abortive attempt. *The Ancestral Footstep*, as it was called, was a theme with unsuccessful and tedious variations that was to dog Hawthorne for the remainder of his career.

What seems to have happened in Rome was that no sooner had he begun writing than he became the hostage of a far more potent subject. His notebooks for the period reveal the germ of what was to become his next full-scale romance, *The Marble Faun*. They also reveal the force and swiftness with which the idea captured his imagination, though he did not actually begin the writing of it until some months later, in Florence.

On April 17, taking his family to the Villa Borghese, Hawthorne had been struck by two sculptured fauns, one of them purportedly a copy from Praxiteles. "I like these strange, sweet, playful, rustic creatures, almost entirely human as they are, yet linked so prettily, without monstrosity, to the lower tribes by the long, furry ears, or by a modest tail; indicating a strain of honest wildness in them. Their character has never, that I know of, been wrought out in literature." An entry made four days later, after a visit to the sculpture galleries of the Capitol, where he had seen what was regarded as the original *Faun* by Praxiteles, was equally enthusiastic: "This race of fauns was the most delightful of all that antiquity imagined. It seems to me that a story, with all sorts of fun and pathos in it, might be contrived on the idea of their species having become inter-mingled with the human race, a family with faun blood in them, having prolonged itself from the classic era till our own days." Hawthrone's careful description of the sculpture — the sturdy, handsome figure, leaning with easy grace against its plinth, the pointed ears nestled in the cropped, curly hair — indicate the posi-bilities he saw in the preposterous merger of man and animal. "The whole person," he wrote, "conveys the idea of an amiable and sen-sual nature, easy, mirthful, apt for jollity, yet not incapable of being touched by pathos. The Faun has no principle, nor could compre-hend it, yet is true and honest by virtue of his simplicity; very capa-ble too, of affection . . ." What the faun represented for the novelist, in the strongest and most attractive terms, was the allegorical image of man — before the Fall, before the irreversible knowledge of evil. Out of that figure, which Hawthorne was to brood over for some months, he was to construct his romance, with all of Rome — both its Christian present and its pagan past — for a backdrop.

Late in May, planning to spend the malarial summer months away from Rome, Hawthorne began making preparations for traveling to Florence. With no experience in the difficult task of bargaining for a *vetturino* to transport the family and the luggage to the Tuscan city, Hawthorne relied on the services of the more practiced Thompson, who finally secured a trustworthy driver. As a precaution, a formal contract was drawn up; the *vetturino* would undertake the eight-day trip — allowing for sightseeing along the way — for a fee of ninety-five scudi, with an additional five crowns for a tip. In the meantime, Hawthorne's German landlord had begun the unpleasant task of taking inventory of the furnishings and household effects at their apartment in the Palazzo Larazani. Hawthorne was sure that he was being charged — to the tune of several scudi — for every chip and crack in the crockery, most of which had been damaged before their arrival in Rome.

Three days before their departure, they had a visit from William Cullen Bryant, his daughter, and a young traveling companion. Hawthorne had met the poet and editor only once before, in Lenox, when Bryant stopped briefly in a coach at his doorway to deposit the visiting Sedgwicks. This time, Bryant, looking gray and tired, more like an ancient farmer than the youthful poet of Hawthorne's imagination, had talked volubly. "My family gathered about him," Hawthorne reported, "and he conversed with great readiness and simplicity about his travels, and whatever other subject came up; telling us that he had been abroad five times and was now getting a little home sick."

They had discussed the Kansas situation, and Hawthorne sensed some of the bitterness of Bryant's views when he spoke of "the triumph of the administration over the free-soil opposition." Hawthorne asked whether Bryant had seen Charles Summer, and Bryant told him that the senator was a much changed man when he had seen him in Paris the year before. Sumner, he said, "had suffered terribly, and would never again be the man he was; he was getting fat; he talked continually of himself, and of trifles concerning himself, and seemed to have no interest for other matters." The poet felt that the shock of the beating had affected his nerves and "extended to his intellect, and was irremediable." He was convinced that Sumner ought to retire from public life, but conceded that no true friend had the courage to tell him so.

Hawthorne had his own condescending view of the senator, though it was tinged by humane considerations. Referring to Bryant's account, Hawthorne wrote, "This is about as sad as anything can be. I hate to have Sumner undergo the fate of a martyr; because he was not naturally of the stuff that martyrs are made of, and it is altogether by mistake that he has thrust himself into the position of one. He was merely (though with excellent abilities) one of the best fellows in the world, and ought to have lived and died in good-fellowship with all the world."

What struck Hawthorne as odd, however, was Bryant's apparent lack of feeling. The poet "was not in the least degree excited about this or any other subject. He uttered neither passion nor poetry, but excellent good-sense and accurate information on whatever subject came up." Bryant, he concluded, was a pleasant man "but rather cold, I should imagine, if one should seek to touch his heart with one's own. He shook hands kindly all round, but not with any warmth of gripe."

On the night before their departure, Hawthorne took Una for a walk to the Piazza del Popolo, crossing and recrossing the Tiber as they went. It was a moonlit night, clear and calm. From St. Peter's, the great bell boomed out into the starry sky. Hawthorne listened while his fourteen-year-old daughter spoke of her love for Rome with what he considered "alarming fervor." He was not quite prepared for Una's confession. "We shall have done the child no good office in bringing her here," Hawthorne noted, "if the rest of her life is to be a dream of this 'city of the soul,' and an unsatisfied yearning to come back." But he decided that nothing "elevating and refining can be really injurious; and so I hope she will always be the better for Rome, even if her life should be spent where there are no pictures, no statues, nothing but the dryness and meagerness of a New England village."

The family's departure on the following morning was an event of unexpected bitterness. Although Hawthorne had given his servant-girl, Lalla, and her mother three weeks' notice, the pair decided they had been cheated and set up a loud wailing, shouting curses and threatening bodily harm. Next, there was unpleasant disagreement with the two men loading the luggage aboard the waiting carriage. Under a rain of abuse, fists raised against the sky, and curses called down from heaven, Hawthorne — so Julian vividly remembered — mounted to the seat next to the driver. His eyes were blazing; he looked straight ahead with grim determination, "smiling in a certain dangerous way that he sometimes had in moments of great peril or stress." He said nothing. The carriage started off, leaving behind Cephas Thompson, who had come to see them off, his son Eddy, close to tears from embarrassment, and, lastly, the screaming Lalla and her mother.

"We drove off," Hawthorne recorded in his journal, "under a perfect shower of anathemas."

◡◠ IV ◠◡

In Florence, early in June 1858, the Hawthornes and Ada Shepard settled into a spacious, ground-floor suite in the Casa del Bello, across the street from the well-known American sculptor Hiram Powers, a long-term resident of the Tuscan city. The rent was $50 a month. Aside from the immense suite of rooms enclosing a small courtyard, there was a garden, "a little wilderness of shrubbery and roses," and a terrace with a small summerhouse and arbor, where Hawthorne could sit "dreaming of a story." Sophia insisted that he take the pleasantest room in the house, overlooking the garden, for a study. Hawthorne planned an ideal regimen for himself. "The weather is delightful; too warm to walk," he wrote, "but perfectly fit to do nothing in, in the coolness of these great rooms. Every day I shall write a little, perhaps — and probably take a brief nap somewhere between breakfast and tea — but go to see pictures and statues occasionally . . ."

He was to see a good deal of his neighbor. Powers, born in Vermont but raised in Cincinnati, still considered himself a Yankee with the proverbial ingenuity. As proof, he produced a Jew's harp he had invented when he was young and the many mechanical devices he had made to assist him in his work. Though well established, Powers had already passed the moment of his greatest fame — when his nearly life-sized *Greek Slave* toured the United States and then became the hit of the 1851 London Crystal Palace Exhibition. An allegorical tribute to the Greek struggle for independence, his nude and manacled female figure was one of the most talked-about and most written-about sculptures of the nineteenth century. Even prudish ministers found it a noble subject, "clothed all over with sentiment, sheltered, protected by it from every profane eye."

Tall, gray, slightly balding, a man of vast curiosity and aggressive opinions, Powers was briskly egotistical, considering himself the only American sculptor fit to touch marble with a chisel. Hawthorne soon learned that Powers was given to the same rivalry and backbiting that characterized other American sculptors in Italy. He complained bitterly of his thwarted attempts to secure commissions from the American government while overrated sculptors like Crawford and Horatio Greenough had been lavishly sponsored. He felt a particular grievance toward Hawthorne's friend Pierce, whom he considered responsible for the fact that a $25,000 appropriation for a sculpture he had offered the nation had never been awarded to him. Hawthorne assured the sculptor that Pierce would have had little to do, personally, with matters relating to the fine arts. Nonetheless, he wrote the former President, who was touring Europe with his wife and expected to meet the Hawthornes in Rome. "If you can set yourself right with [Powers], pray do," Hawthorne wrote Pierce, "for he is a good and sensible (though very sensitive) man, as well as a great artist." (Hawthorne evidently put little faith in Joseph Mozier's contention that Powers himself was to blame, since he had offered the same statue to private patrons for a fifth the price he was asking Congress.)

Powers was an inveterate talker, much of his conversation being about himself, but he had a ready fund of opinions on every topic: religion, spiritualism, Italian cookery, public men. Hawthorne enjoyed Powers' "racy and oracular" conversation. Often, the two men discussed America. Powers had been living in self-imposed exile for two decades; every year, he promised himself a trip back home, but the time passed and he never made it. Hawthorne suspected he would never return. "Like most twenty-year exiles, he has lost his native country without finding another," Hawthorne noted, "but then it is well to recognize the truth, that an individual country is by no means essential to one's comfort." In his studio visits, or on the warm summer nights when the two families sat out on the rooftop of Powers' villa, observing the star-filled sky, listening to the performances of the nearby open-air Teatro Goldoni, Hawthorne began to understand the prejudices of an expatriate. "His long absence from our Country," Hawthorne noted, "has made him think worse of us than we deserve; and it is an effect of what I myself am sensible, in my shorter exile — the most piercing shriek, the wildest yell, and all the ugly sounds of popular turmoil, inseparable from the life of a republic, being a million times more audible than the peaceful hum of prosperity and content."

Among the earliest callers at the Casa del Bello was Robert Browning, who left a card inviting Hawthorne and Sophia to the Casa Guidi, then returned immediately because he had forgotten to give the address. Hawthorne was pleased to see the English poet again, finding him younger than he remembered from their London meeting.

At the Brownings' villa, they had an enjoyable evening. The talk, however, turned to the "disagreeable, and now wearisome" topic of spiritualism. Florence for some time had been agog over the performances of Daniel Dunglas Home, an American actor and spiritualist, one of the great nineteenth-century charlatans. He had been taken up by Mrs. Frances Trollope, the English writer and traveler, who had been a Florentine resident for many years. Home, whose extravagant career had taken him to most of the capitals of Europe, had performed for both Louis Napoleon and Czar Alexander II. At the Tuileries, reportedly, armchairs had floated disconcertingly in midair; at the Russian palace, bells had soared up from tables and pealed in empty space. The Brownings had attended a séance at which a ghostly hand had picked up a clematis wreath and placed it on Elizabeth Barrett Browning's head. Browning maintained that Home had managed the trick with his feet.

Hawthorne took the occasion of his visit to study the Brownings' nine-year-old son, Robert, wearing long curls and lace collars, a somewhat spoiled boy, overly dependent on his mother, yet engaging in an ethereal way. As the father of a sturdy youngster, Hawthorne had misgivings about the fate of the Brownings' son — misgivings that were prophetic, for Pen, as he was called, grew up to become an odd and dilettantish figure, living out his years in Italy as a relic of the great romance of his parents. "I never saw such a boy as this before," Hawthorne observed, "so slender, fragile and sprite-like . . . I should not quite like to be the father of such a boy; and should fear to stake so much interest and affection on him as he cannot fail to inspire. I wonder what is to become of him . . . His parents ought to turn their whole attention to making him gross and earthly, and giving him a thicker scabbard to sheathe his spirit in."

Robert Browning kept up a running conversation with his guests. Hawthorne found what he had to say more "quick-thoughted" and "common-sensible" than he had expected. In the past, he had attempted to read Browning's poems without much success and had complained, "I wish the poets now-a-days would not sing in such devilish queer measures. It bothers me horribly; and as regards these poems, I cannot understand a tenth part of them." Now, it only added to Hawthorne's confusion to find Browning's conversation so clear and purposeful, "since his poetry can seldom proceed far without running into the high grass of latent meanings and obscure allusions."

Elizabeth Barrett Browning seemed even more elfin and spiritual than he remembered her from their London meeting. Her pallor only accentuated her dark, feverishly bright eyes, and her voice, when she spoke, seemed thin and reedy, reminding him of a grasshopper. "Really," Hawthorne observed, "I do not see how Mr. Browning can suppose that he has an earthly wife, any more than an earthly child." He was, nevertheless, impressed by Elizabeth Barrett Browning's benevolence and good will, her headlong support for every just cause. "It seems to me," he ruminated, "there were a million chances to one that she would have been a miracle of acidity and bitterness."

Among the guests that evening were Bryant and his daughter; the poet's wife, overly tired from the journey northward, had remained at their hotel. The little entourage was shortly to leave for Venice. Hawthorne, writing to Cephas Thompson, expressed some alarm over Mrs. Bryant's condition. "I almost fear that she will never see America again," he commented. "I do not think Mr. Bryant realizes how ill she is."

In his journal, Hawthorne set down his final judgment of the American poet, whose character, and seeming callousness, he had tried to analyze earlier. He came to the conclusion that Bryant was "not eminently an affectionate man . . . It is partly the result, perhaps, of his not having sufficiently cultivated his animal and emotional nature; his poetry shows it, and his personal intercourse — though kindly — does not stir one's blood in the least." He suspected that Bryant could hardly appreciate the Brownings' highly emotional verse; it was also his impression that the Brownings, hospitable and cordial to a fault, cared just as little about Bryant's poetry.

After tea and strawberries, the party broke up at ten o'clock, out of deference to Mrs. Browning's poor health. The couple, in fact, were shortly to leave for Normandy, since they considered Florence dangerous in summer. As Bryant was leaving, Elizabeth Browning asked the aged American poet if he planned to make another European trip. Bryant, "not uncheerfully," took hold of his white hair.

"It is getting rather too late in the evening now," he answered, without a trace of self-pity.

Hawthorne had another, very positive glimpse of Browning late in June, just before the Brownings' departure from Florence, at an evening reception given by Isa Blagden, a close friend of the two poets. Miss Blagden, an engaging literary hostess, lived in the Villa Brichieri on the Bellosguardo hill. Hawthorne admired the view from her windows and terrace, high above Florence, and the lofty coolness of the villa's situation. Browning was in a playful mood, teasing Isa Blagden's lap dog, Frolic, and keeping up a babble of bright nonsense. "He must be an amiable man," Hawthorne commented. "I should like him much (and should make him like me) if opportunities were favorable."

Among the other guests that evening, there were two Americans. Francis Boott and his young daughter, Lizzie, who were to become perpetual exiles in Italy and later the friends — and literary property — of Henry James, who installed them in his novel *The Golden Bowl*. Hawthorne also met a Mr. Trollope, the son of Mrs. Trollope, whom he admired. ("America owes more for her shrewd criticisms than we are ever likely to pay," he wrote of her.) He supposed that Trollope was also a writer — "at least, there is a literary man of repute, of this name, though I have never read his works." He was correct — although he had the wrong Trollope. The guest was Thomas Adolphus Trollope, a novelist and historian, though less famous than his younger brother, Anthony. Hawthorne thought the English writer congenial and sensitive but was dismayed to learn that Trollope had lived in Italy for eighteen years. "It seems a pity to do this," he remarked. "It needs the native air to give life a reality; a truth which I do not fail to take home regretfully to myself . . ."

Isa Blagden, too, had been swept up into the new vogue for spiritualism, and much to his chagrin Hawthorne found Sophia and Ada Shepard becoming involved. At a séance at the Villa Brichieri one afternoon, it was discovered that Ada Shepard had unsuspected mediumistic powers. She began writing down, in a bold, flowing hand, messages from the other world, including several from Mother Peabody. Hawthorne recorded the episodes with a show of scientific objectivity: "She sometimes has a perception of each word before it is written; at other times, she is quite unconscious of what is to come next. Her integrity is absolutely indubitable, and she herself totally disbelieves in the spiritual authenticity of what is communicated through her medium." Sophia, however, was convinced that the messages were coming from her mother. "It is very curious and wonderful," she wrote in her diary. After the first encounter, she wanted to be alone with Ada "so that the blessed spirit could say more to me."

Hawthorne could neither believe nor disbelieve; he thought that somehow Sophia's unconscious ideas were being conveyed through Ada Shepard. Still, he thought scientists were guilty of a certain "pig-headedness" in not investigating such phenomena. "My wife's mother is the principal communicant," he noted; "she expresses strong affection, and rejoices in the opportunity of conversing with her daughter. She often says very pretty things . . . but there is a lack of substance in her talk . . . a sentimental surface with no bottom beneath it." He had had similar feelings when Dr. Wilkinson, in London, had showed him examples of spirit writing. "Do I believe in these wonders?" he had asked then. "Of course; for how is it possible to doubt either the solemn word or the sober observation of a learned and sensible man like Dr. Wilkinson? But again, do I really believe it? Of course not; for I cannot consent to let Heaven and Earth, this world and the next, be beaten up together like the white and yolk of an egg."

Through Isa Blagden, Hawthorne was also introduced to another odd spiritualist adventurer, Seymour Kirkup, a minor painter, antiquarian, and historian, who had a reputation as a necromancer, reputedly holding communication with Dante. Kirkup's home in the old Knights Templars' palace on the Arno was crowded with small treasures and manuscripts, books on the occult sciences, and what was purported to be the death mask of Dante. The ancient and doddering Kirkup had greeted them in an old-fashioned frock coat and pantaloons — a good deal cleaner than was customary, evidently, since Miss Blagden had warned Hawthorne that it was "not quite pleasant" to take the old gentleman's hand. With him was a sprite of a child, his four-year-old "adopted" daughter. This was the child of the locally famous Regina, a beautiful young Italian woman, recently dead, who had previously served as Kirkup's spirit medium. Florentine gossip had it that Regina had convinced the dotty old Englishman that the child was his, when, as Hawthorne drily noted, "he did not quite know that he had done anything to bring the matter about." Regina's talent for communicating with the spirits had fortunately been passed on to her daughter. It was through the child, now, that Kirkup kept up his conversations with the departed Dante and the equally dead Regina. Hawthorne thought Kirkup "somewhat crackbrained," simply on the basis of the old man's queer expression — the eyes wild and the eyebrows arched in a state of perpetual surprise. Nevertheless, he enjoyed the visit and was immediately struck with the literary possibilities of the marvelously eerie, elflike child, thrust into her decadent and seedy ambience.

The girl's name was Imogen; Hawthorne thought she might be "put at once into a Romance, with all her history and environment."

The idea was deferred, however; he found it difficult to escape the distractions of Florence, and the weather was not conducive to literary labor. "I feel an impulse to be at work," he complained, "but am kept idle by the sense of being unsettled, with removals to be gone through, over and over again, before I can shut myself up into a quiet room of my own, and turn the key. I need monotony, too — an eventless exterior life — before I can live in the world within." But as early as July 14, he jotted down in his pocket diary that he was "sketching plot" for a new romance, and three days later mentioned beginning a "rough draft." On July 27, he reported more at length in his journal: "I seldom go out now-a-days, having already seen Florence tolerably well, and the streets being very hot, and myself having been engaged in sketching out a Romance — which whether it will ever come to anything, is a point yet to be decided." He complained that "six months of uninterrupted monotony would be more valuable to me, just now, than the most brilliant succession of novelties."

Escaping from the heat of Florence, Hawthorne took new quarters in the Villa Montauto, on the Bellosguardo hill, for the months of August and September. It was a large and capacious villa, "big enough to quarter a regiment," he maintained. One of its notable features was an ancient, battlemented tower with access by way of a creaking and shaky wooden staircase. The grounds of the establishment were laid out with gardens and gravel walks. It came with a staff of servants and a nearby *podere* that supplied the Hawthornes with figs and grapes in abundance. In the evenings, the entire family mounted the tower to enjoy the cool breezes and the spectacular sunset views of Florence. During August, Hawthorne seldom wrote in his journal. Early in September, he confessed that there was little to journalize about: "Furthermore, I usually spend the whole day at home, having been engaged in planning and sketching out a Romance." But he concluded, "I have now done with this for the present, and mean to employ the rest of the time we stay here chiefly in re-visiting the galleries, and seeing what remains to be seen of Florence."

Boasting to James Fields about his moss-covered tower, haunted by the ghost of a heretic monk and inhabited by owls, he claimed, "I hire this villa, tower and all, at twenty-eight dollars a month; but I mean to take it away bodily and clap it into a Romance, which I have in my head ready to be written out." He was, in fact, planning two romances, "one or both of which I could have ready for the press in a few months if I were either in England or America." In salty terms he told Fields, "It is a pity, for I have really a plethora of ideas, and should feel relieved by discharging some of them upon the public."

Although the Hawthornes left Florence on October 1, it was only to travel the short distance to Siena, where they spent nearly two weeks. Hawthorne was intrigued by the medieval city, with its narrow, labyrinthine, cobbled streets, the glum façades of the houses shielding hidden gardens. For a brief moment, he fancied the idea of buying a villa on the outskirts of the city, but decided that the winter winds, sweeping off the mountains, would make the place unbearable.

The house he had in mind was the Villa Belvedere, which an aged Englishman had left to his devoted butler. A spacious house with English-style gardens, it was being rented by William Wetmore Story, who was himself thinking of buying it for a summer residence. Throughout his visits with Story, Hawthorne felt a growing regard, and maybe a bit of envy, for the well-to-do American sculptor, who seemed too richly endowed with talents. Story was a "brilliant person — the fullest of social life and fire — whom I have ever met." As a host, he bubbled and brimmed over with good humor; yet beneath the easy performance, Hawthorne sensed "a morbid sensibility; a pain and care, bred, it may be, out of the very richness of his gifts and abundance of his outward prosperity." That sense, no doubt, had been prompted by a conversation the two men had had before, on Hawthorne's last day in Rome, when the sculptor had spoken of an idea that Hawthorne, too, believed in — the notion "that a piece of good fortune is apt to be attended by an equivalent misfortune, as its shadow, or black twin." Story had told him that for three years he had been living with an inexplicable sense of dread, a fear that "some sorrow would come to counterbalance the prosperity of his present life." But Story's luck never ran out; he remained prosperous, admired, and envied to the end of his career. His real misfortune, perhaps, was that his undeniable facility never deepened into greatness.

∽ V ∾

In Rome, the obliging Cephas Thompson had found them new quarters at 68 Piazza Poli — "such a comfortable, cosy little house, as I did not think existed in Rome," Hawthorne commented. It was not so luxurious as the Villa Montauto, of course, but it was conveniently located near the Trevi Fountain. On quiet nights, Hawthorne could hear the continuous splashing of the water. They had arrived in Rome at midday on October 16, in a flood of brilliant sunshine. In the afternoon, Hawthorne took Rose for a walk in the Medici Gardens, then to the Pincian Hill, where they stood overlooking the Borghese grounds, which looked "more beautiful than ever" under a mild blue sky.

He had not been back in Rome a day when he learned some unpleasant news about Louisa Lander, who was still in America. A diary note, written on October 17, gives only a terse reaction: "Mr. Thompson called before dinner, & spoke of Miss Lander. What a pity!" Precisely what the Salem sculptor had done is a mystery. Perhaps she had spread some disagreeable bit of gossip about a member of the Roman colony while at home, and word had got back to the tight-knit society of Americans in the Eternal City. Given the artistic rivalries involved, she might even have attempted to secure some commission at the expense of a colleague. Perhaps there was some direct connection involving her intimacy with the Hawthornes. Whatever the offense, she was apparently ostracized by certain members of the Roman colony, including the Hawthornes, who, after her return to Rome early in November, evidently refused to see her. Louisa Lander's situation was serious enough that a committee, headed by Story, advised the young woman to go before the American minister to deny the accusations in an effort to clear her name.

Hawthorne's succinct diary entries for the winter of 1858–1859 reveal the story of the sculptor's attempt to regain favor. On November 9, Hawthorne penned a brief entry: "In the evening, Miss Lander & her sister (just from America) called, and were not admitted." An entry on the following day is equally terse: "Miss Lander sent in a card but was not seen." On the 12th, Louisa Lander called at the apartment on the Piazza Poli to leave "some letters & Longfellow's poem," which she had brought with her from America. There is no indication that either Hawthorne or Sophia saw her. An entry on the following day suggests that her call was not accepted, since Hawthorne indicated in his diary that he wrote a note to the young woman and took it to Pakenham and Hooker's bank to leave for her. On the 17th, the sculptor delivered another packet of letters. A last entry dealing with Louisa Lander, written on December 5, indicates that Hawthorne received a note from the young woman in the evening but does not disclose its contents. The entry also mentions that he had sent an answer "by bearer," suggesting that there was some urgency involved. Another Salem sculptor, John Rogers, writing home later that winter about the bust that Lander had made, noted that Hawthorne no longer saw the sculptor and that it was debatable whether Hawthorne would accept the work.

———

Hawthorne had waited until October before returning to Rome, hoping to avoid the danger of Roman fever. Since the damp night air was considered unhealthy, the children were kept indoors, though he and Sophia occasionally took moonlight walks. In what became a ritual each night, Hawthorne played cards with his children. He seems to have settled into a routine of work and leisurely sightseeing. Within a few days after his arrival in Rome, he began working on a new book, noting in his pocket diary the slow progress of the work. "Began to write a Romance," he jotted down on October 25; then on the following days, "I scribbled Romance," "Scribbled Romance poorly," "Scribbled Romance ineffectually."

On November 2, Hawthorne reported in his journal, "Una has taken what seems to be the Roman fever, by sitting down to sketch in the Coliseum." The symptoms were a high temperature and restlessness; Sophia had sat up with her daughter through the night. "It is not a severe attack," Hawthorne wrote cautiously, "yet attended by fits of exceeding discomfort, occasional comatoseness, and even delirium to the extent of making the poor child talk in rhythmic measure, like a tragic heroine." He tried to take some comfort from the medical diagnosis that the fever was seldom dangerous, though likely to recur on later occasions. But Una's illness was to be far more serious, with frequent recurrences over the next six months. Each relapse became more alarming, and each recovery period took longer. In December, Sophia, who had become physically worn and tired, came down ill. No sooner had she recovered than Ada Shepard fell ill, and Sophia was in the position of nursing two invalids. The doctor was making daily and then twice-daily calls. To escape the "hospital," Hawthorne visited Hooker's bank, in the Piazza di Spagna, where he gloomily read the American papers, then strolled through the Pincian and Borghese gardens. He had little heart for his nightly games of whist and old maid with the two younger children, though he tried to maintain some semblance of calm and regularity. At times, over the long winter of recoveries and relapses, he thoroughly despaired of Una's life. It was as if the "black twin" or shadow of misfortune that he had discussed with William Story had fallen across his life.

From November until February 27, when Una appeared to have a brief recovery, Hawthorne wrote nothing in his notebooks. His diaries, however, reveal that he forced himself to work at his new romance — though fitfully and with frequent interruptions. It was a desperate effort to keep his mind occupied and distracted from the fearful possibilities of Una's illness. At the end of the year, he jotted down, "So ends 1858. Since November 25th, I have scribbled more or less of Romance every day; &, with interruptions, from October 26th." On January 30, he noted, "I finished today, the rough draft of my Romance; intending to write it over after getting back to the Wayside." A few days later, on February 3, he wrote James Fields, giving a detailed account of Una's illness. Sophia, he explained, "has worn herself out with watching and anxiety, and has been confined to her bed, some of the time, and the house nearly ever since we got here." He added, "Amid so much domestic trouble, I take some credit to myself for having sternly shut myself up for an hour or two, almost every day, and come to close grips with a Romance which I have been trying to tear out of my mind . . . Portions of it interested me a good deal while I was writing them; but I have had so many interruptions from things to see and things to suffer that the story has developed itself in a very imperfect way, and will have to be revised hereafter."

During the brief remission of Una's illness early in March, Hawthorne took time to enjoy the Roman Carnival with a good deal more fervor than he had the previous year. Hawthorne and his family watched the parades from the balcony of John Lothrop Motley's apartment. The historian of the Dutch republic and his family were spending the winter in Rome. The spectacle — the processions of cavalry, the carriages woven with greenery, the endless streams of merrymakers in fantastic disguises — seemed "strangely like a dream" to Hawthorne. Una was sufficiently recovered to have at least one carriage ride up and down the Corso. Pale and not unattractive, a young woman of fifteen with reddish-gold hair and deep violet eyes, Una received tributes of several bouquets during her excited drive, one of them from the Prince of Wales, who was on a European tour. Hawthorne was pleased. In a letter to Ticknor, he noted that the seventeen-year-old Edward had taken great delight in the affair, pelting and being pelted with confetti as he rode along the Corso. "The poor fellow will not have such merry times in his future life," he added somberly.

Late in March, Una had another relapse. Hawthorne confessed his discouragement in a journal entry on March 23: "I am wearing away listlessly these last precious days of my abode in Rome. Una's illness is disheartening, and by confining my wife, it takes away the energy and enterprise that were the spring of all our enterprises. I am weary of Rome, without having seen and known it as I ought; and I shall be glad to get away from it." The next several weeks proved to be the critical phase of his daughter's illness. Through days and nights of weary waiting, Una was delirious. Friends paid anxious visits; Franklin Pierce, then in Rome, called daily. Sophia reported to her family, "Even dear Mrs. Browning, who almost never goes upstairs, came the moment she heard. She was like an angel. I saw her but a moment, but the grasp of her hand was electric . . . One day there seemed a cloud of good spirits in the drawing-room, Mrs. Ward, Mrs. Browning, Mrs. Story, and so on, all standing and waiting. Magnificent flowers were always coming, baskets and bouquets . . . Everyone who had seen Una in society or anywhere came to ask . . ."

Dr. Franco, their Italian doctor, claimed that unless Una's fever broke, there was little hope for her survival. On April 8, Hawthorne noted in his pocket diary, "A dim morning. General Pierce came early; so did the Doctor. He seems to have very little hope. God help us!" The silent testimony of Sophia's anxiety was the absence of any entries in her diary between April 11 and April 30. For once, her optimism gave way and her faith wavered. When the crisis point came, she had not slept for forty-eight hours. Hawthorne was stretched out in his bedroom. Sophia, standing at the sickroom window, looked out at the deserted city square. She experienced what she felt was a moment of religious transformation. "Why should I doubt the goodness of God?" she asked herself. "Let Him take her, if He sees best . . . I will not fight against Him any more." As she waited, she became conscious that Una's breathing was calmer, more regular, and when she touched her daughter's forehead, she found the fever was subsiding.

The recovery period, however, was long. It was not until late in May that Hawthorne was able to write Ticknor, "We have suffered a great deal of trouble and anxiety from Una's illness; and at one period, we had scarcely no hope of ever taking her out of Rome . . . She has been restored to us, however, and for several weeks past, has steadily and rapidly gained strength . . . Had it been otherwise, I doubt whether we should ever have had the heart to come home without her."

Hawthorne was to regard his winter in Rome as the worst ordeal of his life.

During those anxious weeks of the crisis, Hawthorne had relied on the daily visits of Franklin Pierce. The two friends had taken walks together, visited artists' studios, called on Charlotte Cushman. The former President remained in Rome longer than he had planned, offering what consolation he could. In his worried mood, Hawthorne had been saddened to see "the marks of care and coming age" on his old friend. Pierce — with a slight air of melancholy, perhaps remembering his own dead son — had remarked on what a stout boy Julian had become. "Poor fellow!" Hawthorne noted. "He has neither son nor daughter to keep his heart warm."

They walked together, straying among the Roman ruins, the scenes of ancient history. Pierce talked of his political experiences, which Hawthorne considered "as historic as anything around us." There had been rumors that Pierce might seek the presidency once more, but Pierce flatly rejected the idea. He was "content to let his one administration stand," Hawthorne recorded, "and to be judged by the public and posterity on the merits of that. No doubt, he is perfectly sincere; no doubt, too, he would again be a candidate, if a pretty unanimous voice of the party should demand it." One day, Pierce proudly showed Hawthorne a testimonial letter of appreciation, signed by all his cabinet officers — a rather pathetic personal reward for the terrible burdens of the presidency. Hawthorne was still reluctant to give up his notion that Pierce was a gifted executive, a mover of men. "Certainly he was in his element, as an administrative man," Hawthorne claimed; "not far-seeing, not possessed of vast stores of political wisdom in advance of his occasions, but endowed with a miraculous intuition of what ought to be done, just at the time for action."

In mid April, Pierce and his wife left Rome to continue their tour of Italy, traveling by way of Ancona to Venice. Hawthorne had considered accompanying them but decided to remain in Rome until Una had fully recuperated. In his journal, Hawthorne set down a grateful personal tribute to his friend. "I did not know what comfort there might be in the manly sympathy of a friend," he wrote, "but Pierce has undergone so great a sorrow of his own, and has so large and kindly a heart, and is so tender and so strong, that he really did us good, and I shall always love him the better for the recollection of these dark days." Yet, in an odd conclusion, he seems to have wanted to wipe out his sense of indebtedness. "I do not love him one whit the less for having been President," Hawthorne wrote, "nor for having done me the greatest good in his power . . . If he had been merely a benefactor, perhaps I might not have borne it so well; but each did his best for the other, as friend for friend."

No sooner had Pierce departed than another American politician, Charles Sumner, arrived to spend three weeks with the Storys. Since the brutal attack on him in the Senate, Sumner had suffered from severe physical complaints for which he received only conflicting diagnoses from American doctors. At times, he was racked by frightening chest pains; at others, with unbearable spasms in the head and spine. Sometimes, getting up from a chair, he was forced to drag one foot after the other before he could move with any comfort. In the summer of 1858, the senator had journeyed to Europe to seek advice from European specialists. In Paris, he was treated by a highly recommended quack, Dr. Charles Edward Brown-Séquard, whose theory involved the application of a counterirritant to draw the pain away from the upper regions of the patient's body. Without anesthetic, Sumner was given six treatments of moxa, a combustible substance that was burned on his bare back. For five weeks he could neither lie on his back nor turn over in bed, because of the suppurating wounds. When he suffered an attack of angina pectoris — induced perhaps by his course of treatments — the obliging Dr. Brown-Séquard prescribed belladonna.

Despite mounting pressure at home that he resign, Sumner remained abroad. After the Brown-Séquard treatments he tried the medicinal baths at Aix-les-Bains. But it seems to have been a winter of relaxation in Montpellier that proved the most effective remedy. By March, Sumner was able to write his friend Howe that the pain and the depression were largely over.

His three weeks in Rome — "delicious days" — were a whirlwind of visits, the usual tourist sights, and the inevitable social calls. There were a number of meetings with the Hawthornes. But in his diary, Hawthorne made only mere notations of a call on the senator at the Barberini Palace and an unexpected meeting in the Vatican sculpture galleries. Sophia, in her diary jottings, mentioned a "charming" visit to the Villa Albani with Sumner, Julian, and Mrs. Ward, and a "long call" the senator and Story's daughter, Edith, had made on the convalescing Una.

No sooner had Sumner arrived than he was off, favoring Story with lengthy dispatches. "What I have left undone at Rome haunts me even more than all I enjoyed," he complained to Story. "I think perpetually of pictures and statues unseen . . . Why did I not press you to go with me to the Capitol and the Vatican? . . . You know I am always a learner." His travels northward were an itinerary of encounters with the famous and the fashionable, intermingled with reports on the Austrian invasion of northern Italy. In Turin, he had "passed half an hour" with Cavour, who received him in his bedroom; he had met the Count Bentivoglio, grandson of Manzoni, who assured him that the famous novelist had remained "Italianissimo" under the heels of the Austrians, who had taken Milan. The Marchesa Arconati, Margaret Fuller's old friend, had told him that the Austrian soldiers who had confiscated her properties in Ticino were in such deplorable condition that they could "only live by turning highwaymen." In Paris, after a rest at the Bains Frascati in Le Havre (and a little tour of Normandy and Brittany), he was buying

bronzes and illuminated manuscripts that were "superior to anything in all Boston!" In London, he had accepted far too many invitations to English country houses — "more than enough to fill all the
time until sea-sickness begins." He was not looking forward to his
return to the United States, where he would find himself "in scenes
very different, amidst tobacco-spitting, swearing slave-drivers,
abused by the press, insulted so far as is possible, pained and racked
by the insensibility about me to human rights."

It could hardly have escaped Hawthorne's notice that there had
been a distinct difference between the quiet, forlorn dignity of
Franklin Pierce's visit and the éclat with which Sumner was touring
Europe, a famous champion of the abolitionist cause and an international celebrity, whose medical reports and medical progress were
receiving so much attention in the American press that the *New York
Times* complained the bulletins were arriving with every steamer
and becoming monotonous.

On May 25, the citizen of somewhere else took a final walk in the
Pincian Gardens and the grounds of the Villa Borghese. His feelings
about the ancient city were still mixed. Rome had taken a strange
hold of him, he admitted a few days later: "I seem to know it better
than my birth-place, and to have known it longer; and though I have
been very miserable there, and languid with the effects of the atmosphere, and disgusted with a thousand things in daily life, still I cannot say I hate it — perhaps might fairly own a love for it. But (life
being too short for such questionable and troublesome enjoyments)
I desire never to set eyes on it again."

On the afternoon of the 25th, he and his family made the tiresome
journey to Civitavecchia, where they took the steamer for Leghorn.
Hawthorne had planned to stay over in the Ligurian port for two or
three days so that Una might recuperate before taking the voyage to
Marseilles. From there, they planned to take a leisurely trip up the
Rhone to Switzerland, then on through France to England, where
they would book passage for America. Before their departure,
Hawthorne had already arranged passage for Ada Shepard, who
would be leaving them at Le Havre, returning to the United States
to marry her fiancé, Henry Clay Badger. But at Leghorn, Una
seemed so little affected by her travels that they chanced the
steamer trip to Marseilles, where they arrived on the 29th, putting
up at the Hôtel des Colonies. On the next day, in the Marseilles
railroad station, Hawthorne made a purchase. Somewhat archly, he
recorded in his journal that he had bought "the two volumes of the
Livre des Merveilles, by a certain author of my acquaintance." Two

years before, he had authorized a French translation of *A Wonder-Book*, and he was pleased to discover that it had been printed and illustrated "in very pretty style" by Hachette.

Traveling northward, they stopped at Avignon for several days of sightseeing, then went on, by way of Lyons, to Geneva. There, they took a lake steamer to Villeneuve. Hawthorne's weariness with the endless round of sightseeing found expression in his notebook: en route, they stopped at Coppet, "where Madame de Staël or her father, or both, were either born, or resided, or died, I know not which — and care very little." Outside the dull little village of Villeneuve, they put up at the Hôtel de Byron —"a very grand hotel indeed" with a pretty view of the lake and a glimpse of the Castle of Chillon. On the requisite visit to the storied castle, Hawthorne had been amused to come upon the Hawthorne clan — Sophia, Una, Julian (as well as the amiable Ada Shepard) — all sitting in a row on a bench, sketching the Swiss mountains.

From Switzerland, they recrossed France, stopping at Paris for a few days before moving on to Le Havre and embarking on the channel steamer to Southampton. In Paris, Hawthorne wrote Francis Bennoch, genuinely happy to hear of his English friend's "returning prosperity." He also asked about their mutual friend James Fields, who was then in London with a new wife. (The publisher's first wife, Eliza, had died of tuberculosis in 1851.) In 1854, Fields had married the vivacious, redheaded Annie Adams, and the couple had installed themselves in an apartment on Charles Street that was to become one of Boston's eminent literary salons.

Hawthorne had been eagerly looking forward to the arrival in Europe of his publisher and his new wife; more than once, in his letters, he had complained of Fields's tardiness. Writing to Bennoch, now, he expressed a hope that Fields would remain in London for a while, since he would rather meet him there than in Paris. "I shall stay here only till Tuesday next," he wrote on June 17, "for Paris is a bore to me, and my soul thirsts for sherry and bitter beer, and hungers for a mutton chop. I long for England, just as if I were a native John Bull." He warned his friend, "You will find me travel-worn, shabby (by-the-by, one of the first favors I shall ask of you will be to direct me to a tailor), gray, wrinkled with time and trouble, and nowise improved, except by a moustache which has been the natural growth of Italy. Mrs. Hawthorne says it makes me look like a bandit."

ᜐ VI ᜐ

In London, Hawthorne was immediately caught up in a round of social visits and excursions in the company of Bright and Bennoch and Fields. With Bright, early in July, he visited the House of Commons to hear Lord John Russell, Palmerston, and Disraeli debate on naval appropriations, and to a dinner at the Heywoods' in Connaught Place. On the 12th, the pair made a call on Charles Sumner, who was still in London. (Sumner had been exceptionally friendly to Bright when he was in America.) Hawthorne may have been somewhat reluctant on this occasion, remarking in mean fashion, "As we're neither of us the Lord Chancellor, he won't care about us."

James Fields reported on a breakfast visit Hawthorne had made them in London, accompanied by Julian, whom he found "an interesting boy." "Hawthorne," he noted, "wishes us to take a villa near Florence, where they lived; he said the bells of the city sounded exquisitely there — besides the place was haunted! Talked nervously about his new romance, the muscles of his face twitching, and with lowered voice; he thought some time he might print his journal also."

Unexpectedly, Hawthorne found his brief stay in England lengthened into a year-long delay before returning to America. Fields had arranged for the English publication of Hawthorne's as-yet-unfinished romance, getting £600 for the rights from Smith, Elder & Company. Since foreign writers could secure their English copyrights only by being in residence on the date of publication, Hawthorne decided to remain in England, rewriting the book there and seeing it through publication.

In mid July, he and his family moved to Whitby on the Yorkshire coast, which he hoped would be a suitable spot for working. Whitby, however, proved to be too much a thriving seaside resort for Hawthorne's liking. (A visit to nearby St. Hilda's Abbey, however, apparently provided him with the name for one of the heroines of his romance.) On the 22nd, they moved farther north to the coastal village of Redcar. Writing to his friend Bennoch, Hawthorne described the location: "It is as bleak and dreary a strip of sand as we could have stumbled upon, had we sought the whole world over; and the gray German ocean tumbles in upon us, within twenty yards of our door. But the children like it, and the roses already blow in all their cheeks. It suits my purposes, likewise, and I mean to write all the mornings, and moisten myself with sea spray (not to mention other liquids) in the afternoons and evenings."

Through the late summer and early fall, Hawthorne made steady progress on the new book; the isolation of the spot and the monotony of his days seem to have provided the right circumstances. His terse notations in his pocket diary indicate that, after a day or two of studying the early draft, he had begun serious work on July 26: "At about 10 o'clock, began the Romance in good earnest, and wrote till 3." With unvarying routine, he settled into a program of producing thirty or forty pages a week, writing five or six hours a day. After dinner (3:00 P.M. on weekdays; 2:00 P.M. on Sundays), he and Julian customarily walked along the stretches of deserted beach. While Julian swam, Hawthorne sat in the dunes in the tall eel grass, smoking a cigar, turning over his story in his mind. When the pair made the slow trek back to their lodgings and the waiting family, the sky behind the tiny seaside village had turned dull red. According to Sophia, for relaxation in the evenings Hawthorne read "the stupidest book he can find . . . With the patience of a saint, he pores over the novels of George Prince Regent James . . ." By September 10, he had been able to give "rather more than half" of his manuscript to Sophia to read.

In October, however, Hawthorne and the family moved to Leamington to spend the winter. Writing to Fields on October 10, shortly after the move, Hawthorne noted that Sophia had read portions of the book and "speaks of it very rapturously. If she liked the author less, I should feel much encouraged by her liking the Romance so much. I likewise (to confess the truth) admire it exceedingly, at intervals, but am liable to cold fits, during which I think it the most infernal nonsense. This happens to be the case just at the present moment." On November 8, he wrote a jaunty note in his diary: "Wrote till 5 minutes of twelve & finished the last page of my Romance. 508 manuscript pages."

Sophia commented on the book in a letter to Lizzie: "As usual, he thinks the book good for nothing, and based upon a very foolish idea which nobody will like or accept . . . He has regularly despised each one of his books immediately upon finishing it. *My* enthusiasm is too much his own music as it were. It needs the reverberation of the impartial mind to reassure him that he has not been guilty of a *bêtise*." Later, anticipating a problem, she warned, "Mr. Hawthorne had no idea of portraying me in Hilda. Whatever resemblance one sees is accidental."

Although he had sent the major portion of the manuscript to his English publishers, Hawthorne as usual could not immediately decide on a title. Writing to Fields, who was touring the Continent, he suggested a dozen or more possibilities, including *The Faun of Monte Beni* and *Marble and Life (or Man)* — although none of them particularly satisfied him. He had supplied several possibilities to Smith, Elder & Company as well, but was dismayed when he learned, shortly before publication, that the firm had decided on *Transformation*. Hawthorne, at first railing to Fields against the "pig-headedness" of his English publishers, was then somewhat chagrined to learn that the title was one he had originally suggested himself. Writing to Smith, Elder & Company, Hawthorne claimed, with considerable aplomb, that this was all the better, since "in condemning it, I shall criticize nobody but myself."

Having finished his "moonshiny Romance," with little else to do aside from reading proof, he wrote Fields that he planned to spend the remainder of his time in England "in blessed idleness." The enterprising Fields had inquired about the state of Hawthorne's travel journal. Hawthorne answered that "there is nothing in it that will do to publish."

Evidently on the strength of Hawthorne's praise of Sophia's travel accounts, Fields also wrote to Sophia, suggesting that she become a contributor to the *Atlantic Monthly*, which the firm had recently acquired. It was not a suggestion Hawthorne would likely find agreeable; nevertheless, he wrote Bennoch about it in jovial terms: "I don't know whether I can tolerate a literary rival at bed and board; there would probably be a new chapter in the 'Quarrels of Authors.' However, I make myself at ease on that score, as she positively refuses to be famous, and contents herself on being the best wife and mother in the world."

During the final year in Europe, there had been another sad piece of family news from America. On August 2, 1859, Horace Mann died, apparently of typhoid fever, in Yellow Springs, Ohio. Mann had given up his political career to take up the position of president of the newly founded Antioch College. From the beginning, the school was troubled with financial problems and political factionalism, and in the spring of 1859, officially bankrupt, the institution was auctioned off to a group of Mann's backers. Overworked, pressed by financial worries and the reorganization of the college, he fell dangerously ill with fatigue, fever, and chills. Mary, whose letters to Sophia had recounted the slow decline of her husband, had been burdened as well with the illness of two of her sons. She spent her days moving from one sickroom to another in a state of utter weariness. Mann, feverish and sometimes delirious, his lips swollen so badly that it was difficult for him to speak, had given thought to his last moments. Confronting his doctor, he had demanded, "If I am going to die, I would like to know it. I have many things to say, and it will take some time to say them." Mary had been with him during the last feverish hours, holding him in her arms while his body was racked with fits of shivering. She promised to bury him next to his beloved Charlotte, as he wished; but he had insisted, too, that Mary be buried there when her time came. Even in death, he was too conscientious for the kindness of letting her feel she had been the best beloved. After the solemn funeral rites, at Sophia's urging, Mary and her three boys had moved to Concord to stay at the Wayside.

ᦒ VII ᦒ

With the exception of the expanded 1854 edition of *Mosses from an Old Manse*, which Ticknor & Fields reissued while Hawthorne was consul at Liverpool, *The Marble Faun* was the first new book by the author in seven years. Well before publication, Hawthorne had confessed his nervousness in a letter to Ticknor, claiming he would be appearing before the public with "all the uncertainties of a new author." That worry seems to be reflected in the uneasy preface to the new book, addressed to that conjectural friend, the ideal reader, "closer and kinder than a brother." In it, Hawthorne pleaded the special case of the American writer, doomed to the meager fictional possibilities of a raw country without traditions and a colorful history. "No author," he maintained, "without a trial can conceive of the difficulty of writing a Romance about a country where there is no shadow, no antiquity, no mystery, no picturesque and gloomy wrong, nor anything but a common-place prosperity, in broad and simple daylight, as is happily the case with my dear native land." Though overstated — certainly in his own case — it became one of the more famous dicta of nineteenth-century American literary criticism. "Romance and poetry," Hawthorne asserted, "like ivy, lichens and wall-flowers, need Ruin to make them grow."

But unfortunately, Hawthorne had escaped the constraints of his American prison, had gained the experience of Rome, with its ancient ruins, its alien society and customs, and what an American author might conceive of as its lurking evils, at a point at which his talents, if not his genius, were waning. *The Marble Faun*, in structure and authority, is a less successful novel than *The Blithedale Romance*. It lacks the psychological force and acumen of *The Scarlet Letter*, even the commonplace reality of contemporary life that sustains *The House of the Seven Gables*. True, in writing the book, Hawthorne had been able to draw on his Roman notebooks, full of incident and color, for much of the circumstantial texture of his romance. And he leaned heavily on his recent experiences, his visits to galleries and studios in Florence and Rome, his discussions with American sculptors and painters, for much of the discussion of art and culture that was worked into the book. Critics would refer to it as an "art-novel." Much of the travel-guide aspect of the novel, one suspects, was intended to serve as Melville's technical discussions of whaling had served in *Moby-Dick*, as a kind of ballast for the allegorical nature of the story. But Melville had a keen eye even for the symbolic possibilities of such material. In Hawthorne, much of the Roman lore remains mere backdrop.

The great failure of *The Marble Faun* is his separation of plot and scenery. Hawthorne did not use his setting — as Henry James would use it, taking a hint perhaps from Hawthorne's limitations — to explore the conflict of cultures and classes, the burdens of custom or politics on the individual. *The Marble Faun* is the same high allegory on the "fortunate fall," the loss of innocence, the bitter wisdom of sin, that Hawthorne had written of before in many of his tales and romances; like "Young Goodman Brown," or *The Scarlet Letter*, it could as easily have taken place in the New England forest as in the Borghese Gardens. Rome, "the City of all time and of all the world," added little that was intrinsic to Hawthorne's moral drama.

Yet *The Marble Faun* represents the cleanest and most philosophical exposition of Hawthorne's obsessive theme. Oddly, his escape from the restrictions of the American scene had not extended his range as a novelist; it allowed him only to evolve his subject to its purest refinement. "Every crime destroys more Edens than our own," Hawthorne's unnamed narrator asserts as one of the summary judgments of a lifetime's brooding on the nature of sin. But Hawthorne had not explored the mysteries or the "picturesque and gloomy wrongs" of Roman society in order to come to such conclusions. Unlike Margaret Fuller, who had committed herself to the culture, he had remained essentially a tourist and observer, dispassionate but curious, a man tethered to the closely knit Anglo-American society of Rome and Florence.

Nor did *The Marble Faun* represent any great advance in Hawthorn's fiction-writing techniques. The dramatis personae of the story were rather similar to the casts of characters in *The House of the Seven Gables* and *The Blithedale Romance* — two men, two women, and a sinister interloper. Kenyon and Hilda, his American artists, are simply more talkative, more passive versions of Holgrave and Phoebe, Coverdale and Priscilla. Miriam, like Hester and Zenobia, is a woman with a shadowy past; though innocent, she has been involved in a "mysterious and terrible event." Although the nature of the scandal is serious enough to make Kenyon blanch when he learns Miriam's true name, Hawthorne clearly intended it to remain unspecified. "It only concerns the present narrative," he notes, "inasmuch as the suspicion of being at least an accomplice in the crime fell darkly and directly upon Miriam herself." Much has been made of Hawthorne's references to Guido's painting of Beatrice Cenci and to Miriam's possible connection with the Cenci family, and therefore with the crimes of incest and patricide. (At Miriam's request, Hilda delivers a mysterious package to the Palazzo Cenci.) But those allu-

sions hover like a smoke screen over the novel and are nothing that
Hawthorne gives substantial weight to. The more fruitful implications lie in some conscious or unconscious connection with Mrs.
Henry Field, the former governess in the Duc de Choiseul-Praslin's
household. When Henry Bright, acting on a cue from one of Hawthorne's devoted readers, asked if Miriam had been patterned after
Henriette Deluzy-Desportes, Hawthorne had (somewhat ambigu-
ously) admitted, "Well, I dare say she was . . . I knew I had some
dim recollection of some crime, but I didn't know what." But he
may also have had other, less public, scandals in mind: the vague
rumors about Margaret Fuller and her relationship with the Marchese Ossoli, perhaps. (In Miriam's fictional history there is an
aborted marriage contract with "a certain marchese.") Or perhaps
he had in mind Maria Louisa Lander, the Salem sculptor who seems
to have committed some misdeed that caused her to be ostracized
by the little Roman art colony. But Hawthorne's sense of evil was
always dangerously allegorical to begin with. The moralist who
must find some "unpardonable sin" to certify his sense of evil is
clearly not satisfied with the more banal forms of sinfulness among
his fellow men.

The most difficult character, in fictional terms, is Donatello — the
faun himself. Hawthorne clearly intended him to be a figure of immense appeal: part human, part animal, sensual, handsome, immediate and instinctive in his responses to life. (He was to balk, however, at too-literal readers, who wanted to know whether Donatello's ears were, indeed, pointed and furry like those of the *Faun*
of Praxiteles.) Yet aside from his one, admittedly great, crime —
the murder that motivates the novel's action — Donatello is a rather civilized, parlor version of the natural man. (Even Hawthorne's Concord neighbor, the near-Indian Thoreau, would have
furnished a better, more realistic model — if Thoreau had been more
handsome, less prudish.) Donatello's crime is clearly the result
of his instinctive passions. There had been a witness to the earlier
crime in which Miriam had been implicated — a malign Capuchin
monk who pursues her and clearly has some mysterious hold over
her (a situation that in many respects echoes the relationship of
Westervelt and Zenobia in *The Blithedale Romance*). In a moment of
rage, and out of his love for Miriam — and with Miriam's unconscious prompting — Donatello hurls her tormentor from the Tar-
peian Rock. The crime destroys Donatello's Arcadian innocence:
fleeing to his ancestral estate near Florence, he acquires the penitential wisdom of a civilized man. He decides to return to Rome to face
the penalty. Miriam, too, will take up a penitential life, waiting for
Donatello's release from prison. Hilda, an unfortunate witness to the

murder, is also implicated. Although she is not a Catholic, she finds psychological release from her guilt in a Vatican confessional.

There is a climactic procession in *The Marble Faun* (as there is, too, in *The House of the Seven Gables*, where the alleged murderer, Clifford, in a desperate act of commitment to life and action, tries to fling himself into a motley political procession winding its way down Pyncheon Street). The episode is the Roman Carnival, in which Donatello and Miriam give themselves up to, or are apprehended by, the police. (Hawthorne manages this ambiguous bit of action offstage, merely reporting it by way of an overheard conversation.) The carnival in its tawdry excitement is one of the more successful scenic passages in the book, serving symbolically as "the tumult of life" in which Hawthorne's guilty sinners must plunge themselves in order to begin the expiation of their crime. There is another aspect of the scene that has particular interest. So persistent is the architecture of Hawthorne's imagination, Kenyon must wait for the missing Hilda at a spot opposite a palace with a balcony while the raucous parade streams by. It is a repetition of a similar balcony scene in "My Kinsman, Major Molineux," in which young Robin must wait opposite a mansion with a balcony while a procession of surreal figures — a man with his face painted black and red, a group of wild Indians, and "fantastic shapes without a model" (as well as the penitentially tarred-and-feathered major) — pass by, giving the scene a grim carnival air.

The structure of *The Marble Faun* is like a sculptured frieze-in-the-round. It moves by way of brief and brisk episodes in a circle — "as all things heavenly and earthly do" — from the opening chapter, titled "Miriam, Hilda, Kenyon, Donatello," to the similarly titled final chapter, in which all four principals supposedly have been transformed by their cruel experience. Sculpture, rather than painting, is the operative metaphor for Hawthorne's romance. His sculptor, Kenyon, is clearly intended as the "type" of the artist who, in his art and in his opinions, most nearly expresses the author's views. (Sophia, in a letter to her father, prophetically hit on Hawthorne's puristic equation of sculpture and writing: "Mr. Hawthorne hates exclamations and all sorts of expletives. He likes pure sculpture in talk, as you may suppose from his style of writing.") It is also significant that in his preface, when Hawthorne acknowledges his "thefts" of actual works of art meant to give a realistic texture to his studio scenes, they are works of sculpture: Akers' *Dead Pearl Diver*, Story's *Cleopatra*, as well as the works he avoided borrowing — Hosmer's *Zenobia* and Randolph Rogers' bronze Columbus doors for the Capitol in Washington.

In his perfectly rounded structure, Hawthorne had clearly intended to represent the cathartic change of his characters after their "fortunate" fall. But it is another of the grand failures of the novel that his characters are too unfocused, too lacking in individuality to be of deep concern to the reader. Miriam and Donatello talk volubly about the burdens of penitence and remorse, but Hawthorne is never convincing about the weight of their sorrows. Lacking characters of real dimension, the book has none of the psychological force of *The Scarlet Letter*. Nor is their crime — or their victim — quite credible.

Hawthorne may describe Miriam's dark beauty, her exoticism, but he never renders it, as he did in the smallest detail with Zenobia. Hilda, whose "white wisdom" he meant to praise, is an almost monstrous character. Kenyon, quite accurately, describes her hardened morality as having "the remorselessness of a steel blade." (Sophia had a point in trying to forestall comparisons between herself and Hawthorne's stiffish heroine.) Although Hilda is both a painter and a copyist, as Sophia was, she is unforgivably priggish. Sophia, after all, could overlook the sinner Daniel Webster, content to leave him to God's judgment. Hilda never would. (Her persistent and unbending morality might as easily have been drawn from Lizzie Peabody.)

Kenyon, the most believable but least emotionally involved of the characters, represents a more charitable response in Hawthorne's paradoxical moral drama. Hilda may be changed by the crime; "instructed by sorrow," as Hawthorne describes it, her enthusiasm for painting is critically diminished. "She had known such a reality, that it taught her to distinguish inevitably the large portion that is unreal, in every work of art" — a rather curious form of moral enlightenment. But her rigorous morality has scarcely been mellowed by the experience. Kenyon's views seem to offer an apologia for sin: "Here comes my perplexity . . . Sin has educated Donatello, and elevated him. Is Sin, then — which we deem such a dreadful blackness in the Universe — is it, like Sorrow, merely an element of human education, through which we struggle to a higher and purer state than we could otherwise have attained. Did Adam fall, that we might ultimately rise to a far loftier Paradise than his?"

Hilda's response is uncompromising: "This is terrible; and I could weep for you, if you indeed believe it. Do not you perceive what a mockery your creed makes, not only of all religious sentiment, but of moral law . . . You have shocked me beyond words!" The moral dilemma remains unresolved at the end of the book. That circumstance gave rise to a good deal of dissatisfaction among Hawthorne's readers.

In England, where the book was published as *Transformation* on February 28, 1860, the critical response was generally favorable but also frequently apt in detailing the novel's faults. Taking the cue from the author himself, several of the critics addressed themselves to the special problem of the American writer. The anonymous reviewer of the *London Times* was critical of the tendency of American writers, notably Hawthorne and Poe, to derogate the pragmatic nature of American life, to "revolt against American utilities." He continued, "This impulse induces them to become vagrants in imagination and reality, tourists in the old world of Europe." Somewhat condescendingly, he described Hawthorne as the typical American artist in Rome, "eyes full of innocent wonder, and a heart thumping against his breast." The critic for the *North British Review*, comparing Hawthorne unfavorably with "the author of *Adam Bede*," claimed Hawthorne was too much the "captive" of his imagination. He found in Hawthorne's characterizations "a want of the ease, *abandon*, and lawlessness of life — they are too symmetrical to be natural, too exact to be true. A character may accidentally or incidentally illustrate a law; but the writer who models the character upon the law produces a moral or intellectual monster." The reviewer complained that there was no life in *Transformation*, "only a great deal of very delightful talk about life." Richard Holt Hutton, in a lengthy and carefully reasoned essay in the *National Review*, was also critical of the allegorical bent of Hawthorne's latest work. "The act of sin itself is the only distinct incident of the tale," he complained; "all the rest is either extraneous dissertation on Art, or the elaboration and study of the group of characters requisite to embody this leading idea." What Hutton regretted in both *The Blithedale Romance* and *Transformation* was "the predominance of moral coloring over the definite forms of actual fact." He preferred the better balance of *The Scarlet Letter*. He was particularly harsh about the "general padding" — the "artistic criticisms often powerful, and always subtle, upon Italian art — puffs, not in very good taste, of the works of American sculptors — silly attacks upon nude figures, and the like."

In Hawthorne's view, the most influential criticism of his new book was Henry F. Chorley's review in the March 3 issue of the *Athenaeum*. Chorley, one of Hawthorne's earliest English admirers, was a music and literary critic for the *Athenaeum*. He was also a great friend of Charlotte Cushman's. Strangely, Hawthorne seems not to have met him until July 1859, when he and Sophia were invited to an "aesthetic dinner and tea," at Chorley's London house on Hawthorne's fifty-fifth birthday. In his *Athenaeum* review, Chorley criticized the "inconclusive and hazy" ending of the novel. "Hints," he claimed, "will not suffice to satisfy interest which has been excited to voracity." The fate of Miriam and the faun, he maintained, had been "left too vaporously involved in suggestion." Chorley much preferred the "clear and forcible" last scenes of *The Scarlet Letter*. In passing, he complained of the similarities in character between Miriam and Zenobia, Hilda and Phoebe. Sophia, quick to come to the defense of her husband, wrote the critic a chiding note, protesting that Hilda "can in no wise be related to the enchanting little housewife, whose energy, radiance and eglantine sweetness fill her daily home duties with joy . . ." She added, "I dare say you are laughing (gently) at my explosion of small muskets." Hawthorne added his own rejoinder: "You see how fortunate I am in having a critic close at hand, whose favorable verdict consoles me for any lack of appreciation in other quarters. Really, I think you were wrong in assaulting the individuality of my poor Hilda. If her portrait bears any resemblance to that of Phoebe, it must be the fault of my mannerism as a painter."

Hawthorne seems to have had Chorley's criticism in mind — and to have anticipated further criticisms of the same kind — when he wrote, with some "reluctance," a brief postscript for the second printing of his novel. His explanation in a letter to Ticknor was that it was necessary "to make things a little clearer." In the postscript, published in later printings of the English and American editions, Hawthorne complained, "The idea of the modern Faun . . . loses all the poetry and beauty which the Author fancied in it, and becomes nothing better than a grotesque absurdity, if we bring it into the actual light of day." He clearly would give no assistance to readers who wanted to know "how Cuvier would have classified poor Donatello" or whether he had furry ears. The most he was willing to explain was how and why Hilda had been spirited away and to offer some shadowy but unspecified suggestions as to why a "despotic government" might have concerned itself with Miriam's case. For the rest, the fictional narrator of *Transformation* — and its real author — seemed willing to leave the matter as "clear as a London fog."

American critics, though respectful, were also put off by the vague story line and the considerable amount of travel-writing and aesthetic discussion in *The Marble Faun*. "Plot it has none, nor does any single dominant idea grow through it to the close," the *New York Times*'s reviewer maintained. The *Knickerbocker* magazine provided a parody version of the unsuccessful ending, titled "The Marble Faun: Completed," in which "Father O'Whack, an Irish priest of the Propaganda" took up the duties of proselytizing a possibly sympathetic Hilda.

Hawthorne's favorite critic, E. P. Whipple, in an unsigned essay in the *Atlantic Monthly*, declared it "the greatest of his works," a proof that Hawthorne's genius had "widened and deepened" in the interim since his last-published romance. Still, Whipple unerringly put his finger on one of the real flaws of the book — the bloodlessness of Hawthorne's characterizations. "When Donatello kills the wretch who malignantly dogs the steps of Miriam, all readers think that Donatello committed no sin at all," Whipple wrote, "and the reason is, that Hawthorne has deprived the persecutor of Miriam of all human attributes, made him an allegorical representation of one of the most fiendish forms of unmixed evil." James Russell Lowell gave the book its most unstinting praise in a review published a month earlier in the same magazine. Calling Hawthorne the most "purely original writer" of the nineteenth century, Lowell made flattering comparisons to Shakespeare and Donne, praised the book's atmospheric effects, its air of mystery. Swimming against the stream of critical comment, Lowell maintained that Hawthorne did not draw characters but rather "conceives" them and shows them acted upon by "crime, passion, or circumstance." Then he singled out the quality that in some moments marked Hawthorne's special genius and at other times his fatal flaw — an otherworldliness in his thought and imagination. "He is rather a denizen than a citizen of what men call the world," Lowell explained. "We are conscious of a certain remoteness in his writings . . ."

On the eve of the publication of *The Marble Faun*, writing to James Fields, then in Rome, Hawthorne had been in a reflective frame of mind. "My own opinion," he told his publisher, "is that I am not really a popular writer . . . Possibly I may (or may not) deserve something better than popularity; but looking at all my productions, and especially this latter one with a cold or critical eye, I can see that they do not make their appeal to the popular mind. It is odd enough, moreover, that my own individual taste is for quite another class of works than those which I myself am able to write." Hawthorne confessed to Fields that if he read such books as his own, written by some other writer, he doubted that he would be able to get through them.

Hawthorne had "another class of works" distinctly in mind; he had just been reading them. "Have you ever read the novels of Anthony Trollope?" he asked the publisher. "They precisely suit my taste; solid and substantial, written on the strength of beef and through the inspiration of ale, and just as real as if some giant had hewn a great lump out of the earth and put it under a glass case with all its inhabitants going about their daily business, and not suspecting that they were made a show of."

It was an odd construction for a writer to put on his own case toward the close of a distinguished literary career, since precisely the kind of writing Hawthorne claimed to admire was the kind of writing he had been doing for years, full of telling detail, with a marvelous grasp of the factual moment — in his notebooks.

In his February letter to Fields, Hawthorne had also asked a favor regarding Louisa Lander. Like his artist-heroine, Miriam, the young sculptor was still tainted by scandal. Hawthorne did not want to write her himself — or, as he plainly stated, could not — which suggests that he may have been implicated in the judgment handed down on the Salem woman by the Roman art colony. In his letter to Fields, it was clear that Hawthorne had changed his mind about the portrait bust. "Before you leave Rome," he told his publisher, "I want you to ask Mr. Hooker [the banker] what was the additional amount to be paid upon Miss Lander's bust of me, besides what has been already paid. For reasons unnecessary to mention, I cannot personally communicate with the lady herself; but I should greatly regret to remain in her debt. The amount being ascertained, will you do me the further favor to pay it, whether to Miss Lander or Mr. Hooker. The bust, my friends tell me, is not worth sixpence; but she did her best with it."

In *The Marble Faun*, he had already made his personal judgment about the vanity of human wishes and the egoism symbolized by portrait busts, condemned to linger on, like dusty white ghosts, among a later and uncaring generation. It would be far better if they had been sculptured in snow or were reduced to quicklime at the earliest opportunity. His omniscient narrator muses, "But it is an awful thing, indeed, this endless endurance, this almost indestructibility, of a marble bust! Whether in our own case, or that of other men, it bids us sadly measure the little, little time, during which our lineaments are likely to be of interest to any human being."

Early in the spring, Hawthorne moved his family to Bath, a city he found as "picturesque and interesting" as any he had come upon in England. With its Parisian-style architecture, the houses "adorned with pillars, pilasters and other good devices," with its pleasant Circuses, Crescents, Terraces and Parades, it was a city built for beauty and pleasure rather than business. Hawthorne thought it might be an ideal retirement community for men with modest incomes.

Then, in mid May, leaving Sophia and the children at Bath, Hawthorne took the train to London for a strenuous round of social visits. He stayed with John Lothrop Motley and his wife, who had taken a house at 31 Hertford Street. With the Motleys, he dined with Lord Dufferin; he also lunched with Lady Dufferin, Caroline Norton, and Mr. William Stirling, author of *The Cloister Life of the Emperor Charles V*, with whom he was to dine on Sunday. "Affairs succeed each other so fast," he wrote Sophia, "that I have really forgotten what I did yesterday. I remember seeing Henry Bright, and listening to a stream of babble from his lips, as we strolled in the Park and along the Strand . . . Thou wouldst be stricken dumb to see how quietly I accept a whole string of invitations, and, what is more, perform my engagements without a murmur." He had, he noted, bought a new alpaca umbrella for nine shillings: "Probably, I shall mislay it before my return."

With Henry Bright, he attended another breakfast at Monckton Milnes's, and on the 19th, Bright had taken him, though he was reluctant to go, to the studio of the well-known photographer John Mayall. Unfortunately, Mayall became overexcited by the fame of his sitter, which made Hawthorne doubly anxious — so anxious, in fact, that he clutched at his umbrella "as if it were the last friend left to him." Mayall, snatching it away, commanded, "Now Sir, please to look *intense!*" On the 24th, he went down to Cambridge, where Henry Bright was to receive his master's degree. His rooms in the oldest part of the old Court of Trinity were so dark that he complained, humorously, that he couldn't find his precious umbrella for two days.

Throughout the spring, Hawthorne had been playfully badgering Fields and his wife to return to England, since the couple were planning to make the return voyage with the Hawthornes. He had already booked passage on the *Europa*, sailing from Liverpool on June 16. "I consider it my duty towards Ticknor and towards Boston and America at large," he advised Fields, "to take you into custody and bring you home; for I know you will never come except under compulsion. Let me know at once, whether I am to use force." He was himself having moments of uncertainty. "As regards going home," he confessed in one of his letters, "I alternate between a longing and a dread."

———

On June 16, after a few final days at Mrs. Blodget's in Liverpool, Hawthorne and his family sailed for America. They had been abroad seven years. Hawthorne had seen much of the great world; Sophia had fulfilled her yearning to see the cultural shrines of Europe — the great palaces, the grand museums. Una was now a young lady of sixteen; Julian would become fourteen during the crossing; Rose was nine. It had been a matter of some concern to Hawthorne that so much of their childhood had been spent away from America.

By an odd coincidence, the captain of the *Europa* was Captain Leitch, who had brought them to Liverpool seven years before. By an equally odd coincidence, Hawthorne had made the first journey with one of his publishers; now he was returning with the other. Aboard ship, too, was Harriet Beecher Stowe, internationally famous as the author of *Uncle Tom's Cabin*, whose husband, Calvin Stowe, had been a student at Bowdoin with Hawthorne. Mrs. Stowe had met the Fieldses in Italy and they had become solid friends. On the voyage home, she regaled the company with stories of her New England life.

Only Fields, it seems, was troubled with seasickness during the twelve-day crossing. As a grim form of amusement, Hawthorne thought up queer menus for the ailing publisher — "potted owl with Minerva sauce," "stewed ibis," "livers of Roman Capitol geese." Hawthorne, so Fields recalled, never tired of walking the deck at midnight. He particularly remembered Hawthorne's remarking, "I should like to sail on and on forever, and never touch the shore again."

In Advance of the General Ruin

AFTER THE EXCITEMENT of Europe, Concord was parochial and sleepy in the drowsy heat of midsummer. The family did not pause in Boston when they docked on June 28, but immediately took the train for Concord. Riding to the Wayside in the railroad wagon, past prim white clapboard houses with green blinds, past fields that seemed burned in the shimmering heat, the children had momentary regrets. Julian, recalling the return to his home town, remembered the stifling atmosphere of Concord in summer, the heat simmering until it seemed "as if nothing but a grasshopper could live."

Part of Hawthorne's reluctance to return to Concord was his realization that his house was too small for his growing family. Even before his return, he had commissioned his publishers to find a solution for his problem. "I am really at a loss to imagine how we are to squeeze ourselves into that little old cottage of mine," he had written Fields on one occasion. "We had outgrown it before we came away, and most of us are twice as big now as we were then . . . Pray, have some plan for me before I get back."

Writing to Ticknor in the fall of 1857, he had suggested a possibility. Bronson Alcott had recently acquired the property next to the Wayside. It was a large plot with two houses, and Hawthorne easily recalled it. Anticipating Alcott's usual impracticality even before the Alcotts moved into Orchard House, Hawthorne advised Ticknor to keep an eye on the situation. The two houses, he reasoned, might be converted into a single residence that would suit his purposes. "If [Alcott] should swamp himself by his expenditures on this place," Hawthorne wrote Ticknor, "I should be very glad to take it off his hands; and it seems to me highly probable (judging from the character of the man) that he will ultimately be glad to have me do so. The matter may be ripe by the time we get back to America; but I should feel more inclined to come home if I had the prospect of a more convenient house to come to." As it turned out, the improvident Alcott had managed his affairs with more foresight than usual; the Alcotts were permanently settled in Orchard House when Hawthorne returned.

Back in Concord, Hawthorne wasted no time in arranging for the expansion of the Wayside. He hired two local carpenters, Mr. Wetherbee and Mr. Watts, to build a new wing — a ground-floor library and a bedroom above — with a third-story tower room, twenty feet square, which he planned to use as his study. The positioning of the new wing was unfortunate, thrust up against the terraced hillside so that the library was claustral and dank at most seasons of the year. Nor were Hawthorne's carpenters able to translate his wishes in satisfactory fashion; the floor levels between the existing structure and the new addition did not meet and had to be compensated for by hazardous steps. The tower room, an adaptation of the Villa Montauto tower to the democratic plain-style of Concord, could be reached only by an incredibly steep and awkward climb. Although the small room above the roof level of the house looked out over a splendid view of the Concord fields, it was comfortable only in the spring and fall. In the summer, the heat was unbearable; in the winter, the fireplace with its wood-burning stove gave off such heat that the room was intolerably stifling. Hawthorne had installed a makeshift folding desk in one corner, but he seldom worked at it, preferring his more usual desk-table nearby.

Throughout the late summer and fall, the Wayside was in a state of chaotic disruption; the lawn was covered with unsightly piles of lumber and wood scraps. The sultry air reverberated with the hammering and sawing of Wetherbee and Watts. It was hardly conducive to literary work. By December, however, Hawthorne was writing Francis Bennoch in a mood of anticipation. He had been idle, he complained, since his return to Concord, "but am now meditating a new Romance, which ought to be the most elevated of my productions, since I shall write it in the sky-parlor of my new tower." He wrote, "One of the additions to my house is a little bit of a library and adjacent sleeping room, which I intend for our most honored and welcome guests and have christened by your name — Bennoch's Room. So when you come to see us, you will feel that you are coming home." Time, he claimed, was burying all his English experiences, month by month, "as a sexton throws shovelsfull of earth into a grave. I lose England without gaining America."

For months after the library was completed, the tall, ugly carpenter's Gothic bookcases stood empty. Hawthorne, who had a frugal streak, felt too poor to fill the shelves and began devising comic remedies — silk curtains or rows of painted books — to hide the accusing emptiness. His architectural alterations had cost him a good deal more than he expected, and in December he was forced to write to Ticknor for $550. "This will make the cost of my additions somewhat more than $2000 — the original estimate having been only $500. Well, I suppose, I am fortunate in getting off so cheap; but if I had known how much it was to cost me, I think I should have sold the old house and bought a better one." Later, writing about his architectural renovations to the American writer and diplomat Donald Grant Mitchell, Hawthorne woefully admitted that he had "transformed a simple and small old farmhouse into the absurdest anomaly you ever saw . . . If it would only burn down! But I have no such luck."

It was a period of uncomfortable adjustments. From the vantage point of England, Hawthorne had looked back on the "miserable confusion" of American politics. Writing to Ticknor from Leamington in February 1860, he displayed a callousness bred by distance. "I go for a dissolution of the Union," he had claimed, "and, on that ground, I hope the abolitionists will push matters to extremity." His views were undoubtedly prompted by the headlong course of events following John Brown's bold seizure of the United States arsenal at Harpers Ferry, Virginia, in mid October 1859. Brown's speedy trial, and his subsequent execution on December 2, had polarized American politics. History had left the political parties in disarray; even Charles Sumner, never a Southern sympathizer, found it expedient to remain silent — much to the satisfaction of the newly emerging Republican Party, of which he was a member. With presidential elections coming up, conservative Republicans hoped to play down the abolition issue. Sumner, writing to his friend the Duchess of Argyll after the execution, suggested that Brown was "almost mad" — a judgment on the cautious side, considering that insanity seemed almost endemic in Brown's family, with several members committed to asylums, and a wife and a son who died insane. "Of course his act must be deplored," Sumner told the duchess, but he applauded "the singular courage and character" of the man. In his letter, he took the high ground of many of his contemporaries. "For a practical statesman, believing slavery a wrong, the subject is not without its difficulties," he said loftily. "Not, indeed, that I hesitate to judge the *act;* but how can I refuse my admiration to many things in the *man?*" Fortunately, it had not been necessary to risk his qualified view of Brown in public; his doctors had advised against his taking part in the strenuous congressional debates on the issue.

Hawthorne, in England, could afford to take an even loftier position. He would be content in America, he told Ticknor, if presidential elections and political turmoil were done away with "— and if I could but be deprived of my political rights and left to my individual freedom. The sweetest thing connected with a foreign residence is that you have no rights and no duties . . . I shall never again be so free as I have been in England and Italy."

But the public controversy was brought home to him in very personal ways. While he was in England, in fact, it had arrived at the very doorstep of the Wayside. John Brown had many supporters in Concord, among them the tall, fussing schoolmaster Franklin B. Sanborn, a protégé of Bronson Alcott's. When Brown had been captured at Harpers Ferry, government agents had confiscated letters that clearly implicated Sanborn in the planning of the raid. A congressional subpoena was issued demanding that Sanborn testify in Washington, but the young man refused. In April 1860, agents attempted to arrest Sanborn in Concord in order to bring him to the capital. His neighbors successfully stalled the attackers and hurriedly secured a writ of habeas corpus. Mary Peabody, then living at the Wayside, had contrived a hiding place for young Sanborn in the attic.

Mary was not the only member of the Peabody family in the thick of events. Lizzie, inevitably, had thrown herself wholeheartedly into the cause, journeying to the center of the maelstrom, Richmond, Virginia, to plead with the Virginia governor for the release of one of the conspirators, Aaron Dwight Stevens — without success. Lizzie was always to have the courage of her convictions — an angel marching in where even fools feared to tread. She also stepped up her transatlantic attempts to proselytize her niece Una. Sophia once more objected: "When you get so far out of my idea of right as to talk of its being proper to violate laws sometimes, because we 'can obey higher laws than we break' — this, dear Elizabeth, I used to hear in days past and I consider it a very dangerous and demoralizing doctrine and have always called it 'transcendental slang' . . . I am just on the point of declaring that I hate transcendentalism because it is full of such immoderate dicta."

After his return to Concord, Hawthorne was no more able to escape the political storm than he was able to avoid his Peabody relatives — or his neighbors. Nowhere, in fact, was the death of Brown more devoutly considered an act of martyrdom than in Orchard House. When Bronson Alcott had met Brown several months before the Harpers Ferry raid, he enthusiastically announced, "I think him equal to anything he dares, the man to do the deed . . ." and Alcott was one of the most reverential speakers at the memorial service held in the Concord town hall after Brown was executed. Alcott's daughter Louisa May, twenty-seven and a budding author, recorded the stirring events of that winter with a girlish succinctness. "The execution of Saint John the Just took place on the second," she testified in her diary. "A meeting at the hall, and all Concord was there. Emerson, Thoreau, Father, and Sanborn spoke, and all were full of reverence and admiration for the martyr." Following the attempted kidnaping of Sanborn, she tersely noted, "Great ferment in town. A meeting and general flurry." Louisa's diaries were full of flurries and ferments — it was her breathless style. There were, as well, exclamations of regret that she had not been born a man in such stirring times.

The politics of Concord, transcendental or otherwise, were never to Hawthorne's liking. It was, perhaps, one of the reasons he seldom ventured into Concord society after his return from Europe. Although Sophia and the children went frequently to Orchard House, Hawthorne did not especially encourage the visits of Bronson Alcott, and he usually made a prompt exit when the abrasive Abba Alcott showed up at the Wayside. It is highly probable that Bronson Alcott mistook Hawthorne's aloofness as an instance of shyness. "Nobody gets a chance to speak with him unless by accident," Alcott maintained. "Still he has a tender, kindly side, and a voice that a woman might own, the hesitance is so taking . . ."

Unfortunately, neither Hawthorne nor Sophia could so easily avoid Lizzie Peabody, who was becoming increasingly belligerent and outspoken on the slavery issue — to such a point that Sophia, at least twice, wrote her sister with unusual bitterness: "It is of no avail to dispute about slavery and politics, for there can never be apparently an apprehension of what I mean and say and *my husband* is dangerous ground, for I cannot let anyone be saucy about him to me. It is a matter of supererogation to say he does not study the state of things in this country, for how do you know he does not? But I will not condescend to defend him — though I might say a great deal." A second letter, undated, but evidently written at the height of the turmoil — and twenty-one pages long — was full of recriminations: "How can you tell anything about our innermost life of thought? Is it not arrogant to presume to know, still more deny our yearnings for humanity. Especially how can you know Mr. Hawthorne's sentiments, when he has not communicated with you for twenty years? Why cannot you rest in peace about his sentiments, whatever they may be?" Sophia, who refused to show her husband any of Lizzie's argumentative letters, came down on her sister with unusual severity. "For (whatever you may or may not

recollect)," she wrote heatedly, "you have been in the habit of saying caustic and disagreeable things in reference to him during my
whole married life."

Hawthorne's political views, such as they were following his return, were not communicated to his sister-in-law, but to his English
friend Henry Bright. Bright had written about his recent engagement to Mary Elizabeth Thompson. Hawthorne, replying in mid
December 1860, when talk of secession was at a fever pitch, congratulated Bright heartily and suggested that the couple make a honeymoon trip to America. "If you come soon enough," he advised
Bright, "you will have the pleasure (and I know it would be a great
one to your wicked English heart) of seeing the Union in its death
throes, and of triumphing over me in revenge for all the uncivil
things I used to say about England and her institutions. How queer,
that the rotten old patchwork of your Constitution should be so
likely to outlast all our bran-new contrivances."

He wrote further, "Well, I am ashamed to say how little I care
about the matter. New England will still have her rocks and ice, and
I should not wonder if we become a better and nobler people than
even heretofore. As to the South, I never loved it. We do not belong
together; the Union is unnatural, a scheme of man, not an ordinance
of God . . ." With comic perversity, he asked, "Don't you think England (if we petition her humbly enough) might be induced to receive the New England states back again, in our old Provincial capacity?" He clearly viewed the house of American politics as a
jerry-built structure, ready for the torch.

"Julian (poor little wretch) begins to go to school . . ." Hawthorne
had written Horatio Bridge in September, "for the first time in his
life — his education having hitherto been private." The school in
which the fourteen-year-old boy was enrolled was none other than
that of Frank Sanborn, the abolitionist hero. Sanborn had recently
instituted a progressive coeducational plan; the enrollment of his
school consisted of the children of Concord's more educated citizenry, including Emerson and Judge Rockwood Hoar, Elizabeth's
brother. Hawthorne, who wanted to enroll Julian in Harvard, felt it
was necessary to prepare his son: his advice was "If the boys attack
you, always go for the biggest one!" Sophia remained critical of
Sanborn's coeducational methods; she felt there were too many social occasions — too many dances, picnics, and theatricals — and
not enough serious study. Her son was being introduced to feminine
society at too early an age. "Julian was a sacredly folded bud when
we brought him home to America, with a genuine reverence for

women," she eventually wrote the young schoolmaster, "and now he is forcibly bloomed into a *cavaliere servente* before his wisdom teeth have had time to prick through."

The school had been highly recommended by Ellery Channing. Once again a Concord resident, Channing had sent a belated letter, welcoming Hawthorne "back to the stern and simple fields of this ancient Puritan land." He apologized for his tardiness; "but a traveller," he explained, "is like coffee, and needs to be well settled." Channing not only recommended that Julian attend Sanborn's school, but suggested that Hawthorne should enroll his daughters as well. His letter was probably well intended, but it was slightly tactless. His critical views on the poor upbringing of the Hawthorne children showed through: "Nothing seems to me more unfortunate in this land of activity, than to bring up children in seclusion, without the invaluable discipline that a good school presents."

Hawthorne, however, was very chary of his daughters; neither Una nor Rose was enrolled. Sophia, in fact, wrote Sanborn frankly, "We entirely disapprove of this commingling of youths and maidens at the electric age in school. I find no end of ill effect from it, and this is why I do not send Una and Rose to your school." Hawthorne must have assumed that his decision had been the correct one when, in late September, Una had a recurrence of her Roman fever. Or so Hawthorne believed. His letters to James Fields and Franklin Pierce suggest that the illness involved spells of mental derangement as well as physical symptoms. Writing to Fields on the 21st, he explained, "We are in great trouble on account of our poor Una, in whom the bitter dregs of that Rome fever are still rankling, and have now developed themselves in a way which the physicians foreboded and forewarned us of. I do not like to write about it but will tell you when we meet." He warned, "Say nothing." Several days later, he wrote in a happier frame of mind, full of praise for a Mrs. Rollins of Cambridge, who had treated Una with a new form of electrical therapy. Una was well, he claimed, "her case having yielded at once to the incantations of a certain electrical witch. This Doctor says that the crisis was a most fortunate one and that without it she would have been subject to life-long disease."

On October 9, writing to Pierce, Hawthorne unburdened himself about his greatest fear — that Una might suffer from a chronic mental illness. "All the violent symptoms," he wrote, "were allayed by the first application of electricity, and within two days she was in such a condition as to require no further restraint. Since then, there has been no relapse, and now, for many days, she has seemed entirely well, in mind . . . [Mrs. Rollins] assures us that we need have no apprehension of future mental disturbance, and that we may entertain the most confident hopes of her restoration in all respects — her constitution being remarkably good. I know that you will rejoice with me at these good prospects."

In his dealings with Ellery Channing, after an interval of seven years, Hawthorne must have been deeply aware of how changed their situations were. Ellery was now a widower. Eighteen years before, he and Ellen had been near-interlopers in Hawthorne's honeymoon paradise at the Old Manse. Never a dutiful husband nor a responsible father — although this had never stopped him from giving parental advice — Channing and Ellen Fuller had separated in 1853, when Hawthorne was in England. At the urging of her relatives, the reluctant Ellen had moved to Worcester with the children, staying with her cousin Thomas Wentworth Higginson and his family. Concord neighbors dutifully reported that the usually unsociable Channing had begun dining with the Emersons, boating with Thoreau, and greeting neighbors whom he had hardly acknowledged before.

Although a negligent spouse when Ellen had been at home, Channing became a persistent one after her desertion, writing her ardent and apologetic letters. He also began to take himself seriously as a father, initiating legal action for the recovery of his children. In time, there had been a reunion — much against the advice of the Fuller family. For a brief period, Ellen was to know some happiness and tender affection; Channing had even made the bold step of going to work as an assistant editor for the *New Bedford Mercury*. Never strong or healthy, Ellen had died in September 1856, not long after the birth of her fifth child. Whether Channing was with his wife at the end, or whether he attended the burial services at Mount Auburn Cemetery, is not clear. In time, his children were parceled out among various Fuller and Channing relatives, and as the years passed, Ellery found one reason or another to avoid seeing them. He settled into a prolonged bachelor existence in Concord. Hawthorne saw him with much less frequency. Channing seems not to have minded; his relationships with others were always tenuous in nature. He became something of a Concord character — increasingly eccentric, miserly, cantankerous. Evidently he retained some queer, vestigial sense of past affection for his wife. In 1865, when Channing moved from his Main Street house to smaller quarters on Middle Street, he carried Ellen's dresses from the old home to the new one. He hung them carefully in a closet, where they remained undisturbed year after year, until they fell apart in shreds.

ᕲᘿ II ᕲᘿ

In America, Hawthorne's substitution for the parenthetical literary life he had enjoyed in England was the Saturday Club. Initially, the club had simply consisted of informal meetings held at the Albion House in Boston. By 1856, however, it had evolved into a full-fledged organization with rules and regulations — though of a relaxed and transcendental order. Except for dinners for visiting celebrities or special occasions such as the Shakespeare Memorial of 1864, the meetings consisted of dinners, once a month, at the Parker House. The regular membership included such literary lights as Emerson, Longfellow, Lowell, Oliver Wendell Holmes, and Louis Agassiz. Charles Sumner, who was frequently a guest, joined in 1862 and was followed by the elder Henry James. Hawthorne was elected in absentia, while he was abroad. Writing to Henry Bright, the winter after his return, he described the club enthusiastically as "an excellent institution, with the privilege of first-rate society, and no duties but to eat one's dinners." It was a distinct advantage of the club that one could invite a guest and introduce him to "all our northern notabilities at one fell swoop." At first, Hawthorne attended the meetings with some regularity; it allowed him to renew acquaintances after seven years. "Longfellow has grown younger in appearance," he related to the interested Bright, "but seems not to dress quite so smartly as of yore. Emerson is unchanged in aspect — at least he looks so, at a distance, but, on close inspection, you perceive that a little hoar-frost has gathered on him. He has become earthlier during these past seven years; for he puffs cigars like a true Yankee, and drinks wine like an Englishman."

Yet Hawthorne was also aware that his return to Concord had revived his old reclusive habits, and he hinted as much to Bright. "As for me," he confessed, "I spend a monotonous life, seldom quitting my own hillside and trying earnestly to take root here. I find, however, that I staid abroad a little too long, and as a consequence, have lost my home-feelings for the present, if not forever." In his late years, there was something instinctive and almost irrepressible about Hawthorne's tendency to bolt if he spied visitors coming. He would hurry out the back door of the Wayside to walk along the ridge of the hill among the pines, pacing back and forth. Even in the seclusion of the woods, if he spied someone coming along the road, he would take cover "like a partridge." Over the years, he wore a path along the crest that was still visible long after his death. The very sociable James Fields — whom Hawthorne later proposed for membership in the Saturday Club — was fond of recalling a comic but characteristic example of Hawthorne's inveterate reticence. On a warm and sleepy summer afternoon, the two men were resting on the banks of the Concord River, Hawthorne reciting some half-remembered lines of Thomson's *Seasons,* a poem that had been a favorite since boyhood. There was a sound of approaching footsteps. Hawthorne hurriedly commanded, "Duck! or we shall be interrupted by somebody." Fields could barely suppress his laughter at the thought of two grown men hiding, face down, behind the bushes. Hawthorne, nudging him, whispered in an even more mournful voice, "Heaven help me. Mr. —— is close upon us!"

That Hawthorne, during his last years in Concord, seldom took the path through the woods to the Alcott house was perhaps understandable. That he called so infrequently on Emerson was more unusual. He and Emerson might take walks together or meet at the Saturday Club, but Hawthorne's social calls on his neighbor down the road were few and far between. Edward Emerson recalled one of Hawthorne's rare visits to his father's house. The author was paying an avuncular call on young Ellen Emerson, Una's friend. "Unfortunately," Edward remembered, "she had gone to bed, but [Hawthorne] remained for a time talking with my sister Edith and me . . . To cover his shyness, he took up a stereoscope on the center table and began to look at the pictures. After looking at them for a time he asked where these views were taken." Edward Emerson vividly recaptured the smug astonishment of a child confronted by an incomprehensible elder: "We told him they were pictures of the Concord Court and Town-houses, the Common and the Mill-dam, on hearing which he expressed some surprise and interest, but evidently was as unfamiliar with the center of the village where he had lived for years as a deer or a wood-thrush would be. He walked through it often on his way to the cars, but was too shy or too rapt to know what was there."

In his last years, too, Hawthorne's brooding conservatism, his deepening illness, set him apart from the sociable and liberal-minded members of the Saturday Club. When he attended meetings, he was apt to be taciturn. Henry James left a droll portrait of the author at one of its regular sessions. "Hawthorne isn't a handsome man," James wrote Emerson, "nor an engaging one any way personally: he had the look all the time to one who didn't know him of a rogue who suddenly finds himself in a company of detectives." Yet James had felt a sympathy "amounting to anguish" for the writer and found it impossible to take his eyes off him throughout dinner. "Hawthorne, however, seemed to possess human substance enough and not to have dissipated it away as that debauched Charles Norton, and the good, inoffensive, comforting Longfellow." Hawthorne had seemed like some pathetic Concord owl, brought into daylight and "expected to wink and be lively" in company. "How he buried his eyes in his plate," James commented, "and ate with such a voracity that no person should dare to ask him a question. My heart broke for him as that attenuated Charles Norton kept putting forth his long antennae towards him, stroking his face, and trying whether his eyes were shut." Yet James perceptively had sensed in Hawthorne's behavior something stern and durable that was a reproach to mere sociability. "The old world is breaking up on all hands," he declared; "the glimpse of the everlasting granite I caught in Hawthorne . . . shows me that there is stock enough left for fifty better."

For Hawthorne, as for many Americans, the attack on Fort Sumter served only to steel his energies. Like Henry James, Hawthorne felt the old world was breaking up and a new order was emerging. And like many Americans, he found the prospect exhilarating at first. Writing to Horatio Bridge, still a paymaster general in the navy, Hawthorne was ebullient: "The war, strange to say, has had a beneficial effect upon my spirits, which were flagging woefully before it broke out. But it was delightful to share in the heroic sentiment of the time, and to feel that I had a country — a consciousness which seemed to make me young again. One thing, as regards this matter, I regret, and one thing I am glad of; the regrettable thing is that I am too old to shoulder a musket myself, and the joyful thing is that Julian is too young."

Yet Hawthorne, from the beginning, was never convinced of the purposes of the war. "Though I approve the war as much as any man," he told Bridge, "I don't quite understand what we are fighting for, or what definite result can be expected. If we pummel the South ever so hard, they will love us none the better for it; and even if we subjugate them, our next step should be to cut them adrift." He could never quite view it as a great humanitarian effort to annihilate slavery, only as the inevitable rift in the badly mated politics of the North and the South. "Whatever happens next," he told Bridge, "I must say that I rejoice that the old Union is smashed. We never were one people, and never really had a country since the Constitution was formed."

Quiet Concord had immediately mobilized behind the war effort. On the afternoon of April 19, a company of forty-five young "braves" gathered at the Concord depot, where they were heartened by a speech from Judge Hoar and sent off with a rousing cannon salute. Julian, thrilled by the patriotism of the moment, began drilling regularly with his schoolmates, insisting he would enlist when he came of age. Hawthorne, unable to get down to writing, complained to Ticknor, "I wish I could turn my hand to any useful labor. If I were younger, I would volunteer; but as the case stands, I shall keep quiet till the enemy gets within a mile of my own house."

Louisa May Alcott, who had seen the boys off on that dramatic day, wrote in her diary, "We all seem like one family in times like these . . . I've often longed to see a war, and now I have my wish. I long to be a man; but as I can't fight, I will content myself with working for those who can." Concord matrons and the young girls met weekly to knit and sew for the soldiers. During those first months of the war, Louisa May read Carlyle, gardened, and sewed for the boys. As an extra measure of family patriotism, the Alcotts took in John Brown's daughters as boarders. But as the war days wore on with few Northern victories, Louisa became disheartened. "It seems as if a few energetic women could carry on the war better than the men do it so far," she wrote glumly in her diary.

Hawthorne, too, experienced a letdown. "I wish they would push on the war a little more briskly," he wrote Ticknor. "The excitement had an invigorating effect on me for a time, but it begins to lose its influence. But it is rather unreasonable to wish my countrymen to kill one another for the sake of refreshing my palled spirits; so I shall pray for peace." The unremitting heat of the Concord summer was also weighing him down. In July, Julian, attempting to demonstrate his physical endurance by swimming underwater in the muddy Concord River, fell sick and was confined to bed for several days. The accident provided Hawthorne with a legitimate excuse to take his son to the seashore to recuperate. Late in July, he decided to spend two or three weeks at Prides Crossing, boarding in a cottage near the beaches, not too distant from his sister Elizabeth, who was still living in Beverly. The latest war news made the change of scene all the more welcome. The Northern rout in the first Battle of Bull Run seems to have hardened his mood. Writing to James Russell Lowell, who had invited him to dinner in Boston, Hawthorne declined, but added, "Speaking of dinner, last evening's news will dull the edge of many a Northern appetite; but if it puts all of us into the same grim and bloody humor that it does me, the South had better have suffered ten defeats than won this victory."

Hawthorne and Julian arrived at Prides Crossing on July 27, in a heat wave. They haunted the woods and the seashore and made an excursion to visit Elizabeth, with whom they gathered berries. Writing to Una — "Dear Onion" — he complained that in some inscrutable way, a man had recognized him on the train and had insisted on driving him to the cottage in his carriage, as well as putting "his house, his beach and everything else, at our disposal. Oh ye Heavens! How absurd that a man should spend the best of his years in getting a little mite of reputation, and then immediately find the annoyance of it more than the profit." Writing to Rose a week later, he said, "Tell Mama that I see no newspapers, and do not know, at this moment, whether the Rebels have taken Washington, or what other misfortune may have happened. Almost every hour, however, I hear the noise of drums over the water, from Marblehead or Salem, and very often the thunder of cannon . . . so that I begin to think the war has overspread the whole country except just this little precinct in the neighborhood of West Beach." He conceded, "On the whole, I enjoy this respite from the daily repetition and contradiction of telegraphs about skirmishes, victories and defeats, and could almost be content to remain in the same ignorance till the war is over."

The war, of course, did not go away, and Hawthorne could not remain ignorant of the cost. After the defeats, there came a time of rationalizations and easy metaphors. It was a time to speak of amputations, as if the South were an infected member that needed to be cut away. Hawthorne spoke of it in that fashion, writing to Bridge, who seemed unaccountably optimistic. "My own opinion," Hawthorne countered, "is that no nation ever came safe and sound through such a confounded difficulty as this of ours. For my part I don't hope, nor indeed wish, to see the Union restored as it was. Amputation seems to me much the better plan, and all we ought to fight for is the liberty of selecting the point where our diseased members shall be lop't off." Emerson had used exactly the same terms when writing to James Elliot Cabot soon after the humiliating failure at Bull Run. "The war," Emerson maintained, "with its defeats & uncertainties is immensely better than what we lately called the integrity of the Republic, as amputation is better than cancer. I think we are all agreed in this, and find it out by wondering why we are so pleased, though so beaten and so poor."

The recent defeats tempered Hawthorne's opinions; he became as adamant as his abolitionist colleagues. Henry Bright, expressing the English view that the bloodshed and expense seemed unnecessary, touched a sensitive nerve. Hawthorne, writing in November, seemed to be responding to England at large. He lectured Bright on the necessity of holding on to certain states: "If we stop fighting at this juncture, we give up Maryland, Virginia, Kentucky, Missouri, all of which are fully capable of being made free soil, and will be so in a few years, if we possess them, but not in a hundred years, if we lose them. We give up our Capital too, and retire under a load of disgrace, which to my mind would make national extinction the lesser evil of the two." He asked pointedly, "Cannot an Englishman's common sense help you to see that this is so?"

Hawthorne was not unaware of the mounting casualty lists; a "dearly loved" nephew of Lowell's had been killed, and Oliver Wendell Holmes's son had been wounded in the Battle of Ball's Bluff. Hawthorne reported the news to Bright. Yet in his letter, he took a perversely callous view: "Who cares what the war costs in blood or treasure? People must die, whether a bullet kills them or no; and money must be spent, if not for gunpowder, then for worse luxuries. My countrymen chose to spend themselves and their prosperity in war; and they find, at this very moment, an enjoyment in it worth all their sacrifices. I never imagined what a happy state of mind a civil war produces . . . You will live to see the Americans another people than they have hitherto been; and I truly regret that my youth was not cast in these days."

In the first, bitter winter of the war, Hawthorne, like most of the citizenry of Concord, turned Spartan. "Emerson is breathing slaughter like the rest of us," Hawthorne informed his English friend, "and it is really wonderful how all sorts of theoretical nonsense, to which we New Englanders are addicted in peaceful times, vanish in the strong atmosphere which we now inhale . . . The whole world, on this side of the Atlantic, appears to have grown more natural and sensible and walks more erect, and cares less about childish things. If the war only lasts long enough (and not too long) it will have done us infinite good."

It was a somewhat desperate point of view — a faith arising out of the low ebb of Northern fortunes in the war, an outlook that Sophia seems not to have shared. Writing in her diary on New Year's Day, 1862, she gave an enigmatic weather report: "I heard Mr. Emerson's lecture on War. Furious wind."

Though he might be swept up by the war rhetoric of the times, Hawthorne was distinctly not immune to another very real personal tragedy that had occurred in the summer of 1861, involving his friend Longfellow. On July 9, in the library at Craigie House, Fanny Longfellow had been sealing up a little packet with burning wax. The sleeve of her light summer dress caught fire, and suddenly the whole gauzy dress was afire. Terrified, she ran to her husband in the study. Longfellow, leaping up, tried to extinguish the flames with a rug. It was too small. Fanny broke away in panic; then, desperately, she rushed back to him. Longfellow took her in his arms, trying to shield her face; he was badly burned about the face and arms. Fanny Longfellow lived through the night and into the next day, her pain relieved by ether. On the morning of the 10th, she lapsed into a coma and never regained consciousness, dying a few hours later. Longfellow was heavily sedated with ether and laudanum. In his conscious moments, he feared that he was going insane, begged not to be sent to an asylum. He was too ill to be at his wife's bedside, nor could he attend the funeral services on July 13 — their eighteenth wedding anniversary. "How I am alive after what my eyes have seen," he wrote his sister-in-law later, "I know not. I am at least patient, if not resigned."

Hawthorne could hardly believe his friend's tragedy. His response was almost superstitious; it seemed one more clear case of the shadow of disaster that followed on success. The accident had occurred on his own wedding anniversary. A few days later he wrote to James Fields, "How does Longfellow bear this terrible misfortune? How are his own injuries? Do write, and tell me all about him. I cannot at all reconcile this calamity to my sense of fitness. One would think that there ought to have been no deep sorrow in the life of a man like him; and now comes this blackest of shadows, which no sunshine hereafter can ever penetrate! I shall be afraid ever to meet him again; he cannot again be the man that I have known."

⌒ III ⌒

"I have not found it possible to occupy my mind with its usual trash and nonsense, during these anxious times," Hawthorne wrote Bridge in October 1861, "but as autumn advances, I find myself sitting down to my desk and blotting successive sheets of paper as of yore. Very likely I may have something ready for the public, long before the public is ready to receive it." His optimism was ill founded. The history of his final literary productions is a poignant one. Following his return to America, Hawthorne tried his hand at one abortive romance after another. It was as if he had finally resigned himself to the failure of his "realistic" romances and had surrendered his imagination to his earlier Gothic fantasies — only to find that he could bring nothing in this vein to a satisfactory conclusion, either. In the fragmentary *The Ancestral Footstep*, written in Italy, he had tried to merge the legend of the bloody footprint in Smithills Hall with his theme of the American claimant seeking to recover an English inheritance. Hawthorne's persistence in trying to bond the seemingly disparate elements into a consistent narrative line is an indication of the obsessive nature of his themes. They were, in fact, one theme — and a recurrent one in Hawthorne's fiction. A lost estate and an ancient crime — Eden and the Fall.

The earliest versions, probably begun after the renovations at the Wayside had been completed, had a transatlantic setting — both America and England. A shady old doctor with a penchant for spiders (at first named Etherege, then Grimshawe) lives in a dusty, cobwebby Salem house set next to an old graveyard. He has two wards: a "beautiful boy," who may or may not be the heir of an English estate (Hawthorne's intentions shifted during the retelling); and a young girl with "indistinct remembrances" of an English mansion house and a hospital. (Hawthorne may have borrowed the idea from one of the more impressive segments of Melville's *Pierre*: Isabel's vague recollections of a foreign childhood.) In the English segment, the plot is cluttered with even more Gothic characters: the villainous master of Braithewaite Hall, whose "unpardonable sin" Hawthorne can never quite settle on; an implausible prisoner in a secret chamber and an equally improbable keeper who was a hanged man restored to life by Hawthorne's "powdery" doctor; an aged pensioner, who may or may not turn out to be the true heir.

In time, various elements of the improbable story were grafted onto another impossible theme — that of an immortal man, possessed of a secret elixir. The idea for this variant came from a legend Thoreau had told him about a former occupant of the Wayside who believed he would never die. In the two earliest versions of the immortality theme, Hawthorne's hero — named Septimius Felton, then Septimius Norton — is a brash young American who kills a gay and handsome British soldier, the possessor of the secret formula. (Interestingly, Hawthorne had cast the setting for his story in Concord a century earlier, at the time of another civil war — that between the colonies and the mother country.) When those versions ground down in failure, Hawthorne returned again to his initial concept. In *The Dolliver Romance*, the possessor of the secret elixir is the ancient Dr. Dolliver, the great-grandfather and sole guardian of an elflike child named Pansie.

In these final, abortive attempts at creating a romance, it is as if Hawthorne had wandered into a hall of mirrors in which fragments of his personal life and pieces of his imaginative fantasies were reflected and repeated in bewildering sequence. Dr. Peabody's house on Charter Street, next to the burying ground — a model setting for the first versions — gives way to the Wayside and Orchard House on the Lexington Road in Concord. In his frustrating attempts to come to grips with his problem, bits of his experience are hauled in to give life and impetus to the faltering plot lines: the monstrous spiders of the Villa Montauto; Delia Bacon's imagined evidence buried in a coffin; bitter memories of the Cilley duel, sweetened by a fictional retelling; the story of the British soldier buried by the Old

Manse; recollections of the disreputable Florentine necromancer, Seymour Kirkup, and his sprite-child, Imogen. All of these elements are picked up, worried over, dropped, reconsidered. The course of these last novels is strewn with false starts, rehearsals, attempts to revive a failing enterprise. The mechanics of his fiction had stalled.

Nothing indicates the unhappiness and uncertainty of Hawthorne's frustrated creative impulses — or does so with such poignancy — as the repeated editorial asides that crop up in his "Etherege" manuscript: ironic, caustic, grimly humorous comments about the unsatisfactory performance of the writing, the unmanageable plotting. "The life is not yet breathed into this plot, after all my galvanic efforts," Hawthorne upbraids himself. "Not a spark of passion as yet. How shall it be attained?" Throughout his imaginative life, Hawthorne had found it difficult to define the precise nature of the sin that would correspond to his own deep-seated sense of human sinfulness. In his final romances, his attempts to settle on the nature of a villain's villainy reach an impasse: "Has crept, has sinned, has suffered through all that sordidness, till suddenly raised to this delightful position. Once he had a great temptation to do a horrible thing. Of course, he yielded. Agreeable, brilliant, witty, but heartless and worthless; a man of the world." He complains, "All this amounts to just nothing. I don't advance a step." After a stretch of stilted dialogue, he confesses, "What unimaginable nonsense!" At times, the effort to prime his flagging imagination breaks down into mere lists and bad puns: "Miss Blagden, Miss Ingersoll. Mr. Roberts — Marshall Rynders. President Buchanan of disUnited States." At the outset of a long peroration, he advises himself, "Now for the old pensioner — this origin, pursuit, biography . . . Take the character of Cowper for this man; melancholic, gentle, shy, conscientious, censorious, therefore not acceptable to his neighbours . . . A want of the practical element in his nature . . . In figure, Mr. Alcott." There were moments, in the dazzle of his indecision, when he needed to touch down on the hard earth of fact. "I have not the least notion how to get on," he laments. "I never was in such a sad predicament before . . ." But however much he struggled through each of the failing versions of his enterprise, he could not put his fictional world in order; he remained lost in a thicket of possibilities, unable to find his way out.

Hawthorne was to have an easier time revising the journal notes of his English experiences for publication. But neither was that a literary effort he effectively pursued. Just after his return from abroad, he had worked up a brief essay, "Some of the Haunts of

Burns," which was published in the *Atlantic Monthly* while Lowell was still editor. A year later, after Fields had assumed the editorship, Hawthorne sent a further reminiscence, "Near Oxford," which Fields published in October 1861. By then, Fields was hoping for the serial publication of Hawthorne's novel in progress — the abortive Septimius Felton version of the immortality theme. Fields was enthusiastic about Hawthorne's English articles. The Oxford piece was "admirable," he said; he encouraged Hawthorne to follow it up with an article on English cathedrals. "The sooner the better" was his professional judgment.

Ironically, in the midst of his writing problems, Hawthorne was to meet the prolific and popular English writer whose beef-and-ale novels, with their thick slices of English life, he had professed to admire so heartily. In mid September 1861, Fields gave a literary dinner for the visiting Anthony Trollope. Hawthorne, as well as Holmes, Lowell, and Emerson, was among the guests at a spirited dinner of canvasback ducks and flowing wines. Trollope, red-faced, bespectacled, and balding, was in roaring form. Boasting to his fellow writers, he claimed that he went to work on a novel "just like a shoemaker on a shoe, only taking care to make honest stitches." Day after day, he rose at five in the morning and always wrote his specified number of pages before breakfast.

The talk had then turned to agriculture, and Trollope, in loud good humor, asserted that "England was the only country where such a thing as a peach or a grape was known." Lowell appealed to the silent Hawthorne to defend the honor of the country. With only a slight stirring — "as one sees bubbles rise and send off rings in still water when a turtle stirs at bottom" — Hawthorne had turned and mildly answered, "I asked an Englishman once who was praising their peaches to describe to me exactly what he meant by a peach, and he described something very like a cucumber."

James Fields, writing to Hawthorne a few days later, assured him, "Trollope fell in love with you at first sight and went off moaning that he could not see you again. He swears you are the handsomest Yankee that ever walked the planet."

Between the hazards of the war and his waning interest in his literary occupations, Hawthorne had come to an impasse. He confessed as much to Bridge, in Washington, who had been encouraging him to make a visit to the wartime capital. The invitation was very tempting, Hawthorne replied, but there were obstacles. "For instance," he wrote his friend, "I am not very well, being mentally and physically languid, but I suppose there is about an even chance that the trip and change of scene might supply the energy which I lack. Also, I am pretending to write a book, and though I am no wise diligent about it, still, each week finds it a little more advanced, and I am now at a point where I do not like to leave it entirely." He was also concerned about spending money needlessly "in these hard times," being convinced that the book trade and everybody connected with it would fall to nothing before the war was over.

Franklin Pierce, he mentioned, had paid a recent visit to the Wayside, staying overnight. He and the former President had "mingled our tears and condolences for the state of the country." And he added "Pierce is truly patriotic, and thinks there is nothing left for us but to fight it out, but I should be sorry to take his opinion implicitly . . . He is bigoted as to the Union, and sees nothing but ruin without it." Hawthorne thanked Bridge for sending him a "shaded map of negrodom," one that indicated the proportions of the black and white populations in the Southern states. However bully Hawthorne may have been in his letters to Bright, he was a good deal less sanguine in writing to Bridge. "What a terrible amount of trouble and expense in washing that sheet white," he commented, "and after all I am afraid we shall only variegate it with blood and dirt."

ᜑ IV ᜒ

Early in March 1862, Hawthorne set out on his trip to Washington, accompanied by the obliging William Ticknor. It was a journey that would take him out of his solitude and bring him close to the heart of the war. The pair made slow progress southward; Hawthorne preferred not to travel at night. They stopped at New York and again in Philadelphia. There were persistent rumors that General George McClellan was about to begin his long-delayed peninsular campaign, and Hawthorne looked forward to it with anticipation. He wrote Sophia on the 9th, "The farther we go, the deeper grows the rumble and grumble of the coming storm, and I think the two armies are only waiting our arrival to begin." It was en route from Baltimore that Hawthorne saw unmistakable signs of a nation at war: guards were stationed at all the railroad depots, and along the ridges of the hills he could see scattered military encampments, the tents blackened by the smoke of winter stoves. At every station, eager soldiers passed through the cars, asking for newspapers carrying reports of the battle between the *Monitor* and the *Merrimack*, which had taken place the day before.

At Washington's Union Station, in the darkening evening, they filed out into the street between lines of troops. The military presence was everywhere, in spite of the fact that on the day of their arrival 60,000 men had crossed the Potomac on the March to Manassas. Hawthorne wondered if the time would ever come again, in America, when a man might live a decade without seeing a soldier. It was a question he had no qualms about answering — bluntly — in an article he later wrote about his wartime excursion. "One bullet-headed general will succeed another in the Presidential chair," he speculated, "and veterans will hold the offices at home and abroad, and sit in Congress and the state legislatures, and fill all the avenues of public life."

He and Ticknor put up at Willard's Hotel. Hawthorne was distinctly struck by the miscellaneous Washington types he met in the hotel's corridors and its smoke-filled parlors — businessmen and loafers, office-seekers and minor clerks, army correspondents and petty jobbers, men with dubious inventions for sale. Two thirds of the hotel's patrons were in uniform, improvised or otherwise; a few were grizzled veterans; most were mere "carpet-knights." It was impossible, Hawthorne maintained, not to adopt the habit of the place and order "a mint-julep, a whiskey-skin, a gin-cocktail, a brandy-smash or a glass of pure Old Rye." He noted drily, "The conviviality of Washington sets in at an early hour, and, so far as I had an opportunity of observing, never terminates at any hour."

The unfinished Capitol building, with its scaffolding, its uncompleted dome, presided over the city on the Potomac, giving it a makeshift air. Hawthorne was not alone in finding something improbable about the Washington scene. A young English journalist, Edward Dicey, covering the war for *The Spectator* and *Macmillan's Magazine*, thought Washington was like some extravagant bit of theatrical scenery. "The whole place," he wrote, "looks run up in a night . . . and it is impossible to remove the impression that, when Congress is over, the whole place is taken down, and packed up again till wanted . . . Everybody is a bird of passage at Washington." Hawthorne was to find the alert and enterprising Dicey a welcome companion on some of his later battlefield excursions.

Punctually at nine o'clock one morning, Hawthorne waited in a White House anteroom with a Massachusetts delegation whose function it was to present the President of the United States with an ivory-handled whip that had been made in the home state. Waiting, too, were the brusque and irascible secretary of war, Edwin Stanton, and the more agreeable secretary of the treasury, Salmon P. Chase. The whole improbable democratic assembly of important officials and ordinary citizens waited solemnly while the President finished his breakfast. After a half hour, Hawthorne reported, there was a commotion on the staircase "and in lounged a tall, loose-jointed figure, of an exaggerated Yankee port and demeanor, whom (as being about the homeliest man I ever saw, yet by no means repulsive or disagreeable) it was impossible not to recognize as Uncle Abe." The President shook hands all around and listened patiently to the short speech before the presentation of the gift and the inevitable suggestion for its political use. Lincoln responded with a tactful acknowledgment that he would accept the whip as an emblem of peace, rather than punishment. Hawthorne decided that Lincoln reminded him of a tall, gangling, slightly uncouth country schoolteacher — hardly the chief executive of a powerful nation. Lincoln, dressed in a rusty black frock coat and unbrushed pantaloons, was wearing a pair of carpet slippers; his hair was uncombed. His complexion was dark and unhealthy looking; Hawthorne put it down to the "insalubrious atmosphere around the White House."

The ceremony was brief — part of the nonsense of democratic office. Hawthorne had hoped the President would spin one of his famous backwoods yarns, but none was forthcoming. From his brief encounter, he concluded that Lincoln had "a great deal of native sense, no bookish cultivation, no refinement." He felt the President was undoubtedly "honest at heart," but he wondered, too, if Lincoln was not "in some sort, sly — at least, endowed with a sort of tact and wisdom that are akin to craft, and would impel him, I think, to take an antagonist in flank, rather than to make a bull-run at him right in front." Writing to Una about the meeting, he was noticeably modest: "I have shaken hands with Uncle Abe, and have seen various notabilities, and am infested by people who want to exhibit me as a lion."

On March 15, a day sodden with rain, he took a train trip to Harpers Ferry, eighty miles from Washington. The excursion was paid for by the directors of the Baltimore and Ohio Railroad; but Hawthorne insisted, in writing to Una, that he had paid for it (and "two cold collations") with a speech — though "a very short one." Harpers Ferry was a sea of mud, an "almost fathomless puddle." He visited the old engine house — "rusty and shabby like every other work of man's hands in this God-forsaken town" — that John Brown had seized for his fortress. The building was being kept as a monument to the failure of Brown's insurrection. Hawthorne confessed that he was not one of Brown's admirers; he described the abolitionist, in fact, as a "blood-stained fanatic." Nor could he believe that Brown's death had "made the Gallows as venerable as the Cross" — which was, reportedly, Emerson's view. "Nobody was ever more justly hanged," Hawthorne countered. "He won his martyrdom fairly, and took it firmly." It was his view that Brown had been a mad blunderer and that the state of Virginia had blundered, as well, in hastily executing the abolitionist leader. The Virginia officials would have been better advised to show clemency. But even then, Hawthorne qualified his judgment: "Any common-sensible man, looking at the matter unsentimentally, must have felt a certain intellectual satisfaction in seeing [Brown] hanged, if it were only in requital of his preposterous miscalculation of possibilities." Hawthorne's ruthlessly unsentimental, cool, and considered views estranged him from many of his Concord neighbors. The distance along the larch path between the Wayside and Alcott's Orchard House could scarcely be measured in yards.

Nor, when he saw the pathetic, dumbstruck Confederate soldiers imprisoned, symbolically, in the old engine house, could he rise to the vengeful feelings of many of his contemporaries. His public description of them in an article he was to write for the *Atlantic Monthly* was, perhaps, defensively condescending: "Almost to a man, they were simple, bumpkin-like fellows, dressed in homespun clothes, with faces singularly vacant of meaning, but sufficiently good humored." The Rebels were more "respectful" toward their inquisitive visitors than Hawthorne had expected — "more so," he claimed, "than a rustic New-Englander ever dreams of being towards anybody, except perhaps his minister." Writing to Una, he noted simply, "I made acquaintance with some rebel prisoners, and liked them very much." He did not feel it necessary to infect his children with the prejudices of the hour.

In his letter to Una, Hawthorne also mentioned that he planned to visit Manassas, the capture of which had created a scandal in the administration. Sophia considered General McClellan a hero — largely, it seems, for his literary gifts rather than his tactical successes in the field. She thought McClellan's address to his troops a real gem. "Not one word too much, not one word too little," she was to write Annie Fields. "I conceive an adoring army following the lead of such a ringing of true steel. I lay up this with the President's Special Message, and his Orders, as the only papers I have yet cared enough for to cut from the papers." Her ardor apparently was not affected by the reports her husband sent from Washington. "Tell Mama," Hawthorne wrote Una, "that the outcry opened against General McClellan, since the enemy's retreat from Manassas, is really terrible, and almost universal; because it is found that we might have taken their fortifications with perfect ease six months ago, they being defended chiefly by wooden guns. Unless he achieves something wonderful within a week, he will be removed from command, and perhaps shot — at least, I hope so; I never did more than half believe in him."

It was another rumor in a city of rumors. McClellan was not an engaging public figure, and he seems to have been a stickler in matters of discipline. His orders to the troops against singing the popular "John Brown's Hymn" while on march were frequently defied. Radical abolitionists suspected McClellan's loyalties. His military caution may well have been the result of the deviousness of Washington politics and his faulty intelligence reports. Edward Dicey, one of the shrewder observers of the American scene, felt that McClellan had been kept at his post just because of the too-vocal opposition of the antislavery proponents. Dicey sensed that the New England abolitionists, having elected themselves the national conscience, were more endured than appreciated by the broad American public. Hawthorne was to form a more generous estimate of McClellan after meeting him personally in the course of an excursion into former enemy territory that took in Alexandria, Fort Ellsworth, and McClellan's headquarters in the field.

Along the route to Alexandria, Hawthorne had been dismayed by the dead and rotting carcasses of horses and by the great tracts of woodland that had been utterly devastated. "Fifty years will not repair this desolation," he remarked. "An army destroys everything before and around it, even to the very grass." At army headquarters in a captured seminary, the camp was a bustle of activity. A review of the troops, including some 2000 cavalry, was about to begin. Hawthorne was introduced to McClellan, who was mounted on horseback, wearing a dark blue uniform without epaulets. The general bowed "with a good deal of dignity and martial courtesy, but no airs, nor fuss, nor pretension." Waiting while the review was in progress, Hawthorne could hear the shouts of the men, now nearby, now distant, as McClellan and his aides rode through the ranks. "If he is a coward, or a traitor, or a humbug, or anything less than a brave, true and able man," Hawthorne noted in a change of heart, "that mass of intelligent soldiers, whose lives and honor he had in charge, were utterly deceived . . . for they believed in him, and so did I."

Returning to the train that would take them back to Washington, the party of observers met a dozen or more fugitive slaves — men, women, and children in destitute condition. Dicey, one of the touring group, was struck by the miserable state of the people for whom, presumably, the war was being fought. "Anything more helpless or wretched than their aspect, I never saw," he wrote. "Miserably clothed, footsore, and weary, they crouched in the hot sunlight more like animals than men. They seemed to have no idea, no plan, and no distinct purpose." The little band of fugitives was given money and whatever scraps of food could be found. Dicey overheard one of the men, munching on a crust of white bread, complain, "Massa

never gave us food like that." The journalist reflected, "If their idea
of freedom was white bread and rest, they must have been disappointed bitterly!" Hawthorne, too, came to similar conclusions; he
could not decide whether it would have been more merciful to turn
back the runaway slaves or to urge them northward. "My prevalent
idea," he said, "was that, whoever may be benefited by the results of
this war, it will not be the present generation of negroes, the childhood of whose race is now gone forever, and who must henceforth
fight a hard battle with the world, on very unequal terms." In the
grand scheme of reform, the objects of charity were of less concern
than the charity itself.

Hawthorne made another official visit, this time to Fortress
Monroe in Norfolk Harbor. Bridge and his wife, as well as Ticknor,
were among the official party accompanying Vice-President Han-
nibal Hamlin and "other magnates." The harbor was thronged with
warships and transports. Hawthorne was especially intrigued by the
sight of the ironclad *Monitor* — its round turret rising from a mere
"platform of iron" that was floating at surface level, waves sloshing
over it. The ship, he thought, looked like a "gigantic rat-trap . . .
ugly, questionable, suspicious, evidently mischievous." He was surprised, however, by the convenience of the interior accommodations. Still, he regretted that the *Monitor* seemed to mark the end
of certain forms of naval gallantry. "All the pomp and splendor of
naval warfare are gone by," he complained. "Henceforth, there must
come up a race of enginemen and smoke-blackened cannoneers, who
will hammer away at their enemies under the direction of a single
pair of eyes." Already, there was talk of vessels with armaments that
would fire beneath the surface of the water. There would be no external sign of battle, only a great bubbling and foaming, marking "a
deadly fight going on below — and, by and by, a sucking whirlpool
as one of the ships goes down." He had caught an implausible
glimpse of the future.

The Norfolk trip had been disagreeable; Hawthorne found the
company of the vice-president and the other officials not much to
his liking. "I deserted and came back to Washington with Ticknor,"
he wrote Sophia on April 1. "The party has not yet returned; and I
should not be at all surprised, if the rebels were to catch every
mother's son of them — and daughter, too, for there were a good
many ladies among them. That would be an excellent joke; and
nothing would please me better, if Mr. and Mrs. Bridge were not
among them." He had seen everything of interest in Washington, he
said, and now longed to be home. "It has done me a great deal of
good, this constant activity of mind and body, but being perfectly
well, I no longer need it as a medicine."

Yet he would have to remain in the capital a few days longer, he explained, since he had agreed to sit for a portrait by Emanuel Leutze. The forty-six-year-old artist, recently returned from years in Düsseldorf, was at work on his huge mural commissioned for the southwest staircase of the Capitol building, *Westward the Course of Empire Takes Its Way*. Hawthorne, who visited the artist at the site, was impressed both by the grandeur of the conception and the air of secrecy that hovered about the enterprise. He had had to knock at a rough, temporary door and slip his card underneath before being admitted. It was as if the entire strategy of the war were being planned behind the barricade.

On April 1, the day he had written Sophia, he had begun the first of several sittings; he found the German-born Leutze congenial company. Writing to Fields, he ventured an opinion that his portrait was likely to be "the best ever painted of the same unworthy subject. One charm it must needs have — an aspect of immortal jollity and well-to-doneness; for Leutze, when the sitting begins, gives me a first-rate cigar, and when he sees me getting tired, he brings out a bottle of splendid champagne; and we quaffed and smoked yesterday, in a blessed state of mutual good-will, for three hours and a half, during which the picture made a really miraculous progress." Leutze, he said, was "the best of fellows."

The painting, an oval portrait, reflects the conviviality of the sittings and gives Hawthorne an unusually youthful appearance that belied his age and general physical indisposition — sparkling eyes, an alert expression, the flesh firm and healthy. Hawthorne evidently appreciated the flattering touches; he had been feeling his years. While in the capital, he also visited Mathew Brady's Washington studio and posed for two photographic portraits, probably taken by Brady's assistant, Alexander Gardner. He was far less satisfied with the results. In the seated portrait (there was a standing pose, as well) the eyes have a weary cast and are sunk deep beneath the bushy brows; the hair is frosted with age. Sending a copy to Fields, Hawthorne complained, "My hair really is not so white . . . The sun seems to take an infernal pleasure in making me venerable."

By April 10, after a "very disagreeable journey," he was once more in Concord. On the 13th, he wrote Bridge, "It was a pity I did not wait one day longer so as to have shared in the joyful excitement about the Pittsburg Landing victory and the taking of Island No. 10." Sophia, writing to Annie Fields, claimed that the entire family was in "a state of full paean" over her husband's safe return. "Rose burst out in an original song last evening just as she was going to bed, in the tune of John Brown whose 'soul is marching on' — all in reference to Papa's going and returning from Washington. And I helped and sang too, and as we completed each verse we both almost expired with laughter at our own fun. Just so crazy with joy are we."

In July 1862, the *Atlantic* published Hawthorne's report on his recent excursion, "Chiefly About War Matters," bylined by "A Peaceable Man." Publication had involved some irritating compromises, for which Hawthorne himself was partially to blame. "Chiefly About War Matters" was a literary man's exercise in journalism; its harsher opinions were often swathed in a graceful style. Hawthorne, of course, was writing for home consumption, where a foreign correspondent like Edward Dicey, covering the same topics, could afford to be frank and forthright. Even so, Hawthorne was plainly worried about portions of his article — his descriptions of various public officials, including Lincoln, and probably his mildly charitable account of the Confederate prisoners. Sending the manuscript to Fields early in May, he asked for the publisher's opinion. Fields, about to leave for a business trip to New York, sent the article to the printer without looking it over and without responding to Hawthorne's questions.

Writing to Ticknor on May 17, Hawthorne insisted, "I wanted the benefit of someone's opinion besides my own as to the expediency of publishing two or three passages in the article. I have already spoilt it by leaving out a great deal of spicy description and remark, and whole pages of freely expressed opinion, which seemed to me as good as anything I ever wrote, but which I doubted whether the public would bear. The remainder is tame enough in all conscience, and I don't think it will bear any more castration; but still I don't wish to foist an article upon you that might anywise damage the Magazine."

Nevertheless, Hawthorne went on to make some pointed criticisms of the *Atlantic*'s "political complexion"; the magazine, he claimed, was getting "too deep a black Republican tinge." He warned Ticknor, "There is a time pretty near at hand when you will be sorry for it. The politics of the Magazine suit Massachusetts tolerably well (and only tolerably) but it does not fairly represent the feeling of the country at large; and it seems to me that it would be a good policy to be preparing to respond to another, and wiser, and truer mood of public sentiment."

In his uncertainty, Hawthorne may well have infected his publishers with his own caution. When Fields returned to Boston and duly read the article in page proof, he suggested some revisions and deletions. Writing to Hawthorne, he began tactfully, "I knew I should like it hugely and I do. But I am going to ask you to change some of it if you will. Ticknor & I both think it will be politic to alter yr. phrases with reference to the President to leave out the description of his awkwardness & general uncouth aspect. England is reading the Magazine now & will gloat over the monkey figure of 'Uncle Abe' as he appears in yr. paper." Fields also suggested that Hawthorne delete certain remarks about the Southerners that would "outrage the feelings of many Atlantic readers." Somewhat lamely, he concluded, "The whole article is piquant and tip top in all other respects."

Hawthorne was clearly chagrined, but managed to reply in mild fashion. "Dear Fields," he answered on the 23rd, "I have looked over the article under the influence of a cigar and through the medium (but don't whisper it) of a glass of arrack and water; and though I think you are wrong, I am going to comply with your request. I am the most good-natured man, and the most amenable to good advice (or bad advice either, for that matter) that you ever knew — so have it your own way! The whole description of the interview with Uncle Abe, and his personal appearance must be omitted, since I do not find it possible to alter them, and in so doing, I really think you omit the only part of the article really worth publishing. Upon my honor, it seemed to me to have a historical value — but let it go." He specifically asked that Fields send him proofs of the entire article, since he planned, at some date, to publish it "in all its original beauty." He commented, "What a terrible thing it is, to try to get off a little bit of truth into this miserable humbug of a world!"

It was not the last of his difficulties with wartime journalism. In writing the article, Hawthorne had the notion of adding a few marginal asides — written by an editorial alter-ego who commented disparagingly on the author's views. It was an exercise in ambivalence that confused many of his readers, particularly those who admired the franker comments of the article. Some, like Donald Grant Mitchell, wrote to Hawthorne to protest the editorial intrusions; others, learning that Hawthorne had written them himself, accused the author of both running with the hare and riding with the hounds. Even so, Hawthorne could not quite give up the play-acting. In the October issue of the *Atlantic*, he published a letter to the editor, written in the persona of the aggrieved author complaining about the treatment of his article. "My Dear Editor, You can hardly have expected to hear from me again (unless by invitation to the field of honor) after those cruel and terrible notes upon my harmless article in the July Number. How could you find it in your heart (a soft one, as I have hitherto supposed) to treat an old friend and liege contributor in that unheard-of way?"

By that late date, however, the whole affair had become a stale and overdone joke. Some of Hawthorne's exasperations seems to have spilled over into a letter to Horatio Woodman, a member of the Saturday Club, who had written to say that Hawthorne had misconstrued Emerson's remarks on John Brown. Hawthorne responded, "I am sorry if I misquoted Emerson. I never saw the speech or article in which the phrase appeared, and know no more of it than that single sentence, which reached me in England. Your version of it certainly makes a considerable difference, as allowing the reader or auditor (if he pleases) to put John Brown at a somewhat lower elevation than Jesus Christ." Still, Hawthorne refused to give up his point altogether. "But as a matter of mere taste," he added, "surely, it had better never have been said . . . I wish he [Emerson] would not say such things, and deem him less excusable than other men; for his apothegms (though they often have strange life in them) do not so burn and sting his mouth that he is compelled to drop them out of it."

In the full tide of that spring of 1862, not long after Hawthorne's return to Concord, Henry Thoreau, "the bachelor of thought and Nature," died. The forty-four-year-old poet, naturalist, solitary woodsman had been invalided by the advanced stages of tuberculosis; he died in the Yellow House on Main Street on May 6. Only the year before, for reasons of health, Thoreau had made an extensive, two-month trip. In May 1861, he and Horace Mann, Jr., had traveled westward, by way of Niagara Falls, Detroit, and Chicago, to Redwood, 300 miles up the Minnesota River. There, Thoreau had witnessed an encampment of Sioux, under Chief Little Crow, waiting for their annual payment from the federal agents. With his usual sympathy for the outsider — and his distaste for certain physical aspects of life — Thoreau had found it a somewhat demeaning affair, noting that the "half naked" Indians had performed a dance for the amusement of the visitors. He sensed that the Sioux were "quite dissatisfied with the white man's treatment of them & probably have reason to be so." His observation was prophetic; only a few months after his death, the Sioux, under Little Crow, went on a short-lived rampage that would have ended in the mass execution of the Indians, except for Lincoln's clemency.

Thoreau's western trip was the last long excursion he was able to make. In August, he made a short journey to New Bedford to visit friends; in late September, he saw Walden for the last time. By early winter, he was confined to his parlor-bedroom. Bronson Alcott, visiting on New Year's Day, noted in his journal, "To Thoreau, and spend the evening, sad to find, failing and feeble. He is talkative, however; is interested in books and men, in our civil troubles especially, and speaks impatiently of what he calls the temporizing policy of our rulers; blames the people too for their indifferency . . ." Ellery Channing, in his frequent visits, seems to have ignored the probability of his friend's death. But Thoreau, facing the inevitable, told him, "It is better some things should end." In his last, wearying months, resigned to his fate, Thoreau put his manuscripts in order. With the help of his sister Sophia, he wrote some last essays for the *Atlantic*, stipulating that "no sentiment or sentence be altered or omitted without my consent." With an eye to the future, he also insisted that the copyrights revert to him after the essays had been published. He was cheerful and in good spirits. When one of his aunts asked if he had made his peace with God, Thoreau had primly answered, "I did not know we had ever quarreled." He died at nine o'clock on that May morning, uttering some barely audible words — "Moose," "Indian." It was as if he had been called back, for a moment, from some final wilderness beyond the prosaic streets of Concord.

The funeral services were held in the First Parish Church, the coffin covered with wildflowers. Emerson read the eulogy for his friend, Channing recited a few stanzas written for the occasion, Bronson Alcott read excerpts from Henry's writing. It was a lovely, clear, spring afternoon. The schoolchildren of Concord, given the day off, followed the coffin to the New Burying Ground. Hawthorne and Sophia stood quietly at the graveside with the mourners. From there, they walked together to the Old Manse, where, twenty years before, Thoreau had first called on them.

Hawthorne planned to write a tribute to his dead colleague as a preface to one of his abortive romances — a story that, ironically, dealt with the subject of immortality, the never-completed *Dolliver Romance*. But more than a year after Thoreau's death, writing to Fields, Hawthorne was apologizing for the fact that he had made no progress, either on the novel or the preface. The sketch of Thoreau was necessary, he claimed, "because, from a tradition which he told me about this house of mine, I got the idea of a deathless man, which is now taking a shape very different from the original one." His struggles with the theme of death and immortality prompted some thoughts about a writer's obligations. "It seems the duty of a live literary man," he told Fields, "to perpetuate the memory of a dead one, when there is such fair opportunity as in this case — but how Thoreau would scorn me for thinking that *I* could perpetuate *him*! And I don't think so."

ↄ V ↄ

Whatever its personal embarrassments, "Chiefly About War Matters" gave evidence of the vigor of Hawthorne's style; it also whetted Fields's appetite for more of Hawthorne's discontinued English recollections. In July, Hawthorne sent him the manuscript for "Leamington Spa," and Fields promptly wrote the author, "I don't think even your pen ever did a better thing in its way." Immediately after its publication in the October 1862 issue of the *Atlantic*, Fields reported that he was being stopped in the street by friends who wanted to laugh with him over Hawthorne's description of a fat English dowager. The newspapers were all praising the article, he said, and asking "for more of the same sort." For the December issue, Hawthorne supplied "About Warwick," a casual ramble through the English countryside and English history that brought another round of extravagant praise from his publisher: "That absolutely perfect paper is hailed with delight all over the land . . . Lowell and Longfellow chanted high praises to me last night, and Holmes swears you are the Prince of English writers." Hawthorne's memories of Delia Bacon, "Recollections of a Gifted Woman," appearing in the January number, brought a letter of praise from Harriet Beecher Stowe, who had known Delia Bacon when both of them were schoolgirls. Hawthorne answered with a warm note, grateful for Mrs. Stowe's approval. "It seemed to me almost a pity to disturb her in her grave, after so unfortunate a life," he commented, "and yet there was surely enough in what I knew of her to entitle her to honorable remembrance."

From the beginning of the series, Fields had encouraged Hawthorne to consider making a collection of his English essays. "What a delectable *Book* you are building up out of these capital papers," he had written Hawthorne early. "Let us, Author and Publisher, be thinking of a sleek volume, for pretty soon we shall have made one. *We!*" Fields also supplied some financial incentives by offering to pay $100 for articles of ten pages or fewer and an additional $10 a page for articles longer than ten pages. In the face of his publisher's unstinting praise, Hawthorne was cautious — but appreciative. "I am much encouraged by what you say about the English articles," he told Fields, "— not but what I am sensible that you mollify me with a good deal of soft soap, but it is skillfully applied and effects all that you intend it should."

It had been a weary winter, and his efforts at writing had been hampered by a growing lassitude that was partly due to his pessimistic mood and partly to his increasing physical debilities. The war had been brought very close to home — no more distant, in fact, than Alcott's Orchard House. In a postscript to his January 30 letter to Fields, Hawthorne wrote, "Louisa Alcott has returned from Washington with a Typhus fever which looks very threatening. I am afraid she will not come through it."

Hawthorne's summary note marked the end of the thirty-year-old Louisa's brave but brief service for her country in a time of war. In December 1862, she had received her orders to report to Georgetown, where she would serve as a nurse in the Union Hotel Hospital. The news created a flurry of excitement in the Alcott and Hawthorne households. Sophia had helped mark Louisa's clothing with indelible ink, in preparation for the journey. She wrote Una, who was visiting Ebe Hawthorne in Beverly, "Mrs. Alcott says she shall feel helpless without Louisa, and Mr. Alcott says he sends his only son." Louisa was taking games and all her Dickens books to make the soldiers "jolly." "At supper time," Sophia reported, "Julian came in with the portentous news that the battle has at last begun and Fredericksburg is on fire from our guns. So Louisa goes into the very mouth of the war." Her news about Hawthorne was not encouraging: "Papa has not a good appetite, and eats no dinners except a little potato. But he is trying to write, and locks himself into the library and pulls down the blinds."

Louisa Alcott's letters from Washington were eagerly read in Concord. (Eventually, they were published as *Hospital Sketches*, a volume that added considerably to her reputation as a writer of adventure tales and potboilers.) She had thrown herself into her nursing duties with the boyish aggressiveness that was to characterize much of her life. Rising at six every morning, she dressed by gaslight, then proceeded to the wards to help bathe the patients. The hospital, she reported, was a "pestilence box," overcrowded with wounded and diseased soldiers from the Battle of Fredericksburg; she insisted on opening windows and letting in the fresh air. There was no one in command, she complained, "no competent head, male or female, to right matters, and a jumble of good, bad and indifferent nurses, surgeons, and attendants, to complicate the chaos still more." She helped to feed the injured, wrote letters home for her "big babies." With her reckless devotion to a cause, she came down ill, in mid January, with typhoid and became a patient herself. Bronson Alcott went to Washington, where he waited five days until his daughter was well enough to make the trip home. On the train from Boston to Concord, the couple had met Una. Louisa, in a state of delirium, laid her head on Una's shoulders — "looking ghastly and uprolling her eyes," Sophia reported to Annie Fields, "while she was like a sheaf of flames in Una's arms." Abbie May, the youngest of Alcott's daughters, was now taking her meals with the Hawthornes, as a means of getting her out of the sickroom atmosphere. "For three weeks," Sophia told Annie Fields, "I have done nothing but try to do something for her [Louisa] and her family." She tried to console Mrs. Alcott, who every day poured out her griefs and fears to Sophia.

It was clearly in a depressed mood that Hawthorne wrote Henry Bright, on March 8, apologizing for the long delay in their correspondence. "When society is about to be overturned from its foundations," he explained, "the courtesies of life must needs be a little damaged in advance of the general ruin." It was not easy, he claimed, to write "gossiping epistles when an earth-quake is shaking one's writing table." He attempted to explain his own changed attitude: "You must not suppose . . . that I make myself very miserable about the war. The play (be it tragedy or comedy) is too long drawn out, and my chief feeling about it now is a sense of infinite weariness. I want the end to come, and the curtain to drop, and then to go to sleep. I never did really approve of the war, though you may not have supposed so from the violence and animosity with which I controverted your notions about it, when I wrote last. But you are an Englishman, you know, and of course cannot have any correct ideas about our country . . ."

Bright, a collector of autographs, had requested the signatures of prominent American politicians. Hawthorne had even promised to send him the signatures of "Jeff Davis and other rebels," no doubt expecting them from Pierce. But these had not yet arrived. "When they do," he advised Bright, "I will bundle them all up together, honest men and knaves, wise men and fools (but with very little to choose between them, in my opinion), and will send them by some private conveyance." It was another instance of Hawthorne's view that history was full of collectors' items, like some cabinet of curiosities — or, in this case, like a packet of old letters, the postage for which, undoubtedly, would cost more than "the letters or the men who wrote them" were worth. "Meanwhile," he added, "I enclose a card of Old Abe — an honest man, I do believe, but with extra folly enough to make up for his singular lack of knavery."

The public mood, he informed Bright, was all for continuing the war until the South was utterly defeated. Even the Saturday Club had been infected by that attitude. At the last meeting, there had been a number of military men as guests — generals and colonels, fresh from the battlefield. "The tone of feeling was very patriotic," Hawthorne noted, "the mildest men and most abstract philosophers being, as it seemed to me, the most truculent. Emerson is as merciless as a steel bayonet; and I would not give much for a rebel's life if he came within a sword's length of your friend Charles Norton. For Heaven's sake, don't tell him what I say, or he will turn his weapon against me." Longfellow, too, was of the same opinion, although he had not been attending the club meetings since the "terrible calamity." Hawthorne had met him recently in Ticknor's office: "His hair and beard have grown almost entirely white, and he looks more picturesque and more like a poet than in his happy and untroubled days. There is a severe and stern expression in his eyes, by which you perceive that his sorrow has thrust him aside from mankind and keeps him aloof from sympathy." The poet had become, in Hawthorne's view, a man set apart from normal life, like young Goodman Brown or the Reverend Mr. Hooper with his black veil.

"In other respects," Hawthorne admitted, "you might take him to be very much the same man as formerly. I asked him what he felt about the war, and find him immitigable for its continuance. To say the truth, any man must be sensible of the impossibility of ever bringing it to an end, except by completest victory or direst defeat."

In a very personal way, Hawthorne was to come up against the bitter prejudices of wartime politics. Throughout the spring, he had been turning out his English reminiscences with a diligence that belied his mood and health. His industry was partly due to the continuous encouragement of Fields; mostly, it arose from his need to keep his mind and time occupied with work that went easily and pleasantly when he no longer seemed able to manage the imaginative effort required for fiction. By late spring, he not only had agreed to publish his English reminiscences in book form, but, what was unusual for him, he had come up with a title — *Our Old Home*. He had also written an introductory essay, "Consular Experiences," a reminiscence of his term in office, which he advised Fields to keep "fresh" for the book rather than publish in the *Atlantic*.

With an eye toward publicity and sales, Hawthorne had included, in his consular recollections, his criticism of the diplomatic service and his disagreements with the former secretary of state, General Cass, over the abusive treatment of men in the American maritime service. For liveliness — and undoubtedly for an element of controversy — he gave an account of the disreputable New Orleans minister who had been shipped home after his Liverpool debaucheries. "The article has some features that attract the curiosity of the foolish public," he wrote Fields, "being made up of personal narrative and gossip, with a few pungencies of personal satire." He stressed that aspect: "I am not without hope of drawing down upon myself a good deal of critical severity on this score, and would gladly incur more of it if I could do so without seriously deserving censure. The story of the Doctor of Divinity, I think, will prove a good card in this way."

He had also begun to think of dedicating the book — perhaps to Franklin Pierce, who had, after all, made it possible in the first place by sending him to England. Another possibility was a dedication to his English friend Francis Bennoch. The third option was to have no dedication at all. By July 1, however, writing to congratulate Fields for having advantageously sold the English rights to Smith, Elder & Company, he committed himself to dedicating the book to Pierce, "come what may."

The dedication took the form of a preliminary inscription: "To Franklin Pierce, as a slight memorial of a college friendship, prolonged through manhood, and retaining all its vitality in our autumnal years . . ." This was followed by a short, prefatory letter, "To A Friend," dated July 2, from the Wayside. The tone of Hawthorne's letter was distinctly personal, hardly polemical. In it he stated, somewhat sadly, that his English notes had originally been intended to serve as background material for an ambitious work of fiction that he now seemed incapable of writing. "The Present, the Immediate, the Actual has proved too potent for me," he explained. "It takes away not only my scanty faculty, but even my desire for imaginative composition." His preface, he made clear, was intended "publicly [to] assert a personal friendship between a private individual and a Statesman, who has filled what was then the most august position in the world." In passing, he noted Pierce's steadfast loyalty to the "grand idea" of the Union.

Fields, on receiving the dedicatory letter, was cautious — and prompt in his response. "Your dedication to F.P. has a paragraph in it I should be glad to talk over with you when you come here," he wrote Hawthorne on July 3, "But it is a charming bit of writing, that same dedication." On the 15th, he wrote Hawthorne again: "It is the opinion of wiser men than I am in the 'Trade' that the Dedication & Letter to F.P. will ruin the sale of your book. I tell you this in season that you may act upon it if you elect so to do."

Fields's concern had been prompted by discussions with Longfellow, Emerson, and Judge Hoar, among others. Emerson, thinking the matter over, wrote in his journal that Hawthorne was "unlucky in having for a friend a man who cannot be befriended; whose miserable administration admits but one excuse, imbecility. Pierce was either the worst, or he was the weakest, of all our Presidents." Harsh as Emerson's judgment was, it was the prevailing one among the Concord and Boston literati. Fields had good reason for his misgivings, but he did not try to push Hawthorne too strenuously.

Strictly as a political consideration, Hawthorne's gesture was poorly timed. Immediately after sending his dedication, he had set off for Concord, New Hampshire, to attend a Fourth of July celebration at which Franklin Pierce was to give a major address. On several occasions, Pierce had been an outspoken critic of the war and of the Lincoln administration. Aside from his Democratic prejudices, Pierce had more substantial motives. He was one of the few public men who spoke out courageously against the suppression of free speech and the rights of habeas corpus under Lincoln's wartime administration. In his speech, Pierce particularly remarked on the fate of Clement Vallandigham, a harsh and opportunistic critic of Lincoln's policies, who had been summarily arrested, given a military trial without benefit of habeas corpus, and, on the personal orders of Lincoln himself, banished to the Confederacy. "The mere arbitrary will of the President takes the place of the Constitution," Pierce admonished his holiday audience, as Hawthorne sat next to him on the platform, "and the President himself announces to us that it is treasonable to speak or to write otherwise than as he may prescribe; nay, that it is treasonable even to be silent, though we may be struck dumb by the shock of the calamities with which evil counsels, incompetency and corruption have overwhelmed our country." Pierce, who was no master of political timing, either, had chosen an especially unfortunate moment. As he stood on the platform, blasting the administration, news of the victory at Gettysburg, received by telegraph, was circulating through the audience. It had a markedly souring effect on his public pronouncements.

Time was not kind to Pierce. Less than two weeks later, the brutal New York draft riots erupted. Thousands of draft resisters and sympathizers, protesting the conscription laws and the provisions that allowed the rich to buy their sons out of the draft for $300, tore through the streets, burning and looting. Negroes were hanged from lampposts; a terrified black girl was dragged from an orphanage and beaten to death. Abolitionists — or those suspected of being abolitionists — were assaulted in the streets and barely escaped with their lives. Pierce's speech, circulating in the newspapers, was considered one of the precipitating causes of the violence. Unlike Pierce, Hawthorne was far less concerned about the preservation of the Union, and he appears to have cared little about Lincoln's assumption of unprecedented powers. His appearance on the platform with the former President, however, brought his patriotism into question.

After his return to Concord — and after the reports of the New York riots — Hawthorne sent Fields a lengthy and valiant letter. "I find that it would be a piece of poltroonery in me," he wrote his publisher on July 18, "to withdraw either the dedication or the dedicatory letter. My long and intimate personal relations with Pierce render the dedication altogether proper, especially as regards this book . . . and if he is so exceedingly unpopular that his name is enough to sink the volume, there is so much the more need that an old friend should stand by him. I cannot, merely on account of pecuniary profit or literary reputation, go back from what I have deliberately felt and thought it right to do; and if I were to tear out the dedication, I should never look at the volume again without remorse and shame." He conceded to Fields that he had no wish for martyrdom, and he therefore made some revisions in the wording of the final paragraph — "in such a way that, while doing what I know to be justice to my friend, it contains not a word that ought to be objectionable to any set of readers." The revisions, in fact, only strengthened his tribute to Pierce's faith in the "grand idea of an irrevocable Union" while deleting his own muddled misgivings about the outcome of the war. In his letter to Fields, Hawthorne argued that if his audience was put off by his dedication, then they were "a herd of dolts and mean-spirited scoundrels," and he would not bow down to them even if it did mean the loss of "a thousand or two of dollars."

Annie Fields, who visited the Hawthornes late in July, described the affair in her diary: "It is a beautiful incident in Hawthorne's life, the determination at all hazards to dedicate this book to his friend. Mr. P's politics at present shut him away from the faith of patriots, but Hawthorne has loved him since college days and he will not relent."

Her husband took a more circumspect view.

Hawthorne's letter to Fields had been firm but politic; his letter to Lizzie Peabody on the subject of the dedication was full of frustration and anger. Fields, in a last-minute effort to dissuade the author from making a mistake, had attempted to persuade Ellery Channing to take up the matter with Hawthorne. Channing, unwilling to do so, applied to Lizzie — and Lizzie, with her incorrigible right-mindedness, wrote directly to her brother-in-law. Lizzie's letter has not survived; Hawthorne's response, written on the 20th, plainly expressed his irritation. He was dismayed, of course, to find that a matter he considered private was being "bruited about." "I don't know how Ellery Channing gets his literary intelligence," he said testily. "I supposed that this affair of the Dedication was an entire secret between me and the publisher. Even Sophia did not know it, and I have never whispered it to General Pierce." He assured Lizzie that the dedication would not have the "momentous political consequences" she expected. "I expressly say that I dedicate the book to the friend, and decline any present colloquy with the statesman to whom I address merely a few lines expressing my confidence in his loyalty and unalterable devotion to the Union — which I am glad to have the opportunity of saying, at this moment, when all the administration and abolition papers are calling him a traitor. A traitor! Why he is the only loyal man in the country, North or South. Everybody else has outgrown the old faith in the Union . . . but Pierce retains it in all the simplicity with which he inherited it from his father."

With mounting fervor, he went on, "You do not in the least shake me by telling me that I shall be supposed to disapprove of the war, for I always thought that it should have been avoided, although, since it has broken out, I have longed for military success as much as any man or woman of the North." He was still convinced that the war would only effect, "by a horrible convulsion," what might have been brought about by "a gradual and peaceful change." Even the recent successes of the Union armies would not alter the situation, but only suggest to the Rebels that "their best hope lies in the succor of the Peace Democrats of the North, whom they have heretofore scorned . . ." With that kind of alliance, Hawthorne maintained, the old Union would be restored, and slavery would be "prolonged for another hundred years, with new bulwarks, while the people of the North would fancy that they had got the victory and never know that they had shed their blood in vain . . . In that case, woe to the Abolitionists. I offer you in advance the shelter of the nook in our garret which Mary contrived as a hiding place for Mr. Sanborn." He warned, "Free Soil was never in so great danger as now. If the Southern statesmen manage their matters sagaciously, there may come a revulsion of feeling that would give them more than they ever asked. Do you suppose that the pendulum is not to swing back again?"

That he was supremely irritated by his sister-in-law's meddling was plain. "I admire the valor and generous pertinacity with which you come again to the scratch," he told Lizzie, "offering me the same kind of advice as when I was going to write the Life of Cilley, and the Life of Pierce, and which availed nothing, then as now, because I trusted to my own instinct to guide me into my own right way. I do not write (if you will please to observe) for my letter to be read to others . . ." Wearily, Hawthorne concluded, "The older I grow, the more I hate to write notes, and I trust I have here written nothing now that may make it necessary for me to write another."

Many years later, in 1887, long after Hawthorne's death, Lizzie

Peabody was to explain the circumstances of her letter and Hawthorne's embittered reply. Even at the age of eighty-three, writing to
Horatio Bridge, she could resurrect the long-buried animosities of
the past, claiming that Hawthorne "knew *nothing* about slavery —
he had never been at the South. He never saw a slave or a fugitive
slave. He looked at all anti-slavery literature as beneath the consideration of a reasonable man."

As a means of justifying her remarks about her brother-in-law's
political innocence — and her attempts to save him from himself —
she referred to an incident that had occurred, she said, a week after
Hawthorne's angry letter was written. Understandably, she was
mistaken — the episode had happened two months later, though
Lizzie vividly recalled the details. On September 19, the day on
which *Our Old Home* was published, Bryant's *New York Evening
Post* published an old letter, one that Franklin Pierce had written to
his former secretary of war, Jefferson Davis, in 1860. It had been discovered when Union soldiers ransacked the home of the Confederate
president. In his letter, Pierce had prophesied that in the event of a
war brought on "through the madness of Northern abolitionists . . .
the fighting will not be along Mason & Dixon's line merely. It will
be within our own borders, in our own streets." Widely published in
the Northern papers, the letter was clearly regarded as treasonable
by the abolitionists and more rabid war-supporters. Most of them
felt, as Lizzie explained in a rash of underlining, that Pierce had encouraged Davis "to *secede* & trust that the war would at once be
transferred to the streets of the North, where the Democrats would
fight on the *Southern side.*" Published so soon after the frightening
draft riots, which revealed a lack of support for the war and a
hatred of the abolitionists among the urban poor and the working
classes, the accuracy of Pierce's judgment was particularly un-
forgivable.

"We took Bryant's paper," Lizzie continued in her letter to
Bridge, "and when this copy arrived, it happened Sophia was calling at our house & Mary pointed out this letter to her — & offered to
let her take it home to Mr. Hawthorne. But Sophia exclaimed that it
was 'a forgery *of course,*' & she wondered Mr. Bryant could give it a
place in his paper. About an hour after she returned home, however,
she sent down for it saying, 'Mr. Hawthorne wanted to see the
paper' & we sent it up & from that day to the end of his life — Mr.
Hawthorne never named Franklin Pierce to either *Mary* or *me.*"

Despite the worries of James Fields, *Our Old Home* was a success.
Before publication, Fields reported that advance sales were going

"handsomely" and that a second printing had already been ordered. By September, there were 5500 copies in print. Hawthorne's lively preface and the topical nature of his relationship with Pierce had much to do with the book's popularity; another factor was the sometimes caustic tone with which Hawthorne described English life and English habits — "the little acrimonies of the moment" he had lifted from his English journals. *Our Old Home* suited the mood of many Northern readers who felt that English sympathy with the South only underscored the hypocrisy of England's antislavery sentiments. Considering that most of the articles had appeared in the *Atlantic Monthly,* the book was widely reviewed and praised. The *Albion* pointed out that Hawthorne's criticisms of the English were hardly as biting as those of several generations of English satirists who had written about American manners. The *Boston Transcript* commended the book's "manly truthfulness," and Greeley's *New-York Tribune* found "the solemn pomposity and inflated conceit" of the English tempting game for any humorist. The *North American Review* praised the book's "humor and kindliness" and its exquisite bits of "sky and landscape painting." Comments on Hawthorne's dedication were generally low-keyed; some newspapers found it an unpardonable "intrusion" or simply an indulgence in "pious sentiment." In extolling Pierce, the *Tribune* argued, Hawthorne had mistaken "a windmill for a giant." In reaction to Hawthorne's praise of Pierce's loyalty, Garrison's *Liberator* quipped, "Mr. Hawthorne is good at fiction."

In England, where the book was published simultaneously, the first edition sold out quickly. Some reviewers attributed Hawthorne's acerbity to the usual Northern anti-British sentiments. *Puck,* in a tart and spritely review, claimed that Hawthorne had collected all his "caricatures and libels" while enjoying the hospitality of the country, then waited until the Yankee public would pay good money to see the English abused. It was more incensed with Hawthorne's remark that English girls seemed "all homely alike," compared with the "trim little damsels" of America, and by his description of the fat English dowager, who seemed "solid beef and streaky tallow . . . made up of steaks and sirloins." Hawthorne was referred to as a "Liverpool Lovelace," a "drawing-room idol," and a "lady-killer." The reviewer for *Blackwood's Magazine* charged that during his English visit, Hawthorne had obviously hidden "his true character under a benignant mask." Hawthorne's friend Henry Bright, in an otherwise favorable review in the *Examiner,* remarked, "Nothing, it is true, can be kinder or more generous than the words in which he distantly alludes to individuals; nothing can be more cynical and contemptuous than the expressions he uses of us as a race." Writing privately to Hawthorne, Bright explained, "Don't think me very ungrateful for my abuse of your abuse of English ladies. You see I positively could not help it. An inevitable lance had to be broken, both for the fun of it and the truth of it. It really was too bad, some of the things you say. You talk like a cannibal."

Summing up the British reviews, Hawthorne wrote Fields that the English critics "seem to think me bitter against their countrymen, and it is perhaps natural that they should, because their self-conceit can accept nothing short of indiscriminate adulation; but I really think that Americans have more cause than they to complain of me. Looking over the volume, I am rather surprised to find that, whenever I draw a comparison between the two peoples, I almost invariably cast the balance against ourselves." He made no great claims for *Our Old Home*, finding it "not a good nor a weighty book"; he felt it did not deserve "any great amount either of praise or censure." He was, in fact, weary of the controversy it had aroused. "I don't care about seeing any more notices of it," he told Fields.

He was probably unaware of some of the more bitter private criticisms. Emerson, to whom he sent a copy, told Annie Fields that the book was "pellucid but not deep." In her diary, she noted, "He [Emerson] has cut out the dedication and letter as others have done." Another member of the Saturday Club, Charles Eliot Norton, thought the dedication "the bitterest of satires." "What a blow his friend has dealt to the weakest of ex-Presidents," Norton wrote to George Curtis; he was, he said, "half annoyed, half amused at Hawthorne."

Harriet Beecher Stowe, writing to Fields, exclaimed, "Do tell me if our friend Hawthorne praises that arch-traitor Pierce in his preface and your loyal firm publishes it. I never read the preface, and have not yet seen the book, but they say so here, and I can scarcely believe it of you, if I can of him . . . What! patronize such a traitor to our faces! I can scarce believe it."

In December, Hawthorne performed another act of personal loyalty to his old friend Franklin Pierce. Pierce's wife, Jane, had died on December 2, in Andover. Hawthorne, weak and frail himself, nevertheless journeyed to Boston. There, he stayed overnight with the Fieldses in order to meet with Pierce the next day. The former President was transporting the body of his wife to Concord, New Hampshire, for burial.

Hawthorne, needing some encouragement from his publisher, brought with him the first chapter of *The Dolliver Romance*, "a story which he says he shall never finish," Annie Fields commented in her diary. "J.T.F. says it is very fine, yet sad. Hawthorne says in it, 'pleasure is only pain greatly exaggerated,' which is queer to say the least, if not untrue." Annie Fields thought Hawthorne seemed more ill and nervous than usual, but "as grand as ever, and as true. He does not lose that all-saddening smile, either."

Hawthorne found his old friend "overwhelmed with sadness," needing companionship, and he decided to travel with Pierce to New Hampshire for the burial. After the services, he accompanied Pierce to the small Concord cemetery; they stood, two aged men in the bitter cold, the ground hard and unremitting under their feet. Hawthorne had occasion to remember the "exquisite courtesy" of his friend; in the midst of his grief, Pierce had gently turned up Hawthorne's collar to protect him from the biting winds.

On his return, Hawthorne stopped in Boston to spend another evening with Fields and his wife. Sitting in the book-lined parlor, he had engaged the publisher in a spirited discussion of the *Atlantic Monthly*. Hawthorne acknowledged that it was the most ably edited magazine around, and that it was bound to be successful — except for one hazard. "I fear its politics — beware!" he warned Fields. "What will you do when in a year or two, the politics of the country change?" (It was his only allusion to the effect the bitterness of the political climate had had on him.) Fields answered that he would patiently wait until that time should come.

The sad visit with Pierce and the burial had put him in a reflective mood. As the evening darkened, Hawthorne recalled his boyhood in Maine: the winter nights of skating on Lake Sebago until midnight, the great dark hills hovering above the bright surface of the lake in brilliant moonlight, the long summer days when he roamed the woods in solitude, gun in hand. Lingering over those scenes, he said, "How sad middle life looks to people of erratic temperaments. Everything is beautiful in youth — all things are allowed to it."

↭ VI ↭

The habit of self-reflection, of self-analysis, had provided Hawthorne with the fictive premise for one of his early, ingenious stories, "Monsieur du Miroir," his long, sometimes playful, causerie on his mirror image and alter-ego, that secret sharer who followed him through life. For all its playfulness, the tale had ended on a somber note. Hawthorne's narrator, reflecting on the self-image that seemed to follow him "to the remotest regions and into the deepest privacy," had compared the attempt to escape his "dark twin" to the "hopeless race that men sometimes run with memory, or their own hearts, or their moral selves."

Throughout the long bleak winter of 1863–1864, Hawthorne had little else but time for that unbidden guest who followed him into the privacy of his thoughts. Physically, he was shrunken and worn, subject to fits of seemingly incurable restiveness that were followed by unavoidable fatigue. He had little inclination to read or write. "I have fallen into a quagmire of disgust and despondency with respect to literary matters," he wrote Donald Grant Mitchell. "I am tired of my own thoughts and fancies and my own mode of expressing them." Fields, visiting in January, found Hawthorne sitting before the fireplace, gazing into the flames, his gray dressing gown wrapped round him "like a Roman toga." It had become necessary, so Annie Fields reported in her diary, to protect him against unwanted visitors: "General Barlow and Mrs. Howe had sent word they were coming to call, so Mrs. Hawthorne had gone out to walk (been thrown out on picket-duty, Mrs. Stowe said) and had left word at home that Mr. Hawthorne was ill and could see no one."

Julian, now seventeen and in his freshman year at Harvard, came home on weekends. He was aware that his conversations with his father over the past two or three years had been taking a more serious, though not somber, turn. "Our talks . . ." he recalled, "were of realities, past or to come: wise counsel disguised and illuminated with his unfailing humor." One of the more serious conversations of his first term, evidently, was on the topic of money. Julian had told him of borrowing $10 from James Fields; the incident revealed the granite of Hawthorne's nature. Hawthorne had promptly written to Fields, "Please to record it [the money] against me and don't let the little scamp have any more. An uncle (and your kindness places you in the same category) is a very dangerous member of the family . . . I want him never to be a borrower and to choose to suffer every inconvenience rather than that . . . I have already lectured him on the subject."

Julian also recalled from that final winter a moment of apprehension that he had experienced, once, when he had been reading aloud Longfellow's *Evangeline* to his father. Hawthorne had listened "silently and intently: and, as I read the last verses, a feeling came upon me that there was something in the occasion more memorable than I had thought of, so that I could hardly conclude without a faltering of the voice. That was my fore-glimpse of the truth . . ." But it had only been a brief intuition; afterward, he was convinced his father would improve.

The stalled *Dolliver Romance* weighed heavily on Hawthorne's spirit throughout the winter. Writing woefully to Fields in February, he claimed, "I hardly know what to say to the public about this abortive Romance, though I know pretty well what the case will be. I shall never finish it." It troubled him that the first installment had already been set in print, and he suggested to Fields that an announcement be made in the *Atlantic Monthly,* in the vein of his editorial asides: "Mr. Hawthorne's brain is addled at last, and, much to our satisfaction, he tells us that he cannot possibly go on with the Romance announced on the cover of the January magazine. We consider him finally shelved, and shall take early occasion to bury him under a heavy article." Although the tone was comic, it covered a deep-seated fear of Hawthorne's that his mind had been affected by his apparently consuming illness.

Reverting to a more serious mood, he told Fields that he would not be able to finish his book "unless a great change comes over me; and if I make too great an effort to do so, it will be my death; not that I should care much for that, if I could fight the battle through and win it, thus ending a life of much smoulder and scanty fire in a blaze of glory. But I should smother myself in mud of my own making . . ." He advised Fields, "I am not low-spirited, nor fanciful nor freakish, but look what seem to be the realities in the face, and am ready to take whatever may come." He added a final proviso: "This letter is for your own eye, and I wish especially that no echo of it may come back in your note to me."

In March, however, he was well enough to take a trip southward, accompanied by William Ticknor. Sophia had hoped that the two friends might travel to Cuba; she thought the tropical climate would restore her husband's health. But neither Hawthorne nor Ticknor wanted to make definite plans, preferring to travel south, day by day, in easy stages. On March 28, Hawthorne stayed overnight in Boston with the Fieldses. Annie Fields commented in her diary that Hawthorne's "invalid appearance" had shocked her: "He has become quite deaf, too. His limbs are shrunken but his great eyes still burn with their lambent fire." Hawthorne complained wearily, "Why does Nature treat us so like children! I think we could bear it if we knew our fate. At least, I think it would not make much difference to me now what became of me." He said he regretted that "the good old custom of coming together to get drunk" had gone out of fashion: "Think of the delight of drinking in pleasant company and then lying down to sleep a deep strong sleep." His own sleep was troubled and thin. Through the night, Annie Fields could hear him walking in his room, "heavily moving, moving as if indeed waiting, watching for his fate."

Yet at breakfast Hawthorne had been talkative, discussing his neighbor Bronson Alcott, whom he pronounced "one of the most excellent of men." A few days before, Alcott had asked if there was some misunderstanding between their two families and Hawthorne had told him no, but that it "was not possible to live upon amicable terms with Mrs. Alcott." He added that in "time of illness or necessity," he was sure they would be the best of helpers to each other. "I clothed all this in velvet phrases, that it might not seem too hard for him to bear," Hawthorne said, "but he took it all like a saint."

On the following day, Ticknor and his author took the train to New York, putting up at the Astor House. The weather had turned bad — cold, with a blustering rain "worse than a northeaster." Ticknor's letters to Sophia were encouraging. "I do not think that Mr. Hawthorne suffered any inconvenience from the journey . . ." he wrote on the 30th. "He is looking better, and says he feels very well." On the following day, with the storm continuing, they had remained at the hotel. Hawthorne was eating well: "He seems afraid he shall eat too much, as he says his appetite is good. I assure him he is very prudent . . . He slept well last night, and is evidently gaining strength." On April 3, Ticknor reported that on the next day, weather permitting, they would move on to Philadelphia.

In Concord, Sophia continued to worry. A letter from Horatio Bridge arrived, asking about the postponement of Hawthorne's romance, announced in the *Atlantic Monthly*. In her husband's absence, Sophia unburdened herself of all her anxieties. "Alas, it was no 'author's excuse,' which was published in the Atlantic," she wrote on April 5, "but a most sad and serious truth. Mr. Hawthorne has really been very ill all winter, and not well, by any means, for a much longer time; not ill in bed, but miserable on a lounge or sofa, and quite unable to write a word, even a letter, and lately unable to read." She confessed that she felt "the wildest anxiety about him, because he is a person who has been immaculately well all his life . . . But he has wasted away very much, and the suns in his eyes are collapsed, and he has had no spirits, no appetite, and very little sleep." Hawthorne's "absolute repugnance to see a physician" had been weighing on her "like a millstone." She blamed Concord, wished that they might sell the Wayside and move away: "He needs the damp sea-air for health, comfort and enjoyment." She thought, too, that the war was a contributing cause: "The state of our country has, doubtless, excessively depressed him. His busy imagination has woven all sorts of sad tissues."

From the Continental Hotel in Philadelphia, on April 7, Ticknor sent welcome news. They had had their first real sunshine since leaving Boston and after dinner had taken a drive through Fairmount Park. The ride may have tired Hawthorne and he had gone to bed at nine — although that was his usual practice. At breakfast in the morning, he was "bright" and said that he was feeling better. If Hawthorne was up to it, they might take the train to Baltimore, but they had made no definite plans. "I tell him we will float along and see what 'turns up,' " Ticknor remarked.

The journey had ended in Philadelphia, however. Ticknor, who had given Hawthorne his coat during the carriage ride, had come down with a cold, which became progressively worse, and he was confined to his bed in the hotel. On Saturday, Hawthorne wrote to Fields reporting that a physician had been called in and had "belabored" Ticknor with pills and powders, then "proceeded to cup, and poultice, and blister according to the ancient rule of that tribe of savages." Hawthorne wrote caustically, "The consequence is that poor Ticknor is already very much reduced, while the disorder flourishes as luxuriantly as if that were the doctor's sole object." His room was next to Ticknor's, and, although he was a clumsy nurse and about as useful to his sick friend as "a hippopotamus," he had followed the doctor's orders. He had also made some observations on "medical science and the sad and comic aspects of human misery." He asked Fields to write Sophia and explain the situation; he did not think he would have an opportunity to do it himself.

Early in the morning of April 10, Ticknor died. Hawthorne, in a dazed condition, sat by his dead friend until some member of the family arrived. In his distraught state, he was convinced that death had made a mistake and claimed the wrong man. A Philadelphia acquaintance, a Mr. Childs, had also assisted at the deathwatch; Hawthorne was both touched by the gesture and irritated by Childs's fussing attentions to him.

Returning home, Hawthorne stopped in Boston, staying overnight with Fields. He was still in such a shaken condition that he was unable to eat. Searching for his slippers in his luggage, he inadvertently blurted out, "Oh! I remember, that cursed Childs watched me so I forgot everything." He told Fields that death would not be so terrible if it were not for the undertakers: "It was dreadful to think of being handled by those men."

Arriving in Concord, he found there was no carriage to take him home. In a kind of panic, he had walked the distance to the Wayside, pale and shaking and sweating profusely. "He came back unlooked for that day," Sophia later wrote the Fieldses, "and when I heard a step on the piazza, I was lying on a couch and feeling quite indisposed. But as soon as I saw him I was frightened out of all knowledge of myself — so haggard, so white, so deeply scored with pain and fatigue was the face, so much more ill than I ever saw him before." In the privacy of his home, Hawthorne broke down and wept at the death of Ticknor and the ordeal of the past few days. "There are lines ploughed on his brow," Sophia wrote, "which were never there before." For weeks after, Hawthorne could not rouse himself from a kind of stupor. The memories of the hotel room and the deathwatch, the nightmare journey, hovered behind his glazed and sunken eyes. Sophia read to him. Only once, while she was reading Thackeray aloud, did he manage a fugitive smile.

Early in May, Franklin Pierce visited the Wayside. He was deeply concerned at the feeble condition of his friend, although Hawthorne by then was able to walk — but with marked hesitancy. Pierce suggested that they take a trip together. He had a comfortable carriage and they would make a leisurely journey through the New Hampshire countryside in the burgeoning spring. Sophia, writing Annie Fields about the plan, was optimistic: "I think the serene jog-trot in a private carriage into country places, by trout streams and to old farm houses away from care and news, will be very restorative." On the next day, she wrote Fields, expressing her concern about Hawthorne's health and his unwillingness to see a doctor. She wondered if Fields could secretly arrange for Oliver Wendell Holmes to look at her husband "in some ingenious way . . . as a friend; but with his experienced, acute observation, to look at him also as a physician . . . I wish Dr. Holmes would feel his pulse; I do not know how to judge of it, but it seems to me irregular."

Holmes did, in fact, try to assess Hawthorne's symptoms. He called at the Bromfield House, where Hawthorne was to meet Pierce before beginning their trip on May 12. Hawthorne was not in, but Holmes caught sight of the author coming painfully along the street. The two men walked and chatted; Holmes patiently and unobtrusively questioned Hawthorne about his physical condition. Hawthorne complained of "boring pain, distention, difficult digestion" — most of the symptoms persistent. Holmes noted that Hawthorne looked shrunken and wasted and that his step was very faltering. Hawthorne seems to have mentioned his greatest worry: his fear that his mind might be going, that his inability to work was symptomatic. Holmes quietly convinced him that there was nothing wrong with his mental powers. Hawthorne, he noted, was as hesitant and bashful as always — an "unschooled maiden." But Hawthorne's "calm despondency" about his own condition seemed a bad sign.

Annie Fields, who learned Holmes's private diagnosis, reported it in her diary with the cruel terseness of fact: "O.W.H. thinks the shark's tooth is upon him, but would not have this known."

On May 12, Hawthorne and Pierce began their journey, stopping briefly at Andover. When they reached Concord, the weather was poor, and Hawthorne seemed too feeble to go farther. It was not until the following Monday that they began their slow carriage ride through the countryside, the orchards turning pink and white with bloom. Pierce, who earlier had had hopes for Hawthorne's recovery, began to realize the seriousness of his friend's condition. He suspected, as he later wrote Horatio Bridge, that the seat of the disease was "in the brain or spine or both." He felt it was incurable. Hawthorne had complained of feeling "stupid." Pierce noticed that his mind seemed sluggish but "perfectly clear when roused." It was also noticeable that Hawthorne was walking only with great difficulty and that the use of his hands seemed impaired. On Tuesday, during their ride to Center Harbor, Pierce sensed that Hawthorne was becoming "quite helpless," although the carriage ride seemed to ease his terrible restlessness. On Wednesday, the 18th, Hawthorne insisted on continuing their journey in the afternoon, despite Pierce's suggestion that they remain at the hotel. As they rode along, Hawthorne had pointedly asked if Pierce had read the accounts of Thackeray's calm and quiet death. Pierce acknowledged that he had. In a low voice, Hawthorne remarked, "What a boon it would be, if when life draws to its close, one could pass away without a struggle." When they arrived at the Pemigewasset House in Plymouth, around six that evening, Pierce determined to stay there for the next several days. He planned to write Sophia to ask her and Una to join them.

That evening, Hawthorne took tea and toast in his room, resting and dozing on a couch. The two rooms were adjoining, and when Hawthorne retired at nine, Pierce left the connecting door open. Around one or two o'clock in the morning, he looked in on Hawthorne, who was sleeping peacefully on his side. Two hours later, awakened by a barking dog, Pierce was surprised to find that Hawthorne had not moved at all. Placing his hand upon his forehead and temple, he realized that Hawthorne was dead.

On the May morning that Sophia, planning to accompany her husband to Boston, had walked with him to the waiting carriage, she had broken down and cried. Hawthorne turned his quiet gaze on twelve-year-old Rose and said nothing. Rose Hawthorne was to remember that final glimpse of her father very forcefully many years later. "He hated failure, dependence, and disorder, broken rules and weariness of discipline, as he hated cowardice," she wrote. "I cannot express how brave he seemed to me." She was convinced that her father knew what her mother vaguely suspected, that he would never return. Hawthorne had taken the journey to meet death elsewhere, on the road; his family would not be burdened with the last, demeaning moments of mortality. The news of her husband's death stunned Sophia; with her illimitable faith, she had been hoping there would be a recovery.

On May 21, the body was returned to Concord; the funeral was scheduled for the afternoon of May 23. Sophia experienced a curious feeling of exaltation. "I wish to speak to you, Annie," she wrote Annie Fields in a strange letter — a series of carefully wrought statements extolling the virtues of her dead husband: "A person of a more uniform majesty never wore mortal form. In the most retired privacy, it was the same as in the presence of men." Each precisely modulated sentence, every self-consciously written paragraph, continued the litany: "The sacred veil of his eyelids he scarcely lifted to himself — such an unviolated sanctuary as was his nature, I, his inmost wife, never conceived nor knew."

She wrote, "A tenderness so infinite — so embracing — that GOD's alone could surpass it. It folded the loathesome leper in as soft a caress as the child of his home affections — was not that divine!"

Annie Fields preserved the letter for fifty years. A note in her hand stated, "The original of a precious and extraordinary letter written by Mrs. Nathaniel Hawthorne while her husband lay dead."

On the morning of May 23, Henry Wadsworth Longfellow wrote a hasty note to his friend Charles Sumner. Sumner had heard, first, of the death of a mutual acquaintance, Robert Mackintosh, and then of the death of Hawthorne. On the 21st, he had written Longfellow in the oddly complaining and congratulatory vein in which survivors of the death of a friend greet each other. "One by one, almost in *twos*, they seem to go," Sumner had written. "We shall be alone soon. I forget. I shall be alone. You have children. Life is weary and dark — full of pain and enmity. I am ready to go at once. And still I am left."

Longfellow's reply was calmly detached: "It is only too true. Mackintosh is gone, after being ill all Winter. His disease was dropsy and heart-complaint. Tom went out in the last steamer to look after the family, and to bring them here, if they like to come."

He added, "And Hawthorne too! I am waiting for the carriage which is to take Greene, Agassiz and myself to Concord this bright spring morning to his funeral!" There were further matters: the normal civilities, financial details, congratulations to Sumner on a recent Senate report — the usual business of life. Longfellow also offered a bit of consolation to his old friend: "But do not be disheartened. You have much work of the noble kind to do yet. Let us die standing."

In his letter, Longfellow had mentioned the spring weather; it was to figure prominently in the opening stanza of the graceful lyric he would write to commemorate Hawthorne's funeral.

> *How beautiful it was, that one bright day*
> *In the long week of rain!*
> *Though all its splendor could not chase away*
> *The omnipresent pain.*

The services on that soft May afternoon took place in the Unitarian Church in Concord. The town, as Longfellow recalled it, was "white with apple-blooms"; only the mildest wind sifted through the leafy, green elms along Main Street. The Reverend James Freeman Clarke, who twenty-two years before had married Hawthorne and Sophia, officiated. On the coffin decked with flowers, James Fields placed the uncompleted manuscript of *The Dolliver Romance*. From the church, the slow procession moved to the hilltop plot in Sleepy Hollow Cemetery. There, after the brief words, Franklin Pierce scattered a few final blossoms into the open grave.

As the carriage left the cemetery, Sophia, dazed, caught sight of her husband's colleagues in that uncertain venture, the making of an American literature. Longfellow, Holmes, Whittier, Lowell, and Emerson bared their heads as the carriage passed.

Epilogue

AFTER DEATH came the measured slow-march of public praise. From the beginning, the eulogies and obituaries remarked on the passing of one of the acknowledged masters of American fiction. The distinctiveness of Hawthorne's style, his literary achievements, were extolled. His English reputation was recalled; that recognition was a mark of importance in America's still-scant literary history. Sophia, in her strange, almost exalted grief, took such praise as the confirmation of her lifelong beliefs.

She was not happy, however, about any revelation of her husband's private life. In particular, she was distressed by reports that Oliver Wendell Holmes had been circulating, regarding his brief medical consultation with Hawthorne on a Boston street. His recollections of that sad afternoon meeting were to be published in the July issue of the *Atlantic Monthly*, prefacing the initial episode of *The Dolliver Romance*. Sophia was concerned about any reference to Hawthorne's mental capabilities during the final stages of his illness. Writing to James Fields on May 21, she pleaded, "Dear Mr. Fields, Will you be kind enough to refrain from saying a word to my sister about what Mr. Hawthorne said of fear of not becoming able to — of not being himself as before because on any such suggestion I fear my sister would talk of it to others and inevitably exaggerate and I wish to guard him from a word being said that would have grieved him here — and you know his mind had not yet a shadow — Oh I wish Dr. Holmes would not say he feared it — Why not leave him intact as he is — Oh do try to shield him dear Mr. Fields."

Una, even more disturbed by Holmes's story, added an embittered postscript: "You see this agony is almost too great for Mamma to bear. The thought that a shadow should fall on his clear mind is an arrow all poison in her heart. I shall not easily forgive the person who sent it into her heart. It was too cruel. There would be nothing but peace if it were not for this. Her agitation is terrible this morning. Oh I wish these few days were over."

The English critic Richard Holt Hutton, writing in the *Spectator*, spoke of Hawthorne's "ghostly genius." "He had been called a mystic, which he was not," Hutton declared, "and a psychological dreamer, which he was in very slight degree. He was really the ghost of New England — we do not mean the 'spirit,' nor the 'phantom'; but the ghost in the older sense in which that term is used as a thin rarefied essence which is to be found somewhere behind the physical organization." The metaphor was, in itself, rarefied, but Hutton had his point in attempting to define Hawthorne's habit as a writer of distancing himself from ordinary life and contemporary affairs.

Edward Dicey, writing in the July issue of *Macmillan's Magazine*, recalled the handsome but failing man he had met in Washington and later in Concord. Dicey addressed himself to the complicated problem of Hawthorne's inescapable relationship to the political issues of his time. It was impossible, Dicey contended, for a man like Hawthorne to be "an enthusiastic partisan." The tenor of Hawthorne's mind, his imaginative capacities, put him "altogether out of harmony with the passion of the hour. If he spoke his own mind freely, he was thought by those around him to be wanting in attachment to his country . . . Moreover, if I am to speak the truth, the whole nature of Hawthorne shrank from the rough wear and tear inseparable from great popular movements of any kind. His keen intellect served to show him the weaknesses and vanities and vulgarities of the whole class of reformers. He recognized that their work was good; he admired the thoroughness he could not imitate; but somehow the details of popular agitation were strangely offensive to him." Dicey, to be sure, was unfamiliar with Hawthorne's younger, wandering life, his taste for country taverns and rural fairs. That side of Hawthorne's character would become apparent — though discreetly — only with the publication of his notebooks. Still, Dicey was correct in assessing Hawthorne's aloofness, a quality that made him a perpetual observer rather than a casual joiner. Dicey felt that Hawthorne's sensitivity sometimes "obscured the usual accuracy of his judgment." He related a conversation he had had with the American writer, following Hawthorne's meeting with Lincoln, whom Hawthorne had obviously found a bit coarse and undignified. "Still," Dicey noted, "I can recall how, after he had been describing to me the impression left upon him by his visit to the White House, an eminently characteristic doubt crossed his mind as to whether he was not in the wrong. 'Somehow,' he said, 'though why I could never discern, I have always observed that the popular instinct chooses the right man at the right time.' " After this expression of faith in the democratic process, however, Hawthorne had added a demurrer: "As you have seen Lincoln," he told Dicey, "I wish you could have seen Pierce too; you would have seen a real gentleman . . ."

Hawthorne's American critics were not always so dispassionate on the question of his politics. George William Curtis, in a lengthy assessment that James Fields declined for the *Atlantic Monthly* but which was published in the *North American Review*, fully acknowledged Hawthorne's literary stature, but faulted the political man. Curtis, one of the most articulate spokesmen for the antislavery cause, was thoroughly committed to the progress of the war. He scored Hawthorne's seeming indifference to the issues, noting that in his preface to *The Marble Faun*, while the country had been engaged in a "fierce debate," Hawthorne, with "calm ennui," complained that his homeland offered so few fictional possibilities — no picturesque or gloomy wrongs, only a "commonplace prosperity." "Our great romancer," Curtis claimed, "looked at the American life of his time . . . and could see only monotonous sunshine." Although Hawthorne could produce "harrowing allegories" of the theme of sin in Salem village, he "did not see a Carolina slave-pen or found in it only a tame prosperity." Curtis maintained, "The character of his genius isolated him, and he stood aloof from the common interests. Intent upon studying men in certain aspects, he cared little for man; and the high tides of collective emotion among his fellows left him dry and untouched."

Herman Melville was to write the most private tribute to his fellow author, one that was unclouded by the prejudices of the moment. He had been deeply shocked by the news of Hawthorne's death. Either then, or perhaps a bit later, he wrote a brief lyric, titled "Monody," that was quite different from the gracious but conventional elegy Longfellow had published in the *Atlantic*. The opening stanza of Melville's poem, which was not published until 1891, the year of his own death, suggested a deep personal loss:

> To have known him, to have loved him
> After loneness long;
> And then to be estranged in life,
> And neither in the wrong;
> And now for death to set his seal —
> Ease me, a little ease, my song!

To Melville, Hawthorne still spoke with a sense of directness that might have been overlooked by a general reader. A year after Hawthorne's death, in the anniversary month, Melville, taking up *Mosses from an Old Manse*, the book that had marked their Berkshire meeting, was stirred once again by Hawthorne's plumbing of the depths of human experience. He seems to have felt a particular closeness to the Hawthorne of "Monsieur du Miroir," underscoring two passages. Where Hawthorne's narrator, commenting on his own death, wonders about the fate of his mirror image, "Will he linger where I have lived to remind the neglectful world of one who staked much to win a name . . . ?" Melville, underscoring the final phrase, wrote in the margin, "What a revelation." And where Hawthorne, contemplating the inevitable extinction of the shadowy Monsieur du Miroir, remarks, "He will pass to the dark realm of Nothingness, but will not find me there," Melville noted, "This trenches upon the uncertain and the terrible."

The themes of death and extinction were evidently uppermost in Melville's mind, for he underscored another passage, this one from "The Celestial Rail-road." Hawthorne had described the superb indifference with which the citizens of Vanity Fair met the deaths of their fellow men, who seemed to vanish like soap bubbles in the midst of their activities. The survivors were so accustomed "to such little accidents that they went on with their business, as quietly as if nothing had happened." Poignantly, Hawthorne's narrator adds, "But it was otherwise with me."

Melville, underscoring the final remark, commented, "Nothing can be finer than this." Even from the grave, Hawthorne still had the old power to reach out and touch him personally.

↩ II ↪

In her letters to friends, Sophia suggested that she lived now only for the children. "They are all so bright and good," she wrote Horatio Bridge, "that my life is a thanksgiving for them . . . When they are settled in life, I should like to sleep as *he* did, if God please. Affairs perplex and tire me very much, yet I am in great peace." Rose, she informed Bridge, was enrolled in Dr. Lewis' "famous gymnastic school" in Lexington; Julian was reading logic and metaphysics at Harvard. Una was "keeping up her music and Latin."

At first, Sophia had resisted James Fields's suggestion that she edit Hawthorne's private notebooks for publication in the *Atlantic Monthly*; she felt they were too personal in nature. Writing apologetically to Annie Fields two months after her husband's death, she took refuge in Hawthorne's own metaphor: "The veil he drew around him no one should lift. This is the way I view it now . . . I wish I could gratify you both by doing whatever you desire." In time, however, she relented and under Fields's guidance began editing the journals for publication. In January 1866, selections from Hawthorne's American notebooks began publication in monthly installments in the *Atlantic*.

With her instinctive reticence, Sophia brought a nineteenth-century standard to Hawthorne's sometimes graphic private language. All references to Hawthorne's drinking were deleted from the texts as she copied them. Even mild or comic references to human anatomy — particularly relating to descriptions of the children when they were taking baths or getting ready for bed — were expunged. (Sophia's sense of family privacy was so exacting that when it became a question of publishing Hawthorne's Lenox account, "Twenty Days with Julian & Little Bunny," she felt she had to obtain Julian's consent.) The result was that the picture of Hawthorne as a man who could be down-to-earth in his private moments was considerably altered. In very direct fashion, Sophia tempered the blunter forms of Hawthorne's vocabulary: "pimp" was replaced by "agent"; "whores" was translated as "women." Later critics might complain of editorial tampering, but it was clearly the standard of the age. It was the same standard Hawthorne himself had applied when transcribing his notes into fiction or editing the sometimes saltier versions of his anonymously published stories for book publication.

Sophia yielded, as well, to Fields's suggestion that the material, with additions, should be published in book form. The publication of a two-volume *Passages from the American Notebooks of Nathaniel Hawthorne*, in November 1868, however, seems to have marked the beginning of a serious rift between Hawthorne's widow and his publisher. A disappointing fee for the English rights (Smith, Elder & Company paid only £500, less than Hawthorne had received when he was alive) caused Sophia to question her relationship with the firm of Fields, Osgood & Company, the successor to her husband's old publishing house. Much to her distress, she discovered that the American royalties on her husband's books were steadily decreasing, although Hawthorne's reputation continued to grow and the prices of the books had climbed. Hawthorne's business relationship with Ticknor & Fields had been largely gentleman's agreements, with royalty rates of 10 and 15 percent a volume. Now she discovered that in 1864, Fields, without consulting her, had adopted a flat fee arrangement of twelve cents per copy because of the fluctuating costs of book production during the war. He had made similar arrangements with most of his authors. Some, however, like Gail Hamilton, a popular writer of the time, had begun to conduct a vigorous campaign against the publisher. When Sophia ultimately learned that Gail Hamilton was earning fifteen cents per copy, she began to press the issue. Lizzie Peabody was invited to inspect the company's books, only to report that the arrangement was legal, that it had been agreed to by George Hillard, the administrator for the estate, and that it committed Sophia to the publication of all Hawthorne's works with Fields. Unfortunately, Lizzie also discovered that the sale and demand for Hawthorne's books had been so consistently small that neither the publishers nor the author had averaged "even one thousand a year." But the breach between Sophia and Fields and his wife was never fully healed. When, in 1869, Sophia produced her own journal of reminiscences, *Notes in England and Italy*, it was published by the rival firm, Putnam.

In the fall of 1868, Sophia sold the Wayside and made plans to move to Germany. Julian, whose college education had had some financial assistance from Franklin Pierce, proved to be such a desultory student that at the beginning of his senior year at Harvard, in 1866, he was asked to leave because of his poor academic standing and his many absences. Having next decided on a career in engineering, he enrolled in the Lawrence Scientific School, across the yard from Harvard, but found that its courses were more concerned with geology and zoology than with engineering. His next ambition was to attend the Dresden Realschule, a plan that Sophia agreed to, reasoning that expenses would be a great deal less there. Besides, the city, which had a considerable American colony, had been highly recommended by James Russell Lowell, who knew it well, and by her sister Lizzie, who had visited there. The family sailed in October 1868, aboard the *Deutschland*.

Julian's technical training was delayed by a year because of language difficulties. Although he had been tutored in German by none other than his father's friend Lowell, the lessons had consisted largely of readings in Goethe, which scarcely prepared him for dealing with subjects requiring a technical vocabulary. The family settled into the American colony: Una and Rose took music and drawing lessons; Sophia visited the galleries. The girls made friends with the Lathrops — young Frank and George Lathrop and their mother. Frank was a painter who had studied with Whistler; George was an aspiring poet of nineteen. Their father was a distinguished New York physician. It was in Dresden, too, that Julian met his future bride, American-born May Amelung, twenty-one, whose German-born grandparents had established a lucrative glassworks in Maryland. Within a year, after the completion of his training, Julian returned to New York, where he married "Minne" Amelung in November 1870 and took a position as a hydrographic engineer with the New York Dock Department, working under General George B. McClellan, his mother's Civil War hero. In the meantime, Sophia and her daughters had moved to London.

As it had in the past, an English winter proved hazardous for Sophia. In February 1871, her frail health gave way. Like her mother, she had had a long history of respiratory problems, and this time she came down with what was diagnosed as "typhoid pneumonia." Her breathing became increasingly difficult, and she was treated by attending physicians with ever stronger stimulants — brandy, ammonia, chloroform — which brought only temporary relief. Una and Rose nursed her through the long illness. She lingered on for several weeks, dying on February 26. On Saturday, March 4, the day after Una's twenty-seventh birthday, Sophia was buried in the cemetery at Kensal Green — "on a sunny hillside looking towards the east," Una wrote her absent brother. "We had a head and footstone of white marble, with a place for flowers between, and Rose and I planted some ivy there that I had brought from America, and a periwinkle from papa's grave. The inscription is — *Sophia, wife of Nathaniel Hawthorne*; and on the footstone, 'I am the Resurrection and the Life.' " The ocean that Sophia had once claimed would never separate her from her husband now stretched between them.

In the ensuing years, the publication of Hawthorne's literary remains was taken up by his children, not always with the happiest results. In 1872, Una, who spent most of the rest of her life in England, published Hawthorne's abortive romance, *Septimius Felton*, working from a draft begun by Sophia. Robert Browning assisted her with the text. Never in robust health, suffering from periodic nervous breakdowns, she had nevertheless taken up settlement work in London. She died in September 1877, at the age of thirty-three, while on a visit to a Protestant convent she had been thinking of joining in the little town of Clewer, near Windsor. She was buried in Kensal Green Cemetery beside her mother.

Rose Hawthorne, only months after her mother's death, had hastily married George Parsons Lathrop, who had been sent to England to accompany her and her sister back to the United States. It was an unhappy marriage. Lathrop, a man of unstable character, developed pronounced alcoholic tendencies, which ruined an otherwise brilliant career as an editor and journalist. Early in their marriage, the Lathrops involved themselves in the promotion of Hawthorne's reputation. In 1876, George Lathrop published *A Study of Hawthorne*, drawing on family papers in Rose's possession. The book precipitated a public quarrel with Julian, who protested the invasion of family privacy — although he was later to make use of such papers himself. Rose, who was formally separated from her husband in 1895, was to write her own reminiscences, *Memories of Hawthorne* (published in 1897), making use of many of her mother's letters and diaries. A Catholic convert, she became deeply concerned with the fate of poor people terminally ill with cancer (many with hideous forms of facial cancer) who had been abandoned by their families and were living in deplorable conditions, unable to earn a living or pay for proper hospital care. In 1896, she opened a clinic for such cases in a dingy, two-room flat on the lower East Side of New York. Following the death of her husband, she was received into the Third Order of St. Dominic as Sister Mary Alphonsa in September 1899. Earlier the same year, she had opened St. Rose's Free Home for Incurable Cancer, on Cherry Street, the first of several homes to be established by her growing religious organization. For thirty years she cared for the terminally ill. As Mother Alphonsa, she presided at Rosary Hill Home, the order's second hospital, in Hawthorne, New York. She died peacefully in her sleep, as her father had done, on her parents' wedding anniversary, July 9, 1926, at the age of seventy-five.

Julian, following in his father's footsteps, had a lengthy and prolific career as a writer. For some sixty years, he poured out a stream of romances, novels, critical writings, and reminiscences. As a journalist, he covered the 1897 plague in India, the Spanish-American War in Cuba (in the company of Stephen Crane and Richard Harding Davis), and the McKinley assassination. Throughout his lengthy career he made use of his father's connections and friendships with editors and writers. In 1883, he published a patched-together version of Hawthorne's manuscript drafts on the "American claimant" theme, *Doctor Grimshawe's Secret*. He also produced a number of literary reminiscences of Hawthorne and his circle, and a substantial two-volume biography of his parents, *Nathaniel Hawthorne and His Wife*, published in 1884. Only once in his professional career, it seems, did he let down his guard and acknowledge the difficulties of being Hawthorne's son. "My father is the worst enemy I have," he told a friend. "It would not be so bad if I had chosen a different calling, but whatever I write must always be compared to what he wrote."

At midcareer, in 1908, Julian and a former Harvard classmate, Dr. William Morton, a well-known neurologist, unwittingly became involved in a criminal business venture, the sale of worthless stock in a Canadian mining operation. Hawthorne, eagerly expecting to make a fortune, traded on the family name once more, writing promotional literature and letters for a scheme that reputedly netted some $3.5 million but paid no dividends during the four years of the company's existence. (Another of the front men was the equally prestigious Josiah Quincy, a former mayor of Boston and the secretary of state in Cleveland's administration; the fourth was a professional promoter named Albert Freeman.) In 1912, the four men were indicted for using the mails for fraudulent purposes. After a lengthy trial, Hawthorne and Morton received sentences of one year, Quincy was acquitted, and Freeman managed to escape imprisonment on a technicality. During the trial, the prosecuting attorney branded the defendants as "green goods men," and especially singled out Hawthorne and Quincy for having prostituted "honored names." Despite his conviction, Hawthorne maintained his innocence; a publicized visit to the White House by Mother Alphonsa did not result in a pardon from President Woodrow Wilson. Hawthorne served his full term at the federal penitentiary in Atlanta, Georgia, editing *Good Words*, the prison paper. After his release, he wrote a book about his prison experiences, *The Subterranean Brotherhood*. Hawthorne moved to California and resumed his career as a thoroughgoing literary journeyman. For a number of years he was a contributing writer for the *Star-News* of Pasadena. Despite his earlier humiliations, his eighty-fifth birthday was celebrated with tributes from such literary celebrities as Ellen Glasgow, Lincoln Steffens, H. L. Mencken, and George Bernard Shaw. He died three years later, in his San Francisco apartment, on July 14, 1934.

ᦢ III ᦢ

In 1883, while he was engaged in the research and writing of his biography of his parents, Julian had visited Herman Melville in his home on East 26 Street in New York. Melville had long since disappeared from the American literary scene and was a barely remembered figure. In his last years he published no fiction; only a volume or two of poetry, printed in limited editions and at his own expense. For years he had held a secure but ignominious job as an outdoors customs inspector.

Hawthorne had asked for the meeting in hopes that Melville might still have some of his father's letters, but these, Melville told him "with agitation," had long ago been destroyed. At first, the writer did not seem inclined to talk and only gradually warmed to the younger man, who bore a striking resemblance to his dead father. Julian, who had remembered Melville as robust and vigorous, was saddened by the old man's much-changed appearance. Melville was only a "melancholy and pale wraith of what he had been in his prime." Julian wrote, "His words were vague and indeterminate; and again and again, he would get up from his chair and open or close a window with a stick having a hook at the end, which he kept by him seemingly for that purpose. When I tried to revive memories in him of the red-cottage days — red-letter days too for him — he merely shook his head." Melville, however, did make some passing remarks that struck Julian Hawthorne. "He said several interesting things, among which the most remarkable was that he was convinced Hawthorne had all his life concealed some great secret, which would, were it known, explain all the mysteries of his career."

Julian continued, "It was characteristic in him to imagine so; there were many secrets untold in his own career." Being Hawthorne's son, he was sensitive enough to recognize that Melville had his own buried secrets. But he was also Sophia's son, and, sharing as he did that burden of absolute devotion to the memory of his father, he could hardly acknowledge that Melville might have been right.

Author's Note

Acknowledgements

Notes

Bibliography

Index

Author's Note

Men go through the world each musing on a great fable dramatically pictured & rehearsed before him. If you speak to the man, he turns his eyes from his own scene, & slower or faster endeavors to comprehend what you say. When you have done speaking, he returns to his private music. Men generally attempt early in life to make their brothers first, afterwards their wives, acquainted with what is going forward in their private theater, but they soon desist from the attempt on finding that they also have some farce or perhaps some ear- & heart-rending tragedy forward on their secret boards on which they are intent, and all parties acquiesce at last in a private box with the whole play performed before himself solus.

— Emerson, *Journals.*

I admire the astringency of Emerson's statement. It is not characteristic of his usual optimism. Nor is it representative of that bland image of the man many of us have carried away from surveys of American literature. Yet it is true to the newer Emerson who is coming into focus as a result of recent scholarship. There is, indeed, a mild revolution taking place in the study of nineteenth-century American culture and its seminal figures — one of the benefits of that silent scholarship which is bringing out new and definitive editions of the letters, memoirs, journals, the authoritative editions of the writings, of such figures as Hawthorne, Emerson, and Thoreau, as well as the important but less famous personalities associated with them. The time is coming, I suspect, when nineteenth-century American society will seem as fascinating and complex — if not intellectually so brilliant — as the Paris of the Goncourt brothers.

My routine as a writer is to get up early in the morning, and, after several cups of coffee, start work while the blackened world outside the study windows imperceptibly fills up with light, revealing the familiar forms — the stark trunks of trees, the flat surface of a neighbor's field parched with winter or green with spring — that have become the reassuring landscape of my working hours. But there have been times, after a concentrated spell of writing, when I suddenly became conscious of the blinding glare of noon and began to wonder if the nineteenth century was not becoming more real to me than my own sedentary life. For the past five years, the affairs of Hawthorne and the irrepressible Peabody family, the transient life of John L. O'Sullivan with his green-tinted spectacles and his luxuriant ambitions, the extravagant careers of the actresses Fanny Kemble and Charlotte Cushman, have provided me with something very much like the "private theater" Emerson mentions. Nineteenth-century life began to seem more varied and exciting in its seriousness and its accomplishments, its raw opportunities and spectacular failures, than I had expected. In writing about it, I wanted, if I could, to fix certain scenes in my mind with the vividness of old photographs that, unfortunately, had never happened to be taken: the striking, inconsequential image of Hawthorne and Thoreau, stepping out on an ice floe in the turgid Concord River, for instance, or the glimpse of Hawthorne, as a Civil War correspondent, observing General McClellan as he reviewed his troops. None of those scenes, it was clear, had to be invented. They were available in the documentary sources, if one looked carefully enough; they had already been fixed in prose. As a result, the circumstantial details of nineteenth-century life assumed an increasing importance for me. I had the feeling that if only I could get the context right — the time of the day, the angle of the light, the sounds coming in at the window — I might have a chance of arriving at the truth of Hawthorne's life at some given moment of his time. The context of Hawthorne's life, it seemed to me, had become inseparable from his achievements.

Oddly enough, summary assessments — Hawthorne's "view" of the slavery problem or his opinion of Margaret Fuller, for example — neatly packaged in a paragraph or two and intended to stand for all time as the definitive evaluation of Hawthorne's mind on many subjects, became increasingly unsatisfactory. What Hawthorne (who was a master of ambiguity and evasion) felt on a particular day and in a particular set of circumstances may not have been what he thought on the following morning, much less a year later. I began to think of a biography (or a biographical method) in which everything — the circumstances of the moment, the topical opinions and impressions of the day — would be held in continuous solution, never allowed to crystallize out into falsifying summary assessments. Even the critical evaluations of Hawthorne's writings, I hoped, would be inextricably woven back into the context of his life. That, obviously, was an impossible ideal; in biography as in life, one inevitably makes such judgments — and revises them as one's experience deepens.

Still, it was because of my dissatisfaction with summary evaluations in a one-volume biography (and the distortions they force on the biographer's handling of the lesser lives involved) that I began to think of writing a series of biographies of interrelated figures. What I had in mind was an interlocking sequence of books that would encompass not only the lives of Hawthorne and his family, but would allow me to give a fairer accounting of many of the major and minor personalities with whom Hawthorne was associated. These figures, too — Longfellow, Ellery Channing, Franklin

Pierce, Charles Sumner, Margaret Fuller — were part of the essential context and needed broader treatment if I wanted to avoid falsifying their lives.

The idea, of course, came from Balzac's novel sequence, *The Human Comedy*, in which a minor figure in one book becomes the hero or heroine of another, and hosts of subsidiary characters pass from novel to novel, busily pursuing their careers. But in the way that I envisioned it, I had not come across any example of the method being applied to the practice of biography. For better or worse, my publisher has taken an interest in this biographical project. *Nathaniel Hawthorne in His Times*, is the first volume of an as-yet-untitled quartet, with biographies of Margaret Fuller, Thoreau, and Emerson, I hope, to follow. It is one of those boons a writer dreams of — a serious, long-term work in prospect. It also provides the justification for turning back, once more, to that drama of nineteenth-century life which is, for me, still in performance.

Acknowledgments

DURING THE FIVE YEARS of research and writing of this biography, I have incurred many debts to individuals and institutions. For permission to quote from the necessary Hawthorne papers and related documents, I am deeply grateful to Mr. Manning Hawthorne, literary heir of the Hawthorne family, and to the following institutions for which full citations are provided elsewhere: the Bancroft Library; the Beinecke Rare Book and Manuscript Library; the Henry W. and Albert A. Berg Collection and the Duyckinck Collection of the Manuscripts and Archives Division, both of the New York Public Library; the Boston Public Library; the Bowdoin College Library; the Buffalo and Erie County Public Library; the Chicago Historical Society; the Butler Library of Columbia University; the Cornell University Library; the Essex Institute; the Fruitlands Museums; the Isabella Stewart Gardner Museum; the Historical Society of Pennsylvania; the Houghton Library of Harvard University; the Huntington Library; the Library Company of Philadelphia; the Library of Congress; the Maine Historical Society; the Dawes Memorial Library of Marietta College; the Massachusetts Historical Society; the Abernethy Library of Middlebury College; the Pierpont Morgan Library; the National Archives and Records Service; the New Hampshire Historical Society; the Carl H. Pforzheimer Library; the Owen D. Young Library of St. Lawrence University; the Lucy Scribner Library of Skidmore College; the Trinity College Library, Cambridge, England; the Clifton Waller Barrett Collection, University of Virginia Library.

Books and articles quoted or cited in the text under the usual fair use allowances are all acknowledged in the notes and bibliography. But for permissions for more extensive quotations or, in some instances, borderline cases, I wish to thank the following sources: the *Essex Institute Historical Collections* and its editor, Bryant F. Tolles, Jr., for permission to quote from a variety of articles; the Belknap Press of Harvard University Press for permission to quote from *The Journals and Miscellaneous Notebooks of Ralph Waldo Emerson* and *The Letters of Henry Wadsworth Longfellow*; the Pennsylvania State University Press for permission to quote from *Hawthorne's Lost Notebook, 1835–1841*, transcribed by Barbara S. Mouffe from the original manuscript now in the Pierpont Morgan Library; Cleone Odell Stewart and the Modern Language Association for permission to quote from *The English Notebooks by Nathaniel Hawthorne*, edited by Randall Stewart; David M. Metcalf and Yale University Press for permission to quote from *The Letters of Herman Melville;* Houghton Mifflin Company for permission to quote from *Memories of Hawthorne*, by Rose Hawthorne Lathrop, *Yesterdays with Authors*, by James T. Fields, and *Hawthorne and His Publisher*, by Caroline Ticknor.

My greatest debt, however, is to the Ohio State University Press and the editors of the definitive *Centenary Edition of the Works of Nathaniel Hawthorne*, which I have cited throughout my text.

My indebtedness to individuals is heavy. First and foremost, I am especially grateful to L. Neal Smith, associate textual editor of the *Centenary Edition*, who provided answers to my often nagging queries and supplied typescripts for many of the Hawthorne letters. He graciously offered to check my chapter dealing with Hawthorne's French and Italian experiences against the transcripts of Hawthorne's French and Italian notebooks, which were in the process of being readied for publication by the Ohio State University Press. His help was essential to the research of my book. I must also acknowledge a debt to the late Norman Holmes Pearson, who allowed me to study the transcripts of his long-planned edition of Hawthorne's letters — a task that has now been superseded by the editors of the *Centenary Edition*. Dr. Lola L. Szladits and the staff of the Berg Collection very patiently answered queries and delved into the archives during the course of many visits to the New York Public Library. Donald Gallup, former curator of the Yale Collection of American Literature at the Beinecke Library was unfailingly helpful and encouraging as were staff members Anne Whelpley and Joan Hofmann. I owe special gratitude to Jean G. Johnson and Bill Copeley of the New Hampshire Historical Society and Estelle Rebec of the Bancroft Library for their frequent assistance on research problems.

For their good will in responding to queries, supplying information and clues, tracking down items in obscure publications, and supplying photocopies and illustrative materials, I am grateful to: Dr. Bruce Barker-Benfield of the Bodleian Library; N. A. M. Rodger of the Public Record Office, Kew, Richmond, Surrey; Edmund Berkeley, Jr., and Gregory A. Johnson of the University of Virginia Library; Robert Buckeye of the Abernethy Library; John L. Idol, Jr., of Clemson University; James Lawton of the Boston Public Library; Arthur Monke and Mary H. Hughes of the Bowdoin College Library; Professor Edmund S. Morgan of Yale University; William H. Bond of the Houghton Library; Marcia E. Moss of the Concord Free Public Library; Sandra Scace of the Shaker Community at Hancock, Massachusetts; Robert Nikirk of the Grolier Club; Denis J. Lesieur of the Berkshire Athenaeum; Theodore S. Hope, Jr., of the Browning Institute; Mother M. Angela, O.P., of Rosary Hill Home, Hawthorne, New York; Phyllis E. McLaughlin of the Iowa State Historical Department; Peter Drummey of the Massachusetts Historical Society; Joshua C. Taylor and Meryl Muller of the National Collection of Fine Arts; William F. Stapp of the Photographic Department of the National Portrait Gallery; Paul T. Heffron of the Library of Congress; Michael P. Musick of the National Archives and Records Service;

Archie Motley of the Chicago Historical Society; Mrs. Arthur R. Norton and Marylou Birchmore of the Essex Institute; Harriet McLoone and David Mike Hamilton of the Huntington Library; Joyce Ann Tracy of the American Antiquarian Society; and the writers Herbert Mitgang and Nigel Nicolson.

In my attempts to track down information on the elusive William Symmes and the Private Small from whom Symmes purportedly received Hawthorne's youthful Maine diary, I have been helped by several individuals whom I would like to acknowledge. Norman Simons, curator of the Pensacola Historical Museum and Ernest H. Knight of South Casco, Maine, hunted through local histories and old burial records on my account. D. C. Allard of the Naval Historical Center and Elaine C. Everly and Dale E. Floyd of the National Archives and Records Service searched through ancient Army and Navy records to come up with intriguing pieces for a still unsolved puzzle.

For their many services during the research and writing of this book, I especially thank: John C. Broderick, Rae Brown, John D. Cushing, Lynn Case, Kathleen M. Catalano, Rodney G. Dennis, Mary Doherty, Monroe H. Fabian, Lucretia H. Giese, Dianne M. Gutscher, Mihai H. Handrea, James L. Harwood, Pamela Hoyle, Marvin W. Kranz, Lisa Lieberman, Kenneth A. Lohf, William H. Loos, Ellen D. Mark, Eleanor L. Nicholes, John Pickering, Sally Pierce, Richard S. Reed, Katherine Richardson, Charles Ryskamp, Merton M. Sealts, Jr., Susan Sinclair, Alvin Skipsna, Edward M. Stevenson, Shirley Thayer, Eleanor Tilton, James Tyler, Ross Urquhart, Stuart Wallace, and Senator Lowell Weicker, Jr.

My debts to scholars and biographers of related figures of the period are indicated in the notes. But I want to express my particular gratitude to several writers who have significantly influenced my understanding of Hawthorne's often ambivalent relationships with his contemporaries and who have rescued both minor and major figures from those too-easy generalizations that afflict nineteenth-century American studies: Maurice Bassan, Belle Gale Chevigny, Robert F. Dalzell, Jr., Joseph Jay Deiss, David Donald, Edwin Gittleman, Walter Harding, Joseph Leach, Leo Marx, Frederick T. McGill, Joel Myerson, Stephen Nissenbaum, Martha Saxton, Arthur M. Schlesinger, Jr., Sister Mary Joseph, O.P., the late Randall Stewart, and Louise Hall Tharp. While I disagree with Edwin Haviland Miller's account of the Melville-Hawthorne relationship on particular points, I have found his exploration of Melville's work illuminating in several ways.

I am extremely grateful to the American Council of Learned Societies, which came to my rescue with a much-needed grant-in-aid toward the research expenses of the book, and to the American Philosophical Society, which provided some equally necessary assistance for the same purposes in the final year of writing.

Once more, Augie Capaccio has offered on-the-road assistance during the course of research jaunts.

I am more grateful than I can say to my editor, Jonathan Galassi, who provided the necessary enthusiasm, encouragement, and advice during the lengthy process of writing the book, particularly during those periods of ebbing morale. Helena Bentz is to be thanked for easing the book through production. I am especially grateful for the rigor with which Frances Apt, as copy editor, attacked the manuscript. But I am an impatient scholar (and a poor typist) so I must take full responsibility for any errors of transcription or the misdating of letters and documents that may have occurred during the several drafts of the manuscript that appear to be my normal procedure in writing a biography.

Notes

ABBREVIATIONS

NH   Nathaniel Hawthorne, 1804–1864.

SAH   Sophia A. Hawthorne, 1809–1871.

ECMH   Elizabeth Clarke Manning Hawthorne, 1780–1849.

EMH   Elizabeth Manning Hawthorne, 1802–1883.

LH   Maria Louisa Hawthorne, 1808–1852.

RM   Robert Manning, 1784–1842.

EPPM   Mrs. Elizabeth Palmer Peabody, 1778–1853.

EPPm   Miss Elizabeth Palmer Peabody, 1804–1894.

MTP   Mary Tyler Peabody, 1806–1887.

Centenary   *Centenary Edition of the Works of Nathaniel Hawthorne.* Thirteen volumes to date.

EIHC   *Essex Institute Historical Collections.* Quarterly publication of the Essex Institute.

The italicized words in the sources that follow are the clue names to be found in the notes.

Bancroft Library, University of California, Berkeley, California. *Bancroft Transcripts* refers to Julian Hawthorne's notebook transcripts of letters of Elizabeth Manning Hawthorne to her niece Una Hawthorne, dating from 1861 to 1870.

Yale Collection of American Literature, *Beinecke* Library, New Haven, Connecticut.

The Henry W. and Albert A. *Berg* Collection of English and American Literature in the New York Public Library (Astor, Lenox, and Tilden Foundations), New York, New York. *Cuban Journals, Berg* refers to the bound copies of Sophia (Peabody) Hawthorne's letters to her mother (with additions by Mary Peabody) during her Cuban residence.

Boston Public Library, Boston, Massachusetts.

Bowdoin College Library, Brunswick, Maine.

James Fraser Gluck Collection, *Buffalo* and Erie County Public Library, Buffalo, New York.

Chicago Historical Society, Chicago, Illinois.

Butler Library, *Columbia* University, New York, New York.

Cornell University Library, Ithaca, New York.

Essex Institute, Salem, Massachusetts.

Fruitlands Museums, Harvard, Massachusetts.

Isabella Stewart *Gardner* Museum, Boston, Massachusetts.

Historical Society of Pennsylvania, Philadelphia, Pennsylvania.
Houghton Library, Harvard University, Cambridge, Massachusetts. *Houghton Letter-book* refers to the business transcripts of Hawthorne's letters to his publishers, James T. Fields and William Ticknor.
Huntington Library, San Marino, California.
Library Company of Philadelphia, Philadelphia, Pennsylvania.
Library of Congress, Washington, D.C.
J.S.H. Fogg Collection, *Maine Historical Society*, Portland, Maine.
Dawes Memorial Library, *Marietta* College, Marietta, Ohio.
Massachusetts Historical Society, Boston, Massachusetts.
Abernethy Library, *Middlebury* College, Middlebury, Vermont.
The Pierpont *Morgan* Library, New York, New York.
National Archives and Records Service, Washington, D.C.
New Hampshire Historical Society, Concord, New Hampshire.
Manuscripts and Archives Division, *New York Public Library*, New York, New York.
Pearson Transcripts refers to the transcripts made by the late Norman Holmes Pearson (and others) of Hawthorne's letters and of related Hawthorne and Peabody family letters in preparation for an edition of Hawthorne's letters.
The Carl H. *Pforzheimer* Library, New York, New York.
Owen D. Young Library, *St. Lawrence* University, Canton, New York.
Lucy Scribner Library, *Skidmore* College, Saratoga Springs, New York.
Trinity College, Cambridge, England.
Nathaniel Hawthorne Collection, Clifton Waller Barrett Library, Manuscripts Department, *University of Virginia* Library, Charlottesville, Virginia.

page   MR. HAWTHORNE CALLS AGAIN

3 "And in the evening": Pearson, "Elizabeth Peabody on Hawthorne," 263.
The source of this and further quotations in this chapter is the notebook, written around 1882, in the Morgan Library, which Julian Hawthorne kept in preparation for his biography of his parents. Significant portions of his conversations with his aunt Elizabeth Palmer Peabody, have been published in the Pearson article cited above, as well as in Pearson, "Hawthorne's Duel," both of which were published in *EIHC*.
She was recalling: See MTP to George Peabody, November 16, 1837; Berg.
"new star": Crowley, *Critical Heritage*, 55.
3 "all but Hindoo": Pearson, "Elizabeth Peabody on Hawthorne," 267.
4 "love-disappointment": Ibid., 263.
"brilliant little girl": Ibid., 262.
"clustering locks": Ibid., 263.
"some old 'New-Light' Quaker": Ibid., 261.
5 "But if your brother": Ibid., 263.
Record of a School: The school was Bronson Alcott's controversial Temple School, held in the Masonic Temple on Tremont Street, Boston. It opened in September 1834.
"black hair in beautiful": Pearson, "Elizabeth Peabody on Hawthorne," 264.
"Louisa was quite like": Ibid., 264.
6 "My sister Sophia": Ibid., 265.
"In person she was": J. Hawthorne, *NH and His Wife*, I:49.
7 "The endurance of her physical": Pearson, "Elizabeth Peabody on Hawthorne," 272.
"silent ministry of pain": R. H. Lathrop, *Memories*, 479.
"exercised so strong": J. Hawthorne, *NH and His Wife*, I:180.
"And Miss Sophia": Pearson, "Elizabeth Peabody on Hawthorne," 265.
"In the end": J. Hawthorne, *NH and His Wife*, I:180.
8 "Now dearest, dost thou": NH to SAH, October ?, 1840; Huntington.

10 The Hathorne family: Hawthorne was still using the old spelling when he inscribed his name "Nathaniel Hathorne, Salem, Massachusetts, 1825" on a page of his father's logbook for the ship *America*. The earliest appearance of the Hawthorne signature, apparently, is 1827. See *Centenary*, VIII:583.
William Hathorne, ca. 1607–1681. See *Centenary*, VIII:583.
"waste and howling wilderness": J. Hawthorne, *NH and His Wife*, I:13–24. Hawthorne visited the State Paper Office in July 1856, accompanied by John Gorham Palfrey, who believed the name Samuel Nadhorth to be an anagram for Hawthorne's ancestor, William Hathorne. (See Hawthorne, *English Notebooks*, 383–84.) Mr. N. A. M. Rodger, assistant keeper of the Public Record Office in Kew, England, writes me that the document is still in the archives, signed by Nadhorth, but "there is nothing in the letter to indicate whether or not this might be a pseudonym, and endorsements suggest that it was accepted in London as genuine." Professor Edmund S. Morgan, an authority on colonial America, informs me that Nadhorth is not a name he has come across in period documents. "On the other hand," he notes, "even though New Englanders were fond of playing cute with anagrams in verses, I shouldn't have thought that anyone would try it on a secretary of state."
11 John Hathorne, 1641–1717. See *Centenary* VIII:584. Although various members of the Hawthorne family referred to the witch's curse, the precise nature of it is not clear. The curse that Hawthorne used in *The House of the Seven Gables*, "God will give you blood to drink," is the one Sarah Good pronounced on the Reverend Nicholas Noyes. See Boyer and Nissenbaum, *Salem Possessed*, 8; and Upham, *Salem Witchcraft*, II:270.
"the dreary and unprosperous": *Centenary*, I:10.
Daniel Hathorne, 1731–1796. See Loggins, *The Hawthornes*, 160.
In 1772, after selling the family homestead: Hawthorne mistakenly believed that his grandfather had built the house on Union Street and was rather unforgiving about the sale of the old homestead. See J. Hawthorne, *NH and His Wife*, I:95; also *Centenary*, VIII:595.
12 Nathaniel Hathorne, 1775–1808. See Loggins, *The Hawthornes*, 175.
"remarkable eyes, full of sensibility": Fields, *Yesterdays*, 43.
"a warm-hearted and kindly": Ibid.
"You may tell E.P.P.": EMH to Una Hawthorne, undated fragment; Bancroft Transcripts.
13 On the day of his son's birth: See Nathaniel Hathorne's Log Book for the *Mary & Eliza* (1803–1804); Essex Institute.
"the sternest man": Pearson, "Elizabeth Peabody on Hawthorne," 268.
"Nathaniel Hathorne's Book, Presented": see Hathorne's Log Book, "A Journal of a Passage from Bengal to America" (1795–1796); Essex Institute.
"Coming from eastward": Ibid.
"In the Midst of all": Ibid., page insert.
14 "I remember very well that": EMH to Una Hawthorne, November 12, 1865; Bancroft Transcripts.
Nathaniel Hathorne is virtually never mentioned: The engraving had been made from the portrait by C. G. Thompson.
"might have been taken": *Centenary*, X:76.
"a father's authority": Ibid., 339.
"on the high road": *Centenary*, IX:183.
15 "kindly figure": *Centenary*, V:122.
"He left his family": Obituary notice, *Salem Gazette*, April 20, 1813.
As Cantwell has already pointed out, the same issue carried an obituary notice for Hawthorne's grandmother: "In this town, Mrs. Rachel Hathorne, widow of Captain Daniel Hathorne, aged 79." Coincidentally, Bold Daniel had died on April 19, 1796.

page

"We were indulged": EMH to Una Hawthorne, November 12, 1865; Bancroft Transcripts.

"Nathaniel — O how I am bedear'd": RM to NH, August 14, 1813; Berg.

16 "In five years": NH to ECMH, July 11?, 17?, 1820; Essex Institute.

Richard Manning, 1782–1830.

"As to my lameness": Richard Manning to ECMH, February ?, 1815; Pearson Transcripts.

"quite convenient": NH to ECMH, October 31, 1820; Essex Institute.

17 "nobody to talk to": NH to RM, July 26, 1819; Essex Institute.

Mary Manning, 1777–1841; Priscilla Manning Dike, 1790–1873.

"Take her away!": G. P. Lathrop, *A Study*, 63.

"Stand back, my Lord": Ibid., 64.

"I can't help it": Ibid., 66.

18 "Oh, she'll think": EMH to Una Hawthorne, November 12, 1865; Bancroft Transcripts.

"He never wanted money": Ibid.

When he was nine: On Hawthorne's lameness, see EMH to Una Hawthorne, November 23, 1865; Bancroft Transcripts, and EMH to Fields, letter postmarked December 12, 1870; Boston Public Library.

"It is know 4 weeks": NH to RM, December 9, 1813; University of Virginia.

"I don't know as Nathaniel's foot": EMH to RM, January 12, 1814; Bowdoin.

19 "Nathaniel is no better": Priscilla Manning to Richard and Robert Manning, July 13, 1814; Pearson Transcripts.

"Tell Nathaniel I am much pleased": Richard Manning to RM, November 15, 1814; Pearson Transcripts.

"He was both beautiful": EMH to Una Hawthorne, November 12, 1865; Bancroft Transcripts.

"Be so good Robert": Priscilla Manning to Richard and Robert Manning, August 29, 1814; Pearson Transcripts.

"I never did go": J. Hawthorne, *NH and His Wife*, I:95.

"to live to be twenty-five": EMH to Fields, postmarked December 12, 1870; Boston Public Library.

20 "good health and spirits": Priscilla Manning to Richard and Robert Manning, August 29, 1814; Pearson Transcripts.

"Nathaniel has entirely recovered": ECMH to Richard Manning, January 20, 1815; Bowdoin.

Once, during a blizzard: Hawthorne wrote his Uncle Robert about the recent tragedy in a letter dated March 24, 1819 (Berg). The story of the ballad comes from *Hawthorne's First Diary* by Samuel T. Pickard. The diary, relating events from Hawthorne's years in Maine, has never been found. What were presumed to be transcripts from it were sent to Pickard (editor of the Portland, Maine, *Transcript*) by a man named William Symmes. Through investigation, Pickard learned that Symmes was a mulatto, the natural son of a Maine lawyer, who claimed to have been a companion of Hawthorne's during the Raymond years. Symmes's career was a wide-ranging one; he reportedly served in the merchant marine, spent time in California, and acted as a spy for Colonel La Fayette C. Baker during the Civil War. He purportedly died in Pensacola, Florida, in October 1871. At least, Pickard was sent an obituary to that effect — although he later received further installments of the diary, written by a "friend" of Symmes, but in the same handwriting as the earlier segments. Many of the details in the diary accounts (which were published in the *Transcript*) were considered accurate, and some were remembered by local people. But when the diary was published later in book form, one of the stories — involving a drowning — was obviously an interpolation by Symmes, since it had occurred after Hawthorne left Maine. The story of the diary is a long and complicated one, and some later scholars believe it to be a hoax.

For the past four years, I have been trying to trace the elusive Symmes by way of old army and navy records and burial records. (And I still am.) At this point, I can report only that the circumstantial details of Symmes's story of how he came into possession of the purported diary are corroborated in certain matters. There is a distinct possibility that the original diary existed, but that Symmes tried to "improve" on it.

21 "threatened to kill Louisa": NH to RM, May 16, 1819; Middlebury. Ben Ham, a Raymond, Maine, neighbor, also figures in the disputed Maine diary, another of the circumstantial bits of evidence that tend to lend some credibility to the diary. See Pickard, *Hawthorne's First Diary*, 66ff.
"in Shakespeare": J. Hawthorne, *NH and His Wife*, I:96.
"left much to such": *Centenary*, V:122.
"Those were delightful": J. Hawthorne, *NH and His Wife*, I:96.
"I lived in Maine like a bird": Fields, *Yesterdays*, 113.
22 "Nathaniel [had] a solitary": Mary Manning to ECMH, July 6, 1819; Bowdoin.
"I have begun to go": NH to ECMH, July 26, 1819; Essex Institute.
"I shall never be contented": NH to LH, September 28, 1819; Morgan.
23 "I am extremely homesick": NH to ECMH, March 7, 1820; Essex Institute.
"Though you and I could": NH to LH, March 21, 1820; Essex Institute.
"Then Aunt Mary can't have her": NH to ECMH, March 7, 1820; Essex Institute.
"begun to fit for college": Ibid.
24 "An Author does not write": The handwritten copies of *The Spectator* are in the collection of the Essex Institute.
"almost given up writing Poetry": NH to ECMH, postscript to EMH, October 31, 1820; Essex Institute.
"I dreamed the other night": NH to ECMH, March 13, 1821; Morgan.
"It was enough to have drawn": NH to ECMH, March 6, 1821; Essex Institute.
25 "he might have escaped": Mary Manning to ECMH, May 15, 1821; Essex Institute.
"I did not go to see": NH to ECMH, May 15, 1821; Essex Institute.
"I am quite reconciled": NH to ECMH, March 13, 1821; Morgan.
27 "a slender lad": Bridge, *Personal Recollections*, 4.
"blue-gray sapphires": Elliott, *Three Generations*, 28.
"of carrying his head": Bridge, *Personal Recollections*, 5.
"Are you a man": J. Hawthorne, *NH and His Wife*, I:121.
28 "shy, beautiful soul": *Atlantic Monthly*, July, 1864:98–101.
"He was neither morose": Bridge, *Personal Recollections*, 6.
"great pluck and determination": Ibid., 5.
(The exception, reportedly . . .): A contemporary of Hawthorne's, William H. Foster, who had been a clerk in the Boston & Salem Stage Company, claimed in an article in the *Salem Gazette* (January 7, 1887) that Hawthorne had confessed to writing such an article, although he knew nothing about the subject, and requested that Foster not say anything to Robert Manning, who was awaiting the article. Hawthorne "wouldn't have his Uncle Robert know it for the world." The article in question supposedly appeared in *The Palladium* around 1822. I have not been able to trace such an article in *The New England Palladium & Commercial Advertiser*.
"If anybody is responsible": *Centenary*, XI:4.
29 "Roasted potatoes, butter, salt": Cantwell, *Nathaniel Hawthorne*, 81.
30 On the evening of October 29, 1824: See also Longfellow, *Letters*, I:93, note 1.
31 Even before his graduation: For details of Longfellow's early life and college career, I am indebted to the late Lawrance Thompson's *Young Longfellow*.
"I was an idle student": J. Hawthorne, *NH and His Wife*, I:96.
"My occupations this term": NH to LH, April 14, 1822; Huntington.
"All the card players": NH to ECMH, May 30, 1822; Essex Institute.
"Perhaps he might not": William Allen to ECMH, May 29, 1822; Essex Institute.
"I was full as willing": NH to EMH, August 5, 1822; Essex Institute.
32 "If I had time": NH to LH, May 4, 1823; Huntington.
"I am invited by several": Ibid.
"I am almost dead of homesickness": J. Hawthorne, *NH and His Wife*, I:114.
"I made a very splendid": NH to LH or EMH, fragment, ca. November 1824; Huntington.

page

33 "You ought to give me": NH to EMH, April 21, 1825; Morgan.
"I sincerely sympathize": NH to Mary Manning, November 26, 1824; Huntington.
"made progress in my novel": EMH to Una Hawthorne, fragment, possibly dated February 26, 1865; Bancroft Transcripts.
"Uncle Richard seemed to care nothing": NH to LH, July 14, 1825; Essex Institute.

34 "Yes! — and palms are to be won": Thompson, *Young Longfellow*, 71.

page   THE LONG SECLUSION

36 "It was my fortune": J. Hawthorne, *NH and His Wife*, I:96.
"long seclusion": Ibid., 98.
"I doubt whether so much": Ibid., 97.

37 "If ever I should have": NH to SAH, October 4, 1840; Huntington.
"It was only after": EMH to Fields, December 26, 1870; Boston Public Library.
"were as regular as possible": EMH to Una Hawthorne, fragment, probably dated February 26, 1865; Bancroft Transcripts.
"old ten-gun battery": Hawthorne, *Lost Notebook*, 4. This notebook, long thought lost, was recently discovered by Mrs. Barbara Mouffe and has been published in facsimile, with a transcript by Mrs. Mouffe. Details of Hawthorne's Salem walks are from this source.
"would have been prettier": Ibid., 6.
"a pint bowl": EMH to Una Hawthorne, fragment, probably dated February 26, 1865; Bancroft Transcripts.

38 "No, no, I never": M. A. DeWolfe Howe, *Memories of a Hostess*, 69.
"upon which we differed": EMH to Una Hawthorne, fragment, probably dated February 26, 1865; Bancroft Transcripts.
"The only thing I fear": J. Hawthorne, *NH and His Wife*, I:5.
"Your Papa used to call me": EMH to Una Hawthorne, March 1, 1865; Bancroft Transcripts.
"The only argument": Ibid.
"It is remarkable, but": EMH to Una Hawthorne, June 19, 1868; Bancroft Transcripts.

39 "knows the world marvelously": Pearson, "Elizabeth Peabody on Hawthorne," 266.
"never imagine her in sunshine": NH to SAH, April 17, 1839; Huntington.
"read endlessly": J. Hawthorne, *NH and His Wife*, I:97.
"nor look over the catalogue": EMH to Fields, December 26, 1870; Boston Public Library.
If he claimed to have little interest: For a list of Hawthorne's readings during this period, see G. P. Lathrop, *A Study*, 337.

40 "more delectation out of them": Fields, *Yesterdays*, 63. Hawthorne borrowed volumes of *A Complete Collection of State Trials*, compiled by T. B. Howell and T. J. Howell, from the Salem Athenaeum in February, March, and April 1832. See Turner, *Hawthorne as Editor*, 64.
"strange, pedantic history": *Centenary*, VI:92.
"stalwart Doctor's grandiloquent": *Centenary*, V:122.
"I am not a man": NH to L. W. Mansfield, February 20, 1850; Berg.

41 "the peculiar weariness": Hawthorne, *Lost Notebook*, 13.
"He read a great many novels": EMH to Una Hawthorne, fragment, probably dated February 26, 1865; Bancroft Transcripts.
"might have the pleasure": NH to EMH, October 31, 1820; Essex Institute.
"Of all things, I delight": Fields, *Yesterdays*, 75.

"There was much more": EMH to Una Hawthorne, fragment, probably dated February 26, 1865; Bancroft Transcripts.

42 "unconnected with the world, unconcerned": *Centenary*, III:350.

"seminary of learning": Ibid., 333.

"polished society": Ibid., 343.

"Where was the happiness": Ibid., 350.

"the result of which": Ibid., 353.

43 "The ashes of a hard student": Ibid., 460. Some years later, Hawthorne came upon Nathaniel Mather's gravestone in the burial ground near the Peabody home: "It affected me deeply, when I had cleared away the grass from the half-buried stone and read the name." *Centenary*, VIII: 173, 595.

"calm and quiet bliss": *Centenary*, III:460.

"Many parts of it": Crowley, *Critical Heritage*, 43.

"Purchase it, reader": Ibid., 42.

"The mind that produced": Ibid., 45.

"*Fanshawe* . . . A love story": Ibid., 41.

"no doubt burned it": EMH to Una Hawthorne, fragment, probably dated February 26, 1865; Bancroft Transcripts.

44 "I cannot be sworn": NH to Fields, January 12, 1851; Houghton Letterbook.

"What is more potent": *Centenary*, XI:177.

"One man publishes nothing but": Ibid., 172.

"and he tells me fairly": Ibid., 173.

"I have become ambitious of": Ibid., 172.

"I tell you there is": Ibid., 173.

"My tales! . . . the chimney!": Ibid., 178.

45 "kinder custody": *Centenary* XI:269. According to G. P. Lathrop, in *A Study*, this was Ferdinand Andrews, co-owner, with Caleb Cushing, of the *Salem Gazette*. The story, "Alice Doane's Appeal," which appeared in the 1835 *Token*, was a rewritten and retitled version of the story that Ebe Hawthorne had recalled. The other, "Susan Grey," is presumably one of Hawthorne's lost tales.

"in a mood half savage": Bridge, *Personal Recollections*, 68.

"very dull stuff": *Centenary*, IX:4.

46 "He liked a crowd": EMH to Fields, December 26, 1870; Boston Public Library.

"A great conflagration": Fields, *Yesterdays*, 66.

"I do not know that": NH to Goodrich, December 20, 1829; University of Virginia.

47 "I am obliged to you": Ibid. For details on the *Provincial Tales*, see *Centenary*, IX:489.

"take hold of the work": J. Hawthorne, *NH and His Wife*, I:131–32.

"never see the light": NH to Goodrich, May 6, 1830; Bowdoin (transcript).

"very liberal use": J. Hawthorne, *NH and His Wife*, I:132.

48 "Once a year": Ibid., 97.

"She drinks nothing but": NH to Samuel Manning, August 11, 1829; Essex Institute.

"We did not leave New Haven": NH to LH, August 18, 1829?, a lost letter; G. P. Lathrop, *A Study*, 143–44. Lathrop thought the date of the letter was "probably 1830." But Ebe Hawthorne, writing to Una on December 20, 1865 (Bancroft Transcripts), notes: "I found two or three of your father's [letters] which were written during a short tour in Connecticut with one of our Uncles, in 1831, I think and are very amusing." The *Centenary* editors tentatively relate it to the 1829 trip.

49 Not all of his summer excursions: For an account of Hawthorne's sojourn on Martha's Vineyard, see Turner, *Hawthorne as Editor*, 113. Elizabeth Hawthorne thought the trip to Swampscott occurred "about the year 1833." See EMH to Una Hawthorne, February 14, 1862; Bancroft Transcripts.

"One of your Uncle Sam's": NH to LH, August 17, 1831; Essex Institute. Samuel Manning was traveling for his health. He died on November 17, 1833.

50 "pretty much as if they": Ibid.

"I was making preparations": NH to Pierce, June 28, 1832; Boston Public Library.

"I sincerely congratulate you": Ibid.

51 In September, Hawthorne began his journey: As indicated, the journey to

page

Niagara has been reconstructed from scant documentary and literary evidence. (One wonders, however, if Hawthorne kept a now-lost diary or journal of his Niagara expedition. See discussion of "Fragments from the Journal of a Solitary Man," below.) In the March 1836 issue of the *American Magazine of Useful and Entertaining Knowledge*, which Hawthorne edited, there is an account of a steamboat excursion from Ogdensburg, New York, down the St. Lawrence and "to the other extremity of Lake Ontario." (See Turner, *Hawthorne as Editor*, 58ff.) If this is an account of an actual journey, then Hawthorne would seem to have made another "northern tour." The style of this piece seems quite compatible with Hawthorne's writing, but it is not outside the realm of possibility that he edited and rewrote an article that was on hand when he assumed the editorship of the *American Magazine.*

"passed behind the Great Falling Sheet": Certificate dated September 28, 1832; Beinecke.

Their separate publication represents: Many critics and scholars — probably correctly — associate the "Sketches from Memory" with Hawthorne's abortive *The Story Teller*, a sequence of sketches and individual stories that he had hoped to publish in book form but which he gave to Park Benjamin for serial publication in the *New-England Magazine.* Benjamin published some of the narrative sketches and a connected story, "Mr. Higginbotham's Catastrophe," in the November and December issues of the magazine. Afterward, he dismantled the book, publishing it piecemeal in the *New-England Magazine* and later in the *American Monthly*, of which he became an editor.

My reading of these fragmentary sketches suggests that we may be dealing with at least two separate story sequences. *The Story Teller* fragments (published as "Passages from a Relinquished Work") involve a distinctive group of personalities: the Story Teller himself (as narrator) and his traveling companion, an itinerant preacher named Eliakim Abbott, and such incidental characters as Parson Thumpcushion, Dominicus Pike, and Mr. Nightingale. The "Sketches from Memory," on the other hand, frequently seem very different in character; they contain the straightforward observations of an urbane traveler, rather like the Hawthorne of his later travel journals and diaries.

There is the further problem of a third, complicating sketch, "Fragments from the Journal of a Solitary Man," also considered part of *The Story Teller* sequence, and published in the *American Monthly* of July 1837. This is a patchwork affair, involving a third narrator personality, this one the narrator-friend of Oberon, the fictional author of "The Devil in Manuscript," who reprints passages from a purported journal by the now-dead author. One of the fragments — the most poignant, in fact, "My Home Return" — does refer to both Pike and Nightingale, therefore establishing a connection with *The Story Teller.* Yet this sketch seems below the standards of Hawthorne's usual editing and seems to have been pieced together largely to save some worthwhile fragments of his writing from editorial oblivion.

Arguing against the case for two separate story sequences is the fact that nearly all of the sketches and stories were published by Benjamin, and it seems unlikely that even so diffident an author as Hawthorne would supply the editor with two story sequences to dismantle. (Yet one of the fragments from "Fragments from the Journal of a Solitary Man," for instance, would provide a lead-in for the tale "The Wedding-Knell," which was published in *The Token* for 1837.) It is also quite possible that references that would connect the "Sketches from Memory" with *The Story Teller* had been edited out for publication, which was the case with "My Home Return," portions of which had appeared earlier, as "An Afternoon Scene," in "Sketches from Memory." In default of the original manuscripts ·or letters relating to the matter, the possibilities of *The Story Teller* sequence continue to be intriguing.

"old crystal hills": *Centenary*, X:422.

"the very worst road that ever": NH to ECMH, September 16, 1832; Essex Institute.

52 "a high and abstracted ambition": *Centenary*, IX:327.
"As yet, I have done nothing": Ibid., 328.
"His name and person": Ibid., 333.
"One breeze from the Atlantic": *Centenary*, XI:299. Although the sketch, "The Inland Port," is written as if Hawthorne had visited Burlington on his return trip, his September 16 letter to his mother, written from Burlington, indicates he had stopped there en route to Niagara.
53 "British and American coin": Ibid., 300.
"infinite tribes, overflowing": Ibid., 299.
Traveling south, below Utica: At some point, perhaps on his return trip, Hawthorne visited the ruined fortress of old Fort Ticonderoga, once the scene of historical battles, now opened to the skies, weeds growing in the huge, empty fireplaces. He described it in "Old Ticonderoga" which Benjamin published in the *American Monthly*, February 1836, as an isolated sketch.
"enchanter . . . waved his magic wand": *Centenary*, X:429–30.
"like Poverty personified": Ibid., 432.
"Perhaps these three alone": Ibid., 431.
54 "the sexual division of the boat": Ibid., 436.
"made up of scraps, ill-selected": Ibid., 434.
"Here, in one word": Ibid., 435.
"Here was the pure, modest": Ibid.
55 "My head was close to the crimson curtain": Ibid.
"In spots where destruction": Ibid., 437.
56 "pedestrians, horsemen, stage-coaches": *Centenary*, XI:302.
"some were farmers' taverns": Ibid., 303.
"Never did a pilgrim": Ibid., 281.
"On the contrary": Ibid., 282.
57 "haunted with a vision of foam": Ibid., 284.
"a text of deep and varied meaning": Ibid., 327.
"A recluse, like myself": Hawthorne, *Lost Notebook*, 35.
"shapeless half-ideas": *Centenary*, X:114.
58 "intermediate space, where the business": *Centenary* IX:305.
"on the luxury of wearing out": Ibid., 306.
"In the depths of every heart": Ibid.
"the devils of a guilty heart": Ibid., 307.
"the lights, the music": Ibid., 306.
59 "the table near the fire-place": Ibid., 308.
"As your head falls back": Ibid.
"A lone woman": *Centenary*, X:74.
"My father never went": Ibid., 76.
"I helped your grandfather": Ibid., 77.
60 "Depending upon one another's hearts": Ibid., 88.
"a stern, a sad": Ibid., 89.
"the deep mystery of sin": Ibid., 87.
"for his dying hour was gloom": Ibid., 90.
"secret sin, and those sad": *Centenary*, IX:40.
61 "shrouded in dismal suspicions": Ibid., 49.
"I look around me": Ibid., 52.
"made himself remarkable": Ibid., 37.
"Has it not been well acted?": Hawthorne, *Lost Notebook*, 34.
"So far as I am": *Centenary*, X:33.
"My Kinsman, Major Molineux": Evidently the title of the story was not quite settled at first, since Goodrich referred to it as "My Uncle Molineaux" in his letter of January 19, 1830. (See J. Hawthorne, *NH and His Wife*, I:131–32.) Over a year later, in his letter of May 31, 1831 (J. Hawthorne, *NH and His Wife*, I:132), he wrote of it as "Major Molineaux." Did Hawthorne, prior to publication of the story, feel that the designation "Uncle" was too sensitive — and therefore change it to the more general "kinsman"?
62 "The fair and hospitable dame": *Centenary*, XI:218.

page

"Strange things": Ibid., 220.

63 "first actual discovery": *Centenary*, IV:204. It is an example both of Hawthorne's occasional diffidence as a writer and of the hold of certain ideas upon his mind that he virtually repeats the same insight, some hundred or more pages later, in *The Marble Faun*. See *Centenary*, IV:328.

"an elderly man, of large": *Centenary*, XI:228.

"foul disgrace of a head": Ibid., 229.

"Or, if you prefer": Ibid., 231.

64 "How happy I shall feel": See Hawthorne's letter to his sister on page 24.

page MONSIEUR DU MIROIR

65 "Mr. Horatio Bridge is requested": Bridge, *Personal Recollections*, 48.

"If Nathaniel Hathorne is neither": Ibid., 47.

"Now you are indeed": J. Hawthorne, *NH and His Wife*, I:144–45.

66 That Hawthorne made the bet at just the time: Every student of Hawthorne, I imagine, comes to feel that some fateful experience, either in his youth or perhaps earlier in childhood, opened up for him a deep sense of the sinfulness of human nature — an awareness that permanently altered his view of the world and of human relationships. Even late in his life, Hawthorne could still describe with peculiar force the effects of the initiation of the young into the complexities of evil — the heartsickness that "we may all of us have been pure enough to feel, once in our lives, but the capacity for which is usually exhausted early, and perhaps with a single agony." *Centenary*, IV:328.

In Hawthorne's fictional universe, that midnight knowledge often involves "the sin of some guide whom we have dearly loved." My own theory — though I do not want to burden the text of Hawthorne's life with a purely speculative bit of psychohistory — is that Robert Manning figures in some way in Hawthorne's crucial experience. There is a distinct, though low-keyed animus toward his Uncle Robert revealed throughout Hawthorne's life, something I have tried to underscore in the narrative portions of this biography. It gives a special coloring, I think, to Hawthorne's otherwise innocent remark: "An uncle . . . is a very dangerous member of the family." (Admittedly, the remark was made in a quite different context; see NH to Fields, October 18, 1863 [Houghton], discussed on page 572.)

Yet Hawthorne was also inclined to feel that his Uncle Robert had formed a more accurate estimate of his character than any other member of his family. It is part of the complexity of Hawthorne's response to the "deep mystery of sin" — more so in his fiction than in his life — that he can neither altogether relate to nor altogether disown the sinner. Sin, in fact, is usually presented as an intimate form of knowledge that bonds together both the sinner and the sinned-against.

Having said that, however, I must also point out that in his fiction Hawthorne's animus toward Robert Manning finds a more hostile — and probably unconscious — form of expression. Among the more problematic villains in Hawthorne's stories and romances, there are several who have distinct horticultural associations — as did his Uncle Robert. The sinister Rappaccini cultivates unnatural and poisonous varieties of plants in his evil garden. Roger Chillingworth, the grim prober of the Reverend Dimmesdale's soul, is a specialist in herbs. The hypocritical Judge Pyncheon, so well-respected by his townsmen, has extensive orchards, imports rare varieties of fruit trees, and has bred "two much esteemed varieties of the pear."

Pressed to explain the nature of Hawthorne's critical experience, I would suggest that he may have been subjected to some homosexual assault or seduction, perhaps by his Uncle Robert, during the period when the two were sleeping together. But that, too, is speculation, based on the fact that Hawthorne's theology seemed always to be in search of and hinting at an "unpardonable sin" that he could not precisely name; that he would speak of secret sins that would "look monstrous in the general eye"; and that he was the creator of fictional scientists who, in one way or another, are intent on overthrowing the established laws of nature. My feeling is that Hawthorne's ambivalent attitude toward a possible homosexual complication in his youth also accounts for both the responsiveness and the aloofness of his later relationship with Herman Melville.

"captivated in his fanciful way": EMH to Una Hawthorne, February 14, 1862; Bancroft Transcripts. Later, however (EMH to Fields, December 26, 1870; Boston Public Library), Ebe claimed that Hawthorne's stay in Swampscott had lasted two months.

"Oh Susan, the sugar heart": *Centenary*, IX:628.

"had a very great deal": EMH to Una Hawthorne, February 14, 1862; Bancroft Transcripts.

67 "fluttering in the breeze": *Centenary*, IX:312.

"She kindled a domestic fire": Ibid., 316.

"just such a neat and pretty": *Centenary*, XI:128.

"By-and-by, he'll grow gloomy": Ibid., 130.

68 "cold and passionless": Ibid., 131.

"the weight of its desolate agony": *Centenary*, IX:425.

"handsomest couple": Ibid., 43.

69 "the sad, true tale": Ibid., 319.

"just as the priest": Ibid., 373.

"Courtship is said to be": NH to John Dike, Jr., September 1, 1830; Pearson Transcripts.

"But, after all, the worst": J. Hawthorne, *NH and His Wife*, I:135.

"I shall try your advice": Ibid., 136.

70 "I should not wish to be": NH to Messrs. Carey and Lea, January 27, 1832; Historical Society of Pennsylvania.

"I've been thinking": J. Hawthorne, *NH and His Wife*, I:138.

71 "Thus has this man": Bridge, *Personal Recollections*, 69.

72 "was peculiarly sensitive": Hawthorne, *Works*, XII:258.

"old-fashioned tune": Ibid., 261.

Out of kindness, he also devoted: See Turner, *Hawthorne as Editor*, 216–21.

"I am so busy": NH to LH, January 21, 1836; Essex Institute.

"Daniel Webster drinks": NH to EMH, January 25, 1836; Essex Institute.

73 "Concoct, concoct": Ibid.

"I have written all but": NH to LH [n.d., 1836]; Essex Institute.

"provided always, that it be": NH to EMH, February 10, 1836; Essex Institute.

"My mind is pretty much": NH to LH, February 15, 1836; Essex Institute.

74 "Unless they pay me": NH to EMH, May 12, 1836; Essex Institute.

"manners, customs and civilities": J. Hawthorne, *NH and His Wife*, I:146.

"compelled to this course": Ibid., 137.

"Besides, it is no small": Ibid., 134.

"You have the blues again": Bridge, *Personal Recollections*, 70.

"I fear that you are": Ibid., 72.

75 "I hope to God": J. Hawthorne, *NH and His Wife*, I:138.

"I received your letter": Bridge, *Personal Recollections*, 79.

"unreasonably delayed": J. Hawthorne, *NH and His Wife*, I:146.

76 "I fear you will": Ibid., 142.

"The bane of your life": Ibid., 147.

"I doubt whether you ever get": Ibid.

"And so Frank Pierce is elected": Ibid., 148.

77 "I expect next summer": Ibid., 147.

78 "the fantastic and effeminate men": *Centenary*, X:421.

"a young person of doubtful sex": Ibid., 419.

"I have never read": J. Hawthorne, *NH and His Wife*, I:151.

"As for me": Ibid., 152.

79 "We were not, it is true": NH to Longfellow, March 7, 1837; Houghton.

page
"When I last heard": NH to Longfellow, June 4, 1837; Houghton.
80 "I frankly own": NH to Longfellow, June 19, 1837; Houghton.
"When a new star": Crowley, *Critical Heritage*, 55.
"There is no tradition": Ibid., 58.
"vein of pleasant philosophy": Ibid., 59.
81 "two stories of a darker colour": Ibid., 49.
"My worshipful self": NH to EMH, January 25, 1836; Essex Institute.
"the beautiful simplicity": Crowley, *Critical Heritage*, 53.
"few equals, and with": Ibid., 55.
"A rose bathed and baptized": Ibid., 60.
"national in their character": Ibid., 58.
"for many kinds and classes": Ibid., 62.
82 "of a hardier and more robust": Ibid., 61.
"and making its way": J. Hawthorne, *NH and His Wife*, I:157.
"Your book will do good": Ibid., 153.
83 "To be read fitly": Crowley, *Critical Heritage*, 61.
"mild, shy, gentle": *Centenary*, IX:7.
"They would have been better": NH to Longfellow, June 4, 1837; Houghton.
84 "He is a man of decided genius": J. Hawthorne, *NH and His Wife*, I:154. For details of Reynolds and the expedition, see Haskell, *The United States Exploring Expedition*, and Almy, "J. N. Reynolds: A Brief Biography."
"I think I can do": J. Hawthorne, *NH and His Wife*, I:152.
"But, after all, it will still": Ibid., 153.
"I don't know whether": Ibid., 156.
"It is absolute folly": Ibid., 157.
85 "weak eyes and green spectacles": Longfellow, *Letters*, II:162.
"of the highest rank of magazine": J. Hawthorne, *NH and His Wife*, I:159.
86 The expedition was put under the command of Charles Wilkes: Interestingly, Wilkes's *Narrative of the United States Exploring Expedition* was a source book for Herman Melville, whom Hawthorne later met. It is also quite possible that Melville had read J. N. Reynolds' "Mocha-Dick; or The White Whale of the Pacific," published in the *Knickerbocker* magazine for May 1839. Hawthorne's pay, had he been chosen, would have been $2500 a year plus rations.
"I want you to spend": J. Hawthorne, *NH and His Wife*, I:161.
87 "Are you writing another book?": Ibid., 162.
"Are you seriously thinking": Ibid., 158.
"What has become of your": Ibid., 161.
"If so, we had better": Ibid., 162.
"When you come": Ibid., 163.
88 "It is no use": Ibid., 164.
"So lonely as he is": *Centenary*, VIII:33.
"Je hais — Je hais les Yankees!": Ibid., 34.
89 "polished, yet natural": Ibid., 33.
"the longest space, probably": Ibid., 34.
"as much like the ruins": Ibid., 35.
90 "It is not a little striking": Ibid., 48.
"aged before their time": Ibid., 49.
"knot of whores": Ibid., 58.
"The decanters and wine-bottles": Ibid., 45.
"depressed, neglected air": Ibid., 58.
91 "A man generally places": Ibid., 59.
"Query — in relation": Ibid., 60.
"of Christianity and Deism": Ibid., 58.
"his whole heart — his whole inner man": Ibid., 49.
"We appear mutually to be": Ibid., 43.
92 "Of female society": Ibid., 44.
"not unconscious that some": Ibid., 60.
"the board-built and turf-buttressed": Ibid., 44.

"He is a singular man": Ibid., 61.
93 "bold and fierce as a tiger": Ibid., 62.
"and how it had affected him": Ibid., 61.
"I believe him to be": Ibid., 62.
"full of antique prejudices": Ibid., 72.
"with rather more of the ocean": Ibid., 73.
94 "pride of ancestry": Ibid., 74.
According to Eben, one of English's daughters: Either Ebenezer or Hawthorne himself made a mistake here. A granddaughter of English married a grandson of the witch-trial judge, John Hathorne. The daughter born of this couple was the mother of Hawthorne's relative Suzy Ingersoll, who lived in the "House of the Seven Gables." See explanatory notes, *Centenary*, VIII:584.
"the most arrant democracy": Ibid., 75.
"the folly of tumbling down": *Centenary*, II:2.
"What we call real estate": Ibid., 263.
"One odd, but characteristic notion": EMH to Fields, December 26, 1870; Boston Public Library.
"Four precepts": Hawthorne, *Lost Notebook*, 21.
95 "Follow out the fantasy": Ibid., 19.
"To picture the predicament": Ibid., 22.
"In this dismal and squalid": Ibid., 25.
"Fame — some very humble": Ibid., 36.
"A lament for Life's": Ibid., 33.
"To think, as the sun goes down": Ibid., 34.
"To make one's own reflection": Ibid., 18.
96 "He has been imprudent enough": *Centenary*, X:633. Although these lines appeared in the story when it was published anonymously in *The Token*, Hawthorne — perhaps at Sophia's urging — deleted them, along with a lengthy passage, when it was reprinted in *Mosses from an Old Manse*.
"Here, in my chamber": Ibid., 164.
"If I must needs have": Ibid., 166.
"And when the coffin lid": Ibid., 167.
97 "ferocity of the true blood-hound": Hawthorne, *Works*, XII:255. Hawthorne's essay on Fessenden appeared in the January 1838 issue of the *American Monthly*.
"Indeed, lacking a turn for observation": Hawthorne, *Works*, XII:262.
98 "Dark would have been": Ibid., 262.

page   THE SOPHISTRY OF PASSION

101 "Fate seems to be": *Centenary*, VIII:34.
Lizzie Peabody had issued her invitation: See Pearson, "Elizabeth Peabody on Hawthorne," 263.
"He has lived the life": MTP to George Peabody, November 16, 1837; Berg.
102 "look of entreaty": Pearson, "Elizabeth Peabody on Hawthorne," 265.
Mary Crowninshield Silsbee, 1809–1887; Nathaniel Silsbee, 1773–1850. For details see "Autobiographical Memoir by Nathaniel Silsbee," *EIHC*, January 1899:1–79.
"a great coquette": Pearson, "Hawthorne's Duel," 232.
"a torrent of affectation": Tharp, *Peabody Sisters*, 347.
103 Elizabeth Crowninshield remained a spinster until the age of forty-nine: Hawthorne was to encounter the Mountfords later in Rome, and to see them as touching anomalies in the midst of a carnival atmosphere: "I do not know that I have seen anything queerer than a Unitarian clergyman (Mr. Mountford) who drives through the Corso daily, with his fat wife, in a one-horse chaise, with a wreath of withered flowers and oak-leaves round his hat." Hawthorne, *French and Italian Notebooks*, March 7, 1859.
Jared Sparks, 1789–1866.

page

"because your name is so": EPPm to Sparks, December 26, 1838; Houghton. It is probably the result of Lizzie's meddling nature that there is a very sharp marginal comment on her letter, written in a shaky hand (Mary Sparks's?): "This woman abused the whole thing . . ."

"Star of Salem . . . a woman to whom": Ann Gillam Storrow to Sparks, May 1, 1828; Houghton. For an extended discussion of the relationship of Storrow and Sparks, see Blanshard, "Letters of Ann Gillam Storrow."

104 "little prospect but that": NH to Longfellow, June 4, 1837; Houghton.
"that he was the only human being": J. Hawthorne, *NH and His Wife*, I:170.
"secret spring": NH to O'Sullivan, November 5, 1838; Cornell University Library.
"in the gentlest and most considerate": J. Hawthorne, *NH and His Wife*, I:171.

105 It was not until 1958: See Pearson, "Hawthorne's Duel."
"private and mysterious interview": J. Hawthorne, *NH and His Wife*, I:171.
"vivid affections": NH to SAH, February 7, 1856; Huntington. That Hawthorne's friendship with O'Sullivan did not go deep, one might presume from his remarks: "I like him, and enjoy his society, and he calls up, I think, whatever small part of me is elegant and agreeable; but neither of my best nor of my worst has he ever, or could he ever, have a glimpse." Ibid.

106 "champion her cause": J. Hawthorne, *NH and His Wife*, I:171.
"a frank and generous letter": Ibid., 172.
"It is my purpose to set out": NH to Bridge, February 5, 1838; Bowdoin. Several lines have been excised from the letter.
"not a leg to stand upon": J. Hawthorne, *NH and His Wife*, I:173.
"ample explanations": Bridge, *Personal Recollections*, 5–6. Bridge's recollection was that Hawthorne had gone to Washington. Yet Hawthorne, writing to Lydia Fessenden, the widow of the poet, on April 12, 1838, acknowledging that it had been a "winter of much anxiety and of very little pleasure or profit," remarked that he had "almost entirely given up the idea of going to Washington." University of Virginia.

107 "harsher traits . . . had grown apace": Hawthorne, *Works*, XII:272.
A burning political issue: For details on the circumstances of the Cilley-Graves duel, I have relied on the following: "Report of the Committee on the Late Duel" [1838], 1–8, and "Testimony of Doctor J. M. Foltz, United States Navy" [1838], 3–7; Library of Congress. For background on the political controversies of the period, Schlesinger, *Age of Jackson*, and Cantwell, *Nathaniel Hawthorne*, have proved helpful.

108 "Will not the same desperado": Schlesinger, *Age of Jackson*, 246.
One of these, a duel: See Staples, *Letters of John Fairfield*. Fairfield's letters to his wife contain a good deal of information about Washington political and social life. Duels and prospective duels are mentioned in his letters of January 17, February 27, and June 11, 1836, and January 17 and June 9, 1838.
"facilities to the amount of some $52,000": "Report of the Committee," 1.

109 "I neither affirmed nor denied": Ibid., 2.
"inexplicit, unsatisfactory": Ibid.
"Your note of this date": Ibid.

110 "the highest respect and most kind": Ibid., 4.
"if either of those gentlemen": "Testimony of Doctor J. M. Foltz," 6.

111 "a breach of the highest": "Report of the Committee," 8.
"He died like a hero": Williams to Bridge, February 27, 1838; Bowdoin.
"he loved to sit for whole hours": Hawthorne, *Works*, XII:273.
"I saw how much your brother": J. Hawthorne, *NH and His Wife*, I:165.

112 "I see that you both": Ibid., 166.
"It has fallen to my lot": NH to Longfellow, March 21, 1838; Houghton.
"still a-bed in his Herbert Street": Longfellow Journals, entry March 25, 1838; Houghton.

113 "by various causes": NH to O'Sullivan, April 19, 1838; University of Virginia.
"a person of disputed respectability": Hawthorne, *Works*, XII:274. Hawthorne's sketch of Cilley appeared in the September 1838 issue of the *Democratic Review*.

"A challenge was never given": Hawthorne, *Works*, XII:274.

"Hardly anybody, probably": *Centenary*, VIII:62.

114 "She is something too much": NH to O'Sullivan, April 19, 1838; University of Virginia.

"a good old soul": NH to O'Sullivan, May 19, 1839. See the Grolier Club, *Nathaniel Hawthorne*, 17. The letter is in the collection of Mr. Robert H. Taylor.

"are out of the world": Pearson, "Elizabeth Peabody on Hawthorne," 266.

"What a peculiar person": Ibid., 267.

115 "She is a flower": Ibid.

"But every word": Ibid., 266.

"knowledge of the world": Elizabeth Palmer Peabody?, unsigned review of *Twice-told Tales* in *The New Yorker*, March 24, 1838, 1.

"the most true psychological biography": EPPm to Bridge, June 4, 1887; Bowdoin.

116 "the appearance of the moment": Ibid.

"I complained that there was": Emerson, *Journals*, VII:21.

Jones Very, 1813–1880. For details of Very's life, I am indebted to Gittleman, *Jones Very*.

"angelic Very": R. H. Lathrop, *Memories*, 24.

"They do not understand": Ibid., 25.

"level rays of light": Ibid., 24.

"resignation and acceptance": Gittleman, *Jones Very*, 286.

117 "alone, within a circle": *Centenary*, X:638. Hawthorne deleted the description when he reprinted the piece in *Mosses from an Old Manse*.

"with the Holy Ghost": Gittleman, *Jones Very*, 216.

"with a slightly uneasy": Ibid., 217.

"Such a mind cannot": Emerson, *Letters*, II:165.

"It was a very curious": EPPm to Emerson, December 3, 1838; Essex Institute.

"Louisa came to the door": SAH to EPPm, May 8–13, 1838; Berg.

118 "We were put into": SAH to EPPm, April 26–May 1, 1838; Berg.

What particularly struck Sophia about the painting: Catherine Scollay (1783–1863) was active in Boston and exhibited at the Boston Athenaeum between 1827 and 1843. I have not been able to locate the painting mentioned.

"was not natural": SAH to EPPm, July 23, 1838; Pearson Transcripts. A copy of this letter in the Berg collection is incomplete and deletes a phrase in the Pearson transcript. See SAH to EPPm, July 23, "Monday Morning" [1838]; Berg.

119 "In love-quarrels": Hawthorne, *Lost Notebook*, 58. Hawthorne attributes the observation to his friend David Roberts. The entry appears after December 6, 1837 — that is during the period when he had become acquainted with the Peabody sisters and before his final break with Mary Silsbee.

"on a tour of diversion": "Autobiographical Memoir by Nathaniel Silsbee," *EIHC*, January 1899, 1–79.

"Salem is a hornet's nest": Longfellow Journal, entry March 25, 1838; Houghton.

"forbidden her the slightest use": Mrs. Mary Anne C. Silsbee to Jared Sparks, October 2, 1838; Houghton.

"In my hurry last evening": EPPm to EMH, October 19, 1838?; Essex Institute.

120 ". . . to say that they were evidences": EPPm to EMH [between 1837 and 1842]; Berg.

"In accordance with your exhortations": NH to O'Sullivan, November 5, 1838; Cornell University Library.

122 "A week or two since": NH to O'Sullivan, May 19, 1839; the Grolier Club, *Nathaniel Hawthorne*, 15.

"What a trustful guardian": *Centenary*, VIII:552. Hawthorne's entry is dated "June, 1853," on the eve of his departure for England. The occasion was the burning of "hundreds of Sophia's maiden letters — the world has no more such; and now they are all ashes."

"an event which I am almost sorry": NH to O'Sullivan, May 19, 1839; the Grolier Club, *Nathaniel Hawthorne*, 16.

Sparks was fifty when he resumed: Although garrulous on the subject of history

page

or a visit with Alexis de Tocqueville, Sparks tended to be closed-mouthed about his personal affairs. His private journal entry for May 21, 1839, the day of his marriage, is succinct: "Married to Mary Crowninshield Silsbee at her father's house, Salem." (Sparks's Journal, 1832–1840; Houghton.) By contrast, Longfellow, who met the bridal couple some weeks later, was positively expansive: "Met Sparks and his wife at dinner at Palfrey's. Very pleasant; Mrs. S. once so well known as the fascinating and fashionable Miss Silsbee, is a very attractive woman, with an intellectual style of beauty, which quite leads one captive." Sparks, Longfellow reported, was as gleaming as "Ursa Major." Longfellow Journal, June 15, 1839; Houghton.

"Did I tell you in my last": Pearson, "Hawthorne's Duel," 241.

123 "an inveterate love of allegory": *Centenary*, X:91.

"a voice as rich as": Ibid., 96.

124 "with a bloom so deep": Ibid., 97.

"whether it were a girl": Ibid., 98.

"How often is it the case": Ibid., 109.

"By all appreciable signs": Ibid., 115.

"cares infinitely more for science": Ibid., 99.

Baglioni, convinced that Rappaccini is poisoning: That Hawthorne viewed the poisoning as in some sense a sexual fatality seems clear from an early notebook entry (and a reference within the story itself) to a fable by Sir Thomas Browne concerning an Indian king who sent Alexander the Great "a fair woman, fed with aconites and other poisons, with this intent, either by converse or copulation complexionally to destroy him." Hawthorne, *Lost Notebook*, 85.

125 "No, no, Giovanni": *Centenary*, X:125.

"As he drew near": Ibid., 126.

"Oh, was there not": Ibid., 127.

"surprised, and a little ashamed": Ibid., 98.

"by the subtle sophistry of passion": Ibid., 114.

page   THE QUIET, SILENT, DULL DECENCY OF SALEM

127 "I am tired to death of pen": NH to Catherine Ainsworth, April 12, 1838; University of Virginia.

When Nathaniel Hawthorne first met: For details on the Peabody family and its history, I am indebted to Louise Hall Tharp's two volumes, *The Peabody Sisters of Salem* and *Until Victory*.

129 "a history of suffering": Mann's Journal, July 31, 1837; Massachusetts Historical Society.

130 "Jackson men, Anti-Masons": Messerli, *Horace Mann*, 195.

"The Senate sat today": EPPm to MTP, January 6–7, 1835; Berg.

"rallying point of dissipation": Messerli, *Horace Mann*, 213.

"Not that it would not": EPPm to MTP, September 20–October 6, 1834; Berg.

131 The Peabody sisters and Mother Peabody were incorrigible: The family's prolific habit of writing letters has proved a troublesome boon to historians: original letters and undated fragments of originals, copies (sometimes inexact) and undated fragments of copies, written in one Peabody hand or another, have found their way into archives to plague unwary scholars with variants.

132 "I am going to write a book": MTP to EPPm, May 13–14?, 1834; Berg.

"gentlest and safest horse": MTP to EPPM, January 26, 1834: Berg.

"Sophia continues to take": MTP to EPPM, February 8, 1834; Berg.

"I used to think": MTP to EPPm, May 11, 1834; Berg.

"Again — again — and again": EPPm to MTP. January 16–20, 1835; Berg.

133 "incontinently dosed with drugs": J. Hawthorne, *NH and His Wife*, I:47. Sophia's

mother, who suffered with a persistent cough for much of her life, regularly took small doses of opium to ease her condition. Later in life, however, she wrote her youngest daughter, "For years, I took it in some form or other, but I am now so convinced that the consequences are pernicious, producing irritability of nerves and stupefying headaches that I resolve to use no means but homeopathic." EPPM to SAH, "Mond. January 8," 1844?; Berg. References to Una Hawthorne and Horace Mann, Jr., both of whom were born after January 1844, however, make it clear that the 1844 date is incorrect.

"She was enthusiastic, prone": J. Hawthorne, *NH and His Wife*, I:47.

"I have been trying to clip": SAH to Nathaniel Peabody, March 6, 1853; Berg.

134 "I myself am going to": SAH to EPPm, June 11, 1822; Berg.

She also taught her brothers: See SAP to EPPm, January 18, 1827; Berg.

"We think that your stay": EPP to SAH, July 3, 1827; Berg.

"Well, darling of my heart": J. Hawthorne, *NH and His Wife*, I:67.

135 "regular bodily and intellectual": Walter Channing to SAH, August 12, 1828; Berg.

136 "I ride on horseback": SAH to EPPM, January 13, 1834, Cuban Journals; Berg.

"Every morning there is a golden": Ibid.

"Nothing more can be asked for": SAH to EPPM, May 27, 1834, Cuban Journals; Berg. See Claire Badaracco, "The Night-blooming Cereus."

"I will observe your advice": SAH to EPPM, January 26, 1834, Cuban Journals; Berg.

"I assure you I am very cold": MTP to EPPM, January 26, 1834, Cuban Journals; Berg.

"What think you dearest mother": SAH to EPPM, August 9, 1834, Cuban Journals; Berg.

"My dear one, do not let": EPPM to SAH and MTP. September 9, 1834; Berg.

"sleeps well, and can take": MTP to EPPM, September 14, 1834, Cuban Journals; Berg.

137 "And if you are made well": EPPM to SAH, September 23, 1834; Berg.

"the very spirit of kindness": SAH to EPPM, December 20, 1833, Cuban Journals; Berg.

"He knew better than to expose": EPPm to MTP, August 8?–10?, 1834; Berg.

"I hope you will make out": EPPm to MTP, September?, 1834?; Berg.

"I am thankful": EPPm to MTP, September 20–October 6, 1834?; Berg.

138 "And yet if there is": Alcott, *Letters*, 22.

139 "think less well of many persons": Saxton, *Louisa May*, 83.

"eternal damnation . . . the greatest crime": EPPm to MTP, undated, before August 1836; Massachusetts Historical Society. See also MTP to EPPm, undated, ca. 1836; Massachusetts Historical Society.

140 "I feel more and more": Saxton, *Louisa May*, 86.

"indecent and obscene book": Ibid., 95.

"all I fancy that this": Alcott, *Letters*, 33.

141 "You may ask what": Ibid., 44.

"He not only cannot": Tharp, *Peabody Sisters*, 111.

"I think Mr. Emerson is" SAH to EPPm, [Salem, 1838]; Berg. A transcript of this letter in the Bancroft Library is dated "Sunday, 29th." The month is definitely April.

Her letters were also full of exultant praises: For example, "He is the sublimest of men. The grandest episode in the history of the world, a perfect unity." Transcript of SAH to EPPm, May 26, 1838; Bancroft. Sophia had been reading Jared Sparks's life of Washington.

"I agree with you about": EPPm to SAH, "Sunday–Monday" [1838]; Berg.

"corkscrews, borers, pincers": SAH to EPPm, April 20, 1838; Berg.

142 "But was it not a pity": SAH to EPPm, April 23–25, 1838; Berg.

"he wished he could have": SAH to EPPm, April 26–May 1, 1838; Berg.

"What a beautiful smile": Ibid.

"To be the means": Ibid.

"Last night, after I was left": SAH to EPPm, April 23–25, 1838; Berg.

page
143 "I have been reading of ": SAH to EPPm, May 2–3, 1838; Berg.
"I was lost in a siesta": SAH to EPPm, May 8–13, 1838; Berg.
"I was quite disappointed": EPPm to SAH, "Sunday–Monday," [1838]; Berg. Although this letter is not dated, references to Sophia's previous letter of May 28, and Sophia's response to remarks about Washington Allston, place it, I believe, as June 10–11, 1838.

144 "I feel as if he were a born brother": SAH to EPPm, July 23, 1838; Pearson Transcripts. This portion of the letter is from Pearson's longer transcript of a letter that is incomplete in the Berg collection.
"He said he was not going": Ibid. The notion of dying, nameless, while traveling is one that Hawthorne used in an early story, "The Ambitious Guest."
"He told me . . . that I was the Queen": Ibid.
"He said he had seen you": SAH to EPPm, May 8–13, 1838; Berg.

145 "His first question was": SAH to EPPm, May 14–16, 1838; Berg.
"Mary put E's letter into Scott": SAH to EPPm, [summer, 1838]; Berg.
"Tell E. Hawthorne that": EPPm to SAH, July 31, 1838; Berg.
"A story to show": Hawthorne, *Lost Notebook*, 57; see also *Centenary*, VIII:167.

146 "I do not tell lies": EPPm to SAH, July 31, 1838; Berg.
"Sophia never knew of her sister's engagement": quoted in Carroll A. Wilson, *Thirteen Author Collections*, I:131–32. Mrs. Dall also remarks, "N.H. never allowed his wife to receive the mail. He opened it and read all of E's letters and destroyed what he chose. I have seen his own acknowledgement in writing this in reply to EPP's reproaches or I could not have believed it." The comments about Hawthorne's censorship may have had some basis in actuality, though it may have applied to Lizzie's manuscript on the slavery issue, which Hawthorne had at first returned to Lizzie, and then gave to Sophia when his sister-in-law sent it once more. See page 469.

147 "a certain celestial region": Hawthorne, *Lost Notebook*, 74.

148 "spoke of the trials": *Centenary*, VIII:81.
"perusing their mutual comeliness": Ibid., 86.
"This would be a terrific": Ibid., 90.

149 "Soon, probably, there will be": Ibid., 88.
"but as it is possible": NH to Roberts, July 26, 1838; St. Lawrence.

150 "Fall down, roll down": *Centenary*, VIII:110.
"On the whole, I find": Ibid., 112.
"My study is man": Ibid., 92.

151 "This man was created to shine": Ibid., 587.
"and comes to the tavern": Ibid., 94.
"We talk together very freely": Ibid., 96.
"a dissolute and mirth-making": Ibid., 127.
"We looked through the glass": Ibid., 130.

152 "began to talk with her": Ibid., 145–46.
"Mr. Leach spoke to me": Ibid., 146.

153 "respectably dressed": Ibid., 151.
"How could there be": MTP to Mann, August 26, 1837; Massachusetts Historical Society.
"a young man in this town": Transcript of MTP to Mann, March 3, 1838; Massachusetts Historical Society.
"Seriously, I think a very pleasant": NH to Longfellow, March 21, 1838; Houghton.

154 "Have you blown your blast?": NH to Longfellow, October 12, 1838; Houghton. In this letter, Hawthorne noted of his trip to North Adams, "I have been rambling about since the middle of July till within a week or two past, and have had such pleasant times as seldom happens to a man of my age and experience."
"a strange owl, a very peculiar": Longfellow, *Letters*, II:107.
"Assuredly you have a right": NH to Longfellow, January 12, 1839; Houghton.
"something nearer home": Mann to EPPm, March 10, 1838; Massachusetts Historical Society.

"moral sentiments suited to the class": Messerli, *Horace Mann*, 345.

"In short, there is no end": Dana, *Journal*, I:335.

155 "After I was left alone": EPPm to Mrs. George Bancroft, November 6, 1838; Library of Congress.

156 Whatever her methods, she was successful: According to Mary Peabody, Lizzie informed Hawthorne, and "H. felt very bad when he found he actually got it." MTP to SAH, January 5, 1839; Berg.

"After due reflection": NH to Bancroft, January 11, 1839; University of Virginia.

"I have appointed Nathaniel Hawthorne": Bancroft to Levi Woodbury, January 17, 1839; National Archives.

"I have no reason to doubt": NH to Longfellow, January 12, 1839; Houghton.

157 "I want to know if this looks": Pearson, "Elizabeth Peabody on Hawthorne," 267.

"No testimonial in regard": *Centenary*, IX:568.

"When I was drawing you": This is one of several personal asides to Hawthorne in an eighteen-page journal-letter, relating her Cuban adventures, that Sophia wrote Hawthorne on December 6–7, 1838. University of Virginia.

"S.A.P. — taking my likeness": Hawthorne, *Lost Notebook*, 80.

158 "would never marry at all": Pearson, "Hawthorne's Duel," 232.

page IN THE WIDE DESERT OF THE WORLD

159 "My dearest Sophie": NH to SAH, March 6, 1839; Huntington.

"She said if it was the will": Pearson, "Elizabeth Peabody on Hawthorne," 275–76.

160 "My blessed Dove, Your letter": NH to SAH, July 15, 1839; Huntington.

"I was hardly seated here": R. H. Lathrop, *Memories*, 29.

161 "like Cooper & Hawthorne": Emerson, *Journals* VII:244; also 242.

"I would you could have beheld": Hawthorne, *Works*, IX:224.

"I do think that it is the doom": NH to SAH, March 27, 1840; Huntington.

"I have a mind, some day": NH to SAH, January 1, 1840; Huntington.

"My thoughts sometimes wander back": NH to SAH, November 17, 1839; Huntington.

162 "He has no business, no amusement": *Centenary*, VIII:193.

William Pike, 1811–1876: See *Centenary*, VIII:189–92.

"You will never, I fear": R. H. Lathrop, *Memories*, 154.

"Objects on a wharf": *Centenary*, VIII:193.

"If I write a preface": NH to Longfellow, May 16, 1839; Houghton.

163 "That I have not recently": NH to O'Sullivan, May 19, 1839; the Grolier Club, *Nathaniel Hawthorne*, 15–17.

"Mine own Dove": NH to SAH, April 2, 1839; Huntington.

"to walk half round the world": NH to SAH, April 17, 1839; Huntington.

164 "Oh my dearest, I yearn": NH to SAH, May 26, 1839; Huntington.

"I am tired this evening": NH to SAH, July 24, 1839; Huntington.

"I used to think": NH to SAH, October 4, 1840; Huntington.

"You will always be the same to me": NH to SAH, April 17, 1839; Huntington.

165 "If it were possible": NH to SAH, August 21, 1839; Huntington.

"If we had but a cottage": NH to SAH, postscript to above, August 23, 1839; Huntington.

"Your husband is presently": NH to SAH, August 26, 1839; Huntington.

"Dove, come to my bosom": NH to SAH, September 23, 1839; Huntington.

166 "Ownest Dove, did you get home safe": NH to SAH, October 3, 1839; Huntington.

"Dearest, I beseech you, grant me": NH to SAH, July 30, 1839; Huntington.

"I wish you had read that dream letter": NH to SAH, April 30, 1839, and postscript of, or dated, May 3, 1839; Huntington.

"a sense that something was wanting": NH to SAH, May 26, 1839; Huntington.

167 "warm and voluptuous": Hawthorne, *Lost Notebook*, 66.

page

"I trust it did not 'rekindle' on his return": SAH to Fields, November 6, 1865; Boston Public Library. Whether she was deliberately intending to be misleading, Sophia wrote Fields that it was not until after Hawthorne's return from his North Adams trip "that we first met formally, though he had before known of me through E and my Cuban letters and others which E, unknown to me, had showed him." As her letters to Elizabeth throughout the spring of 1838 indicate, she had seen Hawthorne on many occasions before his trip.

"consumption of the spinal marrow": EPPm note in copies of four letters, SAH to EPPm, May 28 to June 10, 1838; Berg.

168 "I never have thought, you know": SAH to EPPm, May 26, 1838; Berg.

"if this may be called worst": NH to SAH, November 15, 1839; Huntington.

"May God sustain you": NH to SAH, November 14, 1839; Huntington.

"Oh be strong": NH to SAH, November 17, 1839; Huntington.

"Dearest, there is nothing in me": NH to SAH, November 20, 1839; Huntington.

"I came off in the two o'clock": NH to SAH, November 25, 1839; Huntington.

169 "Dearest, for some little time to come": NH to SAH, November 29, 1839; Huntington.

"Sumner is behaving": Donald, *Charles Sumner*, 74.

"What thinks my Dove of this": NH to SAH, October 23, 1839; Huntington.

170 "Altogether I am as happily situated": NH to SAH, November 17, 1839; Huntington.

"My evenings are very precious": NH to SAH, December 2, 1839; Huntington.

"I was invited to dine": NH to SAH, December 5, 1839; Huntington.

"Your husband has received": NH to SAH, December 20, 1839; Huntington.

"Mary and your husband": NH to SAH, December 5, 1839; Huntington.

"I cannot tell you": SAH to NH, December 31, 1839; J. Hawthorne, *NH and His Wife*, I:209.

171 "What a year the last has been!": NH to SAH, January 1, 1840; Huntington.

"Did we walk together": NH to SAH, January 3, 1840; Huntington.

"I want to feel that": NH to SAH, January 1, 1840; Huntington.

"You cannot think how": NH to SAH, January 3, 1840; Huntington.

"Moonlight is Sculpture": Hawthorne, *Lost Notebook*, 82.

172 "I gaze at them by all": NH to SAH, February 7, 1840; Huntington.

"I have met with an immense": NH to SAH, April 22, 1840; Huntington.

"My days have been so busy": NH to SAH, July 10, 1840; Huntington.

"wants a brother": MTP to SAH, January 5, 1839; Berg.

"wasted my precious hours": NH to SAH, July 10, 1840; Huntington.

"Most absolute little wife": NH to SAH, March 15, 1840; Huntington.

"Promise me this": NH to SAH, March 30, 1840; Huntington.

173 "Elizabeth [Hoar] is very well content": Emerson to SAH, May 18, 1840; R. H. Lathrop, *Memories*, 183–84.

"In regard to certain expression": Emerson to SAH, June 3, 1840; R. H. Lathrop, *Memories*, 184–85.

"Would that we could build": NH to SAH, June 22, 1840; Huntington.

174 "a point of union to well-educated": Ossoli, *Memoirs*, 324.

"comprised some of the most": Wade, *Margaret Fuller*, 70.

175 "Do not thou make thyself sick": NH to SAH, July 10, 1840; Huntington.

"Oh there are subjects enough": *Centenary*, VI:292.

176 "By occupying Grandfather's chair": NH to Longfellow, November 20, 1840; Houghton.

"delicate playthings out of the granite": *Centenary*, VI:6.

"If the assembly was disorderly": quoted in Merrill, *Against Wind*, 178.

177 Theodore Parker, in an uncharitable moment: See Swift, *Brook Farm*, 225.

"at this rumor of school or sect": Ibid., 6.

178 "to insure a more natural union": Ibid., 15.

179 "I wished to be convinced": Emerson, *Journals*, VII:407–08.

"The Custom House officers": NH to Roberts, November 15, 1840; Essex Institute.

"Bancroft represented to me": NH to Longfellow, November 20, 1840; Houghton.

180 "Perhaps thou wilt see her":'NH to SAH, November 27, 1840; Huntington.
"any disturbance or displeasure": NH to Bancroft, January 8, 1841; Massachusetts Historical Society.
181 "Methinks all enormous sinners": NH to SAH, March 18, 1841; Huntington.
"Here is thy poor husband": NH to SAH, April 13, 1841; Huntington.
182 "The whole fraternity eat together": NH to LH, May 3, 1841; Huntington.
"Belovedest, I have not yet": NH to SAH, April 13, 1841; Huntington.
"Miss Margaret Fuller might lose": NH to SAH, January 13, 1841; Huntington.
"Thy husband intends to convert": NH to SAH, April 13, 1841; Huntington.
183 "Mr. Ripley was afraid": NH to SAH, April 14, 1841; Huntington.
"Thy husband has milked a cow": NH to SAH, April 18, 1841; Huntington.
184 "in a thick fog": NH to SAH, April 28, 1841; Huntington.
"All this morning I have been": NH to SAH, May 4, 1841; Huntington.
"My life — how beautiful is Brook Farm!": NH to SAH, May 30, 1841; Berg.
"I think this present life": NH to SAH, June 1, 1841; Huntington.
185 "If you only knew how": LH to NH, May 10, 1841; Berg.
"very well dispense with the original": NH to LH, May 3, 1841; Huntington.
"But perhaps it is a modest blush": LH to NH, May 10, 1841; Berg.
"I had not written before": LH to NH, June 11, 1841; Berg.
186 "I have waited for a letter": LH to NH, August 3, 1841; Berg.
"scolding me most pathetically": NH to SAH, August 22, 1841; Huntington.
Perhaps he was feeling all the more guilty: The excursion with Frank Farley was
mentioned as a possibility in a letter to David Mack, dated July 18, 1841 (Pearson
Transcripts). See below.
"He was quite out of his wits": NH to SAH, August 22, 1841; Huntington.
"Thou and I must form other plans": Ibid. Hawthorne had frankly expressed his
doubts about the future of the community in his letter to Mack: "I confess that, of
late, my hopes are never very sanguine. I form my judgment, however, not from
anything that has passed within the precincts of Brook Farm, but from external
circumstances — from the improbability that adequate funds will be raised, or
that any feasible plan can be suggested, for proceeding without a very considerable capital." Although Mack had been one of the signers of the Brook Farm Articles of Association, he became a founder of the Northampton Association in
1842.
187 "I should judge it to be": NH to SAH, September 3, 1841; Huntington.
"I have not written that infernal": NH to Hillard, July 16, 1841; University of
Virginia.
188 "I confess that I have strong": NH to SAH, August 22, 1841; Huntington.
"because such an abominable rascal": NH to SAH, September 10, 1841; Huntington.
"venerable in a three-cornered hat": NH to SAH, September 14, 1841; Huntington.
"I doubt whether I shall": NH to SAH, November 17, 1839; Huntington.
"Sweetest, thou dost please me": NH to SAH, September 10, 1841; Huntington.
189 "cold, chill, sullen": NH to SAH, September 22, 1841; Huntington.
"I am not, nor shall be": NH to SAH, September 27, 1841; Huntington.
190 "Didst thou know what treasures": NH to SAH, September 25, 1841; Huntington.
"From the nature of my office": NH to SAH, September 29, 1841; Huntington.
"I am unwilling": NH to SAH, October 18, 1841; Huntington. Several years earlier, in 1837, Sophia had been "magnetized" by her father's partner, Dr. Fisk. She
had not been put to sleep, but Mary Peabody reported that Sophia had been "extremely soothed" by the treatments. MTP to George Peabody, November 16, 1837;
Berg.
"If she were larger": Centenary, VIII:209.
191 "her intellect is very ordinary": Ibid., 210.
"Margaret Fuller talked of ballads": Ibid., 605.
"It has left a fantastic impression": Ibid., 202.
"The cawing of the crow": Ibid., 214.
"Passing an orchard": Ibid., 215.

page
192 "Fringed gentians": Ibid., 222.
"a very temporary quarrel": EPPm notation on a letter from NH to EPPm, February 19, 1842; Library of Congress.
"Mr. Hawthorne particularly desires": NH to EPPm, June 23, 1841; Library of Congress.
"If Mr. Hawthorne had felt himself solely": NH to EPPm, February 19, 1842; Library of Congress.
193 "unique in their form": Crowley, *Critical Heritage*, 79.
"is characterized by a large": Ibid., 81.
"a pure and living stream": Ibid., 86.
"His *originality*, both of incident": Ibid., 85.
"Mr. Hawthorne's distinctive trait": Ibid., 91.
194 "Surely the book was puffed": NH to Hillard, November 26, 1843; Maine Historical Society.
"I wish the devil had the books": NH to Hillard, May 14, 1844; Collection Donald Henry.
"exquisite sense of what is right": NH to SAH, June 2, 1840; Huntington.
"We are conscious of one another's feelings": NH to SAH, February 27, 1842; Huntington.
"incumbent upon me to offer": EMH to SAH, May 23, 1842; Berg. A second letter from Ebe to Sophia may have helped to alleviate the hurt feelings on both sides: "I dare say we shall and must seem very cold and even apathetic to you, but after you have known us a little while, it may be that you will discover more warmth and sympathy than is at first apparent." EMH to SAH, June 15, 1842; Berg.
195 "Dearest Heart, Thy letter": NH to SAH, May 27, 1842; Huntington.
"some sensation in the forest": Emerson, *Journals*, VIII:53.
"We shall be married in June": SAH to Fuller, May 11, 1842; Houghton.
"If ever I saw a man": Fuller to SAH, June 4, 1842; Berg.
196 "Scarcely had I arrived": NH to SAH, June 9, 1842; Huntington.
"We have left expression": NH to SAH, January 20, 1842; Huntington.
"Thou hast not been out of my mind": NH to SAH, June 20, 1842; Huntington.
197 "I had hoped, as thou knowest": NH to SAH, June 30, 1842; Huntington.
"My Dear Sir": NH to Clarke, July 8, 1842; Houghton.
"Dear, dear Mother, Every step": SAH to EPPM, July 10, 1842; Berg.
"The execution took place yesterday": NH to LH, July 10, 1842; Essex Institute.

page   A NEW ADAM AND EVE
201 "so imminent upon the road": *Centenary*, X:3.
"too remote and dim": Ibid., 4.
"nervous impulse, without purpose": Ibid., 10.
In 1776, the Reverend Emerson: See Edward W. Emerson, *Emerson in Concord*, 4.
202 "from the mere necessity": *Centenary*, X:13.
"the very spot for": Ibid., 4.
"high-backed, short-legged": *Centenary*, VIII:323.
"bad angels": *Centenary*, X:5.
203 "Everything is as fresh": SAH to EPPM, July 10, 1842; Berg.
"Dear Sophie, I could fill sheets": J. Hawthorne, *NH and His Wife*, I:250.
"Say what you will": SAH to EPPM, July 15, 1842; Berg.
"My dearest — I have a thousand": J. Hawthorne, *NH and His Wife*, I:264.
204 "I wish I could be": SAH to EPPM, August 5?, 1842; Berg.
"I housekeep, paint, sew": J. Hawthorne, *NH and His Wife*, I:251.
"My peerless Mother, it sounds": SAH to EPPM, August 30–September 9, 1842; Berg.

"Mr. Hawthorne, who is writing": J. Hawthorne, *NH and His Wife*, I:265.
"abomination of visiting": SAH to EPPM, October 9, 1842; Berg.
205 "N. Hawthorne's reputation": Emerson, *Journals* VII:465.
"I was very naughty": SAH, undated entry [but probably August 2, 1842] from original manuscript of Hawthorne's American Notebooks. (MS MA 580); Morgan. That the quarrel took place on Tuesday, August 2, 1842, seems clear from Sophia's letter to her mother, August 4, 1842 (Berg), in which she describes walking with her husband and lying down on the pine needles.
"We penetrated the pleasant gloom": Ibid.
"A rainy day — a rainy day": *Centenary*, VIII:315.
206 "some ambrosial cow": Ibid., 316.
"Mr. Emerson comes": Ibid.
"such modernisms as astral-lamps": Ibid., 326.
207 "My life, at this time": Ibid., 331.
"I left my Sophie's arms": Ibid., 344.
"one dip into the salt-sea": Ibid., 319.
"I feel somewhat overwhelmed": Ibid., 344.
"All day long, we hear": Ibid., 348.
208 "even the Author of it": Ibid., 349.
"the chief event of the afternoon": Ibid., 334.
"I felt that I was regarded": Ibid.
"from a scruple of his external conscience": Ibid., 335.
"It would be amusing": Ibid., 336.
"It does really seem": Ibid., 337.
209 "without any one salient point": Ibid., 347.
"ugly as sin, long-nosed": Ibid., 353.
"a sort of Indian life": Ibid., 354.
"more exclusive than is": Ibid.
"cloudy and dreamy metaphysics": Ibid., 355.
210 "uncouth and somewhat rustic": Ibid., 353.
"I love Henry, but": Emerson, "Thoreau," *Atlantic Monthly*, August 1862:239.
"being in want of money": *Centenary*, VIII:356.
"as docile as a trained steed": Ibid., 357.
"On the whole, I find": Ibid., 355.
211 "queer and clever young men": Ibid., 357.
"but a poor substitute for Mr. Thoreau": Ibid., 269.
"I think perhaps he will": SAH, entry dated April 23, 1843 (MS MA 580); Morgan.
"I sprang from my husband's embrace": SAH to EPPM, August 22, 1842; Berg.
212 "The house within I like": Myerson, "Margaret Fuller's 1842 Journal," *Harvard Library Bulletin*, July 1973: 325.
"the moon broken in the water": Emerson, *Journals*, VIII:195–96.
"Looking at the moon": Myerson, "Margaret Fuller's 1842 Journal," 324.
213 "year's decay": *Centenary*, VIII:342.
"and smiled to see Margaret": Ibid., 343.
"in spite of his clerical consecration": Ibid.
"What a happy, happy day": Myerson, "Margaret Fuller's 1842 Journal," 325.
"Last evening there was the most beautiful": *Centenary*, VIII:344.
"Dear Margaret, Sophia has told me": NH to Fuller, August 25, 1842; Huntington.
214 "But in doing so": Ibid.
"It is a striking contrast": Myerson, "Margaret Fuller's 1842 Journal," 328.
"I shall never see you": Cantwell, *Nathaniel Hawthorne*, 364.
215 "It needed none, for we": Emerson, *Journals*, VIII:272.
"The Temperance Society": Ibid., 273.
"though like other poets": Ibid., 275.
"powers of persuasion were crippled": Ibid., 274.
"Mr. Emerson held a theological": *Centenary*, VIII:362.
216 "A good old festival": Ibid., 365.
"She made a plum pudding": NH to LH, November 28, 1842; Essex Institute.

page

"sentence by sentence": Ibid. Eliza Leslie's *Directions for Cookery* had first been published in 1828. For a discussion of early cookbooks, see Waverly Root, "The Early American Larder," *Gourmet*, January, 1976; 16ff.

"a rare sight, gliding": R. H. Lathrop, *Memories*, 52.

"figuring dithyrambic dances": Ibid., 53.

"deep snow and steady freezing": SAH to LH, January 4, 1843; Berg.

217 "Mr. Hawthorne is making": Crowley, *Critical Heritage*, 72.

"pink of good nature": SAH to LH, January 4, 1843; Berg.

"My wife is, in the strictest sense": *Centenary*, VIII:367.

"from the midst of many friends": Ibid., 367.

"sighed and groaned": Ibid., 366.

"We have had a delightful": SAH to EPPM, January 12, 1843; Berg.

218 "He is a rather puny-looking man": Cantwell, *Nathaniel Hawthorne*, 375.

"influences both cheering": Fuller to NH, January 16, 1843; Berg.

"I have an immense deal": NH to Fuller, February 1, 1843; Houghton.

219 "I do suppose that nobody ever lived": Ibid.

"the precious heart is gone": SAH to EPPM, February 22–24, 1843; Berg.

"put it in the nicest order": Ibid. Since Sophia's letter was written very shortly after her mother's departure and her mother had stayed two weeks (see SAH to LH, March 5, 1843; Berg), the accident must have occurred shortly after Hawthorne's February 1 letter to Margaret Fuller.

220 "I wish you could see my husband": SAH to EPPM, February 22–24, 1843?; Berg. This letter is catalogued and tentatively dated March 1844 in the Berg Collection, but the Pearson Transcripts designate it as the final portion of Sophia's February 22–24, 1843, letter to her mother, relating to her miscarriage, and I am inclined to accept that dating.

"One grief we have had": *Centenary*, VIII:366. Sophia, in her urge for privacy, inked over or excised most of her own allusions to her miscarriage, as well as certain sentences in Hawthorne's text, including the reference to "our promised child."

"any price for his articles": SAH to EPPM, February 28, 1843; Berg.

221 "If you consider this a fair price": NH to Lowell, December 17, 1842; St. Lawrence.

"I beg you to assure Mr. Lowell": NH to Carter, February 1, 1843; Fruitlands.

"not quite thawed": NH to SAH, March 12, 1843; Huntington.

"that our house was broken open": NH to SAH, March 16, 1843; Huntington.

222 "I expected it to fail": Ibid.

"We cannot very well afford": Ibid.

"I have been looking to receive": NH to Longfellow, November 26, 1842; Houghton.

"I have some scruples of conscience": NH to Longfellow, December 24, 1842; Houghton.

223 "I want very much to see you": Longfellow, *Letters*, II:519. The comet referred to was the "Great Comet of 1843," which had touched off the apocalyptic visions of the Millerite Sect.

"it would be too painful": Horace Mann, Diary, entry March 26, 1843; Massachusetts Historical Society.

224 "I believe no one is quite": MTP to SAH, early April 1843?; Berg.

"the spiritual advantages of change": *Centenary*, VIII:369.

"Slow work, and dull work too!": Ibid., 370.

"What is the use of going": Ibid., 376.

"to extend myself cross-wise": Ibid., 378.

225 "Once in a while, I hear": Ibid., 375.

"My little wife, I know": Ibid., 371.

"Finally, between five and six o'clock": Ibid., 372.

"written in a style": Ibid., 379.

226 "inward thought": SAH, undated entry [following Hawthorne's entry of April 11, 1843] (MS MA 580); Morgan.

"Perhaps a description of the tempest": NH to Bridge, March 25, 1843; Bowdoin. According to the "Abstracts of Service of Naval Officers, 1798–1893" (National Archives), Bridge was appointed to the *Saratoga* on December 7, 1842, and served on it until November 28, 1844.

"I did not come to see you": NH to Bridge, March 25, 1843; Bowdoin.

227 "very graphic and effective": NH to Bridge, May 3, 1843; Bowdoin.

"If you meet with any distinguished": Ibid.

"I by no means despair": Ibid.

228 "are now struggling for the mastery": *Centenary*, VIII:383.

"on the strength of the loveliness": SAH to EPPM, April 20, 1843; Berg.

"Man's accidents": The phrase also appears in their jointly kept notebook as "Men's accidents," *Centenary*, VIII:236. Hawthorne also used it in his Civil War article, "Chiefly About War Matters," but there he added a sardonic marginal note, referring to "little, hard, dry pellets of aphoristic wisdom*/*' See Hawthorne, *Works*, XII:332.

"There never was such an air": SAH to EPPM, April 20, 1843; Berg.

"Yesterday glowed like molten brass": *Centenary*, VIII:387.

A succession of guests descended: See SAH to LH, July 9–14, 1843; Berg.

229 "the voluntary nun, the lady Elizabeth": SAH to LH, June 17, 1843; Berg.

"We shall not put off": SAH to LH, July 9–14, 1843; Berg.

"I have received no money yet": Ibid., NH postscript.

"We were never so happy": *Centenary*, VIII:390.

"I have not felt very well": SAH, entry dated July 9, 1843 (MS MA 580); Morgan. The pages containing Sophia's journal entry had, until recently, been pasted together — the result of her usual sense of privacy.

page   IN THE HALL OF FANTASY

230 "I have written": *Centenary*, VIII:367.

"the next best thing": Nissenbaum, "The Firing of Nathaniel Hawthorne," *EIHC*, April 1978:76.

231 "move Heaven and Earth": NH to O'Sullivan, November 5, 1838; Cornell.

"patriotism and public services": NH to Bridge, March 25, 1843; Bowdoin.

"simplicity of heart": O'Sullivan to Henry Wise, November 24, 1843; Maine Historical Society.

"If I am to send": NH to Lowell?, May 1843?; Berg. Sophia, in letters to Louisa Hawthorne (April 17, 1843) and to her mother (April 20, 1843), referred to Poe's offer as being recent. Berg.

232 "sense of imbecility": *Centenary*, VIII:379.

"It is rather singular": NH to Bridge, May 3, 1843; Bowdoin.

"I am advised that": NH to Griswold, July 2, 1843; Berg.

"Oh, for the $1,300": Tharp, *Peabody Sisters*, 176.

"it can only offer twenty dollars": SAH to EPPM, January 9, 1844; Berg.

233 "at the same valuation": NH to John Frost, March 11, 1844; Library Company of Philadelphia.

"the enormous quantity": Scudder, *James Russell Lowell*, I:99–100.

234 "freaks of idle hearts": *Centenary*, X:331.

"I want my place!" Ibid., 323.

"a woman of unemployed energy": Ibid., 303.

235 "given himself up to despair": Ibid., 302.

"Once upon a time": Ibid., 381. Herman Melville, one of the more extravagant admirers of *Mosses from an Old Manse*, may have found this opening a provocative device. He was to use a very similar gambit for the opening of *Moby-Dick*.

"Let him thank his stars": Ibid., 384.

"all the spice of life": Ibid., 387.

"Be patient — it will come": Ibid., 388.

page

236 "armorers and cannon-founderies": Ibid., 391.

"a brilliant shower of sparkles": Ibid., 395.

"the fatal circumstance": Ibid., 403.

This time, the useless emblems: Until the invention of the neutron bomb, which will demolish the population but leave the real estate intact, Hawthorne's fantasy seemed rather far-fetched.

"with no knowledge of their predecessors": *Centenary*, X:248.

237 "All the perversions": Ibid., 265.

"I have made a law": SAH to EPPM, January 9, 1844; Berg.

238 "Man's intellect, moderated": *Centenary*, X:253.

"excited the wonderment of the people": LH to SAH, March 4, 1843; Berg.

"with now and then a little discourse": J. Hawthorne, *NH and His Wife*, I:274.

"In the papers, it is said": SAH to EPPM, February 4, 1844; Berg.

239 "We can neither of us": SAH to MTP, January 30, 1844; Berg.

"out of the jurisdiction": Mann to "To all whom it may concern", May 3?, 1843; Massachusetts Historical Society.

"I suspect that Mary's baby": J. Hawthorne, *NH and His Wife*, I:275.

"You and Elizabeth are aunts": NH to LH, March 3, 1844; Essex Institute.

"Of my own personal knowledge": Ibid.

"not a red baby": SAH, entry dated April 3, 1844 (MS MA 569); Morgan.

240 "Almost everybody has had": NH to LH, March 15, 1844; Berg.

"I must within no long time": Ibid.

"a very sober and serious": NH to Hillard, March 24, 1844; Maine Historical Society.

"If you want a new feeling": Bridge, *Personal Recollections*, 95.

241 "I wish thy mother": NH to SAH, April 14, 1844; Huntington.

"He has fixed my chamber bell": SAH to EPPM, April 17–18, 1844; Berg.

242 "Mrs. Longlady": NH to SAH, May 27, 1844; Huntington.

"capital story": Wagenknecht, *Mrs. Longfellow*, 110, 112. The entries are dated April 13 and May 25, 1844.

"a boned pirate": F. B. Sanborn, "A Concord Note-Book," *The Critic*, July 1905:79.

"dark and desolate": NH to SAH, May 27, 1844; Huntington.

"so abominably that at last": NH to Hillard, May 29, 1844; Middlebury.

"to my unspeakable relief": NH to SAH, May 29, 1844; Huntington.

"What a gump!": NH to SAH, June 2, 1844; Huntington.

243 "A man of his nice conscience": Ibid. For a more extended portrait of Bradford, see Hawthorne, *English Notebooks*, 75–77.

"in perfect health and absolutely": NH to SAH, June 10, 1844; Huntington.

244 "such little events": *Centenary*, VIII:245.

"the long, melancholy note": Ibid., 248.

"beautiful diversity of green": Ibid., 249.

"harsh, above all other harshness": Ibid., 248.

"Wherever that music comes": Emerson, *Journals*, VII:482. I am obviously indebted here to Leo Marx, who, out of these two episodes, created an entire volume, *The Machine in the Garden*, proving — if it needed proof — that the character of an era can sometimes be captured in its most ordinary moments.

"by the box & the ton": Ibid., 342.

245 "springs up between the feet": Ibid., 420.

"act of incorporation": *Centenary*, X:202.

"This is so unlike": NH to SAH, April 14, 1844; Huntington.

246 "between the cold, lifeless": *Centenary*, VIII:339.

"The people here who are worth": Cooke, *Early Letters*, 192.

"like young Greek gods": Ibid., 21.

"elegant grace which never left him": Ibid., 20.

247 "My regret at not seeing you": Ibid., 192.

"consecrated crank": Stern, *Annotated Walden*, 67.

"coated over merely": Emerson, *Journals*, VII:130; see also 207.

248 "the sublime of mechanics": Emerson, *Journals*, VIII:208.

"small, sour and fierce schemes": Ibid., 210.

"the very model of a community": *Centenary*, VIII:249.

249 "The French have been and are": J. Hawthorne, *NH and His Wife*, I:267.

"It was not a translation": SAH to EPPM, April 6, 1845; Berg.

250 "Indeed, I think it": Cooke, *Early Letters*, 199.

"always morning": Curtis, *Literary and Social Essays*, 47.

"aesthetic tea": Ibid., 43.

"So supreme was his silence": Ibid., 44.

"a few hazy days": Ibid., 42.

"a fine episode in the summer": Cooke, *Early Letters*, 225. For Hawthorne's account of the excursion, see *Centenary* VIII:259–61.

"His own sympathy was so broad": Curtis, *Literary and Social Essays*, 45.

"It was a choice walk": Sanborn, "A Concord Note-Book," *The Critic*, July 1905:80.

"I vaguely remember": Curtis, *Literary and Social Essays*, 25.

251 "I recall little else": Ibid., 26.

"There is no companion": Cooke, *Early Letters*, 254.

The girl had made at least: For details of Martha Hunt's suicide, see the *Concord Freeman*, July 11, 1845:2. Ironically, sixteen years later, Martha Hunt's sister Ellen, also a teacher, committed suicide by drowning herself in the river.

252 "one of the deepest spots": *Centenary*, VIII:262.

"What's this?": Ibid., 263.

"Her arms had stiffened": Ibid., 264.

"which is said to exhibit": Ibid., 266.

253 "spectacle of such perfect horror": Ibid., 263.

"wonderful photograph of the terrible night": SAH to Fields, ca. May 1867; Boston Public Library.

"introduced a series of photographs": *Centenary*, VIII:621.

"For the first time since": R. H. Lathrop, *Memories*, 78.

"Thy letter came this morning": NH to SAH, December 2, 1844; Huntington.

254 "Very probably, your influence": NH to Bridge, November 29, 1844; Bowdoin.

"The good that I get": NH to SAH, December 2, 1844; Huntington.

"He told the most pitiable stories": NH to SAH, December ?, 1844; Huntington.

255 "I shall come back to thee": Ibid.

"Pray tell Lizzie": SAH to EPPM, November 20, 1844; Berg.

"the Blatant Beast": Stewart, *Nathaniel Hawthorne*, 76.

"Polk next and Clay afterward": LH to ECMH, August?, 1844; Pearson Transcripts. In an unrecovered letter to Park Benjamin, dated December 17, 1844, sold at auction in 1921, Hawthorne purportedly expressed himself with some vehemence on the subject of the incoming administration. According to the catalogue paraphrase: "He vigorously attacks the election of Polk to the Presidency. Whole administration is violently attacked. He says that if Texas is annexed, the Union will be broken by a separation between free and slave states; this he regards as inevitable and imminent." Pearson Transcripts.

256 "Bancroft spoke of him": J. Hawthorne, *NH and His Wife*, I:284.

"By manufacturing you thus": Ibid.

"You underrate his disposition": Ibid.

"the hostile party in Salem": NH to Bridge, June 16, 1845; Bowdoin.

257 "considerable progress": NH to Bridge, January 19, 1845; Bowdoin.

"fully equal to one half the profits": Duyckinck to NH, March 21, 1845; New York Public Library.

258 "I look for considerable circulation": NH to Duyckinck, April 7, 1845; New York Public Library.

"I am fit for nothing": NH to Duyckinck, July 1, 1845; New York Public Library.

"He seems to think it preferable": Ibid.

"There is one chance": Ibid.

259 "He is not an agreeable person": NH to Milnes, November 18, 1854; Trinity College, Cambridge.

"Borrowed of Horatio Bridge": *Centenary*, VIII:259.

page
"I saw by a glance": SAH to EPPM, May?, 1845, Sunday; Berg.
260 "I continue to look": NH to Bridge, June 16, 1845; Bowdoin.
"I have said nothing": Ibid.
261 "It was only a freak of fancy": Bridge, *Personal Recollections*, 183–84.
"much more intellect": *Centenary*, VIII:268.
262 "a man of cheerful gossip": Ibid., 270.
"Nathaniel says that room": SAH to LH, August 24, 1845; Berg.
"My dear Sophia": LH to SAH, September 3, 1845; Berg.
263 "as promptly and forcibly": NH to Hillard, September 6, 1845; University of Rochester. See Metzdorf, "Hawthorne's Suit Against Ripley and Dana," *American Literature*, XII:235–41.
"Let it sink, say I": NH to Frank Farley?, n.d.; Beinecke. Since the fragment is undated, it is not clear whether it refers to the first failure of the Brook Farm Association, or to the demise of the community, following a disastrous fire in the newly built phalanstery building on March 3, 1846. See Swift, *Brook Farm*, 36.
"The three years we have spent": SAH to EPPM, September 7, 1845; Berg.
264 "I almost fancy myself criminal": Bridge to NH, September 28, 1845; Bowdoin.
"with flying colors": NH to Bridge, October 7, 1845; Pearson Transcripts.
"great original Thinker": *Centenary*, X:30.
"a poet of deep beauty": Ibid., 31.
265 "The hand that renovates": Ibid., 33.

page   A DARK NECESSITY

266 "Here I am": NH to Duyckinck, October 10, 1845; New York Public Library.
"vociferous cry, Mss! Mss!": Duyckinck to NH, October 2, 1845; Bowdoin.
". . . already, though not a week": NH to Duyckinck, October 10, 1845; New York Public Library. In his reply, Hawthorne also turned down Duyckinck's suggestion that he write a history of witchcraft. "I had often thought of such a work," Hawthorne answered, "but I should not like to throw it off hastily or write it for the sole and specific purpose of getting $500 . . . Perhaps it may be the work of an after time."
"That wretched tale": NH to Duyckinck, December 24, 1845; New York Public Library.
"vagrant progeny": NH to Duyckinck, January 24, 1846; New York Public Library.
"As I never mean to write": Ibid.
267 "We decide on": NH to Duyckinck, February 22, 1846; New York Public Library.
"Louisa complains of the silence": NH to SAH, November 10, 1845; Huntington.
268 "I already love the future": NH to SAH, November 13, 1845; Huntington.
"What a devil of a pickle": NH to Bridge, February 21, 1846; Bowdoin.
269 "some post-office, some custom house": Sumner to Mrs. George Bancroft, January 9, 1846; M. A. DeWolfe Howe, *Life and Letters*, I:264.
"As to Hawthorne": Bancroft to Sumner, January 13, 1846; Ibid., 267.
"will send in for confirmation": Bancroft to George Hood, February 23, 1846; Massachusetts Historical Society.
270 "If you could authorize me": NH to Bridge, March 1, 1846; Bowdoin.
"There is only one solitary": SAH to EPPM, March 22–23, 1846; Berg.
271 "the coat to be": J. Hawthorne, *NH and His Wife*, I:309.
"The delay has really not": NH to Duyckinck, April 15, 1846; New York Public Library.
"a certain Miss Susan Kearney Rodgers": NH to Duyckinck, June 10, 1846; New York Public Library. See also his letter to Duyckinck dated April 30, 1846; New York Public Library.
"dismally in want of money": NH to Duyckinck, April 15, 1846; New York Public Library.

272 "now burdened with decayed wooden warehouses": *Centenary*, I:4.
"such a patriarchal": Ibid., 12.
"Old Lee . . . affirmed": *Centenary*, VIII:281.
"It is a good lesson": *Centenary*, I:26.
"queer vehicle of fame": Ibid., 27.
273 "whom I have found it my duty": NH to Robert J. Walker, May 21, 1846; National Archives.
"A small troglodyte": NH to LH, June 22, 1846, postscript to SAH to LH, June 21, 1846; Berg.
"out of health": SAH to EPPM, March 6, 1846; Berg.
274 "stories to be taken out": NH to Duyckinck, April 15, 1846; New York Public Library.
"I do not pique myself": NH to Duyckinck, April 30, 1846; New York Public Library.
"the most stately street in Salem": Bridge, *Personal Recollections*, 187.
"What a dinner!": Longfellow Journal entry dated October 10, 1846; Houghton.
At Longfellow's insistence: Sophia, in a letter to her mother, November 12–13, 1846 (Berg), noted that her husband's last sitting would be on the 13th and that the sessions were quite long. But this may have been intended to forestall any expectation by the Peabodys that Hawthorne would visit them while he was in Boston.
"Mr. Hawthorne was never so handsome": J. Hawthorne, *NH and His Wife*, I:310.
"we shall not have a cent": SAH to EPPM, November 12–13, 1846; Berg.
275 "Last Friday, we went to see them": SAH to EPPM, September 19–20, 1846; Berg.
"He is still decidedly": Bridge, *Personal Recollections*, 187.
"My husband has no study": Ibid., 188.
276 "rather stale": NH to Duyckinck, June 10, 1846; New York Public Library.
"that could stand, unsupported": *Centenary*, X:34.
"profound treatises on morality": Ibid., 5.
"Unless I could do better": Ibid., 34.
277 "met with good acceptance": NH to Bridge, October 26, 1846; Bowdoin.
"felicity and evanescent grace": Crowley, *Critical Heritage*, 104.
"honestly American": Ibid., 128.
"diseased self-consciousness": Ibid., 136.
"His residence at Concord": Ibid., 135.
"It is a waste": Ibid., 140.
"original at *all* points": Ibid., 91.
"But the fact is": Ibid., 143.
278 "completely overwhelms": Ibid., 145.
"libeling our mothers": Regan, *Poe: A Collection*, 19; quoted in Joseph Wood Krutch, "The Philosophy of Composition."
"forcible-feeble": *Centenary*, X:534.
"the look of oversensitiveness": Carlson, *Recognition of Edgar Allan Poe*, 68.
279 "evident toadyism": *Poe's Complete Works*, III:114.
"too precious to be wasted": Longfellow, *Letters*, III:58.
"most discriminating, philosophical": Scudder, *James Russell Lowell*, I:162.
"Poe, I am afraid": Ibid., 165.
280 "grossly uneducated": Moss, *Poe's Major Crisis*, 195. I am indebted to Professor Moss's volume for untangling Poe's embittered literary affairs and also to his earlier *Poe's Literary Battles*, published in 1963.
"to-day in the gutter, to-morrow": Moss, *Poe's Major Crisis*, 6.
"extraordinary genius": Crowley, *Critical Heritage*, 141.
"the example, *par excellence*": Ibid.
281 "Allegory is at war": Ibid., 150.
"His books afford": Ibid., 146.
"Let him mend his pen": Ibid., 150.
"We observe something which resembles": Ibid., 92. See also Mabbott, *Tales and Sketches*, 451, note 19. Poe was, in fact, a kind of literary Senator McCarthy, a master at making claims of wrongdoing, then weaseling slightly on them, then

page

citing page numbers and alleged similarities (never exactly produced or compared in his texts) that were intended to serve as documentary evidence. On careful examination, most of the charges turned out to be specious. His accusations in this instance were especially unfounded — and the very minor similarities may indicate that he himself had been influenced by Hawthorne's example. Since Poe, admittedly: See Mabbott, *Tales and Sketches*, 422–25, and notes (448–51) for a discussion of the sources.

282 "belonging to the obnoxious class of critics": *Centenary*, X:636.
The deleted sentence reads: "Mr. Poe had gained ready admittance for the sake of his imagination, but was threatened with ejectment, as belonging to the obnoxious class of critics."
"I have read your occasional": NH to Poe, June 17, 1846; Collection of Henry Bradley Martin, quoted in *Centenary*, X:534.
"so all the rooms": SAH to EPPM, September 9–10, 1847; Berg.

283 "He will be as quiet": Ibid.
"I am trying to resume": NH to Longfellow, November 11, 1847; Houghton.
Hawthorne's literary efforts during his three-year term: See *Centenary*, XI:379ff.

284 "The search of an investigator": *Centenary*, VIII:251.
"It had ceased to partake": *Centenary*, XI:99.

285 "It is a tremendous truth": J. Hawthorne, *NH and His Wife*, I:330.
"E. says she thinks": EPPM to SAH, March 7, 1849; Berg.
"At last, by main strength": NH to Webber, February 14, 1848; *Centenary*, XI:383.

286 "friendly service": Longfellow, *Letters*, III:145–46.
Longfellow attempted to return the favor by suggesting that Hawthorne write a history of the Acadians, using newly discovered material that his friend Professor Cornelius Felton would be happy to put at Hawthorne's disposal. Hawthorne declined to take the subject out of the "abler hands of Professor Felton."
". . . [Julian] climbs into a chair": *Centenary*, VIII:402–403.

287 "Sweetest wife, I have nothing": NH to SAH, July 13, 1847; Huntington.
"The more I know him": NH to Duyckinck, March 13, 1847; New York Public Library.
"He eats like an anaconda": NH to SAH, March 15, 1847; Huntington.

288 "I am determined the niggers": McGill, *Channing of Concord*, 103, believes the remark was made during a two-week visit Channing paid in October 1847. But, basing his account on Channing's late recollections, he seems to merge more than one visit into a single occasion. Sophia, in a letter to her mother, October 5, 1846 (Berg), refers to an earlier visit: "We had a visit of one night and a day from Ellery Channing."
"Thou canst have no imagination": NH to SAH, June 19, 1848; Huntington.
"Thou badest me burn": NH to SAH, July 7, 1848; Huntington.
"Tell my little daughter Una": NH to SAH, June 19, 1848; Huntington.
"Thou madest this intelligence known": NH to SAH, June 27, 1848; Huntington.

289 "I did not wish to risk": NH to SAH, July 5, 1848; Huntington.
"Soon — soon": NH to SAH, July 18, 1848; Huntington.
"You would find him": NH to Longfellow, November 21, 1848; Houghton.

290 "The lords of the lash": Donald, *Charles Sumner*, 166.
"I am a bad guest": Emerson to NH, January 12, 1849; Rusk, "Emerson in Salem, 1849," 194.
"I am glad to know": Thoreau to NH, February 20, 1849; Essex Institute.
"a library of nearly 900 volumes": Stern, *Annotated Walden*, 92.
"or perhaps that Indian lecture": NH to Thoreau, February 19, 1849; Morgan.

291 "such a revelation of nature": R. H. Lathrop, *Memories*, 92.
"Mr. Thoreau has risen": Ibid.
"a noble subject": SAH to EPPM, November 19, 1848; Berg.

292 "So wonderfully eloquent": *Centenary*, XI:38.
"Something had been originally": Ibid., 41.
"traitor to a holy cause": Donald, *Charles Sumner*, 184.
"The word *liberty*": Emerson, *The Heart of Emerson's Journals*, 252.

293 "as a reward for political services": NH to Hillard, March 5, 1849; Maine Historical Society.
   "I must confess, it stirs": NH to Longfellow, June 5, 1849; Houghton.
294 "I am turned out of office!": NH to Hillard, June 8, 1849; Maine Historical Society. See also letter to Hillard, June 12, 1849, same source.
   "Do not be troubled": R. H. Lathrop, *Memories*, 93.
   "He has felt in chains": Ibid., 94.
   "The whole contemptible movement": SAH to EPPM, July 4, 1849; Pearson Transcripts.
   "who has proved himself": R. H. Lathrop, *Memories*, 96.
295 "What, that smooth, smiling": SAH to EPPM, July 7, 1849; Pearson Transcripts.
   "explain a piece of mystery": Pearson Transcripts.
   "a person who claimed": NH to Hillard, June 18, 1849. In developing the material for this curious and crucial episode in Hawthorne's political career, I am indebted to Winfield S. Nevins' article in the April 1917 issue of *Essex Institute Historical Collections*, "Nathaniel Hawthorne's Removal from the Salem Custom House," in which the June 18, 1849, letter to Hillard is reprinted (125-27), and the more recent and revised view of the same affair, Stephen Nissenbaum's "The Firing of Nathaniel Hawthorne," in the April 1978 issue of the same periodical. Neither author, however, takes note of the sinuous activities of Horace Conolly or of Hawthorne's dismissal of two inspectors in May 1846, when he replaced them with Burchmore and Haraden (see page 273 of this book). Hawthorne's action seems to contradict his assertion about the mildness of his political tenure.
   "to a gentleman now very prominent": Nevins, "Hawthorne's Removal," 126.
   "a few notices of books": Ibid., 127.
296 "come forward under his own name": Ibid.
   "You never heard such": SAH to EPPM, June 17-21, 1849; Berg.
   The historian William H. Prescott: Writing to Daniel Webster on June 20, 1849, Prescott expressed the opinion that the removal would "bring odium on the government, and on our own party." See Prescott, *The Papers of William Hickling Prescott*, 272-73.
   "I suppose it will be for the best": Nissenbaum, "The Firing," 65.
   "an act of wanton": Ibid.
   "something worse than a crime": Ibid., 66.
297 "I feel pretty well": NH to Longfellow, June 19, 1849; University of Virginia.
   "At about five o'clock": *Centenary*, VIII:428.
298 "Una takes a strong": Ibid., 430.
   "3 o'clock, P.M.": Ibid., 431.
299 "My dearest Mother — Mrs. Hawthorne": SAH to EPPM, August 1, 1849; Berg.
300 "personal and literary friends": Nevins, "Hawthorne's Removal," 119.
   "That gentleman was placed": Ibid., 113.
   "that Zachary Taylor and not James K. Polk": Ibid., 115.
   "There is a Democratic newspaper": Ibid., 117.
301 "worked over into compliant shape": Ibid., 118.
   "with large families": J. Hawthorne, *NH and His Wife*, II:382.
302 "I may be mistaken": Ibid., 383.
   "My purpose is simply": Ibid., 384.
303 "He writes immensely": SAH to EPPM, September 29, 1849; Berg.
   "positively a h——l f——d story": Bridge, *Personal Recollections*, 112.
   "Insincerity in a man's own heart": Hawthorne, *Lost Notebook*, 38.
   "The situation of a man": Ibid., 66.
   "A story of the effects": *Centenary*, VIII:278.
   "a young woman with no mean": *Centenary*, IX:435.
304 "obtrusive sense of change": *Centenary*, I:216.
   "The minister's own will": Ibid., 217.
305 "By thy first step awry": Ibid., 174.
   "the type of shame": Ibid., 79.
   "He thus typified": Ibid., 145.
306 "in a land that afforded": Ibid., 81.

page
"the highest truths": Ibid., 142.
"whether by uttered words": Ibid., 131.
"see the dark problem": Ibid., 132.
"turning her face away": Ibid., 145.
"Here he had studied and written": Ibid., 222.
"But he seemed to stand apart": Ibid., 223.
307 "that stubborn fidelity": Ibid., 259.
"shriek out with the full power": Ibid., 57. Nissenbaum, "The Firing," 57–58, has very ably explored the analogy between Hester's public penance and Hawthorne's political humiliation.
"a stony crust of insensibility": *Centenary*, I:69.
308 "inextricable knot": Ibid., 148. "Crime is for the iron-nerved," Hawthorne asserts in the full passage; "feeble" and sensitive natures such as Arthur Dimmesdale's are forever caught in the "agony of heaven-defying guilt and vain repentance" — certainly, two of the dominant and "inextricable" themes of Hawthorne's fiction.
"When poor Mr. Dimmesdale": Ibid., 143.
"And whither was he now going?": Ibid., 175. "In due course of time . . ." Hawthorne continues, "deadly nightshade, dogwood, henbane, and whatever else of vegetable wickedness the climate would produce" would flourish over Chillingworth's grave. Writing to Longfellow about his political grievances, on June 5, 1849 (Houghton), Hawthorne threatened that where his writing had previously sown "herbs of grace and sweet-scented flowers," it would now produce "nettles, skunk-cabbage, deadly night-shade, wolf's bane, dogwood." His letter to Longfellow had been written before he had actually been turned out of office and before he had begun work on *The Scarlet Letter*. His bitterness about his imminent ouster from office had obviously been carried over into the fictional premises of *The Scarlet Letter* and the character of Chillingworth. It is also another instance of his metaphorical association of evil and horticulture.
"And what was the fire": NH to SAH, May 26, 1839; Huntington. (See page 167.)

page   THE CITIZEN OF SOMEWHERE ELSE
309 "It is either very good": Fields, *Yesterdays*, 50.
He was also a sometime poet: See NH to Fields, November 4, 1848; St. Lawrence. As corresponding secretary for the Salem Lyceum, Hawthorne had invited Fields to deliver one of his poems on the evening of Daniel Webster's lecture — "or on the evening when the Lyceum opens, be the Lecturer who he may."
"I remember that I pressed him": Fields, *Yesterdays*, 50.
"all aglow with admiration": Ibid.
310 "a delicate subject to write upon": NH to Fields, January 15, 1850; Houghton Letterbook.
"Keeping so close to its point": NH to Fields, January 20, 1850; Houghton Letterbook.
"admire your genius and respect": J. Hawthorne, *NH and His Wife*, I:354–55.
311 "I read your letter": NH to Hillard, January 20, 1850; Marietta.
"one end being in press": Bridge, *Personal Recollections*, 110.
"swelled and heaved": Hawthorne, *English Notebooks*, 225.
312 "Here I hardly go out": Bridge, *Personal Recollections*, 112–13.
In joining his fortunes: For details on the Ticknor-Fields business, see Ballou, *The Building of the House*, and Tryon, *Parnassus Corner*. For an account of Fields as an enterprising publisher, see Charvat, *The Profession of Authorship in America*.
313 "the monied men of Massachusetts": Ticknor, *Hawthorne and His Publisher*, 119.
"I do not even know him": NH to Fields, June 17, 1852; Huntington.
"No Irishman need apply": Longfellow, *Letters*, III: 269.
"If they are at the Custom House": Ibid., 292.
The first edition of *The Scarlet Letter*: For details, see *Centenary*, I:xvi.

314 "raise a roar of laughter": Fields to Duyckinck, March 5, 1850; New York Public Library.
"No family of any respectability": Charvat, *The Profession of Authorship in America*, 178.
"We intend to publish your books": Fields to NH, January 14, 1851; Berg. The haste with which *The Scarlet Letter* was published accounts for the mention, in Hawthorne's introduction, of the "briefer articles" that were originally intended to complete the volume.
315 "only sensible ends": Bridge, *Personal Recollections*, 125.
"Nothing is slurred over": Crowley, *Critical Heritage*, 156.
"without an infusion of George Sand": Ibid., 157.
"hardly be prepared": Ibid., 161.
"the greatest production of the author": Ibid., 159.
"always *motived* with a wonderful": Ibid., 158.
"master of such a wizard power": Ibid., 167.
316 "wholly ignorant of Christian asceticism": Ibid., 177.
"There is an unsound state": Ibid., 176.
"the nauseous amour": Ibid., 182.
"by small sneers at Salem": See Lease, "Salem vs. Hawthorne," *The New England Quarterly* XLIV (1971):110–17.
"As to the Salem people": Bridge, *Personal Recollections*, 113.
"the greatest uproar": Ibid., 114.
317 "enmity, or ill-feeling of any kind": *Centenary*, I:1–2.
"Soon . . . my old native town": Ibid., 44.
Ever since his ouster: Sophia's house-hunting activities are described in letters to her mother, September 19 and September 27, 1849 (Berg). Hawthorne's October 23 trip to the Berkshires is recounted in *Centenary*, VIII:293.
"as red as the Scarlet Letter": NH to Burchmore, June 9, 1850; University of Virginia.
In February, by way of her mother: See SAH to EPPM, February 14, 1850; Berg.
318 "immediately lugged into society": NH to SAH, April 26, 1850; Huntington.
"solitary prisoner": *Centenary*, VIII:506.
"middling and lower classes": Ibid., 501.
"with so little care of concealment": Ibid., 504.
319 "I like this painter": Ibid., 497.
"looked dimly out of the canvas": Ibid., 491.
"they are all delusions": Ibid.
It was in Boston: See NH to Burchmore, May 13, 1850; St. Lawrence.
"As it is now merely a matter": NH to Burchmore, June 9, 1850; University of Virginia. "Do ask him about it," Hawthorne continues, "and tell him, too, that whether true or not, I have occasionally the same kind of hankering for him that I have for brandy and water and a cigar."
"If you had any chance": NH to Conolly, June 17, 1850; Bowdoin (transcript).
320 "so harassed in spirit": SAH to EPPM, June 9–16, 1850; Berg.
"Mr. Hawthorne thinks it is *Salem*": SAH to EPPM, August 1, 1850; Berg.
"planted vegetables enough": NH to Burchmore, June 9, 1850; University of Virginia.
321 "the smallest of ten-feet houses": SAH to EPPM, June 23–25, 1850; Berg.
"which can boast of nothing": Ibid.
"Mr. Hawthorne said this morning": SAH to EPPM, September 29, 1850; Berg.
322 "I have not yet tasted the wine": NH to Mansfield, June 17, 1850; Berg.
"her self-important gait": *Centenary*, VIII:294.
"Language — human language": Ibid.
"Indian council-chambers": SAH to EPPM, September 29, 1850; Berg.
"the palest azure": R. H. Lathrop, *Memories*, 128.
"The other afternoon at the lake": SAH to EPPM, September 29, 1850; Berg.
323 "as happy as summer days": SAH to EPPM, August 1, 1850; Berg.
"our most truthful novelist": *Centenary*, VII:169.
"india-rubber rooms": SAH to EPPM, August 1, 1850; Berg.

page

Mlle. Desportes had been the governess: For more on the Praslin case, see Wright, "Hawthorne and the Praslin Murder," *The New England Quarterly*, XV (1942):5–14.

324 "The Autocrat of all the Quacks": *Poe's Complete Works*, III:52.

"George Prince Regent James": SAH to H. A. Bright, September 12, 1859; Beinecke.

"condemned to read any": SAH to EPPM, February 12, 1851; Berg.

Nearby, too, was the tempestuous English actress: Frances Anne Kemble (1809–1893) had married Pierce Butler, a wealthy Philadelphian with slave-operated plantations on Butler's and St. Simon's islands in Georgia. They were divorced in 1849. Kemble's journal of an early tour through the United States had caused as much sensation as that of Mrs. Trollope. The actress's *A Residence on a Georgia Plantation*, published in England in 1861 and detailing the unhappy lives of the Negroes on her husband's plantation, was said to have had some effect in curbing British support for the Confederacy during the Civil War.

"Take your boy": J. Hawthorne, *NH and His Wife*, I:363.

"very prepossessing and lady-like": SAH to EPPM, September?, 1850, Sunday; Berg.

325 "There must first be a close": Hawthorne, *French and Italian Notebooks*, April 22, 1858.

"All I can say is that": NH to Fields, August 23, 1850; Columbia.

"The scene of it": NH to Fields, October 1, 1850; Houghton Letterbook.

"only imaginary inhabitants": *Centenary*, I:44.

326 "As soon as I reached England": Ossoli, *Memoirs*, II:172.

"I find myself in my element": Ibid., 184.

"The more I see": Ossoli, *At Home and Abroad*, 205.

"too dull to carouse": Ibid., 124.

327 "Radical measures of reform": Ibid., 205.

"He aims at political": Ibid., 320.

"It is a time such as": Ossoli, *Memoirs*, II:235.

"My private fortunes": Ibid., 237.

"I should like to return": Ibid., 239.

328 "I forget the great ideas": Ibid., 270.

329 "I see nothing but death": Ossoli, *At Home and Abroad*, 446.

"I dread to speak of Margaret": SAH to EPPM, August 1, 1850; Berg. See also Sophia's letter to Mary Mann, September 9, 1850; Berg.

330 "If they were truly bound": SAH to EPPM, August 1, 1850; Berg.

"Rode with Fields and wife": *Centenary*, VIII:295.

"the violet of the season": Miller, *Melville*, 23.

331 "wildly about": Duyckinck to Margaret Duyckinck, August 6, 1850; New York Public Library.

"well-moistened": Ibid.

"certain destruction": Fields, *Yesterdays*, 53.

332 "I have just got back": Longfellow, *Letters*, III:266.

"talked prose apparently as unconsciously": Miller, *Melville*, 24.

"an earth monster, a perfect Behemoth": Ibid., 26.

333 "Gave them a couple of bottles": *Centenary*, VIII:295.

"Hawthorne is a fine ghost": Duyckinck to Margaret Duyckinck, August 9, 1850; New York Public Library.

"I met Melville the other day": NH to Bridge, August 7, 1850; Bowdoin.

"My hospitality": NH to Bridge, August 18, 1850; Bowdoin.

It is a matter of scholarly debate: One further possibility presents itself: that Melville did indeed write the essay soon after meeting Hawthorne and showed it to Duyckinck, who edited the first segment of it in Pittsfield and mailed it to his office or the printers to be set in type for the August 17 issue.

334 "I never saw the man": Crowley, *Critical Heritage*, 121.

"Yes, it is that flowery Hawthorne": Ibid., 113.

"the visible type": Ibid.

"Ripeness is all": It is no surprise to learn that Melville had underscored this line in his copy of *Lear*. See Matthiessen, *American Renaissance*, 187.

"There are minds": Crowley, *Critical Heritage*, 118.

335 "Let America first praise": Ibid., 119.

"For spite of all the Indian-summer sunlight": Ibid., 115.

"soft ravishments": Ibid., 113.

"infinite height of loving wonder": Ibid., 122.

336 "parity of ideas": Ibid., 125. Another parity between himself and Hawthorne, perhaps, was Melville's "guess" that Hawthorne's books had "sold by the five thousand" — as his own popular books had. That he should have hit on that figure suggests that he had, in fact, talked with either Hawthorne or Fields. At the time of their meeting, *The Scarlet Letter* had gone through two editions amounting to just 5000 copies. Fields was preparing for a third edition of 1000 copies in September.

"For genius, all over the world": Ibid., 121.

"wait an hour": Miller, *Melville*, 31.

"I carried the 'Literary World' ": J. Hawthorne, *NH and His Wife*, I:384.

"Poor Aunty!": SAH to EPPM, September 12, 1850; Berg.

337 "Nevertheless, I must own": NH to Duyckinck, August 29, 1850; New York Public Library.

"lightly but vigorously written": Stewart, "Hawthorne's Contributions to *The Salem Advertiser*," *American Literature*, V (1934):329.

"No writer ever put the reality": NH to Duyckinck, August 29, 1850; New York Public Library.

"I cannot speak or think": Ibid., postscript by Sophia.

338 Like Nathaniel Hawthorne, Herman Melville: For many of the details of Melville's life, I am indebted to such Melville scholars as Charles Anderson, Leon Howard, Jay Leyda, Merrell R. Davis, and William H. Gilman, as well as others whose books and articles are indicated in the bibliography. I am also indebted to Edwin Haviland Miller's *Melville* for its critical investigation of the signs and symptoms of Meville's homoerotic fantasies and yearnings in his writings. As thorough as that examination is, however, I find it a very limited approach to Melville as an author. Nor can I subscribe to Miller's thesis that Melville made a homosexual pass at Hawthorne during the Berkshire period and that this was the reason for Hawthorne's flight from the region and the principal cause of the "estrangement" between the two men. There are too many instances — some of which are indicated in later notes — in which detailed biographical evidence is overlooked, presumably because it does not fit Professor Miller's colorful theory. The thesis, it seems to me, unfortunately reduces what was a complex and creative relationship between the two men to something little better than a seedy sexual adventure.

"fierce, even *maniacal*": Miller, *Melville*, 65.

339 "backward in speech": Miller, *Melville*, 67.

"From my twenty-fifth year": Melville, *Letters*, 130.

340 "Don't you think that the autumn": NH to Longfellow, May 11, 1855; University of Virginia.

"grew to a greenness": Melville, *Letters*, 130.

"What 'reputation' H.M. has": Ibid.

341 "ontological heroics": Ibid., 133.

"Plato who talks thro' his nose": Ibid., 78–79.

"a great, deep intellect": Crowley, *Critical Heritage*, 115.

"the sky above, the sea around": Melville, *Typee*, 1.

"Yes, as everyone knows": Melville, *Moby-Dick*, 24.

342 On September 3, 1850, Melville paid a four-day visit: See *Centenary*, VIII:297.

"even in the afternoon": SAH to MTP, September 9, 1850; Berg.

"a man with a true warm heart": SAH to EPPM, September 4, 1850; Berg.

"very unsatisfactory": SAH to EPPM, September 29–October 3, 1850: Berg.

"tall and erect, with an air": SAH to EPPM, September 4, 1850; Berg.

343 "We have discovered who wrote": SAH to EPPm?, September?, 1850; Berg. So-

page

phia goes on to say: "Since his visit, he drove up one superb moonlight night & said he had bought an estate six miles from us, where he is really going to build a real towered house — an actual tower . . . So we shall have him as a neighbor." The date of the letter can be fixed, at least, as after September 16, when Melville bought his house, and before October 6, when he wrote Duyckinck about moving into Arrowhead.

"too carelessly written": Ibid. Melville complained of one "provoking mistake." Where he had written the "sane madness of truth," the printer had substituted "the same madness of truth."

"In the golden light of evening": Ibid.

"He said the sunny haze": Ibid.

344 "Nothing pleases me better": SAH to EPPm, May 7–10, 1851; Berg.

"a wonderful smile or one powerful word": Ibid.

"the great enchantment of life": Emerson, *Early Lectures*, III:52.

"unites [man] to his race": Ibid.

345 "lingering adherence to the actual": Ibid., 54.

"in elective affinities": Ibid., 52.

"the masterpiece of nature": Emerson, *Essays and Journals*, 167.

"a sort of beautiful enemy": Ibid., 170.

"The only joy I have": Ibid., 169.

346 "head like a moss-rose": Leyda, *Melville Log*, 577. Hawthorne, who also studied the bas-relief in the Villa Albani, had a far different impression: "This is said to be the finest relic of antiquity, next to the Apollo and the Laocoon, but, I could not feel it to be so — partly, I suppose, because the features of Antinous do not seem to me beautiful in themselves; and that heavy, downward look is repeated till I am more weary of it than of anything else in sculpture." *French and Italian Notebooks*, May 10, 1858.

"realized the pure deep love": J. Hawthorne, *NH and His Wife*, I:321.

"As formerly we were connected": Hibben, *Henry Ward Beecher*, 32.

"He was the most beautiful thing": Ibid., 31.

"Bachelors both, we drive": Donald, *Charles Sumner*, 86.

"He is quite in love with Howe": Ibid., 87.

347 "The torrent of affection": Ibid., 92.

"Sumner ought to have been a woman": Ibid., 91.

"have made vows of celibacy": R. Browning, *Dearest Isa*, 26, n.12.

"in point of sex": Leach, *Bright Particular Star*, 196.

"I should be curious to learn": Melville, *Letters*, 78.

348 "It is so true that a woman": Chevigny, *The Woman*, 112.

"Why did Socrates so love Alcibiades?": Ibid., 113.

"She loved me, too": Ibid.

349 "Had the belle of the season": Melville, *Typee*, 170.

"Wherever that great heart": Melville, *Selected Tales and Poems*, 289.

"the sexual feud [that] clogs the aspirant life": Melville, *Selected Tales and Poems*, 410.

". . . Nature, in no shallow surge": Ibid., 408.

page   THIS INFINITE FRATERNITY OF FEELING

351 "I write diligently": NH to Fields, November 3, 1850; Houghton.

"I have been in a Slough of Despond": NH to Fields, December 9, 1850; Houghton Letterbook.

"a new Romance by the author": *Centenary* II:xvii.

"ought to be finished with the minuteness": NH to Fields, November 3, 1850; Houghton.

352 "God will give him": *Centenary*, II:8.
Interestingly, where Hawthorne's contemporaries: For a recent account of the witchcraft trials that suggests an economic basis for the hostility and the hysteria, see Boyer and Nissenbaum, *Salem Possessed.*
"the truth, namely, that": *Centenary*, II:2.
"a very minute fidelity": Ibid., 1.
"to connect a bygone time": Ibid., 2.
"this visionary and impalpable Now": Ibid., 149.
"an absurdity, from beginning to end": NH to Fields, November 3, 1850; Houghton.

353 "My House of Seven Gables": NH to Fields, January 12, 1851; Houghton Letterbook.
"the obscurest man of letters": *Centenary*, IX:3.
"the pale tint of flowers": Ibid., 5.
"communications of a solitary mind": Ibid., 6.
"mild, shy, gentle, melancholic": Ibid., 7.

354 "That side-blow thro' Mrs. Hawthorne": Melville, *Letters*, 118.
"any prim nonsensical house": Ibid., 119.
"of course, buried in snow;": Ibid., 121.
"I think they far exceed": Ibid.
" 'Friend,' replied the little boy": *Centenary*, IX:72.

355 "Still there is something lacking": Melville, *Letters*, 121.
"the blue nectared air": SAH to EPPM, February 12, 1851; Berg.
"Such clear, unclouded eyes": Ibid.
"French, arithmetic, history and geography": J. Hawthorne, *NH and His Wife*, I:376.
"He reads so wonderfully.": SAH Diary, December 26, 1850 — March 14, 1851, entry February 1, 1851; Berg.
"Mr. Hawthorne read me the close": SAH to EPPM, January 27, 1851; Berg.

356 "The House of the Seven Gables has been": SAH to EPPM, February 12, 1851; Berg.
Julian Hawthorne was also to remember: See J. Hawthorne, *Hawthorne and His Circle*, 11.
"the Beautiful": *Centenary*, II:109.
"I do not belong to the dreaming class": Ibid., 235.

357 "selfish in its essence": Ibid., 109.
"a flame which we see": Ibid., 104.
"much smoulder and scanty fire": NH to Fields, February 25, 1864; Huntington.
"I want my happiness": *Centenary*, II:157; see also *Centenary*, X:323.
"Clifford is full of an awful truth": Melville, *Letters*, 124.

358 "In his crude, wild and misty": *Centenary*, II:181.
"in a country where everything": Ibid.
"Though now but twenty-two years old": Ibid., 176.
"Shall we never, never": Ibid., 182.

359 "A Dead Man sits on all": Ibid., 183.
"but of whom, even after much": Ibid., 181.
"Homeless as he had been": Ibid., 177.
"reformers, temperance-lecturers": Ibid., 84.
"has a law of his own!": Ibid., 85.
"lack of reverence": Ibid., 177.
"gift of practical arrangement": Ibid., 71.

360 "one identical tune": Ibid., 163.
"perspiration and weary self-importance": Ibid., 165.
"In short, I make pictures": Ibid., 91

361 But he may also have had in mind: Senator Silsbee had died on July 15, 1850, not long before Hawthorne began work on *The House of the Seven Gables.* See obituaries in the *Boston Advertiser*, July 16, 1820, and the *Salem Gazette*, July 19, 1850.

page

"to ears yet echoing": *Centenary*, II:273.

Nathaniel Silsbee and Daniel Webster, some year before: The dinner, held on August 7, 1834, is recounted in "Autobiographical Memoir by Nathaniel Silsbee," *EIHC*, January 1899:67.

An odd bit of telltale evidence: Consider, for example, the rather overitemized excuses for his not attending his Uncle Robert's funeral in his letter to his sister Louisa, dated October 12, 1842 (Essex Institute): "I cannot, at present, leave Concord for any long space; because my domestic affairs, orchard, potatoes &c, have to be attended to this week, and I have also a guest (Mr. Farley) who has been invited to stay several days — not to mention a literary matter, which must be completed within a specified time."

"two much-esteemed varieties of the pear": *Centenary*, II:231.

"impelled by the species of terror": Ibid., 166. In *The Marble Faun* (*Centenary*, IV:260), another of Hawthorne's characters, the sculptor Kenyon, experiences a similar impulse to throw himself off the tower of Monte Beni. "Have you never felt this strange impulse of an Evil Spirit at your back, shoving you towards a precipice?" he asks Donatello.

"Both impulses might have": *Centenary*, II:166.

362 "strangely enfranchised prisoners": Ibid., 256.

"Meanwhile, looking from the window": Ibid. Speed, of course, is a relative matter. Emerson, for example, notes (*Journals*, IX:119), "The Fitchburg cars run at the rate of one mile in one minute, 45 seconds."

"make himself a prisoner": *Centenary*, II:260.

"A man will commit": Ibid., 263.

"Within the lifetime of the child": Ibid.

363 "ascending spiral curve": Ibid., 259.

"You must take the lead now": Ibid., 266.

"very promising child — kicking": NH to LH, May 20, 1851; Huntington.

"heroic and sublime": NH to EPPm, May 25, 1851; Maine Historical Society.

"proposed they should have but three children": Pearson, "Elizabeth Peabody on Hawthorne," 276.

364 "getting on bravely": NH to EPPm, May 25, 1851; Maine Historical Society.

"more decided drawing of the heart": Ibid.

"Your father, as I see him": Ibid.

"The most inconvenient": NH to LH, July 10, 1851; Pforzheimer.

365 "insane and if not insane": SAH to EPPM, March 8–9, 1849; Berg.

"said nothing absurd or disagreeable": EPPm to SAH, March 23, 1851; Berg.

366 "Who, I pray, is Dwight Currier?": SAH to EPPM, September 29–October 10, 1850; Berg.

"As I sit and look on these mountains": Ibid.

"pitiful hospitality": SAH to EPPm, July 10, 1851; Berg.

"I never intend": Ibid.

367 "How slowly I have made my way": Bridge, *Personal Recollections*, 125.

"Did you feel shy": Ibid, 126.

The book had done well: *Centenary*, II:xxix–xxx; see also Clark, *A Descriptive Bibliography*, 167ff.

368 "the good name of our Ancestors": *Centenary*, II:xxiv.

"Pyncheon jackasses": NH to Fields, June 5, 1851; Buffalo.

"its plot is more complex": Crowley, *Critical Heritage*, 195.

"less ambitious in plan": Ibid., 203.

"The mental nerve": Ibid., 197–98.

"immediate popularity and permanent fame": Ibid.

"helped me to see my book": NH to Fields, May 23, 1851; Houghton Letterbook.

"I thought I could not forgive you": J. Hawthorne, *NH and His Wife*, I:390–91.

369 "a greater sensation": NH to LH, July 10, 1851; Pforzheimer.

"I am going to begin": NH to Fields, July 15, 1851; Gardner Museum.

"At dusk, arrived Herman Melville": SAH Diary, December 25, 1850–March 14, 1851; Berg. Entry March 12, 1851.

"I write to you from the house": NH to Duyckinck, March 14, 1851; New York Public Library.

"Mr. Melville came": SAH Diary, April 11–May 4, 1851; Berg. Entry dated April 11, 1851.

"Herman Melville, from Nath'l Hawthorne": The copy is in the Melville Collection, Harvard College Library.

370 "a pair of *bootees*": Melville, *Letters*, 123.
"The House of the Seven Gables": Ibid., 123–25.

371 "My dear Hawthorne, I should": Ibid., 126.
"It is but nature": Ibid., 127.

372 "The calm, the coolness": Ibid., 128.
"Dollars damn me . . .": Ibid.
"I talk all about myself": Ibid., 129.
"Live in the all": Ibid., 130.

373 "As with all great genius": Ibid., 131.
"babylonish brick-kiln": Ibid., 132.
"Have ready a bottle of brandy": Ibid., 133.
"not a letter, or even a note": Ibid., 135.

374 "How it is I know not": Melville, *Moby-Dick*, 57.
"On the hither side of Pittsfield": *Centenary*, VII:169.
"Herman Melville (whom you praise . . .)": NH to Curtis, April 29, 1851; modern transcript, Houghton. Hawthorne read the book aloud to Sophia, but worried that the descriptions of the dancing-girls "might result in something not altogether accordant with our New England morality; and even now, I hardly know whether we escaped the peril, or were entirely overwhelmed by it. But at any rate, those passages are gorgeous, in the utmost degree."

375 "Melville and I talk": NH to Duyckinck, April 27, 1851; New York Public Library.
"Twenty Days with Julian & Little Bunny": *Centenary*, VIII:436.
"I am strongly tempted": Ibid., 437.
"more wickeder": Ibid., 485.

376 "like a great, awkward": Ibid., 457.
"mortal father ought to be expected": Ibid., 454.
"This is a horrible, horrible": Ibid., 439.

377 "I hope Providence has no intention": NH to Pike, September 2, 1851; Pearson Transcripts.
"To tell you a secret": NH to Fields, September 13, 1851; Houghton Letterbook.
"about time and eternity": *Centenary*, VIII:448.

378 "it was a pain and constraint": Ibid., 465.
"The fact shows that all their miserable": Ibid.

379 "He hates to be touched": SAH to Fields, January 1, 1862; Boston.
"a jolly aspect": *Centenary*, VIII:466.

380 "questions of disputed boundary": R. H. Lathrop, *Memories*, 163.
"What is a garden without": Ibid., 164.
"You stop her, look at": Ibid., 165. Sophia, in writing to Lizzie Peabody on October 2, 1851 (Berg), was probably referring to this episode: "Caroline has made herself strangely disagreeable and crowned her strange behavior with an overt act which I could not have thought possible in a person of good taste, to say nothing of Christian sentiment (but I believe she despises Christ) and decent manners and human friendliness. Mr. Tappan has proved himself most lovely and of the true ideal courtesy and does not share at all in Caroline's hostility. But of course we could not live in the red house any longer at any rate with Caroline at war."

381 "Talking with Mary last night": NH to SAH, September 19, 1851; Huntington.
"Hawthorne has perceived it": Channing to Ellen Channing, October 30, 1851; Massachusetts Historical Society.
"I should think Sophia": Ibid.

page
"What a book Melville has written!": NH to Duyckinck, December 1, 1851; New York Public Library.
"My Dear Hawthorne": Melville, *Letters*, 141.
"Had I been at home": Ibid., 142.
383 "Lord, when shall we be done changing?": Ibid., 143.
384 "Don't think that by writing": Ibid., 144.

page   THE METAL HARDENS

387 "When I write another romance": R. H. Lathrop, *Memories*, 152.
"engage in a longer work": NH to Dwight, November 23, 1851; Beinecke.
388 "a perfect hospital": SAH to LH, December 25, 1851; Berg.
"building a house and locating it": *Centenary*, VIII:313. Hawthorne had earlier touched on this notion in his sketch "Fire-Worship." See *Centenary*, X:146.
It could hardly have been a pleasure: Her visit on December 6, 1851, is mentioned in *Centenary*, VIII:313. His view of Greenwood as a writer is expressed in an undated fragment from a letter to Lizzie Peabody. She had asked him to review one of Greenwood's books, and Hawthorne had responded with the suggestion that Lizzie ought to write the review herself: "I doubt whether anybody else esteems her quite worth the trouble." Sophia, Hawthorne noted, disapproved of Greenwood on "moral rather than literary" grounds. University of Virginia.
"the finest genius": SAH to LH, December 25, 1851; Berg.
"but you shall not have a copy": Ibid., NH postscript.
389 And despite the initial flurry: The first edition of *The Snow-Image*, consisting of 2425 copies, was published in December 1851. *A Wonder-Book* had been issued the month before, in an edition of 3067 copies. See *Centenary*, XI:393, and Clark, *A Descriptive Bibliography*, 183.
"external habits, his abode": *Centenary*, XI:4.
"musty and mouse-nibbled leaves": Ibid., 6.
"These magazine stories": NH to Sartain, December 4, 1851; University of Virginia.
390 "would not write another": NH to Griswold, December 15, 1851; Huntington.
"It really amazed me": Melville, *Letters*, 146.
"And does Mr. Hawthorne continue": Ibid.
391 "Nobody at home": J. Hawthorne, *NH and His Wife*, I:432.
"the temperance-men may preach": *Centenary*, III:175.
"I have got a good cook": J. Hawthorne, *NH and His Wife*, I:432.
"But as you are sweating Romances": Ibid., 433.
392 "Behold, a huge bundle": NH to Whipple, May 2, 1852; Morgan.
"The whole family of Manns": NH to LH, May 16, 1852; Essex Institute.
"certainly, the most romantic episode": *Centenary*, III:2.
"illustrate a theory": Ibid., 1.
"Had he attempted it": Ibid., 2.
393 "set aloof from the possibility": Ibid., 97.
394 "intellectual approbation": Ibid., 79.
"a tolerably educated bear": Ibid., 28.
"I see through the system.": Ibid., 132.
"superior cultivation and refinement": Ibid., 24.
395 "secretly putting weight": Ibid., 25.
"petticoated monstrosities": Ibid., 123.
"the most admirable handiwork": Ibid., 122.
"the gentle parasite": Ibid., 123.
"A female reformer": Ibid., 44.
"a natural indifference": Ibid., 41.
"is never content, unless he can degrade": Ibid., 122.

396 "It often requires but one smile": Ibid., 71.
"But women are always more cautious": Ibid., 28.
"There is nothing parallel to this": Ibid., 33.
"It is all self!": Ibid., 218.
"Did you ever see": Ibid., 60.
"towards the millennium of love": Ibid., 24.
397 "While inclining us": Ibid., 72.
"a tall and well-developed figure": Ibid., 91.
"There is hardly another sight": Ibid., 73.
"Girls are incomparably wilder": Ibid.
"It struck me": Ibid., 15.
398 "the garb of Eden": Ibid., 17.
"a woman to whom wedlock": Ibid., 47.
"A bachelor always feels himself": Ibid., 48.
"I have been exposed": Ibid., 47.
"Their peculiar excellence": Ibid., 35.
399 "maidenly mystery": Ibid., 125.
"a tenderness in his voice": Ibid., 28.
"something of the woman": Ibid., 42.
"There is not the man": Ibid., 133.
"I never said the word": Ibid., 135.
400 "about thirty years old": Ibid., 28.
"rural bowl of milk": Melville, *Letters*, 146.
401 "a friend of mine": *Centenary*, III:51.
402 "the most perfect in execution": Crowley, *Critical Heritage*, 256.
"equally shocking and unnecessary": Ibid., 258.
"an exceedingly bungling way": Ibid., 266.
"too much tenderness for experiments": Ibid., 267.
403 "less capable of love": Ibid., 266.
"just £150 more than I expected": NH to Fields, June 17, 1852; Huntington.
"I hope Hawthorne": *Centenary*, III:xxii.
404 "ultra men of the South": Nichols, *Franklin Pierce*, 200.
"ketch & kill off all *Northern Men*": Douglas, *Letters*, 249.
"I believe there will be": Nichols, *Franklin Pierce*, 201.
405 Mrs. Alcott had bought Hillside: For additional details on Alcott's occupancy, see Saxton, *Louisa May*, 153ff.
"a Shaker in principle": EPPM to SAH, June ?, 1844; Berg.
406 "It is no very splendid mansion": NH to Duyckinck, June 15, 1852; New York Public Library.
"I hardly know whether to congratulate you": NH to Pierce, June 9, 1852; New Hampshire Historical Society.
"It has occurred to me": Ibid. Hawthorne had had a similar idea when Pierce was running for Congress in 1832. Writing to Pierce on June 28, 1832 (Boston Public Library), he said, "It is a pity that I am not in a situation to exercise my pen in your behalf; though you seem not to need the assistance of newspaper scribblers."
407 "being engaged to sit for a portrait": NH to Pierce, June 9, 1852; New Hampshire Historical Society.
"so that my face might": NH to Greenwood, April 17, 1852; Berg. See also Greenwood to NH, April 11, 1852; Essex Institute. I do not know the present location of the miniature, but it seems clear that one was made. According to Sophia, "The summer before we left America, she (Charlotte Cushman) sent a note to Mr. Hawthorne, requesting him to sit to a lady for his miniature, which she wished to take to England. Mr. Hawthorne could not refuse, though you can imagine his repugnance on every account. He went and did penance, and was then introduced to Miss Cushman." SAH to Nathaniel Peabody, January 5, 1854 (copy in Nathaniel Peabody's hand?); Berg.
"intimate through life": NH to Fields, June 17, 1852; Huntington.
408 "fine sentences and sophisticated reasoning": Tharp, *Peabody Sisters*, 220.

page
"admirable" . . . "stooped from the dignity": SAH to EPPM [Concord, 1852]; Berg.

"the greatest work of fiction": Tharp, *Peabody Sisters*, 221.

"Instead of thrusting yourself": NH to Pierce, July 5, 1852; New Hampshire Historical Society.

409 "I am sensible of a very difficult": Ibid.

"Not that I ever did": NH to Longfellow, May 8, 1851; Houghton.

"His sympathies are absorbed": Fanny Longfellow to Sumner [May 1851]; Houghton.

In the spring of 1851: I have been unable to locate any petition that Hawthorne might have signed. It may have been related to the Shadrack Rescue case, involving the arrest of the Plymouth lawyer, Charles Davis, who had aided in the escape of a fugitive slave. Davis was defended by Richard Henry Dana, Jr., and acquitted. See Dana, *Journal*, II: 413ff.

410 "if there should be any right": NH to Burchmore, July 16, 1851; Middlebury. Hawthorne, who had evidently been keeping his eye on Salem politics, had noted that Burchmore had refused to join the coalition of Democrats and Free-Soilers, and commented on it in an earlier letter. See NH to Burchmore, February 11, 1851; University of Virginia.

"Still, whenever I am absolutely cornered": NH to Burchmore, July 16, 1851; Middlebury.

"and shall not show my face": NH to Ticknor, July 24, 1852; Pearson Transcripts.

"I am taking your life": NH to Pierce, July 27, 1852; New Hampshire Historical Society.

"to prevent your coming this summer": NH to LH, June 18, 1852; Essex Institute.

411 "but I hardly think we shall": LH to SAH, July 14, 1852; Berg.

On July 28, in midafternoon: For details of the *Henry Clay* disaster, see the *Salem Gazette* for July 30, August 3, and August 6, 1852.

"an expression of darkness and suffering": J. Hawthorne, *NH and His Wife*, I:457.

"If Elizabeth (my sister) has gone": SAH to EPPM, July 30, 1852; Berg.

"If there is anything immortal": R. H. Lathrop, *Memories*, 199.

412 "I have not the courage": SAH to EPPM, August 5, 1852; Berg.

"It would have been so painful": Ibid.

"But who knows which": Emerson, *Letters*, IV:301.

413 "Take command of the Brigade": Nichols, *Franklin Pierce*, 161.

414 "This story, fabricated": R. H. Lathrop, *Memories*, 203.

"I think you must blaze away": NH to Ticknor, August 25, 1852; Huntington.

"terribly reluctant": NH to Bridge, October 18, 1852; Bowdoin.

"I made an inward resolution": Ibid.

415 "second in dignity": SAH to Nathaniel Peabody, April 3, 1853; Berg.

"Just at this time": NH to Bridge, October 18, 1852; Bowdoin.

"What luck the fellow has!": Ibid.

416 "I love him, and, oddly enough": Ibid.

"All my contemporaries": NH to SAH, September 3, 1852; Huntington.

"This name of 'Hawthorne' seems": Melville, *Letters*, 152.

417 "the craziest fiction extant": Miller, *Melville*, 252.

"I do not, therefore, My Dear Hawthorne": Melville, *Letters*, 157.

"I wish I had": Ibid., 162.

418 "I have no future": Dalzell, *Daniel Webster*, 302.

"a perfect beauty": R. H. Lathrop, *Memories*, 207.

"in the fullness of his power of mind": Ibid.

"I should be grieved to hear": J. Hawthorne, *NH and His Wife*, I:479.

"It will take an aeon": Ibid., 480.

420 "Do not let my name": NH to Burchmore, December 9, 1852; Middlebury. Another of the complications for Hawthorne was that George Loring was running against Hawthorne's friend, Ephraim Miller, the incumbent collector at Salem. See NH to George Loring, February 17, 1853; Middlebury.

"all possible means": NH to Burchmore, March 22, 1853; Beinecke. Hawthorne's suggestion that Burchmore curry favor with the Loring forces seems to have been ill-advised, for Ephraim Miller retained the collectorship, and Burchmore found himself out of favor. In May, still attempting to get Burchmore restored to his old post, Hawthorne was advising him to tell Miller "the simple truth" about his support of Loring. See NH to Burchmore, May 31, 1853; Morgan.

"a poor, miserable, broken": NH to Pike, June 19, 1853; Pearson Transcripts.

"God deliver me from such assistance!": NH to Pike, March 29, 1853; Pearson Transcripts.

421 "There is so much of my paper": NH to Burchmore, March 14, 1853; Morgan.

"has not the requisites": NH to Fields, December 11, 1852; Huntington.

"literary fragrance": NH to Stoddard, March 16, 1853; New York Public Library.

422 "The fact is, I have a friend": NH to Ticknor, February 16, 1853; Berg. The letters of Maria Melville and Allan Melville indicate Hawthorne's efforts with Pierce, Secretary of State William Marcy, and Attorney General Caleb Cushing to get Melville a position—possibly in Honolulu or Antwerp. In June, after Hawthorne's trip to Washington, Cushing wrote to Melville's father-in-law, Lemuel Shaw, suggesting that Melville might be offered a consulship in Italy, perhaps Rome. But Melville declined it because it paid so poorly. See Hayford and Davis, "Herman Melville as Office-Seeker," *Modern Language Quarterly*, X (1949):168–83, 377–88.

"My only hope of [Horatio's] obtaining": NH to Charlotte Bridge, May 18, 1853; Bowdoin.

"I never did anything else": NH to Stoddard, March 16, 1853; New York Public Library. Hawthorne had thought well enough of his earlier volume of children's stories, *A Wonder-Book*, to send a copy to Washington Irving, who had retired to his home, Sunnyside, in New York, after diplomatic service in Spain. Irving responded with an appreciative note, saying he admired Hawthorne's writing as "among the very best that have ever issued from the American press." (Irving to NH, January 29, 1852; Huntington). In July, 1852, Hawthorne sent Irving a copy of his new novel, *The Blithedale Romance*, with more of that "mere twaddle of graciousness" that Henry James noted as being common to authors. In his note, Hawthorne claimed, "Pray do not think it necessary to praise my 'Blithedale Romance'—or even to acknowledge the receipt of it . . . It affords me—and I ask no more—an opportunity of expressing the affectionate admiration which I have felt so long; a feeling, by the way, common to all our countrymen." NH to Irving, July 16, 1852; Beinecke.

423 "I am a terribly heavy guest": NH to Lowell, January 4, 1853; Pearson Transcripts.

"wonderful, and the whole style": SAH to Nathaniel Peabody, February 13, 1853; Berg. The portrait is now in the collection of the New Hampshire Historical Society. As Sophia's letter indicates, it was not completed until 1853. Clark, *A Descriptive Bibliography*, contains on the overleaf a segment of a letter by Healy, describing the sittings.

424 "At the last moment, Mary": EPPm to SAH, January 11, 1853; Berg. Additional details on the death of Mother Peabody are drawn from EPPm to William Logan Fisher, January 26, 1853; Beinecke.

page   OUR OLD HOME

425 "so thin and pale": R. H. Lathrop, *Memories*, 220. J. Hawthorne, in *Hawthorne and His Circle*, 81, mistakenly identifies Silsbee as George Silsbee, "a child of Cambridge and Boston, a man of means, and an indefatigable traveller." But the passenger list for the *Niagara*, published in the *Boston Advertiser*, July 7, 1852, establishes him as William Silsbee of Salem, who was traveling with his companion O. W. Wight, also of Salem. Silsbee, whose wife, Caroline, had died in November 1848, was a friend of the Peabody family (see SAH to EPPm [Salem, early December 1848]; Berg). Sophia was to encounter him a year later, just

page

before his return to America, remarking that he "seems to be a stronger person in every way." SAH to Nathaniel Peabody, August 18, 1854; Berg.

The Mr. Silsbee whom the Hawthornes met during their London stay (see Hawthorne's *English Notebook* entries for November 16 and 19, 1857), discussed on page 479, is almost certainly Edward Augustus Silsbee (1826–1900), the noted Shelley collector and scholar, and is identified as such by Frank P. Stearns in *The Life and Genius of Nathaniel Hawthorne*, 306.

"fling him to the fishes": R. H. Lathrop, *Memories*, 223.

426 "It seems to require more leisure": Ibid., 222.

"a vast pearl": Ibid., 219.

"That, I suppose": Ibid.

"Go away, tiresome": J. Hawthorne, *Hawthorne and His Circle*, 77.

"view with regret": J. Hawthorne, *NH and His Wife*, II:15.

" 'Good!' 'Good!' I exclaimed": Sumner to NH, March 26, 1853; Pearson Transcripts.

"So from all sides": SAH to Nathaniel Peabody, April 3, 1853; Berg.

427 "is quite a lion here": Ticknor, *Hawthorne and His Publisher*, 44.

"old party lines": Ibid., 45.

428 "It is very queer": NH to SAH, April 28, 1853; Huntington.

"Frank was as free and kind": NH to Bridge, December 21, 1854; Bowdoin. Pierce appointed Sanders as an interim United States consul to London in November 1853. But Sanders' publicly expressed opinion that Napoleon III ought to be assassinated, caused Pierce to recall him in 1854.

"It is too bad": NH to Bridge, December 21, 1854; Bowdoin.

"There is really no *distance* now": SAH to Nathaniel Peabody, March 27, 1853; Berg.

"great simplicity and charm": R. H. Lathrop, *Memories*, 220.

429 "It is glorious, glorious": Ibid., 221.

The notebook entries on pages 429–433 are from Hawthorne, *English Notebooks*, 3–38.

433 "peculiar insanity": *Centenary*, V:18.

"I wish you could have heard": NH to Ticknor, May 27, 1855; Berg.

"In my opinion, he has incurred": Hawthorne, *English Notebooks*, 116.

434 "in the Cemetery of Saint James": MH to Mrs. Wilson Auld, August 24, 1853; St. Lawrence.

"For some time past": NH to Sumner, May 23, 1855; Houghton.

435 "If you will let slavery alone": Ibid.

On December 24, 1853: The *San Francisco*, which was carrying troops to California, ran into a violent gale and was wrecked and abandoned in the Gulf Stream. Many of the troops and the crewmen were rescued by passing vessels, most of which were traveling to the United States. The *Antarctic* was Liverpool-bound. Newspaper reports of the wreck and the subsequent investigation of its causes and the conduct of the crew, of charges of mismanagement and robbery aboard ship, kept the story alive for several months. (See the *New York Post*, January 14, 16, 23, and February 27, 1854.) So it was not unusual that the handling of the troops taken to Liverpool was also the subject of a great deal of unfavorable criticism.

436 "Should not Mr. Hawthorne": *Portsmouth Journal of Literature & Politics*, March 4, 1854.

"I hate nothing worse": NH to Ticknor, March 30, 1854; Berg. This was from Hawthorne's covering letter to Ticknor.

"I do not question the propriety": NH to Ticknor, March 30, 1854; Berg. This is from the letter NH asked Ticknor to hold for possible publication.

"I had the old fellow to dine": NH to Ticknor, April 30, 1854; Berg.

"for it is humiliating": NH to Ticknor, May 5, 1854; Berg.

437 "good sense and plainness of speech": Hawthorne, *English Notebooks*, 99.

"I wonder whether he can have": Ibid., 100.

"perfectly quiet and successful": Ibid., 221.

438 At times, Hawthorne warned Fields and Ticknor: See NH to Ticknor, June 27, 1854; Berg.

A letter from Hawthorne to Buchanan: The letter is in the collection of the Historical Society of Pennsylvania.

"aristocratic society": Hawthorne, *English Notebooks*, 315.

"Speaking of Dickens last evening": Ibid., 323. During Dickens' first American tour, in 1842, Hawthorne accepted an invitation to the gala dinner given the popular English author on February 1 at Papanti's Dancing Academy in Boston. He may have attended the dinner, but he made no mention of having met Dickens on that occasion. For the Dickens' dinner, see Johnson, *Charles Dickens*, 374–77, and Dana, *Journal*, I:59.

439 "I should be glad to smoke a cigar": Hawthorne, *English Notebooks*, 554.

"not of a resounding depth": Ibid., 553.

"shuffling along the floor": Ibid., 554.

"I like his books better": NH to Ticknor, April 11, 1856; Berg. Reade, writing to James T. Fields, commented on Hawthorne: "He has an eye like a violet with a soul in it." Reade to Fields, May 23, 1856; Huntington.

"a poem for happy married people": Hawthorne, *English Notebooks*, 620.

"shabby little house": *Centenary*, V:271.

440 "a very thin crust of outward acerbity": Hawthorne, *English Notebooks*, 315.

"heaviest and most awkward": Ibid., 645.

"hereditary prejudices": Conway, *Life of Nathaniel Hawthorne*, 154.

"visiting terms": Conway, "My Hawthorne Experience," *The Critic*, July 1904:23.

"He told me that he was much disappointed in not meeting George Eliot. 'I mentioned my wish to meet her to several ladies in London in whose houses I was a guest, but none of them was on visiting terms with her.' He ascribed this to her irregular marriage to — or relation with — G. H. Lewes."

441 "talked exclusively about Miss Evans": Conway, *Life of Nathaniel Hawthorne*, 194.

"There is no God": Pachter and Wein, *Abroad in America*, 71.

"If you have any little remark": Hawthorne, *English Notebooks*, 77.

"very conversable": Ibid., 376.

"unwholesome modes of life": Ibid.

"Leaving out the illustrious Jenny": Ibid., 377.

442 "Don't call me *Miss Bacon*": Bacon to NH, February 14, 1857; Pearson Transcripts.

Touched by her intensity and dedication: Writing to an English friend, Francis Bennoch somewhat later, Hawthorne claimed, "If I can get out of the scrape with the loss of £100, I shall be satisfied." NH to Bennoch, March 31, 1857; University of Virginia.

"It is no use trying to reason": NH to Bennoch, December 2, 1856; University of Virginia.

443 "of noble blood, and therefore": Hawthorne, *English Notebooks*, 378.

"bird of paradox": Edel, *Henry James*, II:286.

Not long after *Leaves of Grass* was published: Milnes, writing to Hawthorne on June 30, 1856, concluded, "I will not call it *poetry* because I am unwilling to apply that name to a work totally destitute of Art, but whatever we call it, it is a most notable & bold natural truth. There are things in it that read like the old Greek plays." Pearson Transcripts.

"must not be merely good": NH to Ticknor, September 30, 1854; Berg.

"by a very beautiful woman": NH to Milnes, November 13, 1854; Trinity College, Cambridge, England.

444 "I have known Thoreau": NH to Milnes, November 18, 1854; Trinity College, Cambridge, England.

"liked greatly the manners": Hawthorne, *English Notebooks*, 383.

"of that quickly appreciative": Ibid., 381.

445 "We talked, too, of Margaret Fuller": Ibid.

"very simple and agreeable": Ibid., 382.

"He received us with the most frigid": Bright to Robert Temple, September 23, 1852; quoted in Sherman, "Henry Bright in New England," 125.

page

446 "Hawthorne would launch at him": J. Hawthorne, *NH and His Wife*, II:21.
"Here comes De Quincey, begging": NH to Bright, April 4, 1854; Beinecke.
"He can really converse": SAH to Nathaniel Peabody, December 8, 1853; Berg.

447 "Give me the poker": J. Hawthorne, *NH and His Wife*, II:33.
"a head of iron": J. Hawthorne, *NH and His Wife*, I:86–87.

448 "irksome to me beyond expression": NH to Bridge, March 30, 1854; Bowdoin. In his letter, Hawthorne advised Bridge to take a post at the Portsmouth Naval Yard and "let Washington and politics alone."
"Tell the President": NH to Bridge, April 17, 1854; Bowdoin.
"One great part of a Consul's duty": *Centenary*, V:36.
"The position is totally beyond": Ibid., 37.
"Our country wrongs itself": Ibid., 36.
"a hard-featured Jew enough": Hawthorne, *English Notebooks*, 377.
"every old prophet": Ibid., 321.

449 "The English are a most intolerable": Ibid., 97.
"For my part, what few": NH to Longfellow, October 24, 1854; Houghton.
"I am glad of it": Hawthorne, *English Notebooks*, 91.
"These are the truest pages": NH to Emerson, September 10, 1856; Houghton.
"Mr. Hawthorne goes from us": SAH to EPPm, September 29, 1853; Berg.

450 "could easily make up a couple": NH to Ticknor, May 23, 1856; Berg.
"superb brocade, pale-tinted": R. H. Lathrop, *Memories*, 263.
"[Mrs. Heywood] is a sister": Ibid., 266.
"Mr. William Rathbone is a millionaire": Ibid., 235.
"Mr. Hawthorne as chief guest": SAH to Nathaniel Peabody, October 20–23, 1853; Berg.

451 "Not the autocrat of all the Russias": R. H. Lathrop, *Memories*, 230.
"looking so pretty": SAH to Nathaniel Peabody [n.d., 1853]; Berg.
"A boiled turkey": SAH to Nathaniel Peabody, October 23, 1853; Berg.
"cunning workmanship": SAH, to Nathaniel Peabody, October 20, 1853; Berg.
"They look at him as much": R. H. Lathrop, *Memories*, 271.
"his mamma does not wish": SAH to Nathaniel Peabody, November 23–24; 1853; Berg.
"peculiar square form": SAH to Nathaniel Peabody, January 5, 1854 (copy in Nathaniel Peabody's hand?); Berg.

452 "No one hurries in England": SAH to Nathaniel Peabody, August 9, 1853; Berg.
"stereotyped, crystallized": SAH to Nathaniel Peabody, November 23–24, 1853; Berg.
"Yet reforms on every point": Ibid.
"I wish our Senators": R. H. Lathrop, *Memories*, 271.
"the merest petrifaction now": Ibid., 251.
"'Flummery' Mr. Hawthorne": SAH to Nathaniel Peabody, November 23–24, 1853; Berg.
"Mr. Hawthorne replied that it showed": R. H. Lathrop, *Memories*, 290.

453 "to German silver and": SAH to Nathaniel Peabody, September 14, 1854; Berg.
"But, oh, no, dear father": SAH to Nathaniel Peabody, October 4–5, 1853; Berg.
"I wish you could be undeceived": SAH to EPPm, September 29, 1853; Berg.

454 "I have only room": Ibid., postscript.
"that a man has no claim": NH to Hillard, December 9, 1853; Morgan.
"My relations with Bridge": NH to Ticknor, March 30, 1854; Berg.
"I have determined to buy": Ticknor, *Hawthorne and His Publisher*, 136–37.
"When the friend of half a lifetime": NH to Ticknor, January 19, 1855; Berg.

455 "It is marvelous what a difficulty": Ticknor, *Hawthorne and His Publisher*, 137.
"It is impossible, especially": NH to Bridge, April 17, 1854; Bowdoin.
". . . That little bit of Presidential courtesy": NH to Bridge, March 23, 1855; Bowdoin.
"I have not seen half enough": NH to Ticknor, January 19, 1855; Berg.

456 "It looks now as if": NH to Ticknor, April 26, 1855; Berg.
"I shall have about as much": Bridge, *Personal Recollections*, 146.

"It is my instinct": Ibid., 145.
"For Heaven's sake": NH to Pierce, June 7, 1855; National Archives.
457 "It was delightful to see": R. H. Lathrop, *Memories*, 284.
"I have just received your letter": NH to EPPm, January 19, 1855; Pforzheimer.
"I now request that you": Ibid.
"If anything could have softened": SAH to EPPm, January 25, 1855; Berg.
458 "I don't want this money here": NH to Ticknor, February 16, 1855; Berg. Evidently Lizzie's credit was not good, since Hawthorne commented, "I send you back the bill of exchange — the drawer (or at least, the signer) not being in good credit with the Barings."
"If I were easily alarmed": SAH to EPPm, August 17, 1855; University of Virginia.
"Dear E., I hope you will not": NH to EPPm, n.d.; University of Virginia.
"not worse, nor better": NH to Ticknor, September 27, 1855; Berg.
459 "Since I must go away": SAH to NH, September 20, 1855; Berg.
"A gigantic toy": Hawthorne, *English Notebooks*, 238.
"rather poor place of suburban amusement": Ibid., 251.
"irksome and dreary hour or two": Ibid., 258.
460 "My wife behave heroically": Ibid.
"fat sheep, with their woolly heads": Ibid., 270.
461 "I have suffered woefully": Ibid., 271–72.
"It was a foundling": Ibid., 275.
"a strange run of luck": NH to SAH, April 7, 1856; Huntington.
"It quite crushes a person": Hawthorne, *English Notebooks*, 294.
462 "sad, but with an amiable": J. Hawthorne, *NH and His Wife*, II:86. Sophia's description is a remarkably accurate characterization of a portrait of Pedro V, now at the University of Coimbra.
"as big as a center table": SAH to Julian Hawthorne, October 27, 1855; Berg.
"But I remained as obdurate": NH to SAH, December 13, 1855; Huntington.
"that musty old Church of England": Ibid.
463 "He insists on buckling his sword": NH to SAH, November 3, 1855; Huntington.
"Thy letter, my own most beloved": February 7, 1856; Huntington.
"It was a most foolish project": NH to SAH, March 19, 1856; Huntington.
"Thou *never* again shalt go away": Ibid.
464 "It sickens me to look back": NH to Bridge, March 30, 1854; Bowdoin.
"America is a good land": NH to Longfellow, August 30, 1854; Houghton.
465 "redress a great transgression": Donald, *Charles Sumner*, 282.
"supplied no arms of any kind": Ibid., 284. As Sumner's biographer, David Donald, notes, "If the company was technically innocent, its directors and officers individually contributed heavily to supplying the Kansas migrants with rifles."
"the perpetual stench": Ibid., 287.
466 "decreed by Almighty God": Wilson, *Patriotic Gore*, 245.
"he would have done good service": NH to Ticknor, April 11, 1857; Berg.
"I am sorry to perceive": NH to Bridge, March 30, 1854; Bowdoin.
467 "I feel a sorrowful sympathy": Bridge, *Personal Recollections*, 140–41.
"What a storm you have had to face": NH to Pierce, June 7, 1855; National Archives.
"I am sorry Frank has not": Bridge, *Personal Recollections*, 153.
468 "Dear E., I have just received": NH to EPPm, April 20, 1855; Morgan.
"Your letters to me": R. H. Lathrop, *Memories*, 334.
"I do wish, dear Elizabeth": SAH to EPPm, August 7, 1857; Berg.
469 "I do not choose to bother Sophia": NH to EPPm, August 13, 1857; Berg.
The August 13 letter is accompanied by a note on Rosary Hill Home stationery, presumably written by Rose Hawthorne Lathrop, which reads, "Letter of Nath'l Hawthorne to Aunt Elizabeth P. Peabody, who (alas) pestered him to death with letters, until beheaded."
"Upon my word, it is not": NH to EPPm, fragment, October 8, 1857; Berg.
470 "the memory of places": Hawthorne, *English Notebooks*, 410.
"twinkling of an eye": Ibid., 422. Philip Henry Delamotte (1820–1889) had been commissioned as the official photographer of the reconstruction of the Crystal

page

Palace at Sydenham. Prints of the group photograph are in both the Bancroft and Bodleian libraries. Hawthorne also reported that Delamotte had taken an earlier "experimental group of such of us as were there," but neither library has a print of that photograph.

"I have no features": SAH to Annie Fields, December 8, 1861; Boson Public Library.

"But all the rest of us": Hawthorne, *English Notebooks*, 422.

471 "as stupid a place": Ibid., 461.

"agreeable young Scotchman": Leyda, *Melville Log*, 527.

Melville had only Hawthorne's Rock Ferry address: In his *Melville*, Edwin Miller, in order to support his theory that Melville had made a homosexual advance toward Hawthorne that caused Hawthorne to leave the Berkshires, gives the impression that Melville was ashamed to meet with Hawthorne in Liverpool: "Although the most meaningful man in his life was now consul in that city, Melville did not immediately seek him out. He had an older debt to repay. For a day or so he wandered about the city . . . Finally, [Melville] sought out the middle-aged Apollo who for fifteen months had provided him with the security and feeling of well-being he had not known since his father's death. Two days after his arrival he found Hawthorne at the consulate." Miller, *Melville*, 286.

Far from being reluctant to meet with Hawthorne, Melville went out of his way to do so. He arrived in Liverpool on the Saturday afternoon of a rainy weekend. He put himself up in a hotel and had dinner, paid a visit to the Exchange and saw the Nelson statue. Since it was still raining, he spent the remainder of the evening at his hotel. The very next day, Sunday, in the rain, he took the ferry across the Mersey to Rock Park, only to learn that Hawthorne had moved. There was little else he could do except wait for Monday to see Hawthorne at the consulate.

"much the same as he used to do": Hawthorne, *English Notebooks*, 432.

472 "did not grasp very cordially": Ibid., 98.

"has not been well, of late;": Ibid., 432.

"a fine lad": Leyda, *Melville Log*, 529.

"the least little bit of a bundle": Hawthorne, *English Notebooks*, 432.

"Melville, as he always does": Ibid., 432–33.

473 "Good for Constantinople": Leyda, *Melville Log*, 530.

"a fitful and uncertain day": Hawthorne, *English Notebooks*, 433.

"in a small snuggery": Ibid., 436.

"He said that he already": Ibid., 437. As one of his final services for Melville, Hawthorne, on March 20, 1857, signed Melville's contract with Longman's for the publication of *The Confidence-Man*. On his return trip, Melville saw Hawthorne very briefly — on May 4 — during a one-day stopover at Liverpool before sailing for home.

"It will be a great relief": NH to Bridge, February 13, 1857; Bowdoin.

"I wish you would see Pierce": Ibid.

474 "a competent commission of enquiry": Byers, "Consular Despatches of Nathaniel Hawthorne," 310.

"Nobody is so humane": *Centenary*, V:32.

"a perfectly astounding ignorance": Ibid.

"delinquent in the discharge": Byers, "Consular Despatches of Nathanial Hawthorne," 316.

"In making some remarks": Ibid., 312.

"I believe that no man": Ibid., 313.

475 "It is not an exaggeration": Ibid., 315.

"Now it is undeniable": Ibid., 316.

"The note to Lord Napier": J. Hawthorne, *NH and His Wife*, II:161.

476 "What you say with regard to the evils": Ibid., 162.

"almost congealed with cold": Hawthorne, *English Notebooks*, 451.

"better cheered than any other": Ibid., 460.

477 "larger than most Christians get": Ibid., 490.

"As our union has turned out": Ibid., 537.
"I do abhor this mode": Ibid., 540.
478 "On the whole, I think": Ibid., 351.
"Everything that I see": NH to Ticknor, June 5, 1857; Berg.
"Between us, we might write": NH to EPPm, August 13, 1857; Berg.
"ignorant and inefficient": NH to Ticknor, July 30, 1857; Berg.
479 "such a bore as only": Hawthorne, *English Notebooks*, 602; see also Stearns, *The Life and Genius of Nathaniel Hawthorne*, 306.
"architectural order, of which": Hawthorne, *English Notebooks*, 602.
480 Later in his life, settled in Florence: For a more detailed discussion of the Captain Silsbee anecdote, see Edel, *Henry James*, III:218–19.
"He keeps up a manly courage": Hawthorne, *French and Italian Notebooks*, entry January 6, 1858.
"It almost is a hopeless business": NH to Ticknor, January 17, 1858; Berg.
"Here are these journals": NH to Bright, September 21, 1857; Beinecke.

page   THE BURIED PAST

481 "Stretched on sofas, in a state": *French and Italian Notebooks*, January 6, 1858.
"All the dishes were very delicate": Ibid.
482 "snatching with ghostly": Ibid., January 8, 1858.
"great boulder in history": Ibid., January 9, 1858.
"his coat, his cocked hats": Ibid., January 8, 1858.
"their eyes do not win me": Ibid.
"our neighbor across the way": Ibid., January 9, 1858.
"We, who look back": Ibid.
483 "simple, strong, healthy-humored": Ibid.
"a fat-brained, good-hearted": Ibid., January 11, 1858.
"gentlemanly, courteous cool": Ibid., January 12, 1858.
484 "I used to try to imagine": Ibid., January 24, 1858.
"bright young moonlight": Ibid.
"perpetrated unheard of briberies": Ibid.
Fortunately, the family moved: The January 22 entry in Hawthorne's 1858 Pocket Diary (Bancroft) indicates that he took the suite of ten rooms on the second floor at 340 scudi for four months.
485 "a horror of sight-seeing": Van Doren, 219.
"with his feet thrust": Kendall, *Maria Mitchell*, 90.
"If my wits had not been": *French and Italian Notebooks*, February 3, 1858.
486 "Really, it was great nonsense": Ibid., February 13, 1858.
"If the chained tiger-cat": Ibid.
"get down upon paper": Ibid., February 7, 1858.
487 "Whatever beauty there may be": Ibid.
William Wetmore Story, 1819–1895.
"His perplexing variety": Ibid., February 14, 1858.
488 "a grand subject": Ibid.
"full Nubian lips": *Centenary*, IV:126.
"coins, drawings, painted mummy-cases": Ibid., 125.
"fierce, voluptuous, passionate": Ibid., 127.
"the most profoundly wrought": *French and Italian Notebooks*, February 20, 1858.
"with a deep, bright glow": Ibid.
"awful volume of thighs": Ibid., April 22, 1858.
489 "shortish, round and massive personage": Ibid., May 8, 1858.
"like the page of a book": Ibid., May 9, 1858.
"no high aims": Ibid.
"decidedly objected to buttons": Ibid.
"heavy-browed physiognomy": Ibid., February 15, 1858.

page

490 "a sort of pea-jacket": *French and Italian Notebooks*, February 15, 1858.
"delighted with it": NH to Ticknor, April 14, 1858; Berg.
"the finest modelled bust": Ibid.
"to bring Miss Lander's name": Ibid.
"after all but me": Hawthorne 1858 Pocket Diary, entry April 13; Bancroft.
"her farewell visit": Ibid., entry April 15; Bancroft.
"It looked grand but very old": EMH to Una Hawthorne, October 12, 1858; Bancroft Transcripts. The transcript, dated 1859, is obviously in error, since Hawthorne and his family were in England in October 1859.

491 "combination of Daniel Webster": J. Hawthorne, *NH and His Wife*, II:183. One copy of the bust is in the Concord Free Public Library; another in the Essex Institute. One wonders whether Story may have been the "friend" who suggested the changes in the bust.
"harem (scarem)": James, *William Wetmore Story*, I:254.
"very wilful, and too independent": Ibid., 256.
"the police interfered": Ibid., 255.
"need not trouble himself": *French and Italian Notebooks*, April 22, 1858.

492 "doubtless spent a calm life": Ibid., March 14, 1858.
"unworthy of liberty": Eastlake, *Life of John Gibson*, 170.
"The difference between the pre-Raphaelites": *French and Italian Notebooks*, March 14, 1858.
"fifteen years of good work": Ibid., March 11, 1858.
"common-places in marble and plaster": Ibid; see also Gale, *Thomas Crawford*.

493 "miracles of color": Ibid., April 27, 1858.
"I suppose there is a class-feeling": Ibid., May 21, 1858.
"a country shopkeeper": Ibid., April 3, 1858.
"entirely ignorant, even of his own": Ibid. William Wetmore Story, who was critical of Hawthorne for repeating Mozier's story and of Julian for publishing it in his biography, claimed that Mozier's statements were "absolutely without foundation," that Ossoli was "not a man of special ability, but he was a thorough gentleman, of old and distinguished family," that one of his uncles was a monsignor and two of his brothers were in the pope's service in the Guardia Nobile. Story to "My Dear Sir," January 19, 1885; Beinecke.

494 "He could not possibly have had": *French and Italian Notebooks*, April 3, 1885.
"Margaret had quite lost all power": Ibid.
"Thus, there appears to have been": Ibid.

496 "highly essential nuisance": Ibid., March 3, 1858.
"the greatest pictorial miracles": Ibid., May 16, 1858.
"an immortal agony, with a strange": Ibid., March 10, 1858.
"funniest little old fairy": Ibid., April 22, 1858.
"the bearer of the best": Ibid., May 9, 1858.

497 "It was about as queer": Ibid., February 17, 1858.
"If I had a murder": Ibid., February 7, 1858.
"You cannot dig six feet": Ibid., May 8, 1858.
"But Nature has made it": Ibid.

498 "all a humbug": NH, *English Notebooks*, 194–95. The fictional possibilities of the bloody footprint, however, had occurred to Hawthorne a good deal earlier. In one of his American notebooks, we find this: "The print in blood of a naked foot to be traced through the street of a town.": *Centenary*, VIII:239.
In Rome, in the warming spring": See *The Ancestral Footstep, Centenary*, XII:3–89.
"I like these strange, sweet": *French and Italian Notebooks*, April 18, 1858.
"This race of Fauns": Ibid., April 22, 1858.

499 "The whole person conveys": Ibid., April 30, 1858.
"My family gathered about him": Ibid., May 22, 1858.

500 "the triumph of the administration": Ibid.
"This is about as sad": Ibid.
"alarming fervor": Ibid., May 23, 1858.

501 "smiling in a certain dangerous way": J. Hawthorne, *Hawthorne and His Circle*, 332.

"We drove off under a perfect shower": *French and Italian Notebooks*, May 24, 1858. It is also possible that the hostility may have been the result of Hawthorne's tendency to parsimony. Writing to Cephas Thompson on June 11, 1858 (Skidmore), shortly after his journey to Florence, for example, Hawthorne noted that their *vetturino*, Gaetano, had been most excellent but had run short of money on the road and when he asked for another fifty scudi, Hawthorne had refused. At the end of the journey, Gaetano complained that the agreed-upon tip was not enough, and Hawthorne had paid "a scudo or two more, and we parted excellent company." Hawthorne was never the profligate American tourist. "I suppose," he commented, "it is too much to expect of an Italian, to suppose that he will not try to get all the money he possibly can."

"a little wilderness of shrubbery": *French and Italian Notebooks*, June 4, 1858.

502 "clothed all over with sentiment": Gerdts, *American Neo-Classic Sculpture*, 53.

"If you can set yourself right": NH to Pierce, October 27, 1858; New Hampshire.

"racy and oracular" *French and Italian Notebooks*, June 27, 1858.

"Like most twenty-year exiles": Ibid., June 4, 1858.

503 "disagreeable, and now wearisome": Ibid., June 9, 1858.

Daniel Dunglas Home (1833–1886): Home was born in Scotland but came to America at the age of nine. The séance at which the wreath was placed on EBB's head took place on July 23, 1855. In 1864, Home was to be expelled from Florence on charges of sorcery.

"I never saw such a boy": Ibid., June 9, 1858.

"quick thoughted": Ibid.

504 "I wish the poets now-a-days": NH to Ticknor, January 3, 1856; Berg.

"since his poetry can seldom": *French and Italian Notebooks*, June 9, 1858.

"Really, I do not see": Ibid.

"I almost fear": NH to Thompson, June 11, 1858; Skidmore.

"not eminently an affectionate man": *French and Italian Notebooks*, June 9, 1858.

"not uncheerfully": Ibid.

505 "He must be an amiable man": Ibid., June 27, 1858.

"America owes more": Ibid.

"She sometimes has a perception": Ibid., September 1, 1858.

"It is very curious and wonderful": Tharp, *Peabody Sisters*, 263.

506 "My wife's mother is the principal": *French and Italian Notebooks*, September 1, 1858.

"Do I believe in these wonders?": Hawthorne, *English Notebooks*, 617.

"not quite pleasant": *French and Italian Notebooks*, August 12, 1858.

"he did not quite know": Ibid.

507 "I feel an impulse": Ibid., June 13, 1858.

"sketching plot . . . rough draft": Hawthorne, 1858 Pocket Diary, entries July 14 and 17; Bancroft.

"I seldom go out now-a-days": *French and Italian Notebooks*, July 27, 1858.

"big enough to quarter": NH to Fields, September 3, 1858; Huntington.

"Furthermore, I usually spend": *French and Italian Notebooks*, September 1, 1858.

"I hire this villa": NH to Fields, September 3, 1858; Huntington.

508 Although the Hawthornes left Florence: One of the mishaps of the move was that Hawthorne left a leather bag, containing his journal and the manuscript sketch for his romance, under the seat of the railroad car. He was much relieved when it turned up with his luggage the next day. See *French and Italian Notebooks*, October 2, 1858.

"brilliant person — the fullest": Ibid., October 4, 1858.

"that a piece of good fortune": Ibid., May 23, 1858.

"some sorrow would come": Ibid.

"such a comfortable, cosy": Ibid., October 17, 1858.

509 "more beautiful than ever": Ibid.

"Mr. Thompson called before dinner": Hawthorne 1858 Pocket Diary, entry October 17, 1858; Bancroft. On October 21, Hawthorne noted that he, Sophia, and Una

page

had visited Lander's studio (the artist was still absent in America) to see the bust, but he did not give any indication of his dissatisfaction with the changes made.
"In the evening, Miss Lander": Hawthorne, 1858 Pocket Diary, entry November 9, 1858; Bancroft.
"Miss Lander sent in a card": Ibid., entry November 10, 1858.
"some letters & Longfellow's poem": Ibid., entry November 12, 1858.
"by bearer": Ibid., entry December 5, 1858; Bancroft. For additional details, see Idol and Eisiminger, "Hawthorne Sits for a Bust," *EIHC*.

510 "Began to write a Romance": Hawthorne, 1858 Pocket Diary, entries October 25, 26, 27, 28, 1858; Bancroft.
"Una has taken what seems": *French and Italian Notebooks*, November 2, 1858.

511 "So ends 1858": Hawthorne, 1858 Pocket Diary, excised entry, copied by George Parsons Lathrop, March 22, 1874; Bancroft.
"I finished today, the rough draft": Hawthorne, 1859 Pocket Diary, entry January 30, 1859; Berg.
"has worn herself out": NH to Fields, February 3, 1859; Huntington.
"strangely like a dream": *French and Italian Notebooks*, March 8, 1859.
"The poor fellow will not": NH to Ticknor, March 4, 1859; Berg.
"I am wearing away": *French and Italian Notebooks*, March 23, 1859.

512 "Even dear Mrs. Browning": R. H. Lathrop, *Memories*, 370. After a summer in France, the Brownings had returned to Italy and were spending the winter in Rome. The Mrs. Ward whom Sophia mentions may well have been Mrs. Samuel Gray Ward, the beautiful Anna Barker, a recent convert to Catholicism, who was traveling in Europe at the time.
"A dim morning": Hawthorne, 1859 Pocket Diary, entry April 8, 1859; Berg.
"Why should I doubt": J. Hawthorne, *NH and His Wife*, II:210.
"We have suffered a great deal": NH to Ticknor, May 23, 1859; Berg.
"the marks of care and": *French and Italian Notebooks*, March 11, 1859.

513 "as historic as anything": Ibid., March 15, 1859.
"content to let his one administration": Ibid., March 11, 1859.
"Certainly he was in his element": Ibid., March 23, 1859.
"I did not know what comfort": Ibid., April 19, 1859.
Since the brutal attack: See Donald, *Charles Sumner*, 337ff.

514 "delicious days": Sumner to Story, May 14, 1859; Huntington.
"What I have left undone": Ibid.
"passed half an hour": James, *William Wetmore Story*, II:36.
"only live by turning highwaymen": Ibid., 38.

515 "superior to anything in all Boston!": Ibid., 46.
"more than enough to fill": Ibid., 47.
"in scenes very different": Ibid., 45.
"I seem to know it better": *French and Italian Notebooks*, May 29, 1859.
"the two volumes of": Ibid., June 1, 1859. See Conway, *Life of Nathaniel Hawthorne*, 40n.

516 "where Madame de Staël or her father": Ibid., June 12, 1859.
"a very grand hotel indeed": Ibid.
"returning prosperity": NH to Bennoch, June 17, 1859; Beinecke.
"I shall stay here only": Ibid.

517 "As we're neither of us": J. Hawthorne, *NH and His Wife*, II:223.
"an interesting boy": Annie Fields, *James T. Fields*, 60.
"It is as bleak and dreary": NH to Bennoch, July 23, 1859; University of Virginia.
"At about 10 o'clock": Hawthorne, 1859 Pocket Diary, entry July 26, 1859; Berg.

518 "the stupidest book he can find": SAH to Bright, September 12, 1859; Beinecke.
"rather more than half": Hawthorne, 1859 Pocket Diary, entry September 10, 1859; Berg.
"speaks of it very rapturously": NH to Fields, October 10, 1859, Huntington.
"Wrote till 5 minutes of twelve." Hawthorne, 1859 Pocket Diary, entry November 8, 1819; Berg.
"as usual, he thinks": SAH to EPPm, October 20, 1859; Berg.

"Mr. Hawthorne had no idea: SAH to EPPm?, fragment, n.d., 1860?; Berg.

519 "in condemning it, I shall": *Centenary*, IV:xxvii, note 26.
"moonshiny Romance": NH to Fields, February 11, 1860, Huntington.
"in blessed idleness": NH to Fields, November 17, 1859; Huntington.
"there is nothing in it": Ibid.
"I don't know whether I can tolerate": NH to Bennoch, November 29, 1859; University of Virginia.
"If I am going to die": Messerli, *Horace Mann*, 586.

520 "all the uncertainties": NH to Ticknor, March 4, 1859; Berg.
"closer and kinder": *Centenary*, IV:1.
"no author, without a trial": Ibid., 3.

521 "the City of all time": Ibid., 111.
"Every crime destroys more Edens": Ibid., 212.
"mysterious and terrible event": Ibid., 430
"It only concerns the present": Ibid., 431.

522 "Well, I dare say she was": J. Hawthorne, *NH and His Wife*, II:236. The devoted reader was Arthur Penrhyn Stanley, canon of Christ Church and later dean of Westminster.
"a certain marchese": *Centenary*, IV:430.

523 "the tumult of life": Ibid., 453.
"fantastic shapes without a model": *Centenary*, XI:228.
"as all things heavenly": *Centenary*, IV:434.
"Mr. Hawthorne hates exclamations": SAH to Nathaniel Peabody, February 20, 1853; Berg.

524 "white wisdom": *Centenary*, IV:460.
"the remorselessness of a steel blade": Ibid., 384.
"instructed by sorrow": Ibid., 375.
"She had known such a reality": Ibid.
"Here comes my perplexity": Ibid., 460.
"This is terrible": Ibid.

525 "revolt against American utilities": Crowley, *Critical Heritage*, 329.
"eyes full of innocent wonder": Ibid., 330.
"captive . . . a want of the ease": Ibid., 337.
"only a great deal of very": Ibid., 338.
"The act of sin itself": Ibid., 372.
"general padding": Ibid., 384.
"aesthetic dinner and tea": J. Hawthorne, *NH and His Wife*, II:246.
"inconclusive and hazy": Crowley, *Critical Heritage*, 319.

526 "can in no wise be related": J. Hawthorne, *NH and His Wife.*, II:246.
"you see how fortunate": Ibid., 247.
"to make things a little clearer": NH to Ticknor, March 9, 1860; Berg.
"The idea of the modern Faun": *Centenary*, IV:463.
"clear as a London fog": Ibid., 465.
"Plot it has none": Ibid., xxxiii.
"Father O'Whack, an Irish priest": Crowley, *Critical Heritage*, 334.

527 "the greatest of his works": Ibid., 348.
"purely original writer": Ibid., 21.
"He is rather a denizen than a citizen": Ibid.
"My own opinion is that": NH to Fields, February 11, 1860; Huntington.
"Have you ever read the novels": Ibid.
"Before you leave Rome": Ibid.
"But it is an awful thing": *Centenary*, IV:118.
"picturesque and interesting": Hawthorne, *Works*, X:557.

529 "Affairs succeed each other so fast": NH to SAH, May 17, 1860; Huntington.
"as if it were the last friend": J. Hawthorne, *NH and His Wife*, II:257.
"I consider it my duty": NH to Fields, April 26, 1860; Huntington.
"As regards going home": Fields, *Yesterdays*, 88.

530 "potted owl with Minerva sauce": Ibid., 93.
"I should like to sail": Ibid., 92.

531 "as if nothing but a grasshopper": J. Hawthorne, *NH and His Wife*, II:262.
"I am really at a loss": NH to Fields, February 3, 1859; Huntington.
"If [Alcott] should swamp himself": NH to Ticknor, November 5, 1857; Berg.
532 "but am now meditating": NH to Bennoch, December 17, 1860; University of Virginia.
533 "This will make the cost": NH to Ticknor, December 28, 1860; Berg.
"transformed a simple and small old farmhouse": NH to Mitchell, January 16, 1864; Pearson Transcripts. Mitchell, who wrote under the name of Ik Marvel, was the author of *Battle Summer*, an account of the 1848 revolution in France. He initiated the column, "The Easy Chair," in *Harper's* magazine in 1851. Hawthorne had first met him in Washington in April 1853, where he introduced him to Caleb Cushing and was instrumental in Mitchell's subsequent appointment as American consul in Venice.
"miserable confusion": NH to Ticknor, February 10, 1860; Berg.
"almost mad": Donald, *Charles Sumner*, 350. Sumner had met Brown two years before, in 1857, when the abolitionist leader was visiting Boston. Brown had particularly asked to see the coat Sumner was wearing when he was attacked by Preston Brooks. Sumner, who kept the garment, the collar still stiff from his bloodstains, hobbled over to the closet to get it. He handed it to Brown, who stared at it silently and reverentially, as if it were a religious relic.
"For a practical statesman, believing": Ibid., 351.
534 "— and if I could but be deprived": NH to Ticknor, February 10, 1860; Berg.
"When you get so far": Tharp, *Peabody Sisters*, 288.
"I think him equal to anything he dares": Alcott, *Journals*, 316.
535 "The execution of Saint John the Just": Louisa May Alcott, *Life, Letters, and Journals*, 105.
"Great ferment in town.": Ibid., 121.
"Nobody gets a chance to speak with him": Saxton, *Louisa May*, 238.
"It is of no avail": SAH to EPPm, 1861?; Berg.
"How can you tell anything": SAH to EPPm, Friday, 1861?; Berg.
536 "If you come soon enough": NH to Bright, December 17, 1860; Beinecke.
"Well, I am ashamed to say": Ibid.
"Julian (poor little wretch)": Bassan, *Hawthorne's Son*, 26.
"If the boys attack you": Ibid., 27.
"Julian was a sacredly folded bud": Ibid., 28.
537 "back to the stern and simple fields": J. Hawthorne, *NH and His Wife*, II:265.
"We entirely disapprove of this commingling": Bassan, *Hawthorne's Son*, 237, note 80.
"We are in great trouble": NH to Fields, September 21, 1860; Huntington.
"her case having yielded": NH to "Dear Ticknor or Fields," September 27, 1860; Berg.
"All the violent symptoms": NH to Pierce, October 9, 1860; Library of Congress.
539 "an excellent institution": NH to Bright, December 17, 1860; Beinecke.
"As for me, I spend": Ibid.
"like a partridge": Van Doren, *Nathaniel Hawthorne*, 235.
540 "Duck! or we shall be": Fields, *Yesterdays*, 72.
"Unfortunately she had gone to bed": Edward W. Emerson, *Emerson in Concord*, 109.
"Hawthorne isn't a handsome man": The elder Henry James to Emerson, "Sunday Night," 1861?; Houghton. The younger Henry James, who quoted this letter extensively in his *Notes of a Son and Brother*, made extensive literary improvements on the text.
541 "The war, strange to say": NH to Bridge, May 26, 1861; Bowdoin.
542 "I wish I could turn my hand": NH to Ticknor, May 16, 1861; Berg.
"We all seem like one family": Louisa May Alcott, *Life, Letters, and Journals*, 127.
"It seems as if a few energetic women": Ibid., 129.
"I wish they would push on": NH to Ticknor, May 26, 1861; Berg.

"Speaking of dinner": J. Hawthorne, *NH and His Wife*, II:282.

"Dear Onion": Ibid., 289.

543 "Tell Mama that I see no newspapers": NH to Rose Hawthorne, August 5, 1861; Berg.

"My own opinion is that": Bridge, *Personal Recollections*, 170.

"The war with its defeats & uncertainties": Emerson, *Letters*, V:253.

"If we stop fighting": NH to Bright, November 14, 1861; Pearson Transcripts.

544 "Who cares what the war costs": Ibid.

"Emerson is breathing slaughter": Ibid.

"I heard Mr. Emerson's lecture": R. H. Lathrop, *Memories*, 429.

545 "How I am alive": Longfellow, *Letters*, IV:241; see also Wagenknecht, *Mrs. Longfellow*, 242.

"How does Longfellow bear": NH to Fields, July 14, 1861; Huntington.

"I have not found it possible": NH to Bridge, October 12, 1861; Bowdoin.

546 "beautiful boy": *Centenary* XII:96.

"indistinct remembrances": Ibid., 123.

547 "The life is not yet breathed": Ibid., 264.

"Has crept, has sinned, has suffered": Ibid., 268.

"What unimaginable nonsense!": Ibid., 262.

"Miss Blagden, Miss Ingersoll": Ibid., 220.

"Now for the old pensioner": Ibid., 333.

"Take the character of Cowper": Ibid., 335.

"I have not the least notion": Ibid., 286.

548 "The sooner the better": Fields to NH, September 18, 1861; Huntington.

"just like a shoemaker": Scudder, *James Russell Lowell*, II:82.

"England was the only country": Ibid., 83.

"as one sees bubbles rise": Ibid., 84.

"Trollope fell in love with you": Fields to NH, September 18, 1861; Huntington.

"For instance, I am not very well": NH to Bridge, February 13, 1862; Bowdoin.

549 "The farther we go": NH to SAH, March 9, 1862; Huntington.

550 "One bullet-headed general": Hawthorne, *Works*, XII: 303.

"a mint-julep, a whiskey-skin": Ibid., 341.

"The whole place looks run up": Dicey, *Spectator of America*, 61–62.

"and in lounged a tall": Hawthorne, *Works*, XII:309.

551 "insalubrious atmosphere around the White House": Ibid., 310.

"I have shaken hands": J. Hawthorne, *NH and His Wife*, II:310.

"two cold collations": Ibid.

"almost fathomless puddle": Hawthorne, *Works*, XII:325.

"rusty and shabby like every other": Ibid., 327.

"blood-stained fanatic": Ibid.

552 "Any common-sensible man": Ibid., 328.

"Almost to a man, they were": Ibid., 329.

"I made acquaintance with some": J. Hawthorne, *NH and His Wife*, II:310.

"Not one word too much": SAH to Annie Fields, "Tuesday evening," March 18, 1862?; Boston Public Library.

"Tell Mama that the outcry": J. Hawthorne, *NH and His Wife*, II:310.

553 Edward Dicey, one of the shrewder observers: Dicey took a cool view of the New England reformers: "For my own part I was not impressed favorably by what I heard and saw of the Beecher-Stowe Abolitionists. They seemed to me to represent the sickly sentimentalism which is sure to attach itself to any cause however good. I believe that 'Uncle Tom's Cabin' did as much harm, by removing the question of emancipation from the domain of fact into that of fiction, as it did good, by calling public attention to the evils of slavery." *Spectator of America*, 251.

"Fifty years will not repair": Hawthorne, *Works*, XII:318.

"with a good deal of dignity": Ibid., 321.

"If he is a coward": Ibid., 324.

"Anything more helpless or wretched": Dicey, *Spectator of America*, 154.

554 "My prevalent idea": Hawthorne, *Works*, XII:319.

"gigantic rat-trap . . . ugly": Ibid., 336.

page

"All the pomp and splendor": Ibid.

"a deadly fight going on below": Ibid., 338.

"I deserted and came back": NH to SAH, April 1, 1862; Morgan.

555 "the best ever painted": NH to Fields, April 2, 1862; Huntington.

"My hair really is not so white": Ibid. Hawthorne's letter to Ticknor, dated April 20, 1862 (Berg), tends to suggest that Gardner was the photographer: "I wish you would write Derby about my large photograph. You know he promised me (and you too, for that matter) on behalf of Mr. Garden [sic] that I should have a copy — which was my sole inducement for standing, because I knew that Mrs. Hawthorne would like to have it. But on speaking to Garden about it the day before I left Washington, it appeared to me that he did not intend to give the copy."

"It was a pity": Bridge, *Personal Recollections*, 174.

"a state of full paean": SAH to Annie Fields, April 11, 1862; Boston Public Library.

556 Hawthorne, of course, was writing for home consumption: Hawthorne and Dicey may have traded observations about General McClellan, it seems. Hawthorne: "For when before, in all history, do we find a general in command of half a million of men, and in presence of an enemy inferior in numbers and no better disciplined than his own troops, leaving it still debatable, after the better part of a year, whether he is a soldier or no? The question would seem to answer itself in the very asking." *Works*, XII:322. Dicey: "An old Democrat, and a political partisan of McClellan's, in speaking to me, at the period of which I write, about his military capacity, remarked, 'If McClellan was a great general, we should not be discussing, a year after his appointment, whether he really was so or not.' " *Spectator of America*, 244.

"I wanted the benefit": NH to Ticknor, May 17, 1862; Berg.

"political complexion": Ibid.

"I knew I should like it": Fields to NH, May 21, 1862; Huntington.

557 "Dear Fields, I have looked": May 23, 1862; Huntington.

"What a terrible thing it is": Ibid.

"My Dear Editor, You can hardly": *Atlantic Monthly*, October 1862:451.

558 "I am sorry if I misquoted": NH to Woodman, June 22, 1862; Morgan.

"the bachelor of thought and Nature": Emerson, "Thoreau," *Atlantic Monthly*, August 1862:240.

"quite dissatisfied": Meltzer and Harding, *A Thoreau Profile*, 283.

"To Thoreau, and spend the evening": Ibid., 285.

559 "It is better some things should end": McGill, *Channing of Concord*, 157.

"no sentiment or sentence be altered": Meltzer and Harding, *A Thoreau Profile*, 286.

"I did not know we had ever quarreled": Stern, *Annotated Walden*, 136.

"because, from a tradition": NH to Fields, October 24, 1863; Huntington.

560 "I don't think even your pen": Fields to NH, July 24, 1862; Huntington.

"for more of the same sort": Fields to NH, September 24, 1862; Huntington.

"That's absolutely perfect paper": Fields to NH, December 4, 1862; Huntington.

"It seemed to me almost a pity": NH to Stowe, January 4, 1863; Chicago Historical Society.

"What a delectable *Book*": Fields to NH, July 24, 1862; Huntington.

"I am much encouraged": NH to Fields, January 30, 1863; Houghton Letterbook.

561 "Mrs. Alcott says she shall feel helpless": J. Hawthorne, *NH and His Wife*, II:326.

"At supper time": Ibid.

"no competent head, male or female": Louisa May Alcott, *Life, Letters, and Journals*, 143.

"looking ghastly and uprolling her eyes": SAH to Annie Fields, February 20, 1863; Boston Public Library.

562 "When society is about to be overturned": NH to Bright, March 8, 1863; Beinecke.

"The tone of feeling": Ibid.

563 "The article has some features": NH to Fields, April 30, 1863; Huntington.

564 "come what may": NH to Fields, July 1, 1863; Huntington.
"To Franklin Pierce": *Centenary*, V:2.
"The Present, the Immediate, the Actual": Ibid., 4.
"publicly [to] assert a personal friendship": Ibid., 5.
"Your dedication to F.P.": Fields to NH, July 3, 1863; Huntington.
"It is the opinion": Fields to NH, July 15, 1863; Huntington.
"unlucky in having for a friend": *Centenary* V:xxviii.
565 "The mere arbitrary will of the President": Sandburg, *Lincoln: The War Years*,
II:362.
Time was not kind to Pierce: Hawthorne, writing to Pierce on July 26, 1863, noted
that "some spiteful Abolitionist" had sent him a "compendium of abusive paragraphs from the newspapers," all relating to Pierce. "And it seemed to me," he
commented, "that the best method of disappointing his malice was to toss them
aside without reading one of them — which I accordingly did." New Hampshire
Historical Society.
Unlike Pierce, Hawthorne was far less concerned: See, for example, his letter to
EPPm, July 20, 1863 (Houghton): "I do not care a fig what powers the President
assumes at such a crisis as this, if he only uses them effectually."
"I find that it would be": NH to Fields, July 18, 1863; Houghton Letterbook.
566 "It is a beautiful incident": M. A. DeWolfe Howe, *Memories of A Hostess*, 15.
"I don't know how Ellery Channing": NH to EPPm, July 20, 1863; Houghton.
568 "knew *nothing* about slavery": EPPm to Bridge, June 4, 1887; Bowdoin.
"through the madness of Northern abolitionists": *Centenary*, V:xxix.
"to *secede* & trust that": EPPm to Bridge, June 4, 1887; Bowdoin.
569 "the little acrimonies of the moment": *Centenary*, V:5.
"manly truthfulness": Ibid., xxxii.
"solemn pomposity": Ibid.
"humor and kindliness": Crowley, *Critical Heritage*, 391.
Comments on Hawthorne's dedication: The reviews from the *Boston Daily Advertiser* and the *New-York Tribune* are quoted in *Centenary*, V:xxxiii.
"Mr. Hawthorne is good at fiction.": Ibid.
"caricatures and libels": Crowley, *Critical Heritage*, 392.
"all homely alike": Ibid., 393.
"solid beef and streaky tallow": Ibid., 394.
"his true character under a benignant mask": *Centenary*, V:xxxiv.
"Nothing, it is true": Crowley, *Critical Heritage*, 396.
570 "Don't think me very ungrateful": J. Hawthorne, *NH and His Wife*, II:280.
"seem to think me bitter": NH to Fields, October 18, 1863; Huntington.
"pellucid but not deep": M. A. DeWolfe Howe, *Memories of A Hostess*, 15.
"the bitterest of satires": *Centenary*, V:xxviii.
"Do tell me if our friend Hawthorne": Annie Fields, *Authors and Friends*, 184.
"a story which he says": M. A. DeWolfe Howe, *Memories of A Hostess*, 57.
571 "overwhelmed with sadness": Ibid.
"I fear its politics — beware!": Ibid., 58.
"How sad middle life looks": Ibid., 59.
"to the remotest regions": *Centenary*, X:169.
572 "I have fallen into a quagmire": NH to Mitchell, January 16, 1864; Pearson Transcripts.
"like a Roman toga": M. A. DeWolfe Howe, *Memories of A Hostess*, 61.
"General Barlow and Mrs. Howe": Ibid.
"Our talks . . . were of realities": Bassan, *Hawthorne's Son*, 33.
"Please to record it": NH to Fields, October 18, 1863; Houghton Letterbook.
"silently and intently": J. Hawthorne, *NH and His Wife*, II:335.
573 "I hardly know what to say": NH to Fields, February 25, 1864; Huntington.
"unless a great change comes over me": Ibid.
"invalid appearance": M. A. DeWolfe Howe, *Memories of A Hostess*, 62.
"Why does Nature treat us": Ibid., 63.
574 "one of the most excellent of men": Ibid.
"worse than a northeaster": C. Ticknor, *Hawthorne and His Publisher*, 313.

page
"He seems afraid": Ibid., 314.
"Alas, it was no 'author's excuse' ": Bridge, *Personal Recollections*, 189–91.
575 "I tell him we will float along": C. Ticknor, *Hawthorne and His Publisher*, 320.
"proceeded to cup, and poultice": M. A. DeWolfe Howe, *Memories of A Hostess*, 65.
"medical science and the sad": Ibid., 66.
"Oh! I remember": Ibid., 64.
"He came back unlooked for": Fields, *Yesterdays*, 118.
576 "There are lines": Ibid., 119.
"I think the serene jog-trot": Fields, *Yesterdays*, 120.
"in some ingenious way": Ibid., 121.
"boring pain, distention, difficult digestion": *Atlantic Monthly*, July 1864:98–101.
"O.W.H. thinks the shark's tooth": M. A. DeWolfe Howe, *Memories of A Hostess*, 27.
577 "in the brain or spine or both": Bridge, *Personal Recollections*, 177.
"perfectly clear when roused": Franklin Pierce's notes, Hibbard Collection, New Hampshire Historical Society.
"quite helpless": Bridge, *Personal Recollections*, 178.
"What a boon it would be": Pierce to Mrs. Sarah Webster, March 18, 1868; University of Virginia.
"He hated failure, dependence": R. H. Lathrop, *Memories*, 480.
578 "I wish to speak to you, Annie.": M. A. DeWolfe Howe, *Memories of A Hostess*, 70.
"A tenderness so infinite": Ibid., 71.
"The original of a precious": Ibid., 70.
"One by one": Longfellow, *Letters*, IV:412.
"It is only too true": Ibid.
579 "How beautiful it was": Untermeyer, *The Poems of Henry Wadsworth Longfellow*, 397.
"white with apple-blooms": Ibid.

page   EPILOGUE

580 "Dear Mr. Fields, Will you": SAH to Fields, May 21, 1864; Boston Public Library.
"You see this agony": Ibid., postscript.
581 "ghostly genius": Crowley, *Critical Heritage*, 407.
"an enthusiastic partisan": Ibid., 405.
"obscured the usual accuracy": Ibid., 406.
582 "fierce debate": Curtis, *Literary and Social Essays*, 85.
"did not see a Carolina slave-pen": Ibid., 89.
"The character of his genius": Ibid., 83–84.
"To have known him": Melville, *Selected Tales and Poems*, 405.
583 "Will he linger where I have lived": *Centenary*, X:167.
"What a revelation": Leyda, *Melville Log*, 674.
"He will pass to the dark realm": *Centenary*, X:167.
"This trenches upon the uncertain": Leyda, *Melville Log*, 674.
"to such little accidents": *Centenary*, X:202.
"Nothing can be finer than this": Leyda, *Melville Log*, 675.
"They are all so bright and good": Bridge, *Personal Recollections*, 199.
"The veil he drew around him": SAH to Annie Fields, ca. July 1864; Boston Public Library.
584 Hawthorne's business relationship with Ticknor & Fields: For a discussion of the company's contractual agreements, see Ballou, *The Building of the House*, 141–53.
585 "even one thousand a year": Ibid., Ballou, *The Building of the House*, 152.
Julian, whose college education: For many of the details of Julian Hawthorne's later life, I am indebted to Maurice Bassan's *Hawthorne's Son*.

586 "on a sunny hillside": J. Hawthorne, *NH and His Wife*, II:371.

In the ensuing years: The history of the publication of Hawthorne's final manuscripts can be found in the Historical Commentaries of *Centenary*, XII and XIII.

Rose Hawthorne, only months after her mother's death: For details on the life of Rose Hawthorne, I am indebted to Sister M. Joseph's *Out of Many Hearts*.

587 "My father is the worst enemy": Maude Howe Elliot, *Three Generations*, 29.

588 "melancholy and pale wraith": Leyda, *Melville Log*, 782–83.

Bibliography

BOOKS AND PAMPHLETS

Alcott, A. Bronson. *The Journals of Bronson Alcott*. Edited by Odell Shepard. Boston: Little, Brown and Company, 1938.
———. *The Letters of A. Bronson Alcott*. Edited by Richard L. Herrnstadt. Ames, Iowa: Iowa State University Press, 1969.
Alcott, Louisa May. *Louisa May Alcott: Her Life, Letters, and Journals*. Edited by Ednah D. Cheney. Boston: Little, Brown and Company, 1924.
Anderson, Charles Roberts. *Melville in the South Seas*. New York: Dover Publications, Inc., 1966.
Armstrong, Margaret. *Fanny Kemble: A Passionate Victorian*. New York: The Macmillan Company, 1938.
Arvin, Newton. *Hawthorne*. Boston: Little, Brown and Company, 1929.
———. *Longfellow: His Life and Work*. Boston: Little, Brown and Company, 1962.
Ballou, Ellen B. *The Building of the House: Houghton Mifflin's Formative Years*. Boston: Houghton Mifflin Company, 1970.
Bassan, Maurice. *Hawthorne's Son*. Columbus: Ohio State University Press, 1970.
Beecher, Jonathan, and Richard Bienvenu, editors. *The Utopian Vision of Charles Fourier*. Boston: Beacon Press, 1971.
Bode, Carl, editor. *Ralph Waldo Emerson: A Profile*. New York: Hill and Wang, 1968.
Boorstin, Daniel J. *The Americans*. 3 vols. New York: Random House, 1958, 1965, and 1973.
Bowen, Catherine Drinker. *Yankee from Olympus: Justice Holmes and His Family*. Boston: Little, Brown and Company, 1944.
Boyer, Paul, and Stephen Nissenbaum. *Salem Possessed: The Social Origins of Witchcraft*. Cambridge: Harvard University Press, 1974.
Bridge, Horatio. *Personal Recollections of Nathaniel Hawthorne*. New York: Harper and Brothers, 1893.
Brooks, Van Wyck. *The Dream of Arcadia: American Writers and Artists in Italy, 1760–1915*. New York: E. P. Dutton and Company, Inc., 1958.
———. *Literature in New England*. Garden City, New York: Garden City Publishing Company, Inc., 1944.
Browning, Robert. *Dearest Isa: Robert Browning's Letters to Isabella Blagden*. Edited by Edward C. McAleer. Westport, Connecticut: Greenwood Press, 1970.
Burns, Wayne. *Charles Reade: A Study in Victorian Authorship*. New York: Bookman Associates, 1961.
Burton, Jean. *Heyday of a Wizard*. New York: Alfred A. Knopf, 1944.
Calverton, V. F. *Where Angels Dared to Tread*. Indianapolis: The Bobbs-Merrill Company, 1941.
Cantwell, Robert. *Nathaniel Hawthorne: The American Years*. New York: Rinehart and Company, Inc., 1948.

Capers, Gerald M. *Stephen A. Douglas: Defender of the Union*. Boston: Little, Brown and Company, 1959.

Carlson, Eric W., editor. *The Recognition of Edgar Allan Poe*. Ann Arbor, Michigan: University of Michigan Press, 1970.

Cary, Edward. *George William Curtis*. Boston: Houghton Mifflin Company, 1894.

Charvat, William. *The Profession of Authorship in America, 1800–1870: The Papers of William Charvat*. Edited by Matthew J. Bruccoli. Columbus: Ohio State University Press, 1968.

Chase, Richard, editor. *Melville: A Collection of Critical Essays*. Englewood Cliffs, New Jersey: Prentice-Hall, Inc., 1962.

Chevigny, Belle Gale. *The Woman and the Myth: Margaret Fuller's Life and Writings*. Old Westbury, New York: The Feminist Press, 1976.

Christie, John Aldrich. *Thoreau as World Traveler*. New York: Columbia University Press, 1966.

Clark, C. E. Frazer, Jr. *Nathaniel Hawthorne: A Descriptive Bibliography*. Pittsburgh: University of Pittsburgh Press, 1978.

Clement, Clara Erskine. *Charlotte Cushman*. Boston: James R. Osgood and Company, 1882.

Codman, John Thomas. *Brook Farm: Historic and Personal Memoirs*. Boston: Arena Publishing Company, 1894.

Cole, Donald B. *Jacksonian Democracy in New Hampshire, 1800–1851*. Cambridge: Harvard University Press, 1970.

Commager, Henry Steele. *Theodore Parker*. Boston: Beacon Press, 1960.

Connor, Seymour V., and Odie B. Faulk. *North America Divided: The Mexican War, 1846–1848*. New York: Oxford University Press, 1971.

Conway, Moncure D. *Life of Nathaniel Hawthorne*. New York: Haskell House Publishers, 1968. Originally published 1890.

Cooke, George Willis, editor. *Early Letters of George Wm. Curtis to John S. Dwight*. New York: Harper and Brothers, 1898.

Cornell, William M., editor. *Charles Sumner: Memoir and Eulogies*. Boston: James H. Earle, 1874.

Crouthamel, James L. *James Watson Webb: A Biography*. Middletown, Connecticut: Wesleyan University Press, 1969.

Crowley, J. Donald, editor. *Hawthorne: The Critical Heritage*. New York: Barnes and Noble, 1970.

Curtis, George William. *Literary and Social Essays*. New York: Kennikat Press, Inc., 1968. Originally published 1894.

Dalzell, Robert F., Jr. *Daniel Webster and the Trial of American Nationalism, 1843–1852*. Boston: Houghton Mifflin Company, 1973.

Dana, Richard Henry, Jr. *The Journal of Richard Henry Dana, Jr*. Edited by Robert F. Lucid. 3 vols. Cambridge: The Belknap Press of Harvard University, 1968.

Deiss, Joseph Jay. *The Roman Years of Margaret Fuller*. New York: Thomas Y. Crowell Company, 1969.

Dicey, Edward. *Spectator of America*. Edited and with an introduction by Herbert Mitgang. London: Victor Gollancz Ltd., 1972.

Donald, David. *Charles Sumner and the Coming of the Civil War*. New York: Alfred A. Knopf, 1960.

Douglas, Ann. *The Feminization of American Culture*. New York: Alfred A. Knopf, 1977.

Douglas, Stephen A. *The Letters of Stephen A. Douglas*. Edited by Robert W. Johannsen. Urbana: University of Illinois Press, 1961.

Eastlake, Lady [Elizabeth]. *Life of John Gibson, R.A.* London: Longmans, Green and Company, 1870.

Edel, Leon. *Henry James*. 5 vols. Philadelphia: J. B. Lippincott Company, 1953–1972.

Elder, Marjorie J. *Nathaniel Hawthorne: Transcendental Symbolist*. Athens, Ohio: Ohio University Press, 1969.

Elliott, Maude Howe. *Three Generations*. Boston: Little, Brown and Company, 1923.

Emerson, Edward Waldo. *Emerson in Concord: A Memoir*. Boston: Houghton Mifflin and Company, 1889.

Emerson, Ralph Waldo. *The Early Lectures of Ralph Waldo Emerson*. Edited by Robert

E. Spiller and Wallace E. Williams. Cambridge: The Belknap Press of Harvard University Press, Vol. III, 1972.

―――. *Essays and Journals.* Selected and with an introduction by Lewis Mumford. Garden City, New York: Doubleday and Company, Inc., 1968.

―――. *The Heart of Emerson's Journals.* Edited by Bliss Perry. Boston: Houghton Mifflin Company, 1926.

―――. *The Journals and Miscellaneous Notebooks of Ralph Waldo Emerson.* Edited by William H. Gilman, chief editor; Alfred R. Ferguson, senior editor. Cambridge: The Belknap Press of Harvard University Press, Vol. VII, 1969; Vol. VIII, 1970; Vol. IX, 1971.

―――. *The Letters of Ralph Waldo Emerson.* Edited by Ralph L. Rusk. 6 vols. New York: Columbia University Press, 1966.

The Essex Institute. *Charles Osgood (1809–1890).* Catalogue for a Special Loan Exhibition, November 9, 1978–January 14, 1979. Salem, Massachusetts: Essex Institute, 1978.

Fields, Annie. *Authors and Friends.* Boston: Houghton Mifflin Company, 1896.

―――. *James T. Fields: Biographical Notes and Personal Sketches.* Port Washington, New York: Kennikat Press, 1971. Originally published 1881.

Fields, James T. *Yesterdays with Authors.* Boston: Houghton Mifflin Company, 1925.

Fischer, John, editor. *Six in the Easy Chair.* Urbana: University of Illinois Press, 1973.

Gale, Robert L. *Thomas Crawford: American Sculptor.* Pittsburgh: University of Pittsburgh Press, 1964.

Gerdts, William H. *American Neo-Classic Sculpture.* New York: The Viking Press, 1973.

Gittleman, Edwin. *Jones Very: The Effective Years, 1833–1840.* New York: Columbia University Press, 1967.

Goodspeed, Charles E. *Nathaniel Hawthorne and the Museum of the Salem East India Marine Society.* Salem, Massachusetts: The Peabody Museum, 1946.

The Grolier Club. *A Descriptive Guide to the Exhibition Commemorating the Death of Nathaniel Hawthorne, 1804–1864.* New York: The Grolier Club, 1964.

Hale, Edward Everett. *A New England Boyhood and Other Bits of Autobiography.* Boston: Little, Brown and Company, 1900.

Harding, Walter. *A Thoreau Handbook.* New York: New York University Press, 1976.

Haskell, Daniel C. *The United States Exploring Expedition, 1838–1842.* New York: New York Public Library, 1942.

Hawthorne, Julian. *Hawthorne and His Circle.* New York: Harper and Brothers, 1903.

―――. *Nathaniel Hawthorne and His Wife.* 2 vols. Boston: Houghton Mifflin Company, 1884.

Hawthorne, Nathaniel. *The Centenary Edition of the Works of Nathaniel Hawthorne.* 13 vols. to date. General editors: William Charvat, 1905–1966; Roy Harvey Pearce; Claude M. Simpson, 1910–1976. Columbus: Ohio State University Press, 1962–1977. Vol. I, *The Scarlet Letter,* 1971; Vol. II, *The House of the Seven Gables,* 1971; Vol. III, *The Blithedale Romance* and *Fanshawe,* 1971; Vol. IV, *The Marble Faun,* 1971; Vol. V, *Our Old Home: A Series of English Sketches,* 1970; Vol. VI, *True Stories from History and Biography,* 1972; Vol. VII, *A Wonder-Book* and *Tanglewood Tales,* 1972; Vol. VIII, *The American Notebooks,* 1972; Vol. IX, *Twice-told Tales,* 1974; Vol. X, *Mosses from an Old Manse,* 1974; Vol. XI, *The Snow-Image and Uncollected Tales,* 1974; Vol. XII, *The American Claimant Manuscripts,* 1977; Vol. XIII, *The Elixir of Life Manuscripts,* 1977. Vol. XIV, *The French and Italian Notebooks,* is in preparation. I have worked from the typescript of *The Centenary Edition;* quotations in the text are cited by entry date.

―――. *The English Notebooks by Nathaniel Hawthorne.* Edited by Randall Stewart. New York: Russell and Russell, 1962. Originally published 1941, by Modern Language Association of America.

―――. *Hawthorne's Lost Notebook: 1835–1841.* Transcript by Barbara S. Mouffe. University Park, Pennsylvania: Pennsylvania State University Press, 1978.

―――. *Hawthorne's Works.* 13 vols. Boston: Houghton Mifflin Company, 1882.

―――. *Love Letters of Nathaniel Hawthorne.* 2 vols. Chicago: Society of the Dofobs, 1907. Reprinted, with a foreword by C. E. Frazer Clark, Jr., Washington, D.C.: NCR Microcard Editions, 1972.

Hawthorne, Sophia Peabody. *Notes in England and Italy*. New York: G. P. Putnam and Sons, 1869.

Henry, Robert Selph. *The Story of the Mexican War*. New York: Frederick Ungar Publishing Company, 1961.

Heydon, Peter N., and Philip Kelley, editors. *Elizabeth Barrett Browning's Letters to Mrs. David Ogilvy*. New York: Quadrangle / The New York Times Book Company, and The Browning Institute, 1973.

Hibben, Paxton. *Henry Ward Beecher: An American Portrait*. New York: The Press of the Readers Club, 1942.

Holloway, Mark. *Heavens on Earth: Utopian Communities in America, 1680–1880*. New York: Dover Publications, Inc., 1966.

Howard, Leon. *Herman Melville: A Biography*. Berkeley: University of California Press, 1967.

Howarth, William L. *The Literary Manuscripts of Henry David Thoreau*. Columbus: Ohio State University Press, 1974.

Howarth, William L., editor. *Twentieth Century Interpretations of Poe's Tales*. Englewood Cliffs, New Jersey: Prentice-Hall, Inc., 1971.

Howe, Daniel Walker. *The Unitarian Conscience: Harvard Moral Philosophy, 1805–1861*. Cambridge: Harvard University Press, 1970.

Howe, Irving. *Politics and the Novel*. New York: Horizon Press, 1957.

Howe, Julia Ward. *Margaret Fuller*. Boston: Roberts Brothers, 1883.

———. *Reminiscences, 1819–1899*. Boston: Houghton Mifflin Company, 1899.

Howe, M. A. DeWolfe. *The Life and Letters of George Bancroft*. 2 vols. Port Washington, New York: Kennikat Press, 1971. Originally published 1908.

———. *Memories of a Hostess*. Boston: The Atlantic Monthly Press, 1922.

James, Henry. *Autobiography*. Edited by Frederick W. Dupee. New York: Criterion Books, 1956.

———. *William Wetmore Story and His Friends*. 2 vols. published as one. New York: Grove Press, n.d. Originally published 1903.

Johnson, Edgar. *Charles Dickens: His Tragedy and Triumph*. 2 vols. New York: Simon and Schuster, 1952.

Kaul, A. N., editor. *Hawthorne: A Collection of Critical Essays*. Englewood Cliffs, New Jersey: Prentice-Hall, Inc., 1966.

Kendall, Phebe Mitchell. *Life, Letters and Journals of Maria Mitchell*. Freeport, New York: Books for Libraries Press, 1971. Originally published 1896.

Kerr, Howard. *Mediums and Spirit-Rappers and Roaring Radicals: Spiritualism in American Literature, 1850–1900*. Urbana: University of Illinois Press, 1972.

Lathrop, George Parsons. *A Study of Hawthorne*. Boston: James R. Osgood and Company, 1876.

Lathrop, Rose Hawthorne. *Memories of Hawthorne*. Boston: Houghton Mifflin Company, 1923.

Leach, Joseph. *Bright Particular Star: The Life and Times of Charlotte Cushman*. New Haven: Yale University Press, 1970.

Lease, Benjamin. *That Wild Fellow, John Neal, and the American Literary Revolution*. Chicago: University of Chicago Press, 1972.

Lewis, R. W. B. *The American Adam: Innocence, Tragedy, and Tradition in the Nineteenth Century*. Chicago: University of Chicago Press, 1955.

Leyda, Jay. *The Melville Log*. 2 vols. New York: Harcourt Brace and Company, 1951.

Loggins, Vernon. *The Hawthornes*. New York: Columbia University Press, 1951.

Longfellow, Henry Wadsworth. *The Letters of Henry Wadsworth Longfellow*. Edited by Andrew Hilen. 4 vols. to date. Cambridge: The Belknap Press of Harvard University Press, 1966–1972.

Mabbott, Thomas Ollive. *Tales and Sketches, 1831–1842* and *Tales and Sketches, 1843–1849*, Vols. II and III of *Collected Works of Edgar Allan Poe*. Cambridge: The Belknap Press of Harvard University Press, 1978.

Marx, Leo. *The Machine in the Garden: Technology and the Pastoral Ideal in America*. London: Oxford University Press, 1972.

Matthiessen, F. O. *American Renaissance: Art and Expression in the Age of Emerson and Whitman*. London: Oxford University Press, 1974.

McGill, Frederick T. *Channing of Concord*. New Brunswick, New Jersey: Rutgers University Press, 1967.

Meltzer, Milton, and Walter Harding. *A Thoreau Profile*. New York: Thomas Y. Crowell Company, 1962.

Melville, Herman. *The Letters of Herman Melville*. Edited by Merrell R. Davis and William H. Gilman. New Haven: Yale University Press, 1960.

———. *Moby-Dick; or, The Whale*. New York: The Heritage Press, 1943.

———. *Selected Tales & Poems*. Edited by Richard Chase. New York: Holt, Rinehart and Winston, 1966.

———. *The Writings of Herman Melville*, Edited by Harrison Hayford, Hershel Parker, and G. Thomas Tanselle. Evanston, Illinois: The Northwestern-Newberry Edition; *Typee*, 1968; *White-Jacket*, 1970.

Merrill, Walter M. *Against Wind and Tide: A Biography of Wm. Lloyd Garrison*. Cambridge: Harvard University Press, 1963.

Messerli, Jonathan. *Horace Mann*. New York: Alfred A. Knopf, 1972.

Miller, Edwin Haviland. *Melville*. New York: George Braziller, Inc. 1975.

Minnigerode, Meade. *Some Personal Letters of Herman Melville and A Bibliography*. New York: The Brick Row Book Shop, Inc., 1922.

Mitford, Mary Russell. *The Letters of Mary Russell Mitford*. Selected by R. Brimley Johnson. Port Washington, New York: Kennikat Press, 1972. Originally published 1925.

Moss, Sidney P. *Poe's Literary Battles*. Durham, North Carolina: Duke University Press, 1963.

———. *Poe's Major Crisis*. Durham, North Carolina: Duke University Press, 1970.

Nichols, Roy Franklin. *Franklin Pierce*. Philadelphia: University of Pennsylvania Press, 1958.

Normand, Jean. *Nathaniel Hawthorne: An Approach to an Analysis of Artistic Creation*. Translated by Derek Coltman. Cleveland: The Press of Case Western Reserve University, 1970.

Nye, Russel B. *William Lloyd Garrison and the Humanitarian Reformers*. Boston: Little, Brown and Company, 1955.

Ossoli, Margaret Fuller. *At Home and Abroad, or Things and Thoughts in America and Europe*. Edited by Arthur B. Fuller. Port Washington, New York: Kennikat Press, 1971. Originally published 1856.

———. *Love-Letters of Margaret Fuller, 1845–1846*. With an Introduction by Julia Ward Howe. New York: Greenwood Press, Publishers, 1969. Originally published 1903.

———. *Memoirs of Margaret Fuller Ossoli*. Edited by R. W. Emerson, W. H. Channing, and J. F. Clarke. New York: Burt Franklin, 1972. Reprint of 1884 edition.

———. *Woman in the Nineteenth Century*. New York: W. W. Norton and Company, Inc., 1971.

Pachter, Marc, and Frances Wein, editors. *Abroad in America*. Washington, D.C.: National Portrait Gallery, Smithsonian Institution, 1976.

Pessen, Edward. *Most Uncommon Jacksonians: The Radical Leaders of the Early Labor Movement*. Albany: State University of New York Press, 1967.

Pickard, Samuel T. *Hawthorne's First Diary, With an Account of its Discovery and Loss*. Boston: Houghton Mifflin Company, 1897.

Poe, Edgar Allan. *The Works of Edgar Allan Poe*, Vols. III and IV. Boston: Jefferson Press, n.d.

Prescott, William Hickling. *The Papers of William Hickling Prescott*. Selected and edited by C. Harvey Gardiner. Urbana: University of Illinois Press, 1964.

Regan, Robert, editor. *Poe: A Collection of Critical Essays*. Englewood Cliffs, New Jersey: Prentice-Hall, Inc., 1967.

Rogers, Millard F., Jr. *Randolph Rogers: American Sculptor in Rome*. Amherst, Massachusetts: University of Massachusetts Press, 1971.

Rusk, Ralph L. *The Life of Ralph Waldo Emerson*. New York: Charles Scribner's Sons, 1949.

Sandburg, Carl. *Abraham Lincoln: The War Years*. 4 vols. New York: Harcourt Brace and Company, 1939.

Saxton, Martha. *Louisa May: A Modern Biography of Louisa May Alcott*. Boston: Houghton Mifflin Company, 1977.

Schlesinger, Arthur M., Jr. *The Age of Jackson*. Boston: Little, Brown and Company, 1945.

——. *Orestes A. Brownson: A Pilgrim's Progress*. Boston: Little, Brown and Company, 1939.

Scudder, Horace Elisha. *James Russell Lowell*. 2 vols. Boston: Houghton Mifflin Company, 1901.

Shepard, Odell. *Pedlar's Progress: The Life of Bronson Alcott*. Boston: Little, Brown and Company, 1937.

Sister Mary Joseph, O.P. *Out of Many Hearts*. Hawthorne, New York: Published by The Servants of Relief for Incurable Cancer, 1965.

Spencer, Benjamin T. *The Quest for Nationality: An American Literary Campaign*, Syracuse, New York: Syracuse University Press, 1957.

Staples, Arthur G., editor. *Letters of John Fairfield*. Lewiston, Maine: Privately printed, 1922.

Stearns, Frank P. *The Life and Genius of Nathaniel Hawthorne*. Philadelphia: J. B. Lippincott, 1906.

Stern, Philip Van Doren. *The Annotated Walden*. New York: Clarkson N. Potter, Inc., 1970.

Stewart, Randall. *Nathaniel Hawthorne: A Biography*. New Haven: Yale University Press, 1948.

Storey, Moorfield, and Edward W. Emerson. *Ebenezer Rockwood Hoar: A Memoir*. Boston: Houghton Mifflin Company, 1911.

Stowe, Charles Edward, and Lyman Beecher Stowe. *Harriet Beecher Stowe: The Story of Her Life*. Boston: Houghton Mifflin Company, 1911.

Swift, Lindsay. *Brook Farm: Its Members, Scholars, and Visitors*. New York: The Macmillan Company, 1900.

Tharp, Louise Hall. *The Peabody Sisters of Salem*. Boston: Little, Brown and Company, 1950.

——. *Three Saints and a Sinner*. Boston: Little, Brown and Company, 1956.

——. *Until Victory: Horace Mann and Mary Peabody*. Boston: Little, Brown and Company, 1953.

Thomas, Benjamin P., and Harold M. Hyman. *Stanton: The Life and Times of Lincoln's Secretary of War*. New York: Alfred A. Knopf, 1962.

Thompson, Lawrance. *Young Longfellow (1807–1843)*. New York: Octagon Books, 1969. Originally published 1938.

Ticknor, Caroline. *Hawthorne and His Publisher*. Port Washington, New York: Kennikat Press, 1969. Originally published 1913.

Trollope, Thomas Adolphus. *What I Remember*. London: William Kimber and Company Ltd., 1973.

Tryon, Warren S. *Parnassus Corner: A Life of James T. Fields*. Boston: Houghton Mifflin Company, 1963.

Turner, Arlin. *Hawthorne as Editor: Selections from The American Magazine of Useful and Entertaining Knowledge*. Port Washington, New York: Kennikat Press, 1972. Originally published 1941.

Untermeyer, Louis, editor. *The Poems of Henry Wadsworth Longfellow*. New York: The Heritage Press, 1943.

Upham, Charles W. *Salem Witchcraft*. 2 vols. New York: Frederick Ungar Publishing Company, 1976.

Van Doren, Mark. *Nathaniel Hawthorne*. New York: William Sloan Associates, Inc., 1949.

Vincent, H. P., editor. *Melville & Hawthorne in the Berkshires*. Kent, Ohio: Kent State University Press, 1966.

Wade, Mason. *Margaret Fuller: Whetstone of Genius*. New York: The Viking Press, 1940.

Wagenknecht, Edward. *Ralph Waldo Emerson: Portrait of a Balanced Soul*. New York: Oxford University Press, 1974.

Wagenknecht, Edward, editor. *Mrs. Longfellow: Selected Letters and Journals of Fanny Appleton Longfellow*. New York: Longmans, Green and Company, 1956.

Webster, Daniel. *The Letters of Daniel Webster*. Edited by G. H. Van Tyne. New York: Haskell House Publishers, Ltd., 1969. Originally published in 1902.

Whicher, Stephen E. *Freedom and Fate: An Inner Life of Ralph Waldo Emerson*. Philadelphia: University of Pennsylvania Press, 1971.

Whiting, Lilian. *The Florence of Landor*. Boston: Little, Brown and Company, 1905.

Wilson, Carroll A., *Thirteen Author Collections of the Nineteenth Century*. 2 vols. New York: Privately printed for Charles Scribner's Sons, 1950.

Wilson, Edmund. *Patriotic Gore: Studies in the Literature of the American Civil War*. New York: Oxford University Press, 1962.

Woodberry, George E. *Nathaniel Hawthorne*. Boston: Houghton Mifflin Company, 1902.

Woodham-Smith, Cecil. *Queen Victoria*. New York: Dell Publishing Company, Inc., 1972.

Wright, Helen. *Sweeper in the Sky*. New York: The Macmillan Company, 1949.

PERIODICALS

Abernethy, P. L. "The Identity of Hawthorne's Major Molineux," *American Transcendental Quarterly* (Summer 1976).

Almy, Robert F. "J. N. Reynolds: A Brief Biography," *The Colophon* (Winter 1937).

Badaracco, Claire. "The Night-blooming Cereus," *Bulletin of Research in the Humanities*, LXXXI (Spring 1978).

Bassan, Maurice. "Julian Hawthorne Edits Aunt Ebe," *Essex Institute Historical Collections*, C (October 1964).

Byers, John E., Jr., editor. "Selections from the Official Consular Despatches of Nathaniel Hawthorne," *Essex Institute Historical Collections*, CXIII (October 1977).

Blanshard, Frances Bradshaw, editor. "Letters of Ann Gillam Storrow to Jared Sparks," *Smith College Studies in History*, VI (April 1921).

Conway, Moncure D. "My Hawthorne Experience," *The Critic* (July 1904).

Emerson, Ralph Waldo. "Thoreau," *Atlantic Monthly* (August 1862).

Hawthorne, Manning. "Hawthorne and 'The Man of God'," *The Colophon*, II (Winter 1937).

———. "Aunt Ebe: Some Letters of Elizabeth M. Hawthorne," *The New England Quarterly*, XX (June 1947).

Hayford, Harrison, and Merrell R. Davis. "Herman Melville as Office-Seeker," *Modern Language Quarterly*, X (1949).

Holmes, Oliver Wendell. "Nathaniel Hawthorne," *Atlantic Monthly* (July 1864).

Idol, John L., Jr., and Sterling Eisiminger. "Hawthorne Sits for a Bust by Maria Louisa Lander," *Essex Institute Historical Collections*, CXIV (October 1978).

Lease, Benjamin. "Salem Vs. Hawthorne: An Early Review of *The Scarlet Letter*," *The New England Quarterly*, XLIV (March 1971).

Metzdorf, Robert F. "Hawthorne's Suit Against Ripley and Dana," *American Literature*, XII (1940).

Myerson, Joel. "James Burrill Curtis and Brook Farm," *The New England Quarterly*, LI (September 1978).

———. "Margaret Fuller's 1842 Journal: At Concord with the Emersons," *Harvard Library Bulletin*, XXI (July 1973).

Nevins, Winfield S. "Nathaniel Hawthorne's Removal from the Salem Custom House," *Essex Institute Historical Collections*, LIII (April 1917).

Nissenbaum, Stephen. "The Firing of Nathaniel Hawthorne," *Essex Institute Historical Collections*, CXIV (April 1978).

Peabody, Elizabeth Palmer. Unsigned review of *Twice-told Tales*. *The New Yorker*, March 24, 1838.

Pearson, Norman Holmes. "Elizabeth Peabody on Hawthorne," *Essex Institute Historical Collections*. XCIV (July 1958).

———. "Hawthorne's Duel," *Ibid*.

Root, Waverly. "The Early American Larder," *Gourmet*, XXXVI (January 1976).

Rusk, Ralph L. "Emerson in Salem, 1849," *Essex Institute Historical Collections*, XCIV (July 1958).

Sanborn, F. B. "A Concord Note-Book: Ellery Channing and his Table-Talk" *The Critic* (July 1905).

Shaw, Peter. "Fathers, Sons, and the Ambiguities of Revolution in 'My Kinsman, Major Molineux'," *The New England Quarterly*, XLIX (December 1976).

Sherman, William. "Henry Bright in New England: His First Meeting with Hawthorne," *The New England Quarterly*, XLVI (March 1973).

Silsbee, Nathaniel. "Autobiographical Memoir by Nathaniel Silsbee," *Essex Institute Historical Collections*, XXXV (January 1899).

Stewart, Randall. "Hawthorne and Politics: Unpublished Letters to William B. Pike," *The New England Quarterly*, V (April 1932).

———. "Hawthorne's Contributions to *The Salem Advertiser*," *American Literature*, V (1934).

Waggoner, Hyatt H. "A Hawthorne Discovery: The Lost Notebook, 1835–1841," *The New England Quarterly*, XLIX (December 1976).

Wright, Nathalia. "Hawthorne and the Praslin Murder," *The New England Quarterly*, XV (1942).

Index